W9-DBT-992

The Green Guide Hungary

Buda Castle funicular with a view of the Chain Bridge, Gresham Palace, and St Stephen's Basilica, Budapest
© Eloi_Omella/iStock

Regions in the guide:
(see the map inside the front cover)

CONTENTS

© Bence Bezeredy/iStock

DON'T MISS

OUR TOP PICKS

DRIVING TOURS

SEE OUR SELECTION OF ADDRESSES FOR EACH SITE

DISCOVERING HUNGARY

INTRODUCTION TO HUNGARY

UNDERSTANDING HUNGARY

NATURE

HISTORY

FOOD AND WINE

ARTS AND CULTURE

TRADITIONS AND WAYS OF LIFE

PLANNING YOUR TRIP

GETTING THERE

KNOW BEFORE YOU GO

BASIC INFORMATION

ACTIVITIES WITH KIDS

FIND OUT MORE

DON'T MISS

★★★ Worth a special journey ★★ Worth a detour ★ Interesting

★★

Hollókő

This village with its small houses painted white and all perfectly preserved has been on the Unesco World Heritage List since 1987. It maintains the traditions of the Palóc community who live in the region. **See p205.**

© I love takeing photos and i think that is a really great opportunity for me to share them/iStock

© Peter_Horvath/iStock

★★★

Hortobágy National Park

The vast Great Plain, known as the Puszta, is symbolic of freedom for the Hungarian people. Home to numerous species of birds, horses are bred here and graze amid its wild beauty. **See p259**.

© Peter_Horvath/iStock

★★★

Budapest

Hungary's magnificent capital straddles the River Danube. The country's mix of Austro-Hungarian and Turkish heritage blends in perfect harmony in this dynamic city. **See page 30**.

★★

Tokaj and the vineyards

The charming small town of Tokaj is the gateway to a beautiful wine region inscribed on Unesco's World Heritage List. It is just the place to try its delicious wine with notes of quince and apricot. **See p174.**

© gehringj/iStock

© Micolino/iStock

★★★

Pécs

With its Ottoman remains and Early Christian Mausoleum (with Unesco World Heritage status), this vibrant, cultural city in the south of the country is proud of its world-famous Zsolnay ceramics factory and major university. **See p274.**

★★

Szentendre

Just one hour from Budapest, the beautiful city of Szentendre is the artistic and bohemian meeting point of the towns and villages along the Danube Bend. **See p94.**

© Photoservice/iStock

★★

Sopron

At the gateway to Austria, the cinematic backdrop of Sopron has survived the centuries intact, boasting bewitching Baroque palaces and secret passageways. **See p214.**

© julof90/iStock

© Volker Preusser/age fotostock

© Peter_Horvath/iStock

★

Őrség National Park

Within the green triangle of gentle hills that mark the border with Slovenia and Austria lie a number of traditional well-preserved hamlets. Ecotourism at its best! **See p240.**

★★★

Lake Balaton

Beaches and spa resorts, and sunlit vineyards producing delicious wine, this lake has been a magnet for visitors since the 19C. You will find some of the best restaurants in the country here, too. **See p130.**

© nightman1965/iStock

★★

Eger and the Bükk Mountains

With its colorful houses, Baroque churches, and famous red wine, the charming town of Eger lies at the heart of a region of unspoiled nature. **See p183.**

OUR TOP PICKS

Reök Palace, Szeged
© Funkystock/age fotostock

TOP 5 **thermal baths**

1. Széchenyi Gyógyfürdő, Budapest (p62)
2. Gellért Gyógyfürdő, Budapest (p43)
3. Hévízi Tófürdő, Hévíz (p153)
4. Barlangfürdő, Miskolc (p193)
5. Hagymatikum Gyógyfürdő, Makó (p314)

Hagymatikum Gyógyfürdő, Makó
© Tibor Bognár/age fotostock

❤ **Relax beneath the golden dome** of the Turkish Baths in Eger. Built in 1617, they have been magnificently restored. Soak up the magic of an authentic Oriental atmosphere, and enjoy the warm waters that never get cold. **See p188.**

❤ **Admire the superb Art Nouveau exteriors of Szeged**, Hungary's sunniest town. After the terrible flood of 1879, it was completely rebuilt and neo-Baroque and Art Nouveau buildings now line its streets, squares, and gardens. Don't miss Reök Palace, too! **See p307**.

❤ **Discover contemporary Hungarian art** in Debrecen at MODEM (Center for Modern and Contemporary Art). It is the country's largest modern art center after Budapest and holds temporary cutting-edge exhibitions displayed in a bright, light, and innovative building. **See p255.**

Cave Bath, Miskolctapolca
© Brian Jones/iStock

Lake Tisza
© andras_csontos/iStock

❤ **Cycle along the shore of Lake Tisza**, leaving from Tiszafüred on a 34mile/55km cycle path through a gentle, rural landscape. Stop off for a swim along the way or just to relax at the water's edge. **See p264.**

❤ **Step back in time to the ancient world** and explore the Early Christian necropolis in Pécs, where an extraordinary mausoleum with painted burial chambers from the 4C was uncovered beneath the current cathedral. **See p276.**

Budapest viewed from Buda
© Patrice Hauser/hemis.fr

TOP 5 castles

1. Esterházy Palace, Fertőd (p220)
2. Royal Palace of Gödöllő (p120)
3. Almásy-kastély, Gyula (p318)
4. Festetics Palace, Keszthely (p155)
5. Rákóczi Castle, Sárospatak (p179)

Royal Palace of Gödöllő
© posztos/Shutterstock

❤ **Imagine you are an aristocrat for a day** in the magnificent Festetics Palace in Keszthely. Fortunately, its furniture and art collections have been preserved, despite the ravages of the Second World War, and tell the story of the daily lives of a prominent 19C Hungarian ducal family. **See p155.**

❤ **Spend a night in a traditional Palóc house in Hollókő**, a Unesco World Heritage Site. Many of its small, whitewashed houses, decorated inside with embroidery and carved wood, have been turned into vacation accommodation. A delightful rural experience. **See p209.**

❤ **Discover the thatched cottages** of Szenna Open-air Museum, where time itself seems to stand still. People dressed in traditional costume entertain visitors during the summer months. **See p282.**

❤ **Admire the amazing panoramic view** from the terrace of Buda Castle or higher still from the dome of the magnificent Hungarian National Gallery, which occupies a wing of the castle. **See p31.**

Festetics Palace, Keszthely
© Franz Waldhäusl/imageBROKER/age fotostock

Veszprém Old Town
© Iakov Filimonov/Shutterstock

❤ **Discover the city selected as European capital of culture** in 2023. Explore Veszprém's Baroque buildings, historic castle precinct, and palaces transformed into museums. **See p158.**

Café Gerbeaud, Budapest
© Patrice Hauser/hemis.fr

❤ **Enjoy the romance and grandeur of old Hungarian cafés** in Budapest, such as Ruszwurm Cukrászda, where the decor has remained unchanged since 1827 and a hint of Old Europe still hangs in the air. **See p82.**

❤ **Explore the Great Plain in a horse-drawn cart** in Hortobágy, and see egrets, herons, bustards, and storks in these grasslands and wetlands of seemingly endless horizons. **See p259.**

❤ **Try a delicious ice cream** and enjoy a peaceful stroll; always a welcome combination in the sunshine, so why not in Gyula, too? **See p317.**

TOP 5 vineyards

1. **Badacsony** (p148)
2. **Villány** (p287)
3. **Tokaj** (p174)
4. **Eger** (p183)
5. **Sopron** (p214)

Tokaj vineyards
© gehringj/iStock

❤ **Sip some heavenly sweet Tokaji wine**, the color of honey. Thanks to a terroir created by volcanic soil and late harvests, this nectar of the gods has earned Hungary a place on the wine map since the 18C. French king Louis XIV christened it "the wine of kings, and the king of wines." **See p176.**

❤ **Dig deep into Hungarian history** at the National Memorial Garden in Székesfehérvár, the final resting place of kings, among them Stephen (István) I, founder of the Hungarian kingdom. His memory lingers on in the names of many street signs and buildings. **See p164.**

Heron, Hortobágy
© Siegmar Tylla/Zoonar.com/age fotostock

Museum of Applied Arts, Budapest
© Funkystock/age fotostock

❤ **Take a tour of Budapest's Secessionist buildings** and discover some extraordinarily fine interiors, such as in the Museum of Applied Arts, while the collection at the House of Hungarian Art Nouveau has a rich and eclectic charm. **See p47.**

❤ **Spend a night among the vines** in a charming inn in a vineyard in Villány. Explore the winegrowing villages where the rows of small whitewashed cellar buildings offer a chance to linger and taste the wines. **See p288.**

❤ **Remember the Cold War** in Fort Monostor at Komárom. The vast subterranean corridors still house the railway tracks used to transport Russian munitions wagons around what was one of the biggest arsenals of the postwar period. The fort was a secret Soviet location from 1945. **See p236.**

❤ **Walk in the footsteps of King Matthias** as you explore the Renaissance rooms of Visegrád's Royal Palace, before watching brave knights compete in epic jousting combats. **See p104.**

TOP 5 **religious sites**

1. Matthias Church, Budapest (p38)
2. Pannonhalma Abbey (p230)
3. Ják Abbey Church (p243)
4. Majk Camaldoli Hermitage (p237)
5. Esztergom Basilica (p108)

Pannonhalma Abbey
© rusm/iStock

Hercules Fountain, Royal Palace, Visegrád
© Funkystock/age fotostock

Prepare for your trip by finding our top picks on our website
travelguide.michelin.com

Find us also on Facebook®
Facebook.com/MichelinVoyage

DRIVING TOURS

Tokaj and the vineyards in 2 days

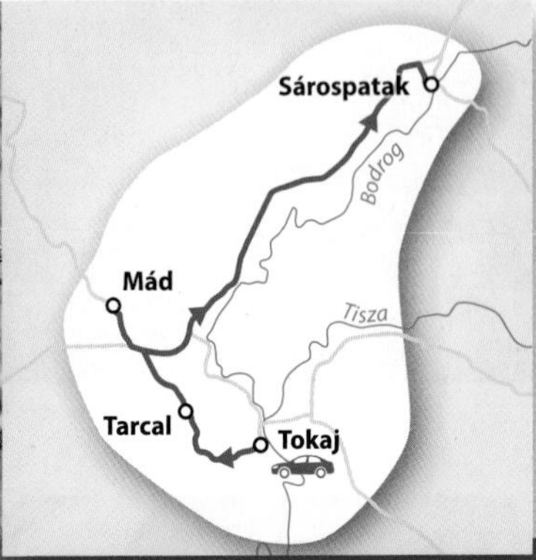

© evryka23/iStock

In brief: 107mi/172km, to tour the whole vineyard area.

Tokaj cellars
© Hungarian Tourism Agency

• D-1 Tokaj

Begin with a visit to the Tokaj Museum (**see p174**). Stop for an in-house roasted coffee (**p182**). Head to the Wine Museum (**p175**) to learn more about the famous local wine and the vineyards that produce it. After lunch at LaBor restaurant (**p181**), visit Rákóczi Pince (wine cellar, **p176**) to taste some Tokaji wine. Round off your day with a stroll through the village or a drive to Tarcal where you can see the huge statue of Christ (**p176**).

Rákóczi Castle
© Bence Bezeredy/iStock

• D-2 The vineyards

Leave Tokaj town and make your way to Mád (**see p177**). Don't miss the synagogue and a delicious lunch at Percze Experience (**p182**). You may like to follow lunch by taking our driving tour of the vineyards or instead make directly for Rákóczi Castle in Sárospatak.

Tip: a car is essential for exploring the vineyards.

Pécs and the vineyards of the south in 3 days

© Digoarpi/iStock

In brief: 88mi/142km, taking in the town, mountains, and vineyards.

• D-1 Pécs

Begin the day in Széchenyi Square (**see p227**), where you can visit the former mosque. Follow this with the Early Christian burial ground (**p276**). Spend the afternoon in the Zsolnay Cultural Quarter, the site of the former ceramics manufacturer (**p280**). Enjoy one of the café-restaurants on the pedestrianized streets in the evening and stay overnight in Pécs.

Tip: the Zsolnay Cultural Quarter is outside the downtown area and has a guesthouse on site.

• D-2 Mecsek Hills

Explore the cave at Abaliget (**see p283**), before enjoying a swim in the lake. Have lunch in Hosszúhetény and then take the road across the mountains to Zengővárkony. Spend the night in the Mecsek Hills (**p284**).

Tip: remember your walking boots to enjoy the lovely trails through the lush Mecsek Hills.

• D-3 The Villány vineyards

Explore the vineyard villages (**see p287**). Start the evening with a wine tasting before dinner and spend the night in situ—accommodation is now available on some estates.

Cairn in the Mecsek Hills
© Sandor91/Shutterstock

The mountains of the north in 4 days

© Lutsenko_Oleksandr/Shutterstock

In brief: 143mi/230km, from Budapest to Miskolc, across the mountains.

• D-1 Mátra Mountains

Leave Budapest in good time to reach Gyöngyös and the Mátra Museum (**see p201**). Carry on across the mountains and stop on Kékestető to enjoy the view (**p202**). Then head to Parád **(p202)** to learn about Palóc culture. A little further on, Sirok Castle will reward you with a wonderful panoramic view over the mountains (**p203**). Return to Eger (**p183**) for the next stage.

• D-2 Eger

Head to the castle first (**see p183**) to see the magnificent view and then explore the center, making sure you visit the Archbishop's Palace (**p186**), the Lyceum (**p186**), and the Minaret (**p188**). Finish the day by relaxing in the Turkish Baths (**p188**) before dinner in Macok bistro (**p195**), where you can taste Eger's world-renowned red wine.

Sirok Castle
© pipoka/iStock

• D-3 Bükk Mountains

Head out to explore the Bükk Mountains (the Bükk National Park), stopping along the way at Bélapátfalva's former Cistercian abbey (**see p190**) and the Lippizaner Stud and Museum in Szilvásvárad (**p190**), where you can also enjoy a trip on a narrow-gauge railway. See the extraordinary Hunguest Hotel Palota in Lillafüred (**p191**), before exploring one of the small caves nearby. Spend the night in Miskolc (**p192**).

Tip: go directly to Miskolc and then take the small train to Lillafüred that runs back and forth between the two several times a day.

• D-4 Miskolc

The busy town of Miskolc is home to Diósgyőr Castle (**see p192**), where you can enjoy a number of events in the summer (medieval jousting tournaments and shows). Just 4mi/7km southwest is the thermal Cave Bath at Miskolctapolca (**p193**), where you can see amazing structures formed by the flow of water over millennia. The beneficial effect of the waters here has been known since the Middle Ages.

Hotel Palota, Lillafüred
© Jana_Janina/iStock

The Great Plain in 6 days

© AndreyGatash/iStock

In brief: 267mi/430km, from Kecskemét to Lake Tisza.

• D-1 Kecskemét

Explore the center of the city on foot, taking in the Great Church and City Hall (**see p323**) and the lovely Art Nouveau exterior of Cifra Palace, which also houses an art gallery (**p325**). Depending on your interests, visit the Leskowsky Musical Instrument Collection (**p327**) or the Hungarian Museum of Photography (**p327**). To prepare for the Great Plain (the Puszta), dine at Kecskeméti Csárda (**p334**), a traditional inn serving local specialties. Spend the night in Kecskemét.

Tip: if you don't have time to make it to Hortobágy National Park, you could visit Kiskunság National Park, 25mi/40km from Kecskemét, where you can get an equally good impression of the Puszta and its traditions (p328).

Klauzál Square, Szeged
© Travelsewhere/Shutterstock

• D-2 Szeged

On the way to Szeged, don't miss Ópusztaszer National Heritage Park (**see p311**). Explore Szeged on foot to see its many Art Nouveau squares and buildings, including the splendid Reök Palace (**p307**) and Gróf Palace (**p310**). Visit the impressive Votive Church (**p308**) and don't miss Klauzál Square (**p307**) and Virág Cake Shop with its tempting sweet treats (**p316**). Szeged is the home of paprika, so don't leave without trying the spicy fish soup at Öreg Kőrössy Halászcsárda (**p315**).

• D-3 Makó and Gyula

On your way to Gyula, stop off in Makó (**see p314**), famous for its striking Organic architecture, which includes the splendid Hagymatikum Thermal Bath. In Gyula visit Almásy Mansion (**p318**). The Hundred-Year-Old Patisserie (**p317**) is a local institution and the perfect place to enjoy a coffee or an ice cream. If you have not already splashed about in the water in Makó, why not head to Várfürdő for a spot of thermal relaxation (**p321**).

• D-4 Debrecen

Make your way back to the city of the Puszta, also known as "Calvinist Rome," and see the imposing Great Reformed Church (**see p250**). Just a stone's throw away, enjoy the lunch menu of the day at the fashionable Ikon restaurant (**p256**). On your way around the city, make time to visit Déri Museum and MODEM (Center for Modern and Contemporary Art), not forgetting the beautiful sculptures at Ferenc Medgyessy Museum (**p255**). Mingle with the locals in the evening in the bars and terraces. Try Roncsbár (**p257**) with its eclectic decor.

• D-5 Hortobágy National Park

The village of Hortobágy (**see p259**) is the gateway to the Great Plain. The Herdsman's Museum and the Round Theater (**p260**) provide a useful introduction, but it is the wildlife of the area that really impresses. Visit the Hortobágy Wild Animal Park and the Máta Stud Farm, then take a trip in a horse-drawn wagon to where you can watch horses galloping "five-in-hand" (**p261**). Do some birdwatching at the Great Fishponds (**p262**) and then enjoy a meal at Hortobágyi Csárda, a traditional roadside inn dating from the 18C (**p264**).

• D-6 Tisza-tó and Tiszafüred

By now you may be in need of slowing down the pace a little, so make your way to Lake Tisza (**see p262**) to relax by the water. But if you can handle some more activity, there are canoes and pedalos for hire, or you can simply go for a swim. If you still have some energy left, visit the cycling center where you can choose between a traditional or an electric bike (**p264**) to tackle the 34mi/55km cycle path from Tiszafüred.

Hortobágy National Park
© CSP_Sziban/age fotostock

The towns and spas of northern Transdanubia in 8 days

© gravisions/iStock

In brief: 435mi/700 km, from the Danube to Lake Balaton

• D-1 The Danube Bend

Leave Budapest and make your way up the west bank of the Danube (**see p92**) to explore the pretty town of Szentendre (**p94**) and two key historic sites: Visegrád (**p106**) and Esztergom (**p108**). For the return trip, head back down the right bank and enjoy the stunning views of the Danube Bend and the riverbank opposite.

• D-2 Győr

On your way beside the Danube, make a stop at Fort Monostor (at Komárom), a key location during the Cold War situated on the border with Slovakia (**see p236**). Have lunch in Győr (**p232**) and spend the afternoon in the historic center (**p227**), stepping back in time in the well-preserved and grand Baroque palaces. Have dinner and stay overnight.

Esterházy Palace, Fertőd
© ARCO/M Klindwort/age fotostock

• D-3 Fertőd–Sopron

On your way to Sopron, visit the magnificent Esterházy Palace at Fertőd, the "Hungarian Versailles" (**see p220**). Have lunch not far from the Austrian border in Sopron (**p225**) and then take a walk around the Old Town (**p214**).

Tip: to extend your day's stay here, you have a choice: a walk in nature at Lake Fertőd or discovering some history in Nagycenk at Széchenyi Mansion. You could also combine the two, of course!

• D-4 Bük–Szombathely

Spend the morning at Bükfürdő (baths, **see p228**) and then have lunch in Szombathely, followed by a walk in the Baroque center (**p245**). On your way to Keszthely, stop off in Ják to see the splendid Romanesque Abbey Church (**p245**).

• D-5 Hévíz and Keszthely

Make a stop at the amazing thermal lake and spa at Hévíz, suspended over the water on stilts and among the most beautiful in the country (**see p153**). Then head to Keszthely on Lake Balaton (**p154**) for lunch, before visiting the well-preserved Festetics Palace (**p155**). Spend the rest of the afternoon in the museums or on the lakeside beach (**p157**). Enjoy dinner and an overnight stay.

• D-6 Lake Balaton

Follow the northern shore of the lake and spend the morning exploring the winegrowing hills of Badacsony (**p148**). Enjoy panoramic views from some of the many tasting venues. After a gourmet lunch, make your way to Tihany Peninsula (**p144**) and its abbey church. Enjoy the view over the lavender fields, and the waters of Lake Balaton. Spend the night here.

Veszprém
© Hungarian Tourism Agency

Tip: Badacsony is known for its pleasant lifestyle, and good accommodation and restaurants.

• D-7 Veszprém

Discover Veszprém, former "city of queens" and European Capital of Culture 2023. There is a wide selection of museums and galleries to be explored within the castle walls (**see p159**). Have lunch, then explore the surrounding area, where you will also find the prestigious Herend porcelain factory (**p160**). Spend the night in Veszprém.

• D-8 Székesfehérvár

Stop en route at Zirc Abbey to see its impressive library (**see p160**). Have lunch and then spend the afternoon in the Baroque center of Székesfehérvár, city of kings (**p164**). Visit the National Memorial Garden, last resting place of many monarchs, then make your way back to Budapest.

Tip: to extend your stay, visit Lake Velence on the way back to Budapest, which is generally less busy than Lake Balaton.

DISCOVERING HUNGARY

Visegrád Citadel overlooking the Danube
© Hungarian Tourism Agency

Budapest and the Danube Bend 1

Michelin national map 732
Budapest, Pest, Komárom-Esztergom counties

St. Stephen's Basilica viewed from Zrínyi utca
© connect11/iStock

BUDAPEST AND THE DANUBE BEND

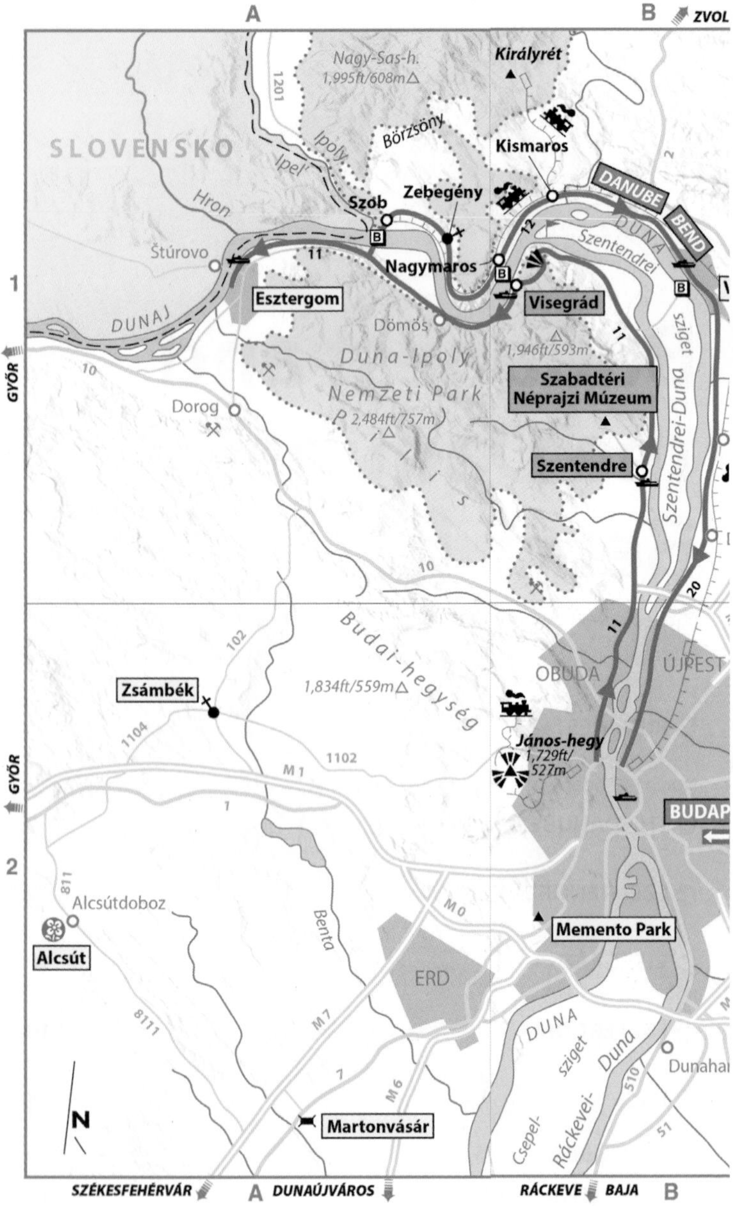

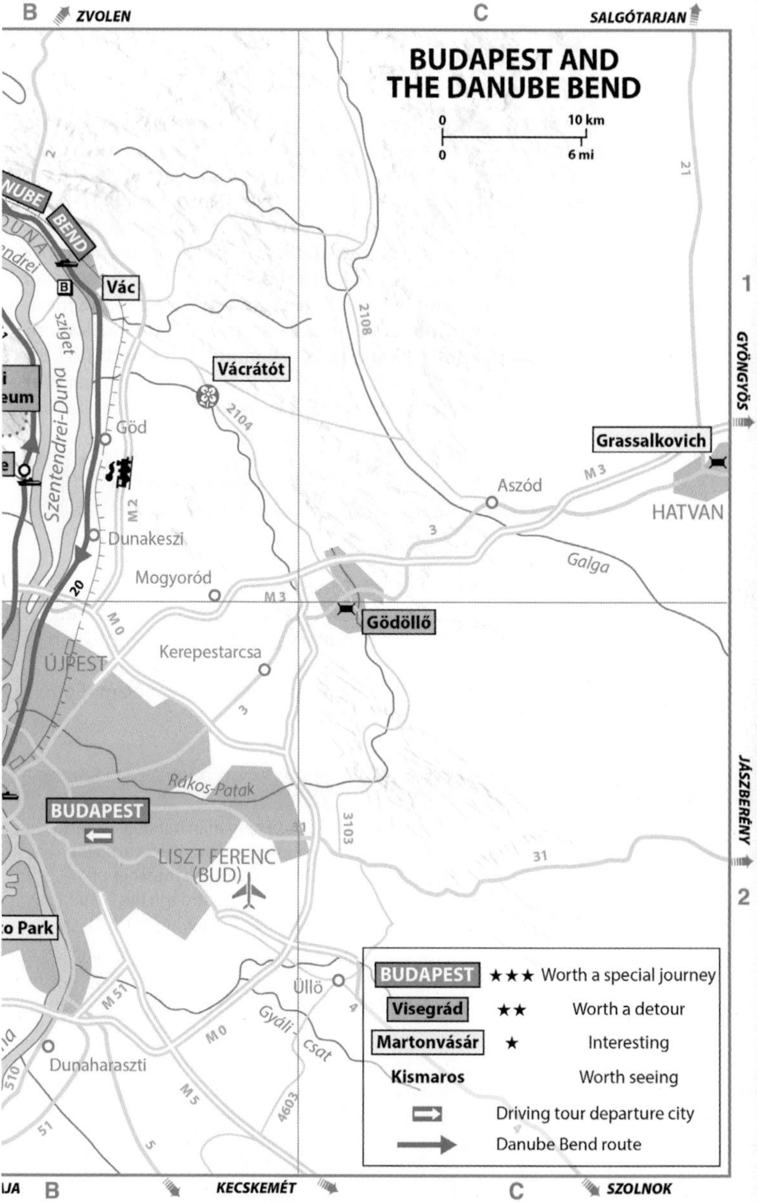
BUDAPEST AND THE DANUBE BEND
0 10 km
0 6 mi
B
ZVOLEN
C
SALGÓTARJAN
1
2
GYÖNGYÖS
JÁSZBERÉNY
KECSKEMÉT
SZOLNOK
DANUBE BEND
DUNA
Szentendrei-Duna
sziget
Vác
Vácrátót
Göd
Dunakeszi
Mogyoród
Kerepestarcsa
ÚJPEST
Aszód
Grassalkovich
HATVAN
Galga
Gödöllő
Rákos-Patak
BUDAPEST
LISZT FERENC (BUD)
Üllő
Gyáli-csat
Dunaharaszti
2108
2104
M2
M3
M0
M5
M51
3103
31
21
20
3
4
5
51
510
4603
BUDAPEST ★★★ Worth a special journey
Visegrád ★★ Worth a detour
Martonvásár ★ Interesting
Kismaros Worth seeing
Driving tour departure city
Danube Bend route

Budapest

★★★

Population 1,749,734 – Budapest county – area code ✆ 1

Arriving for the first time in Budapest, you could be forgiven for a fleeting feeling of dislocation—are you in a Western country or an Eastern one? Are you even sure you are in Europe? Everything seems strange and yet somehow familiar. Today, of course, the city feels European, but it has a certain something else as well. It is the mix of the many diverse elements cherry-picked from other cultures and civilizations that influenced the country down the centuries. These external influences may now be an integral part of Budapest, but it has still retained its own unique identity. Where would it be without its Viennese-style cafés, its Parliament Building resembling London's Houses of Parliament, its superb Turkish baths, or its beautiful Secessionist buildings? It would be just another characterless town instead of a city with a thousand fascinating faces.

ADDRESSES PAGE 73
Stay, Eat, Shopping, Baths, Nightlife, Festivals

INFO:

Tourinform Office: Sütő utca – Pest map H2 (p48–49) Sütő utca 2 (Belváros district, close to Deák Ferenc tér). Open 8am–8pm.

Call center – ✆ (1) 438 8080. Operates 7am–7pm (English).

Tourist info point: Hősök tere – Olof Palme sétány 5 (in the ice rink building). Open 9am–7pm. In high season mobile information kiosks operate in tourist areas (9am–6pm).

BUDAPEST IN 4 DAYS	
Day 1	Buda side: Buda Castle, Hungarian National Gallery, Matthias Church, panoramic view of Pest from the Fisherman's Bastion. Walk through the lanes of Várnegyed. Walk down the hill through the Castle Gardens and Castle Garden Bazaar.
Day 2	Pest side: Parliament Building, St. Stephen's Basilica, Jewish quarter for its synagogues (they will be shut on Saturdays for services). End the day in the Jewish district as it is one of the liveliest in Budapest.
Day 3	Pest side: Andrássy út (State Opera House, Hungarian House of Photography, House of Terror Museum, Franz Liszt Memorial Museum, . . .), Heroes' Square leading to City Park; relax at Széchenyi Baths or visit the Museum of Fine Arts.
Day 4	Divide your time between Buda and Pest, a mix of sightseeing and shopping: Gellért Hill for the view, or relax at Gellért Baths (if you didn't visit Széchenyi Baths yesterday); cross the Danube via Liberty Bridge; Great Market Hall; more shopping in Váci utca, or visit the beautiful Museum of Applied Arts.

Parliament Building by the Danube
© Givaga/iStock

LOCATION:
Regional map B2 (p28–29); town plans: Buda (p37), Pest (p48–49), Budapest (p68–69); Public transport map inside back cover

DON'T MISS:
Budapest's principal attractions: the Buda Castle district; the banks of the Danube and the views across the river, Andrássy út—collectively a Unesco World Heritage Site. Superb baths, such as Gellért and Széchenyi baths. Beautiful museums such as the Hungarian National Gallery.

KIDS:
The funicular to the castle; Budapest Zoo; Városliget Ice Rink and Palatinus Beach and baths on Margaret Island; exploring the Buda Hills on the Children's Railway; Memento Park; an afternoon at the baths.

★★★ Várnegyed (Buda Castle district)

Buda map, p37. Access: BUS 16, 16A, 116 Dísz tér; Tram 19, 41 Clark Ádám tér, then steps or the funicular up to the castle; M 2 Széll Kálmán tér.

★★★ **BUDAI VÁR** (Buda Castle) F2

Built in the 13C, remodeled under the Habsburgs, and then rebuilt after the Second World War, this imposing castle and royal palace complex dominates the hill that rises around 164ft/50m above the Danube. It houses the Hungarian National Gallery, among other cultural sites.

Sikló (Funicular)

Open daily 7.30am–10pm. Ft1,400, round trip Ft2,000 (3–14yrs Ft700/1,100).
The funicular has been operating between Clark Ádám tér and the castle since 1870. Destroyed during the Second World War, a replica was built in 1983, complete with identical wooden cars.

Urban history

ÓBUDA, BUDA, AND PEST

The city was "born" in AD1, when the Romans established a military camp at Óbuda and a civilian city at **Aquincum** (*see p70*) on the right bank of the Danube. The Romans were eventually driven out and replaced by the Huns. Legend has it that it was the brother of Attila, sometimes known as Buda or Bleda, to whom the city owes its name. The settlement continued to develop on the right bank with the building of the first fortress on the rocky outcrop of Buda in the 13C. The population became concentrated across the river in Pest under Ottoman rule in the 16C. The majority of the churches in Buda were converted into mosques during this time and numerous Turkish baths were built. Several hundred years later, in the 19C, Count **István Széchenyi** (1791–1860) initiated a number of urbanization projects, such as the construction of the Chain Bridge and the National Theater (at Pest). He also regulated the flow of the Danube to make it navigable for commercial trade. In 1808 Archduke Joseph, palatine of Hungary and second only to the king in terms of office, set up a commission to improve the urban enviroment in Pest, followed by another in Buda.

THE GOLDEN AGE

At the turn of the 20C, under the Austro-Hungarian Empire, Budapest was a flourishing industrial metropolis and in 1873 Óbuda, Buda, and Pest were officially joined together. The population was boosted by the mass arrival of Jews from Eastern Europe, who settled in the Erzsébetváros area of Pest.

In the face of great economic activity and the proliferation of further urban projects, an international planning competition was launched, with the aim of ensuring the capital was developed in a controlled way. Two major schemes were agreed—the planning of **Andrássy út** (*see p56*) and Nagykörút (Great Boulevard). Regulations were set out in 1894 and the wide-ranging transformation of the city began. In 1896, to mark 1,000 years of the occupation of the Carpathian Basin by the Hungarians, the Millennial Exhibition was held in Városliget (City Park). That year was also memorable for the inauguration of the first subway in continental Europe. The city's golden age peaked in 1902 with the construction of the great **Parliament Building** (*see p46*), which was predominantly inspired by London's Houses of Parliament.

THE DARK YEARS

With the collapse of the Austro-Hungarian Empire in the aftermath of the First World War, the boom years became a thing of the past. During the authoritarian regime of Admiral Miklós Horthy, Budapest recovered a little of its prewar strength. The respite was short-lived, however, as a few years later Nazi domination brought terror to the Budapest ghetto. During the years of the Second World War, all the city's bridges, Buda Castle, and the Old Town were destroyed and would not be rebuilt until the 1960s. In the Communist era, accelerated and forced industrialization brought a fifth of the country's total population into Budapest, a process that resulted in a housing crisis and pollution, problems that still remain today, as they do in many other major cities. As a consequence, in addition to the development of public transport, the city encourages people to travel by bicycle in particular.

Buda Castle
© Remedios/iStock

THE REVIVAL OF THE CITY

Ever since the fall of the Berlin Wall and the establishment of democracy in Hungary, the city has been on the move once again. On a symbolic level, Communist emblems have been removed from official buildings and the names of roads have gradually reverted to their original incarnations. Traffic has been eased by the construction of a ringroad around the city and major projects have been instigated, particularly in the hotel, commercial, and service sectors. An important restoration program has been in progress in both Buda and Pest since the 1990s. A particular example of this can be seen in **Belváros** (between Szabad S. út and József A. utca) and the facelift that Deák Ferenc utca ("Fashion Street") received is thanks to Hungarian businessman Péter Csipak. In **Erzsébetváros** some of the rebuilding work has been financed by foreign investors.

Among contemporary architects the name of József Finta crops up frequently. Before the regime change, he was already well known for having built the grand hotels on the banks of the Danube. József Finta and Antal Puhl Associates designed the Kempinski Hotel Corvinus on Erzsébet tér in a contemporary style that nevertheless resists the more outlandish vagaries of fashion. Another example is the building on Teve utca, which houses the police, again designed by Finta. Opened in 1992 on the banks of the Danube, the **French Institute** was designed by Georges Maurios. Hungarians expressed some regret that the building "turns its back" on the river, but the color of its walls is compatible with its urban setting and its cladding protects it from pollution.

Meanwhile, the 21C launched with notable projects such as **Bálna** (The Whale), a commercial and arts center (*see p66*) and campaigns to restore historic buildings continue to emerge. For example, the prime minister moved into the former Carmelite convent, a stone's throw from Buda Castle, and **Paris Passage** (*see p54*), which had been closed for many years, has been stunningly transformed into a luxurious hotel, the Párisi Udvar.

BUILDING BUDA CASTLE

King Béla IV, who ruled 1235–70, erected the first fortress on the hill above the Danube to protect Buda from a Mongol invasion. The castle was extended during the reign of Sigismund of Luxembourg (r. 1387–1437), but it was primarily during the reign of **Matthias Corvinus** (r. 1458–90) that it enjoyed its golden age. An exceptional king, cultured and with humanist interests and values, particularly in the arts and sciences, he carried out renovations in the Renaissance style.

During the 1686 Siege of Buda, to drive out the occupying Turks, the castle was all but destroyed, while in the 18C and 19C the **Habsburg** rulers sought to turn it into a residence that befitted their royal status. Maria Theresa of Austria began by extending it in a grand Baroque style and in 1890 Franz Joseph entrusted Miklós Ybl and Alajos Hauszmann with the task of remodeling the castle in a neo-Baroque style, despite the fact that by that time Franz Joseph would stay there only rarely.

Szent György tér (St. György Square)

The square lies in front of the castle's main entrance. Just beside it you can see the neo-classical **Sándor Palota** (Sándor Palace), which houses the president of Hungary's official residence and office. The **changing of the guard** takes place in front of the palace every hour, on the hour, between 9am and 5pm. Next door, the building with the classical facade used to be a Carmelite convent. It was dissolved in 1782 and converted. Now restored, it has since become the prime minister's residence.

Castle exterior

A bird of prey with its wings outstretched, holding a sword between its talons, seems on the point of taking flight from a pillar that forms part of the neo-Baroque gate in the castle grounds. It is the mythical **turul** (prononced *too-rool*) bird, the emblem of the Magyar tribes.

Buda Castle's Baroque facade overlooks the Danube and is more than 328yds/300m long with a central dome supported by a series of twin columns. On the large panoramic terrace, pride of place goes to the **equestrian statue of Savoyai Jenő** (Eugene of Savoy), one of the liberators of Hungary from the Turks. Depicted on the pedastal are two scenes from the Battle of Zenta (1697), a surprise defeat for the Turkish forces by the Habsburgs and which heralded the eventual departure of the Ottomans from Hungary.

Continue along the terrace until you are overlooking the river as the **view★★** is superb, with (from left to right) Margaret Island, the Parliament Building, the Chain Bridge, St. Stephen's Basilica, Elizabeth Bridge, Liberty Bridge, and, in the distance, Gellért Hill, the Citadel, and Liberty Statue.

Below (down the steps), is **Várkert Bazár★** (Castle Garden Bazaar), gardens that are once again open to the public. Constructed at the end of the 19C, they were ravaged by bombing in the Second World War and were then turned into a Youth Park during the Communist era. They have now been restored to their former glory and today comprise a series of buildings, gardens, and lawns. The buildings include arcades and promenades designed by the architect Miklós Ybl in a neo-Renaissance style. The Castle Garden Bazaar now also provides a cultural space with areas for temporary exhibitions *(www.varkert-bazar.hu; open Tue–Sun, 10am–5.30pm; info from the glass kiosk in front of the National Gallery; access also possible from the quay: Ybl Miklós tér 2–6, Tram 19). To enter the National Gallery, take the passage to the right.*

The principal attraction of the castle forecourt (look out also for the statue of a groom and horse in the center) is **Mátyás-kút** (King Matthias Fountain)★ which is impossible to miss. This large group sculpture in bronze set against the castle wall is the work of Alajos Stróbl (1904) and shows the king in a hunting scene. It was inspired by a ballad written by Mihály Vörösmarty, a 19C Romantic poet, in which Matthias meets Ilonka, a beautiful young girl, while out hunting.

On the left after the fountain, the internal courtyard is entered through **Oroszlános kapu** (Lions' Gate), the entrance to which is guarded by two stone lions. Stand in the middle of this beautiful paved courtyard to fully appreciate the magnificence of the buildings around you, notably **Országos Széchenyi Könyvtár** (National Széchenyi Library). Cross to the back of the courtyard to the entrance of **Budapesti Történeti Múzeum** (Budapest History Museum, *see p35)* and go down the stairs which lead to the city walls and **Buzogány-torony** (Mace Tower), a remnant of the medieval fortifications. You can leave the castle grounds through an adjacent gate, **Ferdinánd kapu** (Ferdinand Gate) cut into the city wall at this point, and see the semicircular barbican, built in the 14C and 15C.

★★ **Magyar Nemzeti Galéria** (Hungarian National Gallery)

Szent György tér. (1) 201 9082. mng.hu. Open Tue–Sun, 10am–6pm (access to the dome included). Ft3,200 (free with the Budapest Card). Audioguide in English Ft800. Temporary exhibitions Ft3,800 (including the permanent collection). Allow 2–3 hrs for the visit.

Works from the Middle Ages to the end of the 18C have been transferred to the Museum of Fine Arts (*see p59)*. In 2021 the Hungarian National Gallery will move to a new building, designed by the Japanese architectural firm Sanaa, located in the museum center in Városliget (*ligetbudapest.hu/institution/new-national-gallery)*.

The gallery is dedicated to Hungarian art from the 19C to the present day. Among the artists represented are **Mihály Munkácsy** (1844–1900) and **László Paál** (1846–79), who were also great friends. The former studied in Berlin, Munich, and Paris. His painting *Last Day of a Condemned Man* is stark and realistic, whereas his *Woman Carrying Brushwood*, painted while he was staying in Barbizon, south of Paris, is more lyrical. Paál was heavily influenced by the Barbizon School, which is clearly demonstrated in his paintings of landscapes *(Noon, Path in the Forest of Fontainebleau, Landscape with Cows). Luncheon on the Grass* by **Pál Szinyei Merse** is based on one of the Impressionists' favorite themes. The gallery also includes epic works on historical events such as *The Baptism of Vajk* (the future King Stephen I) by **Gyula Benczúr**.

The museum hosts temporary exhibitions, too.

In fine weather don't miss climbing up to the restored **dome**. There is a fantastic 360-degree **view**★★ over Budapest from beneath it *(access from the 3rd and top floor of the museum)*.

★ **Budapesti Történeti Múzeum** (Budapest History Museum)

Szent György tér 2. (1) 487 8871. www.btm.hu. Open Tue–Sun, Mar–Oct, 10am–6pm; Nov–Feb, 10am–4pm. Ft2,000 (no charge with the Budapest Card). Audioguide in English Ft1,200.

This museum takes you on a tour of "Budapest through the ages." Prehistory, antiquity, the Middle Ages, the modern era, and the construction of the castle are all charted in a succession of rooms displaying different collections, including archeological finds, jewelry, ceramics, and objects from everyday life, among many others. Particularly worth seeing is the **Gothic sculpture room** *(first/ground floor)*, which includes some beautiful and striking limestone statues, many of which are displayed with specially designed lighting (pick up a map at the entrance to the room to help you follow the numbering of the displays). A visit to the lower and underground areas of the castle, which date from medieval times, reveals fine ribbed vaulting and an impressive great hall with a tiled stove, which mainly dates from the time of Sigismund of Luxembourg (king of Hungary 1387–1437). And don't miss the **palace chapel**, built in the 14C during the time of the French Angevin dynasty, kings from the House of Anjou, who ruled Hungary 1309–82. Lit by three tall windows, it has a three-part altarpiece in the center.

AROUND THE CASTLE E1–2

After visiting the castle itself, it's nice to soak up the atmosphere with a stroll through the historic district surounding it. There are interesting buildings, along with shops, street food stalls, and restaurants if you start to feel peckish.

Tárnok utca (Treasurer's Street) E1

A busy trading area in the Middle Ages (for German merchants), Treasurer's Street (a reference to the king's chief treasurer) is lined with elegant houses decorated with painted exteriors, attractive balconies, and Baroque ornamentation. It is now very much a tourist street with many shops selling souvenirs, items decorated with traditional Hungarian embroidery, and cafés. Some of the building facades are worth pausing at, such as **No. 14** (Café Tárnok), which dates from the 14C and 15C and was restored in the 1950s.

Arany Sas Patikamúzeum (Golden Eagle Pharmacy Museum) E1

Tárnok utca 18. ✆ (1) 375 9772. semmelweis.museum.hu. Open Tue–Sun, Mar–Oct, 10am–5.30pm; Nov–Feb, 10am–3.30pm (Sat & Sun, 5.30pm). Ft800.

A former merchant's house dating from the 15C, in the mid-18C it became the Golden Eagle Pharmacy as you will see from the wrought iron sign above the door. Today this small museum exhibits objects, jars, and pharmaceutical instruments dating from the 16C–19C. Two of the rooms are particularly interesting—one recreates an 18C apothecary and the other a laboratory that looks more like an alchemist's lair.

A little further along Tárnok utca, look to your left down **Balta köz** (Axe Passage) where you were likely to get your throat cut in the Middle Ages! It is supposedly named for a violent street fight with axes that took place here in the 15C involving members of the powerful Hunyadi family.

Szentháromság tér (Trinity Square) E1–2

The main square of the castle district owes its name to **Szentháromság-szobor★** (Holy Trinity Statue), which stands in the center. This Baroque monument was erected in the 18C to commemorate the plague epidemics of the 17C and 18C. At the time it was customary for survivors to build a monument to the glory of God in gratitude for having been spared.

On the right side of the square you will find the **Matthias Church** with its beautifully intricate stone bell tower and its glazed roof tiles. At the corner of Szentháromság utca is a Baroque palace, **Régi Budai Városháza** (Old Buda Town Hall), built at the end of the 17C by an Italian architect. A bell tower with a clock stands above what was once a chapel. On the same corner, in a niche below an oriel window, a statue of Athena protects the city. In her right hand the goddess holds a sculpted shield emblazoned with Buda's coat of arms. Across the square is a neo-Gothic building that houses the Ministry of Finance.

BUDAPEST

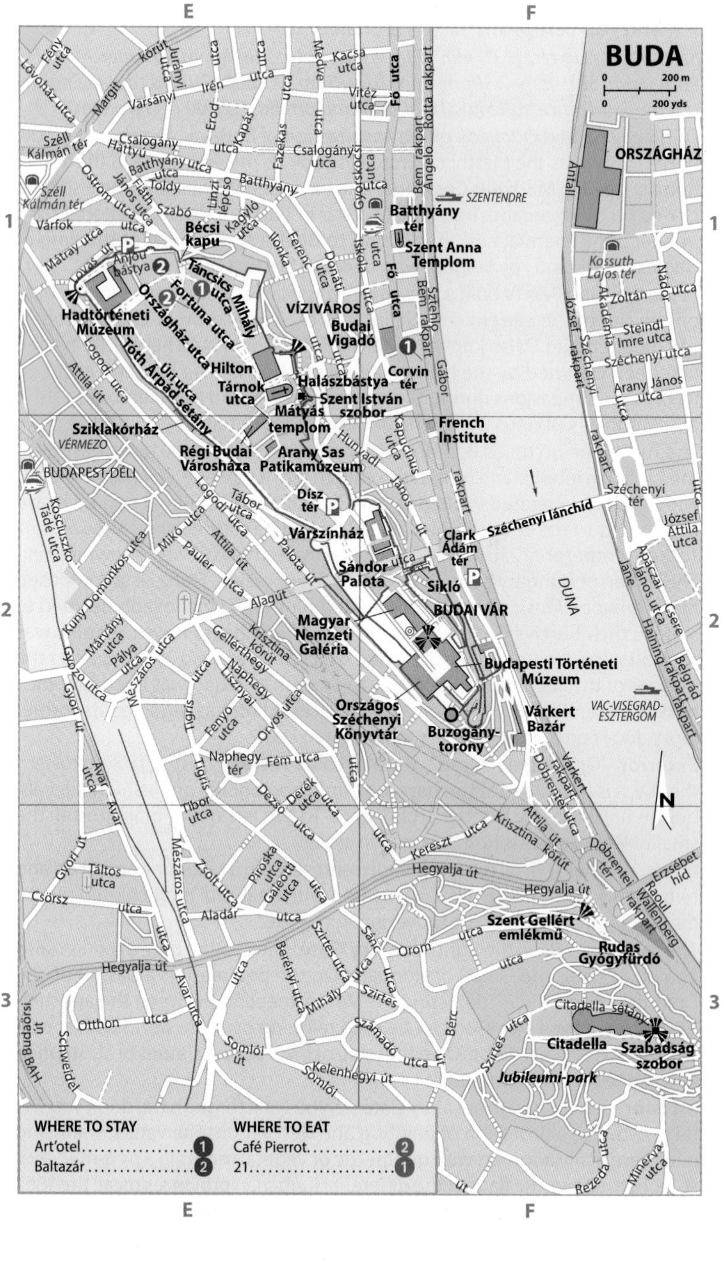
E
F
BUDA
0 200 m
0 200 yds
ORSZÁGHÁZ
SZENTENDRE
Batthyány tér
Szent Anna Templom
Bécsi kapu
Táncsics Mihály utca
Fortuna utca
Országház utca
Úri utca
Tóth Árpád sétány
Hadtörténeti Múzeum
VÍZIVÁROS
Budai Vigadó
Corvin tér
Hilton
Tárnok utca
Halászbástya
Szent István szobor
Mátyás templom
French Institute
Sziklakórház
VÉRMEZŐ
BUDAPEST-DÉLI
Régi Budai Városháza
Arany Sas Patikamúzeum
Dísz tér
Várszínház
Clark Ádám tér
Széchenyi lánchíd
Széchenyi tér
Sándor Palota
Sikló
BUDAI VÁR
DUNA
Magyar Nemzeti Galéria
Budapesti Történeti Múzeum
Országos Széchenyi Könyvtár
Buzogány-torony
Várkert Bazár
VAC-VISEGRAD-ESZTERGOM
Kossuth Lajos tér
Alagút
Hegyalja út
Erzsébet híd
Szent Gellért emlékmű
Rudas Gyógyfürdő
Citadella sétány
Citadella
Szabadság szobor
Jubileumi-park
N
WHERE TO STAY
Art'otel 1
Baltazár 2
WHERE TO EAT
Café Pierrot 2
21 1

★★ **Mátyás-templom** (Matthias Church) E1

Szentháromság tér. ✆ (1) 488 7716. www.matyas-templom.hu. Open Mon–Fri, 9am–5pm; Sat, 9am–2.30pm; Sun, 1pm–5pm. Ft1,800. Guided tour in English, reserve in advance: turizmus@matyas-templom.hu, Ft2,500 (1–5 persons).

Originally named Our Lady of the Assumption of Budavár, the church is now better known as the Matthias Church. It took its present name in the 19C in homage to King **Matthias Corvinus**, who extended the building and also celebrated his two marriages here. The first was in 1461 to Catherine of Podébrady, princess of Bohemia, and the second to Beatrice, daughter of the king of Naples, Ferdinand I of Aragon, who became Matthias's wife in 1476.

In the 13C King Béla IV built a three-nave basilica dedicated to the Virgin Mary on the site of the current church. In 1309 the coronation of Charles Robert of Anjou (Charles I, also known as Károly Róbert) was held here, after he had first been crowned by the bishop in Székesfehérvár. The building acquired its present dimensions during the reigns of Sigismund of Luxembourg (14C) and Matthias Corvinus (15C), who added the south tower.

The Turks, who occupied Buda in 1541 after laying siege to the town, destroyed the Christian interior and turned the church into a mosque, covering the walls with carpets. Liberated in 1686 by the Christian armies, King Leopold I gave the church to the Jesuits. They added Baroque features and in 1867 Franz Joseph, emperor of Austria, and his wife Elisabeth (Sissi) were crowned king and queen of Hungary here. To celebrate the occasion, Franz Liszt composed his *Coronation Mass*, which he conducted himself. Franz Joseph decided to restore the church's Gothic appearance and architect Frigyes Schulek was commissioned to undertake the work, which took around 20 years. After the ravages of the Second World War, further reconstruction was needed, which took another 20 years or so but today the building has regained its former glory and is one of the capital's most visited sites.

Exterior – On the main facade, the **Matthias Tower** soars 262ft/80m toward the sky. It is four-sided at the base, becoming octagonal on the higher levels, before finishing in a slender stone spire. To the left of the main portal, the smaller **Béla Tower** is Romanesque in style.

Above the main portal is a tympanum representing a Madonna and Child and two angels. The church roofs are covered with beautiful multicolored glazed tiles, a common form of roof covering in the 15C.

The south portal (on the right), or **Mary Gate**, dates to the time of Louis I (also known as Louis the Great) of Hungary. On the pediment is a bas-relief, the *Dormition of the Virgin*, depicting the Virgin kneeling between the apostles. At the top of the vault, God can be seen reigning over the world with a royal crown and terrestial globe. On either side of the door are statues of St. Stephen and St. László (King Ladislas I).

Interior – *Enter through the Mary Gate.* As you walk through the door, you will be greeted by a profusion of painting and decoration. The vaults, walls, and pillars are richly adorned with geometric or vegetal motifs in a neo-medieval style. In the nave, the flags of the different Hungarian provinces recall the 1867 coronation. The choir's neo-Gothic high altar has a statue of the Virgin in a mandorla illuminated by golden rays. The Four Evangelists and the Fathers of the Church are represented on the pulpit.

Walk around the church, starting from the left of the choir.

St. Ladislas Chapel – Notable for its frescoes on the life of the saint, a knight-king in the 11C, painted by Károly Lotz.

Holy Trinity Chapel – This contains the sarcophagi of King Béla III of the Árpád dynasty and his wife, Agnes of Antioch.

Matthias Church, Statue of St. Stephen, and Fisherman's Bastion
© Hungarian Tourism Agency

St. Emeric (Imre) Chapel – The chapel has a three-winged altarpiece. On the center panel, the prince-saint Emeric is surrounded by his father, St. Stephen, and his tutor, the archbishop who was canonized St. Gellért (*see p43*).
Baptismal font – This fine example of sculpted stone consists of a basin supported by four columns, each adorned with a lion at its base. The basin is protected by a bronze cover.
Loreto Chapel – The chapel has a magnificent wrought iron door and is dedicated solely to the worship of the Madonna. Look out for the statue of the Madonna and Child, both wearing the Imperial crown of Austria.
Egyháztörténeti Gyűjtemény (Ecclesiastical Art Collection) – *Steps to the right of the choir.* Cross the crypt with its red marble sarcophagus containing the bones of the kings of the Árpád dynasty discovered at Székesfehérvár and the coats of arms of the Knights of Malta (Hospitallers), to reach the chapel of St. Stephen. At the entrance you can see a bust of Empress Elisabeth of Austria (and queen of Hungary) sculpted in Carrara marble, and inside the chapel is the reliquary bust of the saint-king. The stained glass windows depict the saints and the blessed of Hungary. A spiral staircase leads up to the royal oratory where there are photographs of the Holy Crown of Hungary with explanatory panels (in English). Next to it is a gallery displaying sacerdotal vestments and sacred objects such as chalices, patens, and monstrances.

★ **Halászbástya** (Fisherman's Bastion) E1

Behind Matthias Church. www.fishermansbastion.com. Access to the upper level: mid-Mar–Apr, 9am–7pm; May–mid-Oct, 9am–8pm; mid-Oct–mid-Mar, 24hrs access. Ft1,000. Mid-Oct–mid-Mar and outside the visiting hours listed here, no charge.

Built between the end of the 19C and the beginning of the 20C, Fisherman's Bastion is a collection of neo-Romanesque balconies and turrets that might even put you in mind of a fairytale castle. The origins of its name are uncertain but it's likely that it came either from the fishermen's market held nearby in the Middle Ages, or the fishermen's guilds who helped defend the city from the original castle walls. The bastion was built to celebrate the city's millennium in 1896 but it has never been used for defensive purposes. The seven turrets represent the seven Magyar tribes, each chief being commemorated with a statue. Tourists flock here for the spectacular **views★★** from the covered terrace of the River Danube and Pest on the opposite bank. Under the colonnades you will also find a café where you can sip a drink while taking in the panorama. You can also see the colorful roof of Matthias Church from here. If you walk to the end of the ramparts, you will see it reflected in the tinted glass frontage of the adjacent Hilton Hotel. Flights of stone steps at the rear of the church lead down to the Víziváros district *(see p44)*.

Szent István szobor (Statue of St. Stephen) E1
This bronze work by the sculptor Alajos Stróbl (1856–1926) stands in front of Fisherman's Bastion. Hungary's first king, Stephen I, is shown on his caparisoned horse, wearing his coronation cloak and the Holy Crown (St. Stephen's Crown) and holding in his right hand the double apostolic cross symbolizing the country's conversion to Christianity. The halo surrounding his head is an allusion to his canonization in 1083. The imposing neo-Romanesque pedestal is a fine example of sculpted limestone. The bas-reliefs depict important events during his reign.

Hilton Budapest E1
Part of the well known chain, the multiple vertical glass panels in the facade and the hotel's height in sympathy with its surroundings mean this modern design blends in well in an otherwise historic area. It was built on the site of a Dominican convent and incorporates parts of the old building. On the wall of the old St. Nicholas tower, you can see a bas-relief celebrating Matthias Corvinus (it is a copy, the original being in Ortenburg Castle at Bautzen in Germany). The king is shown sitting on his throne with a scepter in his hand with two angels holding the royal crown above his head. You have to enter the hotel lobby to access the **remains of the convent** and its church (view of the Parliament Building, Fisherman's Bastion, and the Buda Castle district).

★★ **Táncsics Mihály utca** (Táncsics Mihály Street) E1
Lined with elegant houses with colorful Baroque and neo-classical exteriors, this street is named after the journalist **Mihály Táncsics** (1799–1884). He was a hero in the struggle for national independence and a staunch supporter of the emancipation of the peasant population. He was imprisoned in 1846 for two years for his radical political views.

★ **Bécsi kapu** (Vienna Gate) E1
Once the second great gate into the city, the Vienna Gate was rebuilt in 1936 as part of the celebrations for the 250th anniversary of the liberation of Buda. A plaque fixed to the inside of the door honors the soldiers of different nationalities who gave their lives in the battles to liberate the city from Ottoman rule. The **Monument to the Recapture of Buda** (1936) depicts an angel portrayed as a woman brandishing the double apostolic cross, symbolizing the victory of the Christian armies raised by Pope Innocent XI. The gate had a different name in the Middle Ages—Szombat-kapu (Saturday Gate)—due to the fact that a market was held in front of it on Saturdays.

★★ **Fortuna utca** (Fortuna Street) E1
Another lovely old street typical of the castle district, with historic buildings steeped in history.

Országház utca (Országház Street) E1

Running parallel with Fortuna Street, this was the city's main thoroughfare during the Middle Ages. Translated into English, "Parliament Street" has been so named since 1790 when Hungary's parliament met in a former Clarissine convent housed at No. 28, today one of buildings belonging to the National Academy of Sciences. Several of the houses (nos. 2, 9, 18, 20, and 22) display Gothic elements.

★ **Hadtörténeti Múzeum** (Museum of Military History) E1

Tóth Árpád sétány 40. ✆ (1) 325 1600. militaria.hu. Open Tue–Sun, 9am–5pm. Ft1,500.

A row of cannons points the way to this museum, which was built in 1830 and is a former barracks. What do you expect to find in a military museum? Well, obviously weapons, uniforms, medals, and so on, so in that respect this museum conforms to type. However, you can also learn about the role Hungary has played in goodwill peacekeeping missions, notably during the Vietnam War. The first floor is devoted to the Hungarian Revolution of 1848 and the War of Independence, along with the Second World War and October 1956 Hungarian Uprising—in other words, all the historic events that have involved the national army to date.

★★ **Úri utca** (Úri Street) E1

Take a walk down the longest street in the castle district with its distinctly tranquil, residential feel to see its many houses with beautiful Baroque facades.

★ **Tóth Árpád sétány** (Tóth Árpád Promenade) E1–2

The promenade runs alongside the medieval castle wall from Esztergom Bastion (a defensive structure in the castle wall) to **Dísz tér**. The promenade's main attraction is the **view** it provides over the western part of Buda and the Buda Hills, as far as Gellért Hill.

The national flag flies over **Esztergom bástya** (Esztergom Bastion), a symbol marking the end of the Turkish occupation. From here the **view** looks across first to part of Buda and then, in the distance, to János Hill.

Anjou Bastion is a little further along and after another row of cannons you reach the tombstone of **Abdurrahman Abdi Pasha**, the last governor of Buda who died at the age of 70 defending the city against the Habsburg soldiers. The monument (identfiable by the stone turban on top) was erected by way of reconcilation by the family of György Szabó, a Hungarian soldier, who was killed on the same spot. The inscription, in both Hungarian and Turkish, reads: "He was a heroic enemy, may he rest in peace."

Sziklakórház (Hospital in the Rock) E2

Lovas út 4/C. ✆ 707 010101. www.sziklakorhaz.eu. Visit by guided tour only: every hour on the hour, 10am–7pm, tours last approx. 1hr. Ft4,000 (reduced price with the Budapest Card).

During the Second World War and again during the 1956 Hungarian Revolution, the warren of caves below Castle Hill housed a remarkable underground hospital. Extending over 2.5mi/4km, it was able to accommodate up to 200 casualties. The kitchens, operating theater, wards, and the infirmary can be seen, as well as a nuclear bomb shelter.

In the years immediately after the Second World War the hospital was rented by the privately owned Vaccine-Producing Institute, which mostly produced a vaccine against typhus. An interesting place to visit that rings the changes from the many Baroque and Art Nouveau buildings in the city.

★★ Gellérthegy (Gellért Hill)

Maps: Buda (p37) & Pest (p48–49). Access: M 4 Szent Gellért tér; Tram 19, 41, 47, 48, 56, 56A Szent Gellért tér. To reach the hill on foot from Pest, take the Liberty Bridge.
Situated between the Elizabeth and Liberty bridges, the wooded Gellért Hill (771ft/235m high) is one of the most recognizable sights on the right bank. In the 19C its slopes were covered with vineyards but they were unfortunately devasted by phylloxera. According to legend, Gellért Hill used to be very popular with witches and wizards who would meet here on sabbath nights. At the foot of the hill, several thermal springs feed the Gellért and Rudas baths, two of the city's most famous bathing complexes.

★★ **Szabadság híd** (Liberty Bridge) H3
Together with the Chain Bridge, this is one of the city's most impressive river crossings. Restored and repainted, and beautifully lit at night, its 362yd/331m span is an outstanding example of ironwork construction. Originally named the Franz Joseph Bridge, it was opened by the emperor himself in 1896 but adopted its current symbolic name in 1946, the year it was rebuilt. The turrets on top of each of the bridge's four piers are decorated with the mythical *turul* bird and at either end the arches bear the Hungarian coat of arms beneath the Holy Crown of Hungary.

★★★ **Gellértfürdő** (Gellért Baths) H3
Kelenhegyi út 4–6. *See also Baths, p88.*
Forming part of the Hotel Gellért building, but managed and run quite separately, this large complex includes swimming pools and thermal baths. It is worth a visit for its **Secessionist** architecture alone. In 1934 the hotel's winter conservatory was replaced by the indoor swimming pool. Beneath the metal and glass dome, which opens up in summer, the indoor pool is lined with columns. They support a mezzanine walkway that looks down over the pool, fronted by pillars covered with Zsolnay ceramic tiles. At one end of the pool there are two small doors, one used to lead to the men's thermal bath *(férfiak)* and the other to the women's bath *(nők)*, but these days the baths are mixed. The baths are beautifully decorated, the blue mosaics, medallions, cherubs, and fountains have all been superbly executed in true **Art Deco** style.
After bathing, you might opt to move on to Gellért Hotel where the tearoom (Eszpresszó) offers excellent pastries, all made in the hotel kitchens. The decor might be in need of a little modernization but this shouldn't spoil the pleasure of sampling the cakes, whether in winter when you're snuggled up in a traditional armchair listening to the pianist, or in summer outside on the terrace under one of the sun umbrellas.

Sziklatemplom (Cave Church) H3
Szent Gellért rakpart 1. (20) 775 2472. Open Mon–Sat, 9.30am–7.30pm. Ft600, including audioguide in English. Built in 1926 and modeled on the sanctuary in the rock at Lourdes in France, the Hungarian Christian community of the Order of St. Paul worshiped at this church until 1951, when the monks were imprisoned by the Communists and the cave was closed. Restored in the 1990s, mass has been celebrated here every day since then.

Szabadság szobor (Liberty Statue) G3
Set on a limestone pedestal, this statue of a woman, 46ft/14m tall and holding a palm leaf at arm's length above her head, seemingly offering it up to heaven, cuts a dignified figure. This colossal monument, similiar to others found in

many Central European countries, was erected in 1947 to commemorate the city's liberation from occupation by Nazi Germany by the soldiers of the Red Army. From the terrace below the statue there is a fine **view★★** of both Buda and Pest across the river. To the right, there is also a bird's eye view of Hotel Gellért and the baths complex, giving you the opportunity to appreciate the architecture of both.

Citadella (Citadel) G3

www.citadella.hu. At the time of writing, the Citadel is closed for an indefinite period. However you can still access the terrace for the spectacular view.
The citadel sits on top of the hill. It was built in 1851 on the orders of Emperor Franz Joseph following the Hungarian revolt against the Austrians in 1848–49. It was used for antiaircraft defense during the Second World War but after the war opened its doors to tourists with a hotel, a restaurant, two cafés, an exhibition of photographs from the period 1850–1945, and a wax museum.
The **Panoptikum 1944** (1944 Wax Museum), which occupies a former air raid shelter, gives you a good idea of how the Citadel was used during the Second World War.
The **view★★★** from the belvedere is superb. Look down on the city below over to Pest on the opposite river bank, and then to the left where, in the distance, Margaret Island, one of the city's great green spaces, is clearly visible.

Jubileumi-park (Jubilee Park) F3

Verejték u. 2. Opened to celebrate the fortieth anniversary of the October Revolution, this well-mananged park is a pleasant place in which to walk, with shaded paths, flower beds, and lawns.

Szent Gellért emlékmű (St. Gellért Monument) F3

Gellért (Gerard in English) was the first bishop of Csanád (in southeastern Hungary) in 1030. He lived during the reign of Stephen I and it was the king himself who asked Gellért to leave San Giorgio Benedictine Monastery in Venice to become tutor to Prince Emeric, the heir to the throne. Gellért's arrival also led to many pagans converting to Christianity. However, it was a revolt by some pagans, in the wake of the death of Stephen in 1038, that led to Gellért's martyrdom in 1046. He is said to have been placed in a barrel and thrown from the top of the hill. Canonized in 1083, St. Gellért is greatly revered in Hungary. The monumental bronze statue (designed by Gyula Jankovits, 1904) stands on the spot where he was martyred, part way down the hill and in front of a neo-classical semicircular colonnade. Gellért, who appears to be blessing the city, holds a cross in his raised right hand. The figure at his feet represents a converted pagan. There is another excellent **viewpoint★★** from here.

★★ **Rudas Gyógyfürdő** (Rudas Baths) F3

Döbrentei tér 9. BUS 5, 7, 8 Rudas Gyógyfürdő; Tram 19, 41, 56, 56A Rudas Gyógyfürdő. *See also Baths, p88).*
There is nothing particularly special about the outside of this building, which was constructed in 1556 by the pasha Mustapha Sokoli. However, step inside and it's a different story. You will find a softly lit octagonal pool lined with marble. It is surrounded by eight columns supporting a Turkish cupola pierced by oculi through which colored rays of light reflect and dance on the water. At each angle is a small basin where the water temperature varies from very cold to very hot. There is also a unique rooftop panorama pool with a view of the Danube.

★ Víziváros (Watertown) EF1–2

Maps: Buda (p37) & Pest (p48–49). Access: M 2 Batthyány tér; if approaching on foot from Pest, cross the Chain Bridge (accessible on the Pest side from M 1, 2, or 3 Deák Ferenc tér).

By the Middle Ages, this district of Buda, the lower part of the city, was already known as "watertown" due to its many thermal springs.

★★ Széchenyi lánchíd (Chain Bridge) F2

The Chain Bridge is the oldest bridge in the city. It is also known as Széchenyi Bridge, after the man who commissioned its construction. This was Count **István Széchenyi**, to whom Budapest owes what is now one of its most iconic landmarks. In December 1820, the young Széchenyi, at the time a captain in the Hussars, learned that his father had died in Buda. Arriving in Pest with the intention of taking the ferry across the Danube to Buda, he found it impossible to cross the river as ice had halted all river traffic. Unable to make the crossing to Buda for several days, the idea of constructing a bridge began to take shape in his mind. Among the designs submitted, the one by British engineers William Tierney Clark and Adam Clark was eventually chosen. The engineers were commisioned to undertake the work and construction took place between 1839 and 1849.

The bridge has a span of 1,247ft/380m and is 52ft/15.7m wide. By using a combination of stone and iron the design achieves a classically beautiful effect. It is particularly beautiful in the evening when the bridge is lit up—the suspension cables between the two pillars in the shape of triumphal arches become garlands of light. At either end, two stone lions stretched out on pedestals proudly keep guard.

Clark Ádám tér (Adam Clark Square) F2

C5 Tram *19, 41 Clark Ádám tér.* Today this is a particularly busy traffic circle used by thousands of vehicles, emerging from, or heading into, the tunnel dug through the hill under the castle. It is the oldest tunnel in the city and leads to the district of Krisztinaváros. The people of Budapest owe this fine piece of civil engineering to **Adam Clark** (1811–66), the English engineer who also oversaw the construction of the Chain Bridge. To the left you can see a sculpture marking **kilometer 0**, the point from where all distances from the capital to the rest of the country are calculated.

Fő utca (Fő Street) F1–2

C3–4 The district's main street is lined with various buildings and it runs parallel to the Danube. **No. 7**, a modern building at the junction with Pala utca, is the **French Institute**, opened in 1992. Across the street a Baroque two-story house with corner turrets houses a French restaurant, the Pavillon de Paris.

At **nos. 30** and **32** you can see a former Capuchin convent and its **church**, just before you reach **Corvin tér**, where there is a row of lovely Baroque houses (nos. 2–5). On the north side of the square is a theater in fine neo-classical style, **Budai Vigadó** (also known as the Hungarian Heritage House) where the Hungarian State Folk Ensemble (Magyar Állami Népi Együttes) often perform—not to be confused with the concert hall in Pest on Vigadó tér (*see p55*). Further down on the right is the neo-Gothic **Calvinist church**, built of red brick.

Batthyány tér (Batthyány Square) F1

M *2 Batthyány tér.* A useful public transport hub, particularly for tourists—metro line 2, buses, trams, and the HÉV suburban train line all connect here.

Chain Bridge, Gresham Palace, and St Stephen's Basilica in the background
© kanuman/iStock

The street is named after count **Lajos Batthyány** (1806–49), a liberal politican who was in favor of reaching a settlement with Austria and was premier of the first Hungarian government in 1848. He resigned from his post following a disagreement with Lajos Kossuth, the leader of the liberal movement, during the 1848 Hungarian Revolution and was executed by the Austrians in 1849 after the revolt collapsed.

Szent Anna templom★ (Church of St. Anne) is an elegant Baroque church that dominates the square with its two identical bell towers. Allegorical statues of Faith, Hope, and Charity can be seen above the main door and in the center of the facade is a statue of St. Anne with Mary. As with all Baroque churches, the interior is decorated in extravagant fashion—in particular the high altar surrounded by marble columns, the frescoes in the dome representing the Trinity, the gilded pulpit adorned with cherubs, and the organ casing.

Near the church, slightly further down, toward the Danube, the **Angelika Restaurant and Café** (*see Taking a Break, p82*) is a former literary café and an ideal place to stop to enjoy a coffee, cake, and the **view** of the Parliament Building across the river.

At **No. 4** Batthyány Square, close to the 19C **market halls**, is the former **White Cross Inn** where plays were sometimes performed. Look out for the reliefs depicting the four seasons and also for the two wrought iron balconies on either side of the main building, Rococo in style on the right and Baroque on the left. The building is entered beneath a porch below street level. The sign for the Casanova bar is a reminder of the famous Italian roué who is supposed to have stayed here toward the end of the 18C, as did Joseph II, Holy Roman emperor, during his visits to Buda in 1783 and 1784.

On the northern side of Nagy Imre tér, the austere brick building that occupies an entire block is the kind that makes people wonder what went on behind its walls. Depending on which period in history is being discussed, the answer is a Gestapo headquarters and prison in 1944, a prison during the Communist regime, and the Military Court of Justice during the 1956 Uprising.

★★ **Király Gyógyfürdő** (Király Baths) G1

Fő utca 82–84. M *2 Batthyány tér;* Tram *19, 41 Bem József tér;* BUS *109 Bem József tér.*

One of the oldest bath houses in the city, it was built in 1565 by Arslan, pasha of Buda during the Turkish occupation. Various architectural features characteristic of the Turkish era are clearly visible, such as the green domes, the tallest of which is topped with a crescent. (*See also Baths, p88.*)

★★★ Lipótváros (Leopold Town)

Pest map (p48–49). Access: M *2 Kossuth Lajos tér;* Tram *2 Kossuth Lajos tér.*

The Lipótváros district is the heart of political and administrative life in the city and takes its name from Holy Roman emperor Leopold II, who ruled Hungary as king 1790–92. Together with Belváros, it forms part of the historical center of Pest. The monuments, leafy squares, and antique shops in Falk Miksa utca in particular make it a very pleasant area to explore on foot.

★★★ **Országház** (Parliament Building) G2

Kossuth Lajos tér 1–3. M *2 Kossuth Lajos tér. (1) 441 4904. latogatokozpont.parlament.hu. A limited number of tickets can be bought on the day at the visitor center to the right of the Parliament Building (access on the lower floor). Open Apr–Oct, 8am–6pm; Nov–Mar, 8am–4pm. Closed during plenary sessions and on public holidays. Ft3,500 for EU citizens on presentation of an identity card or passport, Ft6,700 for non-EU citizens. Tours in English daily, generally at 10am, noon, 1pm, 2pm, and 3pm, but check the website.*

As visitor numbers are restricted, buying tickets online in advance is recommended: *www.jegymester.hu/parlament* (there is an additional charge of Ft200 to buy tickets on site, and the wait can be around an hour in high season).

With one side of the building facing the Danube and another overlooking Kossuth Lajos tér, this colossal structure, which looks like a neo-Gothic cathedral, is in fact the building that houses Hungary's parliament. With its dome, clock towers, pinnacles, spires, colonnades, and galleries, it is very reminiscent of the Houses of Parliament in London or even the cathedral in Milan. It was built between 1885 and 1902 to plans drawn up by Imre Steindl and in 1896 the Hungarian National Assembly sat here to mark the one thousandth anniversary of the founding of the country.

A total of 88 statues portraying Hungarian sovereigns and miliary leaders stand in a solemn line along the building's facades. The symmetrical wings on either side of the central section meet under the dome. They were built when the national assembly split into two chambers—the Deputy Council Chamber (lower house) and the Old Upper House Hall.

Today the Parliament Building is the seat of the president of the Republic (the south wing), the government (the north wing), and the national assembly.

The main entrance is guarded by stone lions that point you in the direction of the Grand Staircase.

Interior – *The guided tour only allows you to see one part of the building.*

Majestic, palatial, awe-inspiring … these are just some of the words that will come to mind when you see the **Grand Staircase** and entrance hall, the decoration of which, made even more splendid by extravagant gilding, is dazzling. On the rib-vaulted ceiling there are frescoes by Károly Lotz entitled *The Apotheosis of Legislation* and *The Glorification of Hungary.*

The **Dome Hall** is a vast circular room with years of Hungarian history represented in statues of sovereigns and the coats of arms of the old Hungarian counties. Also on display are the **crown jewels**★★. To mark 1,000 years since the coronation of Stephen I, they were transferred here from the National Museum. The **Holy Crown** was returned to Hungary by the Americans in 1978. It was sent to America for safekeeping after the Second World War, where it was guarded at Fort Knox. The crown, also known as the Crown of Saint Stephen, which appears on Hungary's coat of arms, is a stunning example of the goldsmith's craft and was probably made in the 11C. The decoration of the lower, Byzantine-inspired section is made up of cloisonné enamel plaques set with precious stones, representing saints and archangels. The Byzantine emperor, Michael VII Doukas, is shown in the center. The upper, Latin part consists of two enameled gold plaques that cross each other and on which Christ in Majesty is shown, as well as portraits of two apostles whose names are inscribed in Latin. The cross on the top is crooked (damaged at some stage during its long history). The silver and rock crystal **scepter** owes its origins to both Egypt and Hungary. The **orb**, with the patriarchal cross on top and bearing the arms of the House of Anjou, dates back to the 14C and the reign of Charles I of Anjou (Károly Róbert). The **sword** was crafted in the 16C by a Venetian workshop.

The statues in the **lobby** or reception room of the **Old Upper House Hall** are allegories of the principal trades of commerce and industry. The council chamber itself is wood paneled and gilded. The president directs the debates between the deputies who sit in rows of seats arranged in a horseshoe shape. In the corridors outside you can see benches reserved for the deputies with numbered cigar holders (each corresponding to a deputy).

"Shoes on the Danube Bank" Memorial G2

Id Antall József rakpart. On the riverbank, to the right of the Parliament Building, is this poignant memorial consisting of a row of 60 pairs of metal shoes. It commemorates the massacre of thousands of Jews by the brutal Nazi-supporting Arrow Cross party during the Second World War *(see p62)*. These executions were often carried out on the quayside and the bodies simply thrown into the Danube.

★ Magyar Szecesszió Háza (House of Hungarian Art Nouveau) H2

Honvéd utca 3. M 2 Kossuth Lajos tér or 3 Arany János utca; Tram 2 Kossuth Lajos tér. ✆ (1) 269 46 22. www.magyarszecessziohaza.hu. Open Mon–Sat, 10am–5pm. Ft2,000.

Unique in Hungary, this museum traces the story of Art Nouveau in the Magyar kingdom *(see p375)*. Housed in the Bedő family residence, an Art Nouveau jewel in its own right, it was built in 1903 by the Secessionist architect Emil Vidor. Spread over three floors are paintings, furniture, and decorative objects that all fight for space, making it feel rather more like an antique shop than a museum, but all the more enjoyable for the richness of the collection and its certain charm.

★ Szabadság tér (Liberty Square) GH2

M 3 Arany János utca.

On the site of a former Austrian Army barracks, this airy public square is surrounded by buildings with grand exteriors, such as **Magyar Nemzeti Bank** (the National Bank of Hungary) and opposite **Tőzsdepalota**, which housed the fomer stock exchange and for a while the Hungarian **national television** service. The two buildings, although quite different, are the work of the same architect, Ignác Alpár.

On the south side of the square is the controversial **A német megszállás áldozatainak emlékműve** (Memorial to the Victims of the German Occupation), erected in 2014. It shows a German Imperial eagle attacking Hungary, depicted

BUDAPEST AND THE DANUBE BEND

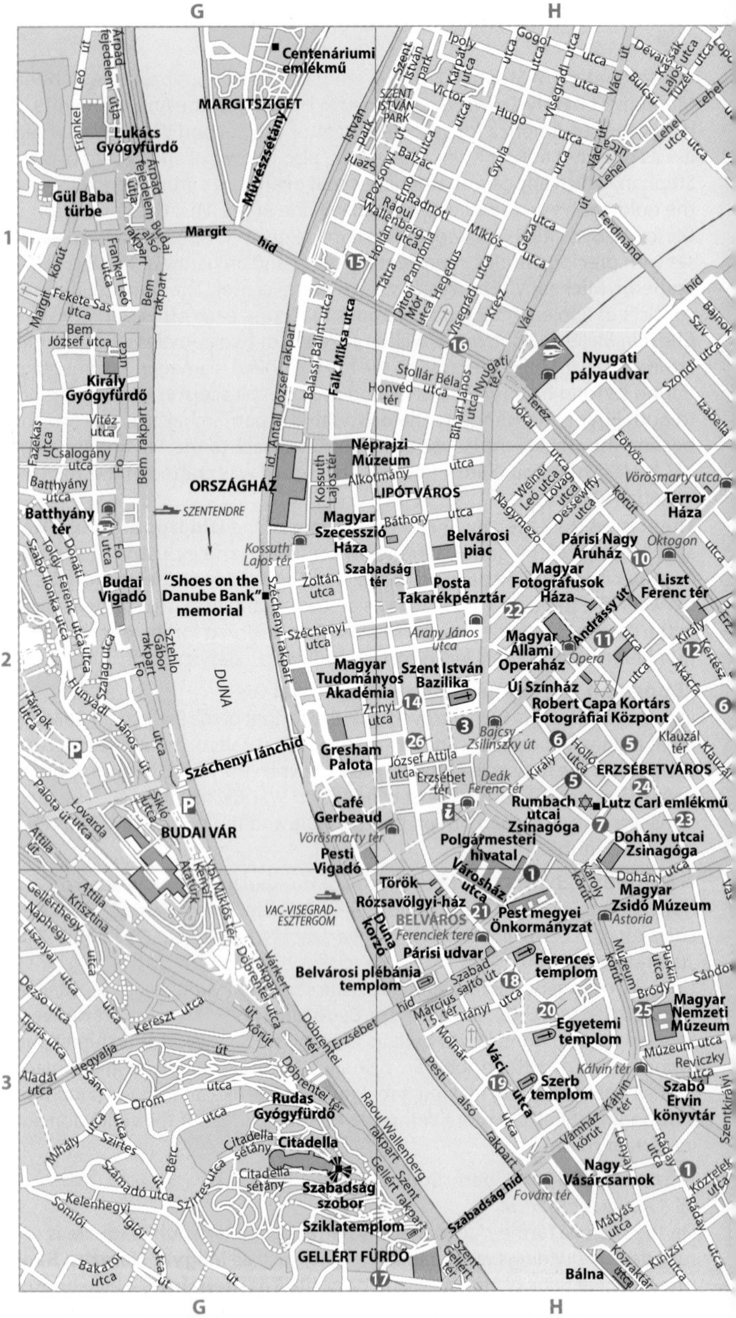

WHERE TO STAY

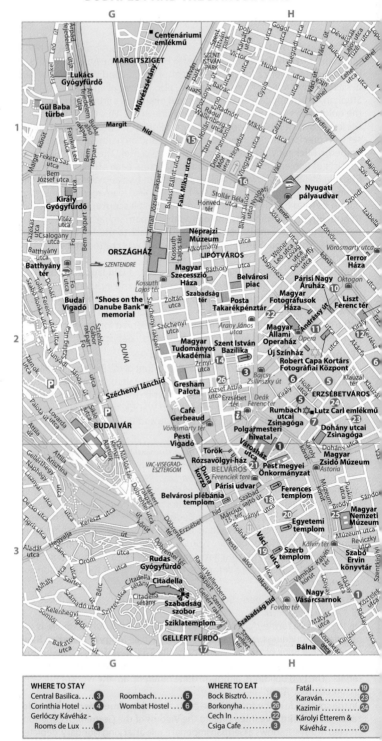

Central Basilica 3
Corinthia Hotel 4
Gerlóczy Kávéház - Rooms de Lux 1
Roombach 5
Wombat Hostel 6

WHERE TO EAT

Bock Bisztró 4
Borkonyha 26
Cech In 22
Csiga Cafe 3
Fatál 19
Karaván 23
Kazimir 24
Károlyi Étterem & Kávéház 20

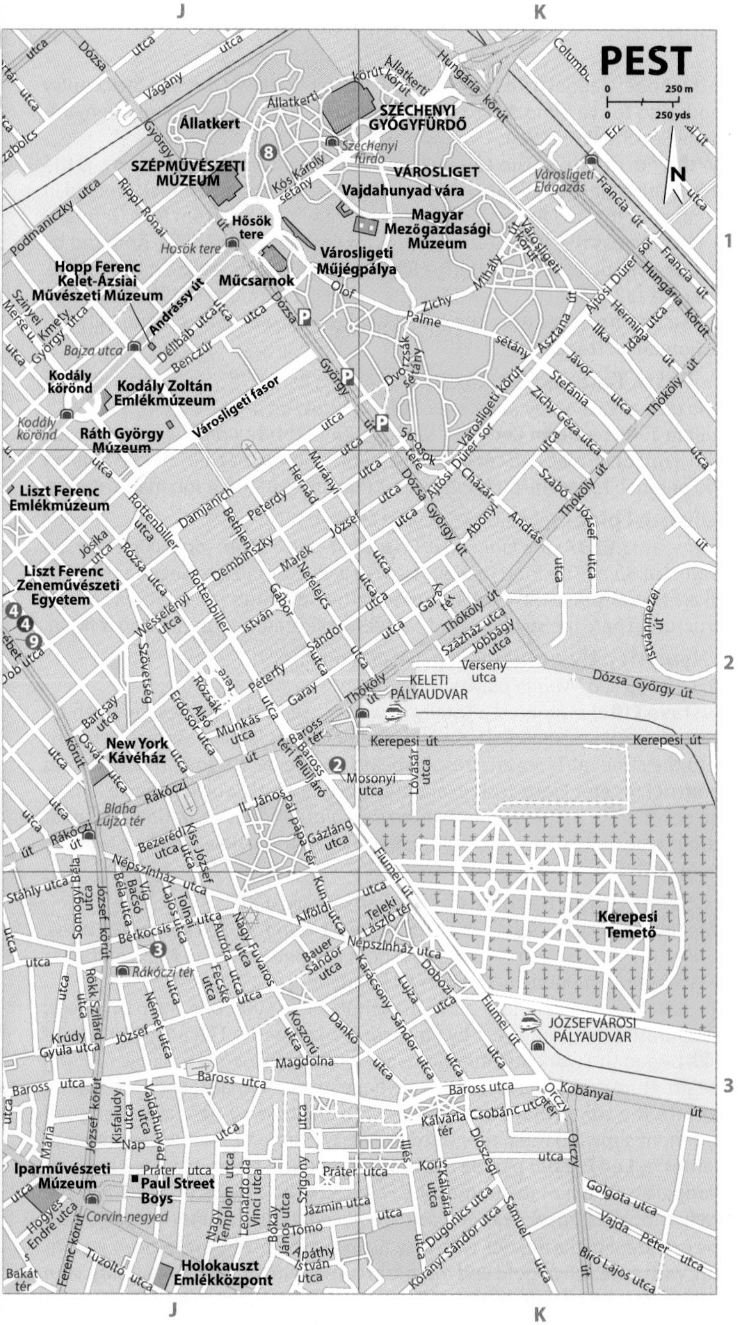

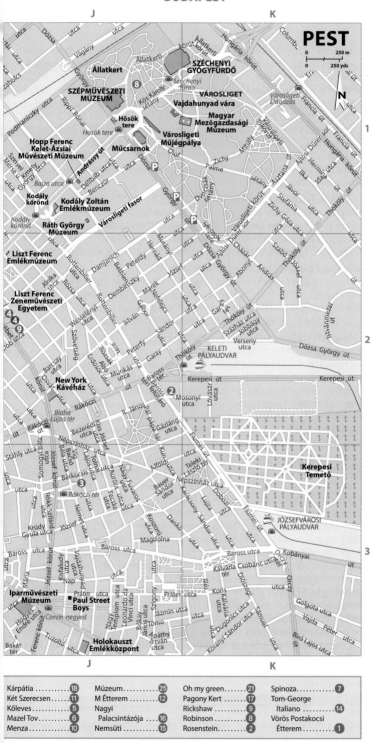

- Kárpátia 18
- Két Szerecsen 11
- Kőleves 5
- Mazel Tov 6
- Menza 10
- Múzeum 25
- M Étterem 12
- Nagyi Palacsintázója 16
- Nemsüti 15
- Oh my green 21
- Pagony Kert 17
- Rickshaw 9
- Robinson 8
- Rosenstein 2
- Spinoza 7
- Tom-George Italiano 14
- Vörös Postakocsi Étterem 1

as the Angel Gabriel. To its critics this seems to play down the way the country tended to turn a blind eye to the deportation of the Jews and the Romanis in the Second World War.

On the north side of the square, surrounded by semicircular lawns, is the only monument in Budapest dedicated to the Soviets, an **obelisk** erected in memory of the Red Army soldiers who liberated the city from Nazi Germany in 1945. Across the street is the **American Embassy**; the USA is honored by way of a statue of General Harry Hill Bandholtz, which is also in the square. After the fall of the short-lived Hungarian Soviet Republic in 1919, the general rescued treasures from the National Museum, which was being pillaged by Romanian troops.

★★ **Posta Takarékpénztár** (Postal Savings Bank) H2

Hold utca 4. M 3 Arany János utca; BUS 15, 115 Hold utca.

Built in 1901 by **Ödön Lechner**, the exterior of this building is very colorful, with a riot of mosiac and ceramic ornamentation; the overall effect is striking and original. Today the building houses the offices of the Hungarian Treasury.

Belvárosi piac (Hold Street Covered Market) H2

Hold utca 13. M 3 Arany János utca. Open Mon–Sat, 6.30am–6pm (Mon 5pm, Fri *10pm, Sat 4pm).* The food market is worth a visit, not just to see the wonderful array of produce on display, but also the building's renovated ironwork structure. There are several good canteen-style eateries on the upper floor.

★ **Nyugati pályaudvar** (Nyugati Rail Terminus) H1

M 3 and Tram 4, 6 Nyugati pályaudvar.

Gustave Eiffel visualized a totally new concept in station design when he created this skilful mix of steel, glass, and brick—its large glass facade opens onto the street at Térez krt. Despite being unable to visit the private waiting room of Emperor Franz Joseph and the lovely Sissi, it's worth taking a look at the ticket office hall *(at the bottom, on the right)*, whose decoration and great height give you an idea of the magnificence of the whole building, waiting room included.

★★ **Szent István Bazilika** (St. Stephen's Basilica) H2

Szent István tér. M 1 Bajcsy-Zsilinszky út or M 1 and 2 Deák Ferenc tér. www.bazilika.biz. Open Mon–Fri, 9am–5pm; Sat, 9am–1pm; Sun, 1pm–5pm. No charge. See website for program of concerts (in Hungarian).

Construction began in 1851 and was completed in 1906, and the basilica was inaugurated that same year by Emperor Franz Joseph. The architect, József Hild, began the work but after his death in 1867 Miklós Ybl took over, giving the structure its colossal, almost overwhelming neo-Renaissance appearance. Set into the somewhat austere exterior is an archway beneath a sculpted pediment showing the Virgin surrounded by Hungarian saints. A number of statues by **Leó Fessler** parade high up around the exterior, including the Four Evangelists (drum of the dome), the Fathers of the Church (towers), and the twelve apostles (apse): *walk around the building starting on the right-hand side.*

The grandeur of the interior, with a layout in the shape of a Greek cross, is startling, with a wealth of gold and marble ornamentation. The dome (315ft/96m high) is decorated with mosaics. On the high altar is a statue of St. Stephen himself sculpted from Carrara marble, with bas-reliefs showing scenes from the saint's life.

The **Chapel of the Holy Dexter** *(to the left of the choir)* displays one of the basilica's most prized treasures. It is a relic believed to be the right hand of St. Stephen and each year on 20 August it is carried in procession to celebrate

Detail of Postal Savings Bank building
© Maurizio Borgese/hemis.fr

the festival for the saint (canonized in 1083), who was also the first king of Hungary, Stephen I (see p109).

Körpanoráma (Panorama Tower) – *Open 10am–4.30pm (6.30pm in summer). Ft600.* Climb up for a superb **panoramic view★★**.

★ **Gresham Palota** (Gresham Palace) G2

Széchenyi tér 5–6. Tram 2 Eötvös tér.

Another example of the Secessionist style in Budapest (1907) and one of the city's most important buildings. It bears the name of a London insurance company, which itself took the name of the founder of the first London Stock Exchange (the Royal Exchange), **Thomas Gresham** (1519–79), who was a financial advisor to Queen Elizabeth I. The facade overlooking Széchenyi tér is decorated with reliefs sculpted in stone. Between the two world wars, artists would meet here at the Gresham Café. Today the palace houses a luxury hotel, the Four Seasons Hotel Gresham Palace.

Magyar Tudományos Akadémia (Hungarian Academy of Sciences) G2

Széchenyi tér 9. Tram 2 Eötvös tér. This is a fine example of a 19C neo-Renaissance building. During the first diet (parliamentary assembly) of 1825–27, Count **István Széchenyi** offered to donate a year's income to build this academy. On the exterior of the top floor are six statues representing the academy's six departments: law, science, mathematics, philosophy, languages, and history. The side facing the Danube features other allegorical statues representing archeology, poetry, astronomy, and political science.

At the corners of the building stand statues of key figures from history, skilled in many different fields: English physicist and mathematician Isaac Newton, Russian scientist Mikhail Lomonosov, Italian astronomer and mathematician Galileo Galilei, Hungarian linguist Gyula Révay, French scientist and philosopher René Descartes, and German philosopher and mathematician Gottfried Leibnitz.

★★ Belváros (Inner City)

Pest map (p48–49). Access: M 3 or 4 Kálvin tér; Tram 47, 49 Kálvin tér; Bus 9, 15, 115 Kálvin tér.

Together with Lipótváros, Belváros forms the historic center of Pest. This district of banks, government departments, businesses, cafés, and restaurants is very lively during the day and its pedestrianized streets are perfect for shopping. During the evening or on Sundays when the traffic is quieter, a stroll along the river here is extremely pleasant.

★ **Szabó Ervin könyvtár** (Metropolitan Ervin Szabó Library) H3

Szabó Ervin tér 1. M 3, 4 Kálvin tér. ℘ (1) 411 5000. www.fszek.hu. Open Mon–Fri, 10am–8pm; Sat, 10am–4pm. Ft1,000.

The Szabó Ervin Library is housed in three adjacent buildings. The principal structure is the magnificent **neo-Baroque Wenckheim Palace**, whose flamboyantly ornate exterior includes impressive wrought iron gates. Despite the fact that it is a working library you can take a look inside if you buy an entrance ticket; you will find yourself in the company of the many students who study here.

On the fourth floor you can peep inside sumptuous boudoirs and ballrooms. The **reading room**★ (smoking room) has beautiful carved wood paneling and a spiral staircase leading to an upper gallery. The cafeteria by the entrance to the library is in the former palace stables.

★★ **Magyar Nemzeti Múzeum** (Hungarian National Museum) H3

Múzeum krt. 14–16. M 3, 4 Kálvin tér. ℘ (1) 338 2122. mnm.hu. Open Tue–Sun, 10am–6pm. Ft2,600 (free with the Budapest Card). Audioguide in English Ft750, from the museum shop. Guided tours in English on reservation. ℘ (1) 327 7749.

Founded in 1802 by Count **Ferenc Széchenyi**, the museum is housed in a neoclassical palace fronted with a very imposing portico of Corinthian columns. The carvings on the tympanum are allegorical depictions of Pannonia (an ancient region of Central Europe that today equates to modern Hungary and parts of Croatia, Serbia, Bosnia-Herzegovina, Slovenia, Austria, and Slovakia), surrounded by the Arts and Sciences. The statue in front of the building depicts the great 19C Hungarian poet **János Arany** (1817–82). Other statues of scholars, poets, and politicians are scattered about the garden around the museum.

On the first (ground) floor, the coronation robe of purple Byzantine silk was a gift from King Stephen I and his wife to the basilica in Székesfehérvár. It dates from the same period as the crown jewels that are displayed in the Parliament Building. Rooms on the first of the upper levels depict key moments in the country's history, from the arrival of the Magyar tribes to the modern post-Communist period. Each era is well illustrated with maps, plans, paintings, and artworks, using items from everyday life including weapons, furniture, and clothes, as well as video footage.

In the room devoted to the era of King Matthias I, the beautiful Gothic choir stalls come from the church at Bártfa (Bardejov in present-day Slovakia). In the next room (covering the Ottoman occupation from the second half of the 16C to the beginning of the 17C), there are more choir stalls, this time from the Franciscan church at Nyírbátor, in eastern Hungary; they represent a highpoint in Hungarian woodworking of the time, particularly notable in the intricate detail of the work. And don't miss the room dedicated to the expulsion of the Turks, which has a ceramic coffered ceiling.

The rooms covering the modern era illustrate the role played by Hungary during this time and its suffering under the grip of dictators such as Miklós Horthy, who allied himself with Hitler's Germany and turned a blind eye to the activities of the sinister Hungarian Nazi party, and Mátyás Rákosi, who engineered the Red Terror during the 1950s. Also covered is the 1956 Revolution, the end of Communism, and the proclamation of the Hungarian Republic on 23 October 1989.

★ **Ferences templom** (Franciscan Church) H3

Ferenciek tere 2. M *3 Ferenciek tere.* The church is entered through a porch with columns on either side and the arms of the Franciscan Order above. The three niches set into the frontage contain statues of St. Peter of Alcantara, St. Antony of Padua, and St. Francis of Assisi. The interior, decorated in the Baroque style, has a single, central aisle. **Franz Liszt** lived for a time in the Franciscan monastery nearby; it is no longer in existence, but the place in the church where he sat when attending mass is marked on one of the church pews. The life of the Virgin Mary is the theme of the ceiling frescoes and the fine pulpit of carved wood is decorated with the twelve apostles.

★ **Egyetemi templom** (University Church) H3

Papnövelde utca 7. M *3, 4 Kálvin tér.*

The Church of St. Mary the Virgin, commonly known as the University Church, has to be the city's most admired Baroque church. It was originally part of a monastery belonging to the Order of St. Paul, the only religious order founded in Hungary in the 13C and abolished in 1782 during the reign of Joseph II. The exterior is very impressive, with a central pediment high up featuring the Pauline Order's emblem and flanked by statues of St. Paul the Hermit and St. Anthony the Hermit. Two towers topped with onion domes, each with a cross, stand on either side. A very fine carved wooden door leads to an interior that is magnificently decorated with frescoes (those on the dome show scenes from the life of the Virgin Mary), marble effects, gilt ornamentation, and carved wood. In the choir above the altar is a copy of the Black Madonna of the Jasna Góra monastery in Poland. The **pulpit★★** was created by the monks, as were the other carved wooden decorations in the church (the confessional boxes, the balustrade of the organ loft, and the pews).

★ **Szerb templom** (Serbian Church) H3

Szerb utca 2–4. M *3, 4 Kálvin tér.*

This 18C Orthodox church is a reminder of the Serbian community that once lived in the area. The church sits behind tall iron gates and high walls; a place full of charm and tranquility.

★ **Váci utca** (Váci Street) H3

M *3, 4 Kálvin tér or* M *3 Ferenciek tere.*

The area around Váci utca is not to be missed, especially the section between Vörösmarty tér and Szabadsajtó út. Váci utca itself is a lively, pedestrianized **shopping street**, with some useful currency exchange kiosks. A little leisurely browsing never goes amiss and you will find shops selling clothes, tableware, items stitched with traditional embroidery, CDs, books, and jewelry. Street musicians, mime artists, and other entertainers add to the general ambience in the warmer months, hoping to receive a few forints for their efforts, as well as stalls selling postcards, guidebooks, and illustrated books about the city.
Váci utca is another street where the occasional glance upward is worthwhile to see some of the **architectural detail**, in particular Nos. 5, 11a (Art Nouveau), 13 (the oldest building in the street in neo-classical style), 15 (a wooden facade), and 18 (ceramic decoration).
On the corner of Váci utca and Régiposta utca, is **Hermész-díszkút** (the Fountain of Hermes). The Greek god Hermes is the messenger of the gods with responsibility for commerce, among other things, appropriately enough

in this area. Other shopping streets that are worth exploring around Váci utca include **Petőfi Sándor utca**, **Párizsi utca**, **Haris köz**, and **Kígyó utca**.

★ **Párisi udvar** (Paris Passage) H3

Petőfi Sándor utca 2–4. M *3 Ferenciek tere.* This passage in the heart of the city is truly unique. The two entrances and the interior are a jumble of different architectural styles—Byzantine, Moorish, Venetian, Renaissance, neo-Gothic, and the inevitable Art Nouveau. In the past the passage housed cafés and small stores, similar to the covered passages that were popular in cities across Europe at the end of the 19C, including Paris from where this one takes its name. However, the passage now forms part of a luxury hotel.

Városház utca (Városház Street) H3

M *3 Ferenciek tere.*

Polgármesteri hivatal (City Hall) is a pink-colored building that was designed by Austrian architect Martinelli during the late Baroque period (after 1710), despite looking more early Baroque in style. It has simple proportions with tall vaulted corridors connecting the rooms and hallways. It was originally a home for disabled soldiers.

Pest megyei Önkormányzat (Pest District County Hall) has occupied this green neo-classical building since 1895. As the plaques in the courtyard will tell you, famous politicians such as Lajos Kossuth and István Széchenyi, and writers such as Sándor Petőfi worked here in the past. There is no charge to enter the courtyard.

Szervita tér (Szervita Square) H3

M *3 Ferenciek tere.* Two buildings with very interesting frontages give onto this tiny square. The lower section of the **former Török Bank** (No. 3) is very modern, made of glass and steel, while the top half has a spectacular allegorical Secessionist mosaic depicting the history of Hungary.

A music store occupies **Rózsavölgyi-ház** (No. 5). It includes a venue for concerts upstairs and features stylized motifs from traditional folklore that anticipate Art Deco (with friezes between the floors). Dating from 1912, the building is by **Béla Lajta**, one of the forerunners of modern architecture in Hungary.

★ **Vörösmarty tér** (Vörösmarty Square) H2

M *1 Vörösmarty tér.* All visitors pass through this square at least once during their stay as its location in the very heart of the pedestrianized area makes it impossible to miss. A **monument to Mihály Vörösmarty** in Carrara marble stands in the center, a man who gave his name to many a street and square in the city. He was a Romantic poet who lived during the first half of the 19C (1800–55) and was fiercely patriotic. On the base of the statue you can see several figures portrayed in the act of reciting verses from his celebrated poem *Szózat* (*Exhortation,* 1840), which became a patriotic song and a kind of second national anthem, sung at the end of ceremonial gatherings.

In summer street musicians, artists, and—if you are brave enough to sit for them—caricaturists who will draw your portait are clustered around the monument and the crowds spill out over the café terraces. It is also here in the square that you will find the famous **Café Gerbeaud★**, a meeting place for the upper echelons of society in the early 20C. The successful Swiss confectioner and chocolate producer Émile Gerbeaud opened it in 1884. Take a look inside, if only to admire its turn-of-the-century charm, or succumb to the temptation of one of the cakes (*see Taking a Break, p83*).

Pest Redout
© Ulrich Reichel/imageBROKER/age fotostock

★ **Pesti Vigadó** (Pest Redout) G2

Ⓜ *1 Vörösmarty tér.* The Pest Redout is a very fine example of the style known as Hungarian Romanticism. The building replaced an earlier concert hall on the site, the short-lived Redoute. Pesti Vigadó was completed in 1864, following plans drawn up by Frigyes Feszl, and was designed as a venue for great ceremonies, concerts, balls, and other spectacular events. It continues as a performance venue today and is one of the best-known concert halls in the city. The side facing the square is punctuated with columns topped with crowns and is extravagantly decorated with sculptures.

★★ **Duna korzó** (Danube Promenade) G2–3

Ⓜ *3 Ferenciek tere.* This tree-lined promenade, which runs alongside the river between Széchenyi tér and Petőfi tér (look for the statue of the poet Sándor Petőfi at one end of a small garden just past the Marriott Hotel), affords the best panoramic view of Budapest, taking in the Danube, Chain Bridge, Elizabeth Bridge, Buda Castle, and Gellért Hill. At night, when everything is lit up, the view is particularly lovely.

★ **Belvárosi plébánia templom** (Inner-city Parish Church) H3

Ⓜ *3 Ferenciek tere.* The oldest church in the Hungarian capital was built on the site of a Romanesque church, in which, according to legend, St. Gellért was buried. With its two symmetrical bell towers on either side of the porch, it is one of the iconic symbols of the city. The building is a mix of several different styles, indicative of the different periods of its construction. For example, the Gothic buttresses that contrast with the Baroque exterior.

As soon as you step inside, your eyes are naturally drawn to the Gothic choir with its cross vaulting, in front of which is a triumphal arch. The Baroque nave is covered by a barrel vault and on the walls that separate the choir from the nave, there are red marble tabernacles. During the Turkish occupation the church was converted into a mosque, a trace of which remains in the form of a mihrab (prayer niche) in the apse to the right of the choir. The pulpit is a fine example of Baroque wood carving.

★★ Andrássy út (Andrássy Avenue)

Pest map (p 48–49). Access: M line 1.

One of the first subway lines to operate in Europe (1896). In spite of its age, it takes only 10min to travel from the center of the city to City Park. Bus 105 runs the length of the avenue. This is the city's most elegant avenue, sometimes dubbed "Budapest's Champs-Élysées." Andrássy út can indeed boast of having some of the city's finest buildings decorated with mosiacs, statues, and friezes, to the extent that together with the Underground (subway), and Heroes' Square, it was listed as a UNESCO World Heritage Site in 2002. Vibrant and lively, with not just numerous stores and boutiques but also theaters, museums, and an opera house, it transforms into a chic residential road after Kodály Köröndn (*see p58*), where it is lined with beautiful villas, opulent private mansions, and buildings decorated with sculptures. Many foreign embassies are also located here.

★★ **Magyar Állami Operaház** (Hungarian State Opera House) H2

Andrássy út 22. M 1 Opera. (30) 279 5677. www.opera.hu. Guided tours daily at 2pm, 3pm, & 4pm (in English). Ft2,500 (short concert included).

The neo-Renaissance opera house was built between 1875 and 1884 by **Miklós Ybl**. Opera goers are greeted by a grand porch entrance with a loggia above. In the two niches on either side of the entrance are statues of the great Hungarian composers **Franz Liszt** (1811–86) on the right and **Ferenc Erkel** (1810–93) on the left. Erkel was a pianist, composer, and talented conductor. He wrote the *Hymnusz*, the Hungarian national anthem, as well as several operas, and conducted the concert given to mark the grand opening of the Opera House on 27 September 1884, when the overture to his opera *Hunyadi László* was played, among other pieces.

The upper part of the building is decorated with a balustrade, upon which are mounted statues of famous composers (including Mozart, Beethoven, Rossini, Wagner, Bizet, Tchaikovsky, and Smetana).

The **interior** is sumptuous with a foyer, "smoker's corridor," auditorium (with frescoes on the ceiling by Károly Lotz depicting the *Apotheosis of Music*), reception room, and a regal staircase resplendent with gilding, wood paneling, frescoes, paintings, and marble ornamentation.

★ **Új Színház** (New Theater) H2

Paulay Ede utca 35. M 1 Opera. Set slightly back from Andrássy út, this is a very impressive reconstruction (1990) of the original building designed by **Béla Lajta** (1909). On the front, at the top, nine gilded ceramic angels hold turquoise cartouches bearing the name of the theater. The interior, a fine example of very early Art Deco, is interesting, unusually blending the colors of cream and blue alongside curved metal grills, mirrors, and chromed light fittings.

★ **Magyar Fotográfusok Háza** (Hungarian House of Photography) H2

Nagymező utca 20. M 1 Opera. (30) 505 0455. maimano.hu. Open Tue–Sun, noon–7pm. Closed public holidays. Ft1,500 (free with the Budapest Card).

The former home and studio of the great Hungarian photographer **Mai Manó** (1855–1917) lies in the heart of the theater district and today houses a photography museum. Temporary exhibitions of work by Hungarian and foreign photographers alike are held in this lovely 19C building, where you can admire a magnificent staircase with an intricate wrought iron balustrade, along with frescoes, stucco work, stained glass windows by Miksa Róth, and a studio beneath a skylight. From the foyer you can see across to the beautiful frontage of the Operetta Theater opposite where Hungarian works and contemporary musicals are staged.

Robert Capa Kortárs Fotográfiai Központ
(Robert Capa Contemporary Photography Center) H2
Nagymező utca 8. M Opera. (1) 413 1310. capacenter.hu. Open 11am–6.30pm. Ft1,500 (free with the Budapest Card). Another example of the Hungarian interest in the art of photography. It was opened in 2013 and named in tribute to the famous Hungarian-born press photographer **Robert Capa** (1913–54), who was awarded the Medal of Freedom by General Eisenhower in 1947 for his work in the Second World War. It is the contemporary counterpart of the nearby Hungarian House of Photography. Temporary exhibitions that change regularly are held here.

Párisi Nagy Áruház (Paris department store) H2
Andrássy út 39. M 1 Opera or Oktogon. Behind this grand Art Deco exterior (1911) is a store that was once patronized by the most stylish women of the city. The former Lotz reception room on the mezzanine level, decorated with frescoes by Károly Lotz, is very grand and is now a Parisian-style café.
On the roof the 360 Bar *(see Bars, p85)* still offers panoramic views over the rooftops, just as it did back in 1911.

Liszt Ferenc tér (Franz Liszt Square) H2
M 1 Oktogon; Tram 4, 6 Oktogon. This shady **square** (in fact, rectangular in shape) encapsulates all the liveliness and energy of a district devoted to entertainment. Cafés, restaurants, and jazz clubs have all opened up here and in summer the terraces tempt passersby to stop and soak up the ambience.

Liszt Ferenc Zeneművészeti Egyetem (Franz Liszt Academy of Music)
Liszt Ferenc tér 8. M 1 Oktogon; Tram 4, 6 Oktogon. lfze.hu/en. H2
This is the main building of the academy founded by the celebrated composer who can be seen seated above the entrance courtesy of a bronze statue by Alajos Stróbl. The opulently decorated **foyer★** *(entrance on Király utca)* is a small Art Nouveau gem, with its gilt mosaic in the style of Klimt, metal medallions, green earthenware tiles, and a fountain, and not forgetting the original cloakrooms. The building underwent extensive renovation work that was completed in 2013.

★★ **Terror Háza** (House of Terror Museum) H2
Andrássy út 60. M 1 Vörösmarty utca. Tram 4, 6 Oktogon. (1) 374 2600. www.terrorhaza.hu. Open Tue–Sun, 10am–6pm. Closed public holidays. Ft3,000. Not suitable for children.
In 1944 this building and several others nearby were the general headquarters of the Hungarian Nazi party and then, between 1945 and 1956, that of the AVO and ÀVH, the Communist state security services. The visit begins on the second floor. The extent of the suffering people endured during these dark times is movingly evoked through the effective use of room reconstructions, documents, propaganda posters, uniforms, witness accounts and personal possessions, and film and audio tracks. Thanks to reconstructions of a train used for deportation and a wire-tapping room, it is as though we are witnesses at a crime scene and the entire exhibition powerfully evokes the atmosphere of the period.
A slow descent by elevator to the basement follows, accompanied by a film in which a torturer describes (with subtitles in English) what was expected

1

of him. In the basement the reconstructed torture chambers make a chilling impression on visitors without actually showing any equipment. In the final room, short films shot by amateurs show the departure of the Russian army from the city. It is revealing to look closely at the faces of the soldiers, they seem almost childlike, as though events have passed them by without knowing why they were there or indeed why they are leaving.

★ **Liszt Ferenc Emlékmúzeum** (Franz Liszt Memorial Museum) J2
Vörösmarty utca 35. M 1 Vörösmarty utca. (1) 322 9804. www.lisztmuseum.hu. Open Mon–Fri, 10am–6pm; Sat, 9am–5pm. Closed public holidays, 26 & 30 Dec. Ft2,000. Audioguide in English Ft700.
A reconstruction of the small service apartment in the old Academy of Music building where **Franz Liszt** lived for the last five years of his life (1881–86), when he would spend winters in Budapest. The rooms are presented as they were in Liszt's time, who by then had become very famous. The bedroom, office, and living room contain his personal possessions such as tuning forks, a pair of spectacles, letters, a hat, walking stick, gloves, a rosary, a prayer book given to him by the pope, and a portrait of his daughter Cosima. In the sitting room you can see the Bösendorfer piano which was the artist's favorite. A concert is held every Saturday at 11am (included in the price of the ticket).

Kodály körönd (Kodály Circus) J1
M *1 Kodály körönd.* Four identical buildings form this elegant circus (with a traffic intersection in the center). To emphasize its perfect symmetry, each of the four segments of lawn in the center contains a statue of one of the freedom fighters who were engaged in the struggle against the Ottoman Turks.

Kodály Zoltán Emlékmúzeum (Zoltán Kodály Museum) J1
Andrássy út 89. M 1 Kodály körönd . (1) 352 7106. kodaly.hu/museum. Open Wed–Fri, 10am–noon, 2pm–4.30pm (Sat 11am–2pm), visits by appointment only . Closed Aug. Ft1,500.
Along with Béla Bartók, **Zoltán Kodály** (*see p324*) had a great influence on 20C Hungarian music. The apartment where he lived from March 1924 until his death in March 1967, contains many of the great composer's personal possessions, such as his pianos, library of books, writing desk, and music scores. You will also discover his less well-known talent as a potter; a collection of his pots and vases is displayed in the dining room.

Hopp Ferenc Kelet-Ázsiai Művészeti Múzeum (Ferenc Hopp Museum of Asiatic Arts) J1
Andrássy út 103. M 1 Bajza utca. (1) 469 7762. hoppmuseum.hu. Open Tue–Sun, 10am–6pm. Ft1,200 (free with the Budapest Card). Guided tours in English on reservation (weekdays only). Ft10,000.
Ferenc Hopp (1833–1919) was an optician but also one of Hungary's great travelers, donating to his country objects he brought back from his many expeditions to Asia. The museum is in his former villa and exhibits Hopp's collection on rotation with other objects acquired in the years since the museum's founding. It includes exhibits from as far afield as Mongolia and Korea.

Városligeti fasor (Városliget Alley) J1
M *1 Bajza utca.* This tree-lined street provides an alternative route to Andrássy út if you are on your way to Városliget (*see p59*). It takes you through a residential area and contains some beautiful Art Nouveau villas that are well worth seeing. When you reach City Park, look out for the large **memorial to the 1848 and 1956 uprisings**.

★ **Ráth György Múzeum** (György Ráth Museum) J1
Városligeti fasor 12. M 1 Bajza utca. ✆ (1) 416 9601. www.imm.hu. Open Tue–Sun, 10am–6pm. Ft2,000 (reduced price with the Budapest Card).
Bought in 1901 by György Ráth, the first director of the Museum of Applied Arts, this villa reopened its doors as a museum in fall 2018. Having once been an annex to the Ferenc Hopp Museum (*see opposite*), it now houses a selection of the Art Nouveau collection from the Museum of Applied Arts (currently closed, *see p65*).

★★ Városliget (City Park)

Pest map (p48–49). Access: M 1 Hősök tere.
Városliget, along with Margitsziget (Margaret Island), is very popular in summer. Families come here in search of a shady spot and some fresh air in which to relax or walk, or to visit the baths, which are among the most beautiful in Budapest … and in winter they come to skate on the lake.

Hősök tere (Heroes' Square) J1
A huge square with the Museum of Fine Arts on one side and the Hall of Art on the other. Heroes' Square was designed by architect Albert Schickedanz and over the years has become a great assembly point for mass demonstrations or public celebrations.
At one end of the square is **Millenniumi emlékmű**★ (Millennium Monument). As the name implies it commemorates the one thousandth anniversary of the Magyar conquest and was unveiled in 1896. The central column is 118ft/36m high and carries a statue of the Angel Gabriel standing on a globe and bearing the Hungarian crown and an apostolic cross. An imposing group of sculptures depicting Prince Árpád on horseback accompanied by six other Magyar tribal chiefs are arranged around the plinth. The curved colonnade to the rear is divided into two symmetrical sections, on top of which are allegorical statues representing Labor and Wealth (on the left) and Knowledge and Glory (on the right), facing the chariots of War and Peace. Between each pair of columns are statues of historical figures (kings and princes) who left their mark on the country's history. Beneath each one is a relief sculpture depicting a scene from their life. The figures include Stephen I, Béla IV, Louis the Great, Matthias Corvinus, Gábor Bethlen (prince of Transylvania), Ferenc II Rákóczi, and Lajos Kossuth, hero of the 1848–49 Revolution.

★★★ **Szépművészeti Múzeum** (Museum of Fine Arts) J1
Dózsa György út 41 (Hősök tere). M 1 Hősök tere. ✆ (1) 469 7100. www.szepmuveszeti.hu. Open Tue–Sun, 10am–5.30pm. Ticket office closes at 5pm. Ft3,200 (free with the Budapest Card). Audioguide in English Ft800.
The modern art collections (after 1800) are exhibited at the Hungarian National Gallery (*see p35*).
Renowned for its painting collection in particular, the museum boasts an entrance that is as impressive as the exhibits inside behind a colossal portico made of eight Greek-inspired Corinthian columns (the pediment is a replica of the one on the Temple of Zeus at Olympia).
The historic halls have been restored, including several that had been closed for a number of years but are now open again to the public, thus increasing the exhibition space available. It has therefore been possible for the collection of Hungarian old masters, previously on display at the National Gallery (*see p35*), to become part of the Museum of Fine Arts collection once more.

Museum of Fine Arts
© Hungarian Tourism Agency

Hungarian Baroque Art (1600–1800) – Jakab Bogdány and Ádám Mányoki are two of the most famous exponents of the portraits of aristocrats and still lifes that evoke the Baroque style of the courts so well. A special hall is dedicated to 18C sculptures, religious paintings, and funerary portaits, with monumental works and richly decorated retables.

The Baroque art of Vienna is represented by Austrian Franz Anton Maulbertsch, a highly successful painter and engraver during the Austro-Hungarian Empire.

European Art (1250–1600) – Examples of work by the great European schools dating from the 13C to the end of the 16C provide an impressive overview of the art of the period.

Italian Painting – The Quattrocento (15C) is represented by Domenico Ghirlandaio *(St. Stephen)* and Gentile Bellini *(Portrait of Caterina Cornaro, Queen of Cyprus)*. Works from the following century include those by Leonardo da Vinci (an equestrian statuette attributed to him), Raphaël, Titian *(Portrait of Marcantonio Trevisani),* Veronese *(Portrait of a Man),* and Tintoretto. The Baroque rooms bring together works by Tiepolo, in particular.

German Painting – Among the exhibits, look out for a 15C masterpiece by Hans Holbein the Elder *(The Dormition of the Virgin)*. The German Renaissance is represented by Albrecht Dürer *(Portrait of a Young Man)* and Lucas Cranach the Elder.

Flemish Painting – From the 16C you will find work by Hans Memling, Gerard David *(The Nativity)*, Bruegel the Elder, and masterpieces by Rubens, Van Dyck, and Jordaens. You can also see one of the museum's more recent acquisitions—*Portrait of Princess Mary* (eldest daughter of King Charles I of England) painted in 1641 by Van Dyck.

Spanish Painting – Notable works include El Greco's *Mary Magdalene*, his much darker painting *The Agony in the Garden of Gethsemane,* and also *The Lunch* by Velasquez. Goya's *Young Woman with a Pitcher* is another example of the genre. Paintings by Murillo *(The Infant Jesus Distributing Bread to Pilgrims)* and Jusepe de Ribera, known for his powerful realism, complete this school.

Other treasures in the museum include the remarkable pieces in the department of **Egyptian antiquities**, the **Greek and Roman antiquities**, the **collections of 20C art** (Victor Vasarely, Simon Hantaï, Pablo Picasso, among others), and not forgetting the section devoted to **European sculpture**.

Műcsarnok/Kunsthalle (Hall/Palace of Art) J1

Dózsa György út 37. M 1 Hősök tere. ✆ (1) 460 7000. www.mucsarnok.hu. Open Tue–Sun, 10am–6pm (Thu, noon–8pm). Ft600/2,900 depending on visit (free with the Budapest Card). Shop and café (open Tue–Sun, 10am–11pm).

On one side of Heroes' Square, facing the Museum of Fine Arts, this building resembles a Greek temple. It holds temporary exhibitions only. An immense **statue of Stalin** (26ft/8m high) used to stand nearby but this major symbol of Soviet oppression was torn down and destroyed during the uprising on the night of 23 October 1956 (*see p361*).

Néprajzi Múzeum (Museum of Ethnography) J1

www.neprajz.hu. The museum was originally housed in the former Royal Court of Cassation in the Lipótváros district, but the space was too cramped and it closed in December 2017 in preparation for its reopening in the new museum hub in Városliget. See the website above for details.

The ethnographic collection is particularly large, providing a good insight into rural communities from the 18C to the beginning of the 20C, before the Treaty of Trianon (1920) sealed the fate of Hungary after the First World War (*see p354*). Local culture, fishing, crafts, fairs and markets, family life, and traditional festivals are illustrated with photographs, costumes, and objects from everyday life.

1

Állatkert (Zoological Garden) J1

Állatkerti krt. 6–12. M 1 Széchenyi Fürdő. ✆ (1) 273 4900. www.zoobudapest.com. Open May–Aug, 9am–6pm (Fri–Sun, 7pm); Apr & Sept, 9am–5.30pm (Fri–Sun, 6pm); Mar & Oct, 9am–5pm (Fri–Sun, 5.30pm); Jan–Feb & Nov–Dec, 9am–4pm (24 & 31 Dec, 1pm). Ft3,300, children Ft2,200 (reduced price with Budapest Card).

Opened in 1866, this is one of the oldest zoos in the world. Entry is through a large doorway flanked by two stone elephants. Inside you can see more than 500 mammals, 700 birds, and 1,500 reptiles and fish. The original Art Nouveau buildings were restored—the elephant house looks like a palace from an Arabian fairy tale—and the animal facilities updated in the 1990s.

Városligeti Műjégpálya (Városliget Ice Rink) J1

Olof Palme sétány 5. M 1 Hősök tere. ✆ (1) 363 2673. www.mujegpalya.hu. Ice rink: hours and ticket prices vary, see website.

This 193,750sq ft/18,000sq m open-air ice rink, the largest in Europe, has been a favorite with locals since the end of the 19C. The lake, which freezes over naturally in winter, gave way to an artifical ice rink in 1926, becoming one of the capital's unmissable attractions. In spring it becomes a boating lake once more.

★ **Vajdahunyad vára** (Vajdahunyad Castle) J1

M 1 Hősök tere or Széchenyi fürdő. ✆ (1) 422 0765. www.vajdahunyadcastle.com. Courtyard accessible 24hrs.

This castle is an eccentric mix of styles. Built for the 1896 Millennial Exhibition, it was designed to illustrate Hungary's varied architectural history, which explains why Roman, Gothic, and Baroque can be found side by side. The main section was inspired by Hunedoara (Corvin) Castle (formerly Vajdahunyad) in Transylvania, in present-day Romania. Approaching via the bridge over the lake

THE JEWISH COMMUNITY IN BUDAPEST
The Jews arrived mainly from Central Europe during the 17–18C and settled first in Buda in the castle district. The early years were difficult for this "foreign" community, until Holy Roman emperor Joseph II signed an Edict of Tolerance (1783) giving the Jews the same rights as Christians. In the second half of the 19C, the Jews settled in Pest, a law having been passed allowing them to own land. By the end of the century, the Jewish community was 170,000 strong and one of the best integrated in Europe. However, after the First World War, a wave of anti-semitism broke out. By 1938 and now allied with Nazi Germany, Hungary passed anti-Jewish laws and the situation worsened in 1944 after the Germans entered Hungary. By the end of 1944, the Jews in the capital had been confined to a ghetto, while those elsewhere were murdered or deported by the Arrow Cross, the Fascist party that came to power in October of that year. It is estimated that some 90 percent of Hungary's 600,000 Jews died during the war.

and through a gatehouse, you arrive in the courtyard, where on the left is the **Jáki Chapel**. Above the chapel entrance are statues of the twelve apostles, very reminiscent of the 13C equivalent in the church of the old Benedictine abbey at Ják in western Hungary. In front of the Baroque part of the castle is a strange figure, seated on a marble bench, whose features are hidden under a hood. This bronze statue (1903) by Miklós Ligeti is entitled **Anonymous**, a scribe at the court of King Béla III (12C) whose identity is unknown. There is another sculpture to look out for, a bust of Béla Lugosi, the Hungarian-American actor who made the role of Count Dracula his own in the original 1931 film; it stands in a niche on the corner of an exterior wall.

The castle houses the **Magyar Mezőgazdasági Múzeum** (Museum of Hungarian Agriculture), which covers the history of working the land, raising livestock, fishing, hunting, forestry, and viticulture up to the present day. *www.mezogazdasagimuzeum.hu. Some signs in English. Open Tue–Sun, 10am–5pm. Ft1,600.*

★★★ Széchenyi Gyógyfürdő (Széchenyi Baths) JK1

Állatkerti krt. 11. M *1 Széchenyi fürdő.* *(See also Baths, p 88.)*

The baths are said to be one of the largest thermal spring complexes in Europe and the site is certainly vast and as Baroque as you could wish for with gilding, frolicking cherubs, and statues languishing in the sun. Spend a day with the children, lounge around with friends, play chess by the pool, or paddle in one of the dozen or so pools … there is something for everyone. Outside is a large swimming pool (164ft/50m), a thermal water pool (100°F/38°C), an activity pool, and naturist areas on the terraces, not forgetting a restaurant to satisfy appetites sharpened by so much activity. It looks even more extraordinary in winter, when snow covers the pools and clouds of steam drift over the entire area giving it a fairy-tale appearance. There are also several smaller pools indoors, including thermal and immersion pools and an underwater traction pool.

When you leave, walk around to the opposite side of the building where you will see the grand entrance to the thermal hospital where time seems to have stood still. Discovered in 1897, the Széchenyi springs are the deepest and warmest in the city (167°F/75°C).

★ Erzsébetváros (Old Jewish Quarter)

Pest map (p48–49). Access: M 2 Astoria, M 1 Deák Ferenc Tér; Tram 47, 48, 49 Astoria; BUS 7, 9 Astoria.

Roughly bordered by Károly körút, Erzsébet körút, Dohány utca, and Király utca, the best way to explore the old Jewish quarter is on foot to soak up its unique atmosphere. It is also the fashionable haunt of Budapest's young people who crowd into its "ruin bars," the delapidated buildings reinventing the local nightlife.

★★ Dohány utcai Zsinagóga (Dohány Street Synagogue) H2

Dohány utca 2. M 2 Astoria; trolleybus 74 Nagy Diófa utca. ✆ (1) 413 5584. www.jewishtourhungary.com. Open Sun–Fri: May–Sept, 10am–8pm (Fri 4pm); Mar, Apr & Oct, 10am–6pm (Fri 4pm); Nov–Feb, 10am–4pm (Fri 2pm). Closed Sat & Jewish holidays. Ft5,000 (reduced price with the Budapest Card). Guided tour in English, daily at 10.30am.

Able to accommodate 3,000 people, this is the **largest synagogue** in Europe (and the second largest in the world after Temple Emanu-El in New York). It was built between 1854 and 1859 from plans drawn up by the Viennese architect Ludwig Förster. Inspired by Byzantine and Moorish architecture, it is a large building of light-colored brick, decorated with ceramic tiles, with onion domes on top of two towers either side of the main entrance. The interior is magnificent with two tiers of wooden galleries around the perimeter and lit by two great chandeliers, each weighing 1.7 tons/1.5 tonnes. Note the richness of the decoration and, in particular, the vaulted ceiling and Ark of the Covenant, where the sacred Torah is kept, the parchment scroll bearing the Law of Moses.

Magyar Zsidó Múzeum (Hungarian Jewish Museum) – The history and traditions of the Hungarian Jews are illustrated with objects, manuscripts, textiles, and paintings.

Raoul Wallenberg Emlékpark (Raoul Wallenberg Holocaust Memorial Park) Approximately 2,000 people are buried here, to the rear of the Dohány synagogue, where a weeping willow (*Tree of Life*) sculpted in steel by **Imre Varga** (1991) honors the memory of the Hungarian Jews murdered during the Second World War. A plaque is dedicated to the Righteous Among the Nations, including **Raoul Wallenberg**, the Swedish diplomat who risked his life to provide safe passage for tens of thousands of Jews. In 1945, after Budapest had been liberated from the Nazis by the Red Army, he was arrested and taken to the USSR where he disappeared. In 2000 his execution by the Soviet authorities was finally acknowledged by the Russians, although he was only declared officially dead by the Swedish government in 2016.

Lutz Carl emlékmű (Carl Lutz Memorial) H2

You will find this moving memorial outside **No. 12 Dob utca** in the former Budapest ghetto. It depicts the figure of a man lying on his back, trying to get up by asking an angel for help. It is a tribute to **Carl Lutz** (1895–1975), a Swiss diplomat who rescued many Jews, risking his own life in the process.

★ Rumbach utcai Zsinagóga (Rumbach Street Synagogue) H2

Rumbach Sebestyén utca 11–13. M 2 Astoria. Currently closed for building work but you can view the exterior. Built between 1869 and 1872, this is an early work by the Viennese architect Otto Wagner. The brick facade with its tall archways and two towers resembling minarets (similar to those on the Dohány Street Synagogue) has a Moorish feel, as has the richly decorated interior.

★ **New York Kávéház** (New York Café) J2

Erzsébet krt. 9–11. M 2 Blaha L. tér. www.newyorkcafe.hu. Open 9am–midnight.
The building was constructed between 1891 and 1895 for the New York Life Insurance Company as their Budapest office. In the early 20C the New York Café that opened on the first (ground) floor was a favorite haunt of journalists, writers, and poets, but it later fell into disrepair. However, the building has been completely restored and is now a luxury hotel, of which the café remains part.

Kerepesi Cemetery and Ferencváros

Pest map (p48–49).

If you are interested in Secessionist architecture, you won't want to leave Budapest without visiting the Museum of Applied Arts. And if you have sufficient time, Kerepesi Cemetery and the streets of Ferencváros are also interesting to walk around. A working-class district in the 19C, today Ferencváros is a laid-back area popular with families due to its proximity to the Danube, its public gardens, and bustling market. Finally, don't miss the Museum of Contemporary Art. It's a little eccentric, but you'll be won over by its wealth of modern exhibits that represent all aspects of the Hungarian Avant-garde.

★ **Kerepesi Temető** (Kerepesi Cemetery) K2–3

Fiumei út 16. M 2, 4 Keleti pályaudvar. Open Nov–Feb, 7.30am–5pm; Mar, 7am–5.30pm; Apr & Aug, 7am–7pm; May–Jul, 7am–8pm; Sept, 7am–6pm; Oct, 7am–5pm. No charge.
This landscaped cemetery was opened in 1847. Here, among the elegant tree-lined avenues is where you will find the bourgeoisie of the Austro-Hungarian Empire and the party bosses of the Communist era. Some of the tombs are an excuse for indulging in architectural fantasies (such as the headstone of statesman József Antall or the sweep of cherubs on the effigy of Lujza Blaha, a famous Hungarian actress and "the nation's nightingale"). Several other notable figures are buried here, among them the poets Mihály Vörösmarty and József Attila, along with the politicians Ferenc Deák, Lajos Batthyány, and Lajos Kossuth. It is one of the largest park cemeteries in Europe and provides photographers with infinite possibilities for capturing creative images. Close to the main entrance is the small **Piety Museum** that illustrates Hungarian death rituals with a collection of hearses, catafalques, and funeral urns *(open Mon–Fri, 9am–5pm; Sat, 10am–2pm; no charge).*

★ **Holokauszt Emlékközpont** (Holocaust Memorial Center) J3

Páva utca 39. M 3 Corvin-negyed. ✆ (1) 455 3333. hdke.hu. Open Tue–Sun, 10am–6pm. Ft1,400 (reduced price with the Budapest Card). Audioguide in English Ft850. Not suitable for children.
The Holocaust Memorial Center is both a museum and a research center with an educational vocation. It presents the Holocaust in Hungary in a way that at times makes difficult but compelling viewing—tracing the journeys of victims (both Jews and Romanis) from at first being deprived of their rights through to their extermination—via modern media (audio, film projections, interactive terminals, and so on). A synagogue hosts temporary exhibitions.

Paul Street Boys J3

Práter utca 11–15. M 3 Corvin-negyed. This bronze sculpture of boys playing a game of marbles depicts a scene from the eponymous novel written by Ferenc Molnár (1878–1952), Hungary's most popular author. It was unveiled in 2007 to mark the centenary of the book's publication.

Great Market Hall
© Paolo Paradiso/iStock

★★ **Iparművészeti Múzeum** (Museum of Applied Arts) J3

Üllői út 33–37. M 3 Corvin-negyed. www.imm.hu. Closed for renovation until end 2020.

Opened in 1896 on the occasion of Hungary's millennium celebrations, the building itself is another of the city's unmissable sights. The architect **Ödön Lechner** (his statue stands in front of the museum), dubbed the "Hungarian Gaudí," designed it in the Secessionist style, the Hungarian arm of Art Nouveau in which an Eastern influence is more evident (*see p375*). Step back and look up to see the beautiful decoration of the roofs and facades with ceramic tiles featuring floral and animal designs. Equally impressive is the ceiling in the entrance hall, which is a riot of flowers.

The rest of the interior is a little more subdued but still extremely fine. Beneath a large, glass atrium, lies a great hall with a mezzanine floor edged with dazzling white colonnades and balustrades around the perimeter. The museum's collection includes hundreds of European Arts and Crafts objects, arranged under five broad categories: porcelain, ceramics, and glassware; paper making, leather, bookbinding, and decorated paper; textiles; wood, carpentry, and cabinet making; metal and ironwork.

A selection of the museum's holdings is also on display at the **Ráth György Museum** (*see p59*).

★★ **Nagy Vásárcsarnok** (Great Market Hall) H3

Vámház krt. 1–3. M 4 Fővám tér. www.piaconline.hu. Open Mon 6am–5pm; Tue–Fri, 6am–6pm; Sat, 6am–3pm.

The central market in any city is usually one of the places tourists love to wander around, making them feel they are part of the local life, and the market in Budapest is no exception.

The exterior of this brick building, with its neo-Gothic towers, roofs of Zsolnay majolica, arches, and a clock on the central section, draws your attention straight away. It looks more like a railway station or a strange church/palace

FROM RABBIT TO MARGARET ISLAND

The Romans living in the neighboring city of Aquincum (*see p70*) would come to the island to cure their ailments in its thermal waters. During the Middle Ages, when it was a hunting ground for the kings of the Árpád dynasty, it was known as the Island of Rabbits.

In the 12C religious orders built several monasteries here and in the 13C, after having suffered defeat at the hands of the Mongol invaders, **King Béla IV** vowed that his daughter Margit (Margaret) would devote her life to God as soon as the country was liberated. True to his word, he built a convent for Dominican nuns—the ruins of which can still be seen—and sent his daughter there, who was then aged just nine. The Turkish occupation of the 16C and 17C led to the destruction of the religious buildings and the island remained uninhabited until the end of the 18C when it became the property of Joseph, archduke of Austria and palatine of Hungary, who transformed it into a vast public park.

hybrid. It was built at the end of the 19C as one of five covered markets designed by the architect **Samu Petz**. The municipal authorities had decided to replace the previous open-air markets, which were considered harmful to health due to the unpleasant odors they emitted. Inside you find yourself in a great hall of iron and glass with lofty ceilings. The first (ground) floor is full of stalls piled high with colorful fruit and vegetables, strings of garlic, garlands of chili peppers, plus huge salamis. Depending on what you are hoping to buy, it's worth comparing prices as you may find they are cheaper the further in you go from the entrance. Local spririts are also on sale, such as the celebrated apricot brandy *(barack pálinka)* and Unicum liqueur. On the upper level, a gallery runs around the perimeter of the hall where there are bars and stalls selling food, handicrafts, Hungarian wines, and several offering a wide range of table linen embroidered with motifs from Hungarian folklore.

★★ **Bálna** (The Whale) H3

Fővám tér 11–12. M 4 Fővám tér. Tram 2 Zsil utca. www.balnabudapest.hu. Open 10am–8pm (Fri–Sat, 10pm).

This vast glass-fronted **shopping and cultural center** opened in 2013 after considerable controversy over its shape. Budapest residents soon nicknamed it Bálna (whale), which stuck. If its contemporay outline radically alters the view of the Danube at this spot, it has nevertheless blended seamlessly into the landscape, not least because it sits on the remains of two renovated older buildings. Inside the "belly" are several boutiques and very nice restaurants, with a terrace overlooking the river, perfect for lunch or an aperitif before dinner. The **Új Budapest Galéria** (New Budapest Gallery), an exhibition space devoted to contemporary art, also has a home here. *(1) 388 6784. budapestgaleria.hu. Open Tue–Sun, 10am–6pm. Ft1,000 (free with the Budapest Card).*

★★ **Ludwig Múzeum Budapest**

(Ludwig Museum of Contemporary Art)

At MÜPA, Komor Marcell utca 1. HÉV 7 Közvágóhíd. Tram 1, 2 Közvágóhíd. (1) 555 3444. www.lumu.hu. Open Tue–Sun, 10am–6pm. Ft1,600 permanent collection (free with the Budapest Card). Budapest map(p68–69) C3, near Rákóczi hid (bridge).

The Museum of Contemporary Art moved from the Royal Palace to **MÜPA** (the Palace of Arts) to take advantage of the facilities and amount of space offered by this new arts complex. It occupies three floors with a total exhibition space of more than 29,063sq ft/2,700sq m. The first two floors are devoted to temporary exhibitions of works by Hungarian and foreign artists. The permanent collection, gifted by Irene and Peter Ludwig (a German industrialist and passionate collector—notably of Picasso, with 800 of his paintings, the largest collection in the world), is exhibited on an upper floor. The museum always tries to promote the work of Hungarian artists and the collection is not limited to the Ludwigs' donation as it continues to acquire other works. Among the best-known exponents of global trends in modern art exhibited here are, alongside Picasso (three later works), Roy Lichtenstein, Jean Tinguely, Frank Stella, Joseph Beuys, Robert Rauschenberg, Claes Oldenburg, Andy Warhol, and Jasper Johns. Also included is a work by Yoko Ono—a white chessboard on a white table. The Hungarian Avant-garde (1956–58) has not been forgotten, nor a new generation of artists including László Bartha, Béla Kondor, and István Mazzag, among others.

★★ Margitsziget (Margaret Island)

Maps: Budapest (p 68–69) & Pest (p48–49). Access: via the south of the island Tram 4, 6 Margitsziget/Margit híd; HÉV 5 Margit híd; M 3 Nyugati pályaudvar. Via the north of the island: Tram 1 Népfürdő utca/Árpád híd. To explore the island itself: BUS 26.

Two bridges provide access to the northern (Árpád Bridge) and southern (Margaret Bridge) ends of the island, which is 1.6mi/2.5km long and 0.3mi/500m wide. A green haven of peace far from the din of traffic (cars are not permitted on the island), it is rightly considered one of the most beautiful parks in the capital.

Margit híd (Margaret Bridge) BC1–2

The bridge was designed by French engineer Ernest Goűin; work began in 1872 and was completed in 1876. Unusually, the bridge consists of two spans that join at the tip of Margaret Island at an angle of 150 degees. Stand in the middle of the bridge looking south down the river to take in the **view★** of the Danube spanned by the Chain Bridge; on the right you can see Buda Castle and the Matthias Church and on the left, Pest and the Parliament Building. In the distance are Gellért Hill and the Liberty Statue.

Centenáriumi emlékmű (Centennial Memorial) G1

Close to the fountain marking the island's southern tip is the Centennial Memorial, a distinctive bronze sculpture shaped like a flame, which was unveiled in 1972 to mark the amalgamation of Buda, Pest, and Óbuda. A curious mix of objects are depicted on the inside of the memorial, including a ship's rudder, a propeller, and a cog wheel.

Palatinus strand (Palatinus Beach) B1

Facing the Buda side of the city, the vast complex of **Palatinus fürdő** (Palatinus Strand Baths, open all year, with indoor pools, *see p89*) includes several pools, a wave pool, and a lido, with some nice grassy areas for sunbathing. Needless to say, it gets pretty crowded in summer.

Művészsétány (Artists' Promenade) B2–C1

Lined with busts of famous Hungarian musicians, writers, and artists such as Franz Liszt, Ferenc Erkel, and Mór Jókai, the promenade runs across the center of the island, shaded by large plane trees, and leads to a neo-Romanesque chapel. Close by, the **rose garden** in the center of the island is a fragrant and charming place in which to wander (from May onward).

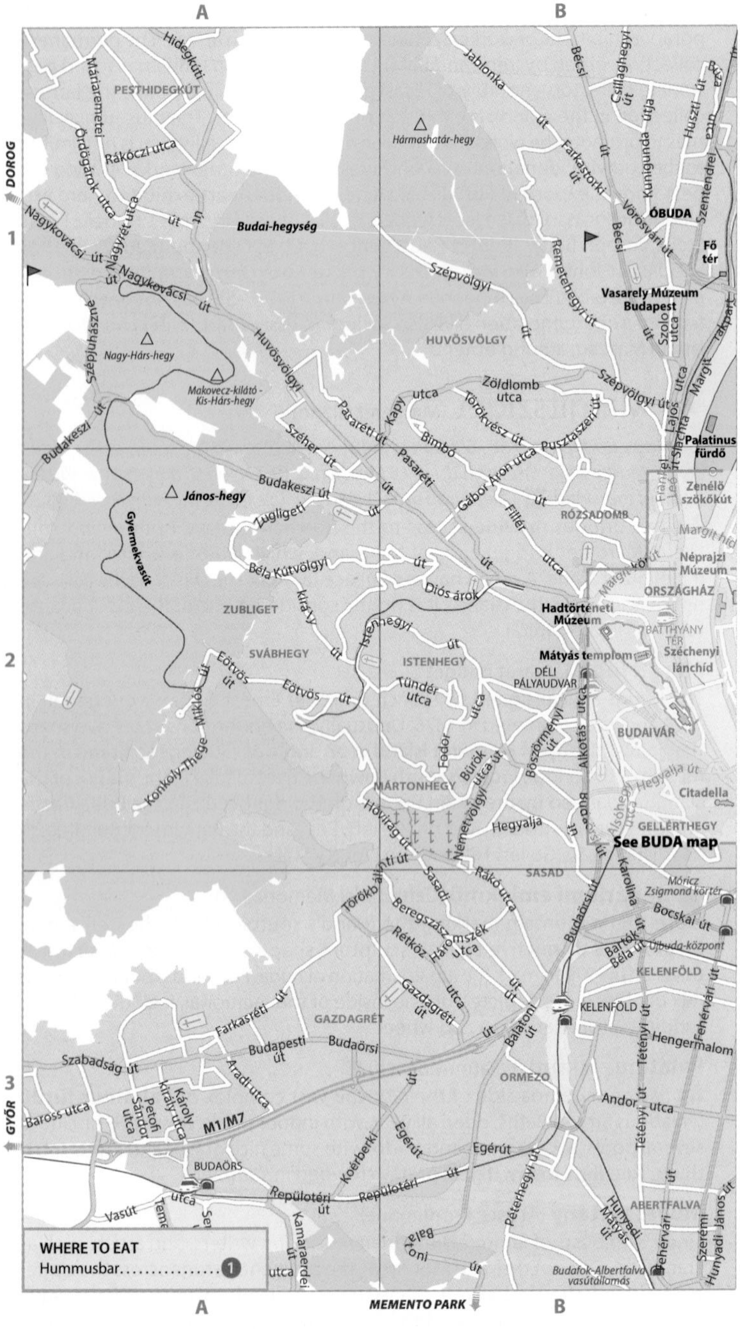
A
B
DOROG
GYŐR
MEMENTO PARK
1
2
3
PESTHIDEGKÚT
Hidegkúti
Máriaremetei
Ördögárok utca
Rákóczi utca
Nagykovácsi út
Nagyrét utca
Budai-hegység
Hármashatár-hegy
Jablonka út
Bécsi út
Csillaghegyi út
Kunigunda útja
Huszti út
Szentendrei
Farkastorki út
Vörösvári út
ÓBUDA
Fő tér
Vasarely Múzeum Budapest
Remetehegyi út
Szépvölgyi út
Szolo utca
Margit
HUVÖSVÖLGY
Nagy-Hárs-hegy
Makovecz-kilátó - Kis-Hárs-hegy
Szépjuhászné
Hűvösvölgyi
Zöldlomb utca
Törökvész út
Kapy utca
Pasaréti út
Bimbó
Pusztaszeri út
Lajos utca
Palatinus fürdő
Budakeszi út
Széher út
János-hegy
Gyermekvasút
Zugligeti
Gábor Áron utca
Fillér utca
RÓZSADOMB
Zenélő szökőkút
Margit híd
Béla Kútvölgyi út
Király út
Diós árok
Margit körút
Néprajzi Múzeum
ORSZÁGHÁZ
ZUBLIGET
Hadtörténeti Múzeum
Istenhegyi út
BATTHYANY TÉR
SVÁBHEGY
ISTENHEGY
Mátyás templom
Széchenyi lánchíd
DÉLI PÁLYAUDVAR
Eötvös út
Tündér utca
Alkotás utca
Böszörményi út
BUDAIVÁR
Fodor utca
Bürök utca
Konkoly-Thege Miklós út
MÁRTONHEGY
Hegyalja út
Citadella
Németvölgyi út
Hóvirág út
Alsóhegy utca
GELLÉRTHEGY
See BUDA map
Rákó utca
SASAD
Móricz Zsigmond körtér
Törökbálinti út
Sasadi
Beregszászi
Háromszék utca
Rétköz
Budaörsi út
Karolina
Bocskai út
Bartók Béla út
Újbuda-központ
KELENFÖLD
Gazdagréti út
Farkasréti út
GAZDAGRÉT
Budaörsi
Balatoni út
KELENFÖLD
Tétényi út
Fehérvári út
Hengermalom
Budapesti út
Szabadság út
Aradi utca
ORMEZŐ
Károly király utca
Petőfi Sándor utca
Baross utca
M1/M7
Andor utca
Egérút
BUDAÖRS
Koérberki
Repülőtéri út
Péterhegyi út
Vasút utca
Kamaraerdei út
Balatoni út
ABERTFALVA
Hunyadi Mátyás út
Szerémi
Hunyadi János út
Budafok-Albertfalva vasútállomás
WHERE TO EAT
Hummusbar................1

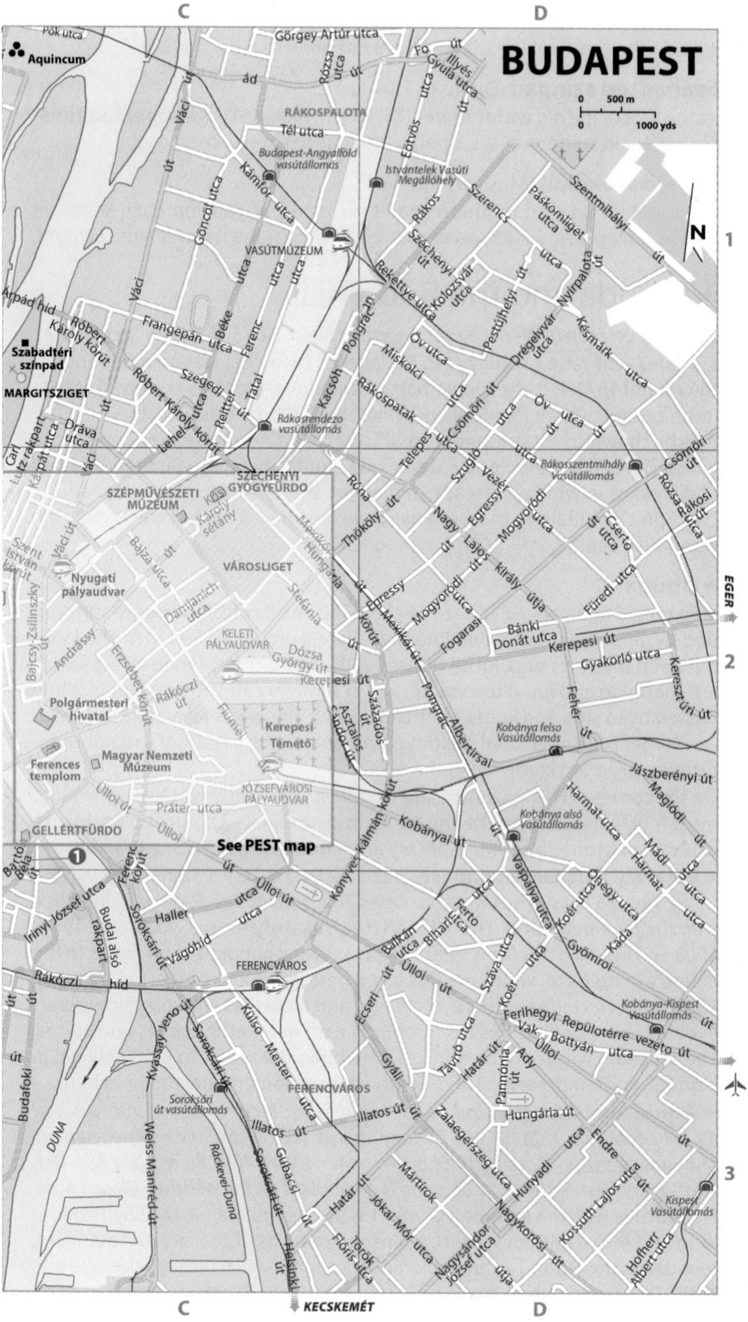
BUDAPEST
0 500 m
0 1000 yds
N
C
D
1
2
3
Aquincum
Pók utca
Görgey Artúr utca
Rózsa utca
Fő út
Illyés Gyula utca
RÁKOSPALOTA
Tél utca
Budapest-Angyalföld vasútállomás
Istvántelek Vasúti Megállóhely
Eötvös utca
Váci út
Kámfor utca
Göncöl utca
VASÚTMÚZEUM
Szerencs
Páskomliget utca
Szentmihályi út
Rákos
Széchenyi út
Rekettye utca
Kolozsvár utca
Pestújhelyi út
Nyírpalota út
Késmárk utca
Drégelyvár utca
Árpád híd
Róbert Károly körút
Frangepán utca
Béke utca
Ferenc
Szabadtéri színpad
MARGITSZIGET
Szegedi út
Reitter
Tatai
Kacsóh Pongrác
Miskolci
Öv utca
Rákospatak
Csömöri út
Rákosrendező vasútállomás
Lehel utca
Dráva utca
Carl Lutz rakpart
Kárpát utca
Telepes utca
Szugló
Vezér
Rákosszentmihály Vasútállomás
Rózsa utca
Rákosi út
SZÉCHENYI GYÓGYFÜRDŐ
SZÉPMŰVÉSZETI MÚZEUM
Kós Károly sétány
Róna
Thököly út
Nagy Lajos király útja
Egressy út
Mogyoródi út
Cserto utca
Szent István körút
Nyugati pályaudvar
Bajza utca
VÁROSLIGET
Mexikói
Hungária körút
Füredi utca
EGER
Bajcsy-Zsilinszky út
Andrássy
Damjanich utca
Stefánia
Fogarasi
Bánki Donát utca
Kerepesi út
Gyakorló utca
Erzsébet körút
KELETI PÁLYAUDVAR
Dózsa György út
Mexikói út
Pongrác
Keresztúri út
Rákóczi út
Polgármesteri hivatal
Fiumei
Kerepesi Temető
Asztalos Sándor út
Századas út
Albertirsai
Fehér út
Kobánya felso Vasútállomás
Jászberényi út
Ferences templom
Magyar Nemzeti Múzeum
JÓZSEFVÁROSI PÁLYAUDVAR
Üllői út
Práter utca
Könyves Kálmán körút
Kobányai út
Harmat utca
Maglódi út
GELLÉRTFÜRDO
See PEST map
Kobánya alsó Vasútállomás
Vaspálya utca
Mádi utca
Ferenc körút
Bartók Béla út
Irinyi József utca
Budai alsó rakpart
Soroksári út
Haller utca
Vágóhíd utca
Balkán utca
Bihari út
Ferto utca
Koér utca
Óhegy utca
Kada utca
Gyömrői út
Rákóczi híd
FERENCVÁROS
Ecseri út
Száva utca
Kobánya-Kispest Vasútállomás
Ferihegyi Repülőtérre vezető út
Vak Bottyán utca
Kvassay Jenő út
Külső Mester utca
Gyáli út
Távíró utca
Határ út
Ady
Budafoki út
Soroksári út vasútállomás
Pannónia út
Hungária út
DUNA
Illatos út
Zalaegerszeg utca
Endre út
Weiss Manfréd út
Ráckevei-Duna
Gubacsi út
Mártírok útja
Hunyadi utca
Kossuth Lajos utca
Kispest Vasútállomás
Határ út
Jókai Mór utca
Nagykőrösi út
Török Flóris utca
Nagysándor József utca
Hofherr Albert utca
Helsinki út
KECSKEMÉT

Domonkos kolostor (Dominican Convent) C1
The ruins of the convent where Princess Margaret lived can be seen amid the trees in the center of the island *(see box p66)*.

Szabadtéri színpad (Open-air Theater) C1
At the foot of the old **water tower** (187ft/57m high, 1911) is an **open-air theater**, where in summer plays, operas, and dance shows are staged.

Zenélő szökőkút (Musical Fountain)
The fountain is at the southern end of the island, as you approach Margaret Bridge. It plays at intervals, accompanied by music, and is illuminated at night.

★ Óbuda and the Buda Hills

Budapest map (p68–69). Access: north of Buda. HÉV 5, direction Szentendre.
This area—or rather suburb—in Budapest's District III was an independent town until 1873. It is the oldest part of Budapest, the Romans having made it the capital of their Pannonia province. Back then it was a military city, but nearby they also established a "civil" city called Aquincum, the remains of which can still be seen today *(see below)*. Not far away, the Buda Hills are an idyllic place in which to escape and all the better for being so close to the city. You can breath in the fresh air while enjoying stunning views over the Hungarian capital.

★ Óbuda BC1

★ **Fő tér** (Fő Square) – *HÉV 5 Szentlélek tér.* This small **cobbled square** surrounded by affluent Baroque buildings has quite a provincial feel to it. The lanes between the rows of colorful houses with their old-fashioned street lamps are charming and good to explore, and in summer cafés and restaurants lure passersby to stop and linger on their terraces. This peaceful area soon makes you forget the impersonal buildings erected nearby as part of a major urbanization program launched in the 1960s.
On the corner of Hajógyár utca and Laktanya utca, you might be surprised to meet four ladies, each sheltering beneath an umbrella. This **group sculpture** was cast in bronze by contemporary artist **Imre Varga** (1923–2019).
★ **Vasarely Múzeum Budapest** – *Szentlélek tér 6. HÉV 5 Szentlélek tér; Tram 1. (1) 388 7551. www.vasarely.hu. Open Tue–Sun, 10am–5.45pm. Ft800 (free with the Budapest Card).* The artist **Victor Vasarely** (born Győző Vásárhelyi, 1908–97) lived in Paris from 1930 but gave several hundred of his works to the country of his birth, which are displayed here in the Zichy Mansion building. The exhibits include paintings, drawings, and tapestries and show how his art evolved using optical illusion combined with geometric shapes and colors. The museum was renovated in 2017 enabling the works to be displayed in a bright, contemporary setting. Temporary exhibitions are also held here.
★ **Aquincum** – *Szentendrei út 139. HÉV 5 Aquincum then 15min walk or Bus 134 Záhony utca; Bus 134, 106 Záhony utca. (1) 250 1650. www.aquincum.hu. Museum open Apr–Oct, 10am–6pm; Nov–Mar, 10am–4pm. Ruins open Apr–Oct, 9am–6pm. Rest of the year: opening is dependent on the weather. Closed Mon. Ft1,900 (free with the Budapest Card).* The site covering an area 656yds/600m long and 437yds/400m wide contains the remains of the city of Aquincum, founded in the 1C, and an archeological museum. Aquincum's golden age was in the 2C and 3C, when it was full of tradesmen and craftsmen and bustled with activity. At that time the combined populations of Óbuda and Aquincum totaled more than 60,000. In the year AD124 Aquincum became a *municipium*

Aquincum
© Jule_Berlin/iStock

under the Roman emperor, Hadrian, meaning it was governed according to its own laws while still remaining under Rome's authority. In AD194, under Emperor Septimus Severus, the city became a Roman colony. At the end of the 4C, Aquincum came under attack by invaders from the east. The city went into decline and in the 5C the Huns delivered the final blow. The Romans abandoned it but not before making a treaty with the new ruler, Attila.

The **ruins** clearly show the layout of the city on a grid plan, a network of sewers and pipes, and the foundations of various buildings. Opposite the museum there were public baths and a great covered market *(macellum)*, with craftsmen's workshops, merchants' stalls, and houses.

At the far end of the site, in a small building (a former bathhouse that was part of a private house), a fragment of a mosaic floor depicting wrestlers has been uncovered. A few steps to the left, another small building, with a sundial at the entrance, contains more fine mosaics.

Retracing your steps toward the museum, you will see a shrine to Mithras, the Persian sun god, who was worshiped by first the Greeks and then the Romans, and also the Painter's House, a reconstruction of a 3C home.

Two buildings house exhibitions. The first, near the entrance, explores the history of Budapest since the Paleolithic era and includes a large number of items that were excavated on site, such as statues, bas-reliefs, coins, pottery, and tools, along with other everyday objects. Temporary exhibitions are also held here. Virtual games allow players to do battle against a gladiator, which will please the children. The second building, the furthest away, also mounts temporary exhibitions.

Budai-hegység (Buda Hills) A1–2

This lovely green landscape lies to the west of Buda, just a few miles from the city which can be stifling on very hot days. For locals and tourists in search of fresh air, the Buda Hills offer footpaths through the woods, picnic areas, and some lovely views.

★ **Gyermekvasút** (Children's Railway) – *Széchenyi-hegy and Hűvösvölgy. Tram 56, 56A, 59B, 61 toward Hűvösvölgy as far as Városmajor, then the cogwheel railway (tram 60) to Széchenyi-hegy. ✆ (1) 397 5394. www.gyermekvasut.hu. Usually operates 9am–6pm (times vary according to season). Closed Mon (except in summer). Train ride Ft1,400 round trip, children Ft700.*

The Children's Railway (Gyermekvasút) or Pioneer's Railway (the Pioneers was the name of the youth movement created in the Communist era) is a delightful attraction. One way of getting to the Children's Railway lower terminus is by taking the small cogwheel railway (officially tram 60) outside the Danubius Hotel Budapest—the hotel is easy to spot as it is in the form of a tall rotunda *(Szilágyi Erzsébet fasor 47)*. Get off the cogwheel railway at its upper terminus (Széchenyi-hegy) and walk toward the television transmitter, near to which you will find the small Children's Railway Station. Apart from the engine driver, who is an adult, the whole railway is staffed by children (ticket sales, station master, departure signaling) dressed in regulation uniforms; they greet each arrival and departure with a military-style salute. The route (7.5mi/12km), which is mainly through wooded areas, is very enjoyable. There are several stops along the way and you can get off at any of them if you feel like stretching your legs. To go back down the hill from the terminus at Széchenyi-hegy, take bus 158 or tram 56 as far as Széll Kálmán tér.

János-hegy (János Hill) – *BUS 291 to Nyugati pályaudvar, Zugliget terminus, then the* **Libegő** *(chairlift). ✆ (1) 391 0352. bkk.hu. The timetable varies according to daylight hours (high season, 9am–7pm). Ft1,200 round trip (free with the Budapest Card).*

János Hill is the highest point in Buda (1,726ft/526m). At the top, take the road to the right that climbs up to a neo-Romanesque observation tower from where there is a magnificent **panoramic view★★**.

It is also possible to reach the tower via the Children's Railway. Get off at János-hegy Station and take the path that heads up through the countryside *(30min walk)*.

South of Budapest Regional map (p28–29)

★ Memento Park B2

9.3mi/15km south of the center of the city. M 4 Kelenföld pályaudvar, then BUS 101 or 150 to Memento Park (15–30min journey); direct bus from M Deák tér at 11am (look for the hostess on the pavement opposite the Ritz-Carlton hotel); Ft4,900 entrance ticket included. ✆ (1) 424 7500. www.mementopark.hu. Open 10am–7pm. Ft1,500 (children Ft1,200): reduced price with the Budapest Card. Brochure-map in English (Ft600). Guided tour in English daily at 11.45am (Ft1,200).

This is quite unlike anything you've ever seen before. A large number of statues and group sculptures that were erected during the Communist era (1945–89) were taken down and then relegated to this park that was specially created for the purpose. Monuments dedicated to the glory of the era and its leading figures—from workers' movements and the Soviet-Hungarian pact to the Hungarian Brigade who fought in the Spanish Civil War—the collection is certainly impressive and keen photographers are in for a treat.

At the entrance, you can't miss the inevitable Trabant, the iconic car that was manufactured in East Germany in the former Soviet Bloc.

In the cinema *(opposite the entrance)* films are screened on the secret services and their methods of rough justice. In the store you can buy Soviet passports, posters, magnets, mugs, and other memorabilia bearing Communist symbols.

ADDRESSES IN BUDAPEST

See maps: Buda (p37) & Pest (p48–49)

Tel. area code 1

USEFUL INFORMATION

Embassies

In the event of problems, contact your embassy.
Basic Information p411.

Emergency numbers

112 police, ambulance, fire service.
Doctor 24hrs (Főnix SOS) – *203 3615.*
Pharmacy 24hrs – Teréz Patika. *Teréz krt. 41. 311 4439.*
SOS dentist – *317 6600.*

GETTING THERE

Liszt Ferenc International Airport is 14 mi/22 km southeast of the city center. Only **Terminal 2** (which is divided into 2a and 2b) is currently in operation.
Info – *www.bud.hu*

Bus and metro

The cheapest options to go from the airport to the city center:
Bus 100E direct to Deák Ferenc tér *(1hr journey)*, every 20min between 5am and 1.20am. Special fare rate Ft900.
Bus 200E to Kőbánya-Kispest, the southern M3 terminus. Then take metro line M3 (blue) via Deák Ferenc tér. Departs every 8–12min during the day and 25min evenings; operates 4am–11pm. Ft530 (transfer ticket, *see p74*).
Night bus 900 to Dél-Pesti Autóbuszgarázs (bus terminus), between 11pm and 4am.
For the city center, get off at the Bajcsy-Zsilinszky út stop and change to the 950 or 950A bus. Ft530 (transfer ticket, *see p74*).
In each case, buy tickets from the BKK office in the arrivals hall of Terminal 2.

Airport minibus/shuttle

The easiest and most comfortable option if this is your first visit. The minibus will drop you off wherever you want in the city and there is no extra charge for luggage. Operates 24hrs, departs every 30min.
Reserving 24hrs ahead is advised: *www.minibud.hu*. Buy tickets at the miniBUD counter in the arrivals hall. The price depends upon the number of passengers (guide prices in euros: €19.50/US$22 for 1 person, €10.60/US$12 per person for 2, €7/US$8 per person for 3 passengers, …).

Taxi

Főtaxi is the airport's official taxi service. Look for their yellow booths near the exit from Terminal 2. Allow around Ft7,600 to the center (you can also pay in euros, around €24/US$26).
Info – *222 2222. www.fotaxi.hu*

GETTING AROUND

Budapest has a very efficient public transport system operated by BKK. You can access timetables and maps at **www.bkk.hu/en**. Buses, trams, and trolley buses generally circulate between 4.30am and 11pm, and the metro operates until 11.50pm (Friday & Saturday until 0.30am for lines M2 and M4). Night buses operate outside these hours.
Key public transport hubs:
– In Buda: Batthyány tér and Széll Kálmán tér
–In Pest: Deák F. tér and Blaha L. tér

Public transport map: inside back cover

Tickets

Tickets cannot be purchased on trams or trolley buses but they are sold in metro stations (**M** sign), newspaper kiosks, and BKK booths in the main transport hubs and terminuses. However, you can buy them on board buses.

Tickets are sold in single units (Ft350) or in booklets of 10 (Ft3,000) and are valid for all forms of public transport within Budapest. Single tickets bought on the bus cost Ft450. Tickets must be validated before travel for each journey (look for orange, yellow, or red machines – you may have to pull the black slot frame down to validate tickets on red machines). Validate your ticket at the entrance to the metro, but inside buses, trolley buses, HÉV suburban trains, and trams. Always retain your ticket in case of inspection during or at the end of the journey.

There are no turnstiles on the metro but often a white line on the floor, if you cross this line without a validated ticket you could be fined. Travel cards are checked at the metro entrance.

You can use the same single ticket on the metro for any number of line changes for up to 80min from validation. You don't need to validate for each line change, but if you exit the system and return within 80min, you must buy a new ticket.

To **transfer** between types of transport (bus, tram, metro, HÉV suburban train, and trolley bus) on a single journey you need the more expensive transfer ticket (Ft530). Note it is valid for one transfer only per single journey.

Travel cards allow limitless travel within the boundaries of Budapest: 1 day (Ft1,650), 3 days (Ft4,150), 1 week (Ft4,950).

Budapest Card (see opposite).

EU seniors (over 65) can travel free on public transport on presentation of a valid form of ID.

Inspections are made regularly throughout the day; the inspectors generally wear red armbands rather than a uniform. On the spot fines for traveling without a ticket are high (from Ft8,000).

Metro

The 4 lines in Budapest are differentiated by color: M1 yellow, M2 red, M3 blue, and M4 green. M1 (known locally as the "small underground") was the first underground railway in continental Europe and follows Andrássy út above ground, linking the downtown area to City Park (Városliget). Opened in 2014 and ultra modern, line M4 links Keleti pályaudvar (the city's eastern rail terminus) with the residential district Kelenföld in the south, via Szent Gellért tér.

Doors open and close automatically and the name of the next stop is announced.

Lines 1, 2, and 3 all pass through Deák Ferenc tér.

The two need-to-know signs are *bejárat* (entrance) and *kijárat* (exit). The different metro lines are indicated by color and destination on each platform. Some stations are very deep so the escalators can be steep, not to mention speedy. Take care in the rush hour.

Bus and trolleybus

Buses are blue and trolley buses red. Buses with a black number stop at all stops, but those with a red number or showing the letter "E" are express buses, which skip some. Each stop is labeled with its name and times are given on blue signs (generally between 5 and 15 minutes frequency, depending on the time of day). Stops are sometimes announced. Push the button near the door to signal that you want to get off, particularly in the evening.

Tramways (Villamos)

Tram carriages are yellow (with a couple of exceptions) and travel the length and breadth of the city. Stops are sometimes announced. There are two night lines. The lines serving the most popular tourist areas are:

– **4** and **6**: runs along the Grand Boulevard to Széll Kálmán tér.

– **2**: hugs the Danube on the Pest side from Közvágóhíd to Jászai Mari tér (near the bridge and Margaret Island).

– **19**: runs along the Danube on the Buda side via Batthyány tér.

– **60**: the cogwheel railway. (**Fogaskerekű**) is popular with locals and links the Buda Hills with Városmajor.

River bus

The BKK transport company runs three routes, generally every 30 to 60 minutes, between 6.30am and 8.30pm. Tickets cost Ft750 (from ticket machines, BKK booths, or from the crew) and are validated by the crew. For timetables, see: bkk.hu/en/timetables/

- **D 11** (weekdays only): Újpest (Árpád út)/Kopaszi-gát.
- **D 12** (weekdays and weekends): Rómaifürdő/Kopaszi-gát.
- **D 14** (weekdays) south of the center of the city, runs straight across the river from one bank to another: Királyerdő (on Csepel Island) and Molnár-sziget (in the Soroksár district of Pest).

HÉV suburban trains

The following lines operate (the first name indicates the departure station in Buda or Pest):

– **5**: Batthyány tér (M 2)/ Szentendre.

– **6**: Közvágóhíd/Ráckeve;

– **7**: Boráros tér/Csepel.

– **8**: Örs vezér tere (M 2)/Gödöllő.

– **9**: Örs vezér tere (M 2)/Csömör.

Taxis

Taxis (licensed taxis are yellow and should display the tariff and their license number) are plentiful (operating as companies or independently). Ask the price at the start of your journey and keep an eye on the total. Beware of scams.

The following companies are reputable. Their company name should appear on the car door or on the luminous sign on the roof. Hailing a taxi in the street is not recommended (usually a lot more expensive). Phone for a taxi instead. Beware of unlicensed taxis *(see p423)*.

City Taxi – *211 1111.*

Főtaxi – *222 2222.*

Budapest Taxi – *777 7777.*

6X6 Taxi – *666 6666.*

Bicycles

Motor vehicles are prohibited on Margaret Island making it the perfect place for cycling. Bike hire is available near the southern end of the island. You can also book a guided tour by bike.

The city launched its **public bike-sharing network** in 2014: MOL Bubi (molbubi.bkk.hu). Bikes (green) are available from a number of docking stations, mostly on the Pest side. Allow Ft500/24hrs, Ft1,000/72hrs, Ft2,000/1 week.

SIGHTSEEING

Budapest Card

It makes sense to invest in a **Budapest Kártya/Budapest Card** if you plan to visit museums and want to enjoy unrestricted travel on public transport within the city boundaries. When traveling outside them, you must buy an extension ticket from your departure point while presenting your Budapest Card. The card's benefits include:

– Free unlimited travel on the public transport system, including metro, bus, trolleybuses, trams, HÉV suburban trains (but excluding both the Buda funicular and the chair lift on Mount János in the Buda Hills).

– Free entry (or reduced price) for a number of museums and cultural attractions.

– Discounts for tickets to certain shows, in some shops, restaurants, cafés, pubs, and swimming pools.

– Discounts at some car hire firms and for bike hire on Margaret Island (Margitsziget).

The Budapest Card can be purchased at the airport, from Tourinform offices, in the major metro stations, travel agents, and online at: **budapest-card.com**, with a 5 percent discount.

Prices – *Ft6,490/24hrs, Ft9,990/48hrs, and Ft12,990/72hrs.* Make sure you date and sign your card. A small explanatory booklet is supplied with the card.

www.budapestinfo.hu/card-info

Guided tours

A number of companies offer **walking tours**, some themed. Information is available from Tourinform.

Absolute Walking Tour – *269 3843. absolutetours.com.* Offers themed walks (3hrs, guide price in euros from €36/US$40), along with cycle and Segway tours.

Yellow Zebra Bikes – *Sütő utca 2. M 1, 2, or 3 Deák Ferenc tér. 269 3843. yellowzebrabikes.com.* Bike tours (4hrs including a café stop, guide price in euros around €28/US$31). Walking tours are also available.

BudaBike Tours – *70 242 5736. www.budabike.com. Reserve min. 1 day in advance.* Five tours of 2–3hrs (guide price in euros €25–30/US$28–33), including one at night.

Big Bus Tours – *Andrássy út 3. M 1 Bajcsy-Zsilinszky út . 235 0078 . eng.bigbustours.com.* Tours include hop on/hop off with 26 stops and audioguides. 2-day pass available, guide price in euros €24.30/US$27. Reduced price with the Budapest Card.

City Tour – *Andrássy út 2. M 1 Bajcsy-Zsilinszky út. 374 7073. www.citytour.hu.* Hop on/hop off; guide price in euros for a 2-day pass €24/US$27. Reduced price with the Budapest Card.

Cityrama – *Báthory utca 22. 302 4382. www.cityrama.hu.* Tours usually last 3hrs (€25/US$28). A tour in a Trabant (3hrs), the famous East German car that became symbolic of the Eastern Bloc, leaves at 10.30am from the Cityrama office or from your hotel (if in the center), with or without an English-speaking driver (you need your driver's license if you opt to drive). Guide price in euros for a private tour for 2, around €120/US$133.

RiverRide – *Széchenyi tér. 332 2555. riverride.com.* An amphibious vehicle takes you through the city and then onto the River Danube. From Ft9,000.

Legenda – *Pier no 7. Vigadó tér. M 1 Vörösmarty tér. Tram 2 Vigadó tér. 317 2203. www.legenda.hu.* A 70-minute cruise from Ft3,900.

Mahart PassNave – *Belgrád rakpart. M 4 Fővám tér. Tram 2 Fővám tér. 484 4013. www.mahartpassnave.hu.* Dinner from Ft10,900 (reduction with the Budapest Card).

STAY

Most of Budapest's hotels are at the higher end of the market price-wise and it is not always easy to find cheap rooms in the downtown area, although things are improving. Renting an apartment, even for one night, is an alternative (www.airbnb.com). For a vacation with a difference, you could stay with a local (www.wimdu.com).

Buda or Pest—which is best? On the Buda side (west/right bank), the atmosphere is fairly relaxed and peaceful, with lovely views of the Danube. The Pest side (east/left bank) is more lively.

Prices – The rates given here are the minimum for a double room in high season, bearing in mind that prices can rise during vacations and when the Formula 1 Grand Prix is in town (late July–early Aug).

Várnegyed

SPLASH OUT

2 **Baltazár** – Buda map E1 – *Országház utca 31. BUS 16, 16A, 116 Bécsi kapu tér; M 2 Széll Kálmán tér. (1) 300 7051. baltazarbudapest.com. P Ft6,500/day. 11 rooms Ft29,000/55,000.* A charming boutique hotel with very comfortable rooms, each decorated in a different style. A calm ambience and an excellent restaurant with a terrace and a nice wine bar.

Víziváros

A TREAT

1 **Art'otel** – Buda map F1 – *Bem Rakpart 16–19. M 2 Batthyány tér; Tram 19, 41 Halász utca. (1) 487 9487. artotelbudapest.com. P Ft5,180/day. 156 rooms Ft35,300/48,270, Ft4,860.* Situated by the river, near the castle and the commercial district in the heart of the city. There are views of the Parliament Building and the Chain Bridge.

Lipótváros

SPLASH OUT

3 **Central Basilica** – Pest map H2 – *Hercegprímás utca 8. M 1 Bajcsy-Zsilinszky út. (1) 328 5010. www.hotelcentral-basilica.hu. 37 rooms Ft30,800/55,000.* Located in the historic center, near the basilica, a hotel that represents good value for money; a clean and welcoming environment.

Belváros

A TREAT

1 **Gerlóczy Kávéház Rooms de Lux** – Pest map H3 – *V. Gerlóczy utca 1. M 3 Ferenciek tere; M 2 Astoria. (1) 501 4000. www.gerloczy.hu. 19 rooms Ft28,800/52,440, Ft3,885.* Just a few steps from the River Danube, this tiny hotel with a café annex has a Belle Epoque aura. Retro charm, but with attention to detail and modern facilities.

Erzsébetváros

BUDGET

6 **Wombat Hostel** – Pest map H2 – *Király utca 20. M 1 Bajcsy-Zsilinszky út. (1) 883 5005. www.wombats-hostels.com. 112 rooms Ft21,000/24,250 and dormitories Ft4,530/6,800, Ft1,600.* A good example of youth hostel-style accommodation, but a little more designer-led than is usual, housed in a former 4-star hotel. The rooms and dormitories are spotless. Good for those on a budget despite being a bit noisy at times.

1

A TREAT

5 Roombach – Pest map H2 – *Rumbach Sebestyén utca 14. M 1, 2 or 3 Deák Ferenc tér. ✆ (1) 413 0253. roombach.com. P Ft4,850/day. 98 rooms Ft35,200/41,700 ☕.* Ideally located in the heart of this busy and popular district; you can walk from here to the city's major sites. The rooms are small but comfortable and clean. A friendly welcome and a varied buffet breakfast.

SPLASH OUT

4 Corinthia Hotel – Pest map J2 *Erzsébet körút 43–49. M 1 Oktogon; Tram 4, 6 Király utca. ✆ (1) 479 4000. www.corinthia.com. P Ft5,800/day. 383 rooms Ft44,000/91,800 ☕, ✂ Bock Bisztró.* This legendary hotel dating back to 1896 has been completely renovated. Up until the Second World War it was *the* place to stay in Budapest. Its elegant and grand Belle Epoque exterior now conceals a contemporary interior that is super luxurious. There is also a spa and wellness center with a recently refurbished swimming pool.

EAT

There are many simple but good restaurants in the **Belváros** district, on Ráday utca (M 3 or 4 Kálvin tér). Near **Andrássy út**, on Liszt Ferenc tér (M 1 Oktogon), restaurants stay open till very late in the evening. Those in the **Erzsébetváros** district on Dob utca (M 1, 2, or 3 Deák Ferenc tér) are a good bet. At lunchtime, most restaurants offer good value set menus *(mai menü)* as well as à la carte. Our price ranges correspond with the restaurants' main menus or fixed price menus. For a wider selection of restaurants, consult the *Guide Michelin: Main Cities of Europe* by scanning the QR code here.

Six of the 26 Budapest addresses have been awarded Michelin stars.

Várnegyed

A TREAT

2 Café Pierrot – Buda map E1 – *Fortuna utca 14. M 2 Széll Kálmán tér. ✆ (1) 375 6971. www.pierrot.hu. Open noon–midnight. Ft11,820/18,740.* Traditional cooking and fine dining in elegant surroundings, with a subtle nod to Pierrot in the decor. A pleasant garden in which to eat in fine weather.

1 21 – Buda map E1 – *Fortuna utca 21. M 4 Széll Kálmán tér. ✆ (1) 202 2113. 21restaurant.hu. Open noon–11.45pm. Ft8,800/12,000.* Eat on the terrace during the day and inside in the evening, in a friendly bistro atmosphere. The chef fuses traditional Hungarian cuisine with more contemporary flavors.

Gellérthegy

BUDGET

17 Pagony Kert – Pest map H3 – *Kemenes utca 10. M 4 Szent Gellért tér. ✆ (31) 783 6411. www.pagonykert.hu. Open 10am–10pm. Ft5,430/6,770.* In a small street near Gellért Baths, this lovely outdoor café is open in summer in the garden *(kert)* of a former pool complex. Some tables are even laid out in the (now empty) pools. Fresh, simple, and delicious food with a particularly tasty homemade lemonade. A great venue in fine weather.

1 Hummusbar – Budapest map p68–69, C2 – *Bartók Béla út 6. M 4 Szent Gellért tér. ✆ (70) 376 1776. hummusbar.hu. Open 11am–10pm (Sat & Sun,* *noon–10pm). Around Ft3,300.* One of a chain of restaurants offering Middle Eastern food (there are over a dozen in the capital). On the menu: pitas, *shakshuka* (an egg-based dish), falafels, and hummus, of course. Delicious, healthy, and good value.

Víziváros

BUDGET

16 **Nagyi Palacsintázója** – Pest map H1 – *Batthyány tér 5.* M *2 Batthyány tér. www.nagyipali.hu. Open 24hrs. Ft290/990.* One of a chain of pancake houses, this place is perfect for lunch on the go and is very popular with the locals. Food is served all day: *sós rakott tejföllel* (lasagne with a pancake base and sour cream), *mákos* (sweet pancakes with poppy seeds), *meggyes* (morello cherries), and *almás* (apple). Take your food up to the mezzanine level from where you can gaze out at the busy square (Batthyány tér) and beyond that the Danube.

Lipótváros

BUDGET

15 **Nemsüti** – Pest map G1 – *Jászai Mari tér 4/b.* M *3 Nyugati pályaudvar;* Tram *4, 6 Jászai Mari tér. (70) 621 1123. nemsuti.hu. Open Mon–Fri, 10am–6pm.* Before heading off to explore Margaret Island, stop at this sandwich bar famous for serving the best vegetarian food in Budapest. Choose from salads and soups, along with more substantial dishes and delicious cakes, plus fruit juices.

A TREAT

14 **Tom-George Italiano** – Pest map H2 – *Október 6 utca 8.* M *1 Bajcsy-Zsilinszky út. (20) 266 3525. www.tomgeorge.hu. Open 11.50am–midnight. Ft8,800/23,600.* Near the basilica, this restaurant has a contemporary feel and serves fusion food in a stylish interior. Fresh, creative dishes with an eye on Hungary, Asia, and the Mediterranean.

13 **Borkonyha** – Pest map H2 – *Sas utca 3.* M *1 Bajcsy-Zsilinszky út. (1) 266 0835. www.borkonyha.hu. Open Mon–Sat, noon–midnight. Closed Sun & public holidays. Ft11,300/17,100. Tasting menu Ft23,000.* An elegant, modern, and airy bistro near the basilica, where Hungarian wines (over 200 in total, many of them served by the glass) are paired with good dishes based on local produce.

Belváros

BUDGET

21 **Oh my green** – Pest map H3 *Petőfi Sándor utca 10.* M *3 Ferenciek tere. (1) 321 0448. (30) 575 1180. www.ohmygreen.hu. Open Mon–Fri, 9am–7pm (Sat, 10am–5pm). Under Ft3,300.* If the thought of Buddha bowls, chia seeds, and goji berries whets your appetite, head for this place, with its attractive, warm, contemporary interior and ultra-healthy snacks that burst with flavor.

AVERAGE

20 **Károlyi Étterem & Kávéház** – Pest map H3 – *Károlyi Mihály utca 16.* M *2 Astoria. (1) 328 0240. www.karolyietterem.hu. Open noon–11pm. Ft7,500/11,100.* In a lovely elegant and historic setting—the courtyard of the town house of the counts of Károly, shaded by huge trees. The menu is essentially Hungarian but includes the odd nod to other European cuisines. A pianist generally plays from 7pm.

19 **Fatál** – Pest map H3 – *Váci utca 67.* M *3, 4 Kálvin tér;* M *3 Ferenciek tere. (1) 266 2607.*

www.fatalrestaurant.com. Open noon–midnight. Ft7,100/9,100. No card payments. People are usually quite happy to queue to eat here on account of its unique atmosphere. Design-wise: a long cellar with a vaulted ceiling, communal tables, a jolly, country feel. Food-wise: the generous and substantial dishes are served on wooden boards *(fatál)* or directly in the pots and pans that cooked them. Watch out for the vast portions though.

A TREAT

25 **Múzeum Kávéház és Étterem** – Pest map H3 – *Múzeum körút 12 . M 2 Astoria. (1) 338 4221. muzeumkavehaz.hu. Open 6pm–midnight. Closed Sun and public holidays. Ft8,400/12,900.* In business since 1885, this is a good choice for lovers of traditional Hungarian cooking (pike-perch fillet à la Múzeum, trout, Hortobágy pancakes, etc.). Inside you'll find a Belle Epoque interior with faïence tiles, wood detailing, and high ceilings.

18 **Kárpátia** – Pest map H3 – *Ferenciek tere 7–8. M 3 Ferenciek tere. (1) 317 3596. www.karpatia.hu. Open Mon–Fri, 11am–11pm; Sat & Sun 5pm–11pm. Ft10,900/19,000.* A classic central address in Budapest and a city landmark on Ferenciek Square. This restaurant has been serving contemporary and traditional Hungarian food since 1877. With faux medieval decoration typical of the late 19C.

Andrássy út

BUDGET

22 **Cech In** – Pest map H2 – *Lázár utca 7. M 1 Opera; M 3 Arany János utca. (20) 298 9929. Open Mon–Sat, 4pm–1am. Under Ft1,900. No card payments.* Specializing in Czech beer, this friendly bar near the opera serves hearty Central European food at good prices, eaten at the counter or in the wood-paneled dining room.

AVERAGE

12 **M Étterem** – Pest map H2 – *Kertész utca 48. M 1 Opera or Oktogon, Tram 4, 6 Király utca. (1) 322 3108. metterem.hu. Open Tue–Sun, 6pm–midnight. Ft5,400/7,700.* A stone's throw from the Music Academy, Hungarian cooking is served at reasonable prices. An arty and cosmopolitan clientele.

11 **Két Szerecsen** – Pest map H2 *Nagymező utca 14. M 1 Opera. (1) 343 1984. ketszerecsen.hu. Open 8am–midnight (Sat & Sun, 9am–midnight). Ft7,400/11,500.* This local bistro enjoys a central location, a pleasant atmosphere, and a clientele of regulars. It doesn't quite extend to fine dining but its soups, salads, and Hungarian meals with a French twist hit the spot very nicely. You can eat on the terrace in summer.

10 **Menza** – Pest map H2 – *Liszt Ferenc tér 2. M 1 Oktogon; Tram 4, 6 Oktogon. (1) 413 1482. www.menza.co.hu. Open 11am–midnight. Ft6,000/11,000.* It is hard to miss this place on the popular Liszt Ferenc tér. Good Hungarian dishes are served in a 1950s socialist cafeteria-style interior. Usually packed and therefore noisy, but no complaints about the food or service.

9 **Rickshaw** – Pest map J2 – *Corinthia Hotel, Erzsébet körút 43–49. M 1 Oktogon; Tram 4, 6 Király utca. (1) 479 4855. www.rickshaw.hu. Open Wed–Sun, 6pm–11pm. Ft5,600/9,400.* This restaurant in the luxury Corinthia Hotel is said to serve the best Asian food in Budapest. People flock here to taste Thai, Malaysian, and Chinese cooking, as well as excellent sushi prepared by the Japanese chef. Elegant Zen decor.

Városliget

A TREAT

8 **Robinson** – Pest map J1 – *Városligeti tó.* M *1 Széchenyi Fürdő. ✆ (1) 422 0222. www.robinsonrestaurant.hu . Open noon–11pm. Ft11,023/14,589.* Situated right next to the water, on a wooded island in the lake in Városliget (City Park). Robinson offers the chance to escape the city noise and try Hungarian and Mediterranean cuisine while gazing across the lake to Vajdahunyad Castle. A guitarist plays to accompany dinner.

Erzsébetváros

BUDGET

24 **Kazimir** – Pest map H2 – *Kazinczy utca 34.* M *1, 2, or 3 Deák Ferenc tér. ✆ (20) 354 5533. ✆ (1) 798 5747. bistro.kazimir.hu. Open Mon–Sun, 10am–4am. Menu Ft1,490.* Opposite the Orthodox synagogue, this restaurant serves food with an emphasis on tradition. A warm welcome and frequent (free) jazz concerts at 9pm).

☺ 23 **Karaván** – Pest map H2 – *Kazinczy utca 18.* M *2 Astoria or Blaha Lujza tér. Open 11.30am–midnight.* Street food reaches Budapest. A small open-air venue with several vans serving food to take away or eat in at one of the tables provided: burgers, salads, pancakes, pasta, hot dogs, cold meats, Indian vegetarian dishes, ice cream.… There's something for everyone.

AVERAGE

7 **Spinoza** – Pest map H2 – *Dob utca 15.* M *1, 2, or 3 Deák Ferenc tér. ✆ (1) 413 7488. www.spinozahaz.hu. Open 8am–11pm. Ft5,600/9,200.* In the heart of the Jewish quarter, schnitzels and traditional Hungarian cuisine (a pianist plays from 7pm). A breakfast menu is available all day. There are regular performances in the small theater at the rear. A Klezmer concert (the traditional music of the Ashkenazi Jews) on Thursdays from 7pm with a 3-course meal, Ft12,000.

6 **Mazel Tov** – Pest map H2 – *Akácfa utca 47.* Tram *4, 6 Erzsébet körút. ✆ (70) 626 4280. mazeltov.hu. Open daily 11am–1am (Fri & Sat 2am). Ft5,270/6,730.* Delicious Israeli street food (*shawarma* sandwich) or something more elaborate (lamb with grilled aubergine) served in a very pleasant atrium. There's a jazz group in the evening and brunch on Sundays. Reservation essential if you don't want to eat in the less appealing dining room next door.

5 **Kőleves** – Pest map H2 – *Kazinczy utca 41.* M *1, 2, or 3 Deák Ferenc tér. ✆ (1) 322 1011. www.kolevesvendeglo.hu. Open Mon–Wed, 8am–11pm; Thu & Fri, 8am–midnight; Sat, 9am–midnight; Sun, 9am–11pm. Ft7,430/9,250.* The atmosphere here is relaxed and cosmopolitan. The menu offers a small selection of Jewish-influenced dishes (as you'd expect, given its location in the Jewish quarter), adapted to modern tastes. Vegetarians and those wanting only "light bites" will enjoy the salads and appealing meat-free dishes.

4 **Bock Bisztró** – Pest map J2 – *Corinthia Hotel, Erzsébet körút 43–49.* M *1 Oktogon;* Tram *4 or 6 Király utca. ✆ (1) 321 0340. www.bockbisztro.hu. Open daily, noon–midnight (closed public holidays). Ft7,700/13,400.* An elegant restaurant with Art Deco touches, although the atmosphere is more like a small bistro. Classic Hungarian cuisine mixed with lighter dishes, tapas, cheese, and cold cuts. Attentive service.

Near Kerepesi Cemetery

AVERAGE

3 **Csiga Cafe** – Pest map J3 – *Vásár utca 2.* M *4 Rákóczi tér.* ✆ *(30) 613 2046. Open 8am–11.45pm. Ft5,300/6,100.* This small café with the snail logo *(csiga)* attracts a loyal clientele for its cosy ambience, music, and excellent but reasonably priced menus—already quite a rarity in a district that is heading upmarket.

2 **Rosenstein** – Pest map J2 – *Mosonyi utca 3.* M *2, 4 Keleti pályaudvar;* Tram *24, 6 Keleti pályaudvar.* ✆ *(1) 333 3492. rosenstein.hu. Open Mon–Sat, noon–11pm. Ft6,500/13,100.* Tucked away in a small street, serving Hungarian and modern Jewish dishes (soups, roasted foie gras, Lake Balaton fish, venison, goose), this restaurant also serves a fine selection of wines, including some good Villányi (red). The menu in 5 languages comprises a substantial 28 pages.

Ferencváros

AVERAGE

1 **Vörös Postakocsi Étterem** – Pest map H3 – *Ráday utca 15.* M *3, 4 Kálvin tér.* ✆ *(1) 217 6756. www.vorospk.hu. Open 11.30am–midnight. Ft5,200/11,400.* Another place to try in this street brimming with restaurants, many of which serve dishes with an international influence. However, this place is notable for serving exclusively Hungarian food, including typical meat dishes.

TAKING A BREAK

What better or more typical way to while away a few hours in Budapest than by enjoying a coffee and a deliciously rich cake in one of the many **cukrászda** (cake shop/tea salon).

Várnegyed

Ruszwurm Cukrászda
Szentháromság utca 7. ✆ *(1) 375 5284. www.ruszwurm.hu. Open 10am–6pm.* With Biedermeier decor and its delicious *krémes* (a sort of vanilla slice), this is one of the oldest tearooms in Hungary (Sissi, aka Empress Elisabeth of Austria would visit in the 19C). One of the busiest tea salons, locals and tourists line up patiently for a table in the charming small dining room, which has remained unchanged since 1827. Cake and old-school nostalgia, what's not to like?

Víziváros

Angelika Kávéház – *Batthyány tér 7.* M *2 Batthyány tér;* Tram *19, 41 Batthyány tér.* ✆ *(1) 225 1653. www.angelikacafe.hu. Open 9am–11pm (midnight in summer). Closed 24 Dec.* Located near the Danube, with a terrace boasting a great view of the Parliament Building on a sunny day. There are also pleasant rooms inside where you can taste one of the many cakes and pastries, including the house speciality, Angelika torta (a sort of sponge cake with chocolate and vanilla).

Andrássy út

Művész Kávéház – *Andrássy út 29.* M *1 Opera.* ✆ *(1) 343 3544. muveszkavehaz.hu. Open Mon–Sat, 8am–9pm; Sun & public holidays, 9am–9pm.* This café is certainly one of the most expensive in town but you can't beat the location on this smart and chic avenue. It has a deliciously retro interior (wood, marble, chandeliers) and the list of particularly tasty cakes and pastries provides the perfect excuse to stop and let time go drifting by … just for a little while at least.

Mai Manó Kávézó – *Nagymező utca 20.* Ⓜ *1 Oktogon. ✆ (1) 269 5642. Open 8am–1pm.* A North African-style café near the house of the famous photographer Mai Manó. Velour banquettes in mint-tea green, carpets, and a profusion of cushions complete the intimate look. It's nice to relax here with a drink.

Belváros

Gerbeaud – *Vörösmarty tér 7–8.* Ⓜ *1 Vörösmarty tér. ✆ (1) 429 9000. www.gerbeaud.hu. Open 9am–9pm.* The city's most famous tearoom was bought in 1884 by renowned Swiss confectioner Émile Gerbeaud. Hugely popular with tourists from around the world, the address is still an institution today, even if the quality of the cakes is a little uneven. Choose one at the counter and it will be brought to the table.

Fruccola – *Kristóf tér 3.* Ⓜ *1 Vörösmarty tér. ✆ (1) 430 6125. fruccola.hu. Open Mon–Fri, 7am–9pm; Sat, 8am–9pm; Sun, 8am–7pm.* Unusually for Budapest, this place serves excellent fresh fruit juices. Get your daily vitamin hit with a mix of pineapple, cilantro (coriander), spinach, lemon, and orange juice. Cakes, sandwiches, and salads, too.

Erzsébetváros

☺ **Fröhlich Kóser Cukrászda** – *Dob utca 22.* Ⓜ *2 Astoria or Blaha Lujza tér. ✆ (1) 266 1733. www.frohlich.hu. Open Mon–Thu, 9am–6pm; Fri, 9am–2pm; Sun, 10am–6pm. Closed Sat.* Known for its Jewish pastries and therefore extra busy during Jewish festivals, this small Ashkenazi café serves (according to those in the know) one of the best *flódni* in town, an apple cake with nuts and poppy seeds. A warm welcome; a perfect place for breakfast or a snack.

Café New York – *Erzsébet krt. 9–11.* Ⓜ *2 Blaha Lujza tér;* Tram *4, 6 Wesselényi utca. ✆ (1) 886 6167. www.newyorkcafe.hu. Open 8am–midnight.* This legendary café is worth a visit just for the experience. A brunch menu (buffet until 11am) that is family-friendly (no charge for under 8s) is served in the downstairs bar. Otherwise, prices are a bit high, with tea for two around Ft25,000.

SHOPPING

Falk Miksa utca in Lipótváros is *the* street for antique hunters. In the Belváros district, luxury brand outlets stand alongside more touristy shops, particularly in the famous **Váci utca** and the surrounding streets.

Lipótváros

Anna Antikvitás – *Falk Miksa utca 18–20.* Ⓜ *2 Kossuth Lajos tér;* Tram *2 Országház. ✆ (1) 302 5461 or (20) 935 0374. www.annaantikvitas.com. Open Mon–Fri, 10am–6pm; Sat 10am–1pm.* Pieces in bronze, hand-embroidered tablecloths, and glass and porcelain items (1750–1940) are packed into this charming store. All hail from Austria, Hungary, and the historic Transylvanian region. The prices are a little more affordable than in many similar shops in the street.

ÜVEG/HÁZ – *Sas utca 5.* Ⓜ *1 Bajcsy-Zsilinszky út. ✆ (30) 548 6376. www.uveghazbudapest.com. Open Mon–Sat, 11am–6pm.* Elegant designer jewelry and accessories, including handmade items at reasonable prices.

Andrássy út

Sugar! –*Paulay Ede utca 48.* Ⓜ *1 Opera. ✆ (1) 321 6672. www.sugarshop.hu. Open Tue–Sun 10.30am–10pm; Mon, noon–10pm.* Giant lollipop trees, candy bears, and windows full of brightly colored cakes. This incredible confectioners is a modern Alice in Wonderland treasure trove of candies and sweets, with its immaculate white walls and colorful counters. Eat in or take out the sugary delights. Even the washroom is worth a visit (no spoilers as to why, though).

Belváros

Paloma – *Kossuth Lajos utca 14. M 3 Ferenciek tere. (20) 961 9160. palomabudapest.hu. Open Mon–Fri, 11am–7pm; Sat, 11am–3pm.* Discover the work of a number of Hungarian designers under one roof: jewelry, bags, clothes, hats. A dozen shops occupy two floors around a lovely courtyard that is also home to a café. Sometimes used as the backdrop for various events.

Herend Porcelain Manufactory – *József Nádor tér 11. M Deák Ferenc tér. (20) 241 5736. (1) 317 2622. www.herend.com. Open Mon–Fri, 10am–6pm; Sat, 10am–2pm.* This shop is the Budapest outlet for the famous Hungarian porcelain manufacturer Herend. Great ideas for quality Hungarian gifts or souvenirs to take home.

Magma – *Petőfi Sándor utca 11. M 3 Ferenciek tere. (1) 235 0277. www.magma.hu. Open Mon–Fri, 10am–7pm; Sat, 10am–3pm. Closed Sun & public holidays.* This boutique-gallery gives Hungarian artists and designers the chance to show their wares: furniture, tableware (ceramics and porcelain), jewelry (pretty rings in colored glass), elegant bags, some inspired by Hungarian folklore.

Szamos Gourmet Ház – *Váci utca 1. M 1 Vörösmarty tér. (30) 570 5973. szamos.hu. Open daily, 10am–9pm.* This excellent chocolatier is particularly known for its marzipan creations. A good place to buy gifts for the sweet-toothed or to sample something on the spot in the café, where they also serve breakfast and snacks.

Paprika – *Vörösmarty tér 1. M 1, 2, or 3 Deák Ferenc tér. (20) 365 6600 or (30) 674 1331. www.paprikamarket.hu. Open daily 10am–8pm (Fri & Sat 9pm).* Sachets of paprika, marzipan chocolates, wine from Tokaj, porcelain jewelry, embroidery; a treasure trove for the dedicated souvenir hunter on the trail of all things Hungarian.

Rózsavölgyi és Társa – *Szervita tér 5. M 3 Ferenciek tere, 1 Vörösmarty tér . (1) 318 3500. www.rozsavolgyi.hu. Open Mon–Thu, 10am–10pm; Fri & Sat, 10am–8pm (closed Sun).* One of the largest record stores in Budapest selling a wide range of classical and Hungarian folk music, among other recordings.

Erzsébetváros

Printa – *Rumbach Sebestyén utca 10. M 1, 2, or 3 Deák Ferenc tér. (30) 292 0329. printa.hu. Open Mon–Sat, 11am–8pm.* Near the Rumbach Street Synagogue, this concept store is art gallery, café, and designer shop all in one. Decked out in black and white, it offers a good selection of silk screen prints and posters by emerging artists, and limited edition clothes and accessories made from sustainable materials. Support young local artists and take home some interesting and cool souvenirs.

Ferencváros

Nagy Vásárcsarnok (Great Market Hall) – *Vámház krt. 1–3. M 4; Tram 2 Fővám tér. (1) 366 3300. www.piaconline.hu. Open Mon, 6am–5pm; Tue–Fri, 6am–6pm; Sat, 6am–3pm.* The famous indoor market is held in beautifully renovated halls that date from 1897. On the first (ground) floor are a number of stalls selling traditional folklore products and food—strings of paprika, garlic, and onions, wine, alcohol, and the famous local salami. You can also buy products from the famous Hungarian brand Pick. Upstairs, the gallery is full of stalls selling fast food and local crafts. Beware of the odd "tourist trap" though.

Flatlab – *Baross utca 3. M 3, 4 Kálvin tér. ✆ (30) 949 4286 or (30) 627 8790. www.flatlab.hu. Open Mon–Fri, 1pm–8pm.* Located near the Hungarian National Museum, this showroom in a minimalist apartment highlights pieces from young designers whose workshops are also on the premises (fashion, design, and graphics). There's a range of things to buy by local creators, including designer items, gadgets, and clothes. A good place for ferreting out unique pieces or limited editions.

BARS

Gellérthegy

Palack Wine Bar – *Szent Gellért tér 3. M 4 Szent Gellért tér. ✆ (30) 997 1902. www.palackborbar.hu. Open daily, noon–midnight (Mon, 11pm; Sun,10pm).* An excellent spot to try Hungarian wines while nibbling on some tapas of salami or cheese in a relaxed atmosphere. Tasting evenings and concerts are also available.

Raqpart – *Jane Haining rkp. M 1 Vörösmarty tér; Tram 2 Eötvös tér. ✆ (30) 732 4751. raqpart.hu. Open Jun–Sept, noon–1am (Fri & Sat, 3am).* The rather spectacular location (right by the Chain Bridge on the banks of the Danube) makes this open-air bar (only open in summer) one of the best places for a drink while watching the sun set over the castle and river. Electro disco beats meet wooden tables and decking. Come here for lunch or dinner as well.

Andrássy út

360 Bar – *Andrássy út 39. M 1 Opera. ✆ (30) 356 3047. 360bar.hu. Open Sun, Tue, Wed 2pm–midnight; Thu–Sat 2pm–2am (closed Mon).* This is Budapest's most beautiful rooftop bar, on top of the old Párizsi Nagyáruház department store. It is the perfect spot for an aperitif while watching the sun go down. Enjoy the same views in winter, but this time cocooned inside a transparent heated igloo. Chilly weather never felt so cozy.

Boutiq'Bar – *Paulay Ede utca 5. M 1 Bajcsy-Zsilinszky út. ✆ (30) 554 2323. www.boutiqbar.hu. Open Tue–Thu, 6pm–1am; Fri & Sat, 6pm–2am.* Said by many to serve the best cocktails in Budapest. Most of them are house specials, but the bartenders will mix you a classic of your choice upon request, from daiquiris to cosmopolitans.

Erzsébetváros

Doblo Wine & Bar – *Dob utca 20. M 2 Astoria. ✆ (20) 398 8863. www.budapestwine.com. Open Mon, Tue, Fri, Sat, 2pm–2am; Wed, Thu, Sun, 2pm–1am.* If you didn't already know that Hungary is a winegrowing country, this dynamic wine bar is an excellent opportunity to discover the country's very diverse winegrowing regions, to try the dry and sweet wines of Tokaj, but also the fruity red wines of Szekszárd. And if you are an afficionado, you will be delighted by the wide range on offer. Either way, you should also enjoy the bar's elegant bohemian atmosphere.

NIGHTLIFE

The area in and around Andrássy út is home to two superb musical venues, the **State Opera House** and the **Academy of Music**. In the south of the city, the arts complex **MÜPA Budapest** offers a good program of theater, dance, and music, worthy of the best international venues. For something a little more lightweight, head for the Petőfi Bridge area, on the Buda side, where **A38**, a Ukrainian ship transformed into a cultural center, is moored. And make sure you include a visit to a **romkocsma**, a "ruin bar," one of the alternative bars and cafés set up in abandoned buildings in the Jewish district. Check out the website dedicated to them: ruinpubs.com. For more information on the various line-ups and programs, see the printed information on site and the websites of the different venues, where you can often book online. Alternatively, head to one of the ticket offices in the city or to the venue itself for tickets.

Ticket Express Hungary (TEX) – in Bálna (see p66). M *4 Fővám tér;* Tram *2 Zsil utca.* *(30) 505 0666. www.eventim.hu. Open Mon–Fri, 10am–6pm; Sat 10am–3pm.*

Ticketpro – *Károly krt. 9.* M *1, 2, or 3 Deák Ferenc tér.* *(1) 555 5515. www.ticketpro.hu.* *Open Mon–Fri, 9am–9pm; Sat, 10am–2pm. Tickets are also available online.*

Gellérthegy

Szatyor Bar – *Bartók Béla út 36.* M *4;* Tram *6 Móricz Zsigmond körtér.* *(1) 279 0291. www.szatyorbar.com. Open Tue–Sat, noon–1am; Sun & Mon noon–midnight.* A slightly off-the-wall atmosphere that lends itself to long, late-night conversations. A good venue in which to see local bands from Budapest.

A38 – *Petőfi bridge. Moored container ship, Buda side.* Tram *4, 6 Petôfi híd.* *(1) 464 3940. www.a38.hu. Open daily 8am–10pm.* Disco, restaurant *(open Mon–Sat, 11am–11pm)*, concert hall (capacity 700), and exhibition hall, this former cargo ship is one of the city's top nightlife venues specializing in live music, with an eclectic schedule of pop, rock, jazz, and electro. Anchored on the Buda side, downstream from Petôfi Bridge, there's a great view of Pest's south bank from its deck.

Víziváros

Hagyományok Háza (Hungarian Heritage House) – *Corvin tér 8.* M *2 Batthyány tér.* *(1) 225 6049/225 1012. hagyomanyokhaza.hu. To book* *225 6056 (Mon–Thu, noon–6pm; Fri, 10am–2pm).* Performances by the Hungarian State Folk Ensemble, founded in 1951.

Lipótváros

Duna Palota – *Zrínyi utca 5.* M *1, 2, or 3 Deák Ferenc tér.* *(1) 235 5500. www.dunapalota.hu.* The shows start at 8pm, alternating between three internationally renowned folk ensembles. You can also opt to take a Danube dinner-cruise after the show.

Budapest Jazz Club – *Hollán Ernő utca 7.* M *3 Nyugati pályaudvar;* Tram *4, 6 Jászai Mari tér.* *(1) 413 9837 or 798 7289. bjc.hu/home/. Open Mon–Thu, 10am–midnight (Fri & Sat 2am); Sun 4pm–midnight).* The most famous jazz club in Budapest has live shows every day by Hungarian and international artists from 8pm. Arrive before and eat or enjoy a glass of wine in the café or bistro.

Morrison's 2 – *Szent István krt. 11. Tram 4, 6 Jászai Mari tér. ✆ (1) 374 3329. www.morrisons2.hu. Open Mon–Sat, 5pm–5am; Sun, 7pm–5am.* A lively music bar with five dance floors, billiards, and karaoke. Daily concerts.

Andrássy út

Magyar Állami Operaház (State Opera House) – *Andrássy út 22. M 1 Opera. ✆ (1) 332 7914. ✆ (1) 814 7100. www.opera.hu.* One of the most prestigious opera houses in Europe with performances in a neo-Renaissance palace (1884) decorated with frescoes painted by the greatest Hungarian artists of the time. The biggest names in music play here. Performances are also held in the Erkel Theater *(János Pál pápa tér 30).*

Liszt Ferenc Zeneművészeti Egyetem (Franz Liszt Academy of Music) – *Liszt Ferenc tér 8. M 1 Oktogon. ✆ (1) 462 4600. zeneakademia.hu.* Founded by the Hungarian composer himself in 1875, the academy remains the capital's premier concert venue. It occupies a beautiful Art Nouveau building with stained glass windows, mosaics, and sparkling crystal chandeliers. Audiences are rewarded with performances by the best symphony orchestras in the country at very affordable prices. And if you're nearby at rehearsal time, you may hear some of the music escaping from the building, so why not linger for a brief free concert!

Erzsébertváros

Szimpla Kert – *Kazinczy utca 14. M 2 Astoria. ✆ (20) 261 8669. szimpla.hu. Open noon–4am (Sun, 9am–4am).* Reclaimed furniture, exposed pipes, and industrial ducting lit by small colored lamps, with a pretty courtyard: this is a genuine *romkocsma*. Szimpla Kert has become something of an institution, but go for a drink and to enjoy the music rather than to eat. DJs and live music (from 8pm) in the evening.

Ellátóház – *Dob utca 19. M 1, 2, or 3 Deák Ferenc tér. ✆ (20) 527 3018. Open Mon–Wed & Sun, 5pm–midnight; Thu 5pm–2am, Fri & Sat 5pm–5am.* Located in the Jewish quarter, this ruin bar is a central venue for drinks, music, concerts and parties.

Outside the center

MÜPA Budapest – *Komor Marcell utca 1. HÉV 7; Tram 1 Közvágóhíd. ✆ (1) 555 3000. www.mupa.hu. Open 10am–6pm. Generally closed 2nd week Jul–3rd week Aug, check website.* This cultural arts complex has been offering a diverse program of excellent quality since it opened in 2005 (opera, contemporary dance, jazz, world music). Artists of international standing play here as does the Hungarian National Philharmonic Orchestra. Free concerts are given several times a week by the students from the Conservatory of Music.

BATHS

Gellért Baths – *Kelenhegyi út 4. Entrance in the road to the right of the hotel. M 4; Tram 19, 41, 47, 48, 56, 56A Szent Gellért tér. ✆ (1) 466 6166. gellertfurdo.hu. Open 6am–8pm. From Ft5,900.* The baths might be in need of a little refurbishment but they are housed in one of the city's most spectacular buildings. The complex includes a resort area (pool with wave machine, solarium, sauna, bar, restaurant, a great indoor pool) and a thermal baths section, which is the most interesting from an architectural point of view, and includes 2 baths (96–100°F/36–38°C), a cold bath, saunas, and a hammam. Massages

1

are available and there's a VIP spa. The thermal waters are said to be particularly good for rheumatism and osteoarthritis.
(*See also p42.*)

Rudas Baths – *Döbrentei tér 9. Tram 19, 41, 56, 56A Rudas Gyógyfürdő. (1) 356 1322. en.rudasfurdo.hu. Women: Tue. Men: Mon, Wed, Thu, Fri till 12.45pm. Mixed: Fri from 1pm, Sat & Sun. Open 6am–8pm, see website for more detailed opening times. From Ft3,700.* This authentic Turkish bath comprises thermal pools (60–108°F/16–42°C) and a separate outdoor panorama pool (84°F/29°C) on the roof above the wellness section. A number of different types of massage are available (firming, aroma, exfoliating, relaxing, ...).
(*See also p43.*)

Király Baths – *Fő utca 84. M 2 Batthyány tér; Tram 19, 41 Bem József tér. (1) 202 3688. fr.kiralyfurdo.hu. Open 9am–9pm. From Ft2,600.* These small Turkish baths are thermal only (97°F/36°C) and are housed beneath the domed roof, offering a hammam, sauna, massages, and pedicures. Minimum age 14. (*See also p44.*)

Lukács Baths – *Frankel Leó út 25–29. Tram 17, 19, 41 Szent Lukács Gyógyfürdő. (1) 326 1695. en.lukacsfurdo.hu. Open 6am–10pm. From Ft4,300. Sauna world: supplement, Mon pm–Fri, Ft600; Sat & Sun, Ft800.* There tend to be fewer tourists here, but instead locals who are regulars and people taking a cure. Refurbished in 2012, there are 2 outdoor pools and a sundeck. Inside there are 5 thermal pools (72–104°F/22–40°C). Sauna World contains an infrared sauna and a Himalayan salt wall.

Széchenyi Baths – *Állatkerti körút 11. M 1 Széchenyi fürdő. (1) 363 3210. www.Széchenyibath.hu. Open 6am–10pm. From Ft6,000.* In the heart of Városliget (City Park). Outside you'll find a thermal whirlpool, an Olympic-size swimming pool, a thermal pool (100°F/38°C), solarium, and restaurant. Inside there are several baths, from cold to very warm. Treatments and massages are provided in booths. (*See p62.*)

Veli bej Baths – *Árpád Fejedelem útja 7. Tram 17, 19, 41. (1) 438 8587. (1) 438 8400. Open Mon–Sat, 6am–noon, 3pm–9pm; Sun, 9am–11.45am, 3.30pm–8.45pm. From Ft2,240, (prices increase in the afternoon).* The largest Turkish baths in Budapest, with 5 pools (central pool 97–100°F/36–38°C). Steams baths with aromatic oils, sauna, jacuzzi, swimming pool, jet massage. Massages can be booked at the entrance. A café is accessible from the baths. Minimum age 14.

Dagály Baths – *Népfürdő utca 36. M 3 Forgách utca; Tram 1 Népfürdő utca/Árpád híd. (20) 375 2658. en.dagalyfurdo.hu. Open 6am–8pm. From Ft2,900.* Outdoor thermal baths. Ten baths of varying sizes and temperatures (79–97°F/26–36°C). Also on offer are whirlpools, a lazy river, underwater aqua massage, waves, geysers, a children's pool, sauna, and massages and other treatments.

Dandár Baths – *Dandár utca 5–7. Tram 2, 24 Haller utca/Soroksári út. (1) 215 7084. en.dandarfurdo.hu. Open Mon–Fri, 6am–9pm; Sat & Sun, 8am–9pm. From Ft2,000.* Completely refurbished in 2014. Indoor thermal baths (68–100°F/20–38°C). Massages are available.

ACTIVITIES

Palatinus Strand – *Margitsziget. BUS 26. ☎340 4500. en.palatinusstrand.hu. Open 8am–8pm. From Ft3,200.*
Not thermal baths, but rather the largest open-air bathing area in Budapest, with 11 swimming pools (including one with waves), a "slidepark" for surfers and a beach. The water is 71–97°F/22–36°C. And if you'd like a change from swimming, you can also play football, beach volleyball, and tennis. Four interior pools are open all year round. (*See also p67.*)

EVENTS AND FESTIVALS

April

Spring Festival – Classical and contemporary music, theater, opera, operettas, folk music, Hungarian and foreign ballet, film. *www.btf.hu/events*

May–June

Jewish Art Festival – Concerts, poetry readings, and theater in multiple locations across the city, incuding the Columbus Ship. *zsidomuveszetinapok.hu*

Mid-June

Danube Carnival – An international dance and music festival (classical, contemporary, traditional Hungarian folk, world music).
dunakarneval.hu

Night of the Museums – Around 20–25 June. Free access to museums and entertainment. 6pm–1am. *muzej.hu*

July

Open-air film festival – Daily, 4.30pm–11pm. Films are projected in front of the Parliament Building.

July–October

Sparties – Spa parties ("sparties") are held on Saturday evenings at Széchenyi Baths.
www.bathsbudapest.com

August

Sziget Festival – Mid-August. A Woodstock/Glastonbury-style music festival with a dozen stages lasting a week. It attracts young people from around the world to Óbuda Island in search of good music. *www.szigetfestival.com*

Festival of Folk Arts – Held in Buda's Castle District. The city celebrates its birthday with a firework display on 20 August. *www.mestersegekunnepe.hu*

September

Wine Festival – Second week of the month. A celebration of wine, with auctions, tasting, a harvest procession, and concerts on the terraces of Buda Castle.
www.aborfesztival.hu

European Heritage Open Days – Third weekend of the month. Access to a number of locations usually closed to the public with conferences and concerts.

October

CAFé Budapest Contemporary Arts Festival – Experimental contemporary art festival (music, film, exhibitions).
www.cafebudapestfest.hu

December

Christmas markets – Venues in the center of the city.

Opera Gala and Ball – A big, glamorous event held on New Year's Eve.
www.opera.hu

The Danube Bend

(Dunakanyar)

★★★

Pest and Komárom-Esztergom counties

The Danube is known as the Duna in Hungarian and the Danube Bend (or Curve) as the Dunakanyar, a picturesque and beautiful landscape. It may not be blue, as in the Strauss waltz, but this stretch of the river easily lives up to its romantic reputation. From its source in the Black Forest in Germany, it flows from west to east, crossing southern Germany, northern Austria, calling in on Bratislava, and then forming the border between Slovakia and Hungary. As it wends its way north, bypassing Hungary's Gerecse Mountains and touching Esztergom, it drops down between the Pilis and Börzsöny mountains, then swings south between forest-covered hills before passing Vác and Szentendre in the famous Danube Bend. All that remains for Europe's second longest river is to glide on through Budapest, before descending further south and crossing the Great Plain, leaving Hungarian territory just south of Mohács on its way to the Black Sea.

LOCATION:
Regional map AB1 (p28–29).
North of Budapest, Rte 11 (west bank) or Rte 2; Rte 12 (east bank).

DON'T MISS:
The Danube Bend landscape—to enjoy it fully, take a river cruise. The views from the vantage point of Visegrád Citadel are a must.

TIMING:
It is possible to take a day river cruise through the Danube Bend from Budapest, stopping off in a town or two along the way, depending on the boat's timetable. If you want to see everything, then allow a more leisurely 2/3 days, either by car or public transport.

The Danube Bend by boat

Pest side: pier at the end of Vigadó tér; Buda side: at the end of Batthyány tér (only for the Budapest–Szentendre–Visegrád–Esztergom line).

Traveling by boat from Budapest is a great way to see the magnificent sweep of the river and enjoy the quite different view of the landscape on either side from the water. Depending on the cruise, you can stop off at Szentendre, Vác, or Visegrád, but we recommend going all the way to Esztergom (allow a whole day).

Mahart PassNave

(1) 484 4000. www.mahartpassnave.hu.

Budapest–Szentendre–Visegrád–Esztergom line (5hrs 20min) – *Mid-Apr–end Aug, Tue–Sun; Sept, Sat. Outward: departs Vigadó tér (Budapest) 9am, Szentendre 10.30am, Visegrád 12.20pm, Esztergom 2.20pm. Return: departs Esztergom 4pm, Visegrád 5.40pm, Szentendre 7pm; arrives Vigadó tér (Budapest) 8pm. Stops at: Leányfalu, Tahitótfalu, Nagymaros, Dömös, Zebegény. Budapest to Esztergom Ft3,820, round trip Ft5,720 (prices vary if you stop at other places).*

Express Budapest–Vác–Visegrád–Esztergom line (1hr 30min) – *End Apr–end Sept, Tue–Sun (except 20 Aug). Board 30min before departure. Outward: departs Vigadó tér (Budapest) 10am, Vác 10.40am, Visegrád 11am, Esztergom*

The Danube Bend viewed from Visegrád Citadel
© Hungarian Tourism Agency

11.30am. Return: departs Esztergom 5pm, Visegrád 5.30pm, Vác 5.50pm, arrives Vigadó tér (Budapest) 6.30pm. Budapest to Esztergom Ft5,300, round trip Ft8,000 (prices vary if you stop at other places). In summer cruises also depart from Visegrád and Esztergom, info on the company website.

★★★ Day cruise to Esztergom

Board the boat at Budapest in the morning. You will probably find yourself in the company of plenty of other tourists and families on a day out, but the boats are comfortable and the trip should be highly enjoyable. The atmosphere is usually relaxed and friendly, and some boats have a bar on board for drinks and snacks (only on the Budapest-Szentendre-Visegrád-Esztergom line). Once you are clear of the northern suburbs of the capital, you soon reach **Szentendre Island**. From here the boats continue past the island via either the left arm of the river (the Szentendre side) or the right arm (the Vác side), depending on the cruise line. The boats stay close to the shore for a few peaceful miles as they drift northward between sandbanks and flocks of birds. The towns of **Szentendre** and **Vác** go out of their way to welcome visitors; the quaysides and the clock towers of their Baroque churches beckon and you have the chance to spend a few pleasant hours strolling through the towns, unless you plan to return another day and continue on the cruise. The medieval **Visegrád Citadel**, surrounded by fortified walls, soon appears perched high on its hill, looking spectacular, with the Börzsöny Mountains opposite. After Visegrád the views become truly picturesque as the Danube begins its famous **bend** between the Börzsöny and Pilis mountains, flanked by hillsides covered with forest that pile one on top of the other in unforgettable panoramas. Finally, the boat arrives at the monumental **Esztergom Basilica**, which marks the end of your trip to the Hungarian/Slovakian border.

After drifting along amid the peaceful river landscape, arriving back in Budapest at the end of the afternoon is magical as the Parliament Building comes into view on one side, and Buda Castle on the other, with the bridges spanning the river ahead of you.

The Danube Bend by car Regional map (p28–29)

Round trip from Budapest (87mi/140km). Allow 1 day. See the Regional map p28–29 for the route.

To cross from one side of the river to the other, try taking the ferry. Everybody else does! To go to work, to the market, to visit friends … it's like catching a bus. The trip may only last a few minutes but it is an inescapable part of life along the Danube. There are three that operate, from south to north and from the left bank to the right bank: Vác–Szentendre Island (Tahitótfalu), Nagymaros–Visegrád, and Szob–Pilismarót. Departures generally every hour.

★★ THE WEST (RIGHT) BANK TO ESZTERGOM AB1

Leave Budapest by the Danube's right bank and take Rte 11, direction Szentendre. The road crosses Óbuda and large residential areas before passing the Roman ruins at Aquincum.

The right bank of the Danube is the most interesting of the two thanks to three unmissable towns: Szentendre, Visegrád, and Esztergom, each one steeped in history. Route 11 soon leaves the banks of the river to follow the Szentendrei-Dunaág, the arm of the Danube that flows between Szentendre Island and the west bank of the river, to the outskirts of Szentendre. As you approach Visegrád the full width of the Danube comes back into view.

★★ Szentendre *(see separate entry, P94)*

★★ Visegrád *(see separate entry, p104)*

The Pilis Mountains that rise behind Visegrád are very popular with hikers. A favorite spot from which to set off is the village of **Dobogókő**, which is the highest point in the mountains of the Danube Bend and offers one of its most striking panoramas to those energetic enough to climb up on foot.

★★ Esztergom *(see separate entry, p108)*

★ THE EAST (LEFT) BANK BACK TO BUDAPEST AB1

From Esztergom rejoin Rte 11 in the opposite direction. At Basaharc, turn left down a small road and take the ferry to return to the left bank of the river (Pilismarót–Szob shuttle ferry).

You can return to Budapest down the left bank of the Danube *(Rte 12)*. The road cuts into the side of the hills overlooking the river, with views across to the bank opposite in places. This side of the river might be less interesting in terms of places at which to stop off, but its views of the Danube are striking and hiking paths into the countryside start at intervals along the way, particularly in the Börzsöny Mountains.

Late in the afternoon on sunny days, the light is particularly beautiful, giving the landscape a special radiance. Look out for the many grand houses that once belonged to the aristocracy. They built homes here to take advantage of the lovely setting and the forests that offered plenty of opportunities for hunting.

Szob

This small town is at the border with Slovakia, just where the border heads north away from the Danube.

Börzsöny Múzeum *Szent László utca 14. ✆ (27) 370 408. www.museum.hu. Open Thu–Fri, 9am–4pm; Sat & Sun, 9am–5pm. Ft600.*

The museum opens a window onto the everyday lives of the people living in

the Börzsöny Mountains and around the Danube Bend through objects found during archeological excavations, along with the region's flora and fauna.
Continue beside the Danube on Rte 12.

Zebegény

This small village in a lovely setting has become a favorite destination for people in search of a little peace and quiet, particularly those from the city on weekends. Look out for the **parish church** *(in Petőfi tér),* designed by architect Károly Kós. It dates from 1909 and is Art Nouveau in style. The highly decorated interior is inspired by folk art and above the altar the apotheosis of the Holy Cross is entwined with garlands of flowers.
Zebegény was the permanent home of Hungarian painter **István Szőnyi** (1894–1960), whose house and studio have been turned into a **museum** where many of his works are can be seen, some of which immortalize previous inhabitants of the village. It now houses an art school offering free courses in drawing, painting, ceramics, and enameling to young people. *(Bartóky utca 7. ℘ (27) 620 161. www.szonyimuzeum.hu. Open Mar–Oct, Tue–Sun, 10am–6pm; Dec–Feb, Fri–Sun, 10am–4pm. Ft900. Guided tours in English available.)*

Nagymaros

A village that is famous for its red fruits and the cultivation of raspberries, which are collected to make delicious jams and syrups.
If you have some energy to spare for a detour, a marked hiking trail *(trail sign horizontal blue stripe on a white background, 1hr)* sets off from the village center and leads through the forest to the Juliánus Kilátó (lookout tower) from where there is a superb **panorama** of the Danube Bend.

Kismaros

kiralyret.bloglap.hu. Departures: Apr–Oct, 10am, noon, 2pm, 4pm, 6pm (May–June, Sat & Sun, public holidays, also 9am & 11am); Nov–Mar, Sat & Sun and public holidays, 10am, noon, 2pm, 4pm, and 6pm. Ft900 (Ft1,400 round trip).
Small forest railway – This is one of the oldest light railways in Hungary. Trains leave Kismaros, the southern terminus, on a 30-minute journey to Királyrét in the Börzsöny Mountains. The train's wooden benches rattle and shake as you travel through the lovely landscape, across woodland and meadows, and past farms.
Királyrét (King's Meadow) – A number of pleasant walking trails suitable for all levels set off from here. King's Meadow is a popular place for families who come to picnic and enjoy nature (there are also a couple of restaurants). You can fish in the lake Királyréti Horgásztó and watch the turtles—if you can spot them—in Bajdázó-tó (lake). You can also call in at **Hiúz Ház** (Lynx House Visitor Center, *open Fri, 9.30am–3pm; Sat & Sun, 9.30am–4pm*) and see an interactive exhibition of the local fauna and flora.
Börzsöny Mountains – The mountains were the favorite hunting grounds of King Matthias Corvinus and the aristocracy. Although relatively modest in height—the tallest peak is no more than 3,281ft/1,000m—they are still an imposing sight when viewed from the River Danube. People from Budapest come to the mountains in particular for the small resorts on the southern slopes that look down on the great river. The northern slope, on the other hand, which descends to the Slovak border, has very few places where it is possible to break your journey.

★ **Vác** *(see separate entry, p115)*
Rte 20 leads back to Budapest, crossing the industrial suburb of Újpest.

1

Szentendre

★★

Population 26,447 – Pest county – area code ✆ 26

Just a short distance from Budapest, a trip to Szentendre is almost obligatory for everyone staying in the Hungarian capital. Its romantic appearance and picturesque Danube setting have helped to make it popular with artists, who have been finding inspiration here since the 19C. Post-Impressionism, Constructivism, Surrealism, the Avant-garde, the town has seen the emergence of most art movements and trends. Its popularity with tourists has done nothing to spoil its charm. There is no doubt that this delightful town is so appealing because it is Hungary just as we like to imagine it—narrow cobbled streets, elegant small houses painted in bright colors, and, looking upward, a host of onion domes. Szentendre fairly bristles with churches, seven in total, of which four are Orthodox. After seeing the sights, you might like to take things easy and take advantage of the proximity of the Danube to go canoeing or just relax on the town's riverside beach equipped with all amenities.

ADDRESSES PAGE 102
Stay, Eat, Shopping, Events and Festivals

INFO:
Tourist Office – Szentendre map A2 *Dumtsa Jenő utca 22. ✆ 317 965. iranyszentendre.hu. Open daily 10am–6pm.* Information, maps, tickets for Danube cruises, gift shop.

LOCATION:
Regional map B1 (p28–29); Szentendre map (p97)
14mi/22km north of Budapest via Rte 11, on the right/west bank of the Danube.

PARKING:
Parking is available in the center of town on the Danube embankment (charges apply); parking close to Rte 11 at the corner of Duna korzó, no charge (Rózsakert parkoló, southern entrance to the town).

DON'T MISS:
Fő tér (the main square) and the small streets adjacent to it; the interior of the Serbian Church; an evening stroll by the Danube; Hungarian Open-air Museum.

TIMING:
Stay 1–2 days in Szentendre, especially if you visit the Hungarian Open-air Museum.

KIDS:
Marzipan Museum; Hungarian Open-air Museum.

Walking tour Szentendre map, p97

From the HÉV station, take Kossuth Lajos utca.

This pretty town inevitably gets busy during high season—solo travelers, groups of friends, families on holiday or having a weekend away. Tour parties stride through the streets and narrow lanes, ice cream in hand, while the shopkeepers stand outside their stores trying to convince passersby to come

Fő Square
© trabantos/Shutterstock

and take a look inside. As dusk falls, and in the evening when it is illuminated, the Duna korzó (Danube Promenade) is a popular place for a stroll by the river. The eleven **museums that form the Ferenczy Museum Center (FMC)** all have the same opening hours and ticket prices, as follows: *(20) 779 6657. muzeumicentrum.hu/en/. Open Tue–Sun, 10am–6pm. Ft1,400. Combined ticket for entry to all the museums Ft1,700.*

★ Ferenczy Múzeum (FMC) A2

Kossuth Lajos utca 5. Part of the FMC (see above). The Ferenczy family has its place firmly established in the pantheon of Hungarian artists. At the end of the 19C, **Károly Ferenczy** (1862–1917) began to paint outdoors, influenced by the Impressionists, and ultimately became a leading member of the Nagybánya artists' colony. Ferenczy painted in a number of different materials and styles and was very productive. In this museum you can see not just Károly's paintings but also the work of his three children: family portraits by his eldest son Valér (1885–1954), bronze and wood sculptures by his second son Béni (1890–1967), and tapestries by his daughter Noémi (1890–1957). There is a magnificent view of the Danube from the balcony. Pajor Mansion (18C), which houses the museum, also stages temporary exhibitions of modern art.

Marcipán Múzeum (Marzipan Museum) A2

Dumtsa Jenő utca 12. Open Mon–Fri, 9am–7pm; Sat & Sun, 10am–7pm. Ft600. This small museum, entered through the back of the Szamos café-pastry store, will delight children. While almond paste as a soft, sweet treat has plenty of fans among the not so young, too, it's fair to say no one would expect to find it molded into works of art. Master confectioners have created a number of colorful tableaux of varying sizes, demonstrating the precision of their work, patience, and dedication. The Budapest Parliament Building, Emperor Franz-Joseph and Empress Sissi, along with Michael Jackson, Princess Diana (life-size models of the latter two, weighing around 60lb/133kg each and involving up

SERBIA AND ITS ARTISTS

The Serbian community – The Serbian settlement dates back principally to 1690 when the Turks occupied Belgrade, the capital of present-day Serbia. Protected by Holy Roman emperor Leopold, they enjoyed various privileges and a community of around 6,000 Serbs was established at Szentendre. Joined later by more of their countrymen, the Serbs formed their own enclave in the town, preserving their traditions and their Orthodox religion. The 18C was Szentendre's golden age. Hungarians, Serbs, Greeks, and Dalmatians united to transform the town into a flourishing center for trade. Each community built homes and places of worship. The exterior of the churches took on the appearance of the Baroque churches of the West while remaining faithful to their own denomination. This is why today you can find several Orthodox churches in this small town in an otherwise Catholic area.

An artists' colony – Szentendre has long been on the wish list of Budapest artists looking to move to the country without being too far from the capital. The first artists' colony (Művésztelep) was established here in 1926, welcoming Constructivists and Post-Impressionists who had been rendered stateless. These painters had previously been working in an artists' colony at Nagybánya, which became part of Romania (and was renamed Baia Mare) after the Treaty of Trianon. The driving force behind the creation of the Szentendre School, which was orientated toward Surrealism and the Avant-garde, was Lajos Vajda *(see p99)*.

Another colony was established in the 1970s and a decade later the town became a rallying point for the Hungarian "neo-Avant-garde." Today art is exhibited in numerous galleries all over the town and during the **Art Capital festival** *(see Events and Festivals, p103)*.

to 340 hours of work), Mozart, characters from the Muppet Show, and many others will amaze you. The exit is through the store.

Barcsay Múzeum A2

Dumtsa Jenő utca 10. Part of the FMC, see p95. The Constructivist painter **Jenő Barcsay** (1900–88) lived and worked in this house for many years. Today it is a museum displaying many of his works, including paintings, sketches, and mosaics.

★★ Fő tér (Fő Square) A1–2

This cobbled square—the main square in Szentendre—is more triangular than square in shape. Several of the lanes leading off it head down toward the Danube. In the center is a **plague cross**, similar to those seen in many Hungarian towns. It was erected in 1763 by the Serbian merchants' association to commemorate the town being spared from a plague epidemic. Boutiques and restaurants line the square, the outdoor terraces of which are of course crowded with visitors on sunny days.

★ Kmetty Múzeum A2

Fő tér 21. Part of the FMC, see p95.

Located in a former merchant's house, this museum is devoted entirely to the painter **János Kmetty** (1889–1975). During his first trip to Paris in 1911, he was influenced by artists such as Cézanne, which would become apparent in his first landscape paintings. He subsequently met Lajos Kassák and the group of artists known as the Activists. He taught fine arts in Budapest and, from 1930

SZENTENDRE

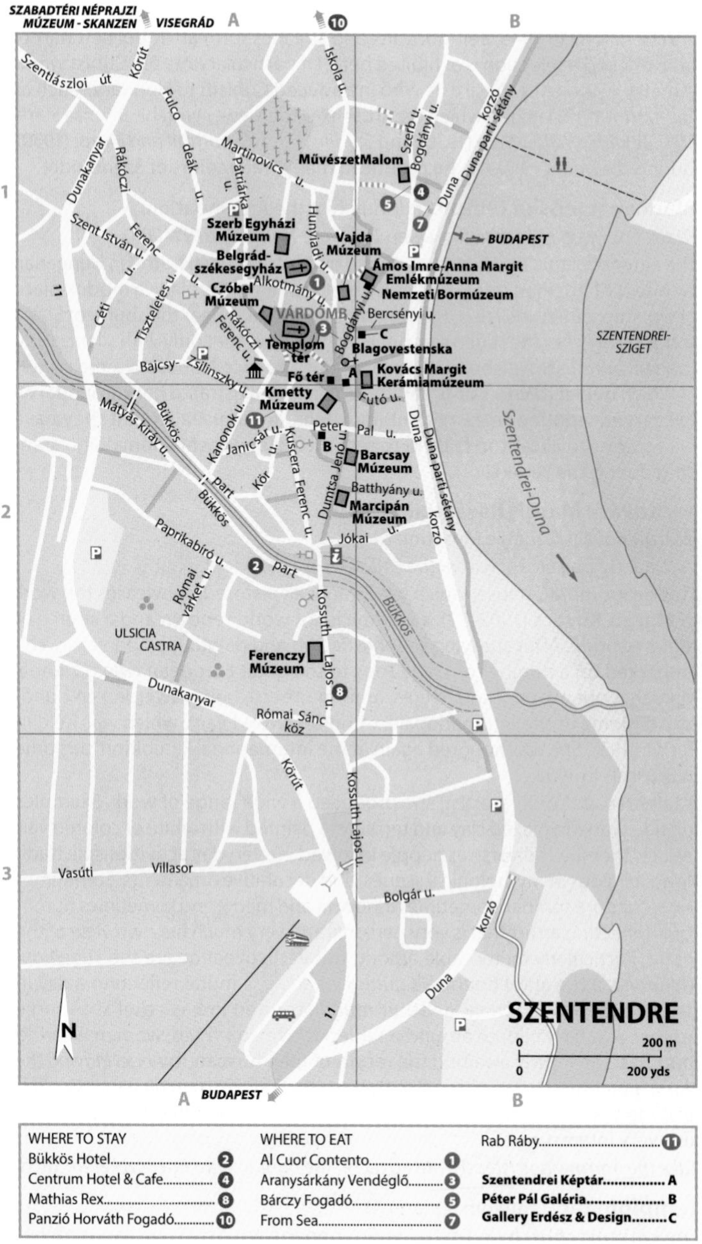

WHERE TO STAY	WHERE TO EAT	Rab Ráby........ 11
Bükkös Hotel........ 2	Al Cuor Contento........ 1	
Centrum Hotel & Cafe........ 4	Aranysárkány Vendéglő........ 3	**Szentendrei Képtár........ A**
Mathias Rex........ 8	Bárczy Fogadó........ 5	**Péter Pál Galéria........ B**
Panzió Horváth Fogadó........ 10	From Sea........ 7	**Gallery Erdész & Design........ C**

onward, spent his summers at Szentendre, becoming a member of the local artists' colony in 1945. Self-portraits and still lifes form an important part of his work and a selection is exhibited here. Of particular note are Cubist works (Kmetty was one of the artists who introduced Cubism to Hungary), such as *Self-portrait* (1911–17), in which the artist fixes the viewer with his intense stare, *Still Life with a Yellow Vase* (1930), and *Still life with Self-portrait and Mirror* (1930). During the years 1940–50, he produced many watercolors of Szentendre.

Blagovesztenska templom (Church of the Annunciation) A1

Fő tér. Entrance in Görög utca. Open Tue–Sun, 10am–5pm. Ft400.

The exterior of this 18C church, designed by **András Mayerhoffer** (a Hungarian architect of Austrian origin), gives no hint that it is a Serbian Orthodox place of worship, but inside it is a different matter. You may hear the sound of Slavic songs rising from the sanctuary, but even if you are met only with silence, you can still admire the elaborate funishings and Rococo iconostasis, the panels of which depict mainly saints painted against an illustrated background. The tall carved wooden seats, resembling stalls, are unusual in that they have raised arms to allow the faithful to rest their elbows while remaining standing during the service.

★★ **Kovács Margit Kerámiamúzeum**

(Margit Kovács Ceramic Museum) B1

Vastagh György utca 1. Part of the FMC, *see p95.*

This beautiful 18C house, which has been well restored, showcases the work of **Margit Kovács** (1902–77), a ceramicist of world renown and a source of regional pride. After studying graphic design and painting on porcelain, she embarked on a number of study trips to the great European cities (Vienna, Munich, Copenhagen, and Sèvres, among others), being awarded an honorary diploma at the International Exhibition (World Fair), which was held in Paris in 1937. She was honored again at the International Exhibition, this time in Brussels in 1958.

A talented and prolific artist, she produced a wide range of work. Examples include works in glazed clay and terracotta painted with white or colored varnish on themes as diverse as people involved in everyday activities, folk traditions, religious or mythological scenes, and decorative ornaments. Sometimes the results are somber, sometimes innocent and merry, and sometimes humorous, reflecting an art that is very personal and very much her own view of the world. Particularly memorable among this vast collection are the *Kugelhopf Madonna*, a beautiful figurine; *Country Wedding*, a mural reflecting a day in peasant life; *Large Family*, another mural sculpted in bas-relief showing a mother and her children around a table; *Fishermen's Wives*, women wearing long coats anxiously awaiting the return of their husbands; *Angel Playing the Harp*, a painted and varnished sculpture; and unvarnished sculptures such as *Pottery with Bagpipe Player*. A video that shows the artist hard at work is also very interesting.

Take the narrow lane (steps) from Fő tér on the right toward Rákóczi Ferenc utca.

Templom tér (Templom Square) A1

The **catholic church** dedicated to St. John the Baptist (Szent János plébánia templom) occupies a large part of this square on top of a low hill. The most visible sections of the exterior date from the beginning of the 14C. The interior is Baroque with painted wooden altars decorated with statues, also in wood. The painted frescoes in the choir are modern, by members of the Szentendre artists' colony.

The **Czóbel Múzeum** is in one of the buildings lining the square, looking over toward the church. It exhibits the works of **Béla Czóbel** (1883–1976), a Hungarian painter and member of the Paris School, who divided his time between Budapest and the French capital, where he worked with the Post-Impressionists and Fauvists. A talented portrait painter, Czóbel focused on painting women. His portraits are diverse, the colors bright, and his paintings full of lyricism and a certain mystery. He was the first Hungarian painter to have a museum dedicated to him in his own lifetime.

Belgrád Szerb ortodox székesegyház

(Serbian Orthodox Church) A1

Entrance on Alkomány utca. Open Tue–Sun, 10am–6pm. Ft700 (including museum).
The church was named for the Serbian refugees from Belgrade who built it in the late 18C. The steeple soars skyward above its red walled exterior. The entrance is through a Rococo carved oak door, behind which lies a highly ornate Baroque interior. The beautiful **iconostasis★** has gilded ornamentation and paintings that depict the saints, and above, the life of Jesus.
It is possible to attend an Orthodox service—hearing the Gregorian chants and litanies performed by the priests is a lovely and atmospheric experience.

Szerb Egyházi Múzeum (Serbian Museum of Ecclesiastical Art) A1

Next door to the Serbian church. 312 399. Open May–Sept, Tue–Sun, 10am–6pm; Mar–Apr & Oct–Dec, Tue–Sun, 10am–4pm; Jan–Feb, Fri–Sun, 10am–4pm. Ft700 (including the church).
The exhibits are displayed over two floors (explanations in English and Hungarian). Look out for the iconostasis from the Buda Serbian Orthodox Church (19C), an 18C carved wooden tomb attributed to Teodor Phelonin Grunkoviæ, several grand 18C papal robes, and Serbian and Russian icons, as well as an incunable (a very early printed document) in four volumes dating from the end of the 15C.
Take Alkomány utca, a small street leading downward. Turn left into Hunyadi utca.

★ Vajda Múzeum A1

Hunyadi utca 1. Part of the FMC, see p95, currently closed for renovation work.
Lajos Vajda (1908–41) was an important figure in 20C Hungarian painting. Before settling in this bourgeois apartment in the 19C, he spent four years in Paris (1930–34), where he studied with Fernand Léger. His work reveals a number of influences—traditional art, religious symbols, Cubism, Surrealism, and later, Abstract art. When Nazism and Stalin were on the rise, his subjects became the darkness of nature and the human soul. His paintings are somber and disquieting, while his self-portraits have a mystical feel in the style of modern icons. The museum and its garden also display work by contemporary artists based in Szentendre.
Return to Alkomány utca. The small street named Ferenczy Károly leads to Bogdányi utca.

Nemzeti Bormúzeum (National Wine Museum) B1

Bogdány utca 10. bor-kor.hu. Tastings and sale of Hungarian wines.
Part of the restaurant Labirintus (meaning Labyrinth) building, the wine museum introduces visitors to Hungary's 22 winegrowing regions in a beautiful vaulted cellar. Wine (4,000 bottles) from around 150 different producers is also on sale, with cellarmen on hand to give advice to prospective buyers, as well as some rare vintages from the museum's own cellar (requiring a budget to match!).

1

Ámos Imre – Anna Margit Emlékmúzeum (Ámos Imre – Anna Margit Memorial Museum) B1

Bogdányi utca 10. Part of the FMC, see p95, currently closed for renovation work.

A leading figure in Hungarian art, **Margit Anna** (1913–91) and her husband **Imre Ámos** (1907–44) were two charismatic artists. Margit's boldly colorful paintings have recurring themes of Nazism and the Holocaust while Imre's Surrealist paintings reveal a dreamlike world. Their home, which has become a museum, is all the more poignant because Anna's remains were laid to rest here. You will see her simple stone tomb in the courtyard when you arrive. Although both artists were Jewish, only Margit surived to live on into old age while Imre died in a concentration camp.

GALLERIES AND OTHER VENUES HOLDING TEMPORARY EXHIBITIONS

In addition to the museums dedicated to major artists in Szentendre, a number of other venues in the town showcase works of art both past and present. They include:

Szentendrei Képtár (Szentendre Gallery) A1

Fő tér 2–5. Part of the FMC, see p95.

Established in 1978 on the first floor of a former office building, for a long time this was the only art gallery in the area. Today its position in the center of Szentendre makes it a key venue for temporary exhibitions.

MűvészetMalom (ArtMill) B1

Bogdányi utca 32. Part of the FMC, see p95.

In 1998, following a collaboration between the town and the Szentendre Art Foundation, this former 19C flour mill was transformed into a large display space (over three levels) devoted to temporary exhibitions of modern art.

Péter Pál Galéria A2

Péter Pál utca 1. 311 182. Open 10am–6pm. No charge.

The gallery aims to approach the traditional applied arts in a contemporary way. There are displays of embroidery, carpets, curtains, ceramics, place mats, and glassware, among other things, all handmade in a contemporary style. Temporary exhibitions by local or international artists are also held here.

Gallery Erdész & Design B1

Bercsényi utca 4. (30) 941 7896. www.galleryerdesz.hu. Open 10am–6pm.

The upper floor displays work—principally paintings and sculptures—by artists with Szentendre connections (Korniss, Vajda, Barcsay). The first (ground) floor is where Hungarian and foreign designers exhibit and sell their work, including silver rings by Péter Vladimir and decorative glasswork by Márton Horváth.

Excursions Regional map (p28–29)

★★ **Szabadtéri Néprajzi Múzeum** (Hungarian Open-air Museum) B1

2.5mi/4km north of Szentendre, follow directions to "Skanzen," turning left off Rte 11. Address: Sztaravodai út 75. Parking (Ft900/day). By bus (bus station next to HÉV railway station), www.volanbusz.hu. Buses every hour Mon–Fri, every two hours Sat & Sun, from bus stop 7. Parking (Ft900/day).

502 537. www.skanzen.hu. Open Apr–beg Nov, Tue–Sun, 9am–5pm; Mar & Nov open on certain days, check for details. Ft2,000. To get around inside the museum: a 1930s-style train Ft500/day; bike or scooter hire Ft600/day.

Interior of one of the houses, Open-air Museum
©H. Payelle/Michelin

Allow a full day to visit the museum and take part in some of the activities. There is a café and a restaurant at the museum entrance, a wine bar (in the Northern Uplands museum section), and a bakery (the Great Plain section).
Opened in 1967 at the foot of the Pilis Mountains, which form part of the **Duna-Ipoly Nemzeti Park** (Duna-Ipoly National Park), this is the largest open-air museum in Hungary. Its aim is to preserve traditional Hungarian architecture by selecting existing buildings from the different regions, dismantling, and then reconstructing them here where the public can visit them. Today there are more than 300 buildings to see arranged in regional units over an area of 148 acres/60ha; they provide a unique insight into rural life in Hungary from the second half of the 18C to the first half of the 20C.
This charming and fascinating museum aims to preserve a traditional world that has now all but disappeared in the face of urbanization and modernization. You can look inside the buildings, some very humble and some more grand, many of which have been laid out to form streets or squares with a church, schoolroom, store … just as they would have been before being transported here. Eight Hungarian regions are represented: Northern Hungary, Northern Uplands (Tokaj, Gyöngyös, Mád), Upper Tisza, the Alföld (Great Plain), Southern Transdanubia, Upper Balaton/Bakony, Western Transdanubia, and Kisalföld (Little Plain). Each region/village has themed exhibitions and different workshops where craftspeople demonstrate various traditional skills (tannery, candlemaking, breadmaking, cookie making, wool spinning, woodworking, syrup making). Animals complete the scene, such as the famous Hungarian cattle (Great Plain), with their long curved horns.
In the Upper Tisza village look out for the Calvinist church with its painted interior and wooden belfry, as well as the rotary mill driven by horses. In the Great Plain the thatched houses combine living accommodation, storage sheds, and stables all under one roof. In the Kisalföld region, a votive chapel marks the beginning of a main street lined with houses, while in the Balaton region the houses are built from volcanic rock with cellars for storing wine.

ADDRESSES IN SZENTENDRE

See Szentendre map p97

ARRIVAL/DEPARTURE

Train – HÉV 5 from Budapest, Batthyány tér *(departures every 30min, 40min journey).*

Bus – *www.volanbusz.hu.* From Árpád hid Bus Station in Budapest *(bus line 880/882, 30min journey).*

Boat – the Mahart Passnave line from Budapest – *℘ (1) 484 4000. www.mahartpassnave.hu. 1hr30min journey. Ft2,540 (round trip Ft3,820).*
Mid-Apr–Sept, Tue–Sun: departs from Vigadó tér, Budapest, at 2pm, from Batthyány tér at 2.10pm; returns at 4.30pm.
Mid-Apr–Jun & Sept–Oct, Tue–Sun: departs from Vigadó tér at 10.30am, from Batthyány tér at 10.40am; returns at 9.30pm.
Jun–Aug, Tue–Sun: departs from Vigadó tér at 6pm, from Batthyány tér at 6.10pm; returns at 9.30pm.
Mid-Apr–Aug, Tue–Sun; Sept, Sat only: departs from Vigadó tér at 9am; returns at 7pm.

STAY

BUDGET

10 Panzió Horváth Fogadó – A1, off map – *Daru piac 2. ℘ 313 950. www.horvathfogado.hu.* P *4 rooms (including 1 family room). Ft12,600/19,400. ☕ Ft1,500.* A 10min walk from the center of town, this guesthouse is in a quiet area. The rooms are simple but well appointed. You will be welcomed by a charming couple who are happy for you to use their garden in fine weather.

AVERAGE

8 Mathias Rex – A2 – *Kossuth Lajos utca 16. ℘ 505 570. www.mathiasrexhotel.hu.* P *12 rooms and studios. Ft16,500/29,500. ☕.* This elegant guesthouse is near the station and the downtown area. The rooms are light and modern and there is a terrace for breakfast, which is hearty and provides a good choice. Good value for money.

4 Centrum Hotel & Cafe – B1 – *Bogdányi út 15. ℘ 302 500. www.centrumhotelszentendre.hu.* P *7 rooms. Ft16,000/35,000. ☕ Ft1,500.* This small hotel is in a lovely location on the Duna korzó. It also has a café and bar.

SPLASH OUT

2 Bükkös Hotel – A1, off map – *Bükkös part 16. ℘ 501 360. www.bukkoshotel.hu.* P ✕ *22 rooms, Ft31,500/44,000. ☕ Restaurant.* A peaceful boutique hotel (for adults only) beside a small river with views of the town's bell towers. The rooms are spacious, modern, and well-equipped. The spa offers a welcome retreat after a day out.

EAT

BUDGET

1 Al Cuor Contento – A1 – *Alkotmány utca 5. ℘ (30) 359 8778. Ft1,490/2,590.* If you feel like a change from Hungarian cuisine, why not eat Italian? This is a great little place, run by an Italian, of course. He knows how to charm his clientele with pasta dishes cooked *al dente* in the style of his homeland, which are accompanied by delightful wines from small producers.

7 From Sea – B1 – *Tinódi köz (a small street linking Bogdányi út with Duna korzó). Ft1,700/4,300.* In this small street leading down to the river in one direction, try the simple fish and seafood dishes served at one of a handful of tables. Everything is very fresh and tasty.

11 **Rab Ráby** – A2 – *Kucsera Ferenc utca 1. ✆ 310 819. www.rabraby.hu. Ft1,700/4,000.* Despite an interior overflowing with antiques and collectibles, from earthenware plates and vintage posters, to armor and farm implements, you will still be able to eat authentic Hungarian cuisine with a choice of well-prepared dishes, many of which feature goose meat. A small patio to enjoy on sunny days.

5 **Bárczy Fogadó** – B1 – *Bogdányi utca 3. ✆ 310 825. From Ft2,500.* This restaurant in an 18C building specializes in Serbian and Hungarian cuisine. Once through the entrance and away from the noise of the road, the decor is rustic, with whitewashed walls and traditional blue tablecloths (produced by a method of dyeing cloth indigo-blue, a speciality of the town of Győr, *see p227*).

AVERAGE

3 **Aranysárkány Vendéglő** – A1 – *Alkotmány utca 1. ✆ 301 479. www.aranysarkany.hu. Ft3,100/5,900. Menus Ft4,100/7,900.* Keep an eye out or you might miss the entrance to this restaurant in a small, steep street. The food is delicious and the prices reasonable.

TAKING A BREAK

Szamos – *Dumtsa Jenő utca 12. ✆ 310 545. szamosmarcipan.hu. Open 9am–7pm (Sat & Sun, 10am–7pm).* Budapest's famous chocolate maker has a café in Szentendre. It's somewhere not to be missed if you fancy a great cup of coffee and a pastry served in traditional Viennese style (interior design included). A real treat.

SHOPPING

Shop till you drop in Bogdányi, Bercsényi, Alkotmány, Szerb, or Dumtsa Jenő utcák (streets).

Kovács Kékfestő – *Bogdányi utca 36. ✆ 314 388. www.kekfestokovacs.com. Open 10am–6pm.* Devoted entirely to selling fabric dyed indigo-blue, a Kovács family specialty, the technique having been passed from father to son and daughter since 1878. Whether you are looking for small items or clothing, the quality is excellent.

Szakrális Szövőműhely – *Szerb utca 2. ✆ (70) 380 8534. www.szakralis-szovomuhely.hu. Open 11am–6pm.* You can see the three looms that Brigitta Bicseki uses every day to produce beautiful fabrics that are made into shawls, tablecloths, and rugs, proof of her great skill and craftsmanship.

EVENTS AND FESTIVALS

Spring Festival – April. Theater productions and concerts.

Art Capital – End May–end Aug. An art festival showcasing work by Hungarian and international artists. Exhibitions are also held in the town museums. *www.artcapital.hu*

"Day and Night" – Last Sat & Sun in Aug. Exhibitions, workshops, themed walks, street music, film screenings, theatrical performances.

Wine and Jazz Festival – *Last Sat & Sun in Sept.* Wine fair, concerts, wine-themed walks, tastings.

Visegrád

★★

Population 1,840 – Pest county – area code ☏ 26

The name Visegrád is of Slavic origin, meaning "the acropolis" or "the upper castle," and the citadel that looks down on the river below is one sight on the Danube Bend that is not to be missed. The town itself is surrounded by forested hills where King Matthias would go hunting. Today the hunters and noblemen have been replaced by walkers and visitors, who come to enjoy the rich heritage of this town of kings.

ADDRESSES PAGE 107
Stay, Eat, Events and Festivals

INFO:
Tourist Office – *Duna-parti út 1. ☏ 397 188. www.visitvisegrad.hu. Open Tue–Sun, 10am–4pm.*

LOCATION:
Regional map B1 (p28–29).
25mi/40km north of Budapest via Rte 11, on the right (west) bank of the Danube.

PARKING:
Large car park on Rte 11 in the center of the town.

DON'T MISS:
The palace below, the citadel above.

TIMING:
Allow 1 whole day to visit Visegrád.

KIDS:
Budding knights will be wide-eyed at the sight of medieval tournaments being reenacted in the town's three "castles" (the Royal Palace, Solomon Tower, and the Citadel).

Walking tour

★ **Királyi Palota** (Royal Palace)
Fő utca 29. ☏ 597 010. www.visegradmuzeum.hu. Open Tue–Sun, 9am–5pm. Ft1,300.

In its heyday this 15C palace, one of the largest in Hungary, had 300 rooms. Although many are now in ruins, the main building was reconstructed in the 20C. The palace became derelict after the Turks destroyed much of it during their occupation. However, after years of research and excavation work (see the exhibits of crockery, weapons, tools, fragments of ornamentation on the first/ground floor, panels in English), archeologists were able to identify the remains of part of the palace and reconstruct it. What we see today is only a small part of what was once here, but it still provides a good idea of how splendid the palace once was. As it was the residence of the kings of Hungary for more than two centuries, the palace was the epicenter of the kingdom on many occasions, until the court was moved to Buda in 1410. It later became the summer residence of King Matthias during his reign *(see box opposite)*.

The building is on the slope of the hillside and is laid out on terraces over several levels, part way between the lower town and the citadel. Today it is possible to visit the first (ground) floor and two other floors where rooms have been recreated and furnished (banqueting hall, King Sigismund's bedroom,

Renaissance apartments, and the royal kitchen). Some decorative Renaissance elements can be seen, including two fountains—the famous **Oroszlános kút** (the red marble Lion Fountain), the first monumental sculpture to be created outside Italy, and the **Herkules kút** (Hercules Fountain), decorated with the coat of arms of Matthias Corvinus, in the pretty ceremonial courtyard, which is enclosed by colonnaded galleries.

The **gardens**, which have also been reconstructed, include a simple enclosed garden, an orchard, and a relaxing area with a fountain.

Tournaments with knights on horseback take place in summer (*see Events and Festivals, p107*).

Salamon-torony (Solomon Tower)

Salomontorony utca (steps to the right of Hotel Vár). 597 010. www.visegrad.hu. Open May–Sept, Wed–Sun, 9am–5pm. Ft700.

Situated at the foot of the citadel, to which it is linked by the fortified castle wall, the hexagonal Solomon Tower was built during the reign of Béla IV as a lookout for possible invaders. At more than 98ft/30m high and with walls almost 26ft/8m thick, it is a very solid piece of defensive construction. Inside, on several levels, are exhibitions tracing the history of Visegrád.

Tournaments between knights on horseback and medieval displays are regularly organized here.

1

★★ Fellegvár ("The castle in the clouds," the Citadel)

Accessible on foot, a 30min steep walk uphill (there are two forest paths: from the Solomon Tower, signs with a blue cross on white background; or to the left of the post office, signs with a horizontal blue line on a white background). Alternatively, access by car via the scenic road (parking Ft300/day).

A PALACE THAT ROSE FROM THE ASHES

The Romans built the first fortress on the site that would become Visegrád in the 4C. By around the turn of the 10C, the Slavs were in residence here and they named it Visegrád. Two hundred and fifty years later, by which time the kingdom of Hungary had been founded, **King Béla IV** (r. 1235–70) ordered a residential keep (Solomon's Tower) to be built by the river at the foot of the hill and a citadel on top. When King Charles I (r. 1308–42) conquered Visegrád a century later, he installed himself in the citadel. Charles was succeeded by Louis I of Anjou (r. 1342–82) who decided to add a lower section to the fortress, transforming several existing buildings into a proper palace (with a chapel, gardens, and fountains). After this, Sigismund of Luxembourg (r. 1387–1437) expanded the palace but in around 1410 moved the royal court permanently to Budapest. Several decades later Visegrád became a summer residence that **Matthias Corvinus** (r. 1458–90) went on to transform into an opulent Renaissance palace.

Matthias and his queen, Beatrice, brought in Italian Renaissance artists who enriched the palace with fountains, lavish decorations, and gardens. They received distinguished guests here, among them a papal legate who described Visegrád Palace as "an earthly paradise." The arrival of the Turkish armies led to the destruction of the palace and the remains were used as a source of stone for other building work. Over time its former glory and importance were forgotten and all traces of the building were lost. It wasn't until 1934 that **Frigyes Schulek** (the architect behind Fisherman's Bastion in Budapest) found the site and began to uncover the ruins.

Fellegvár Citadel
© Hungarian Tourism Agency

398 101. www.visegrad.hu. Open Apr–Sept, 9am–6pm; Mar & Oct, 9am–5pm; Nov, 9am–4pm; Dec–Feb, Fri–Sat, 10am–4pm. Closed 24 Dec. Ft1,700.
Situated at a height of 1,148ft/350m and built between 1240 and 1255, the citadel is associated with two important events. The first was in November 1335 when King Charles I (Károly Róbert) hosted the **Congress of Visegrád** here, at which the kings of Poland and Bohemia and the knights of the Teutonic Order agreed to join forces in an anti-Habsburg alliance. This made it possible to establish a new route that bypassed Vienna and facilitated trade between Central Europe and the East (see the display in the castle outbuildings).
The second concerns the coronation regalia, which was kept at the castle until 1440 when the Holy Crown was stolen by one of Elizabeth of Luxembourg's handmaids—on Elizabeth's orders—and taken to Székesfehérvár, where she intended to crown her son Ladislas V. Ladislas did indeed become king, but not until he was elected king of Hungary four years later and today the crown is kept at the Parliament Building in Budapest.
It is quite a climb up to the castle, but the sight that greets you on arrival is pretty much unchanged from the one admired by the kings and queens of long ago. Visegrád's main attraction is without doubt the **view★★★** from the citadel. It is here that the Danube Bend as a descriptive term really makes sense. Marking the border between Slovakia and Hungary for around 62mi/100km, the river meanders between the Börzsöny and Pilis mountains before bending around and flowing on toward the Hungarian capital. Directly opposite you can see the town of Nagymaros *(see p93)*.
The tower houses several exhibitions: the history of the citadel's construction; medieval arms and armor; and the traditional activities of the inhabitants of the citadel and the surrounding area, such as hunting, fishing, and so on.
During the summer months, various **shows and demonstrations** (tournaments, reenacted battles, archery, …) are held either within the citadel itself or beside its walls.

ADDRESSES IN VISEGRÁD

ARRIVAL/DEPARTURE

Bus – Bus line 880/882 operates between Budapest and Visegrád *(journey time 1hr 15min via Szentendre)*; departures roughly every 30min. *www.volanbusz.hu*

Boat – Mahart Passnave line from Budapest – *(1) 484 4000. www.mahartpassnave.hu. Mid-Apr–Aug, Tue–Sun; Sept, Sat only: departs from Budapest, Vigadó tér at 9am; returns at 5.40pm. Journey time 3hrs 20min. Ft3,180 (round trip Ft4,760). End-Apr–Sept, Tue–Sun: departs from Vigadó tér at 10am; returns at 5.30pm. Journey time 1hr. Ft4,300 (round trip Ft6,500).*

STAY

AVERAGE

Honti Panzió and Hotel Honti – *Duna-parti út. 398 120. www.hotelhonti.hu.* P *Panzió: 7 rooms, Ft19,440/22,680. Hotel: 23 rooms, Ft29,160/38,880.* Looking a little like a Swiss chalet, Hotel Honti is near the main street, but set back from the road, which protects it from too much noise. Modern bedrooms with balconies. A nice spa and outdoor pool. Honti Panzió (guesthouse) shares the same facilities (access to the spa and pool) while being less expensive.

Butikhotel Visegrád – *Mátyás Király út 61. (20) 388 0676. butikhotelvisegrad.hu/en/nyitolap_en/. 12 rooms. From Ft26,000.* Opened in 2019, this small hotel is on the road leading to the citadel, not far from the town center, but surrounded by trees. Comfortable rooms with a balcony and air-conditioning. A hot tub and sauna. Breakfast is buffet style, with two nearby restaurants recommended for dinner (shuttle bus available).

EAT

BUDGET

Kovács-kert Étterem – *Rév utca 4. 398 123. www.kovacs-kertetterem.hu. Ft1,100/3,000.* This restaurant serves very generous portions of Hungarian cuisine. Whether eating in the dining room or on the terrace, service is prompt and comes with a smile. A Visegrád address that we'd recommend.

Sirály Étterem – *Rév utca 15. 398 376. www.siralyvisegrad.hu. Ft2,200/4,500.* A large restaurant in the center of town, which welcomes groups as well as Hungarian families and tourists passing through. The food (Hungarian cuisine) is hearty, the menu is in English, and the welcome is warm.

EVENTS AND FESTIVALS

International Palace Games – Mid-July over 3 days. The Visegrád Congress of 1335 is remembered and celebrated over three days in summer. The courtyard of the Royal Palace is transformed into a setting for medieval tournaments and contests. Mounted knights, musicians, dancers, flag and spear throwers come from all over Central Europe and gather at the Royal Palace. In medieval costume, wearing breastplates and carrying halberds, they make a fantastic sight.

Esztergom

★

Population 27,840 – Komárom-Esztergom county – area code ✆ 33

At the point where the Danube flows from west to east past Esztergom, it still forms the border between Slovakia and northern Hungary. Once past the town, the border parts company with the river and heads north, while the river makes a sharp, 90-degree turn to form the famous Danube Bend (Dunakanyar) and carries on flowing south. It was at Esztergom that Stephen, the first king of Hungary and founder of the modern state, was crowned in 1000. Stephen divided the country into ten bishoprics and decreed that it would be the archbishop of Esztergom who would crown all future monarchs, a tradition that was maintained from that time onward and the royal family were resident in the town until the 13C. Today, Esztergom is the seat of the Catholic Church in Hungary.

ADDRESSES PAGE 113
Stay, Eat, Taking a Break

INFO:
There is no tourist office at Esztergom. See the website www.esztergom.hu

LOCATION:
Regional map A1 (p28–29); Esztergom map (p111)
Northwest of Budapest: 30mi/49km on Rte 10; 42mi/67km on Rte 11, which skirts the Danube via Szentendre and Visegrád.

PARKING:
Car parks at the foot of the basilica or near the Mária-Valéria Bridge.

DON'T MISS:
The basilica and the castle.

TIMING:
Allow a fairly short day to visit.

KIDS:
The Danube Museum and its interactive exhibits.

Discover Esztergom map (p111)

The location

Thanks to the two hills **Vár-hegy** (Castle Hill) and **Szent Tamás-hegy** (St. Thomas Hill), the terrain of the town is quite varied. A narrow arm of the Danube, the Kis-Duna (Little Danube), flows a short way inland, separating the tranquil **Prímás-sziget** (Primate's Island) from the rest of the town at the edge of Víziváros (Watertown). A 10-minute walk from the basilica leads to the bridge (Kossuth Lajos híd) that crosses to the northern end of the island. The ferry that operates between Hungary and Slovakia and the boats going down the Danube toward Budapest depart from the island.

VÁR-HEGY (CASTLE HILL) A1

★ **Szent Adalbert Főszékesegyház** (Esztergom Basilica)
✆ (20) 268 1553 www.bazilika-esztergom.hu. Open Apr–Sept, 8am–7pm; end Mar–end Apr & Oct, 8am–6pm; Mar, 8am–5pm; rest of the year, 8am–4pm. Main building no charge, crypt Ft300, treasury Ft900, panorama hall Ft300, the dome Ft700. Combined ticket Ft1,500.

Esztergom Basilica and Castle
© Funkystock/age fotostock

In the 19C the imposing Cathedral of our Lady of the Assumption and St. Adalbert (Esztergom Basilica), replaced a church originally founded by King Stephen I dedicated to the saint. It was destroyed during the course of fighting

THE FOUNDING OF THE HUNGARIAN STATE AND CHURCH

Home to the royal family for three centuries and the religious capital of Hungary, Esztergom has been the center of Hungarian Catholicism for more than a thousand years and remains the seat of the archbishop primate of Hungary.

The town keeps alive the memory of **Grand Prince Géza**, the supreme Magyar chieftain and a key member of the ruling Árpád dynasty. After having raised an army, he established his seat of power at Gran (subsequently named Esztergom) and reigned there from 972 until 997. His son Vajk, baptized István (Stephen), ruled as prince from 997 to 1000, before being crowned the first king of Hungary on Christmas Day of that year. Once crowned, **Stephen I** asserted his authority. He settled part of the nomadic population, forcing every tenth village to build a church and support a priest. He founded two archbishoprics and built a basilica. He also introduced the concept of openness and tolerance.

Having chosen the Western form of Christianity over the Greek Church (Eastern Orthodoxy), first Géza and then his son Stephen I, placed Hungary at the heart of Europe, making it one of the most advanced bastions of Western civilization. Esztergom thrived—its golden age lasted from the end of the 12C to the middle of the 14C, with the king entertaining numerous foreign rulers. However in the mid 13C, following the Tartar invasion, King Béla IV transferred the royal seat to Buda. The archbishop remained in the town, moving into the Royal Palace. Subsequent archbishops welcomed renowned European scholars and artists, making Esztergom a major cultural center that rivaled the capital.

against the Turks and only the chapel, built by Cardinal **Tamás (Thomas) Bakócz**, survived the vicissitudes of war. The cardinal's fame is not solely due to having built the chapel, but also to having been entrusted with the leadership of a crusade against the Turks that in 1514 descended into a peasant's revolt. This was because, some said, Bakócz regretted not having succeeded in becoming pope. What remained of the chapel was dismantled (into 1,600 pieces) at the beginning of the 19C and removed from its original site to be reconstructed next to the present basilica. The **Bakócz Chapel★** is one of the oldest remaining examples of Renaissance art that exists outside Italy. Built of red marble, it was created by Tuscan sculptors.

The new basilica, designed by Pál Kühnel and János Packh, was completed in 1869 by Joseph Hild, architect of Eger Cathedral Basilica, in the neo-classical style seen today. The foundation stone was laid in 1822 and work continued for nearly 50 years, with the building being consecrated in 1856. **Franz Liszt** composed and conducted the mass known as the *Gran Mass* (Gran being the German name for Esztergom) for the occasion.

The basilica is an integral part of the Esztergom landscape. You can't miss it thanks to its imposing size (387ft/118m long, 154ft/47m wide, with a facade of 318ft/97m and a total height of 328ft/100m) and its position perched on the hilltop towering over the Danube. Various artists had a hand in its decoration and inside is a copy of Titian's *Assumption of the Virgin*, said to be the largest picture ever painted on canvas; the original is in Venice.

Crypt – Hungary's cardinals have been buried in this crypt since Ambrus Károly, prince archbishop of Esztergom, was interred here in 1809. Cardinal **Mindszenty**, primate of Hungary, who took refuge in the American Embassy after the events of 1956 and died in exile Vienna in 1971, also lies here. It was not until 1991 that he was buried at Esztergom as he had expressed the wish not to be interred in Hungary until after the last Soviet soldier had left the country. The two statues standing guard representing Mourning and Eternity, lit by candles, add atmosphere.

Treasury – *60 steps.* Many sacred objects used for religious celebrations are on display. Included in the opulent collection are ceremonial robes, chalices, ciboria, crucifixes, and patens. Of particular note is the Baroque chalice that belonged to Holy Roman empress Maria Theresa, the monstrance of Garamszentbenedek, King Matthias's gold calvary cross encrusted with enamel, as well as many Italian, Byzantine, and Hungarian items that are steeped in history.

Panorama Hall – An initial flight of 120 steps leads to the upper level of the basilica, where there is a small exhibition about its construction as well as a café where you can have a drink while you survey the town through a large arched window.

Dome – The 400 steps of a narrow spiral staircase climb up to the base of the dome from where there is a 360-degree **view** over the Danube Bend, Esztergom, and the Slovakian town of Štúrovo across the river.

★ Magyar Nemzeti Múzeum Esztergomi Vármúzeuma

(Esztergom Castle Museum)

✆ 500 095. www.varmegom.hu. Open Apr–Oct, 10am–6pm; Nov–Mar, 10am–4pm; Tue–Sun. Ft1,600.

Built at the end of the 12C during the reign of King Béla III, the castle (the former **Royal Palace**) is situated on the southern part of the plateau. It was largely destroyed by the Turks in the 16C, but started to come to life again in 1930 when archeological excavations began. After King Béla IV moved the

ESZTERGOM

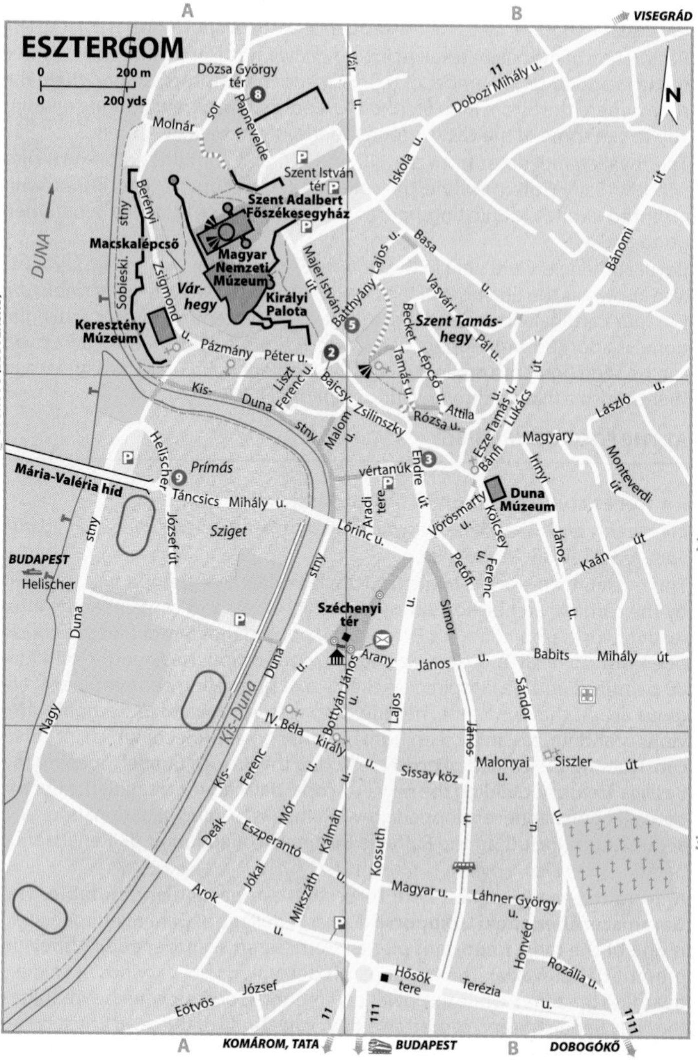

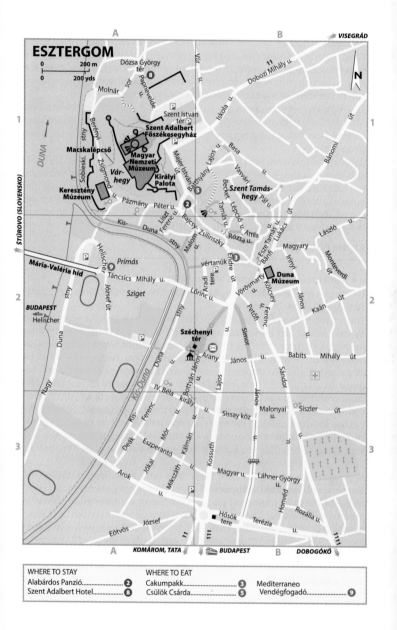

WHERE TO STAY
- Alabárdos Panzió 2
- Szent Adalbert Hotel 8

WHERE TO EAT
- Cakumpakk 3
- Csülök Csárda 5
- Mediterraneo Vendégfogadó 9

royal seat to Buda, it became the residence of the archbishops of Esztergom. Restoration of the palace resulted in the uncovering of interesting architectural features and today a number of rooms are open to visitors, among them the room where the future King Stephen was born. Transparent flooring enables you to see some of the castle's foundations as you walk over them.

The royal chapel dates from the 11C and 12C and contains an original rose window. Early Gothic in style, the columns in the chapel are decorated with sculpted capitals depiciting figures that symbolize the struggle between good and evil.

Royal audiences were held in the Double Chamber (15C) on the upper level, also known as the Chamber of Virtues. It is decorated with frescoes depicting the four cardinal virtues and is attributed to a Florentine master, while the dome is adorned with signs of the zodiac. A reproduction of the Holy Crown can be seen here (the original is in the Parliament Building in Budapest) and there is also a marble throne dating from the 12C.

AT THE FOOT OF VÁR-HEGY (CASTLE HILL) A1

★★ Keresztény Múzeum (Christian Museum)

Mindszenty tér 2. www.keresztenymuzeum.hu. Open Mar–Dec, Wed–Sun, 10am–5pm. Ft 900. Allow 2hrs for visit.

This museum, one of the largest diocesan museums in Europe, was founded by the cardinal archbishop **János Simor** (1813–91) and contains some interesting works from different European Schools. János Simor had previously been bishop of Győr, where he began his collection. He brought with him 80 paintings and was inspired by the idea of promoting contemporary religious art. At the same time, he sought to restore some of Esztergom's previous grandeur, as can be seen from his other great projects, which included constructing the cathedral porch, restoring the Bakócz Chapel, opening the Basilica Treasury, building the new episcopal palace, and creating the library. His collection has never stopped growing thanks to important donations and acquisitions (including the Raffaele Bertinelli collection of 63 Renaissance paintings in 1878).

Among the many exhibits are three that are particularly notable. The **Garamszentbenedeki Úrkoporsó** (Easter Sepulchre of Garamszentbenedek) is one of the most important pieces, from Garamszentbenedek Abbey (in present-day Slovakia). The upper part is decorated with carvings of soldiers guarding the tomb, while the lower part mounted on four wheels symbolizes the Holy Sepulchre and carried an effigy of the body of the dead Christ (a carved wooden statue that today is kept in Garamszentbenedek Abbey) during the Easter processions. The beautiful sepulchre (11ft/3.25m high, 7ft/2.26m long, and 3ft/1m wide) was created in 1480 and has been restored several times since then.

The second highlight of the museum is a **Romanesque statue** (Cologne, 1170) of a woman carrying an earthenware jar (perhaps Mary Magdalene); her deep sorrow is poignantly visible in the finely sculpted contours of her face. And thirdly, *Ecce Homo* painted by **Hans Memling** between 1470 and 1480, is one of the wonders not just of the museum but also of the entire Dutch School. A bound Christ is depicted displaying his wounds, seeming to manifest a radiant serenity as he looks upon the world with compassion. Despite its small size, the painting is compelling.

Macskalépcső (Cat Steps)
A fork in Berényi Zsigmond utca.
It's easy to miss this tiny alley with a charming name that turns into a steep flight of nearly 200 steps leading up to the basilica. The climb might be tough but the views over the Danube are superb!

THE LOWER TOWN AB2

★ **Széchenyi tér** (Széchenyi Square) AB2
Surrounded by beautiful buildings, some housing cafés and shops, the square is a lively place, with the statue of the Holy Trinity in the center. At one end is the 17C Baroque town hall; the hook where the executioner's sword was permanently suspended can be seen on the balcony, a reminder of the town's right to mete out tough justice. Among the various architectural styles, you can see Rococo at Nos. 7 (1768) and 24 (1780), Early Baroque (end of the 18C) at No. 15, Classicist (1802) at No. 19, and Romantic at Nos. 3 (1862) and 21 (1860).

Mária-Valéria híd (Mária-Valéria Bridge) A2
This **bridge** crosses the Danube, linking Esztergom in Hungary with Štúrovo in Slovakia. It also provides one of the best views of the basilica.

Duna Múzeum (Danube Museum) B2
Kölcsey utca 2. ☏ 500 250. Open Wed–Mon, May–Oct, 9am–5pm; rest of the year, 10am–4pm. Ft700. Allow 1hr for visit.
Faced with the sometimes capricious natures of the Danube and the Tisza, one of its major tributaries, Hungarians have had to come up with solutions to a number of problems. Equally, they have taken advantage of these two rivers to harness the power of water. The museum explains the part water plays in the natural world and how people have used it down the centuries. Press a button and water flows and wheels turn—you don't need to speak Hungarian to grasp the essentials.

ADDRESSES IN ESZTERGOM

See Esztergom map (p111)

ARRIVAL/DEPARTURE

Train – From Budapest-Nyugati Station *(journey time 1hr 30min).* It is a 15min walk to the town center from Esztergom Station, or you can take bus no. 1.

Bus – *www.volanbusz.hu.* Bus line 880/882 operates between Budapest and Esztergom *(journey time 2hrs via Szentendre and Visegrád).* Departures roughly every 30min.

Boat – Mahart Passnave line from Budapest – *☏ (1) 484 4000. www.mahartpassnave.hu*
Mid-Apr–Aug, Tue–Sun; Sept, Sat only: departs Budapest, Vigadó tér at 9am, from Batthyány tér at 9.10am (journey time 5hrs 20min); returns at 4pm (journey time 4hrs). Ft 3,820 (Ft5,720 round trip).
End Apr–Sept, Tue–Sun: departs from Vigadó tér at 10am; returns at 5pm. Journey time 1hr 30min. Ft5,300 (Ft8,000 round trip).

STAY

AVERAGE

2 **Alabárdos Panzió** – A1– *Bajcsy-Zsilinszky utca 49. ✆ 312 640. alabardospanzio.hu.* *17 rooms, Ft16,000. 7 apartments (min 3 night stay) Ft30,000/39,000. Ft1,500.* This well-kept guesthouse is centrally located, with clean rooms, each furnished in a different style. There is an attractive interior courtyard where guests can sit outside in the fresh air.

8 **Szent Adalbert Hotel** – A1 – *Dózsa György tér 1. ✆ 541 972. www.szentadalbert.hu. 38 rooms, Ft18,470/21,710 .* A very quiet hotel, close to the basilica in the residential area of Castle Hill. The interior garden cannot be seen from the road, which adds to the hotel's tranquil atmosphere. Rooms are basic but clean. The hotel also welcomes pilgrims (dormitories).

EAT

BUDGET

3 **Cakumpakk** – B2 – *Bajcsy-Zsilinszky utca 15. ✆ 30 811 6069. Open noon–8pm (Fri & Sat, 11pm; Sun, 10am–8pm). Ft1,950/3,690.* Most of Esztergom's restaurants are quite traditional in design but this one is sleeker and more contemporary, serving mainly hamburgers with interesting combinations of ingredients. However, they also serve some traditional dishes, too.

9 **Mediterraneo Vendégfogadó** – A2 – *Helischer utca. ✆ 311 411. www.mediterraneo.hu. Open 8am–10pm. From Ft2,400.* This restaurant is a little off the tourist beat, but is in a pleasant location on Primate's Island. The cuisine is Mediterranean-inspired but there are also Hungarian dishes. The food is fresh and tasty. Half-portions are available.

AVERAGE

5 **Csülök Csárda** – B1 – *Batthyány Lajos utca 9. ✆ 412 420. csulokcsarda.hu. Open noon–10pm. Ft2,690/4,690.* The specialty here is knuckle of pork (incidentally, also the name of the restaurant), but there are many other tempting Hungarian specialties. Meals are served in the building's vaulted cellar. A good wine list.

TAKING A BREAK

There are plenty of cafés with terraces on **Széchenyi tér**.

Rondella Presszó – *In the gardens behind the basilica. ✆ 20 776 9962.- Open Tue–Sun, 9am–5pm.* This is a good place at which to stop off after visiting the basilica: coffees, a good selection of drinks, pastries, cakes, and ice creams. The terrace is very popular in fine weather.

Vác

★

Population 32,728 – Pest county – area code ✆ 27

Although less opulent than Esztergom and perhaps less picturesque than Szentendre, this town on the Danube, one of the oldest in Hungary, is still well worth a visit. It has been a Roman Catholic bishopric since the 11C. Vác's position on the east/left bank of the river already sets it apart from the other towns of the Danube Bend popular among tourists, making it a little quieter as a result. The beautiful Baroque architecture in its center is of particular note, the many buildings in this style being a legacy from the bishops of the 18C. Today, this small historic town retains its prosperous, tranquil air.

ADDRESSES PAGE 119
Stay, Eat, Shopping, Sports and Activities

INFO:
Tourist Office – *Március-15 tér 17. ✆ 316 160. www.turizmusvac.hu. Open 9am–5pm.*

LOCATION:
Regional map B1 (p28–29). On the left bank of the Danube, about 22mi/35km from Budapest via Rte 2.

PARKING:
No parking in the center. There are some spaces (charges apply) along the Danube Corso, or there is a large parking lot at the railway station.

DON'T MISS:
Március 15 tér; a walk along the Danube Corso as the sun is setting.

TIMING:
A full day is sufficient in which to see the town and visit the Vácrátót Botanical Garden.

KIDS:
Providing they are not too young or of a very sensitive nature, children are likely to be fascinated by the mummies in the museum.

Walking tour

★ **Március 15 tér** (March 15 Square)

Part of the square (which tapers at one end) is lined with single-story Baroque houses. In the center you can see the remains of the foundations of the Church of **Szent Mihály** (St. Michael's Church)—the **crypt** is all that is left to look around today *(open Tue–Sun, 10am–6pm, Ft500; combined ticket including entry to Memento Mori and Pannonia Ház Ft2,200; buy tickets at Memento Mori, see p116)*. Right next to it is a small pavilion from where the crystal clear notes of a set of bells chime out every hour.

Work on building **Városháza** (City Hall) at No. 11 began in 1736, although it was not completed until the visit of Empress Maria Theresa in 1764. The building is well proportioned and decorated with a wrought iron balcony and sculptures representing not only Justice and Hungary's coat of arms, but also the Migazzis, an important local family. Christoph Anton Migazzi (1714–1803) enjoyed Maria Theresa's patronage and was bishop of Vác and archbishop of Vienna.

THE MUMMIES OF VÁC

In 1994, when a team of specialists and artists were getting ready to begin work on the restoration of Vác's Dominican church, they were forced to delay to allow scientists to investigate a discovery that was—to say the least— intriguing. Workmen had uncovered a hidden staircase that led to a crypt, the existence of which was previously unknown. In it they discovered more than 200 coffins stacked on top of each other up to the ceiling and inside were perfectly preserved bodies. The wood shavings inside the caskets had absorbed the bodily fluids, while an ambient temperature of 46–52°F/8–11°C had led to the natural mummification of the human remains. And not only human—a cat and a bird, both of which had no doubt been accidentally shut in the crypt, had met the same fate… Some of the mummies are on display at Memento Mori *(see below)*.

Fehérek temploma (Church of the White Friars)
On one side of Március 15 tér you will see the Dominican Church of the Virgin Mary, or "church of the whites," named for the white habits worn by the monks of the Dominican Order. Inside the 18C church, the single nave (typical of monastery churches) is resplendent with Rococo decoration, although the monastery itself was never built.
Behind the church is a **market** *(piac)* built in the Organic style *(see p375)* by László Sáros. You will find all kinds of produce on sale (fruit, vegetables, honey, cold meats *(open 6am–4pm, Sat 1pm)*.

Memento Mori – Tragor Ignác Múzeum
Március-15 tér 19. 200 868. muzeumvac.hu. Open Tue–Sun, 10am–6pm (Nov–Mar, 5pm), Ft1,200; combined ticket including entry to the St. Michael crypt and Pannonia Ház Ft 2,200.
The rooms on the first (ground) floor trace the history of the town and its churches. One room features some of the 262 occupants of the coffins discovered in the crypt of the Dominican church, who were residents of Vác and died between 1750 and 1810.
Three of the famous **mummies** were found in a former cellar in the basement and everything (or almost everything) was preserved, including clothes, skin, and tufts of hair. The beautifully painted coffins are proof of the devotion of the living for their dead. A side room displays rosaries and crucifixes, some made of wax (quite unique), that were found in the coffins.

Köztársaság út (Köztársaság Street)
Continuing in a westerly direction from Március 15 tér, the street is lined with beautiful buildings, sometimes partly hidden by the foliage on the trees.

Pannónia Ház – Tragor Ignác Múzeum (Pannonia House)
Köztársaság út 19. 200 868. muzeumvac.hu. Open Tue–Sun, 10am–6pm (Nov–Mar, 5pm). Ft1,200, combined ticket, including entry to Memento Mori and Pannonia Ház Ft2,200.
Built around an internal courtyard garden, this branch of the museum brings together several interesting collections. One is an unusual array of more than 400 **cast-iron pans** made between 1850 and 1950 in Germany, the Czech Republic, Austria, Russia, and Hungary. Another displays the work of sculptor, painter, and printmaker **Gyula Hincz** (1904–86), including paintings, illustrations for children's books, drawings, and sculptures. His style evolved through Figurative art, Abstraction, and Surrealism, using vibrant colors.

Church of the White Friars, March 15 Square
© H. Payelle/Michelin

Finally, you can see the work of ceramicist **István Gábor** (1891–1984), regarded as the founder of the modern ceramic movement in Hungary, following in the footsteps of Margit Kovács (*see p98*) and Géza Gorka. More than one thousand objects are on display (plates, vases, decorative items, and more). Works by István Gábor can also be seen in the courtyard garden, as well as some of Andrea Vertel's playful ceramic figures.

Diadalív (Triumphal Arch)

The arch or **kőkapu** (stone gate) is situated at the end of Köztársaság út and was erected by Bishop Migazzi on the occasion of Empress Maria Theresa's visit. It is the only such arch in Hungary.

Theresianum

Today the Theresianum building is a prison, but it began life as an academy attended by the children of Hungary's noble families. Given to the town of Vác by Maria Theresa, it was named Theresianum in her honor. After the collapse of the 1848–49 Revolution, the building was converted into a prison. In the 20C, between the two world wars, Miklós Horthy, who was at the time regent of Hungary, turned it into the toughest and most secure penitentiary in the country; political prisoners were incarcerated here. It was retained as a prison during the Communist era without relaxing its harsh disciplinary regime. Among those held here was a certain Abraham Lajbi (or Ludwig Hoch), who managed to escape. Better known under the name of **Robert Maxwell**, he became a press baron in the UK and met a tragic end in 1991 (under mysterious circumstances), when he fell from his luxury yacht and drowned.

★ Danube Corso

This long promenade beside the Danube is a popular place for a stroll or a picnic on sunny days. If you time it right and the weather is clear, the sunset is breathtaking, with the rolling hills of the Danube Bend in the distance. In summer the river cools the atmosphere and, as it flows by, seems to bring with it a gentle breath of fresh air for the benefit of the promenaders. Between

Liszt Ferenc sétány and Ady Endre sétány (at the bottom of Eszterházy utca), there is a jetty from where you can catch the ferry (which also takes cars) to Szentendre Island.

Piarista templom és rendház (Piarist Church and Convent)

Köztársaság út.

The **Column of the Holy Trinity** (18C) announces the Piarist Church (18C), which was originally Baroque but was then rebuilt in a more eclectic style. The Piarists are a Catholic educational order founded in the early 17C.

Vác Cathedral

Konstantin tér. Open Mar–Nov, Mon–Sat, 10am–noon, 2pm–5pm.

The entrance to this imposing neo-classical cathedral is through a portico with six Corinthian columns attributed to the French architect Isidore Canevale, who had taken over the work begun by two Austrian architects, Franz Anton Pilgram and Johann Hausmann. Inside, the cupola is decorated with a fresco by Franz Anton Maulbertsch representing the meeting between the Virgin Mary and St. Elizabeth. In a small garden with trees, across the cathedral fore-court, you can see the yellow walls of **Püspöki Palota** (the former Bishop's Palace). A market known as the "episcopal" market selling fresh local produce and crafts takes place on Thursdays.

Ferences templom (Franciscan Church)

This small Baroque church is the oldest in Vác and the small square alongside it (Géza király tér) marks the center of the medieval town. The remains of King Géza I are buried here. The pulpit was sculpted by a Franciscan brother to represent the four cardinal virtues (Justice, Prudence, Strength, and Temperance).

Excursions

Regional map (p28–29)

★ **Vácrátóti Nemzeti Botanikus Kert** (Vácrátót National Botanical Garden) B1

6mi/10km southeast via Rte 2104. Bus 314, direct from Budapest or Vác; get off at Vácrátót Botanikus kert. ✆ (28) 360 122. www.botanikuskert.hu/en. Open Apr–Oct, 8am–6pm; Nov–Mar, 8am–4pm. Glasshouses open Tue–Thu and Sat & Sun, 8am–3.45pm; Fri 8am–1.15pm. Ft1,000.

Gardeners and botanists in particular will be in seventh heaven here, but you don't need to be a horticulturalist to enjoy this lovely peaceful place where the accent is on trees as well as plants and flowers. Founded by Count Sándor Vigyázó in 1870, it was originally an extensive English garden spread over 67 acres/27ha. **Vilmos Jámbor**, a botanist and landscape gardener, transformed it into a place for study and scientific research, but without detracting from its charm. More than 12,000 varieties are grown in the gardens in conditions reflecting their natural habitat, while elegant glasshouses nurture less hardy palms, cacti, and orchids.

ADDRESSES IN VÁC

ARRIVAL/DEPARTURE

Train – From Budapest-Nyugati Station *(journey time 25min)*. It is a 10min walk to the center of town from the station.

Bus – Bus lines 300, 302, and 303 operate between Budapest and Vác *(journey time 1hr)*. Departures roughly every 30min. *www.volanbusz.hu*

Boat – Mahart Passnave line from Budapest – *(1) 484 4000. www.mahartpassnave.hu. End-Apr–Sept, Tue–Sun: departs from Budapest, Vigadó tér at 10am; returns at 5.50pm. Journey time 1hr 40min. Ft3,300 (round trip Ft5,000).*

STAY

AVERAGE

Bellevue Vendégház – *Eszterházy utca 12. (70) 676 6816. www.bellevuevac.hu. 4 rooms & 1 apartment (up to 6 people), Ft16,000/26,000.* Near the town center and the Danube Corso. The rooms are immaculate, housed in two buildings on a road leading down to the Danube, with views of the river or the garden, or even both. The only disadvantage is they do not serve breakfast.

Vácz Hotel – *Honvéd utca 14. (30) 388 7746. www.vachotel.hu. P 14 rooms, Ft 21,900/25,900.* A brand new hotel in a building you can't miss as it is painted red, a 10min walk from the center of town. The rooms are modern and comfortable. Breakfast is hearty, offering plenty of choice, with some organic produce.

EAT

BUDGET

Magora Vegán Étterem – *Március 15 tér. 20 277 5267. magora-vac.hu. Open 8am–8pm (Sun, 11.30am–8pm). Around Ft2,200.* Vegetarians/vegans will be delighted to discover this place, which is in a good location in the town's main square. It serves soups, salads, main dishes, and veggie burgers, as well as pastries and cakes for when you want a break from sightseeing.

AVERAGE

Remete Pince – *Fürdő utca 3. 302 199. etteremvac.hu. Open noon–10pm. Ft2,500/4,000.* Fine Hungarian cuisine is served in this gastronomic restaurant, a short distance from the Danube Corso. The terrace is on a pedestrianized street which is a big plus. Vegetarian dishes are also available.

SHOPPING

Váci Curia – *Március 15 tér 20. 307 238. curia.hu. Open noon–10pm (Fri & Sat, midnight; Sun, 8pm).* A wine bar where you can discover quality Hungarian wines produced by both big and small winegrowers, with a choice of snacks to accompany them. A collection of some 2,500 bottles is on display in the wine museum *(open Mon–Sat, 2pm–6pm, Ft600).*

SPORTS AND ACTIVITIES

Cyling

EuroVelo 6 This cycle route crosses Europe, connecting the Atlantic Ocean with the Black Sea, taking in Hungary and nine other countries. The section between Vác and Szob is one of the best cycling routes in the country.

Around Budapest

There is plenty to see in Budapest, enough to keep you busy for several days, but it would be a shame to miss some key sites that are not far from the city. However, since public transport links are not always direct, access by car can be the most practical option. A Baroque palace, a neo-Gothic castle, lovely gardens, and a beautiful Romanesque church are all just a few hours from the capital.

ADDRESSES PAGE 125
Eat, Events and Festivals

LOCATION:
Regional map (p28–29)
Our suggested excursions are within a radius of 37mi/60km maximum around Budapest.

TIMING:
Each of the sites could be visited on a day trip. But as Gödöllő and Hatvan are close together, as are Alcsút and Zsámbék, you could combine them.

KIDS:
Gödöllő Palace, 3D exhibition in the stables, Brunszvik Castle park.

Excursions around Budapest Regional map (p28–29)

★★ **Gödöllő Királyi Kastély** (Royal Palace of Gödöllő) C2

17.5mi/28km northeast of Budapest. M 2 to Örs vezér tere, then HÉV 8 to Gödöllő Szabadság tér (journey time 50min).

28 410 124. www.kiralyikastely.hu. Open Apr–beg Nov, Mon–Thu, 9am–5pm; Fri–Sun,10am–6pm; Nov–Mar, 10am–4pm (Sat & Sun, Christmas vacation, 5pm). Ft2,600 (children Ft1,500). Audioguide in English Ft800. No charge for visiting the park.

The Royal Palace of Gödöllő, which covers over 18,2991sq ft/700sq m and has 69 acres/28ha of parkland, is considered Hungary's most important Baroque palace. Above the main entrance is a dome, below which an elegant wrought iron balcony rests on four pairs of red marble pillars decorated with Ionic capitals.The Grassalkovich coat of arms is proudly displayed in the center of the balustrade *(see opposite)*. The layout is unusual in that it has seven wings extending to the rear from either side of the main entrance, interconnecting one with another at angles of 90 degrees. The royal apartments have been painstakingly restored and an exhibition pays hommage to Empress Elisabeth.

Princess Marie Valerie, Elisabeth's fourth child, was nicknamed the "Hungarian Child" because she was born in Buda Castle. Marie Valerie was educated according to the customs of the Hungarian court and spent a lot of time with Sissi during her stays at Gödöllő.

One section is devoted to the Grassalkovich era, illustrating the palace's Gothic period, and houses a theater dating from that time. Rooms that you can see include the Grand Hall which houses a large ballroom, and the (separate) reception rooms of Franz Joseph and Sissi, all sumptuously decorated.

The **Baroque theater** and Miklós Horthy's bunker can only be visited as part of a guided tour; tours in English are available: *(28) 410 124 or visit informacio@kiralyikastely.hu. Charges apply.*

Gödöllő, Sissi's Palace

THE GRASSALKOVICH FAMILY

It was the great Hungarian nobleman Count **Antal Grassalkovich I** (1694–1771) who began building the Royal Palace of Gödöllő, entrusting its planning to architect **András Mayerhoffer**. The first stage of its construction (1741–49) saw the completion of the chapel, two corner towers at either end of the front facade, a hippodrome, and five of its wings. Construction of the final two wings began in 1760, along with several rooms for living quarters. The count's son, Antal Grassalkovich II, carried out more modifications between 1782 and 1785. He replaced the corner towers with the two pavilions with sloping mansard roofs and he also built a theater. Following in his wake, Antal Grassalkovich III began further alterations but his death in 1841 marked the end of the male line of the family. The estate passed to the female line, then came into the ownership of Baron György Sina in 1850, and then was bought by a Belgian bank in 1864.

THE GOLDEN AGE OF FRANZ JOSEPH AND SISSI

The palace hosted royalty when **Maria Theresa**, empress of Austria and queen of Hungary, stayed here in 1751 on a visit to the first Count Grassalkovich, but it was not until over a century later that it enjoyed its true golden age. The Hungarian state assumed ownership of the palace in 1867. After six months of renovation work under the direction of architect **Miklós Ybl**, it was offered to Emperor Franz Joseph and Empress Elisabeth (Sissi) for their coronation as king and queen of Hungary. The royal family loved coming to Gödöllő to relax in spring and autumn, far from the protocol and etiquette of the Viennese court. Sissi was particularly fond of the palace where, as an accomplished horsewoman, she could ride in the surrounding woods. Hunting with hounds, horse racing, parties, receptions, concerts … there is no doubt that many happy days were spent at Gödöllő. The local population very quickly took Sissi to their heart. A very different type of court from the one in Vienna to which she was accustomed grew up around the empress. She was not bound by strict rules here and as Franz Joseph only spent short periods of time at the palace, Sissi was the star around which everything revolved. After her tragic assassination in Geneva in 1898, Franz Joseph's visits became even less frequent, the last being in 1911. His successor, Charles I of Austria, who ruled Hungary from 1916 to 1918 as King Charles IV, only stayed in the palace once.

REVIVAL, DECLINE, AND RESTORATION

In 1919 the palace became the seat of the military high command of the short-lived Hungarian Republic of Councils, before being occupied by Romanian troops. In 1920, with the coming to power of Miklós Horthy as regent, the estate once more became the summer residence of Hungary's head of state and saw a revivial of its heyday with receptions, parties, and hunts being organized for distinguished guests. During the Second World War, German troops plundered the palace and then Soviet troops turned it into a military hospital and used it as a barracks after burning all the furniture. In 1990, when the Russians finally left, the Palace was in a sorry state and a long campaign to restore it began. It was in 1996 that the Palace at last opened its doors to visitors once more.

The stables house an interactive **exhibition of equestion culture**. Hunting and equestrian sports were enjoyed by the artistocracy until the beginning of the 20C. Everything is in Hungarian but you can view a film in English (reserve ahead). *Open Thu–Sun, 10am–6pm. Ft1,000 if you have already purchased a ticket for the palace, Ft1,400 if not.*

A walk in the park (no charge to enter) makes a pleasant end to the visit.

★ **Grassalkovich-kastély – Széchenyi Zsigmond Vadászati Múzeum** (Grassalkovich Mansion – Zsigmond Széchenyi Hunting Museum), at **Hatvan** C1

Hatvan is 37mi/60km northeast of Budapest by Hwy M3. Kossuth Lajos ter 24. (37) 541 900. vadaszatimuzeum.hu. Open Tue–Sun, 9am–5pm. Ft1,600. Abandoned for many years, the Grassalkovich Mansion, built at Hatvan by Count **Antal Grassalkovich I** between 1754 and 1757, has risen from the ashes once more. The Baroque mansion, much of which has been restored to its former glory, now houses a well-presented museum dedicated to hunting, fishing, and forestry management in Hungary. Traditions that have been handed down throughout the entire Carpathian Basin are explored here, with exhibits on fauna and flora, fishing and hunting techniques, weapons, animals, trophies, and utensils for preparing and cooking meat. They explain how hunting evolved over the years, from initially being a means of subsistence into an aristocratic pastime and on to its continued pursuit today. Also covered is how different animal species are monitored and preserved. There is a fine collection of trophies and an exhibition on Count Széchenyi, who in his day was also an accomplished hunter.

Interactive areas let you try your hand at archery, or go on a virtual hunt (with a laser) after rabbits, foxes, and wild boar.

If you prefer to leave the animals in peace, you can walk in the park and the gardens, which have also been restored.

★ **Brunszvik-kastély** (Brunszvik Castle), at **Martonvásár** A2

21mi/33km southwest of Budapest by Hwy M7. Parking in front of the reception area at the Agroverzum (science center), Brunszvik utca 2. It was in 1785 that Count **Antal Brunszvik** built Martonvásár as his family seat, before it was transformed in 1870 into the neo-Gothic castle with a touch of Scottish baronial hall thrown in that you see today. It is surrounded by a lovely park with majestic trees and is now occupied by the Agricultural Research Institute of the Hungarian Academy of Sciences.

Beethoven Múzeum – *(22) 569 500. martonvasar.hu. Open Apr–Oct, 10am–6pm; Nov–Mar, 10am–5pm. Ft1,400 (children Ft800).* Two rooms document the occasions the great composer stayed here. Of particular interest are letters exchanged between the composer and the daughters of the Brunszvik family. You can also see a lock of his hair and learn about Beethoven's pieces connected with Hungary—it all makes for an interesting visit.

Park – *(22) 569 563. martonvasar.hu. Open spring–fall, 9am–6pm; winter, 10am–4pm. Ft2,800.* This is a beautiful English-style park and a lovely place for a walk. In the center there is a small lake with an island, where concerts of works by Beethoven are staged every summer. What could be more romantic?

Royal Palace of Gödöllő
© Hungarian Tourism Agency

A FAMILY THAT MADE ITS MARK

The great composer **Ludwig van Beethoven** often stayed at Brunszvik Castle. The cultured and outgoing Brunszvik family were also very liberal in outlook. Ferenc, one of Count Antal Brunszvik's children, befriended Beethoven and was one of the few people who were on familar terms with the complex and at times difficult composer. It is said that Beethoven fell in love with Ferenc's sister Jozefin, composing his sonatas *Clair de lune* and *Appassionata* for her. Friends of Ferenc also asked Jozefin to ask Beethoven to compose something to mark the opening of the German theater in Budapest; he duly obliged with the *King Stephen Overture* and the *Ruins of Athens Overture*.

Theresa, another of Antal Brunszvik's children, became a follower of the Swiss educational reformer Johann Heinrich Pestalozzi and was also in touch with the like-minded Welsh social reformer Robert Owen, who opened the first nursery school in Britain in 1816. Theresa founded the first nursery school in Budapest, where a statue commemorates her contribution to the wellfare of young children.

★ Alcsúti Arborétum A2

33mi/52km west of Budapest by Hwy M1 and Rte 811.

(22) 353 219. www.alcsuti-arboretum.hu. Open Mar–Sept, 10am–6pm; Oct–Feb, Thur–Sun,10am–6pm. No charge.

This park in the English style planted with trees and covering 99 acres/40ha surrounds the remains of Alcsútdoboz Palace (only the entrance portico, the chapel, and a number of follies remain). Hungarians enjoy coming here in all seasons but the park is particularly attractive in the fall when the leaves change color and in spring when the first flowers begin to appear below the tree canopy (snowdrops, crocuses, daffodils).

The palace was built in the 19C for Archduke Joseph (1776–1847), palatine of Hungary and the brother of Holy Roman emperor Francis II. Joseph worked hard to improve and develop Pest, including the Lipótváros area; he helped improve sewerage and public hygiene, supported the building of a national museum, as well as being responsible for the landscaping of Margaret Island and the building of a railway line between Budapest and Vác.

In addition to the palace, he planted the arboretum with more than 300 species of trees that can still be seen today. One cedar of Lebanon is 170 years old—the oldest in Hungary.

★ Zsámbéki Romtemplom (former Zsámbék Church) A2

19mi/30km west of Budapest by Hwy M1.

It is not possible to enter the remains to look around, but you can view the exterior. The outline of the ruins of this church against the sky, badly damaged during the Turkish occupation, makes for a striking image. It was built in the first half of the 13C and stands alone on a hill overlooking a plain and the town of Zsámbék. The church was part of a Premontre monastery, founded by the Aynard family, who were originally from France. It is a very fine example of late Romanesque style, anticipating the forms of early Gothic art—ribbed vaulting, pilasters with capitals and hook-shaped decorations, with tall, slender proportions. The Western facade consists of a portal flanked by two towers between which is a rose window.

Ráckeve B2, off map
30mi/47 km south of Budapest on Rte 6.
Eötvös utca 1. (24) 429 747. www.tourinform.rackeve.hu.
This peaceful small town is situated on Csepel island, in Pest county. It is worth making a detour here to see the 15C church, which prides itself on being the only Baroque Orthodox church in the entire country.

★ **Nagyboldogasszony templom** (Serbian Church) – *Viola utca. (24) 423 277. Open Apr–Oct, Tue–Sat, 10am–noon, 2pm–5pm; Sun, 2pm–5pm). Nov–Mar, Sat 10am–noon, 1pm–4pm; Sun 1pm–4pm.* The blue and white bell tower standing outside offers no clue as to the surprise hidden inside the church—an extraordinary interior, literally covered in decoration in the Orthodox tradition from floor to ceiling. It was built in the 15C for the significant Serb community who lived in the city, fleeing the Ottoman occupation in the south.

ADDRESSES AROUND BUDAPEST

EAT

AVERAGE

Gödöllő

Solier Cafe – *Dozsa György utca 13. (20) 396 5512. solier.hu. Restaurant Ft3,000/4,900, menu Ft7,900.* A choice of two places in which to eat at the one address—something substantial in the formal restaurant (well-prepared Hungarian meals), or a snack in the café (homemade cakes and some pretty good savory snacks, such as gougères with cheese, potatoes, or tomatoes, and cheese puffs).

Hatvan

Grassalkovich Étterem – *Thurzó utca 16. (37) 744 444. grassalkovichetterem.hu. Ft2,850/4,850.* The restaurant is in the grounds of the Grassalkovich Mansion, not far from the Hunting Museum. Aside from traditional Hungarian cuisine, you also have the chance to try not just game but also fish dishes (catfish, in particular) with wild herbs.

Zsámbék

Nyárfás Étterem – *Nyárfás utca 2. Szépia Bio & Art Hotel restaurant. (23) 919 100. www.szepiahotel.hu. Ft2,500/4,000.* Chef István Kozma likes adding Italian twists to Hungarian cuisine and his customers like it, too. He's not afraid to use more unusual ingredients such as pearl millet and barley, or even tofu. Vegetarians will feel at home here.

EVENTS AND FESTIVALS

Gödöllő Palace

See www.kiralyikastely.hu for program details.
Festival of Chamber Music – March.
Baroque Palace Days – Second weekend of August. Dance displays, equestrian shows, and concerts in the palace.
International Harp Festival – October.

Brunszvik Castle, Martonvásár

Beethoven Concerts – Last three Saturdays in July. *www.filharmonikusok.hu*

Lake Balaton 2

Michelin National Map 732
Veszprém, Fejér, Zala, and Somogy counties

Pier on Lake Balaton, Keszthely
© Jon Arnold Images/hemis.fr

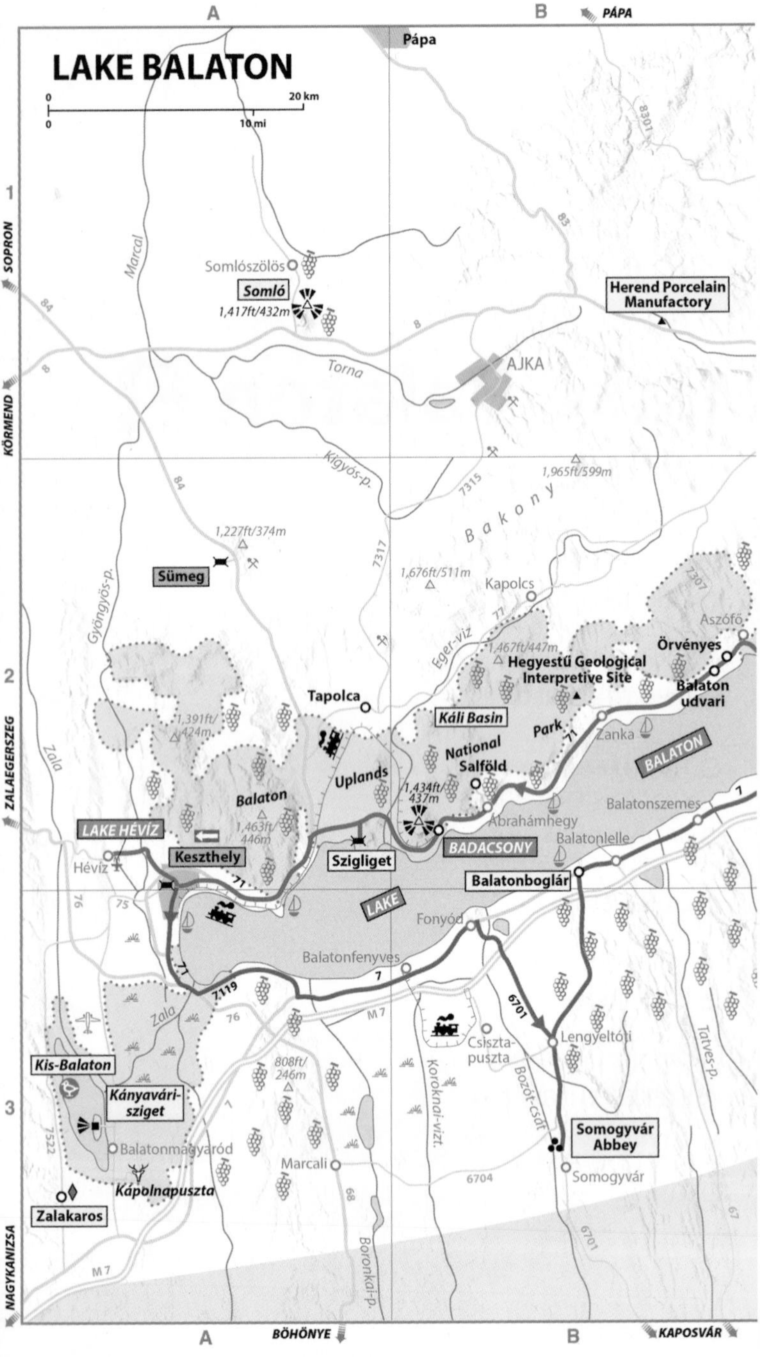
LAKE BALATON
0
20 km
0
10 mi
A
B
PÁPA
Pápa
1
2
3
SOPRON
KÖRMEND
ZALAEGERSZEG
NAGYKANIZSA
BÖHÖNYE
KAPOSVÁR
Marcal
Somlószőlős
Somló
1,417ft/432m
Herend Porcelain Manufactory
AJKA
Torna
Kigyós-p.
1,965ft/599m
Bakony
1,227ft/374m
Sümeg
1,676ft/511m
Kapolcs
Gyöngyös-p.
Eger-víz
1,467ft/447m
Hegyestű Geological Interpretive Site
Aszófő
Örvényes
Balaton udvari
Tapolca
Káli Basin
1,391ft/424m
National
Park
Zanka
BALATON
Salföld
Uplands
Balaton
1,434ft/437m
Ábrahámhegy
Balatonszemes
LAKE HÉVÍZ
1,463ft/446m
Keszthely
Szigliget
BADACSONY
Balatonlelle
Hévíz
Balatonboglár
LAKE
Fonyód
Balatonfenyves
Zala
Csisztapuszta
Lengyeltóti
Kis-Balaton
808ft/246m
Kányavári-sziget
Koroknai-vízt.
Bozót-csat.
Tatves-p.
Somogyvár Abbey
Balatonmagyaród
Marcali
Somogyvár
Kápolnapuszta
Zalakaros
Boronkai-p.

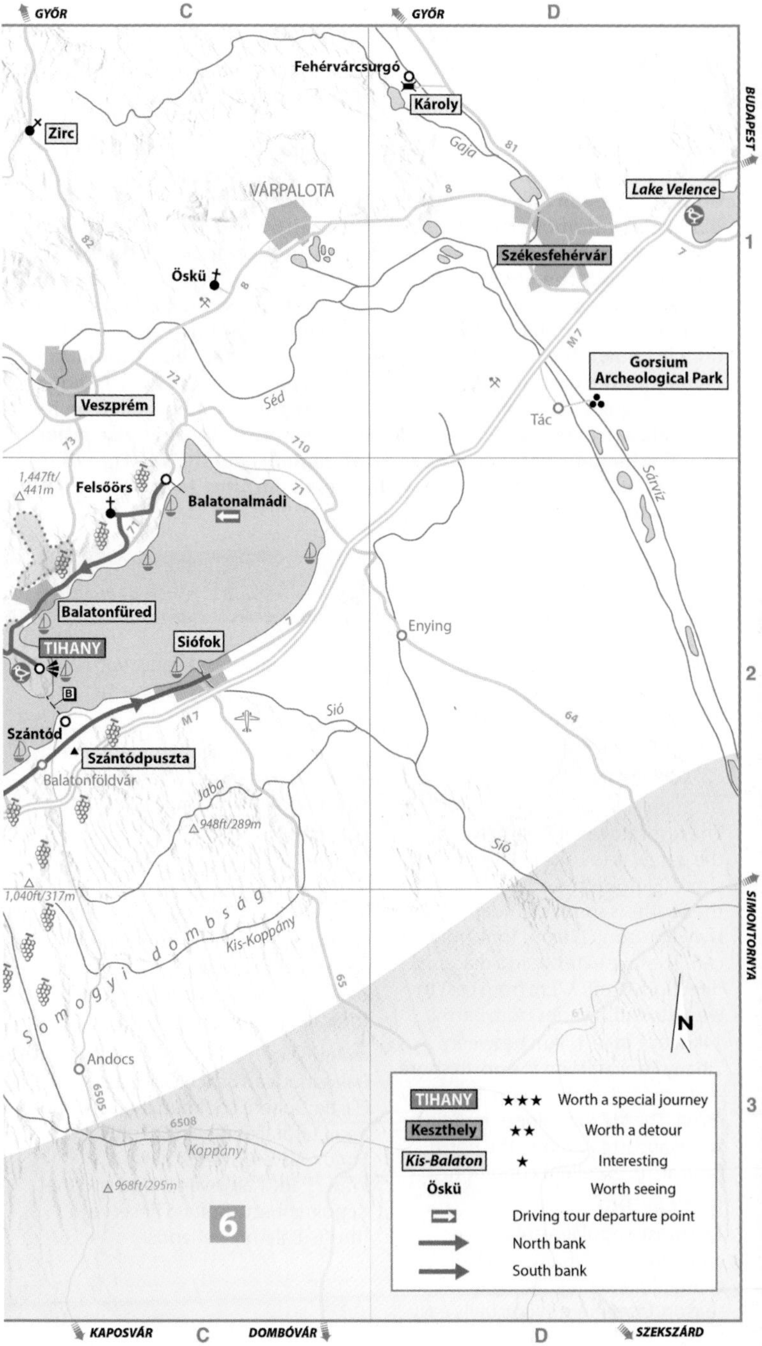
GYŐR
C
GYŐR
D
Fehérvárcsurgó
Károly
BUDAPEST
Zirc
Gaja
81
VÁRPALOTA
8
Lake Velence
82
1
Székesfehérvár
7
Öskü
8
M7
Gorsium
Archeological Park
Veszprém
72
Séd
Tác
73
710
1,447ft/441m
Felsőörs
Balatonalmádi
71
Sárvíz
71
Balatonfüred
7
Enying
TIHANY
Siófok
2
B
M7
Sió
64
Szántód
Szántódpuszta
Balatonföldvár
Jaba
948ft/289m
Sió
1,040ft/317m
SIMONTORNYA
Somogyi dombság
Kis-Koppány
65
61
N
Andocs
6505
3
6508
Koppány
968ft/295m
6
TIHANY ★★★ Worth a special journey
Keszthely ★★ Worth a detour
Kis-Balaton ★ Interesting
Öskü Worth seeing
Driving tour departure point
North bank
South bank
KAPOSVÁR
C
DOMBÓVÁR
D
SZEKSZÁRD

Lake Balaton

★★★

Veszprém, Zala, and Somogy counties

Warm, turquoise waters in the heart of Transdanubia? That's the magic of Lake Balaton, one of the largest lakes in Europe, which breathes a little of the Caribbean into the center of the European continent. Stretched out like an enormous chili pepper (what else!) between the old manorial town of Keszthely in the west and the very popular beach resorts at its northern end, the undisputed star of the Hungarian tourist industry can be reached comfortably in just two hours along the highway from Budapest. A popular holiday destination for nearly two centuries, the lake is known locally as the "Hungarian Sea." It has seen Hungarian history unfold gradually around it, from the palaces of the Belle Epoque to Communist vacation resorts. While the region has long relied on its lakeside attractions, today it is keen to demonstrate what else it has to offer, including its six winegrowing regions and the winegrowing villages, hillsides riddled with caves, small Baroque towns and their castles and spas.

ADDRESSES PAGE 136
Stay, Eat, Sports and Activities, Events and Festivals

INFO:
Most localities around the lake have a Tourinform Office stocked with brochures & maps.

LOCATION:
Regional map AC 2–3 (p128–29)
The resort town of Balatonfüred, the gateway to Lake Balaton's north shore (Siófok is the equivalent for the south), is south of Budapest on Hwy M7 (81mi/130km, 1hr40 min by car). The lake extends in a diagonal direction 48 mi/77km from east to west. Its width varies from 8.6 mi/14km to 1 mile/1.5km between Tihany Peninsula on the north shore and Szántód on the south (linked by ferry). The M7 runs along the south shore and Rte 71 along the north. Both are in excellent condition.

PARKING:
The most popular resorts (Balatonfüred, Tihany, and Siófok) charge for parking during the high season. Elsewhere, it is usually easy to park and often free away from the main sights. Make sure you have some change handy for the meters.

DON'T MISS:
The north shore, with its magnificent vine-covered slopes offering splendid views of the lake.

TIMING:
Allow at least three days to complete a circuit of the lake without feeling rushed; two days along the north shore and one for the south. A week will allow you to stop off at a resort or do some wine tasting, with time for walking or cycling.

KIDS:
Balatonudvari Beach; Szigliget Castle; Sphere Lookout; the Tourist and Cultural Center in Szántód; Siófok Water Tower; Zalakaros Water Park; Kányavári Island and the Kápolnapuszta Buffalo Reserve in the Kis-Balaton wetlands.

The Hungarian Sea

The lake's name comes from the Avar word *blatno*, meaning "stagnant water" in reference to its marshy areas, which are still present today, especially around Tihany. Lake Balaton's waters and reedbeds have long been a source of sustenance, providing fish and game. Thanks to the lake's beauty and the special light, it became a popular retreat for Hungarians escaping the towns and cities. In the 16C it also formed a kind of natural border separating the Habsburgs from the Turks, while in the 18C, Germans, Croats, and Slovaks settled in the region. At the end of the 18C, Balatonfüred and Hévíz started taking shape as attractive resorts where wealthy families from Buda, Pest, and Austria would spend their summers.

The **rail link from the south**, which connects Budapest to the Adriatic coast (the port city of Rijeka, or Fiume in Italian), passes the southern shoreline of Lake Balaton and was was built in 1861. The rail line that passes the northern shore dates from 1909. It was at this time that the lake, part of which had been backfilled, acquired its present shape and the tourism industry started to develop. In the years just after the First World War, 50,000 to 60,000 people were vacationing regularly at Lake Balaton, but by the eve of the Second World War, the figure had risen to nearly 250,000.

Communist riviera – The socialist regime that became established in Hungary after the Second World War strove to develop a form of mass tourism that would benefit the workers. This led to the **nationalization** of existing facilities, the expropriation of existing holiday villas, and the construction of vacation centers. Alongside the centers opened by workers' organizations or companies, some areas, such as the Balatonaliga resort, were reserved for party members. Inside this protected complex, the hierarchy remained intact. The amount of space allocated to a visitor and the quality of the service and facilities available depended entirely on their status. The construction of large blocks for social housing dates from this era, many of which, in the 1990s, were turned into hotels.

And today – The Balaton region continues to play a key role in Hungary's tourism industry. After Budapest, it is the most visited area in the country. Each year more than 1.8 million tourists spend time in the various resorts on and around the banks of the lake or in its hinterland. On long weekends during the high season, the people of Budapest swell the ranks of the German tourists, who make up the largest number of visitors. The success of this region, sometimes called the "Hungarian sea," is due of course to the nature of its environment and microclimate, but also to the facilities on offer, which all contribute toward making this area one huge lakeside resort. Holidaymakers in search of a rest and the chance to unwind, or those keen to take part in more energetic recreational activities, can find around 100 beaches dotted about the lake and all kinds of facilities at a range of prices.

The lake is also not the only point of interest in the region, the hinterland is very pleasant and picturesque. The **Kis-Balaton** wetlands (*see p135*) are to be found at the western end of Lake Balaton, while not far away the charming town of **Keszthely** and its splendid and well-preserved palace are also interesting to explore.

Another extensive stretch of inland water, **Lake Velence** (*see p167*), is situated halfway between Budapest and Lake Balaton. It is a haven for environmentalists and nature lovers.

Around the lake Regional map (p128–29)

The north and south shores of the lake are very different. The areas around Balatonfüred in the northeast have a timeless quality about them. On the north shore, a succession of Baroque churches, Art Nouveau "kiosks," stately villas, colorful wooden pavilions on stilts, and fragrant gardens lead down to Tihany Peninsula. A few miles further on is the resort of Badacsony, set against a backdrop of green mountains, with vineyards on the lower slopes. Walkers also come here to explore the area's natural parks with their geological curiosities and hot springs, and places where you can eat and drink alfresco are dotted around.

Hungarians come from all over the country to both shores to relax and swim. If you like to swim in shallow waters, head for the south shore, but experienced swimmers may prefer the north shore, where the lakebed shelves more steeply just a few yards out.

During summer, the entire shoreline is extremely busy and it can be difficult to find accommodation in the larger towns, so if you are in search of some peace and quiet it's a good idea to try the villages.

★★ THE NORTH SHORE AC2

69mi/111km from Balatonalmádi. See the Regional map p128–29 for the route. From Budapest, leave Hwy M7 at exit 90 toward Balatonfüred, then follow Rte 71, which passes the east end of the lake.

This shore offers more variety than the south. You'll find several beach resorts here, but also vineyards that cling to the volcanic slopes and produce some very pleasant white wines.

Balatonalmádi C2

The first major resort on the northern shore approaching from the east is dominated by the cliff of Balatonakarattya. Balatonalmádi has been earning its place as a destination of choice here since around 1870. On sunny days the town is busy from first thing in the morning with outdoor activities at its fine, sandy beach and in its sailing clubs. From the center of town, brown signs reading "Óvári kilátó" point the way to a high point *(about 1.5mi/2.5km by car)*, where a **lookout tower** *(kilátó)* offers a beautiful view of the lake. It is the first of many opportunities for fine panoramic views, since one of the charms of the north shore lies in its hills, like a series of balconies looking down over the lake.

Felsőörs C2

Set back a little from the lake, this village, with its small red sandstone **Római katolikus plébániatemplom** (Roman Catholic parish church, 13C), is the perfect excuse to wander through the surrounding vineyards. Local quarries supplied the stone that has lent color to the exterior of the buildings: black from basalt and volcanic rock, white from limestone, and red from sandstone.

Return to Rte 71 which runs along the shoreline around the lake.

★ Balatonfüred BC2

See p141. Continue on the main road.

Rte 71 loops around the foot of Tihany Peninsula. To access the peninsula itself, take the main road off Rte 71.

★★★ Tihany BC2

See separate entry, p144.

If you don't have time to drive right around the lake but want to get across to the south shore, a **ferry** (which takes cars) leaves from the end of the peninsula *(15min crossing, see p136)*. The queue grows quickly in summer, but departures are frequent. Nearby restaurants and cafés can help to pass the waiting time pleasantly.

Örvényes B2

Apart from the water mill, which is still working *(Szent Imre utca 3)*, this charming village with its white houses is worth a stop for its **small beach** (grass) equipped with facilities *(Platán Szabadstrand, Fürdő utca)*. Shaded by sycamore trees and patrolled during the season *(Jun–Sept, 10am–8pm)*, it has the added bonus of offering a view of Tihany Peninsula.

Balatonudvari B2

Stop off at the cemetery *(temető)* on your right as you enter the village to see the heart-shaped tombstones (late 18C–early 19C).

Another of the village's attractions is the municipal **beach**, where the shallow water makes it an ideal place for families to splash about.

★★★ **Badacsony** B2

See separate entry, p148.

★ **Káli Basin** B2

See separate entry, p150.

★ **Szigliget vár** (Szigliget Castle) A2

Signposted from the entrance to the village. Parking at the base of the castle. Open Jul–Aug, 8am–8pm (check for other months). No entrance charge while the castle is being restored (ticket office closed during restoration work).

A cobbled path and steps lead up through woodland to this 13C castle, which is perched on **Vár-hegy** (Castle Hill, 784ft/239m). The view extends across the vineyards, the lake, and the village below, and it is hard to imagine that this was once an island. There are a few swings and other play equipment for children.

A shop selling homemade ice cream, regularly ranked among the best in Hungary, lies near the start of the path to the castle *(see Taking a Break, p139)*.

★★★ **Lake Hévíz** A2

See separate entry, p153.

★★ **Keszthely** A2

See separate entry, p154.

THE SOUTH SHORE AC2–3

76.5mi/123km from Keszthely. See the Regional map p128–29 for the route. Follow Rte 71. Leave Keszthely along the southern shore of the lake.

"What's the best thing about the south shore? Its view of the north shore!" as the locals like to joke. The south shore is home to a number of Hungarian lakeside resorts—Fonyód, Balatonboglár, Balatonlelle, Balatonszemes, and Balatonföldvár follow one after the other, all looking fairly similar and packed with people in the summer, culminating in Siófok, which is where young Hungarians like to party. But here and there you can still see old farmhouses with roofs thatched with reeds, typical of this lakeside region and still resisting the pressures of tourism. *Take Rte 6701 from Fonyód toward Kaposvàr.*

★ **Szent László Nemzeti Emlékhely** (Ruins of the Benedictine Abbey), at **Somogyvár** B3

Besliahegy 64. ✆ (70) 197 9902. Visitor center open Jun–Aug, 10am–6pm; check times for rest of the year. Ft1,200.

To ring the changes from the lakeside resorts, try a detour to see these ruins deep in the Hungarian countryside. In 1091 King Ladislas I called on the Benedictine monks of the Abbey of St. Gilles in France to create this monastery. From the impressive ruins that have been uncovered, it is possible to gauge the original size of the church, indicating a building that was 197ft/60m long and 79ft/24m wide. A visitor center provides information about the history of the site.

Make a U-turn to rejoin Rte 7 toward Balatonboglár.

★ **Balatonboglár** B2

With a population of 6,200, Balatonboglár is typical of the lakeside resorts on the south shore and has a row of grassy and sandy beaches, bordered by no shortage of accommodation. Long, tree-lined paths hug the lake and complete the picture, while a little further back from the water, beautiful houses sit among the trees.

★ **Gömbkilátó** (Sphere Lookout) *Kilátó utca. ✆ (30) 351 4476. Charges apply for parking. Open summer, 9am–9pm; rest of year hours vary. Ft300 (3–18 yrs Ft250).*

This unusual lookout point inside a sphere constructed from 240 steel triangles, offers a fine view of the lake and the hills of the north shore. Lit up at night, it is one of Lake Balaton's iconic sights. The wooded hill on which the lookout stands is now an adventure park, with a treetop rope course, karting, café-restaurant, among other attractions.

Continue on Rte 71 for 17.5mi/28km.

Szántód C2

This holiday town has the distinction of being situated at the narrowest point of the lake, where is it just 1 mile/1.5km wide. The **ferry** that makes the crossing to Tihany Peninsula opposite is based here (*see p136*).

★ **Szántódpuszta Majormúzeum** (Szántódpuszta Tourist and Cultural Center) – *Signposted from the center of town. ✆ (30) 447 82 16. szantodpuszta.hu. Open Jun–Aug, 8.30am–6pm; mid-Apr–end May, hours vary (closed Sept–mid-Apr). Ft900.*

The extensive wooded park houses an open-air museum of well-restored 18C and 19C rural buildings. Linked by shaded paths, some of the buildings feature small exhibitions on farming life, including animal enclosures and an aquarium where you can see the different types of fish found in Lake Balaton. Horseriding and horse-drawn carriage rides are also available.

Continue on Rte 71 for 9.5mi/15km.

It is virtually impossible to tell where one resort ends and the next begins in the stretch between Szántód and Siófok; the area is deserted off season but packed in summer.

★ **Siófok** C2

Fő tér 11 (at the base of the water tower). ✆ (84) 696 236. Open Mon–Fri, 8am–6pm; Sat, 9am–1pm.

Tucked away between two rocky outcrops, Siófok is the ultimate lakeside town with a main beach that attracts up to 13,500 people a day in summer (*see Sports and Activities, p140*). Popular with families, young Hungarians also congregate here, attracted by its concerts, dance clubs, and nighttime

Entrance of the Evangelical Church, Siófok
© GluckKMB/iStock

bars (including many along Petőfi sétány, a path near the waterfront), which have swallowed up most of the last traces of its late-19C elegance.

Víztorony (Water Tower) – *Fő tér 11. Open daily, Jun–Sept, 9am–midnight; rest of year hours vary. Ft850 (children Ft350).* This all-concrete, 147.5ft/45m monument dating from 1912 is the town's symbol, with a tourist information center at its base, and a lookout and revolving café on top.

Kálmán Imre Emlékház (Imre Kálmán Museum) – *Kálmán Imre sétány 5. (84) 311 287. Open Tue–Fri, 10am–5pm; Sat, 9am–1.30pm. Ft500.* The original building, where composer of operettas **Imre (Emmerich) Kálmán** (1882–1953) was born, no longer exists, but the town has established a commemorative house here. It displays the belongings and sheet music of this Jewish artist, who fled the Nazis and settled in the United States in 1940.

Evangélikus templom (Evangelical Church) – *Fő utca 220, Oulupark (10min walk from the town center).* An interesting example of contemporary (1990) Organic architecture (the exterior looks like a giant owl), the church was designed by Hungarian architect Imre Makovecz.

★ Around Kis-Balaton Regional map A3

The **Kis-Balaton** (Little Balaton) wetlands, once part of the main lake, are now separate due to the accumulation of alluvial deposits from the Zala river. This lends a regal serenity to its 8,649 acres/3,500ha, with reed beds and stretches of shallow water. Known for its rich birdlife, the Kis-Balaton is now a protected natural area.

★ Zalakaros

22.5mi/36km southwest of Keszthely on Rte 75, then Rte 7522.

One of the jewels of the many Hungarian thermal spas, this peaceful little town has undergone enormous development since the discovery of a hot spring here in 1962. The original **thermal bath** is now at the center of a gigantic water park, which has therapy pools and water slides, wave pools, wellness facilities, hot tubs ... altogether numbering around 60 attractions for the whole family (*see p139*). Zalakaros is all about thermal tourism, and is particularly popular with Czech, German, and Austrian visitors. You will find all the normal resort facilities here and perhaps even still have time for a little relaxation.

Kápolnapuszta Buffalo Reserve and lake

6.2mi/10km northeast of Zalakaros. (70) 228 2864. bfnp.hu/en/buffalo-reserve-kapolnapuszta. Open daily, Jun–Aug, 9am–6pm; Apr, May, Sept, Oct 9am–5pm; Nov–Mar, 9am–4pm. Ft800 (3–14 yrs Ft500).

You can see the water buffalo from along a walkway of about 1.2 mi/1km and some are tame enough to be stroked. Horse-drawn carriage rides are also often available (on reservation) and there's a playground for children.

★ **Kányavári-sziget** (Kányavári Island)

4.5mi/7km northwest of Kápolnapuszta. Info: kisbalaton.hu.

This small island is the only part of the Kis-Balaton wetlands that is open to the public. After parking your car (charges apply), take a wooden footbridge across to the island. Trails lead to a lookout tower, children's playgrounds, small beaches, and picnic areas with facilities.

ADDRESSES AROUND LAKE BALATON

If you are visiting off-season, check opening times in advance. In general venues start opening in May, when the lake is warm enough for swimming, but many close again at the end of September when it starts getting colder. However, there is still plenty going on around the lake at the start of fall.

TRANSPORT

From Budapest

Train – Several departures daily from Déli Station in Budapest to Balatonfüred (north) and Siófok (south). Allow 1.5/2hrs for the fastest trains *(about Ft2,800)*. There are also connections from Pécs, Győr, and Sopron. *mavcsoport.hu/en*

Bus – Buses connecting the capital with Lake Balaton leave from Népliget Bus Station in Budapest. Allow 3hrs journey time *(about Ft2,800)*. There are also bus connections from Pécs, Győr, and Sopron. *volanbusz.hu/en*

Around the lake

Car – This is the most practical way to explore the region in any depth, although by bike is good, too (*see Sports and Activities, p140*). You can head off the beaten track and discover the hinterland of the lake, which is not as easy by train or bus.

Bus – *menetrendek.hu*. Numerous buses connect the various towns in the region. Quick and frequent, they can be more convenient than trains for getting around the lake.

Train – *mavcsoport.hu/en*. The lake is quite well served by two railway lines, one along the north shore to Tapolca, the other along the south shore to Keszthely. The two lines don't link up, but there is a connection between them.

Ferry – *balatonihajozas.hu. End Jun–beg Sept, 6.40am–11.20pm, departures every 40min; rest of year hours vary. Ft700/foot passenger, Ft400/bicycle, Ft1,900/car.* The ferry operates as a shuttle service between Tihany and Szántód throughout the year, with more departures during the high season, which helps to avoid congestion on the roads.

STAY

Balatonalmádi (north shore)

AVERAGE

Villa Millennium – *Mikszáth utca 5. ✆ (30) 461 02 29. villamillennium.hu. Ft23,900 ☕.* With a lively splash of color in the decor and a contemporary interior, this is quite unlike many traditional guesthouses and has been completely renovated. It occupies the handsome villa that housed the first guesthouse in the vicinity. A lovely garden is an added bonus.

Balatonszepezd (north shore)

A TREAT

Sir David Castle – *Nyár utca 2. ✆ (30) 98 95 800. sirdavidcastle. com. 6 rooms & 4 apartments, Ft26,600 ☕.* The distinctive yellow exterior with castle-like turrets gives this architectural folly its charm. Built by an ethnologist in 1906, it was recently converted into a small hotel by an Italian businessman. There's also a garden and (small) swimming pool. As it is located outside the center, it is ideal for those traveling by car.

Siófok (south shore)

A TREAT

Hotel Kentaur – *Akáfa utca 1. ✆ (84) 350 001. hotelkentaur.hu. 35 rooms, Ft26,600/32,400 ☕.* In a pretty residential street and with a garden, this well-maintained, family-run hotel and restaurant is simple and comfortable. Although the rooms could benefit from improved soundproofing, you can still find some peace and quiet.

SPLASH OUT

Jókai Villa Hotel – *Batthyány utca 2. ✆ (84) 506 798. jokaivilla. com. 12 rooms, Ft32,400/38,600 ☕.* Named in honor of the writer Mór Jókai (1825–1904), who spent his last summer here, this beautiful and majestic villa (1897), close to the center of town and the beaches, still has its Belle Epoque charm. A nice garden as well.

EAT

The free *We Love Balaton* and *Funzine* booklets (in English) list good offers and the latest places to visit. Also free from the tourist offices are maps of places to eat. Locals eager to practise their English may also be willing to give you the names of their current favorite gastronomic spots. They can be a valuable source of information as the eateries here tend to change hands frequently.

Paloznak (north shore)

BUDGET

Sáfránkert Vendéglő – *Fő utca 1. ✆ (70) 431 2050. homolapinceszet.hu/safrankert-vendeglo. Open Thu–Sun, noon–9.30pm. Ft2,290/4,290.* You need to make a small detour between Balatonalmádi and Balatonfüred to reach the center of this charming village where a winemaker has opened a small, simply decorated gourmet bistro and wine bar. The small menu chalked on a slate focuses on local produce and house wines. The cooking style is Hungarian while at the same time embracing modern trends.

2

Csopak (north shore)

AVERAGE

☺ **Bisztró Szent Donát** – *Szitahegyi utca 28. ✆ (20) 928 1181. szentdonat.hu. Open Oct–May, Thu–Mon, noon–9pm. Ft3,990/4,990.* Situated between Balatonalmádi and Balatonfüred, this elegant restaurant was established in 2014 on the family wine estate of the same name. Its main attractions are its elegant food and a terrace with a superb view over the vineyards and the lake.

Szigliget (north shore)

AVERAGE

Bakos Attila Vendéglője – *Iharos utca 4. ✆ (87) 461 210. Open Wed–Sun, noon–9pm. Ft2,950/4,250.* The walls of this restaurant are covered floor to ceiling with paintings and photos, which makes for an absorbing few minutes even if you only study those near you! Enjoy solid country fare on checkered tablecloths, including "Hoffman" carp stews, catfish, and other lake specialties. A large beergarden-style terrace for fine weather.

Zánka (north shore)

AVERAGE

☺ **Neked Főztem Gasztrokocsma** – *Fő utca 7. ✆ (70) 365 1003. restu.hu/neked-foztem. Open summer, noon–9pm. Ft2,950/4,290.* Situated between Tihany and Badacsony, what's not to like about this small country restaurant? Its food transcends its Hungarian roots, using modern techniques to produce lighter and even tastier results. The beautiful large terrace is overlooked by the nearby church steeple, which only adds to its appeal. Reservation recommended as it's often full.

Zamárdi (south shore)

AVERAGE

Paprika Csárda – *Honvéd utca 1. ✆ (87) 461 210. Open 10am–10pm (Fri & Sat, 11pm). Ft2,450/4,950.* A practical choice as it is open year-round (unlike the majority of places on the south shore). This vast restaurant in one of Siófok's neighboring towns occupies a traditional building with a shaded terrace. The menu offers an impressive array of specialties from pan-seared foie gras to catfish. Our advice is to stick to the simpler dishes, which are often the best.

Balatonszemes (south shore)

AVERAGE

Kistücsök Étterem – *Bajcsy Zs. utca 25. ✆ (84) 360 133. Open noon–10pm. Fixed price menu (5 courses) Ft9,900. A la carte Ft3,490/4,990.* It is no accident that this name keeps appearing on lists of the best restaurants in Lake Balaton; the owner is Balázs Csapody and the restaurant has been an undeniable success thanks to chef Jahni László who has been in charge of the kitchen here for 27 years. A culinary landmark, with affordable prices from a Western European perspective.

Siófok (south shore)

BUDGET

Rozmaring Kiskert Vendéglő és Pizzéria – *Akácfa utca 53. ✆ (30) 694 0949. Open Wed–Sun, noon–9pm. Ft1,290/3,990.* The locals love this Italian restaurant, which claims to serve the best Neapolitan pizza in Lake Balaton. Grills and specialty pasta dishes are also on the menu, which is short but full of tasty offerings. Reservation recommended.

TAKING A BREAK

Two of the region's great pleasures are dining alfresco lakeside and sipping drinks in the vineyards, again alfresco. The vineyards are a long-standing institution, especially on the north shore where the best sit high up on the hills with superb views. Many offer tastings of the estate's wines and often simple dishes to accompany them (cheese and cold meats).

A warning for those traveling by car: Hungary operates a zero tolerance policy regarding drink-driving. In other words, it's best for designated drivers to leave sampling the wines for a day when somone else is at the wheel.

Balatonalmádi (north shore)

BÁRmikor – *István sétány 4–6. (30) 263 79 49.* Quite literally the "whenever you want" bar. This open-air venue is right at the water's edge. The local hipsters like its repurposed furniture, large terrace (with some shade), and fruit *fröccs*, a cocktail made with wine and sparkling water, along with snacks and tapas platters to nibble with their drinks.

Paloznak (north shore)

Homola Borterasz – *Vincellér utca. (70) 431 2050.* Young Hungarians love this open-air wine bar in a natural setting among the vineyards. DJ nights compete with peaceful afternoons relaxing on the estate's terraces, or on deckchairs with a view of the lake in the distance.

Badacsonyörs (north shore)

Csendes Dűlő Szőlőbirtok – *Hegyalja út 43. (70) 295 5110. Open 11am–7pm (Sat & Sun, open till later).* This wine bar is famous for its terrace and magnificent view of the vineyards, with the lake as a perfect backdrop. It has also adopted the trend for deck chairs that has recently spread to many local wine bars—ideal for taking a break, glass in hand, while contemplating the landscape.

Szigliget (north shore)

Várkávézó – *Kisfaludy utca 26. (30) 622 2094.* Situated near the path leading up to Szigliget Castle, ice cream connoisseurs just have to try the homemade variety in this modest tea room, said to be among the country's best. The pistachio ice cream, among other flavors, has won a barrage of prizes. Just between us, the cakes aren't bad either. A real treat!

BATHS

As elsewhere in Hungary, the thermal baths and water parks are one of the lake's great attractions. *See Hévíz (p153).*

Zalakarosi Fürdő – Regional map A3 – *Termál út 4. Ft2,800/4,400 per day, depending on whether you want to use all or part of the water park.* This bathing complex is the most popular and best adapted to the needs of families in the Balaton region. Apart from the thermal bathing facilities, it contains many water-themed attractions (including numerous water slides and a wave pool).

SPORTS AND ACTIVITIES

Swimming

Even though there are plenty of other things to do around the lake, the numerous beaches are still the main attraction between May and September. On the next page you will find some of our favorites:

2

Sajkodi Strand, Tihany – *At the southwest entrance to the peninsula, north shore.* Plenty of trees providing shade and steps at intervals down into the water. A very popular grass beach.

Lidó Strand, Vonyarcvashegy – *5mi/8km east of Keszthely, north shore.* A range of water-based activities are available in the nearby village of the same name (water skiing, windsurfing, …). A sandy beach with areas of grass.

Diási Játékstrand – *3mi/5km east of Keszthely, north shore.* All sorts of outdoor games are available (including giant chess, mini-golf, and pétanque). An area of grass.

Fonyód strand – *6mi/10km east of Balatonboglár, south shore.* With a beautiful view of the volcanic mountains on the north shore, this beach is also one of the few that has a stretch of sand.

Main Beach, Siófok – *Next to the port, south shore.* Packed in summer, there's even a stretch of sand complete with palm trees.

Hiking and Cycling

Hiking – Lake Balaton's walking trails (suitable for all levels) are another of its great attractions. Some run along beside the lake, others lead up into the vine-covered hills, others still explore the many geological curiosities of this formerly volcanic region. You can find information on the most scenic paths at the tourist offices.

Cycling – A cycle path (130.5mi/210km) runs right around Lake Balaton, thanks to which in just a few years the lake has become one of Hungary's most popular cycling destinations. Places to hire bikes are dotted around the perimeter of the lake, but the rates are more or less identical. Expect to pay around Ft500/hour and Ft2,500/day. The website **balatonbike.hu** *(in English)* lists routes that are suitable for all levels.

Most trains allow you to take your bike on board for a small fee.

EVENTS AND FESTIVALS

Zamárdi

Balaton Sound – One of the biggest electronic music festivals in Europe takes place on the beach over 5 days in early July. *balatonsound.com*

Szigliget

Castle Festival – The castle comes to life for 2 days in mid-June with tournaments, falconry, and chivalrous knightly exploits. *szigligeti-var.hu*

Paloznak

Jazzpiknik – Three days of music at this open-air location at the beginning of August. Local wines and food are available to accompany the cool jazz sounds. *jazzpiknik.hu*

Balatonfüred

★

Population 24,114 – Veszprém county – area code ✆ 87

This charming and elegant spa town is the oldest resort on the lake's northern shore. The great and the good of Hungarian society have been coming here for more than two centuries, when bathing in the lake would be accompanied by a therapy based on the Balaton mud. Water treatments are available at the cardiology hospital based here, but the spa waters are actually alkaline and mineral rather than medicinal. In the early 19C, when tourism on the lake was in its infancy, the town already boasted several hotels and was a cultural center with its own theater. It also had a port at which the steamer lines of the day would call in. Today, for many, it remains a place to see and be seen, stylish and fashionable, a kind of Hungarian Saint Tropez bathed in sun, with a turn-of-the-century nostalgia.

ADDRESSES PAGE 143
Stay, Eat, Sports and Activities, Events and Festivals

INFO:
Tourist Office – *Blaha Lujza utca 5. ✆ 461 210. Open summer, Mon–Sat, 9am–7pm, Sun 10am–4pm; rest of year hours vary.* In a small old building in the historic center.

LOCATION:
Regional map C2 (p128–29)
Although the city is fairly spread out, its historic center, bordered by Tagore Promenade, can easily be explored on foot.

PARKING:
Finding a parking spot can be a challenge in high season. Keep your eyes open and some change handy.

DON'T MISS:
An evening stroll along Tagore Promenade; the small History Museum; a swim in the lake.

TIMING:
Half a day is enough to cover the essentials. With more than 3.5mi/6km) of beaches, all the facilities of a lakeside resort are on offer. Balatonfüred makes a pleasant and convenient base if you want to go on trips into the surrounding area.

KIDS:
The small History Museum; Lóczy Cave; the lake beach (*see Sports and Actitivies, p143).*

Walking tour

Balatonfüred's reputation owes much to the people associated with it, such as actress and singer **Lujza Blaha** (1850–1926), nicknamed "the nightingale of the nation," and the writer **Mór Jókai** (1825–1904). Both had houses here, attracted by the beauty of the locality, the gentle climate, and the trees that offer a protective barrier against the wind. The buildings that began to spring up in the town at the beginning of the 19C also contributed to its renown, while notable figures of the time (poet Sándor Kisfaludy, physician István Huray) did a great deal to help modernize the town. Its social life revolved around the Horváth House and the annual Anna Ball, attracting illustrious names such as Lajos Kossuth, István Széchenyi, and Wesselényi Miklós.

The lake is an ideal place for sailing, a sport that was introduced here at the end of the 19C and reportedly sparked by two gentlemen from Britain. It soon flourished and between May and November still attracts both amateur and seasoned sailors—boats are constantly sailing back and forth and not a day seems to pass in summer without some form of regatta taking place.

★ **Tagore sétány** (Tagore Promenade)
All Balatonfüred comes out at dusk to walk along this shaded lakeside promenade, named in honor of the Indian writer and Nobel Prize winner **Rabindranath Tagore** (1861–1941). In 1926, recovering from heart problems at the sanitarium here, he planted a linden tree in gratitude. His statue now sits watching benevolently over the activity at the adjacent marina.
At the end of the promenade, turn right into Vitorlás tér and carry on up Jókai Mór utca where you will find the circular **Kerektemplom**, a Catholic church built in the late 19C, and looking as if it was modeled on Rome's Pantheon.

Jókai Emlékház (Mór Jókai Memorial House)
Honvéd utca 1. ✆ 950 876. Open Wed–Sun, 10am–6pm. Ft650.
Mór Jókai (1825–1904) was a prolific novelist known as Maurus Jokai in the English-speaking world, who could count Britain's Queen Victoria among his admirers. His magnificent villa strives to preserve the historical setting in which Jókai—sometimes compared to Dickens—wrote most of his work.

Városi Múzeum (History Museum)
Blaha utca 3. ✆ 580 041. Open Wed–Sun, 10am–6pm. Ft650.
The town's small but informative history museum uses archive photos, works of art, toys, and everyday objects (including a collection of glasses for spa guests) to transport you back to Balatonfüred's golden age; by the 18C it was already being hailed as a spa town.

★ **Gyógy tér** (Gyógy Square)
The **Kossuth Lajos forrás** (Lajos Kossuth drinking water fountain), erected in 1800, stands in the center of Gyógy ("Cure") Square. Between 1 May and 30 September, you can sample the water of Balatonfüred here. In the 18C the waters of the carbonated springs were mixed with sheep's milk and used to treat stomach problems. The therapeutic properties of these waters for treating heart problems in particular were discovered at the end of the 19C.

Szanatórium
Gyógy tér 2. The Szanatórium was erected in 1810 as a convalescent home and now houses the **State Hospital of Cardiology**. Beneath the building's arcades, you will find commemorative plaques bearing the names of many of the famous intellectuals, artists and politicians who were treated here

Anna Grand Hotel
Gyógy tér 1. The Anna Grand Hotel is famous for having hosted the **Anna Ball**, the resort's star social event. The ball was first held in 1825 for the daughter of a rich family who spent their summers in Balatonfüred *(see opposite)*.

Lóczy-barlang (Lóczy Cave)
2mi/3km north of the town center (5min drive or 30min walk). Öreghegyi út. ✆ (30) 491 0061. bfnp.hu/en/loczy-cave-balatonfured. Visit by guided tour only (about 30min). Open mid-Mar–Sept, 10am–6pm. Ft600.
Created by limestone erosion, these caves are among the many unusual geological curiosities of the region.

ADDRESSES IN BALATONFÜRED

TRANSPORT

Train – Station: *Castricum tér. mav-start.hu.* Frequent trains in summer to/from Budapest *(3hrs, around Ft2,800)*, and also connections with Tapolca, Veszprém, Keszthely, Hévíz.
Bus – Bus station: *next to the train station.* To Tihany *(30min, around Ft300)*, Keszthely *(1hr, around Ft1,300)* and Budapest *(3hrs, around Ft2,800).*
Ferry – *balatonihajozas.hu.* A shuttle service in summer to Tihany, Siófok, Csopak, Balatonalmádi.

STAY

A TREAT

Gombás Kúria – *Arácsi út 94 (30min walk from the lake). ✆ (30) 9317 522. gombaskuria.hu.* P. *11 rooms, Ft22,700/26,000.* This converted former 18C wine estate bulding has retained its character. The simple but comfortable rooms enclose a pleasant garden; a paddling pool for children.

SPLASH OUT

Club Hotel Füred – *Anna sétány 1–3. ✆ 482 411. clubhotelfured.hu. 43 rooms, around Ft60,000 1/2 board.* In summer the prices of this popular family hotel soar, but it's a great place to stay. Situated beside the lake and inside a lovely wooded park. Various water activities are on offer, including swimming in the lake or the large private pool.

EAT

BUDGET

Kredenc Borbisztró – *Blaha Lujza utca 7. ✆ (20) 518 9960. kredencborbisztro.hu. Open summer, noon–10pm (Sat & Sun 11.30pm); rest of year hours vary. Ft1,990/2,990.* A good place in which to discover vintage wines. This cozy wine bar has a good central location, with a terrace on the street. Concerts some evenings.

AVERAGE

Baricska Csárda – *Baricska dűlő. ✆ 950 738. baricska.hu. Open Thu–Sun, noon–10pm. Ft2,690/7,390.* A little touristy, but this traditional tavern among the vines is still charming; a terrace where you can enjoy classic Hungarian meals. Romani musicians add to the atmosphere *(Fri & Sat, evenings; Sun, at noon).*

TAKING A BREAK

Karolina – *Zákonyi Ferenc utca 4. ✆ 583 098. karolina.hu. Open summer, 8am–midnight; rest of year hours vary.* Locals and tourists flock to this large tea room run by three brothers. A spacious terrace, delicious cakes, and concerts at weekends.

SPORTS AND ACTIVITIES

Swimming – Of the town's three beaches, our favorite is **Kisfaludy Strand**, which is clean and well equipped. A charge is made for entry during the high season *(balatonfuredistrandok.hu; open summer 8.30am–7pm).*

EVENTS AND FESTIVALS:

Anna Ball – 26 July, Anna Grand Hotel. A glamorous ball where the parade of guests is a spectacle in itself; dressed in period costumes, they bring back to life the aristocratic spirit of the town's golden age.

Tihany

★★★

Population 1,369 – Veszprém county – area code ✆87

A little over three miles/five kilometers long, this undulating, wooded peninsula reaches out into the turquoise waters of Lake Balaton as though trying to touch the shore opposite. This lovely area is dominated by the twin bell towers of the Benedictine Abbey Church, famous for its Rococo interior. The charter concerning the abbey's founding is the oldest surviving document in old Hungarian (the original is now at Pannonhalma Abbey). It is the cultural treasure of the small Tihany village, from where a short walk steers you away from the crowds to 988 acres/400 hectares of the oldest nature reserve in Hungary. Known for its hiking trails and geological formations, its geysers and basalt cones are more suggestive of Iceland than Central Europe. In summer, the heady scent of lavender gives the whole scene an air of enchantment.

USEFUL ADDRESSES PAGE 147
Stay, Eat, Taking a Break, Sports and Activities

INFO:
Tourist Office – *Kossuth Lajos utca 20. ✆ 538 104. www.bfnp.hu/en/tihany-peninsula-and-vicinity. Open Mon–Fri, 9am–5pm; Sat & Sun, 10am–4pm.* Stocked with numerous brochures *(including Funzine* and *WeLoveBalaton)* and a walking map of the peninsula.

LOCATION:
Regional map C2 (p128–29)
Tihany map (p146)
Five miles/8km southwest of Balatonfüred and 24mi/39km northeast of Badacsony on Rte 7, which loops around the foot of the peninsula.

PARKING:
The parking lots (mostly in Tihany village with a few elsewhere, charges apply) fill up quickly in summer. Have change ready for the parking meters (no card payment).

DON'T MISS:
The abbey; the views of the lake from the top of the village; a walk in peaceful natural surroundings.

TIMING:
Two hours will be enough to explore the village and its abbey; allow a day if you add in a hiking trip.

KIDS:
Echo Hill; Lavender House.

The village

Situated 1.2mi/2km inside the peninsula, huddled on the eastern slope of a plateau at a modest altitude of 262ft/80m, pretty Tihany village dates back to the 11C, when King András (Andrew) I of Hungary founded the Benedictine Abbey and the village grew up around it, a time when the inhabitants mainly earned their living from fishing and as ferrymen. Fortified with a castle in the 13C, the village resisted a series of attacks by the Turks, but in the end it was the Habsburgs who in 1702 destroyed the castle, of which only a few ruins remain today.

You can reach the abbey via the small streets that lead up the hill from the main street lined with souvenir shops.

Benedictine Abbey by Lake Balaton
© Dronandy/iStock

★★ **Bencés apátság** (Benedictine Abbey Church)

✆ 538 200. tihanyiapatsag.hu. Open summer, Mon–Sat, 9am–6pm; Sun, 11.15am–6pm; rest of the year hours vary. Ft1200 (low season Ft800).

The two towers of this lovely old abbey church are visible from a good distance. Founded in 1055, it was built as a royal necropolis and the **tomb of King András I** lies in the heart of the Romanesque crypt. The 11C church was destroyed in 1702, so the elegant building that you see today dates from the 18C. Imposing in size from the outside, inside the interior doesn't disappoint, showcasing the work of Austrian cabinetmaker Sebastian Stuhlhof, who created the altar, sacristy, and a beautiful organ in the Baroque and Rococo styles of the time. The superb frescoes on the ceiling are by the 19C artist Károly Lotz.

Abbey Museum – *Combined ticket including abbey.* This small museum housed in an 18C building attached to the church, completes a visit to the abbey with an exhibition on **Charles IV**, emperor of Austria and the last king of Hungary (r. 1916–1918), who waited in vain in Tihany to be restored to his throne.

Before leaving, walk around to the other side of the abbey for a great **view★★** of the lake from the lookout on the garden side. The abbey also hosts **concerts** in the summer, often featuring organ music.

The footpath Pisky sétány is on the left side of the abbey (as you face the lake) and leads to a group of small houses with thatched roofs. During summer they form a sort of small **open-air museum** attached to some shops *(open May–Sept, 10am–6pm; Ft800/600). Continue up the Pisky sétány.*

Visszhang-hegy (Echo Hill)

Signposted.

The hill lies at the end of Pisky sétány. Famous for its echo that at one time would repeat up to 16 times, the acoustics have since been altered by new buildings in the immediate vicinity. The echo might not last quite so long these days but it's still fun to try out.

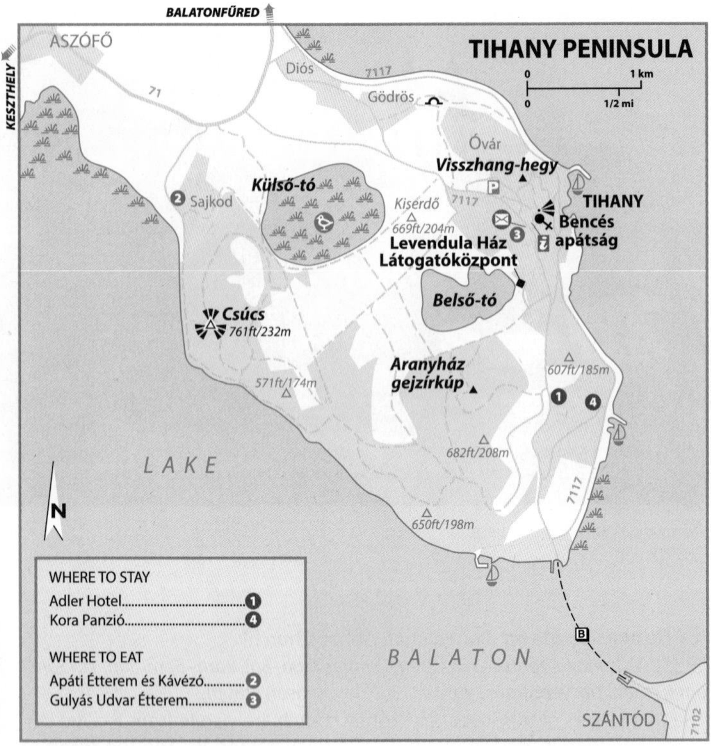

The peninsula

The road to the village runs alongside a marshy area called **Külső-tó** ("outer lake"). Further on, lavender fields surround **Belső-tó** ("inner lake," with a surface area of around 74 acres/30ha) some 82ft/25m above Lake Balaton.

★ **Levendula Ház Látogatóközpont** (Lavender House)
Major utca 67. ✆ 53 8033. bfnp.hu/en/lavender-house-visitor-centre-tihany. Open summer, 9am–6pm; rest of the year hours vary. Ft1,200.
This small modern visitor center beside Belső-tó presents the history of the peninsula in an interesting way, tracing its evolution from its volcanic origins to the lavender fields that grow here today. Activities, a maze, and a walkway along the edge of the water make it a fun spot for families.

Hiking and cycling

Three well-marked trails enable you to roam the peninsula on two feet or two wheels, while always finding your bearings in relation to the towers of the abbey above. The tourist office provides brochures with useful, up-to-minute routes. One of them runs alongside a **volcanic geyser field** where more than a hundred basalt rock formations reveal where geysers such as the one named Aranyház (Gold House) once gushed out of the ground and were solidified as a result of volcanic eruptions.
Another trail climbs to the top of **Csúcs-hegy** (Csúcs Hill, 761ft/232m), in the north-west of the peninsula, from where there is a superb **view**★★ *(about 2hrs walk from the abbey).*

ADDRESSES IN TIHANY

TRANSPORT

Buses run between the village of Tihany and Balatonfüred Station *(up to 20 per day during summer)*. There is a useful bus stop near to where the **ferry** connecting Tihany to Szántód docks *(p136)*.

STAY

A TREAT

1 **Adler Hotel** – *Felsőkopaszhegyi utca 1/A. (87) 538 000. adler-tihany.hu. .13 rooms & 2 apartments, Ft26,900/28,500* . This small, well-run hotel and restaurant is on a quiet road 1 mile/1.5km from the heart of the village. A hot tub, small outdoor pool, and sauna add to its attractions. Bikes are available free of charge.

4 **Kora Panzió** – *Halász utca 5. (20) 9443 982. tihanykora.hu.* P *6 rooms, Ft22,700/26,000* . In a quiet wooded area near the lake, 1.25mi/2km from the village, this small guesthouse wins you over with its cleanliness and pretty garden with a small pool. There's a barbecue area also.

EAT

BUDGET

2 **Apáti Étterem és Kávézó** – *Romkápolna utca 2 (Sajkod). (30) 566 7356. apatietterem.hu. Open Fri–Sun, 11am–9pm. Ft1,850/3,990.* Just off Rte 71, among trees at the foot of the peninsula, the homemade pizzas served here are said to attract foodies from all over Hungary. Other dishes worth the detour include a tempting foie gras with wine jelly. There's a nice terrace and play equipment for children.

AVERAGE

3 **Gulyás Udvar Étterem** – *Mádl Ferenc tér 2. (87) 438 051. gulyasudvar.hu. Open summer, 11am–10pm; rest of year hours vary. Ft2,800/4,400.* If you are looking for Hungarian specialties, take a seat in this traditional tavern near the bottom of the steps leading to the abbey. Goulash, braised pork with cabbage, fried carp, and strudel, they're all here, including food grilled on the barbecue on the terrace in the evening.

TAKING A BREAK

Rege Cukrászda – *Kossuth Lajos utca 22. (30)166 4431. www.apatsagicukraszda.hu. Open Mon–Thu, 10am–7pm; Fri–Sun, 9am–9pm.* Don't miss this tea room in the heart of Tihany village. Its reputation doesn't just come from the wonderful view of the lake—the homemade cakes are excellent and the savory options are just as good.

Levendula – *Kossuth Lajos utca 31. (30)166 4431. www.levendulafagylaltozo.hu. Open summer, 10am–6pm (Fri–Sun, 7pm).* Opposite the abbey as you head downhill, this ice cream parlor is highly recommended by locals for its classic flavors as well as for its more unusual ones (lavender or … camembert!).

SPORTS AND ACTIVITIES

Sail & Surf – *Rév utca 3 (in the Club Tihany vacation complex, 1.25mi/2km outside the village). (30) 22 789 27. wind99.com.* Venture out onto the lake's shallow waters to take up (or go back to) windsurfing. This club is a local institution, with instructors who are proficient in English.

Badacsony

★★★

Population 2,082 – Veszprém county – area code ℘87

Mount Badacsony's distinctive silhouette (it is actually an ancient volcano) stands proudly above the vineyards that roll down its slopes overlooking Lake Balaton. Several grape varieties thrive here on the basalt-rich hillsides, an invitation to wander through the lovely vineyards dotted with beautiful estate houses. Head to the summit for the superb view (of course!). The partly surfaced road up to the top is lined with wineries with cellars that offer tastings.

ADDRESSES PAGE 151
Stay, Eat, Shopping, Events and Festivals

INFO:

Tourist Office – *Park utca 14. ℘ 531 013. west-balaton.hu. Open summer, Mon–Fri, 9am–7pm; Sat & Sun, 10am–7pm; rest of year hours vary.* A hiking trail starts in front of the tourist office.

LOCATION:

Regional map B2 (p128-29)

Rte 71 becomes Balatoni út where it circles around the town. The hiking trails are accessed north of this road, after having crossed the railway line (with your back to the lake).

DON'T MISS:

The climb up Mount Badacsony; the open-air tasting areas in the vineyards; Sümeg and its castle.

TIMING:

One day for the main attractions.

KIDS:

Sümeg Castle; Tapolca Caves.

Discover

Badacsony can refer to the village, the lakeside resort, the wine region, and the mountain. Overlooking the lake from a height of 1,437ft/438m, the volcanic mountain is a real local landmark, offering hikers the chance for some great walks with wonderful **panoramas★★**. One of the best-known trails *(2mi/3.2km)* leads to Kisfaludy-kilátó (Kisfaludy Observation Tower), one of the tallest observation towers on the lake, which provides a particularly fine **view★★** of the lake and the volcanic rock formations. You can stop at a

THE LOCAL NECTAR

The quality of Hungary's wines is well known, and those grown on the slopes of Badacsony often rate highly on lists of the country's best. The Romans were already growing vines here 2,000 years ago. With a Mediterranean-style microclimate and a basalt subsoil on which the vines thrive, the terroir prides itself on producing a delicious local wine, **Olaszrizling** (which translates as "Italian riesling"), as well as other top-quality wines: **Szürkebarát**, **Furmint**, and **Kéknyelű**. You can taste the finest vintages in the many beautiful lime-washed cellars bordering the surfaced path that leads to the top of the mountain.

St. George Hill
© Patrick Frilet/hemis.fr

vineyard for a tasting on the way. Most have terraces that enjoy panoramic views (see p152). But if you find the thought of the climb a little intimidating, much of it can be done by car.

Excursions Regional map (p128–29)

★★ **Sümeg** A2

20.5mi/33km northwest on Rte 71, then Rte 84.

Lajos utca 15. 550 276.

The view is picturesque and pretty: an adorable little town huddled under a 13C castle perched high on a hill.

★★ **Sümeg vár** (Sümeg Castle) – *sumegvar.hu. Open summer, 9am–7pm; rest of year hours vary. Ft1,500 (6–14 yrs Ft800).* This castle became a symbol of national resistance against the Turkish occupation in the 16C. Construction began in the 13C and annexes were added in the 15C. The major projects that followed began while the country was still occupied (the bishop of Veszprém took refuge here). The castle is worth a visit, as much for the enjoyable historical reenactments as for the **views**★ it offers of the extinct volcanoes of Tapolca. And there's a children's playground in the main courtyard.

On your way back down from the castle, don't leave without having a quick look at the town itself, with its narrow streets lined with low houses and especially the **Plébániatemplom** (parish church, *Bíró Márton utca 3; open Mon–Sat, 8am–3.45pm*). Sometimes called the "Rococo Sistine Chapel," the church contains **frescoes** ★★ by **Franz Anton Maulbertsch**, an Austrian painter whose work adorns the walls of many 18C churches in Hungary.

In keeping with the medieval atmosphere, look out for the local entertainment specialty— **tournaments in historical costume** held in an arena at the foot of the castle *(daily, mid-Jul–mid-Aug; rest of the year Wed & Sat).*

★ **Káli Basin** (Káli-medence) B2

Northeast of Badacsony.

This area is sometimes known as the Tuscany of Hungary. The basin and valley occupy an area of land roughly shaped like a diamond between **Salföld** *(7mi/11km from Badacsony on Rte 71)* in the south and **Kapolcs** *(16mi/26km from Salföld on Rte 77)* in the north. Covered with lavender fields, orchards, and vineyards, and interesting geological formations, it is now a protected area inside the **Balaton-felvidéki Nemzeti Park** (Balaton Uplands National Park), a Unesco Global Geopark. An interpretive center is currently under construction in Salföld, but for now it is pleasant just to wander from one village to another, especially since the quality of restaurants is on the rise, as old farms are taken over by young chefs aiming to inject new life into the local cuisine.

Hegyestű Geológiai Bemutatóhely (Hegyestű Geological Interpretive Site) *Hegyestű or Needle Hill is between Monoszló and Zánka). 555 294. bfnp.hu/en/hegyestu-geological-visitor-site-monoszlo. Open summer, 9am–7pm; rest of year hours vary. Ft800 (3–14 yrs Ft500).* Apart from providing a good view of the old basalt quarry, this small visitor center explains the geological heritage of the area and the strange shape of "Needle Hill."

Tapolca A2

9.5mi/15km north of Badacsony.

Tapolca is a small, pretty town with a historic center at the foot of Szent György-hegy (St. George Hill), built around a small lake fed by two subterranean springs, which have carved an impressive underground labyrinth out

ANCIENT GEOLOGICAL FORMATIONS

The mountains north of Lake Balaton tell the geological story of several million years. Each has its own characteristics that make it unique. Volcanic activity at the end of the Pannonian era created conical mountains. The flat tops of Badacsony, Szent György (Saint George), and Csobánc hills make them look rather like gigantic coffins. They are bordered by interesting basalt columns or organ formations. The extraordinary Badacsony Stone Gate (Kőkapu) is formed by two great basalt towers.

of the rock. Part of this network of corridors, which lies under the center of the city, can be visited by boat. The cave system also lies partly beneath the town's hospital and a 4-star hotel. Hotel guests can visit the cave to enjoy the benefits of its microclimate.

★ **Tavas-barlang** (Lake Cave) – *Kisfaludi utca 2. ✆ 412 579. Open summer, 9am–8pm; rest of year hours vary. Ft2,200 (3–14 yrs Ft1,500).* There are two sections to the cave: In one you can enjoy therapeutic treatments. If you feel as though your breathing has improved, it should come as no surprise—patients come here for speleotherapy, the breathing in of the mineral-enriched air. In the other section, you can drift in a boat through the illuminated caves across the stunningly clear karst water.

Somló-hegy (Somló Hill) A1

23.5mi/38km north of Tapolca on Rte 8.

Welcome to the smallest wine region in Hungary on a plain a few miles from **Somlójenő**; its vines are sheltered by the slopes of Somló ("hat of God") Hill (1,417ft/432m). Neglected during the Communist period, new vines were planted and production, mainly white wines, was restored in the early 2000s. **Climb** up for a beautiful **panoramic view★** from Szent István lookout.

2

ADDRESSES AROUND BADACSONY

STAY

Badacsonytomaj

AVERAGE

Óbester Panzió – *Római út 203. ✆ (30) 213 02 25. obester.hu. 8 rooms & 2 apartments Ft19,900/23,900.* Run by a Hungarian-Swedish family with their dogs and cats, this old farmhouse surrounded by vineyards is one of our favorites. Rooms with just the right mix of simplicity and mod cons look out over the tranquility of the vineyards and the lake. Barbecues on summer evenings. Numerous books on the region to leaf through on the small landscaped terraces in the beautiful garden.

Around Somló-hegy

SPLASH OUT

Kreinbacher Birtok – *Somló-hegy, 8481 Somlóvásárhely. ✆ (88) 236 420. kreinbacher.hu. 16 rooms from Ft32,000. Tasting menu Ft7,990/10,990. A la carte Ft2,990/5,990.* A hotel, wine bar, restaurant, and winery all rolled into one, this estate is notable for its ultra contemporary architecture, with its various estate buildings placed boldly but neatly within the landscape. The elegant food from the restaurant adds the finishing touch.

EAT

Badacsonytomaj

AVERAGE

Muskátli Étterem – *Balaton utca 2. ✆ 471 167. muskatli-vendeglo.hu. Open 9am–8pm. Ft2,090/4,890.* A small traditional village tavern offering honest and hearty family food: tripe stew, fried foie gras, *galuskával* (a Hungarian pasta dish). A good local address, open all year round.

Around the Káli Basin

AVERAGE

Kővirág – *Fő utca 9/A. 8274 Köveskál. ✆ (70) 418 7713. kovirag.hu. Open summer, noon–10pm; rest of year hours vary. Ft3,200/6,700. 6 rooms from Ft19,000.* A good restaurant with accommodation. Stylish and contemporary, without entirely relinquishing tradition.

BARS

The terraces on the wine estates are a must. Surrounded by vines, they are invariably picturesque. There is usually some food on offer to accompany the wine tastings, ranging from simple to more elaborate. The terraces are usually open in the warmer months from 11am to 7pm, later on weekends.

Badacsonyörs

Csendes Dűlő Szőlőbirtok – *Hegyalja út 69. ✆ (70) 295 5110. csendes-dulo.hu.* A terrace with panoramic views under a thatched roof. A well-regarded, family-run estate. Hot dishes can sometimes be ordered.

Badacsonytomaj

Laposa Birtok – *Római út 197. ✆ (20) 7777 133. bazaltbor.hu.* One of the most beautiful panoramic terraces, along with some creative dishes to accompany the wines. In summer Sunday lunch can be ordered in advance.

Németh Pince – *Római út 135. ✆ (70) 772 1102. nemethpince.hu.* A family-run estate that can boast of producing some award-winning wines that can be tasted here. They are very proud of their late harvest wines and the sweet Badascony ice wine, where the grapes are harvested when the temperature drops below zero.

Káptalantóti

Istvándy Pincészet – *Hegymög dűlő. ✆ (70) 361 8421. istvandy.hu.* Another very pretty terrace perched high up in the vineyards, where you can enjoy good food and wines from the estate.

SHOPPING

Káptalantóti

Liliomkert Piac – *Open Sun, 9am–noon.* One of the most well-known farmers' markets in Hungary. Some people drive hours in order to soak up the atmosphere here and buy cheeses, *pálinka,* and strudels.

EVENTS AND FESTIVALS

Valley of the Arts Festival, Kapolcs – *muveszetekvolgye.hu.* One of Hungary's oldest arts festivals (since 1989) offers live performances in three picturesque villages, centered around Kapolcs, over 10 days in July. Theater groups, circus skills, music and dance in courtyards, churches, and community spaces.

Lake Hévíz

★★★

Population 4,633 – Zala county – area code ✆83

It would be an understatement to say that the star of this small town is its thermal lake; in English "Hé-víz" means "hot water." It is famous throughout Europe and beyond for its therapeutic properties. Up to a million people each year seek the benefits offered by the spa complex here. Mounted on stilts in the center of the lake and reached by a walkway, it is in an extraordinary setting. In cold weather steam rises from the surface amid the drifting water lilies, adding a mysterious, almost magical quality, especially when the wild ducks, which stop off at Hévíz in winter, take to the air.

ADDRESSES PAGE 156
Stay, Eat, Taking a Break, Sports and Activities

INFO:
Tourist Office – *Rákóczi utca 2. ✆ 540 131. heviz.hu. Open Mon–Fri, 9am–5pm; Sat & Sun, 10am–3pm.* In the main pedestrian street. Information about the town, including accommodation and activities available in the area. Bicycle hire available.

LOCATION:
Regional map A2 (p128–29)
Hevíz is located 6.2mi/10km northwest of Lake Balaton. Lake Hévíz is in the center of a park and surrounded by woodland, 550yds/500m south of the main pedestrian street.

PARKING:
There is parking in the town and around the lake (charges apply).

DON'T MISS:
A swim in the lake.

TIMING:
Half a day will allow you to enjoy the lake at your leisure.

KIDS:
In Keszthely, the English-style gardens of the castle and the lake beaches *(see Sports and Activities, p157)*.

2

Discover

Lake Hévíz lies hidden inside a large wooded park that is closed to the public, but which can be accessed via the spa complex that manages it. Buy the "visitor's ticket" if you don't want to bathe (although that would be a shame).

★★★ **Hévízi Tófürdő** (Thermal lake and spa)
Dr. Schulhof Vilmos utca 1. ✆ 342 830. spaheviz.hu. Open May–Aug, 8.30am–7pm; rest of year hours vary. Visitor's ticket (no bathing) Ft1,000; bathing included Ft3,200 (3hrs), Ft3,900 (4hrs), Ft5,500 (1 day). Towel hire Ft400. A restaurant on site.
The largest thermal lake in the world, with a surface area of 11 acres/4.4ha, it is fed by a spring that produces 108 gal/410 liters per second, enough to completely renew the water of the lake every 28 hours. You can swim whatever the season; the temperature here varies from 71°F/22°C in winter to 95–100°F/35–38°C in summer. The spring supplying the lake is hot, rising from a depth

A LITTLE HISTORY

Popular since ancient times, the therapeutic properties of the lake were apparently already known to the people of the Stone Age. It was **Count György Festetics**, however, from an aristocratic landowning family, who really launched Hévíz as a spa town in 1795. It gradually became popular, with a few "miracle" cures to help along its reputation. Hévíz grew as a spa between the two world wars, but really started to take off in 1970 when a number of hotels were built, mostly offering spa therapies, but also eye and dental care.
A traditional Hévíz cure takes advantage of centuries-old therapeutic traditions, natural thermal waters, and medicinal mud. The treatments are based on bathing in the lake, together with balneotherapy and physio-therapeutic treatments, including a weight bath developed by the Hungarian rheumatologist Dr. Károly Moll.

of 124ft/38m at temperatures between 100°F/38°C and 107°F/42°C. In winter, a light cloud of steam rises above the water and is visible from several miles away. Then the locals say the lake is "smoking its pipe."
The first buildings were erected in the late 18C. Today the pavilions mounted on stilts look a little like a fairy-tale palace. If you would like to bathe in the lake but are not feeling very energetic, you can use a flotation device. Many spa goers make use of one in order to relax totally in the warm water, so that they can enjoy and fully benefit from bathing. You can rent one at the park entrance when you buy your ticket but they are also available to buy at the many nearby shops. The spa complex also includes the St. Andrew's Hospital for Rheumatology and Rehabilitation.
Bathing in the lake for more than 30 minutes is not recommended, unless on medical advice. The water is also not recommended for children under 12 years of age. There is a non-thermal swimming pool reserved for children on the banks of the lake in high season.
For visitors passing through, a dip in the water is fun, but those here for their health can expect to derive the following benefits:
Physical – The water is warm so you can enter it without any of the unpleasant (or exhilarating, depending on your frame of mind) effects on the body when encountering a sharp drop in temperature. The muscles can therefore relax while bathing. The hydrostatic pressure is excellent for the venous and lymphatic system, helping to reduce edema and swelling.
Chemical – The composition of the water is balanced in negative and positive ions and other dissolved substances recommended for rheumatism, musculoskeletal problems, osteoporosis, and so on.
Peat – The lakebed consists of a thick layer of peat which forms medicinal mud. Slightly radioactive, it has various components, including organic compounds that have a mild antibacterial effect. No pathogens can therefore live in the lake water.

Excursions Regional map (p128–29)

★★ **KESZTHELY** A2

7mi/10km from Hévíz, at the western end of Lake Balaton.
Kossuth Lajos utca 30. 314 144. west-balaton.hu. Open summer, 9am–7pm (Sat & Sun, 4pm); rest of year hours vary.

Aerial view of the Hévíz thermal lake and spa
© Hungarian Tourism Agency

With its quiet lanes lined with pastel-colored buildings, this small but significant town is Lake Balaton's cultural hub and has retained an elegant and appealing traditional aspect. It is famous for its **Baroque palace** that was built for the Festetics family, a key branch of the Hungarian nobility, originally from Croatia. Begun in 1745, the construction of the palace—the third largest such building in Hungary after Fertőd and Gödöllő—took more than a century. By 1945 it was one of the few castles/palaces that had not been destroyed or looted, making it a unique relic of the Hungarian aristocracy.

2

★★ **Festetics-kastély** (Festetics Palace)

Helikon Kastélymúzeum. Kastély utca 1. ✆ 314 194. helikonkastely.hu. Open July & Aug, Mon–Sun, 9am–6pm (Wed 9am–noon); May, Jun & Sept, Mon–Sun, 10am–5pm; Oct–Apr, Tue–Sun, 10am–5pm. Palace and coach museum: Ft2,700. Castle and all exhibitions: Ft3,900. Parking (charges apply).

This now houses the Helikon Palace Museum. As you wander through its rooms, you could be forgiven for thinking there is a slightly British feel about the place. In fact the building was extended by Duke Taszilo Festetics between 1883 and 1887. His wife, the Scottish Lady Mary Victoria Douglas-Hamilton, contributed her ideas to the design. If time is tight, make sure you visit the library. You'll pass through a succession of many rooms on the way, most with their original interiors, including coffered ceilings, a monumental carved staircase, Rococo furniture, and works of art, recreating the life of an aristocrat in the 18C and 19C. All thanks to a Soviet army officer, who saved the palace from looting at the end of the Second World War by walling up the points of access.

★★ **Helikon Library** – This is one of the most famous in Hungary, along with the library of Zirc Abbey (*see p160*). It was founded in 1799 by **Count György Festetics** (1755–1819), possibly the most notable member of his family. An enlightened patron of the arts and versed in the sciences, he created the Georgikon, Europe's first agricultural college. Hence among the 86,000 volumes are many books on agriculture and livestock. The library's Greek-sounding name was dreamed up by the count, who was passionate about Greek literature; he also began the Helikon literary festivals.

English Garden – English landscape architect Henry Ernest Milner was commissioned to redesign the garden in the naturalistic English style in 1889. Children will enjoy the small area with farm animals. Some glasshouses also.
Carriage museum *At the bottom of the English garden.* A fine collection of horse-drawn carriages, as used by the aristocracy and the local people.
Exhibits on **hunting** and **historic model railways** are also to be found in buildings within the castle grounds.

The town

Amazon Ház (Amazon House Visitor Center) – *Kastély utca 15. ✆ (83) 314 194. Open Jul & Aug, Mon–Sun, 9am–6pm; May, Jun & Sept, Mon–Sun, 10am–5pm; Oct–Apr, Tue–Sun, 10am–5pm. Ft1,300.* In the former Hotel Amazon, a fascinating window onto the past, filled with many period objects (trunks, travel irons, hand luggage, ...), this recently opened museum takes us on an aristocratic Grand Tour between the 17C and 19C, which launched the fashion for tourism. You can also learn about the first tourists on Lake Balaton.
Walk up Kossuth Lajos utca, a pleasant pedestrian street.
Fő tér (Fő Square) – The town hall (Polgármesteri Hivatal) on the main square, dates from the end of the 18C.
Magyarok Nagyasszonya templom (Church of Our Lady of Hungary) – In the Gothic style, the church contains some 14C and 15C frescoes, discovered during restoration work. Count György Festetics is buried in the crypt.
Georgikon Majormúzeum – *Bercsényi Miklós utca 65–67. ✆ 311 563. elmenygazdasag.hu. Open summer, 9am–5pm (Wed 8pm); rest of year hours vary. Ft600.* Founded by Count György Festetics, the Georgikon Institute (the agricultural college) was housed here until 1848. The building now contains this museum dedicated to the history of the institute, along with winegrowing and agriculture.
Balatoni Múzeum (Balaton Museum) – *Múzeum utca 2. ✆ 312 351. balatonimuzeum.hu. Open 9am–5pm: June–Aug, daily; Apr, Oct & Nov, Mon–Fri; May & Sept, Mon–Sat. Ft900.* This Baroque revival (1928) building houses a museum dedicated to the geological and ethnographic history of Lake Balaton. A slide show illustrates the Kis-Balaton wetlands area (*see p135*).

ADDRESSES IN HÉVÍZ AND KESZTHELY

TRANSPORT

Train – As there is no train station in Hévíz, rail travelers arrive at **Keszthely Station** (on Mártírok utca), from where there are frequent bus departures for **Hévíz Bus Station** *(journey time 15min)*. From Keszthely Station, there are rail connections to Budapest *(journey time about 3hrs)*, Pécs, Tapolca, Győr, and Sopron.

STAY

As it caters mainly to spa visitors, Hévíz town offers a variety of 3- and 4-star hotels. Some of the hotels are classified as spa and/or therapeutic hotels offering thermal therapy and spa or wellness services.

Hévíz

SPLASH OUT

Ensana Thermal Hévíz – *Kossuth Lajos utca 9–11. ✆83 889 444. 203 rooms. Ft34,000/38,000.*

www.ensanahotels.com/thermal-heviz/en/the-hotel. A few minutes' walk from Lake Hévíz, this hotel has a spa and bathing complex, with 6 pools (indoor and outdoor) and a sauna world. There is also a program of sports, including walking and bike tours, tennis, Nordic walking, and horse riding. The spa offers various treatments including balneotherapy.

Keszthely

BUDGET

Ilona Kis Kastély Panzió – *Móra Ferenc utca 22. ✆ 312 514. 6 rooms, Ft12,900* ☕. Like something out of a fairy tale, the rooms of this guesthouse are hidden away under a turreted roof. The slightly unusual decoration is more than made up for by the lovely garden, the kindness of the owners, and the proximity of the beach, just 220yds/200m away.

AVERAGE

Hotel Bacchus – *Erzsébet Királyné útja 18. ✆ 378 566. bacchushotel.hu.* ✕. *26 rooms, Ft24,000* ☕. Ideally located near the castle and Lake Balaton, this quaint hotel has a restaurant in its old cellars and even a small private wine museum with over 1,000 objects to do with winemaking.

EAT

Hévíz

AVERAGE

Öreg Harang Borozó – *Zrínyi utca 181 (1.5mi/2.4km north of the thermal lake spa). ✆ (30) 927 9011. oregharang.hu. Open 3pm–10pm. Ft2,390/5,690.* A superb country tavern and restaurant set among the vines of an estate. The atmosphere is all the warmer for being able to enjoy homemade specialties here. Meals are taken seated on wooden benches and often end with the clinking of glasses of *pálinka*.

Keszthely

BUDGET

Jóbarát Vendéglő – *Martinovics utca 1 (1.25mi/2km east of the castle). ✆ 311 422. jobaratvendeglo.hu. Open 11am–10pm. Ft1,990/3,500.* Recommended by the locals, this slightly out-of-the-way tavern is charming for its simple, country atmosphere, with a ceramic stove in the center, and its house specialties, including *dödölle* (a kind of Hungarian gnocchi) and *tócsni* (potato pancakes).

TAKING A BREAK

Keszthely

Marcipán Múzeum – *Katona József utca 19 (signposted from the castle). ✆ 319 322. Open Wed–Sun, 10am–6pm. Ft180.* A fun marzipan museum that is actually the back room of a cake shop, where the couple who own it display their crazy creations, including a marzipan replica of the castle. As a bonus, there is a small tea room with good cakes and homemade elderberry syrup.

SPORTS AND ACTIVITIES

Keszthely has two main **beaches**, Helikon and Városi; both charge for entry during the high season *(8.30am–7pm, Ft800/400)*. However, the amenities are good and are suitable for children, especially Városi Strand (the municipal beach), which has a slide pool. Equipment for windsurfing and kitesurfing is available for hire as well.

Veszprém

★

Population 59,754 – Veszprém county – area code ✆88

The charming university town of Veszprém, the "city of queens" lies in the Bakony Valley. It is about to become a lot more famous as in 2023 it will be European Capital of Culture. All the queens of Hungary were traditionally crowned here by the archbishop of Veszprém, after the coronation of Queen Gisela, wife of Stephen I, the first Christian king of Hungary. The chasuble in which Stephen's coronation mass was celebrated was also embroidered here. On top of a rocky peak looking out over the Séd river, the historic center of Hungary's first episcopal seat lies inside the walls of its castle and contains a number of former mansions that have now been turned into museums and galleries. The area around the castle is particularly well preserved.

ADDRESSES PAGE 163
Stay, Eat, Taking a Break, Sports and Activities

INFO:
Tourist Office – *Óváros tér 2.* ✆ *404 548. veszpreminfo.hu.* Leaflets, maps, ticket sales, souvenir shop.
For information about Veszprém as European Capital of Culture: *2023veszprem.hu/en/*

LOCATION:
Regional map C1 (p128–29)
Veszprém is 10.5mi/17km north of Lake Balaton (from Balatonfüred). The historic center lies inside the castle walls; the modern center is based around the pedestrianized street Kossuth Lajos utca, which is close by.

PARKING:
There are plenty of spaces; charges apply around the perimeter of the historic center, no charge elsewhere.

DON'T MISS:
A stroll around the castle precinct with its museums and galleries.

TIMING:
One day is enough to see Veszprém, but the city can also be a good base for day trips in various directions.

KIDS:
Veszprém Zoo (*see Sports and Activities, p163*).

THE CITY OF QUEENS

How has Veszprém managed to acquire this name? To trace its origins, we have to go back to the 11C, and the time when **King Stephen I** founded the bishopric and had the fortress built here. His wife, Queen Gisela, the daughter of Henry II, duke of Bavaria (c. 980–1059), was crowned in the fortress and Veszprém was said to be her favorite city. All the queens of Hungary were subsequently crowned here by the archbishops of Veszprém in Gisela's wake and the town became a favorite royal residence. Completely destroyed in the 17C by Turkish troops, Veszprém as you see it today was rebuilt in the 18C.

In 1911, nearly one thousand years after her death, Gisela was beatified by Pope Pius XI in recognition of her great devotion and good works.

Walking tour

★ **THE OLD TOWN**

Leave the car in Óváros tér (Óváros Square, parking 7am–5pm, charges apply). Concentrated along a single street, the historic precinct inside the castle walls can be explored on foot, entering via **Hősök kapuja**, Heroes' Gate. However, just before you go through into the historic center, you might like to pause at the **Tűztorony** (Fire Watchtower, *open 9am–5pm, Ft800*), and climb to the top to get your bearings and for a **panoramic view** ★★ over the city and its surroundings, including the Bakony Mountains.

Some information signs in English are dotted around the castle precinct.

Vár utca (Castle Street)

This rather grand and winding street (note the entranceways tall enough to take carriages) begins at Heroes' Gate. Look out for the building at No. 21 designed by Jakab Fellner, the aristocratic Esterházy family's architect, who also built the **Bishop's Palace** at No. 16, one of the masterpieces of Hungarian Baroque *(not open to visitors).*

★ Modern Képtár (Gallery of Modern Art)

Vár utca 3–7. 561 310. www.muveszetekhaza.hu/hu/vizit. Open May–Oct, Mon–Sat, 10am–6pm; Nov–Apr, Mon–Sat, 10–5pm. Ft800.

Housing the László Vass Collection, this is a pleasant surprise, with an interesting collection of modern art and design, including works by Bernar Venet, Gerrit Rietveld, Günther Uecker, and Christo, along with screen prints by Aurélie Nemours and nesting tables by Josef Albers, a notable member of the Bauhaus.

2

★ Dubniczay Palota (Dubniczay Palace)

Vár utca 29. 560 507. www.muveszetekhaza.hu/hu/vizit. Open May–Oct, Tue–Sun, 10am–6pm; Nov–Apr, Tue–Sun, 10am–5pm. Ft1,000.

The Baroque rooms of this beautiful renovated mansion hold an interesting collection of **Hungarian contemporary art** (the Carl László Collection) where you can discover the work of around 30 artists, assembled since the 1980s by a private collector. In the garden, a modern all-brick annex (the **Tegularium**) displays a collection … of 1,400 bricks. All made in Hungary, from Roman times to today. There is little information in English, unfortunately.

Salesianum

Vár utca 31. szalezianum.hu. Open Jun–Aug, daily, 9am–5pm; Sept–May, Tue–Sun 9am–5pm. Ft1,200 (combined ticket including the cathedral Ft1,500).

Reopened to the public in 2016 after restoration work, this beautiful palace houses the town's tourist center. An exhibition traces the life of **Márton Padányi Biró** (1693–1762), a powerful bishop in the Hungarian church who lived here. It also houses the workshops of a violin maker, a candlemaker, a small café (the only place where you can eat inside the castle walls (*see Taking a Break, p163*), and a herb garden.

Szent Mihály Bazilika (St. Michael's Cathedral Basilica)

Open beg May–mid-Oct, Tue–Sun, 10am–5pm (closed during mass). Ft500 (combined ticket including the Salesianum Ft1,500).

Founded in the 11C, the cathedral has been destroyed and rebuilt several times since then, the last occasion being in 1910. Only the Romanesque **crypt**★ has survived and is worth a visit. You will see people prostrating themselves before a relic, the arm bone of Queen Gisela, the Bavarian wife of King Stephen. It was brought back from Germany, where she is buried, in 1996. Several other remains are visible nearby under a transparent dome, from the 10C **St. George's Chapel** (Szent György kápolna).

★ **Gizella-kápolna** (Gisela Chapel)
☏ 426 095. Open May–Oct, 10am–6pm; by appointment rest of the year.
Discovered during construction work in the 18C, judging from the Byzantine-inspired frescoes of the apostles on the walls, this chapel is thought to date from the 13C, making the frescoes some of the oldest in Hungary.

Gizella Királyné Múzeum (Queen Gisela Museum)
☏ 426 095. Vár utca 35. Open 10am–5pm. Ft400.
This museum displays sacred objects from the treasure of the bishopric and Christian works of art. **Szent István ferences templom** (St. Stephen's Church), belonging to the Franciscan order, stands next to the museum.
Vár utca terminates at the city walls, with a view to Benedek-hegy (St. Benedict Hill), one of the city's 7 hills, and the viaduct that spans the River Séd. Look out for the stone statues of King Stephen and Queen Gisela, which were erected in 1938 to commemorate the 900th anniversary of Stephen's death. They stand watch on the parapet night and day, looking out regally over the city.

Excursions Regional map (128–29)

★ **Herendi Porcelánmanufaktúra** (Herend Porcelain Manufactory) B1
9.3mi/15km west of Veszprém on Rte 830. Kossuth Lajos u. 140. ☏ 261 518. herend.com. Open beg Apr–Oct, daily, 9.30am–6pm; Nov–Mar, Tue–Sat, 10am–4pm (closed 3rd wk Dec–3rd wk Feb, check website for details). Minimanufactory, incl. guided tour in English, and Porcelain Museum Ft3,500.
Herend porcelain has been gracing prestigious tables for nearly two centuries. At the time the factory was created in 1826, Japanese and Chinese porcelain was extremely expensive. Thanks to its advanced techniques, however, Herend was able to compete with them, securing orders from the nobility of Europe, including Britain's Queen Victoria. Nationalized in 1948, the factory was bought back by its workers in 1992. It is flourishing once again, as can be seen from the modern complex opposite the historic museum. The brick buildings housing the **Minimanufactory** surround a small square with an ornamental pond where the porcelain-making process is demonstrated, while the most beautiful pieces are on show in the **Porcelain Museum**. Don't leave without visiting the **store**: the pieces are very beautiful, and are priced accordingly.

Ösküi kerektemplom (Öskü Round Church) C1
11mi/18km northeast of Veszprém on Rte 8.
Take a short detour into the countryside to this most unusual church, a large mushroom-shaped building overlooking the village of Öskü. It is one of the few circular churches in Europe. The domed roof and choir date from the 15C while the walls date from the 11C.
Opposite the church is a small park with a table, wooden benches, and a stream. A good place for a picnic if it's lunchtime.

★ **Zirci apátság** (Zirc Abbey) C1
15.5mi/25km northeast of Veszprém on Rte 82.
Another small historic town in the Bakony Mountains, Zirc is especially

St. Stephen's Church and Holy Trinity statue, Veszprém
© I love takeing photos and i think that is a really great opportunity for me to share them/iStock

noteworthy for its fully working Cistercian abbey, whose vast facade comes as something of a surprise when wandering around the town center, which is much more modest in size *(parking in the adjoining streets, no charge).* **Welcome center** *593 675. zirciapatsag.hu. Open Tue–Sun, 9am–5pm (Nov–Apr, 10am–4pm). Guided tours every hour. The library and church are visited by guided tour only (1hr) Ft800/person (combined ticket Ft900); visitor center Ft1,000; arboretum Ft800; all inclusive ticket Ft2,900.* You have to walk through the welcome center (part shop, part ticket office) in order to join the guided tour. Bear in mind that the schedule is strict and the tours are conducted in Hungarian.

★ **Library** – If time is tight, this should be your priority. Tucked away on the first floor of the main building, it is the abbey's literary treasure trove and is admired for its superb marquetry, the work of a local cabinetmaker (1857), and for its collection of 65,000 volumes containing a wealth of rare manuscripts, some 70 examples of very early printed matter (books, pamphlets), a Bible in nine languages, and a text of the French Constitution presented to Louis XVI in 1791 by the French revolutionary assembly. One of the oldest celestial globes in the world (1630) is also on display, based on the observations of the Danish astronomer Tycho Brahe.

On your way out, you can visit the highly ornate abbey **church**, which contains frescoes by the Austrian **Franz Anton Maulbertsch** (1724–96) above the high altar and the south altar, an artist little known outside the German-speaking world. The modern **visitor center** is very interesting and traces the history of the site from 1182 to the present day, but most of the information is in Hungarian only. Finally, there is a large **arboretum** behind the abbey, which is planted with rare species.

Pápa B1, off map

31mi/50km northwest of Veszprém (28mi/45km west of Zirc).

Márton István utca 10. (89) 777 047. Open Mon–Fri, 9am–5pm, Sat 9am–noon.

While this charming town is mostly known for its distinctive textiles, the heir to

THE BLUE DYE DIASPORA

Until the 16C, textiles dyed blue were the preserve of an elite few. Obtained from the plant *Isatis tinctoria* (woad) cultivated in Germany, the dye was complicated and expensive to produce. However, everything changed in the 16C, when Dutch traders began to import the indigo plant from Asia. It revolutionized the production of blue textiles to the point where it threatened the German dye industry. To protect it, the government clamped down on weavers' workshops that used imported indigo. Threatened with death, some emigrated to more welcoming countries, forming the "blue dye diaspora." And so it was that **Johann Friedrich Kluge**, fleeing German Saxony, set up Pápa's first factory in 1786. Over the years the Kluge family expanded its business and perfected its production techniques, keeping up with customer demands and following scientific and technical discoveries, leading to the development of what at the time was a cutting-edge industry. It was nationalized in 1956. Today there are still a dozen or so cities in Hungary that carry on this process, producing beautiful textiles with contrasting patterns printed on blue backgrounds.

a long Hungarian tradition (*see box p162)*, its small historic center is notable for its Baroque architecture. It was also an important center for Protestantism in the late Middle Ages, although today the most interesting of the town's churches is the Catholic church in the main square.

★★ **Kékfestő Múzeum** (Blue Dye Fabric Museum) – *Március 15 tér 12. (89) 324 390. kekfestomuzeum.hu. Open Apr–Oct, Tue–Sun, 9am–5pm; Nov–Mar, Tue–Sat, 10am–4pm. Ft900.* The Kluge family's *kékfestő* (blue-dyed fabric) factory has been turned into a museum. The equipment on display seem about to start up; all that is missing is the steam, the fabrics dripping with dye, and of course the workers. You can also see the laboratory where research and development were carried out, and at the end of the visit, an exhibition of designs by 20C artist Irén Bódy, (1925–2011), who worked in the applied arts and made superb use of this printing technique. A shop at the museum entrance sells textiles in short lengths or made up into clothes, purses, and so on.

★ **Esterházy-kastély** (Esterházy Castle) – Pápa owes its Baroque appearance to Count Károly Esterházy, bishop of Eger and Vác, who had this castle built by Jakab Fellner and József Grossmann. Today it is occupied by cultural institutions and the chapel has been turned into a library. The ceiling frescoes are the work of Josef Ignaz Mildorfer, an 18C artist from the Viennese court.

Fő tér – Several Baroque houses line this main square. See nos. 12, 21, and 23.

Nagytemplom (Great Church) – Jakab Fellner and Jozsef Grossman, the two architects responsible for Esterházy Castle, also designed this Roman Catholic church dedicated to St. Stephen, known locally as "the big church." Inside are frescoes by Franz Anton Maulbertsch representing St. Stephen. Unusually, for Hungary, the Stephen in question is Christianity's first martyr. Any representations of Saint Stephen in Hungary are usually of King Stephen I, also known as King Saint Stephen, rather than Saint Stephen, the first Christian martyr, who died in AD36.

ADDRESSES IN VESZPRÉM

TRANSPORT

Train – Station *(Veszprém vasútállomás)*. Around 20 trains a day leave Budapest for Veszprém *(the fastest take 1hr25min)*, but there are also direct rail links with Herend *(14min)* and Győr *(2hrs)*.
Bus – Bus station *(Volán Autóbuszállomás): Jutasi út 4.* There are frequent buses to Sümeg, Keszthely, and Siófok *(2hrs)*, Budapest *(2hrs15min)*, Tapolca *(1hr)*, and Herend *(20min)*.

STAY

BUDGET

Sommerhaus – *Diofa utca 13 (0.7miles/1.1km from the citadel). 3 rooms. Ft11,000/13,000.* Situated on a quiet side street in the center of town. All the rooms in this charming guesthouse (maximum 2 guests per room) have a kitchenette with a refrigerator and kitchenware.

A TREAT

Oliva Hotel – *Buhim utca 14. 403 875. oliva.hu. Ft2,190/3,990. 20 rooms, Ft24,000.* This hotel is usefully situated just 220yds/200m from the historic district center. Clean and functional rooms in an old building that has been renovated. The restaurant is excellent.

EAT

BUDGET

Marica Kávéház – *Kossuth Lajos utca 5. (70) 634 2403. Open 10am–10pm (Fri–Sat, 1am). Ft1,490–2,990.* This small, unpretentious, contemporary café-restaurant in the pedestrian street of the modern town center (220yds/200m from the castle) serves burgers, pizzas, and salads and is a magnet for students. Good homemade lemonades.
Fricska Gastropub – *Miklós utca 10. 794 331. Open 10am–11pm (Fri & Sat, 1am). Ft1,290–2,200.* Situated among the greenery in a beautiful garden beside the Séd river at the foot of the castle hill, this restaurant is worth the (small) detour. The atmosphere is a mix of beergarden and open-air bistro, and the food is based on grilled meat and burgers.

TAKING A BREAK

Mackó Cukrászda – *Megyeház tér 2. (30) 782 5232. Open 7am–7pm (Sat–Sun, 9am).* Hungarians love this sort of traditional tea room, and this one in particular is popular for the quality of its cakes and homemade desserts (its *île flottante* is sumptuous). Savory bites are on offer at lunchtime.
Szaléziánum Kávézó – *Hegyalja út 69. szalezianum.hu/tea-es-kavehaz. Open 10am–6pm.* A pocket-size café, the only place to eat inside the castle. Enjoy cakes and small sandwiches in the garden when the weather is fine.

SPORTS AND ACTIVITIES

Zoo – *Kittenberger Kálmán utca 17. (30) 699 0870. veszpzoo.hu. Open May–Sept, 9am–6pm; rest of year hours vary. Ft3,300 (2–18 yrs Ft2,300).* The animals come from all over the world. Children will enjoy the playgrounds and a new "Dino Park" dedicated to dinosaurs, with life-size models.

Székesfehérvár

★★

Population 97,382 – Fejér county – area code ✆22

From the highway between Budapest and Lake Balaton, Székesfehérvár might look like an industrial town full of large accommodation blocks, but take a chance on stopping off and you will be well rewarded. The Baroque center is dotted with beautiful churches, museums, and pleasant streets lined with café terraces. For Hungarians, Székesfehérvár is near sacred, the place where kings have been crowned for centuries and where Stephen I, the most famous of all, lies at rest. Many visitors pass this city by without a second glance. Don't be one of them!

ADDRESSES PAGE 168
Stay, Eat, Taking a Break, Baths

INFO:
Tourism Office – *Oskola utca 2–4. ✆ (23) 537 261. turizmus.szekesfehervar.hu. Open daily, Jul–Aug, 9am–6pm (Sat & Sun, 10am–4pm); rest of year hours vary.* Stock up here on maps and brochures. The staff are very competent. Free wifi.

LOCATION:
Regional map D1 (p128–29)
Székesfehérvár is halfway between Budapest and Balatonfüred. The center of town occupies a sort of triangle between the streets Mátyás Király körút to the west, Várkörút to the east, and Budai utca to the south.

PARKING:
The historic center is pedestrian only, with parking spaces at the perimeter (charges apply). The nearest free parking area is Palotai utca, northwest of Mátyás Király körút.

DON'T MISS:
A stroll through the narrow streets of the Baroque downtown; the National Memorial; the Deák Collection.

TIMING:
A day should be long enough to visit the main points of interest while enjoying the gentle pace of this small town, which is easily explored on foot.

KIDS:
The beaches of Lake Velence.

Walking tour

THE OLD TOWN

Start at Városház tér.

The **town hall** (Polgármesteri Hivatal) stands in this pleasant square lined with café terraces, opposite the **Franciscan church**. The Bishop's Palace (Püspöki Palota) was built in the Zopf (late Baroque) style in the early 19C, using stones from the royal palace and the remains of the medieval basilica.

Access the National Memorial/Medieval Ruin Garden via Koronázó tér.

★ **Középkori Romkert** (National Memorial/Medieval Ruin Garden)
✆ 317 572. szikm.hu/kiallitohelyek/nemzeti_emlekhely. Open 9am–5pm. Ft700.
One of Hungary's principal historic sites, it holds the remains of the basilica founded by **Stephen I** (also known as King St. Stephen, Szent István király).

Bory Castle
© bartoshd/iStock

A total of 37 kings of Hungary were crowned and some 20 are buried here, including Stephen I himself, who lies in the white marble sarcophagus at the entrance. The basilica was destroyed in 1601 when gunpowder being stored in the building by Turkish troops exploded, an event that resulted in the ruins you see today.

Return to Városház tér and turn left down Kossuth utca.

★ **Kossuth utca** (Kossuth Street)

A charming and lively street with interesting passageways leading off into interior courtyards, it successfully integrates contemporary concrete architecture into the historic setting. At the intersection with Táncsics Mihály utca you'll find **Árpád Fürdő** (*see p169*), which stand alongside a pink building in the Secessionist style.

Turn right toward Arany János utca.

Szent István székesegyház (St. Stephen's Cathedral)

Closed for renovation until 2022.

The cathedral, with its prominent twin towers at the front, was built in the 18C on the site of a 13C church where King Béla IV was crowned in 1235. The Baroque building you see today is the work of court architect Franz Anton Hildebrandt, while Johann Cimbal painted the frescoes on the ceiling. King **Béla III**, a key member of the ruling Árpád dynasty in the 12C, and his wife Agnes of Antioch are at rest in the crypt.

Outside, on the north wall, the Christ on the Cross is dedicated to the victims of the 1956 Hungarian Uprising. The city's coat of arms can be seen above the main portal.

Szent Anna kápolna (St. Anne's Chapel)

The only surviving building from the medieval period (1470), this small and sober chapel stands modestly opposite the cathedral. Inside, look out for the 18C Baroque altar.

Walk down Arany János utca toward Szent István ter.

THE ROYAL CITY

At one time Székesfehérvár was, after Esztergom, the largest city in the Kingdom of Hungary and home of the kings who, from Stephen I in 1038 until János (John I) Szapolyai in 1540, were crowned and buried here. Stephen I ordered his palace to be built in Székesfehérvár, along with the cathedral, designed by Italian architects. The crown jewels and the national archives were also kept in the city.

The city was the scene of a key event in the history of the Hungarian monarchy. In 1222 King András (Andrew) II issued the **Golden Bull**, a charter laying down the rights and duties of the nobles and the limitations of the king's power. It was in effect the first Hungarian constitution and the equivalent of England's Magna Carta. It can also be seen as a predecessor of the Declaration of Human Rights. Designed to respond to the pressure of the barons, whose cooperation the king needed, it recognized their right to rebel against their sovereign without being punished for treason, if the king were to abuse his power.

In 1543 Székesfehérvár fell into the hands of the Ottoman invaders and the cathedral and palace were ransacked and the royal tombs desecrated. The Turks destroyed much of the city, but eventually left around 1688. However, reconstruction work was not completed until the end of the 18C. The railway contributed to the development of the city in the 19C and by the Second World War the city had become an important rail hub. As a result, serious fighting broke out between the occupying Germans and the invading Russians, causing the city to suffer major damage once more, although the historic center was not so badly affected. After the war, thanks to its strategic position, Székesfehérvár became an industrial center for aluminum, the manufacture of buses, and the assembly and production of televisions. The population doubled in less than a decade, the reason for the extensive residential blocks dotted around the city.

Szent István tér (St. Stephen's Square)

The **equestrian statue of St. Stephen** stands proudly on a plinth in the center of this pleasant landscaped square.

To return to Városház tér, walk back up **Megyeház utca**, looking out for the two late-18C Romantic revival houses at nos. 7 and 11. The interior courtyards hint at the charm and tranquility of urban life here.

Cross Városház tér and continue on Oskola utca.

★ **Deák Gyűjtemény** (Deák Collection)

Oskola utca 10. ✆ 329 431. deakgyujtemeny.hu. Open Tue–Sun, 10am–6pm. Ft700.

If you only have time to visit one of the town's museums, be sure to make it this one. This beautiful 18C house holds an interesting collection of **Hungarian paintings** from the early 20C to the 1960s. The 600 works were gathered by the collector Dénes Deák (1931–1993), who bequeathed them to the city along with some sculptures (in the basement).

Return to the main pedestrian street, Fő utca.

★ **Fekete Sas Patikamúzeum** (Black Eagle Pharmacy)

Fő utca 5. ✆ 315 583. Open Tue–Sun, 10am–6pm. Ft700.

You can still see the original beautiful wooden fittings in this former Jesuit pharmacy (18C)—carved by a Jesuit brother—which also displays all the instruments and vessels used by pharmacists at that time. It was in use until 1971.

★ **Nepomuki Szent János templom** (St. John of Nepomuk Church)
Built by the Jesuits (1745–51), this church was subsequently taken over by the Cistercians. Inside, frescoes cover all the walls and vaults. Look out for the carved and gilded wooden pulpit from the 18C. In the **sacristy** you can see further examples of the fine handiwork of the Jesuit brothers—beautifully carved oak and linden wood furniture in the Rococo style.

★★ **Szent István Király Múzeum** (King St. Stephen Museum)
Országzászló tér 3. ✆ 315 583. szikm.hu. Open Tue–Sun, 10am–6pm. Ft700.
The museum displays a collection of Roman stones and sculptures, the most important pieces of which come from the Roman city of Gorsium (*see below*), on the first (ground) floor. The upper level is devoted to the archeological history of the region from prehistory to the end of the Turkish occupation.

BEYOND THE OLD TOWN

Old Serbian Quarter
Take Ady Endre utca, and then Tobak utca to Rác utca.
Serbs settled in this area in the 16C under the Ottoman occupation. Rác utca (Serbian Street) harks back to this period, where a row of 12 restored tradi tional houses with thatched roofs forms a small open-air museum (Palotavárosi Skanzen; *✆ 315 583; open May–Oct, Mon–Fri, 9am–5pm; Ft700).*
The church (Rác templom) contains a beautiful 18C **iconostasis**★★ (wall/ screen of icons and religious paintings).

★ **Bory vár** (Bory Castle)
Head north from the center, take Szekfü Gyula, cross junction onto Berény út, cross road onto Béla út, turn right after the cemetery into Bicskei utca, then take Máriavölgy utca to reach Bory tér. bory-var.hu/en. Open daily 9am–5pm. Ft1,800.
This unusual building mixing various styles was created by **Jenő Bory** (1879–1959), an architect and sculptor who was born in Székesfehérvár. For over 40 years he spent his vacations building this amazing structure with his own hands.

2

Excursions Regional map (p128–29)

★ **Gorsium Régészeti Park** (Gorsium Archeological Park), at **Tác** D1
In Tác, 9.5mi/15km south of Székesfehérvár on Hwy M7 (exit 70 toward Tác). ✆ 315 583. szikm.hu/kiallitohelyek/gorsium. Open daily, Apr–mid-Oct, 10am–6pm; mid-Oct–Mar, Tue–Sun, 8am–4pm. Ft1,200. A large on-site parking lot.
About 1.2mi/2km from the village, these are the remains of the Roman city of Gorsium-Herculia. A modern concrete building contains a museum that traces the history (in Hungarian) of this Roman city that once had a population of up to 7,000 before it was destroyed by barbarians in 260. You can walk around the excavated city (work began in 1958) and make out its various streets (including a row of shops) and buildings such as the governor's palace and two basilicas. At the edge of the site you will find a **theater** that could seat 1,200 spectators. The city was abandoned once the Romans left and the stones were reused to build houses in nearby areas, including in Székesfehérvár.

★ **Velencei-tó** (Lake Velence) D1
6mi/10km east of Székesfehérvár on Rte 7.
Tópart u. 47, at Velence. ✆ (30) 974 2566. velenceturizmus.hu.

A smaller version of Lake Balaton that is not as well known to foreign tourists. This nature reserve is particularly enjoyed by birdwatchers (part of the lake is covered with reedbeds). The south shore has been developed as a resort area. Its shallow water, and **beaches** of sand and grass are popular with families, although the choice of accommodation and restaurants is a little limited.

★ **Károlyi-kastély** (Károlyi Castle), at **Fehérvárcsurgó** D1

In Fehérvárcsurgó village, 12mi/19km east of Székesfehérvár on Rte 81. Petőfi Sándor utca 2. ✆ (21) 311 0422. Visit by guided tour only (1hr) in English and Hungarian. Open 10am–5pm. Ft1,500.

A vast building in stark contrast to the small village in which it is located. Renovated by the Franco-Hungarian descendants of one of the great noble families, it is in elegant French-style grounds. Sadly, the interior has been damaged over the years, but the owners managed to retrieve the property after it was confiscated at the end of the Second World War. They set about renovating it and today the building's main function is as a hotel-restaurant *(see below)*.

ADDRESSES IN SZÉKESFEHÉRVÁR

TRANSPORT

Train – Station: *Beké tér (1.25mi/2km southeast of Városház tér)*. There are several connections to/from Budapest *(1hr)*, Balatonfüred *(1hr2min)*, and Siófok *(34min)*.

Bus – Station: *Piac ter 4–8*. The journey times are more or less the same as by train, but the bus station is in the center of town.

STAY

BUDGET

Belváros Vendégház – *Arany János utca 21. ✆ (70) 293 9333. belvarosvendeghaz.hu. 6 rooms, Ft13,000 ☕. Private parking nearby (charges apply).* This guesthouse offers simply furnished and immaculate rooms in a pretty house in the historic center. All have a private bathroom. Worth considering also since it is centrally located accommodation at a very reasonable price.

AVERAGE

Szent Gellért Hotel – *Mátyás Király krt. 1. ✆ 510 810. szentgellerthotel.hu. 39 rooms, Ft22,000 ☕. Brewery open 10am–10pm.* Clean and recently renovated, this fairly nondescript but comfortable hotel is in the quiet but historic downtown area. As a bonus, there is a reputable brewery on the ground floor which serves award-winning craft beers. A wellness roof terrace with a Finnish sauna that is open all year round.

Fehérvárcsurgó

A TREAT

Károlyi-kastély – *Petőfi Sándor utca 2. ✆ (21) 311 0422. karolyikastely.accenthotels.com/en. ✕ Ft2,550/5,650. 22 rooms, Ft24,300 ☕.* A very grand hotel! A castle formerly belonging to members of the Austro-Hungarian aristocracy, turned into a hotel with a French touch added by the Franco-Hungarian owners, descendants of the original proprietors. Hungarian and French food is served in the restaurant.

EAT

BUDGET

Rosetta Étterem – *Szent István tér 14. ✆ 806 008. Open 11.30am–10pm (Fri & Sat, midnight). Ft1,000/2,000.* Situated at the corner where two streets converge and looking out on a beautiful shady square, this restaurant and its lovely terrace have a touch of *la dolce vita* about them, and not just on the plate.

Perte Bistro – *Lakatos utca 2. ✆ (70) 331 7831. Open 8am–10pm. Ft1,000/3,000.* When the weather is fine, the large terrace that looks out onto Városház tér beckons. At other times, the modern interior is just as inviting. Very generous servings, although the food could be a little more elegant. Good homemade drinks (lemonade, smoothies, for example).

A TREAT

67Sigma Étterem – *Oskola utca 2–4. ✆ (20) 970 4997. Open Mon–Sat, 11.30am–10pm. Ft4,000/9,800.* In a Baroque house in the historic center, with a newly decorated interior, this elegant restaurant is a haunt for local foodies who appreciate the precision of the cooking and balanced flavors that combine to produce Hungarian haute cuisine.

TAKING A BREAK

Damniczki Cukrászda – *Fő utca 3. ✆ 340 283. damniczki.hu.* Previously located outside the center of town, this cake shop, ice cream parlor, and tea room all rolled into one made the sensible decision to open this new branch in the middle of town. Choose from around 30 flavors of homemade ice creams and sorbets, including the "raspberry-wine" flavor which received an award in a national competition in 2013. The homemade cakes are also popular among those with a sweet tooth.

Pátria Kávéház és Étterem – *Városház tér 1. ✆ 397 089. www.patriakavehaz.hu. Open 9am–10pm (Fri & Sat, midnight).* Benefiting from the sun from noon onward on fine days, the beautiful terrace of this historic café next to city hall calls for a coffee or a quick meal break. Its central location close to all the points of interest makes it a useful spot at which to stop off.

BATHS

Árpád Fürdő – *Kossuth u. 12. ✆ 814 400. fehervar-arpadfurdo.hu. Open 9am–10pm. Ft3,900/day.* Built in 1905 and renovated in 2010, these Art Nouveau baths have retained some of their period charm—colonnades and frescoes around one of the pools, carved wooden booths. The facilities on offer include a Turkish bath, sauna, and a salt room.

Tokaj and the Mountains of the North 3

Michelin National Map 732
Borsod-Abaúj-Zemplén, Heves, Nógrád counties

Tokaj vineyards, Mád
© Hungarian Tourism Agency

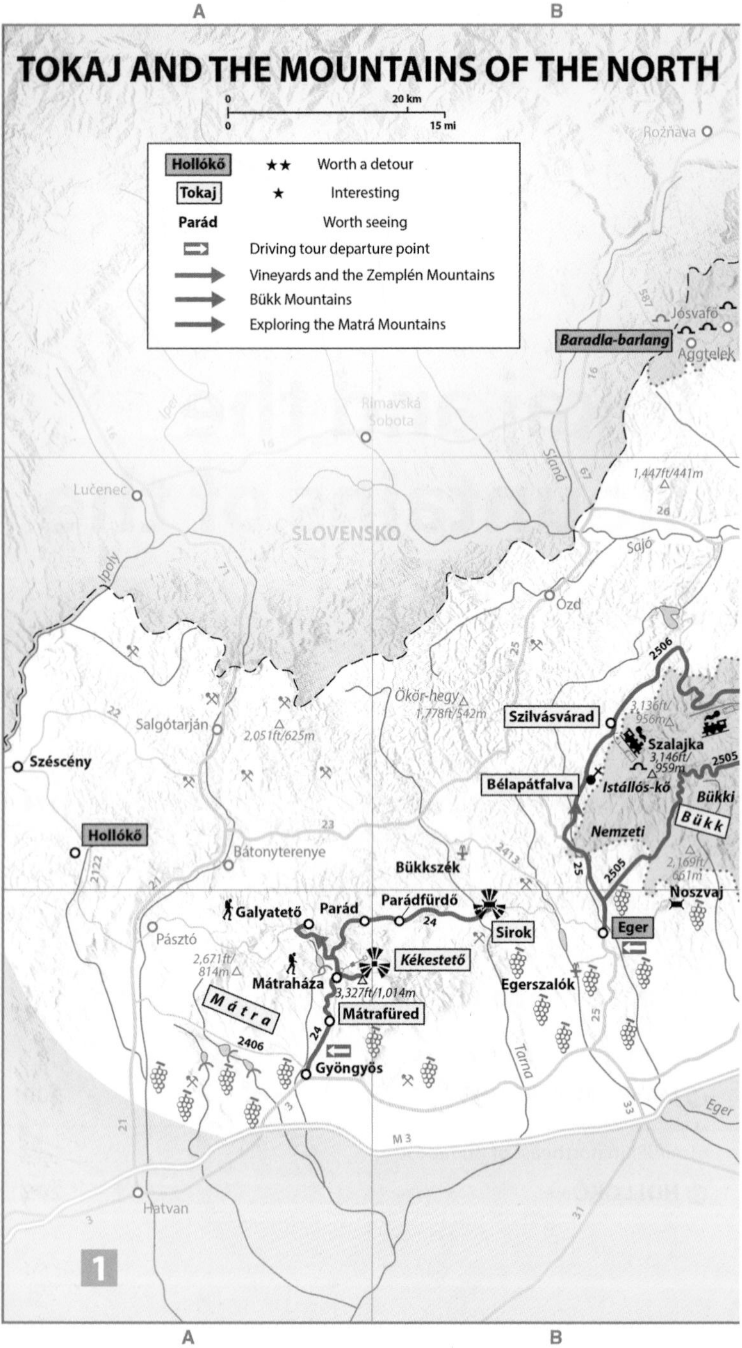
TOKAJ AND THE MOUNTAINS OF THE NORTH
Hollókő ★★ Worth a detour
Tokaj ★ Interesting
Parád Worth seeing
Driving tour departure point
Vineyards and the Zemplén Mountains
Bükk Mountains
Exploring the Matrá Mountains
0 20 km
0 15 mi
A
B
1
2
3
ZVOLEN
BUDAPEST JÁSZBERÉNY
Rožňava
Jósvafő
Baradla-barlang
Aggtelek
Rimavská Sobota
Lučenec
SLOVENSKO
Ipoly
Ipeľ
Slaná
Sajó
1,447ft/441m
Ózd
Salgótarján
2,051ft/625m
Ökör-hegy
1,778ft/542m
Szilvásvárad
3,136ft/956m
Szalajka
3,146ft/959m
Szécsény
Bélapátfalva
Istállós-kő
Bükki
Nemzeti
Bükk
2,169ft/661m
Noszvaj
Hollókő
Bátonyterenye
Bükkszék
Galyatető
Parád
Parádfürdő
Sirok
Eger
Pásztó
2,671ft/814m
Kékestető
Mátraháza
3,327ft/1,014m
Egerszalók
Mátra
Mátrafüred
Gyöngyös
Tarna
Eger
M3
Hatvan
1

TOKAJ AND THE VINEYARDS

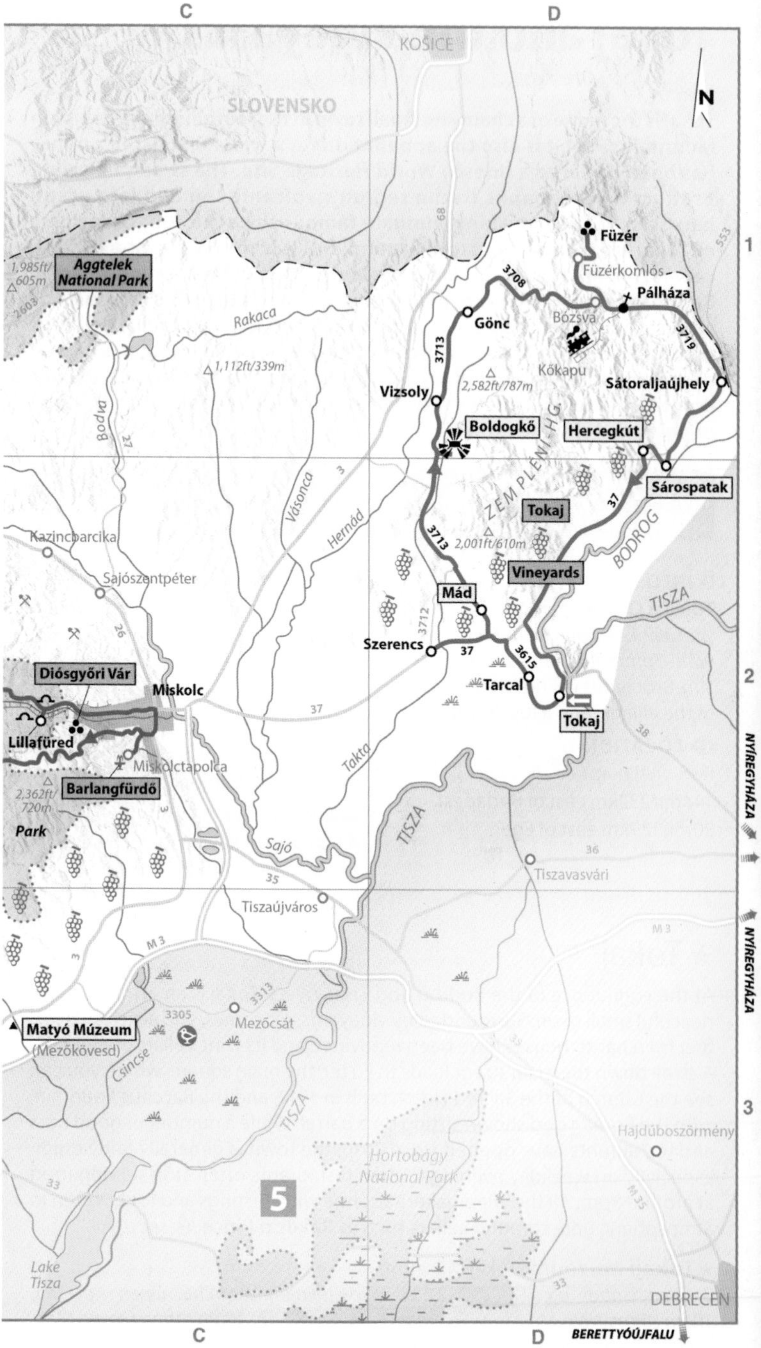

Tokaj and the vineyards★★

Population 4,155 – Borsod-Abaúj-Zemplén county – area code ✆ 47

Tokaj is the name of a charming small town in the foothills of the Zemplén Mountains, but it is also the appellation for a winemaking region that has been declared a Unesco World Heritage Site. The sweet, rich wine produced here thanks to the region's volcanic soil and late grape harvests, has been making Hungary famous since the 16C. The streets of Tokaj are pleasant to stroll around, but it is the museums and wine cellars that are the real attraction, along with the surrounding villages. Before setting off, there are two important Hungarian words to master if wine tasting is likely to be part of your visit: *bor* (wine) and *pince* (cellar). A boat trip on the River Tisza will complete your stay, enabling you to pass a few very agreeable days here. And if you come in spring and summer, don't forget to look out for the storks that make their nests on the tops of poles and chimney stacks.

ADDRESSES PAGE 180
Stay, Eat, Events and Festivals, Sports and Activities

INFO:
Tourist Office – *Serház utca 1. ✆ 3 352 125. Open Mon–Fri, 9am–5pm; Sat, 10am–2pm. Closed Sun.* Brochures in English, street plan of the village, and a tourist map.

LOCATION:
Regional map D1–2 (p172–73)
144mi/232km east of Budapest.
80mi/129km east of Eger.

PARKING:
Some free spaces in the town center.

DON'T MISS:
The Tokaji Museum; tasting wine in a cellar; the synagogue in Mád.

TIMING:
Allow a day for Tokaj and one or two more days to explore the local area.

KIDS:
A boat trip or kayaking on the river (*see Sports and Activities, p182*).

★ Tokaj

At the confluence of the Bodrog and Tisza rivers, Tokaj is an attractive and peaceful small town. Surrounded by vineyards, pine trees, and acacias, its former merchants' houses have been renovated and its wine cellars opened up. A stroll down the main street leads to Fő tér, the main square, where you can see the Church of the Sacred Heart, built in 1912, and the Bacchus Fountain, with the Roman god shown sitting on a barrel. While a number of good bars and restaurants have opened since 2010, the town is generally fairly quiet, especially on weekday evenings, when restaurants often stop serving food at around 8pm. All the winemakers arrange wine tastings and tours, often in atmospheric underground cellars such as **Rákóczi Pince** (*see p176*).

★ **Tokaji Múzeum** (Tokaj Museum)
Bethlen Gábor utca 7. ✆ 352 636. www.tokajimuzeum.hu. Open Apr–Oct, 10am–6pm; Nov–Mar, Tue–Fri, 9am–5pm; Sat & Sun, 10am–4pm. Closed Mon. Ft1,000 (combined with the World Heritage Wine Museum, Ft1,600). Guided tour in English Ft5,000 per group (reservation recommended).

Tokaj town
© Bence Bezeredy/iStock

The museum is in an attractive residential building dating back to 1790, which was once owned by a Greek merchant—by the turn of the 18C, trade in Tokaji wine across Europe was already brisk. As with every other building in the region, this one boasts a splendid cellar where items relating to the wine trade are displayed, including Gönc barrels, bottles of different ages and vintages, and tools and equipment used in the winemaking and bottling processes. There is also a table on which *aszú* grapes (those affected by noble rot) were sorted. A display on the first (ground) floor explores the region from a geological and historical perspective, while the next floor houses a collection of religious items, including a small prayer desk inlaid with ivory, a monstrance, several carved and painted wooden crucifixes, and a collection of icons, including a small triptych. You can also see the reconstructed living quarters of a Greek merchant, who was involved in dealings with the corporation of winegrowers and producers. There is an exhibition of everyday items from the last century (furniture, crockery, fabrics, …) on the upper floor.

★ **Világörökségi Bormúzeum** (World Heritage Wine Museum)
Serház utca 55. ✆ 552 050. www.bormuzeum.eu. Open Apr–Oct, 10am–6pm; Nov–Mar, Tue–Fri, 9am–5pm; Sat & Sun, 10am–4pm. Closed Mon. Ft1,000 (combined ticket with the Tokaji Museum, Ft1,600).

This modern, interactive museum explores the history and culture of the region's renowned wines. You can learn how Tokaji wine has been a useful tool in diplomacy—negotiations were sometimes sweetened in more ways than one with the judicious offering of barrels of the wine. There is also information about great wine regions elsewhere in Europe that have similarly been listed as Unesco World Heritage Sites.

Nagy Zsinagóga (Great Synagogue)
Serház utca 55. ✆ 552 000. Entrance at the rear of the building; ask for the key at the reception of the Ede Paulay Theater nearby.

This impressive synagogue, or rather former synagogue, was built in the 19C when there was a well-established Jewish community in the area. However,

"A WINE FOR KINGS AND THE KING OF WINES"

A quote from King Louis XIV of France describing the renowned Tokaji wine around 350 years ago, when it became the tipple of choice for the crowned heads of Europe. It owes its flavors to the region's volcanic and loamy soils in particular, and to long-established winemaking traditions. The local Continental climate, in which very hot summers last right up until the beginning of fall and misty mornings are followed by sunny days, make the grapes sweeter and produce **botrytis** ("noble rot"), facilitating a late harvest. The *aszú* grapes, picked by hand, one by one (often harvested three or four times), are then soaked in grape juice in full fermentation or in young wine from the same year. The liquid is then transferred to oak barrels. The minimum maturation period is 18 months.

Once bottled, the wine must remain in bottle for at least one year. The traditional process consists of double fermentation of the selected fruits in oak barrels and in cellars dug out of the volcanic rock, where the temperature fluctuates between 50–53.6°F/10–12°C. Only those wines achieving a sugar content of 4.2oz per 2.11 US pints/120g per liter of wine can qualify as **Aszú**.

the Jews did not return to worship here after the dreadful days of the Second World War and the Holocaust. The synagogue has now been entirely renovated and is used as a conference hall and cultural center.

Cellar tours and wine tasting

★ **Rákóczi Pince** – *Kossuth tér 15. ✆ 352 408. www.rakoczipince.hu. Open Jul–Aug, 11am–8pm; Sept–June, Fri–Sun, 11am–5pm. Cellar tour and tasting of 5 wines from Ft3,700.* You will find the building housing this, the town's oldest cellar, in front of the statue of Bacchus on the main square. Built at the turn of the 15C, it has belonged to kings and princes, and while the barrels now on display no longer contain wine, the vast Hall of Knights is certainly worth a look.
Hímesudvar Pincészet – *Bem utca 2. ✆ 352 416. www.himesudvar.hu. Open 10am–6pm. Cellar tour and mini-tasting of 5 wines from Ft 1,990.* A warm welcome in a building dating back to the 16C that was formerly a hunting lodge. You can also order cheese to go with the excellent white wines.
Demeter Zoltán Pincészet – *Vasvári Pál utca 3. ✆ (20) 806 0000. www.demeterzoltan.hu. By appointment.* Since creating his cellar in 1996, this winemaker, who speaks excellent English, has devoted his life to promoting the Tokaji wine region. His love of wine and the region is evident.

Driving tour Regional map (p172–73)

★★ VINEYARDS AND THE ZEMPLÉN MOUNTAINS D1–2

107mi/172km round trip. Allow a day or perhaps even two to visit all the sites listed. See the route marked on the Regional map.
Leave Tokaj on Rte 3615 heading toward Tarcal.

Tarcal D2

This village boasts the tallest statue of Christ in Europe (28ft/8.5m high). From the center of the village, it takes at least 20min to climb the steps to the top of the hill, but having made it, you can stand next to the immense, white granite figure and enjoy the beautiful view of the vineyards and surrounding countryside. *At the northern end of the village, turn left on Rte 37 for Szerencs.*

Szerencs D2
This small town of barely 10,000 inhabitants nevertheless made its mark on Hungarian history in the struggle against Habsburg domination. Built in the 16C on the remnants of a 13C abbey, the castle changed hands several times before ending up in the possession of the aristocratic Rákóczi family, *voivodes* (princes) of Transylvania. It was here that Sigismund Rákóczi (who was proclaimed prince in defiance of the Habsburgs) was interred in a red sarcophagus that you can still see in the **Calvinist** church on the market square. The attractively restored **castle** now houses local council services, a library, a theater, a youth hostel, and the **Zempléni Múzeum** *(open 10am–5pm, Ft600)*, a small museum with displays of old postcards and local history.
Rejoin Rte 37, before taking a left turn onto Rte 3713.

★ **Mád** D2
This village is attracting an increasing number of visitors thanks to its excellent wine, artisan produce (cheese, soap, and honey), and its Jewish heritage. It is also home to many of the region's most charming hotels and restaurants *(see Addresses, p181).*
★ **Synagogue** – *Táncsics utca 38. (30) 925 1808. Open 9am–4pm. Ft 500 (including an exhibition about the Jewish community in Mád, Ft900).* This synagogue, built in a Baroque style in 1795, is one of the most beautiful in Hungary and was used by the village's Jewish residents for 150 years. The Jewish community was more or less wiped out in the concentration camps of the Second World War and the synagogue was left to slowly decay before being renovated in 2004, thanks to American benefactors. An exhibition exploring Mád's Jewish history is to be found in the old schoolhouse and rabbi's residence, with some particularly moving filmed contributions from the few descendants of former inhabitants. *Continue along Rte 3713.*

★ **Boldogkő vára** (Boldogkő Castle) D1
Open 9am–4pm (May–Sept, 8pm). Ft1,300. A medieval restaurant in the fortress. Perched precariously on a rocky peak, this 13C castle can be seen from a good distance and enjoys a splendid panoramic view across the Zemplén Mountains. The interior houses several exhibitions, including an interesting collection of lead soldiers. A number of events are held here in summer.
Continue along the road, heading north for 3.75mi/6km.

Vizsoly D1
The first Bible in Hungarian was produced at the printing works in this village in 1590. It was translated by Gáspár Károli, a pastor from Gönc, and is also notable for being the first work to be printed in the Hungarian language.
★ **Printing Museum** – *Szent János utca 82–84. www.vizsolyibiblia.hu. Open June–Sept, 9am–6pm; Oct–Apr, 10am–4pm. Ft 900.* This small museum traces the history of printing in Hungary from the 16C. The panels are in Hungarian but a guide is available in English. The first Bible in Hungarian that is on display is in fact a copy.
Református templom (Reformed Church) – The church is right beside the museum and has been well restored. It houses some fine, very old frescoes, some of which date back to the 13C, while even the most recent were painted before the end of the 15C. The designs were covered up with white rendering when the Calvinist reforms were imposed, resurfacing only in 1940.
The road passes through a green and undulating landscape for its entire length; you will be driving right around the Zemplén Mountains.

Boldogkő Castle
© Hungarian Tourism Agency

Gönc D1

You are now in "cooper country"—the "Gönci barrel" has become the volumetric unit for **Tokaji Aszú** wine. The region is also famous for the variety of apricots from which the local brandy *(pálinka)* is made.

Follow the road through Bózsva and then take a left turn, continuing through Nyíri and Füzérkomlós to the castle parking lot.

Füzér vára (Füzér Castle) D1

Open 10am–6pm. Ft 2,000.

The small village of Füzér boasts a 13C fortress perched on a rocky crag high above. Extensive renovation was carried out in 2012 and the restored rooms now transport visitors back to medieval times. The path from the parking lot up to the castle is fairly steep (550yds/500m), but the splendid view is worth it.

Pálháza D1

After visiting the village's **Református templom** (Reformed Church), you could take a short trip on a **narrow gauge railway**. The Pálházi State Forest Railway winds its way through the forest to Kőkapu, where there is a hotel with a restaurant in a pretty setting near a lake (a trip of 5mi/8km).

Sátoraljaújhely D1

This town on the Slovakian border has links with the Rákóczi family, as well as with the language reformer Ferenc Kazinczy (a museum and his mausoleum; he campaigned to replace German with Hungarian as the country's official language). In the center the tree-lined Kossuth Lajos tér offers a chance for a break on its café terraces and ice cream parlors. Kossuth, the famous political reformer, is said to have made a speech from the balcony of No. 5.

Rte 37 loops back on itself around the Zemplén Mountains.

★ Sárospatak D1

ℹ Szent Erzsébet utca 3. Open Tue–Sat, 8am–4pm.

As the intellectual center of Calvinism and the active cultural heart of the region in the 16C, Sárospatak came to be known as the "Athens of Hungary."

Looking out over the River Bodrog and its tributaries, it also became famous for being part of the Rákóczi family's landholdings, whose most celebrated member was Ferenc II (*see box below*).

★★ **Rákóczi vár** (Rákóczi Castle) – *Szent Erzsébet utca 19. Open Tue–Sun, 10am–6pm. Castle Museum, Ft700 (including a guided tour of the Red Tower in English, Ft2,000; min. 7 persons, otherwise Ft14,000; reservation required in summer only). A nice café.* The restored area open to the public is only one part of the fortress. The oldest part is the **Vörös torony** (Red Tower), a medieval keep. The name derives from the fact that it was originally covered in red plaster. The Perényi family had the 13C castle rebuilt in a Renaissance style at the turn of the 16C, adding a palace which was subsequently redesigned and occupied by the Rákóczi family until 1711. A wooden bridge leads to the entrance near the base of the Red Tower, inside which a museum explores the history of the Rákóczis, with displays of costumes, furniture, weapons, crockery, and pictures. There are nice views of the town, the surrounding countryside, and the River Bodrog from the roof of the tower.

A round balcony window in one corner of the castle, on the upper level, contains an enclosed, semicircular gallery known as the Sub Rosa Balcony after the rose-shaped keystone in the ceiling. Conspirators in the struggle for independence from the Habsburgs met in secret beneath it in the 17C and the expression *sub rosa* (beneath the rose) has come to mean any agreement made in secret.

★ **Szent Erzsébet templom** (St. Elizabeth's Church) – *Szent Erzsébet utca 13.* This building dates back to the end of the 15C and was awarded minor basilica status in 2008. Originally a Roman Catholic church, it has since been converted by the Reformed Church. Inside is a plaque commemorating St. Elizabeth, a

FERENC II RÁKÓCZI, PRINCE OF TRANSYLVANIA

The fifth prince of Transylvania, Ferenc (Francis) II, was born in 1676, shortly before the death of his father Ferenc I. The latter was preoccupied with the future of his wife, Countess Ilona Zrínyi, after his death and duly arranged for her to marry Imre Thökölywhen the time came. Thököly was leader of the Kurucs, the partisans who took up arms against the Austrians in response to Habsburg oppression. It was Thököly who introduced Ferenc to military life, and Ferenc and his mother spent three years in a besieged fort at Munkács. Ferenc married in 1694, after which he returned to his native region and, despite pressure, at first refused to rebel against the Austrians. But faced with the violence of the repression and the treatment meted out to the peasants, he resolved to lead the revolt against the Habsburgs. Ferenc was an honest and decent man, cultured and curious, dividing his time between his responsibilities of state and the pleasures of life. His writings reflect a mind drawn to meditation, aware of social conditions. An esthete and a gourmet, he was a great connoisseur of the Tokaji wine produced by local winegrowers. He attracted the attention of both Peter the Great of Russia and Louis XIV of France, but their interest in his affairs proved to be short-lived and Ferenc found himself alone in his struggle with the Habsburgs. Eventually his troops drifted away and Ferenc was obliged to go into exile. It took him to Russia, Poland, and France, and in 1717 he arrived in Turkey to solicit the aid of the sultan, who gave him asylum and a place to live in a small town on the shores of the Sea of Marmara. It was here that he died in 1735, having devoted his remaining years to theology, meditation, writing, and carpentry.

native of the town who died in 1231 at the age of 24, having devoted her last years to the poor; she is still greatly venerated in both Hungary and Germany.
Református Kollégium (Reformed College) – *Rákóczi utca 1.* Sárospatak owes at least some of its reputation as the so-called Athens of Hungary to this college founded in 1531. In 1650 Zsuzsanna Lorántffy, the wife of György Rákóczi, invited János Amos Comenius, a Czech humanist and educational reformer, to organize the college's teaching program, and he remained here for four years.
★★ **Könyvtára** (Reformed College library) – *Open 9am–5pm (Sun, 1pm). Nov–Mar, closed Fri afternoon, Sat & Sun. Donation requested.* This splendid library houses some 450,000 works (in Greek, Hebrew, Latin, and Hungarian). The beautiful long reading room contains a stunning trompe l'oeil ceiling and paintings at either end representing the Arts and Sciences. A wooden gallery supported on oak columns runs around the perimeter of the upper part of the room. The Rákóczi family made their printing machinery available to János Amos Comenius, enabling him to publish works in Latin and the first illustrated textbook for children, *Orbis Pictus*. In the wake of the persecutions of the Counter Reformation, the college was saved when King George II of England interceded with the Viennese court. Well-known Hungarians who studied here include Hungarian language reformer Ferenc Kazinczy and the statesman Lajos Kossuth, among many others whose busts and statues have been erected in the grounds called the **Iskolakert** (school garden).

★ Hercegkút D1

The village is known for the highly unusual Gomboshegyi Cellars, part of the Unesco Tokaj Historic Cultural Landscape. The triangular entrances lead into two- or three-tier cellars beneath turf roofs, used to store wine since the 18C.
Remain on Rte 37; you will reach Tokaj town again, 20mi/33km to the south.

ADDRESSES IN THE TOKAJI WINE REGION

GETTING THERE

Train – A frequent service operates daily between Budapest-Keleti Station and Tokaj *(journey time around 5hrs, Ft3,950).*

STAY

There are few hotels in this region, but guesthouses are numerous. You will need a car if you stay near rather than actually in Tokaj.

Tokaj

BUDGET

Paulay Guesthouse – *Hajdú köz 11. ✆ (20) 451 7789. www.paulayborhaz.hu. 3 rooms & 1 family apartment, from Ft10,500.* A guesthouse in the heart of the village run by a couple who also produce their own wines. It is the birthplace of Ede Paulay, 19C playwright and former director of the National Theater. The rooms are delightful and you can taste the wines as well as homemade jams and honey.

AVERAGE

Toldi Fogadó – *Hajdú köz 2. ✆ 353 403. www.toldifogado.hu.* *13 rooms, Ft16,900. Ft1,500.* A comfortable and welcoming hotel in an ideal location in the village. It includes a nice spa area with a small swimming pool, jacuzzi, and sauna. Good food, too.

LaBor Kvártély – *Bethlen Gábor utca 1. (70) 883 8888. www.laborbistro.hu. 6 rooms, Ft17,900/25,900.* This charming old house was attractively restored in 2018. A narrow staircase leads to the country-style rooms on the upper level; the cheaper rooms on the next floor up have dormer windows and are just as cosy. A (free) bottle of wine in every room.

Tarcal

A TREAT

Gróf Degenfeld Castle Hotel – *Terézia kert 9. 580 400. www.hotelgrofdegenfeld.com. 20 rooms, from Ft30,000.* With its furniture in the Empire style and a setting in the heart of parkland and vineyards, this rather grand hotel cultivates a 19C atmosphere. The rooms are enormous and comfortable, and the wine made by the owners is one of the few organic Tokaji wines available. A swimming pool, too.

SPLASH OUT

Andrássy Rezidencia Wine & Spa – *Fő utca 94. 580 015. www.andrassyrezidencia.h. 41 rooms, from Ft41,000, and 1/2 board.* The splendid swimming pool, plunge pool in a small grotto, and jacuzzi make it worth splashing out on the only 5-star hotel in the area. Treatments and massages using grape-based products in the VinoSense Spa.

Mád

BUDGET

Napudvar Vendégház – *Batthyány utca 29. 348 050. www.lesko-tokaji.hu. 3 rooms, Ft13,000.* The owners of this charming guesthouse cultivate vines (along with flowers and aromatic plants) in their pretty garden. An excellent breakfast with homemade jams.

SPLASH OUT

Hotel Botrytis – *Batthyány utca 12–14. 348 017. www.hotelbotrytis.com. 6 rooms, from Ft 32,000.* This boutique hotel with its contemporary decoration attests to the growth of tourism in the village of Mád, where the local wine and fine restaurants prove consistently popular.

EAT

Tokaj

BUDGET

LaBor – *Bethlen Gábor utca 1. (70) 883 8888. Open 9am–9pm (Sun, 5pm). Closed Mon. Lunch menu Ft1,500, main courses in the evening Ft1,300/3,300.* This chic bistro has become the restaurant of choice in Tokaj. Popular at lunchtime for its reasonably priced seasonal menu. Light and delicate Hungarian cuisine such as chicken breast with grilled vegetables, apple, celeriac mash.

Bonchidai Csárda – *Bajcsy-Zsilinszky utca 21. 352 632. Open 10am–10pm. Ft1,200/5,100.* Bonchidai's broad terrace on the banks of the River Tisza is very pleasant in summer, and you can expect to be served generous helpings of classic Hungarian food.

Mád

BUDGET

Első Mádi Borház – *Hunyadi utca 2. 348 007. Open 8am–10pm (Sun, 8pm). Ft1,800/3,200.* It's impossible to miss this wine bar at the entrance to the village. To accompany the wine, try some delicious homemade terrines with onion or peach chutney, or duck breast served with sweet potato mash. It's also the perfect place to take a break for a coffee.

AVERAGE

Percze Experience – *Árpád utca 70. ✆ (20) 464 2222. Open Wed–Sat, 10am–10pm; Sun, noon–3pm, reservation only. Main courses Ft2,490–3,990.* Enjoy sophisticated Hungarian dishes and taste the owner's excellent wines in contemporary surroundings, with a beautiful view of the village. Delicious desserts are on offer, including apricot clafoutis.

Sárospatak

BUDGET

Ristorante Collegno – *Szent Erzsébet utca 10. ✆ 314 494. Open 11am–11pm (Sun, 10pm). Ft1,250/2,400.* An Italian restaurant in a cellar with a vaulted ceiling; very popular with the locals.

A Boros – *Rákóczi utca 21. ✆ 658 200. Open noon–10pm (Fri–Sat, midnight; Sun, 4pm). Closed Mon. Ft2,000–3,500.* The young and dynamic team serve local wines and cheeses, but you could opt for the homemade hamburgers or fish & chips. Airy, modern surroundings with a pleasant terrace in a small courtyard.

TAKING A BREAK

Tokaj

Tokaji Kávépörkölő Manufaktúra és Kávéház – *Bethlen Gábor utca 10. ✆ 552 008. Open 9am–7pm (Sat & Sun, 8pm).* Whether you choose an espresso or a latte, the coffee, which is roasted in-house, is delicious. But, if you would like a change from coffee, try a rooibos tea or a hot chocolate to go with the homemade cakes. Wine tastings are also available (*Ft1,800 for 4 mini glasses*).

BARS

Tokaj

Prés Wine Bar – *Rákóczi utca 30. Open 4pm–midnight (sometimes closed in low season).* This hip wine bar is the new place of choice in which to try the local vintages and chill out, glass in hand, in the cellar beneath a vaulted ceiling. A small menu of tasty snacks is also on offer.

SPORTS AND ACTIVITIES

Tokaj

Kayak and boat trips

Vízisport Turistaház – *Tiszapart (an area on the opposite riverbank, across from Tokaj village). ✆ 552 187 .www.hajokirandulas.hu.* You can hire kayaks and small motorboats (no license required) or take a river cruise on the Tisza from here.

Bicycle tours

Tokaj Tourist Office – *See* Info, *p174.* *Ft2,000/day.*

Vízisport Turistaház – *See above. Ft2,000/day.*

EVENTS AND FESTIVALS

Grape harvest festival – A celebration at the beginning of October that lasts 3 days (including wine tastings, concerts, processions in traditional costume, a market, …).

Bor, mámor, Bénye festival – Each August, in the gardens of Erdobénye *(north of Tarcal, off Rte 37)*. A dozen winemakers open their gardens, houses, and cellars for the weekend. Live jazz, folk, and world music, while watching artists, artisans, and performers. bormamorbenye.hu/en/

Eger and the Bükk Mountains★★

53,436 population – Heves county – area code ✆ 36

Known as the Baroque pearl of the north, Eger is a beguiling city nestling between the Bükk and Mátra mountain ranges. These protect it from the north winds and ensure a good climate for the cultivation of the vines that produce the famous Egri Bikavér wine (Bull's Blood of Eger). The story goes that István Dobó, hero of the struggle against the Turks in the 16C, gave the wine to his troops to give them strength during the Siege of Eger. And it can still be enjoyed today on one of the many terraces that line Dobó István tér and the pedestrian streets, where brightly painted facades and Gothic, Baroque, neo-classical, Rococo, and Art Nouveau buildings combine to form a delightful backdrop.

ADDRESSES PAGE 194
Stay, Eat, Baths, Bars, Events and Festivals

INFO:
Eger Tourist Office – Eger map B2 – *Bajcsy-Zsilinszky Endre utca 9. ✆ 517 715. www.visiteger.com. Open 8am–5pm (Jul–Aug, 6pm); Sat & Sun, 9am–1pm; Sept–Jun, closed Sun; Nov–Mar, closed Sat.* Stocked with brochures in English and city maps.

LOCATION:
Regional map BC2–3 (p172–73); Eger map (p184)
83mi/134km northeast of Budapest.

PARKING:
Parking is available in the city center.

DON'T MISS:
The castle; the Archbishop's Palace; the Turkish Baths.

TIMING:
Allow two days.

KIDS:
Fortifications of the castle and Eger Astronomy Museum; see the horses at the National Stud; a narrow-gauge railway excursion to Szilvásvárad; Diósgyőr Castle in Miskolc; Bükkszék Baths with family facilities (*see p196*).

3

★★ Eger Eger map (p184)

The castle is a good place to begin your visit to Eger. It is easy to spot as it looks down over the city. Access is via Dózsa György tér, which will take you to the base of the ramparts, from where a short but steep path leads to the south gate and the enclosed area behind the fortifications. The rest of the city's historic center is easy to negotiate on foot.

★★ **Dobó István Vármúzeum** (István Dobó Castle Museum) B1

Vár 1. ✆ 312 744. www.egrivar.hu. Open daily, 10am–6pm (Nov–Mar, 4pm). Castle museums Ft1,700 (Casemates and the Wax Museum, Ft500 extra each). Audioguide in English, Ft400. When the museums are closed, the pathway around the castle is accessible 8am–10pm (Nov–Mar, 6pm), Ft850. A café and the celebrated 1552 Restaurant are in the courtyard.

Construction of the castle began in 1248 in order to protect Eger against Mongol invasion. It became a beacon of Hungarian patriotism during the siege of 1552 (*see p187*). The pathway around the castle can be accessed

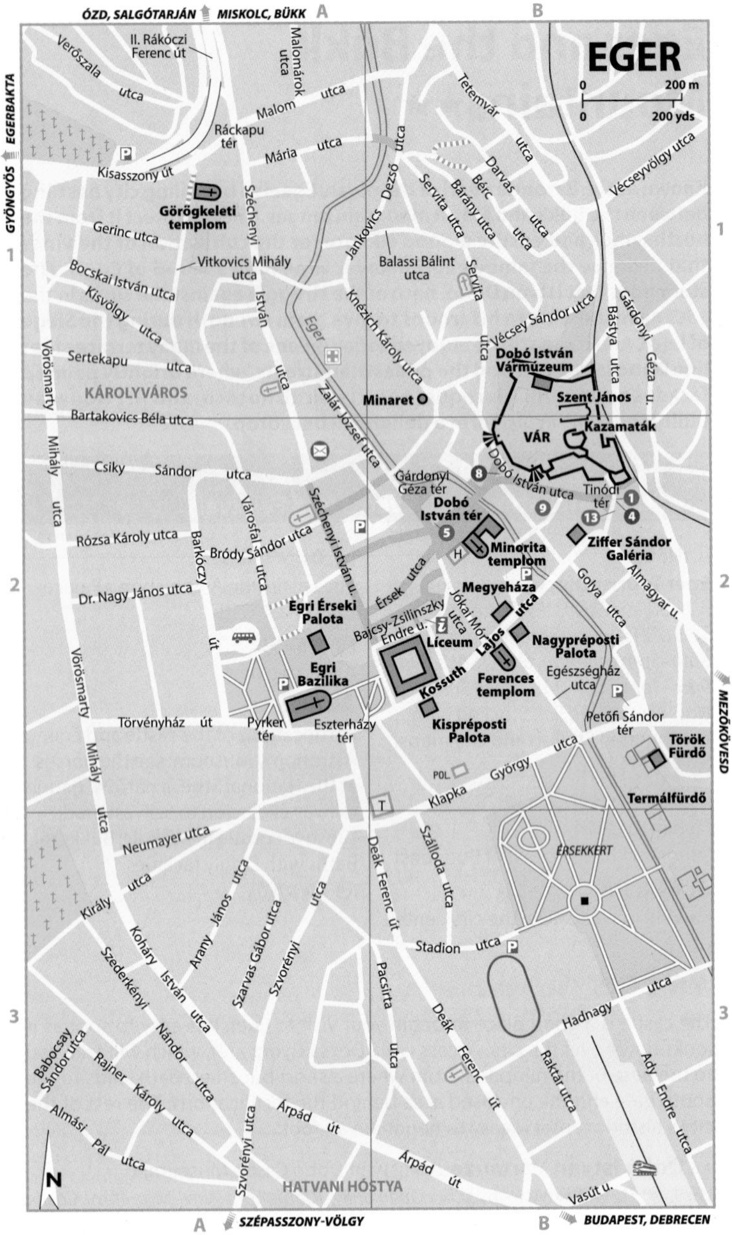
EGER
0 200 m
0 200 yds
ÓZD, SALGÓTARJÁN
MISKOLC, BÜKK
GYÖNGYÖS EGERBAKTA
MEZŐKÖVESD
SZÉPASSZONY-VÖLGY
BUDAPEST, DEBRECEN
A
B
1
2
3
Verőszala utca
II. Rákóczi Ferenc út
Malomárok utca
Malom utca
Ráckapu tér
Mária utca
Kisasszony út
Görögkeleti templom
Gerinc utca
Vitkovics Mihály utca
Bocskai István utca
Kisvölgy utca
Sertekapu utca
KÁROLYVÁROS
Bartakovics Béla utca
Csiky Sándor utca
Rózsa Károly utca
Dr. Nagy János utca
Vörösmarty Mihály utca
Széchenyi István utca
Jankovics Dezső utca
Tetemvár utca
Darvas utca
Bérc
Bárány utca
Servita utca
Balassi Bálint utca
Vécseyvölgy utca
Vécsey Sándor utca
Knézich Károly utca
Eger
Zalár József utca
Minaret
Dobó István Vármúzeum
Szent János
VÁR
Kazamaták
Bástya utca
Gárdonyi Géza u.
Gárdonyi Géza tér
Dobó István utca
Dobó István tér
Tinódi tér
Minorita templom
Ziffer Sándor Galéria
Városfal utca
Bródy Sándor utca
Barkóczy út
Széchenyi István u.
Érsek utca
Egri Érseki Palota
Bajcsy-Zsilinszky Endre u.
Jókai Mór utca
Megyeháza
Líceum
Lajos utca
Kossuth
Nagypréposti Palota
Golya utca
Almagyar u.
Ferences templom
Egészségház utca
Egri Bazilika
Kispréposti Palota
Törvényház út
Pyrker tér
Eszterházy tér
Petőfi Sándor tér
Török Fürdő
Termálfürdő
POL
Klapka György utca
ÉRSEKKERT
Neumayer utca
Király utca
Arany János utca
Szarvas Gábor utca
Szvorényi utca
Deák Ferenc út
Szálloda utca
Stadion utca
Pacsirta utca
Hadnagy utca
Koháry István utca
Szederkényi Nándor utca
Babocsay Sándor utca
Rajner Károly utca
Almási Pál utca
Árpád út
Raktár utca
Ady Endre utca
Vasút u.
HATVANI HÓSTYA
N

WHERE TO STAY		WHERE TO EAT			
Imola udvarház Dessert	4	BrumBrum	1	Il Padrino Pizza Club	9
Senator Ház	8	Főtér	5	Macok	13

for some great panoramic **viewpoints★★** across the city. Along the way you will see the grave of Géza Gárdonyi, the author of *Eclipse of the Crescent Moon*, a set text in Hungarian schools that recounts the story of the Siege of Eger by the Turks.

Ruins of Szent János (St. John's Cathedral) – Construction of the cathedral began in the 11C, proof of the importance of Eger at the time. After the Romanesque building was destroyed by the Mongols, work on reconstruction, this time in the Gothic style, began again at the end of the 15C, only to be halted by a fire. An explosion in a gunpowder store in 1552 put paid to what remained of the cathedral, leaving the ruins that you can still see today within the castle complex.

★★ **Kazamaták** (Casemates/Blockhouses) – Beneath the cathedral ruins lies an impressive network of underground corridors and rooms carved out of the rock. This was the only place of safety during the sieges of the city, and it was also a useful place to store cannons and munitions. An ingenious device kept track of the movements of any attackers trying to tunnel their way in—chickpeas balanced on the taut skins of drums reacted to the slightest movement of the air or ground caused by enemy excavations. The two underground areas accessible to the public feature a contemporary display using film and video animation. The exhibits include finds from excavations at the castle, such as cannons and cannonballs from the 16C and 17C.

Gótikus Püspöki Palota (Gothic Bishop's Palace) – Pay tribute to the intrepid Captain Dobó when you visit the Heroes' Hall on the first (ground) floor of the old Bishop's Palace, a splendid structure dating back to the 15C. You can also see pieces of furniture, historical items, tapestries, and interactive displays and dioramas illustrating the different eras in the history of Eger Castle.

Tömlöcbástya (Jail) – This rather gloomy cellar and former prison includes instruments of torture and execution from medieval times.

Panoptikum (Wax Museum) – A small museum housed in a vaulted cellar in a corner of the castle complex features life-size wax models of the people who shaped its history, including of course, the renowned Captain Dobó.

CITY CENTER AB2

Take Tinódi Sebestyén tér, walking down from the castle, then turn onto Kossuth Lajos utca and cross Eger patak (a stream).

Kossuth Lajos utca (Lajos Kossuth Street) B2

Several buildings in this street are worth a look for their exteriors, although only a few are open to the public.

★ **Megyeháza** (Regional County Hall) – No. 9. The building dates back to the 1750s and was designed by a Viennese architect. Its two great wrought iron gates are by Henrik Fazola, master locksmith and factory owner, and feature representations of the three theological virtues (Faith, Hope, and Charity).

Nagypréposti Palota (Palace of the Grand Provost) – No. 16. A Baroque building housing the regional library.

Ziffer Sándor Galéria – No. 17. This gallery bearing the name of the well-known 20C painter born in Eger, Sándor Ziffer, occupies the old Orthodox synagogue and holds temporary exhibitions.

Ferences templom (Franciscan Church) – A Baroque church with a single nave, built in the mid-18C from the remains of a Turkish mosque.

★ **Kispréposti Palota** (Palace of the Vice Provost) – No. 4. A Rococo creation built in 1758 with a carved stone exterior of elegant windows and niches, and a wrought iron balcony over the entrance.

Egri Bazilika (Eger Cathedral Basilica) A2
Pyrker János tér 1. ✆ 515 725. Open 8am–6pm. Donation of Ft300.
Organ recital (30min): May–Oct, Mon–Fri, 11.30am (Sun 12.45pm). Ft800.
Eger's Cathedral Basilica is a vast neo-classical structure built in 1836 to designs by József Hild, the architect responsible for the cathedral at Esztergom. Access is via an imposing staircase lined with statues (St. Peter and St. Paul to the left, St. Stephen and St. Ladislas to the right). A great portico of six Corinthian columns topped by a pediment fronts the entrance. The interior is a little somber, but features a ceiling and cupola decorated with frescoes.

Líceum (Lyceum) B2
Eszterházy tér 1. ✆ 520 400. The Lyceum is one of the oldest educational institutes in Hungary and is now the headquarters of the Károly Eszterházy University of Applied Sciences. It is housed in a complex of buildings constructed in the Zopf style in the 18C and arranged around a beautiful large interior quadrangle; the library and astronomical observatory are particularly interesting.
★★ **Library** – *Upper level. Open Tue–Sun, 9.30am–3.30pm (Oct–Mar, closed Sun). Ft1,000.* Founded by Bishop **Charles Esterházy**, the archdiocesan library opened on 28 December 1793 and its shelves now hold more than 130,000 volumes that range from medieval manuscripts and early printed books to works from the 16C, 17C, and 18C, and even a letter written from Vienna by Mozart to his sister after their father had died. The Regency interior was created in oak by a local craftsman. Note also the superb painted ceiling by **Johann Kracker**, depicting a meeting of the Council of Trent in Italy, which met between 1545 and 1563 and was a major part of the Counter Reformation, changing the face of the Roman Catholic Church. It was to be Kracker's last work and was completed with help from his son-in-law. It depicts 132 key figures of the Catholic Church of the time, and the painter himself even makes an appearance in the form of a mustachioed warrior holding a lance.
Astronomy Museum – *6th floor. Open Feb–mid-Mar & Nov–mid-Dec, Sat & Sun, 9.30am–1pm; mid-Mar–Oct, Tue–Sun, 9.30am–3pm. Ft1,300 (including the camera obscura).* This small museum in the so-called Magic Tower features a range of 18C measuring instruments from the time when the observatory was the best-equipped in Eastern Europe. A fascinating place for astronomy enthusiasts, the tower also includes a planetarium, a room of interactive experiments, and a camera obscura.
Camera obscura – *9th floor, admission included in the Astronomy Museum entry ticket.* The mystery of this darkened room (1776) is revealed in the form of a panoramic view of the city reflected onto a table in real time by a system of mirrors—an 18C version of a webcam!
Take a right as you leave the Lyceum, returning to Széchenyi István utca, a charming pedestrianized street lined with cafés.

★★ **Egri Érseki Palota** (Archbishop's Palace) A2
Széchenyi utca 3. ✆ 517 356. www.egriersekipalota.hu. Open Tue–Sun, 10am–6pm (Oct–Mar, 4pm). Ft1,800, including audioguide in English. There's a café inside (Ft100 discount on presentation of admission ticket).
The 18C palace was renovated and repurposed as a splendid museum in 2016. The Baroque building houses a magnificent collection of ecclesiastical items, including 15C chalices, liturgical vestments, and the case belonging to Archbishop József Samassa, who was made cardinal in 1905, containing objects for celebrating mass. The private apartment occupied by the archbishops who

A city symbolizing Hungarian patriotism

The region has been inhabited since the Neolithic period; the ancestors of the Hungarians that moved into the Pannonian Basin settled here in the valley of the River Eger (Ohře in Hungarian; although the name Eger is commonly used, it is in fact German). **King Stephen I**, who in the 11C used Hungary's ecclesiastical districts as the basis for his administration of the country, made the area a bishopric with its seat at Eger. However, when the Mongols invaded in 1241, the city was razed to the ground and deserted by those inhabitants who had not been massacred or kidnapped. The area was gradually repopulated by families arriving from Western Europe; these new residents hailing from France, Italy, and points further north helped to turn Eger into a city of culture, strongly influenced by Renaissance ideas.

ISTVÁN DOBÓ, A HUNGARIAN HERO

Born around 1500, István Dobó was a Hungarian landowner and distinguished army captain of good character. He commanded a series of fortresses before taking over the Eger garrison in 1549. As the Turks began to extend their empire ever further into Hungarian territory, he recognized the danger and realized the defenses of the city would have to be reinforced. When the Turks came to besiege Eger in 1552, Dobó had just 2,000 soldiers with whom to defend the city against some 100,000 Turks, but despite the incredible odds he succeeded in repelling their advance, thanks to some wine and the women of Eger, if the legend is to be believed *(see box p188)*. His exploit sealed Dobó's reputation as a bona fide hero and turned Eger into a symbol of Hungarian patriotism. István Dobó is celebrated throughout the city, in particular in the main square, which bears his name and is home to a statue in his memory.

Despite their fabled strength and undeniable courage, the citizens of Eger were eventually unable to prevent the Turks from taking over in 1596; on this occasion, the defenses were manned by foreign mercenaries who surrendered without a shot being fired at the promise of being spared and set free. The bargain was not kept, however, and some were massacred and the rest imprisoned. For 90 years Eger remained under the rule of the Turks, who built mosques and baths here, the remains of which can still be seen today, including the minaret on Knézich Károly utca *(see p188)*.

THE VARYING FORTUNES OF THE HISTORIC CENTER

The year 1687 saw the **liberation of Eger** from the occupying Turks, who were given safe passage to leave the city after a siege lasting four months. By 1690 Eger had between 3,000 and 4,000 inhabitants. The Habsburg emperor Leopold I had the castle blown up at the turn of the 18C, fearing that the fortified city could become a stronghold for rebels clamoring for Hungarian independence. **Ferenc (Francis) II Rákóczi** was the ill-starred hero of this struggle, providing justification for Austrian fears *(see box p179)*.

A century later, in 1800, a part of the center of the city went up in smoke in a fire and it was rebuilt once more with a new skyline featuring the Cathedral Basilica, the third largest church in the country.

lived here has been decorated with period furniture. The art collections on display belong to the church and to the city of Eger. Look out for the delicate frescoes of birds rediscovered during restoration work in 2013 in the small room with a cupola that once housed cages of rare birds. You can also see Empress Maria Theresa's coronation cloak.
Turn right into Szent János utca.

★ **Dobó István tér** (István Dobó Square) B2
Local and national hero István Dobó's statue stands in the center of the square. He was defender of the city and conqueror of the Turks (*see p187*).
Minorita templom (Minorite Church)– *Donation Ft300.* The **church of the Minorite Friars**, seamlessly integrated among the apartment buildings on the south side of the square, is a beautiful example of Baroque art and took 15 years to complete, starting in 1758. Above the high altar is a painting by Johann Kracker depicting the Virgin Mary and St. Anthony of Padua.
Follow István Dobó utca toward the minaret.

★ **Minaret** B1
Knézich Károly utca. ✆ 70 202 4353. Open 10am–6pm (Oct–Apr, 5pm). Ft400.
This last remaining trace of the Turkish presence in Eger is in a good state of preservation. This is the 14-sided tower (131ft/40m high) from which the call to prayer rang out when the Ottoman Turks were in occupation here. Ninety-seven spiral steps climb up to a small balcony with a beautiful view.
To round off the afternoon, head back through the center of the city to the fountains of the lovely Archbishop's Garden and then on to the Turkish Baths.

★★ **Török Fürdő** (Turkish Baths) B2
Fürdő utca 3-4. ✆ 510 552. www.egertermal.hu. Open Mon–Tue, 4.30pm–9pm; Wed–Thu, 3pm–9pm; Fri, 1pm–9pm; Sat & Sun and public holidays, 9am–9pm. Ft2,200 for a 2.5hr session. To just take a look inside, Ft500.
These baths, built in 1617 during the Turkish occupation, have been magnificently restored. People come here to relax and chat in an intimate setting, just as they did in the time of the Ottoman Empire. Taking a dip in one of the six pools beneath the splendid cupola covered with 200,000 sheets of gold leaf is a must. A good place to try an authentic Turkish bath experience, especially given that these baths are generally less busy than those in Budapest.

WINE AND STRONG WOMEN

The Turks besieged Eger in 1552, when it is said that more than 100,000 well-equipped invaders, led by Grand Vizier Ahmed and Ali, pasha of Buda, surrounded the town. In stark contrast, the commander of the Hungarian troops, **István Dobó**, had just 2,000 soldiers at his disposal. Dobó decided to open up the wine cellars and tap the barrels to fortify his bearded warriors, who then set about offering the Turkish fighters a "warm welcome" without even politely wiping their mouths. Their red beards and lips led the Sultan's men to think that the Hungarians drew their strength from drinking bull's blood *(egri bikavér)*, a name that stuck and came to be used for the wine produced in Eger.
The women of Eger were determined to stand by their menfolk. They made food and served the wine for the soldiers. They also boiled up oil and pitch and poured it down onto the assailants, earning the expression "strong as an Eger woman!"

Eger Cathedral Basilica
© nightman1965/iStock

OUTSIDE THE CITY CENTER AND THE SURROUNDING AREA

Görögkeleti templom (Serbian Orthodox Church of St. Nicholas)
Eger map A1 (p184)
Széchenyi utca 55. On top of a small hill, about half a mile from the center.
Holy Roman emperor Joseph II allowed the Serbs to build this church in the late 18C on condition that it would be located outside the city walls (no longer in existence). The reward for those who make the trip here comes in the form of a beautifully carved wooden **iconostasis★** made of 60 painted panels.

3

Szépasszony-völgy (Valley of the Beautiful Woman)
Eger map A3, off map (p184)
Around 1 mile/1.5km southwest of the downtown area; bus shuttle service in summer (details at the tourist office).
Wine lovers should not miss a trip to the so-called Valley of the Beautiful Woman, where several dozen cellars have been dug out of the rock, to sample the famous Bull's Blood, a strong fruity wine. In high season, you can take a seat on the terraces of the cellar-wine bars, which also serve small snacks to stave off hunger.

Egerszalók Regional map B3 (p172–73)
5.5mi/9km southwest of Eger via Rte 25
This village is on the tourist map for its hill of salt, an amazing sight, created through the action of hot spring water emerging from the subsoil of the volcanic mountain range after a well was dug in 1961. They were looking for oil or gas at the time, but what came spurting out instead was medicinal thermal water at a temperature of 149°F/65°C. This natural phenomenon was incorporated into the thermal baths at the Saliris Resort in 2007 (*see p196*).

De La Motte-kastély (De La Motte Castle), at **Noszvaj** Regional map B3
6.5mi/11km northeast of Eger. Dobó István utca 10. Open 10am–4pm. Ft1,000.
Noszvaj is known for its plum jams, but also as being the location of De La

Motte Castle, built in the Baroque style in 1778 and so-named because one of its first chatelaines entered into a second marriage with a Frenchman, a certain Monsieur de la Motte. While it may look more like an elegant country house, the interior is worthy of its castle moniker with, in particular, frescoes on the ceiling depicting gods from Greek mythology.

★ **Matyó Múzeum** (Matyó Museum), at **Mezőkövesd** C3

14mi/22km southeast of Eger. Szent László tér 8. Open Tue–Sun, 9am–5pm (Nov–Mar, 3pm). Ft800. Information panels in Hungarian but brochure in English.
The small town of Mezőkövesd contains this museum dedicated to the traditions of the Roman Catholic **Matyó people**, who were part of Hungarian folk culture in the 18C and 19C. Their story is told through photographs, costumes, and furniture. Their art features floral motifs embroidered on clothes and painted on furniture and crockery. These pretty designs were inscribed on Unesco's Intangible Cultural Heritage list in 2012.

Driving tour Regional map (p172–73)

★ **BÜKK MOUNTAINS** BC2–3

91mi/147km circular tour from Eger. See the route marked on the Regional map. Allow a day.
As this area is also a national park, the Bükk Mountains have retained their natural and wild beauty. Walking through the forests of oak and beech, you feel a long way from civilization and the cosmopolitan city of Budapest. The region was once covered by the sea and the mountains were formed by the accumulation of calcareous deposits that turned into limestone over the course of millennia, which explains the ease with which water can seep down through the brittle rock and form incredible caves here.
Head north from Eger along Rte 25, then turn right onto Rte 2506, a few minutes after Szarvaskő.

★ **Bélapátfalva Abbey** B2

Open May–Sept, Tue–Sun, 9am–6pm; Oct–Apr, Tue–Sun, 10am–4pm; closed Nov–Dec. Ft550 including audioguide.
The Cistercian abbey is located a little way outside the small town of Bélapátfalva from which the abbey takes its name. It has survived almost intact in a small green valley in the limestone hills that provided the stone for the abbey and now supply a cement plant. In a clearing surrounded by trees, the location is beautiful; the peacefulness seems as total as it must have been when the abbey was founded in 1232. Monks lived here until the 16C; they cleared the forest and dug out a pond for fish during the lean times, but the Turks and religious wars chased the brothers out. It was not until the 18C that the bishop of Eger had the chapel restored, prompted by the religious fervor of a local hermit. The organ pipes, pulpit, sacristy, high altar, and side altars all date from this time. The marks of 35 master masons have been identified at different points in this well-preserved Romanesque building.
The road continues north through attractive wooded surroundings.

★ **Szilvásvárad** B2

This town is known for its connections with the famous **Lipizzaner**, the magnificent horses that originally came from Slovenia, with a breeding line that dates back to the 16C and which was supported by the Habsburg nobility. With their intelligence, strength, and powers of endurance, Lipizzaner are used in dressage at the highest level. Riders at the celebrated Spanish Riding School in Vienna are trained on Lipizzaner horses.

Állami Ménesgazdaság (National Stud and Museum) – *Egri utca 16. www.menesgazdasag.hu/en/. Open 9am–noon, 1pm–4.30pm. Ft1,200.* Visitors can tour the stud and visit the Lipizzaner Museum (pictures, drawings, and photos of the most famous horses from past years) and a carriage exhibition. However, the highlight is the opportunity to see the horses themselves in one of the shows or at ease in the fields. Szilvásvárad is also a center for carriage driving with two, three, or even up to seven horses in hand. The horses look magnificent in their harness. On summer weekends, you can attend dressage demonstrations or riding classes, or take a carriage ride.

Narrow-gauge train excursion – *Open Jun–Aug, 8.30am–6pm, departures every hour. Single ticket Ft 900.* Children (and adults) will enjoy taking the train from Szilvásvárad into the forest. Climb into one of the open carriages for a delightful 15min trip through the woodland, where you can catch glimpses of waterfalls and streams through the trees. Get off at **Szalajka** to visit the **Forest Museum** and **Istállóskő Cave**, one of the locations in Hungary where Paleolithic pottery has been discovered. Look out for the pretty **Fátyol waterfall**, where the water tumbles down a gentle gradient. Take the train back to Szilvásvárad or return on foot, a pleasant walk amid the peace and quiet of the forest that takes around 2hrs.

Continue along Rte 2506 heading north. Take a small road to the right shortly before reaching Dédestapolcsány. Drive through Mályinka and take a left at the next fork; the road is not very well maintained, so do drive carefully.

Lillafüred C2

The town of Lillafüred is officially part of Miskolc *(see p192)*, almost 7.5mi/12km away. A **small train** runs back and forth *(6 departures/day, journey time 30min)* between the two: in Lillafüred catch it from behind the Hotel Palota and in **Miskolc** on Dorottya utca.

Situated at the meeting point of two valleys, the Szinva and the Garadna, Lillafüred is named after the wife of András Bethlen, a politician who enjoyed visiting the region in the late 19C. The name of the wife in question was Lilla Vay, and the place was dubbed Lillafüred ("Lilla's baths"). It is noted for its pretty natural setting but also for the amazingly glamorous **Hotel Palota**, built in a neo-Gothic style between 1927 and 1930. Its turrets peep out from among the surrounding trees just like a fairy tale castle, and it looks fabulous lit up at night. In 1920 Hungary lost substantial territory after the Treaty of Trianon *(see p354)*, particularly in this northern region. The result was a desire to conjure up the splendor of bygone ages (the legacies of Matthias Corvinus and Louis the Great) and build this luxury hotel, which became a significant project in the interwar years. This vision of the glory days of Hungary features in the paintings and stained glass windows in the hotel, where you can make out famous characters from Hungarian history.

The Communist regime then took it over, including its nationalist images (some of which were replaced), turning the building into a vacation center for members of the National Council of Trade Unions. Today the Hunguest Hotel Palota is open to everyone once more. Despite renovation work in 2009, you might still see some traces of its previous occupants here and there while having a snack or lunch *(see Addresses, p195)*. The hotel is located at the far end of **Hámori tó** (Hámori Lake) in an area that offers plenty of opportunity for walkers to stretch their legs. There are several **caves** not far from the hotel: Anna-barlang, Szeleta-barlang, and **István-barlang**, which is considered the most beautiful.

Miskolc C2

Széchenyi utca 16. (46) 350 425. www.hellomiskolc.hu. Open 8.45am–4.30pm (Sat 9am–2pm). City map and brochure in English.

Although it is now the fourth-largest city in the country, Miskolc did not even exist in the days of the Austro-Hungarian Empire. Initially there were just a few villages here, but with the Treaty of Trianon having placed Hungarian industrial sites and railroads in Czechoslovakia, a need arose in the interwar period to develop a new industrial area, which was further expanded during the Communist era. The long avenues lined with large housing developments are a little short on charm at first sight, but the center of the city, with its castle and museums, and the nearby thermal baths are worth a stop. **Széchenyi utca**, a pedestrian and tram route in the heart of Miskolc, is very busy during the day due to its stores and many cafés. You can also see a number of private villas of different styles, some of them in a poor state of repair.

The **Nemzeti Színház** (National Theater) on the corner of Déryné utca was built in 1850 to replace the first Hungarian language theater (built 1823), which had been destroyed in a fire. You might like to pop into the **Magyar ortodox templom** (Hungarian Orthodox Church, Deák tér 7), built in a late Baroque style between 1785 and 1787 by Greek refugees who had fled from the Turks. It boasts a 53ft/16m high iconostasis made up of 84 icons and an image of Our Lady of Kazan (presented by Catherine the Great of Russia when she passed through on her way to Vienna), and a crucifix brought from Mount Athos (1590) by Greek refugees.

The **Avasi református templom** (Gothic Protestant Church of Avas, *Papszer utca 14*) is also interesting. Built in the 13C and burned down by the Turks in 1544, the originally Gothic church was then rebuilt in 1560. There is a painted wooden interior and the pews are decorated with Rococo floral motifs. The separate belfry, dating back to 1557, features a Renaissance gallery.

★★ **Diósgyőri vár** (Diósgyőr Castle) – *Vár utca 24. www.diosgyorivar.hu. Open 9am–6pm (Nov–Mar, 5pm). Ft1,500 including audioguide in English).*

The castle was built for **Louis the Great** in the second half of the 14C. Imagine it at the time of its construction when, unlike today, it was surrounded by trees in the middle of a forest; it was very popular among the nobility for the abundant game in the area. It was known as the Castle of Queens and Louis conducted diplomatic negotiations here. The castle changed hands several times during the war for independence against the Habsburgs under Ferenc II Rákóczi at the start of the 18C, but eventually lost its strategic importance, was abandoned, and slowly fell into disrepair. Restoration did not begin until many years later, in the 1950s.

Designed on a square layout, there is a square tower at each corner; you can climb to the top of one of them for some great views. In summer the central courtyard hosts a range of different events. The castle was completely renovated in 2014 and furnished with modern pieces in the style of period furniture. You can see a room filled with armor, another with with trophies and stuffed animals, a herbalist's room full of scented plants, the queen's bedchamber, a dining hall, and a chapel, all equipped with interactive information panels *(in English, see the website for the program).*

Herman Ottó Múzeum (Ottó Herman Museum) – *Görgey Artúr utca 28. Open Tue–Sun, 9am–5pm. Ft3,200 (including admission to the Pannonian Sea Museum).* The largest museum in the city has thousands of exhibits, among them a collection of 200 pictures, drawings, and statues by Hungarian artists working between the end of the Baroque period and the advent of Art Nouveau. It

Diósgyőr Castle
© Hungarian Tourism Agency

is named after Ottó Herman, the Hungarian polymath and pioneer of natural history research. The museum has several buildings in the city but the Pannonian Sea Museum is in a new part of the main building

Pannon-tenger Múzeum (Pannonian Sea Museum) – *Görgey Artúr utca 28. www.pannontenger.hu. Open Tue–Sun, 9am–5pm. Ft2,800 (including admission to the Herman Ottó Museum, Ft3,200).* This natural history museum has some extremely well-preserved, 7-million-year-old swamp cypresses that were discovered locally in 2007, at a depth of 215ft/65m. There are also mineralogical and geological displays.

3

★★ **Barlangfürdő** (Cave Bath), at **Miskolctapolca**

In Miskolctapolca, 4.5mi/7km southwest of Miskolc. barlangfurdo.hu. ✆ (46) 560 030. Open 9am–8pm. Ft2,600. Also spa treatments and massages (from Ft2,200). A café inside.

People have been aware of the curative properties of the waters at Miskolctapolca since the Middle Ages. Springing up from a depth of 2,952ft/900m, the radioactive water is slightly carbonated and gushes out of the ground in a cloud of bubbles at a temperature of around 86°F/30°C. All kinds of conditions are treated in the Cave Bath, in particular heart palpitations, stomach complaints, and mental and physical exhaustion. The air in the cave is very humid, which is also good for respiratory problems, in particular complaints such as asthma and bronchitis. The highlight of a visit to this large thermal spa complex for most people is the chance to take a dip in a cave carved out by water, one of the few of its kind in Europe. The water snakes through various channels and basins and into seven pools where the temperature varies between 84° and 95°F/29° and 35°C. It is a truly unique experience. You can also sit beneath the bubbling water for a natural shoulder massage. The many outdoor pools are also very popular on fine days.

Return to Eger, 37mi/60km to the southwest of Miskolc.

Barlangfürdő, Miskolctapolca
© bjonesphotography/iStock

ADDRESSES IN EGER AND BÜKK MOUNTAINS

See Eger map (p184)

GETTING THERE

Train – There are numerous train departures from Budapest-Keleti Station to Eger *(journey time around 3hrs, Ft2,520/3,840)*.
Bus – Plenty of bus connections from Budapest *(journey time 2hrs30min, around Ft2,600)*.

STAY

Eger

AVERAGE

4 **Imola Udvarház Dessert** – B2 – *Tinódi tér 4. (30) 207 8085. www.imolaudvarhaz.hu. - 7 rooms, Ft19,900/21,000 & 6 apartments, Ft26,000/38,000* . This boutique hotel is lovely and in a perfect location at the foot of the castle. The rooms are light and modern, with suites available for familes. There are two excellent restaurants next door (Macok and Brumbrum, *see opposite*) that are part of the same group.

A TREAT

8 **Senator Ház** – B2 – *Dobó István tér 11. 320 466. www.senatorhaz.hu. 11 rooms, Ft18,500/23,400* . This guesthouse is ideally situated in a pretty 18C building in the heart of the city. The hall and breakfast room are full of old photos and vintage objects, but the attractive bedrooms have been brought right up to date. The restaurant has a good reputation and serves Hungarian cuisine

Miskolc

A TREAT

Öreg Miskolcz – *Horváth Lajos utca 11. (46) 550 550. www.oregmiskolcz.hu. 25 rooms Ft25,900* . Stay in a modern building that was constructed in 2005 but in an Art Deco style. It has comfortable rooms close to the historic center of the city.

EAT

Eger

BUDGET

9 **Il Padrino Pizza Club** – B2 – *Fazola Henrik utca 1. ✆ 786 040. Open 11am–10pm. Pizza from Ft1,140.* A great place for pizza lovers in a small, cozy, and informal room on an upper level. Established in 1991, it's definitely the best in town and lots to choose from.

AVERAGE

5 **Főtér** – B2 – *Dobó István tér. ✆ 817 482. www.fotercafe.hu. Open 10am–10pm . Ft1,690/5,390.* Try traditional Hungarian cuisine (pan-fried foie gras or pork ragout) at this restaurant in the heart of Eger; they also do several local vegetarian dishes such as breaded cheese (camembert style) with blueberry jam.

1 **BrumBrum** – B2 – *Tinódi tér 4. ✆ 516 180. Open Wed–Sun, 11am–11pm (Sun,10pm). Ft2,700/5,500.* The younger sibling of Macok, the restaurant next door, is a little cheaper, but has equally contemporary and playful surroundings with images of bears on the walls. The menu features a delicious Turkish-style eggplant caviar and some Hungarian dishes that are lighter than those you might find elsewhere, leaving enough room for dessert. Reservation essential at weekends.

A TREAT

13 **Macok** – B2 – *Tinódi tér 4. ✆ 516 180. Open noon–10pm (Fri–Sat 11pm, Sun 6pm.) Ft2,790/6,900.* The city's most fashionable spot serves a reinterpretation of Hungarian and international cuisine; the dishes are inventive and well-presented, and the surroundings contemporary. A terrace and an impressive selection of wines. Reservation recommended in high season.

Lillafüred

BUDGET

Mathias – *Hunguest Hotel Palota. ✆ (46) 331 411. www.hotelpalota.hu. Open noon–4pm. Ft2,900/4,200.* Try some traditional Hungarian cooking in a fairy tale castle setting, not forgetting to admire the nine stained glass windows celebrating the cities that have made Hungarian history.

Miskolc

BUDGET

Pizza Kávé Világbéke – *Széchenyi István utca 19. ✆ (70) 608 6886. Open Tue–Sun, 9am–10pm (Sat, 11pm; Sun, 6pm). Ft490/1,290.* A contemporary look for a restaurant in the busiest part of the city serving excellent pizza by the slice, including the "Magyaros," a local delicacy with caramelized onions, salami, and paprika.

Szilvásvárad

BUDGET

Szalajka Fogadó – *Egri utca 1. ✆ (36) 564 020. Open noon–8pm (Fri–Sat, 9pm). Ft1,590/3,450.* This Hungarian inn (it also has rooms for accommodation) on the main road in the village is a good place to stop for lunch, with generous portions and a terrace that is open during the summer.

TAKING A BREAK

Eger

Manooka Kávézó – *Bajcsy-Zsilinszky utca 17. ✆ 796 60. www.manooka.hu. Open 8am–6pm, (Sat & Sun, 3pm).* Tucked away in a tiny courtyard, a place to relax and

chill serving good coffee, freshly pressed fruit juices, and bagels. There's a play area for toddlers.
Marján Cukrászda – *Kossuth Lajos utca 28 . ✆ 312 784. Open 9am–7pm.* A contemporary-style tea room with a large terrace that is just the place to try a cake or a bowl of ice cream.

BARS

Eger

Petrény Winery – *Dobó István tér 10. ✆ (70) 329 3398. Open 10am–10pm (Fri–Sat, 1am).* A wine bar where you can try a bottle from Petrény, one of Eger's famed vineyards, or explore more of these robust wines with a wine-tasting of 5 or 6 vintages selected by the manager. You can also order a plate of cheese or charcuterie to go with them.
Artiszt Wine & Spirit – *Széchenyi István utca 16. ✆ (30) 494 8200. Open 10am–10pm (Fri–Sat, 2am; Sun, 9pm).* Depending on the time of day, you can have a cappuccino at one of the tables outside on this lively pedestrian street or a glass of Eger wine from the St. Andrea cellars inside.
Gál Tibor – *Csiky Sándor utca 10. ✆ (20) 852 5002 .www.galtibor.hu. Open Tue–Sun, 10am–7pm (Sat, 11pm; Sun, 1pm).* Gál Tibor, a winemaker of some renown, has opened a very nice contemporary wine bar and tasting room in his winery. A tasting of four wines (2.5floz/70ml glass from Ft2,500).

BATHS

See Eger map (p184)

Eger

Török Fürdő (Turkish Baths) – *See p188.*
Termálfürdő (Eger Thermal Spa) – B2 – *Petőfi tér 2. ✆ 510 557. www.egertermal.hu. Open 8am–8pm (Sept–May, 9am–7pm). Water slides open June–Aug, 10am–6pm. Ft2,200 (children over| 4 years Ft1,800).*
This large baths complex features numerous indoor and outdoor swimming pools, thermal spring pools, and water play areas.

See Regional map (p172–73)

Egerszalók

Saliris Resort Spa – B3 – *Forrás utca 6. ✆ 688 600. www.salirisresort.hu. Open 10am–8pm. Ft3,400 for 3hrs.* This large spa (and hotel) complex has 17 indoor and outdoor pools, saunas, jacuzzis, water play areas for children, and the amazing natural feature, the Salt Hill.

Bükkszék

Bükkszék Fürdő (Bükkszék Baths) – B2 – *Fürdő utca 10. ✆ (30) 500 3437. www.bukkszekfurdo.hu. Open 9am–7pm.* A thermal spa complex 15mi/24km northwest of Eger with a water slides, a grass beach area, and open-air swimming pool.

Miskolctapolca

Barlangfürdő (Cave Bath) – *See p193.*

EVENTS AND FESTIVALS

Eger

Egri Bikavér Ünnep (wine festival) – The town celebrates its famous Bull's Blood wine over 3 days in mid July.

Miskolc

Bartók Plusz Operafesztivál (Bartók Plus Opera Festival) – For a week in mid June, the city is held spellbound by opera events that feature artists from all over the world.

Aggtelek National Park

Aggteleki Nemzeti Park

★★

Borsod-Abaúj-Zemplén county – area code ✆ 48

Spectral white limestone rocks are dotted about amid bucolic meadows, forests, and lakes, a perfect habitat for rare plants and insects. The karst caves, carved out by water over the course of millennia, are an integral part of the park and form a fascinating underground network of caverns that are its great attraction. The exceptional nature of the park led to it being inscribed on the Unesco World Heritage List in 1995.

ADDRESSES PAGE 198
Stay, Eat, Sports and Activities

INFO:

Tourist Office – In front of the entrance to Baradla Cave in Aggtelek. ✆ *503 000. Open 8am–4pm.*

LOCATION:

Regional map BC1 (p172–73)

Situated 68mi/109km northeast of Eger and 37mi/60km north of Miskolc.

PARKING:

Parking (no charge) in front of the cave entrances.

DON'T MISS:

A visit to Baradla Cave.

TIMING:

The park can be visited as a day trip from Eger or Miskolc.

KIDS:

Baradla Cave.

Baradla Cave
© Gudella/iStock

Discover Regional map (p172–73)

★★ **Baradla-barlang** (Baradla Cave) B1
www.anp.hu. Three guided tours, all in Hungarian, each leaving from a different entrance. Main entrance in the village of Aggtelek: 0.6mi/1km tour, taking 1hr. May–Sept, 10am, noon, 1pm, 3pm, 5pm; Oct–Apr, 10am, 1pm, 3pm; Ft2,400. Jósvafő entrance: 0.9mi/1.4km tour, 1hr. May–Sept, 11am & 4pm; Oct–Apr, 2pm; Ft2,200. Vőrős-tó (Lake Vőrős) entrance, exiting at Jósvafő village: 1.4mi/2.3km tour, 1hr40min. May–Sept, 10am, noon, 2pm, 4pm; Oct–Apr, 10am, noon, 2pm; Ft2,700.
The main entrance to Baradla Cave is the busiest, but the tour route is easy to negotiate and is suitable for all ages with plenty of interesting things to see. The temperature remains constant throughout the year (between 48°F and 50°F/9°C and 10°C), so take a sweater, even in summer. You may not understand what the guide is saying, but the many rock formations speak for themselves, including stalactites and stalagmites, columns (formed when a stalactite meets a stalagmite), and drapery formations on the walls.
Having reached the deepest part of the cave (295ft/90m), you will arrive at the Concert Hall, where music is played in order to demonstrate the excellent acoustics. Concerts are held here in summer *(see www.anp.hu for the program)*. The other tour routes are less popular but are just as interesting. Note that the route entering at Jósvafő village also passes through the Concert Hall, and the third route, which is slightly more physically challenging, runs along the bed of the Styx, the underground river named after the river of Hades that formed the boundary between heaven and earth in Greek mythology. It can fill up a little after heavy snow or rainfall.

Aggteleki Nemzeti Park (Aggtelek National Park) BC1
There are also plenty of places where you can explore the park above ground—walking trails through the forest, between the karst rock formations, and around the lakes (download guides in English, www.anp.hu). In spring the meadows are full of flowers, thousands of anemones in particular.

ADDRESSES IN AGGTELEK

STAY

BUDGET

Nomád Baradla Hostel and Campground – *Baradla oldal 1. ✆ 350 005. www.szallas-aggtelek.hu.* ✕ P *28 chalets, Ft4,000/12,000.* Wooden chalets (rather Spartan) sleeping 4–6 people are scattered through the park right up to the main entrance of the cave. A camping area and a hostel with 9 rooms. Bicycle hire.

Tengerszem Hotel és Étterem – *Situated near the Jósvafő cave entrance. ✆ 30 318 1853. www.tengerszemhotel.hu.* ✕ *18 rooms, Ft9,000* ☕. You can expect a warm welcome in this large Swiss-style chalet with its beautiful view of the surrounding countryside. The rooms are basic but clean.

EAT

The two hotels listed have restaurants: **Nomád Baradla** opens 8am–6pm; **Tengerszem** is open 11am–9pm (Nov–Mar, 7pm).

SPORTS AND ACTIVITIES

Kúria Hucul Lovasbázis – (equestrian center) – *Táncsics utca 1. Jósvafő. ✆ 350 052. anp.hu.* Take a ride in a carriage or on horseback. Reservation required.

An extraordinary underground world

The Aggtelek–Jósvafő karst caves are on (or rather beneath) Hungarian soil, while the section that extends into Slovakia is known as the Domica Cave. The entire Baradla-Domica Cave System is over 15.5mi/25km in length, with the Hungarian section being the longest (12.5mi/20km). Over the course of time some 300 caves have been cut into the karst limestone mountains in the **Bódva Valley** (an area of 77sq mi/200sq km). They are home to a biosphere that has been protected since 1985, when the area was designated a national park. Numerous streams appear and disappear into the sinkholes (*barlang* in Hungarian) that are characteristic of karst landscapes, some of which are filled with water forming small lakes.

Millions of small crevices allow the slightly acidic surface water to enter and dissolve the limestone, which is studded with soluble substances. As it seeps through the rock, the water deposits a tiny part of the material it is carrying, which eventually builds up to create the rock formations that make this underground world so magical. In places the water has created sequences of terraces, draperies, columns, and corridors, settling into silent, still pools in other places.

ROCKS CREATED MILLIONS OF YEARS AGO

The formation of this natural phenomenon dates back more than 200 million years and some sediments are more than 4 million years old. The presence of humans in the caves has been verified and dated to around 35,000 years ago, while the oldest document to mention the structure is a map of the area made in 1794, when the first visits to the caves were made in the early 1800s. The cave-dwelling flora and fauna is typical for karst areas, with several rare species being identified by the Aggtelek speleologists/biologists, including around 20 species of bat, but also Mesoniscus graniger, a kind of woodlouse that is white, as it lacks any pigment, and is also almost blind.

THE CAVES OF HUNGARY

Hungary has created nine national parks, five of which have caves that are a great draw for tourists. In addition to Aggtelek National Park, there are the national parks of Bükk and the Balaton Uplands, as well as the Duna-Ipoly National Park (the area around the rivers Danube and Ipoly) and the Duna-Dráva National Park (the area around the rivers Danube and Dráva). Some of the caves qualify as medicinal, with exceptional climatic conditions that can promote the treatment of bronchial diseases.

Of the 3,000 natural caves that are protected, 125 benefit from special preservation measures and 26 are more than half a mile (over a kilometer) in length, with the longest being Baradla in Aggtelek (12.5mi/20km) and Pálvölgyi (7mi/11km), which lies beneath the Budapest suburb Rózsadomb (Rose Hill). Budapest is the only capital city in the world to have more than 18mi/30km of caverns beneath its streets. Nine caves have been opened up to the public, while five are open to specialist cave explorers.

Some of the cave watercourses supply cities with drinking water, such as in Pécs, or have been consecrated, such as the Chapel of the Order of St. Paul in Gellért Hill Cave in Budapest (*see p42*).

The Mátra Mountains

★

Heves county

The Mátra Mountains are a popular excursion from the city, providing a good opportunity to get into the wilds of nature just an hour's drive from Budapest. The highest peak in the country is here—the 3,327ft/1,014m summit of Kékestető. Popular activities include skiing in winter and walking or taking a spa cure during the rest of the year.

ADDRESSES PAGE 204
Stay, Eat, Taking a Break, Sports and Activities

INFO:
Gyöngyös Tourist Office – *Fő tér 10. ☏ 37 311 155. Open Mon–Fri, 8am–4pm (closed Sat & Sun).* Maps and brochures about the town and the Mátra Mountains in English.

LOCATION:
Regional map AB3 (p172–73)
50mi/81km east of Budapest along highway M3. The mountains are only an hour's drive from Budapest but are deep in the countryside.

DON'T MISS:
The view from Mount Kékes, the highest point in Hungary; the House of the Holy Crown in Gyöngyös.

TIMING:
Allow a day, or more if you intend to go walking.

KIDS:
Mátra Museum; Parád Coach Museum; Sirok Castle; Oxygen Adrenalin Park in Mátrafüred.

Driving tour Regional map (p172–73)

★ EXPLORING THE MÁTRA MOUNTAINS

A circular tour of 43.5mi/70km; see the route marked on the Regional map. Allow a day.

Gyöngyös A3

While the name might mean "pearl," unfortunately the new part of town has lost some of its luster, although it has retained its crafts and industry and is a center for business. However, situated in the heart of a winemaking area, Gyöngyös is the gateway to the local region and there are sights to see in the old part of town.

Fő tér is the pedestrianized main square; it is lined with Baroque and Art Nouveau buildings, which you can admire from a seat at a pavement café. Fő tér is also where you can see two statues: one of Károly Róbert (Charles I, 1288–1342), who granted Gyöngyös municipal status, and "Huszár," in memory of the 6th Hussar Regiment. At the northern end of the square you will find, on the right, **Szent Bertalan templom** (St. Bartholomew's Church, undergoing renovation for an indefinite period). Despite the Baroque decoration added in the 18C, this is considered Hungary's largest Gothic church. If you walk to the rear of it, you may hear a lilting melody emerging from a beautiful Baroque building that was once a school run by the Jesuits, now the music conservatory.

★ **Szent Korona Ház** (House of the Holy Crown) – *Szent Bertalan utca 3. www.szentbertalankincstar.hu. ☎ (37) 300 072. Open Tue–Sat, 10am–5pm. Ft600.* Across the road from the church, this small 18C Baroque palace derives its name from the fact that the Holy Crown was hidden here during the Napoleonic Wars. The museum, which was completely renovated in 2014, now houses the **Treasury of St. Bartholomew's Church**, with 43 magnificent items in gold on display, including some chalices and ciboria dating back to the 15C. They were hidden away for safekeeping from Soviet troops during the Second World War by three priests and it was not until the 1960s that the last of the trio revealed their hiding place on his deathbed. There is also an exhibition of old missals, liturgical vestments, and statues, including the poignant *Sadness of Christ* from the 18C.

Mátra Múzeum – *Kossuth Lajos utca 40. www.matramuzeum.hu. ☎ (37) 505 530. Open Tue–Sun, 9am–5pm. Mansion and natural history exhibition, Ft1,100 each, or Ft1,500 for admission to both.* The former Orczy Mansion and its grounds are now the setting for the Mátra Museum (a branch of the Hungarian Museum of Natural History), which was renovated and redesigned in 2009. The first thing to greet you on entering is the star of the collection: Bruno, the skeleton of a young mammoth discovered in 1947. Several rooms upstairs are dedicated to examining local history from a wide variety of perspectives, including an exhibition of fossils and minerals typical of the Mátra Mountains, a history of hunting, and a display about the terrible fire of 1917, which destroyed the entire town (of the 20,000 inhabitants, 8,000 were rendered homeless).

In a natural history museum in a new building in the grounds, a life-size artificial oak tree rises up through its three levels, where dioramas present different natural habitats. There is also a fine collection of insects, in particular a host of butterflies, and many stuffed animals, but in the Palm House you can also see several live species, including lizards (bearded dragons), small iguanas, and chameleons in aquariums and tanks.

Leave Gyöngyös, heading north along Rte 24.

★ Mátrafüred A3

A **narrow-gauge railway** connects Gyöngyös to Mátrafüred *(open Apr–Oct, Ft1,000).*

This spa town and health resort situated at 1,115ft/340m is equally popular in summer and winter with the citizens of Budapest, not to mention German

HIGH GROUND

The great faultline, reponsible for many of the Hungarian thermal springs, extends from the northern shores of Lake Balaton, continues through Budapest, and carries on toward the southern flanks of the Mátra Mountains. It runs alongside a series of hills that form a ridge; as you head east of the Danube and the ridge begins to transform into mountains, you find you are in Upper Hungary. From the uplands of Börzsöny, passing through the Mátra Mountains on the way to Bükk, the elevation of the land rarely exceeds 3,280ft/1,000m. However, at 3,327ft/1,014m above sea level, **Mount Kékes**, in the heart of the mountains, is Hungary's highest point. The uplands forming Upper Hungary are partly sedimentary and partly volcanic, as are the Mátra Mountains. There is, however, a central axis running from Parád and Galyatető to Gyöngyös that crosses the mountains and makes traveling easy. The entire Mátra Mountains area is covered with magnificent beech forests.

and Austrian visitors. It is a good starting point for forest excursions and walking trips, with a wide range of different skiing and hiking trails of varying lengths, all well signposted. The local council promote "adventure" tourism, so you can hire bicycles, monster bikes, segways, and quad bikes *(see Sports and Activities, p204)*.

Mátraháza A3

At 2,427ft/740m, this small village is at an even higher altitude than Mátrafüred. Mátraháza boasts all the features of a health resort and winter sports center, with numerous trails for walkers and skiers starting and finishing here (in good years there is snow on the ground in January and February).
After leaving Mátraháza, turn right at the post office.

★ Kékestető (Mount Kékes) AB3

Hungary's highest peak is at an altitude of 3,327ft/1,014m; the summit rock is painted in the colors of the Hungarian flag. For an even better **panoramic view** of the area, climb up to the observation platform of the television tower on top of the mountain *(open 9am– 4pm, Ft700; café on upper floor)*. The view to the south stretches as far as the Great Plain and in clear weather northward to the Tatra Mountains. Various hiking trails and paths start from here.
Return to Rte 24 and continue heading north. Take a left turn after 1.8mi/3km.

Galyatető A3

This is another small health resort where there are also good hiking trails. One gray stone building in particular may pique your curiosity—the **Nagyszálló** ("Grand Hotel"), still in business today as the Grandhotel Galya, was a luxury home before the Second World War, but under the Communist regime was reserved for trade union members and used to entertain "comrades" from abroad. Around 550yds/500m north of the hotel, you will find **Galya Kilátó** *(a 100ft/30m observation tower, Ft200)* from where you can get a great view of the Mátra Mountains.
Return to Rte 24 and carry on toward Parád.
Before you reach Parád, about halfway along the road from the junction with Route 24 from Galyatető to Parád (about 3mi/5km), you can sometimes smell the **sulfurous springs** of the village of Parádsasvár before they come into view on the left. The bottled mineral water is used to treat digestive and stomach complaints and can be bought at the side of the road.

Parád A3

Palócház (Palóc House) – *Sziget utca 10. Open Tue–Sun, 10am–4pm (Sun, 2pm). Ft300.* This traditional Palóc house, painted white and roofed with thatch, provides a glimpse into the daily lives of the Palóc, a people from the Mátra Mountains. Worth a look if you are not going to Hollókő *(see p205)*.

★ **Kocsimúzeum** (Coach Museum)– *Kossuth Lajos utca 21. Open Tue–Sun, 9am–4pm. Ft 600.* The Coach Museum is housed in the stables of Count Károlyi's castle. This interesting and decorative building contains both the museum and the stables themselves, where you can occasionally catch a glimpse of the horses used to draw the carriages on festive occasions. The museum has a display of the various stages of manufacture of a horsedrawn vehicle, involving a number of different trades, from wheelwrights to saddlers, not to mention farriers, painters, carpenters, and cabinet makers. After the trades have been explained, there is an exhibition of farm wagons, carts, open-topped chara-bancs, various carriages—both luxurious and more modest—as well as sleds

Hiking in the Mátra Mountains
© Viktor Loki/Shutterstock

for journeys in winter. Detailed models give a real insight into the intricacies of making these vehicles that were used for anything from traveling and discreet trysts to the pomp and ceremony of parades. You will also discover that it was the Hungarians who invented the first coach in the small town of Kocs; the word *kocsi* ("coach" in Hungarian) was taken from the name of the town and adapted as "coach" in English and *coche* in Spanish.

Parádfürdő (Spa and wellness center) B3

Nor far from the Kocsimúzeum, you will find Parádfürdő attached to the Erzsébet Park Hotel and restaurant *(see Addresses, p204)*, where you can stay or just get a bite to eat. It is a therapeutic thermal spa center, but the waters are reserved for thermal hospital patients only.

Continue along Rte 24.

★ **Siroki vár** (Sirok Castle) B3

Open Apr–Oct, 10am–6pm; Nov–Mar, 9am–4pm. Ft1,000. Parking Ft400. Brochure in English about the castles of the region, including Sirok, Ft1,200.

Having parked your car at the foot of the hill, allow around 15min to walk up the fairly steep path to the castle, which dates from the 14C. Strategically sited between the Mátra and Bükk mountains, this fortress was built to protect the garrison at Eger 12mi/20km away. There are stories of a tunnel that links the two, although no one has ever found it. The Turks were successful in capturing Sirok Castle after the fall of Eger in 1596. A docu-drama shot in the castle *(around 15min, subtitles in English)* depicts the life of the Turkish soldiers who occupied the site for almost a century. The castle was destroyed at the turn of the 18C and lay in ruins for some time before being restored and opening its doors to the public in 2015. The **panoramic view**★★ over the Bükk and Mátra mountains and the peak of Kékestető and, to the north, the mountains of Slovakia, is simply splendid.

ADDRESSES IN THE MÁTRA MOUNTAINS

GETTING THERE

You will need a car to get here and to move around once you're here.

STAY

Mátrafüred

A TREAT

Residence Ózon – *Üdülőtelep 2. ✆ 37 506 000. ozon.hotel-residence.hu/en. Ft29,000/57,000.* Situated at the foot of Mount Kékes, of which some rooms have a view, this is a large hotel (with a conference center) with good facilities, including several pools (one reserved for children), a sauna world (Finnish and aroma saunas, also an outdoor sauna and jacuzzi). The hotel restaurant offers both tasty Hungarian and international dishes.

Parádfürdő

A TREAT

Erzsébet Park Hotel – *Kossuth Lajos utca. ✆ 36 544 40. www.erzsebetparkhotel.hu.* *100 rooms, from Ft30,000.* A hotel and thermal spa housed in the new wing of what was once a private residence built at the end of the 19C. The treatments on offer here include a *mofeta*, a "dry" bath in carbonic gas, but only under medical supervision. Or you can choose instead to enjoy the (indoor and outdoor) swimming pools, sauna, and jacuzzi.

EAT

The hotels listed above all have restaurants where you can stop for lunch.

Gyöngyös

AVERAGE

Bori Mami – *Belváros tér 7. ✆ 30 830 934. borimami.hu. Open Mon–Fri, 8am–9pm; Sat, 8am–11.30pm; Sun, 9am–9pm. Ft2,390/11,900.* Currently the area's go-to restaurant where, from breakfast to dinner, you can enjoy sophisticated Hungarian cooking made with local produce. There is also a small selection of pasta dishes and vegetarian options.

TAKING A BREAK

Gyöngyös

Lipóti Pékség és Kávézó – *Fő tér 10. Open Mon–Sat, 6.30am–6pm (Sat, 1pm).* This bakery-café is a perfect place in which to grab a bite on the hoof (sandwiches, filled croissants, and other snacks). Try the *tönkölyös*, an excellent cake with nuts and plums.

SPORTS AND ACTIVITIES

Mátrafüred

High-Tech Sportok Bázisa – *Parádi utca 8. ✆ 20 443 4444. www.hsb.hu. Open 9am–5pm.* This agency organizes excursions into the Mátra Mountains by jeep, segway, bicycle, and so on.

Oxygen Adrenalin Park – *Halfway between Mátrafüred and Kékestető. ✆ 37 316 480. www.adrenalin-park.hu. Open May–Aug, 9am–7pm; Nov–Mar, 10am–4pm. Limited service in winter. Ft600. An extra charge for some rides and activities.* With a zip wire, bouncy castle, bobsleigh track, and quad bikes, this large adventure park in the forest has all sorts of activities for all ages.

Hollókő

★★

Population 341 – Nógrád county –area code ☏ 32

This picturesque village in the heart of the Cserhát Mountains lies on a hillside surrounded by vineyards. It is a huddle of around sixty small houses, with limewashed earthen walls, surrounded by wooden balustrades. Visiting the well-preserved and maintained village of Hollókő is like stepping into an old photograph. It has been a Unesco World Heritage Site since 1987 and is the ideal place to learn about the culture of the Palóc people who live in the region. Many of the houses have been turned into small museums or bed and breakfast accommodation.

ADDRESSES PAGE 209
Stay, Eat, Shopping, Events and Festivals

INFO:
Tourist Office – *On the village parking lot. ☏ 20 568 0545. Open 10am–6pm.* Brochure and village map in English. You can also buy a ticket that includes admission to the castle, museums, and wine tastings here *(Ft3,500).*

LOCATION:
Regional map A2 (p172–73)
61mi/98km northeast of Budapest.

PARKING:
A large parking lot at the bottom of the road to the castle (charges apply).

DON'T MISS:
The small museums in the Palóc houses and the castle.

TIMING:
Allow a day.

KIDS:
The Palóc Playhouse and the Museum of Palóc dolls.

★★ The village

Leave the car at the big parking lot at the top of the village and return on foot to Kossuth Lajos utca, the main cobbled street, which leads to the church.

Szent Márton templom (St. Martin's Church)

The church is a small white building, on top of which is a wooden belfry and a shingle roof. If you happen to turn up in time for a service on a Sunday, you may bump into a woman in traditional costume, with a bodice and skirt embroidered with multicolored flowers, a jacket in pink edged in green (or green edged in pink). The headdresses, always very colorful, are in different styles and include a white embroidered bonnet on which can be worn a scarf arranged as a crest or a fan-shaped coronet. *Take Petőfi Sándor utca to the right of the church, which will take you down and back to Kossuth Lajos utca, from where you can make your way back up to the village.*

The village streets

The museum houses are generally open Mar–Oct, 1am–6pm; opening times may be more restricted out of season.

The old village of Hollókő Ófalu was the first location in Hungary to be designated a Unesco World Heritage Site. All the houses are positioned perpendicular

The Palóc

The people who have long been associated with this region are an ethnic minority originally hailing from Slovakia, known as the Palóc (pronounced "palots"). In the 1930s, when the village of Hollókő was still difficult to reach, Viola Tomori, a Hungarian sociologist, conducted a study of the inhabitants of the village, who lived off the land, relying on the surrounding countryside for all their resources. She drew a range of conclusions from her observations, in particular about the male/female relationships. Palóc culture held that marriage and love were two separate things and that the conflict between a person's feelings and their best interests was one of the most difficult problems a family had to face. Almost all the traditional songs of the Palóc are about love and are full of amorous expression; the decoration and arrangement of their clothes are all designed to attract attention, such as the multiple embroidered petticoats that bulk out the skirts of the women, also demonstrating their wealth. The women's varied and colorful headdresses are also designed to draw attention.

FAMILY HIERARCHY

Family structures are very important and this hierarchy is expressed in the location of the houses. A family's first house is erected beside the road, with their descendants building their own house behind the first, thus forming a line of houses stretching back. The oldest family—the one highest up in the village hierarchy—always occupies the house right beside the road. The village officials are elected and paid by by the villagers.

A COMMUNITY THAT ENDURES

Its remote location has protected the village from development, allowing it to preserve, intact to the present day, the appearance that earned its Unesco classification. Thanks to this recognition and the tourism that it generates, the residents of Hollókő have been able to keep their employment options open (such as offering hospitality to visitors and accommodation). While the majority of them now live in modern houses in the new village (right next door to the old one), they continue to practice traditional activities in Hollókő, including pottery, weaving, breadmaking, and cheesemaking. Visitors are able to explore a living community, not just a village preserved "in aspic" and enjoy the chance to immerse themselves in 19C rural life.

FOLK FESTIVALS

The modern Palóc no longer wear traditional dress while going about their everyday life, but they do wear their costumes on various occasions, such as during the Easter Festival, on 20 August (St. Stephen's Day), and at weddings, to the evident delight of tourists and photographers. The men wear boots, tight black pants, embroidered linen shirts, ribbons knotted round their waists, and traditional black hats, while the women don embroidered skirts and up to eight petticoats, and tie ribbons in their hair. The festival held at Easter lasts three days, with concerts, dance recitals, and—as tradition demands—the men arming themselves with buckets of water with which to soak the women!

Main street, Hollókő village
© Funkystock/age fotostock

to the street. Different parts of the village have been destroyed by fire over the years (1874, 1886, and 1896), but each time the villagers have rebuilt identical copies using the traditional techniques. The thick walls stand on stone foundations. The frames are wooden, as are the gables, below which a small porch juts out under the eaves. The passageway that allows you to pass from one room to the next along the house is also sheltered by the eaves of the roof. The gardens are separated from each other and from the street by wooden paling fences.

The village does not look exactly as it did in the past; the roofs were originally thatched, animals no longer wander the streets, and the house fronts and gardens are now decorated with geraniums and flower baskets. That said, the interiors that are open to the public are as they would have been back in the day, with painted furniture featuring hand-drawn floral garlands and any number of embroidered accessories, such as cushions, tablecloths, and quilts, making for a jolly and cheerful atmosphere.

3

Palóc play-house

Kossuth Lajos utca 53.

Open-air activities for small children in the yard of the playhouse, while families can enjoy games together indoors. Pretty wooden toys are for sale.

★ Postamúzeum (Post Museum)

Kossuth Lajos utca 80. Ft500.

Find out about the evolution and development of the postal service. Telegraph and other communication equipment is also on display, including an old telephone exchange, stamps, and postcards.

★ Falumúzeum (Village Museum)

Kossuth Lajos utca 82. Ft400.

This charming building houses an exhibition of tools, baskets, kitchen utensils, embroidered fabrics, and painted plates.

Forgách Castle
© Gudella/iStock

★ **Guzsalyas** (Museum of Weaving and Traditional Palóc Dress)
Kossuth Lajos utca 94. Ft400.
An exhibition of looms, embroidery, and folk dress.

★ **Babamúzeum** (Museum of Palóc Dolls)
Kossuth Lajos utca 96. Ft400.
Around 200 porcelain dolls dressed in beautifully detailed and colorful folk costumes are on display in the cabinets here.

★ **Hollókő vár** (Hollókő Castle)
The castle has to be accessed on foot; just over a 10min walk, either from the parking lot at the top of the village or along a small path (signposted Vár) leading off from Kossuth Lajos utca at the bottom of the village. 60 508 2454. Open Mar–Oct, 10am–5.30pm. Ft900. Café with a terrace.
Built in the 13C and destroyed at the turn of the 18C, the castle has now been restored and some rooms reimagined, such as with a reconstruction of a medieval kitchen and wax figures in contemporary dress. The comprehensive information panels are in Hungarian. Situated on a small hill, there is a lovely view out over the surrounding countryside and its sheltered vineyards—a green oasis of peace and quiet that is perfect for picnicking.

Excursions Regional map (p172–73)

Szécsény A2
10mi/16km northwest of Hollókő.
This small town close to the Slovakian border is surrounded by the northern hills, a region traditionally associated with hunting. Rather than reaching for your rifle, you may be lucky enough to catch sight of a fine stag moving through the deep forest nearby at the end of summer. With a little luck (and a lot of patience) you may also see wild boars, roe deer, and even mouflons, wild sheep with elaborate horns.
The beautiful Baroque houses are the main attraction of the village itself, which their owners have restored with great care. **Forgách-kastély** (Forgách Castle) is a beautiful Baroque manor, painted yellow and white and decorated with stucco that conceals the last remnants of the old medieval fort, of which only a few walls and a corner tower are left.

ADDRESSES IN HOLLÓKŐ

GETTING THERE

Driving from Budapest is the simplest solution, but if not possible, there is a direct **bus** connection from the capital that runs every day.

STAY

AVERAGE

Hollóköves Guesthouses – *Reception at Kossuth utca 50. 20 325 8775. www.hollokoves.hu. Seven houses at various locations in the village, from Ft16,000* . Stay in one of the delightful houses in the village, a good solution for families. Furnished in the traditional Palóc style, each has a kitchen and a bathroom, and a generous breakfast is served at Hollóköves Kávézó (*Kossuth utca 50).*

SPLASH OUT

Castellum Hotel Hollókő – *Sport utca 14. 21 300 0500. www.hotelholloko.hu.* *68 rooms, from Ft37,000* . This modern hotel at the top of the village has beautiful rooms with contemporary interiors and bay windows; some have a terrace looking out over the valley. A lovely swimming pool and spa, and a small play area for children, billiards, and bowling.

EAT

The restaurants close at 6pm or 7pm, apart from the restaurant in the Castellum Hotel, which stays open until 10pm.

BUDGET

Muskátli – *Kossuth utca 61. 32 379 262. Open Wed–Sat, 11am–6pm (Sun, 5pm). Closed Mon & Tue. Ft2,200/3,100.* The charming courtyard of this traditional building is just the place to try Palóc soup, harking back to when this was the main local dish.

TAKING A BREAK

Hollóköves Kávézó – *Kossuth utca 50. 20 626 2844. Open 8.30am–5.30pm.* The large terrace is a great place for a coffee or tea, served with a smile.

Kalácsos – *Kossuth utca 70. Open 9am–5pm.* This delicious bakery also serves coffee and other drinks. Take a seat at a table outside to try an apple or poppyseed *rétes* (Hungarian strudel).

Cheesemaker – *Petőfi utca 3. Open 9am–5pm.* Gyöngyi and László Horváth make their cheeses by hand. Add some bread from the baker's and you have a ready-made picnic for your expedition into the countryside.

SHOPPING

Several souvenir stores sell magnets, embroidered tablecloths, ceramics, and brandy.

Fakanalas – *Kossuth utca 65. Open 10am–6pm.*A selection of wooden toys and kitchen utensils.

EVENTS AND FESTIVALS

Easter Festival – For three days in April, Hollókő is one long round of church masses, concerts, and parades in traditional Palóc dress. Accommodation should be booked well in advance if you intend to visit at this time of year.

DEO TRINO & UNI
POTENTI SAPIENTI
BONOQUE

Sopron and the Little Plain 4

Michelin National map 732

Győr-Moson-Sopron, Komárom-Esztergom, Vas counties

Fire Tower and Holy Trinity Column in Fő Square, Sopron

© Tibor Bognár/age fotostock

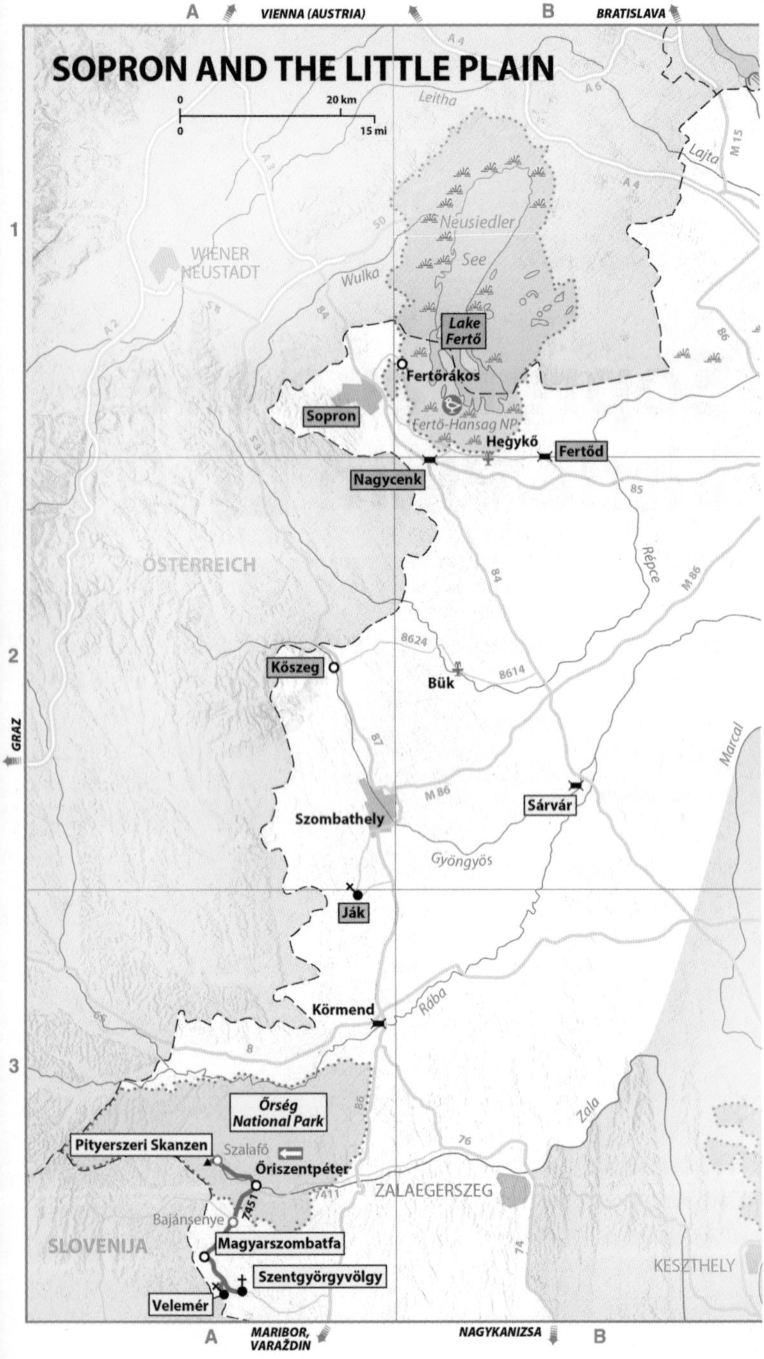
SOPRON AND THE LITTLE PLAIN
0 20 km
0 15 mi
A
B
1
2
3
VIENNA (AUSTRIA)
BRATISLAVA
GRAZ
MARIBOR, VARAŽDIN
NAGYKANIZSA
Leitha
Lajta
Neusiedler See
Wulka
WIENER NEUSTADT
Lake Fertő
Fertőrákos
Sopron
Fertő-Hansag NP
Hegykő
Fertőd
Nagycenk
ÖSTERREICH
Répce
Kőszeg
Bük
Marcal
Sárvár
Szombathely
Gyöngyös
Ják
Körmend
Rába
Őrség National Park
Pityerszeri Skanzen
Szalafő
Őriszentpéter
ZALAEGERSZEG
Zala
Bajánsenye
Magyarszombatfa
SLOVENIJA
Szentgyörgyvölgy
Velemér
KESZTHELY
A 4
A 6
M 15
A 3
A 2
S 4
S 31
50
84
85
86
M 86
8624
8614
87
8
76
7411
7451
74

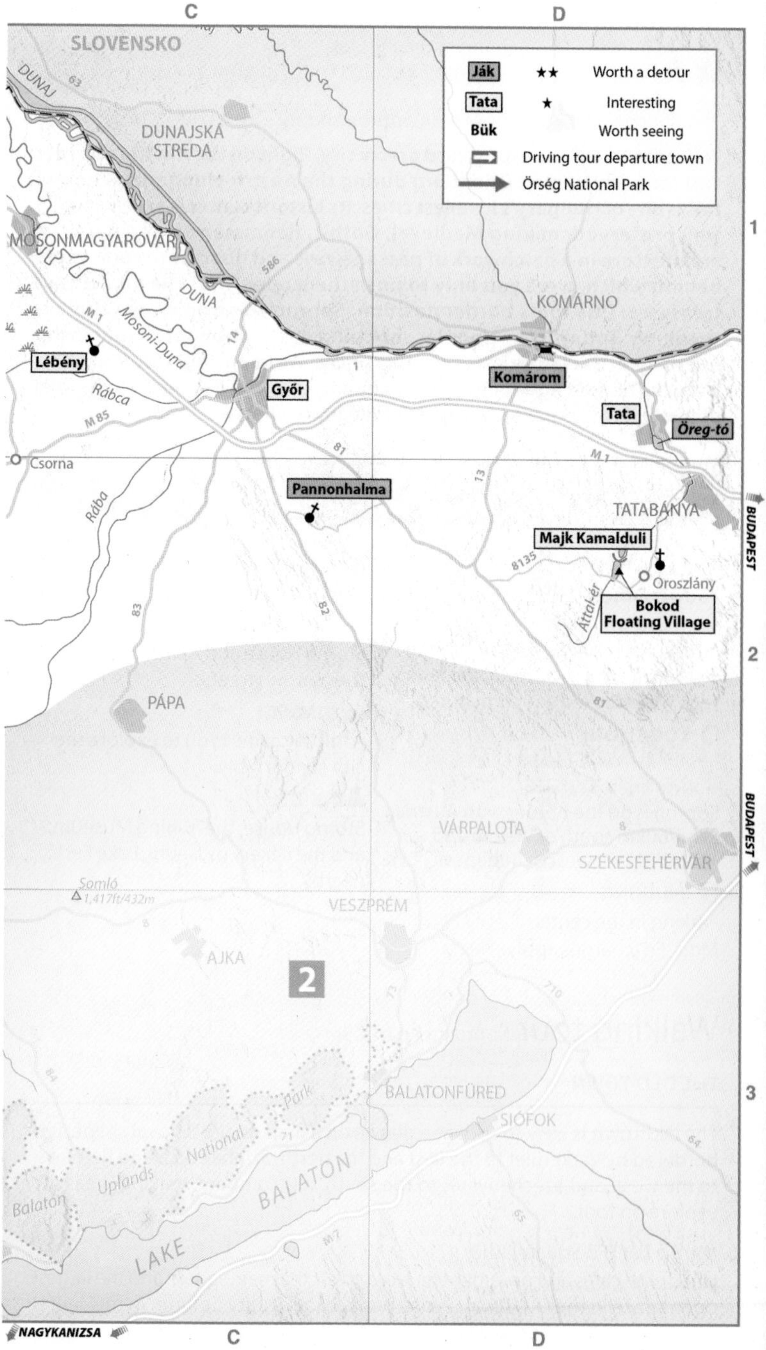
C
D
SLOVENSKO
DUNAJ
DUNAJSKÁ STREDA
Ják ★★ Worth a detour
Tata ★ Interesting
Bük Worth seeing
Driving tour departure town
Őrség National Park
1
MOSONMAGYARÓVÁR
DUNA
Mosoni-Duna
KOMÁRNO
Lébény
Győr
Komárom
Rábca
Tata
Öreg-tó
Csorna
Rába
Pannonhalma
TATABÁNYA
BUDAPEST
Majk Kamalduli
Oroszlány
Által-ér
Bokod Floating Village
2
PÁPA
VÁRPALOTA
BUDAPEST
SZÉKESFEHÉRVÁR
Somló
1,417ft/432m
VESZPRÉM
AJKA
2
BALATONFÜRED
SIÓFOK
3
Balaton Uplands National Park
LAKE BALATON
NAGYKANIZSA
C
D

Sopron

★★

Population 64,454 – Győr-Moson-Sopron county – area code ✆ 99

Welcome to a picture-postcard pretty city. Right on the Austrian border and formerly named Odenburg during the Austro-Hungarian Empire, this is one of Hungary's loveliest cities. Its historic center is exceptionally well preserved, mixing Medieval, Gothic, Renaissance, and Baroque architecture in a patchwork of passageways and doors into courtyards behind which, were you only to push them open, must lie all kinds of treasures. Due to its border position, Sopron was originally German-speaking. Today it is a popular shopping destination for neighboring Austrians attracted by its reasonable prices. An important cultural center from the Middle Ages until the Renaissance, Sopron has retained its love of festivals and spectacles, which take place all year round.

ADDRESSES PAGE 225
Stay, Eat, Baths, Events and Festivals

INFO:
Tourist Office – Sopron map, B2
Szent György utca 2. ✆ 951 975. turizmus.sopron.hu. Open Jun–Sept, 10am–6pm; check times for the rest of year. Well stocked with brochures.

LOCATION:
Regional map A2 (p212–13); Sopron map B2 (p218)
Sopron is on the border with Austria, 37mi/60km south of Vienna and 134mi/215km west of Budapest.

PARKING:
Parking in the center Mon–Fri (charges apply); underground parking is available below Petőfi tér (charges apply).

DON'T MISS:
Storno House and a stroll through the narrow streets.

TIMING:
A full day allows you to explore the city comfortably.

KIDS:
Storno House; the Mining Museum; and the Bakery museum; Lake Fertő nearby.

Walking tour Sopron map (p218)

THE OLD TOWN

The Old Town is easy to spot at a glance on a map due to its oval shape. It is bordered by Várkerület to the east and the north, Színház utca and Petőfi tér to the west, and Széchenyi tér to the south. It is compact, making it easy to explore on foot.

★★ **Fő tér** (Fő Square) AB2
Lined with cafés and pavement terraces, this is the main square and the largest open space in the Old Town. Pause beside Holy Trinity Column in the center (a "plague column" erected in 1701) and take a 360-degree look around you to admire some of the beautiful buildings.

Fő Square and the Fire Tower at night
©SzB/iStock

★ **Tűztorony** (Fire Tower) B1–2

☎ 311 327. tuztorony.sopron.hu. Open mid-Jun–Sept, 10am–8pm (rest of the year, 6pm). Ft1,200 (children Ft300). Information about the city's museums can be found on the first (ground) floor.

This symbol of the city is also its tallest building (190ft/58m). It acquired its name from its function as a watchtower, protecting the city from the danger of fire, invasion, and strangers trying to bring wine into the city. Today it is open to visitors, providing a bird's-eye view of the rooftops and layout of the Old Town as well as a **panoramic view★** over the surrounding area and across to the foothills of the Austrian Alps. The tower stands on Roman foundations and is constructed in several different styles. The square base with its 7ft/2m thick walls is 12C. The round tower with an arcaded balcony dates from the 16C. The Baroque pinnacle was added in 1680. From the balcony, the view toward Fő tér is dominated by the roof of City Hall.

4

Városháza (City Hall) B2

Not open to visitors. This was built at the end of the 19C in the Eclectic style. In addition to the conventional municipal service departments, the building houses 15,000 works and 5,000 medieval documents, charters, royal edicts, and fragments of manuscripts, some of which date back to 1381.

★ **Storno-ház** (Storno House) B1–2

Fő tér 8. ☎ 99 311 327. sopronimuzeum.hu. Open Tue–Sun, 10am–6pm. Ft1,000.
Welcome to the historic home of the Storno family. During the 19C this middle-class family of Italian origin were responsible for restoring many of Sopron's monuments. The Stornos were keen art lovers and lived in this 15C building (remodeled in the Baroque style in the 18C) from 1875. The house had hosted many famous guests before their arrival, including King Matthias in 1482. As you walk around the richly furnished and decorated rooms on the upper level it feels as though the building is still a home—floorboards creak, the windows glazed with "bottle glass" let in faint light, the table is set, and the beds are made, as if the people living here had only left the day before (the

Prosperity and independence

The Celts were the first to establish permanent settlements in the region. They were followed by the Romans, who in 1C built a camp on the site that they named **Scarbantia** and were to remain here for more than three centuries. Scarbantia was elevated to the status of *municipium*, meaning that the townsfolk could enjoy the same benefits as Roman citizens. Two important trade routes passed through the town—the Amber Road that ran from the shores of the Baltic to Italy and the north-to-south transcontinental route across Central Europe. This useful strategic position soon boosted the town's importance. Toward the end of the 4C, Emperor Valentinian reinforced the town's defenses, but they were eventually breached and from the 5C onward the town was invaded by one army after another. Avars, Germans, Slavs, and finally Magyars installed themselves in Sopron, building their defensive walls high (16ft/5m thick and 49ft/15m tall) so that by the 11C the town was able to resist the advancing forces of Peter the Hermit during the First Crusade.

ROYAL CITY AND "CIVITAS FIDELISSIMA" (MOST LOYAL CITY)

In 1277 Sopron was awarded the charter of a royal city, which allowed it to trade free of the rules and restrictions of the local lords. Once again the town reinforced its defenses, encircling itself with ramparts and erecting 34 towers and dungeons to protect the population that by now numbered some 22,000. Protected by these fortifications, trade and business prospered. The emerging class of merchants and craftsmen made Sopron a thriving center with a forward-looking society that attracted artists and scientists from abroad. The first high school was established in Sopron in 1557; two centuries later, in 1722, the works of Haydn were printed here; and in 1769 a theater was opened. During this time the city was also adding to its number of educational institutions, notably creating a senior school dedicated to forestry management that still exists today in the form of the university's Faculty of Forestry.

That Sopron is still part of Hungary today, despite the outcome of the Treaty of Trianon in which Hungary's borders were redefined, is entirely due to the will of the people. In 1921 they voted in a referendum to reject the treaty's revision of borders, which had placed Sopron in Austria, and instead asked to remain in Hungary. That is why, when viewed on a map, the border does a little loop around Sopron, which is just 4mi/6km from the Austrian border.

FREEDOM ON THE MENU

On 19 August 1989 Sopron was the first place in which the Cold War's Iron Curtain was breached. On that day an immense picnic (the Pan-European Picnic) was held on the Austrian-Hungarian border, in a peaceful demonstration organized by several European associations, during which the barbed wire was symbolically cut. For the three-hour duration of the picnic, the border crossings remained open and 600 citizens of the former-GDR, mainly families, were able to cross to the West in front of the guards, who looked on impassively. Hungary, which was already in the process of dismantling its borders, finally opened them on 11 September 1989. Today, a monument (2009) and a park (2011)—the Páneurópai Piknik Emlékpark—commemorate the event on the actual picnic site at Fertőrákos, a few miles from Sopron (*see p220*).

family in fact moved out in 1984). To complete the visit, there is an exhibition on the upper floor about Sopron from the 16C to the present day. Among the exhibits is the piano that **Franz Liszt** played as a child *(additional ticket Ft700).*

Fabricius-ház (Fabricius House) AB1–2

Fő tér 6. ✆ 311 327. sopronimuzeum.hu. Open Tue–Sun, 10am–6pm. Ft800.

Standing on the remains of Roman walls, Fabricius House was built in the 18C. The building houses three exhibitions, among them a history of the Amber Road, the ancient trading route transporting amber to the Mediterranean. You can also see rooms that have been recreated to depict the daily life of a patrician family in the 17C. They are worth seeing for the sheer number and quality of the everyday objects on display, including priceless furniture, travel chests, tiled stoves, and, among the kitchen equipment, a spit-roaster that can be operated at several different speeds.

In the atmospheric Gothic brick-vaulted basement you will find Roman stone sarcophagi, as well as three large statues of Jupiter, Minerva, and Juno, discovered during the construction of City Hall.

Patikamúzeum (Pharmacy Museum) B2

Fő tér 2. sopronimuzeum.hu. Open Apr–Oct, Tue–Sun, 10am–2pm. Closed rest of the year. Ft500.

The present building might only date from 1850, but the Angel Pharmacy originally occupied the site in the late 16C. Now a museum, you can see numerous objects from the building's original incarnation—jars of blue glass and enameled earthenware pots for storing unguents, lotions, and potions away from the light. The exhibits have been supplemented by those from other pharmacies. Look out for the marks that indicate their origins. Jars from the Angel Pharmacy bear the mark of an angel, those from the Lion Pharmacy (established in 1623), a lion, and so on. A book belonging to the Bayer company, containing the formula for aspirin, is also on display.

Kecske templom (Goat Church) AB2

Templom utca 1. The popular name of Sopron's most famous church is commemorated in the sculpture of the head of a goat and a kid, perhaps inspired by the legend that a goatherd found some treasure that helped finance the church's construction. The Franciscan Order began building the church at the end of the 13C, with work continuing until the beginning of the 15C. The monastery was later occupied by the Benedictine Sisters, which is why it is also known as the Benedictine Church. The high altar painting is by **István Dorfmeister** (1729–97), whose work can be found in numerous Hungarian churches. He lived in Sopron and remains one of the great masters of Baroque painting. You can also see a tabernacle dating from the end of the 15C and a pulpit from the same period. The beautiful **Chapter Hall** has pointed Gothic vaulting, while faded frescoes decorate the walls. You can also see some grotesque stone carvings, reminding the faithful of their many sins. In the 16C the church was the seat of five diets (assemblies) and three queens were crowned here, as well as several kings, including Ferdinand III.

Központi Bányászati Múzeum (Mining Museum) A2

Templom utca 2. ✆ 312 667. sopronimuzeum.hu. Open Apr–Oct, Wed–Sun, 10am–2pm. Closed rest of the year. Ft500.

This Baroque building, formerly the home of the Esterházy family, whose coat of arms is shown above the door, stands opposite the Goat Church. Today it houses the Mining Museum and features, in particular, the village of Brennbergbánya, which came to prominence in the 18C for its coal deposits

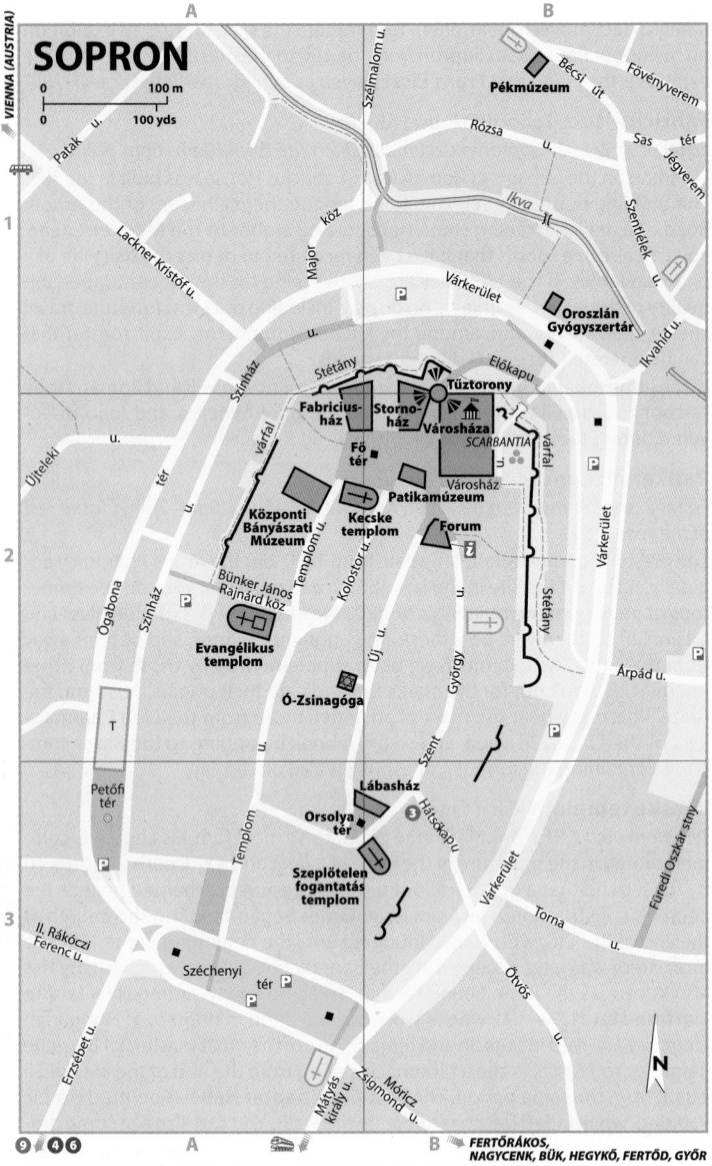

WHERE TO STAY

Sopronbánfalvi Kolostor Hotel és Étterem....... 4

Vadászkürt Panzió....... 6

WHERE TO EAT

Cézár Pince....... 3

Vadászkürt Étterem....... 9

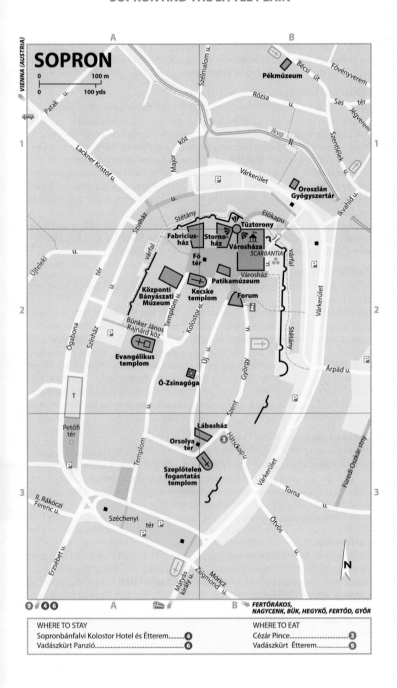

and remained a key mining site for 200 years. The museum offers a fascinating insight into mining techniques, both ancient and modern.

No. 4 Templom utca is a fine building housing the **Erdészeti Múzeum** (Forestry Museum). The house has an interesting history in itself; **Joseph Haydn** (1732–1809) gave several chamber music concerts here (at the time Hadyn was the Esterházy family's court composer and orchestra director, *see p220*). It was also here in 1921, after unrest in the region, that the representatives of the Allied Powers (France, Russia, and the UK) oversaw the results of the referendum demanded by the people of Sopron. The majority voted to remain in Hungary (rather than become part of Austria), involving a revision to the Treaty of Trianon.

Evangélikus templom (Lutheran Church) A2

Large enough to accommodate 3,000 worshipers, on several levels, this church was built in 1782–83 and is the largest in Sopron. It then had to wait 80 years for its steeple to be added, since Holy Roman emperor Joseph II had forbidden the building of bell towers on Lutheran churches. The church bell later played an important role: it was this bell that informed the inhabitants that they could remain Hungarian after the referendum (*see p216*). The organ has three keyboards, 52 registers, and 1,860 pipes, making it the largest in Hungary. God the Father and St. Michael surrounded by six angels sit on top. *Walk down Templom utca and take Fegyvertár utca on the left.*

Orsolya tér (Orsolya Square) AB3

The neo-Gothic Church of St. Ursula occupies one side of this small square. The Mary Fountain, in the center of the square, dates from the 16C. **Lábasház** (Arcade House), at No. 5, is fronted with the arcade that gives it its name and regularly mounts temporary art, local history, and ethnographic exhibitions (*311 327, sopronimuzeum.hu/en, opening hours vary according to the exhibitions, check in advance).*

★ **Ó-Zsinagóga** (Old Synagogue) A2

Új utca 22. Open Apr–Oct, Tue–Sun, 10am–6pm. Closed rest of the year. Ft800

Rediscovered and restored in 1967, this medieval synagogue (14C), abandoned for many years, witnessed the changing fortunes of Sopron's Jewish community. Jews had lived in Sopron since the 9C and numbered around 1,300 families by the time they were driven from the city in 1526. A plaque at No. 28 records that in 1944 all Sopron's 1,600 Jews were sent to extermination camps.

4

Pékmúzeum (Bakery Museum) B1

Bécsi út 5. 99 311 327. sopronimuzeum.hu. Open Apr–Sept, Tue–Sun, 2pm–6pm. Closed rest of the year. Ft500 (children Ft250).

This historic 17C bakery is now a museum, but smells of bread and pastry still seem to pervade the air.

Excursions Regional map (p212–13)

★★ **Fertő tó** (Lake Fertő) B1

6mi/10km north of Sopron. Take the road toward Tómalom, Sopronkőhida.

Fertő-Hanság National Park Visitor Center (in the small Kócsagvár building complex, at the edge of the village of Sarród, near the park; 17mi/28km southeast of Sopron). 537 620. ferto-hansag.hu. Open Mar–Aug, Mon–Fri, 8am–6pm; Sat & Sun, & public holidays, 9am–6pm. Rest of the year, check in advance. The Visitor Center complex also has accommodation (see Addresses, p225).

Lake Fertő straddles two countries—in Austria, where the majority of the lake lies, it is known as the Neusiedlersee. Unesco designated it a World Heritage Site in 2001 under the joint name Fertő/Neusiedlersee Cultural Landscape. On the Hungarian side its banks are protected by the **Fertő-Hanság Nemzeti Park** (Fertő-Hanság National Park), a paradise for cyclists and walkers and dotted with charming lakeside villages, vineyards, wetlands, and reedbeds. For years the local inhabitants made a living from fishing and agriculture, but now it is the tourists, attracted by the fully navigable lake's shallow waters, who drive the local economy.

With plenty of places to stay and things to do, the village of **Fertőrákos** makes an ideal base from which to explore around the lake. Don't miss the **Kőfejtő★** (quarry), which was in operation between 1628 and the 1940s. The quarrying has left behind a series of otherworldly caverns and colonnades, making an interesting setting for the concerts and plays that are held here during the summer months. There is a great view over the lake from the nature trail that winds through the area above the quarry.

In a completely different vein, Fertőrákos was also the place where the Pan-European Picnic was held in August 1989 (*see p216*). The **Páneurópai Piknik Emlékpark** commemorates the event with panels recounting what happened on that historic day (*paneuropaipiknik.hu*).

The road winds down toward Üdülőtelep, past expanses of reedbeds at the lake's edge. In summer the cooler lakeside area is popular with those keen to escape the heat. The lake, whose waters mysteriously vanished in the 19C before reappearing equally mysteriously, is also a haven for birds and birdwatchers. Look out for the unusual houses with thatched roofs mounted above the water on stilts, linked by wooden walkways.

★★ **Esterházy-kastély** (Esterházy Palace), at **Fertőd** B1–2

15mi/24km east of Sopron. 537 640. eszterhaza.hu. Visit by guided tour only (about 50min): 1pm in English, in Hungarian at all other times. A brochure in English is available at the entrance. Open Jun–Sept, 9am–6pm. Rest of the year, check in advance. Ft2,000.

There's a touch of the great European palaces of Versailles and Schönbrunn about this immense Baroque building and grounds with their immaculate

PRINCELY PATRONAGE

Prince Miklós Esterházy was a cultured man who wanted to fill his home with music, commissioning an opera house and a chapel for his palace. To provide the music, he employed not just an orchestra but also the famous Austrian composer **Joseph Haydn** (1732–1809) as his "chapel master." Haydn agreed to compose exclusively for the prince and became the court composer. As well as being responsible for the musical scores, he ran the orchestra, looked after the instruments, and played music himself. This arrangement gave Hadyn security, while also enabling him to still retain a degree of independence. The prince died in 1790 but his son Antal proved less interested in music. Despite this Haydn was retained on a salary although he no longer had any duties. He made his way to England and was soon was busy writing the *London Symphonies. Many more quartets, masses, and oratorios followed*. His prolific talent was such that Mozart said: "He can do everything, play games and shock, provoke laughter and the deepest emotion."

Lake Fertő
© Dietmar Najak/age fotostock

flowerbeds. It was built by Prince Miklós (Nicholas) Esterházy between 1762 and 1766, who had been inspired by the French king Louis XIV's palace, which he had visited during his foreign travels on behalf of the Habsburgs. On his return, as heir to the vast Esterházy family estates (371,000 acres/150,000ha in this region alone!), the prince, assisted by architect Melchior Hefele, commissioned the palace's construction on an estate bequeathed to him by his father, transforming the hunting lodge that was already there. Miklós, also known as the "Magnificent" for his generous dedication to the arts, continued improving the building until his death in 1790, even creating Esterháza village to house the palace servants and the craftsmen working on its construction. The Rococo building has 126 rooms and symmetrical wings enclosing a large courtyard fronted by three enormous wrought iron gates. Behind these, two wings curve around in a semicircle, completing the enclosure of the courtyard (aligned exactly north to south). Opposite the gates, across the courtyard, the main (southern) part of the palace is accessed by two flights of stairs that meet on a large balcony. The facade here looks out over the park and the gardens. Thanks to major renovation work undertaken after the Second World War, the main rooms of the palace were restored and you can still see some of the original stoves and pieces of furniture.

Esterházy Palace was built in the fashionable style of the era. On the first (ground) floor there is a "Chinese bedroom" that is more than 200 years old; its laquered panels are unique in Hungary. The Sala Terrena was the summer dining room and has a floor of dazzling, cool, white Carrara marble, while the floral frescoes on the ceiling bear the initials of Prince Miklós.

On the upper floor, the ceremonial hall and concert room, often still in use today, give a hint of the luxurious life of that bygone era, especially the spectacular parties hosted by Prince Miklós. Music, dance, games, hunting, ballet, and banquets … the festivities would continue into the night, lit by thousands of lanterns carried by peasants and the sky bright with fireworks bursting overhead. Miklós entertained many distinguished guests here, among them Queen Maria Theresa and the German writer Goethe. The guest list emphasized the wealth and privilege of the host but also aroused envy and criticism of the vast sums spent, to the extent that in 1766 the women living in the area around the estate protested and demanded the canceling of the tithe the local people had to pay.

★★ **Széchenyi-kastély** (Széchenyi Mansion), at **Nagycenk** B1–2

7.5mi/12km south of Sopron by Rte 84. Kiscenki utca 3. 360 023. szechenyi orokseg.hu. Open Apr–Sept, Tue–Sun, 10am–6pm. Rest of the year, check in advance. Ft1,400. Audioguide Ft500.

The village of Nagycenk is known for its links to the Széchenyi family who built their family seat here at the end of the 18C. István Széchenyi frequently stayed at the mansion where he could work in peace. When he died, he was buried at Nagycenk and his mausoleum attracts a constant stream of visitors, both Hungarian and from overseas. Severely damaged during the Second World War, the mansion has since been rebuilt. Today it houses the Széchenyi Museum and a stud farm. Beside it is a church, designed by **Miklós Ybl** (1814–91), one of the leading Hungarian architects of the 19C.

★ **Széchenyi István Emlékmúzeum** (István Széchenyi Memorial Museum) – This museum dedicated to István Széchenyii's life (*see opposite*) is housed in Széchenyi Mansion.

As the written information is in Hungarian, pick up an audioguide in English at the entrance. The lifestyle of the aristocratic Széchenyi family in the 19C is explored here via the rooms on the first (ground) floor.

The house is luxurious, but still far from the opulence of Esterházy Palace. István Széchenyi was more concerned about the future of his country and the everyday lives of Hungarians than with keeping up appearances. It was a trait inherited from his father, who had already contributed to and helped found the National Library and the National Museum. István took over the running of the estate in 1820 and, wanting to turn it into a model farm, gave away part of the land to the peasant farmers.

On the upper floor you can learn about the works commissioned and instigated by Széchenyi. The house was already lit by gas, and he went on to install modern bathrooms with flushing toilets. A stud farm adjoining the western end of the house is proof of his passion for horses. Horse-drawn carriage rides and carriage driving are available every day between 10 am and 4 pm.

Sárvár B2

36mi/58km south of Sopron by Rte 84.

Sárvár is a small spa town, whose waters are fed from springs that surge up from a depth of 6,500ft/2,000m. It benefits from two medicinal waters: one (181°F/83°C, chlorinated) treats joint, gynecological, and dermatological complaints; the other (109.4°F/43°C, ionized alkaline) is suitable for the treatment of joint and locomotive ailments, as well as neuropathic syndromes. Sárvár is also the location of the castle of Countess **Erzsébet Báthori** (Elizabeth Báthory), wife of Count Ferenc Nádasdy II, lord of Nádasd and Fogarasföld. She was imprisoned in Čachtice Castle (in present-day Slovakia), where she died in 1614. You can see her portrait in the gallery at Nádasdy Castle.

★ **Nádasdy vár** (Nádasdy Castle) – *Várkerület utca 1. (95) 320 158. nadasdy-muzeum.hu. Open Tue–Sun, 9am–9pm. Ft800.* Dating from the 16C, the castle is hexagonal in shape around a central courtyard. It belonged to the forward-looking and cultured Nádasdy family who installed at Sárvár the printer that issued the first book in Hungarian, a translation of the New Testament (16C). Nádasdy Castle now houses a cultural center and a museum. On the upper

István Széchenyi

Known as "the Greatest Hungarian" in his home country, Count István Széchenyi (1791–1860) earned this accolade by putting all his energy and part of his fortune to the service of his country, building up its economy, and elevating it to the status of a developed nation. Learning of even just a few of his many accomplishments, you realize that this title was not bestowed lightly.

POLITICS AND PATRONAGE

A career soldier and a Habsburg supporter, Széchenyi took part in the wars against Napoleon. At the same time, he became involved in the work of the Hungarian national assembly (1825–27) and offered a year of his income in order to found the **Academy of Sciences**, commissioning the building near the Chain Bridge in Budapest that still houses the academy today.

ENGINEER, BUSINESSMAN, AND MAN OF ACTION

Széchenyi put in place several important civil engineering projects in his lifetime. The entire area of land between the Danube and Tisza rivers was prone to flood regularly. Széchenyi tackled this problem by regulating the flow of the rivers. He also realized that the great Danube was not being used to its full potential, so he set about improving navigation on the river, so that it could be opened up to commercial steam-powered shipping. He was also involved in improving land transport and communication. He introduced the resurfacing of roads with tarmac, a technique he brought back from his travels in England, and was involved with the early railway in Hungary.

The count also demonstrated entrepreneurial skills, setting up the Danube Steam Navigation Company in 1831, the Pest Roller Mills in 1837, and the Commercial Bank of Hungary in 1841. In addition, he was the driving force behind the building of the vital crossing over the Danube, the Chain Bridge, between Buda and Pest in the capital, as well as the National Theater, and the tunnel through Castle Hill in Budapest.

REVOLUTION AND PERSECUTION

Although a former supporter of the Habsburgs and long opposed to political reformer Lajos Kossuth, Széchenyi eventually joined Kossuth (minister of finance) in Hungary's first elected government in 1848 as minister of public works and transport, but the unrest and the fear of an armed struggle became too much for him. He retreated to a mental health institution in Döbling where he remained until the end of his life. Toward the end of the 1850s, he wrote a satirical work on the repressive system of the Habsburg occupation, the "Bach regime" (named after the minister of the interior of the time), which led to him being questioned by the Viennese police and accused of conspiracy. Tragically, he committed suicide in 1860.

Fearing demonstrations, the Viennese police ordered his funeral to take place a day earlier than had been announced. Despite this, 6,000 people were present and over three days more than 50,000 people came to pay their respects to the man whom Lajos Kossuth, in spite of the differences between them, had declared "the Greatest Hungarian."

THE HUSSARS

The hussars are part of the Hungarian army and are a unit of light-cavalry soldiers that has been in existence since the 15C. In battle, the lightly armed hussars would emerge from the ranks of the heavy cavalry to disrupt and spread fear among the enemy but without directly confronting them. The hussars would then withdraw behind the heavy cavalry once more, to bide their time until it was the moment to attack and harass the enemy again. Their success was such that in the 16C they were considered a "typically Hungarian weapon," and their tactics were ultimately adopted by the rest of the armies of Europe.

In the 17C and 18C, the Hungarian light cavalry was considered the best in the whole of Europe. Their fearsome reputation over the years has been enriched by the many stories and legends surrounding their exploits.

floor, the main part of the museum explores the life of the hussars through uniformed models, armor, weapons, and so on. Also on this floor, don't miss the richly painted and decorated **Knights Hall★**. The ceiling frescoes dating from the middle of the 17C are the work of Hans Rudolf Miller and show scenes from battles against the Turks. The paintings on the walls are 18C and feature bibical scenes by István Dorfmeister.

Sárvár Arborétum – The arboretum (opposite Nádasdy Castle and its grounds), was originally part of the castle park but fell into disrepair. It eventually found its way into the hands of its final owner Ludwig III of Bavaria, who planted many trees and did much to develop the arboretum in the late 19C. Today it's a pleasant place in which to enjoy a quiet and relaxing stroll among the old and venerable trees, labeled both in Hungarian and Latin.

★★ Kőszeg A2

29mi/47km south of Sopron, first by Rte 84 and then 8627.

Situated very close to the Hungarian-Austrian border, Kőszeg seems to be trapped in a time warp. You could quite easily believe that it had been built as the set for a film about the history of Hungary, since the old medieval city has been perfectly preserved. The historic center lies behind the remains of the town walls and defensive ditches, designed mainly to protect it against Turkish invasion. The fortifications were so effective that even Süleyman the Magnificent, after a month of laying siege to this small town, had to give up and halt his advance toward Vienna. The church bells in Kőszeg ring out every day at 11am to mark the retreat of the defeated Ottoman troops, who left the city on 30 August 1532 at 11am.

Entry into the old city is through **Hősök kapuja** (Heroes' Gate), which commemorates the brave soldiers who struggled against the Turks and leads to **Jurisics tér★** (Jurisics Square). Surrounded by well-preserved medieval houses, the town hall is the old city's only Baroque building.

Jurisics vár (Jurisics Castle) – *Jurisics Miklós Várműzeu. ☎ (94) 360 113. jurisics-var.hu. Open Tue–Sun, 10am–5pm. Ft1,600 (children Ft1,000).* Built at the end of the 13C, it was remodeled in the Renaissance and Baroque styles during the 16C and 17C. Inside, the museum recounts the exploits of **Miklós Jurisics**, the military leader who led the resistance against the Turkish insurgencies of 1532. A bronze statue with his effigy stands in the courtyard of this attractive castle.

ADDRESSES IN SOPRON

See Sopron map (p218)

ARRIVAL/DEPARTURE

Railway station – *Állomás utca 2.* A 10min walk from the historic center. Direct connections with Budapest *(2hrs45min)* and Győr *(1–2hrs).*

Bus station – *Lackner Kristóf utca 9.* A 10min walk from the center. Connections with Fertőd (every hour), Győr (every 2hrs), and Veszprém (4 buses/day).

STAY

Reserve well in advance if you visit during the Volt Festival.

AVERAGE

6 **Vadászkürt Panzió** – A3, off map – *Udvarnoki utca 6. 314 385. vadaszkurt.hu. 4 rooms. Half-board on request.* Known for its restaurant *(see below right)*, this large guesthouse with its walls painted apple green overlooks a small garden. It is one of the best places to stay in Sopron, so reserve early if you want to stay here and enjoy the lavish breakfast with its homemade jams.

A TREAT

4 **Sopronbánfalvi Kolostor Hotel és Étterem** – A2, off map – *2mi/3.5km west of Sopron center. Kolostorhegy utca 2. 505 895. banfalvakolostor.hu. 17 rooms, Ft25,000/40,000 depending on the room. see overleaf.* Gorgeous! Tucked away in the wooded hills around Sopron, this 17C monastery is now a retreat and a hotel. You will feel at peace in the simply furnished bedrooms, some in the monks' former cells, where their books have been preserved.

Around Lake Fertő

BUDGET

Kócsagvár – *Rév-Kócsagvár, Sarród. (06) 99 537 620. ferto-hansag.hu. 10 rooms, Ft3,700 per person per night.* This unusual building complex, which curls around and looks a little like a snail shell seen from above, was designed by Imre Makovecz, one of the exponents of Organic architecture *(see p375).* Inspired by the style of the local fishing villages, the roof is thatched with reeds. The accommodation is a little reminiscent of a youth hostel, but each room has its own bathroom.

Horváth Ház Panzió – *Fő utca 194–196, Fertőrákos. 355 368. horvathhazpanzio.hu. 15 rooms, Ft14,000/16,000.* This charming guesthouse is in a quiet part of the village's main street. There's a café, an inner courtyard and garden, and you can hire bikes (a secure bike park).

EAT

BUDGET

3 **Cézár Pince** – B3 – *Hátsókapu utca 2. 311 337. cezarpince.hu. Open 4pm–midnight (Sun, 11pm). Ft1,100/1,350.* With its blue and white striped exterior and impressive entrance, this place cuts a real dash. It is renowned for the quality of its wine list and its platters of cold meats and cheeses; diners sit together at long wooden tables, surrounded by old winemaking equipment. A patio for sunny days.

9 **Vadászkürt Étterem** – A3, off map – *Udvarnoki utca 6. 314 385. vadaszkurt.hu. Open Tue–Sat, 11am–10pm; Sun, 11am–4pm. Ft2,500/4,200.*

The ideal place to discover the wines of Sopron, and the surrounding area, thanks to their fine cellar built up over 30 years. The traditional, flavorsome local dishes are an added bonus. Specialties include game (venison, pheasant, wild boar) and fish (pike-perch and carp).

Sopronbánfalva Étterem – *Kolostorhegy utca 2. ✆ 505 895. banfalvakolostor.hu. Open 6pm–9pm (Sat & Sun, noon–3pm). Ft2,500/4,200.* Elegant beneath its fresco-painted ceiling, the monastery's restaurant *(see Stay)* is worth a detour, possibly more for its ambience than its fine dining. Its setting is superb, a heritage gem in the countryside.

TAKING A BREAK

Kultúrpresszó – *Várkerület 96. ✆ 30 299 6140. kulturpresszo.hu. Open Sun–Fri, 8am–7pm; Sat, 8.30am–8pm.* Sopron's youth congregate in this genial small café and coffee-roaster's. A good choice of sandwiches, bagels, and homemade cakes to accompany your coffee. A great little place with a terrace in summer. Locally made T-shirts for sale, too.

Zwinger Kávéház – *Várkerület 92. ✆ 340 287. Open 9am–8pm.* Tucked away at the bottom of one of the charming hidden passageways in the old part of Sopron, this ice cream parlor is a magnet for its deletectable homemade ices sold by weight. Don't forget to factor in the candy toppings, which add extra weight.

IN THE EVENING

Gambrinus – *Fő tér 3. Open 10am–11pm (Fri–Sat, midnight).* This conveniently located tavern has become a tourist trap, but with its view over Sopron's main square it is still a great place to drop in for a drink. As a plus, it serves food all day long, which is quite unusual in Hungary.

BATHS

See Regional map (p212–13)

Hegykő – B1–2 – *Saratermal.hu* This spa, 12mi/20km southeast of Sopron, is fed by water that gushes from the ground at a temperature of 131°F/55°C. Recommended for joint pains, it attracts people in search of a cure or wishing to boost their general well-being. Both indoor and outdoor baths.

Bükfürdő – *bukfurdo.hu* Situated 28mi/45km southeast of Sopron, the springs that feed this spa are said to be the most abundant in Hungary. Renowned for easing muscular disorders. With 34 swimming pools, slides, a spa, and sauna, this enormous thermal spa complex covers 35 acres/14ha.

EVENTS AND FESTIVALS

Volt Festival – 4 days end-Jun–beg-Jul, Sopron. One of Hungary's biggest rock and electro music festivals, with an international lineup. *volt.hu/en*

Haydn Festival – 3 days in September. Esterházy Palace in Fertőd honors the composer and musician, who led the palace court orchestra for many years.

WINERIES

The Sopron area produces mainly red wines. Notable wineries include:

Pfneiszl: pfneiszl.hu
Luka: lukawine.com
Weninger: weninger.com/hu
Raspi: raspi.hu
Taschner: taschnervin.hu
Linzer-Orosz: linzerorosz.hu

Győr

★

Population 130,094 – Győr-Moson-Sopron county – area code ☏ 96

Like some other Hungarian cities, Győr does a good job of concealing its riches. You have to pass some rather featureless industrial suburbs before the "city of the three rivers" reveals its hidden delights—a well-restored Baroque center with numerous museums at the point where the Mosoni-Duna, an arm of the River Danube, meets the Rába and Rábca rivers in the lower part of the Old Town. After Pécs and Sopron, Győr is said to be the Hungarian city with the greatest number of ancient buildings, some dating back to the 13C. This makes it just the place to unearth a cornucopia of architectural treasures.

ADDRESSES PAGE 232
Stay, Eat, Baths, Events and Festivals

INFO:
Tourist Office – Győr map B2 – *Baross Gábor út 21 (upstairs). ☏ 311 771. latogatokozpontgyor.hu; gyor.hu. Open Mon–Fri, 9am–6pm (Sat, 4pm; Sun, 2pm).* Besides the usual visitor information, there is a small exhibition on local history, a baggage store, and small shop.

LOCATION:
Regional map C1 (p212–13); Győr map (p228). Győr is 55mi/88km east of Sopron. Approaching from Vienna or Budapest (the city is halfway between the two), the main road into Győr is Szent István út; turn off left opposite City Hall, down Aradi vértanúk útja to get to the Old Town.

PARKING:
Parking in the Old Town (charges apply, ticket machines); no charge in the modern part of the city.

DON'T MISS:
The Baroque center, its narrow streets and museums.

TIMING:
Győr has much more to offer than is initially apparent. Allow at least one full day.

Walking tour Győr map (p228)

THE OLD TOWN

Renting a bike from one of the public docking stations is a practical and fun way of getting around *(fee payable; information from the tourist office or gyorbike.hu).*

Széchenyi tér (Széchenyi Square) B1
This cobbled square in the heart of the Old Town has been well restored. The Column of St. Mary (1686) in the center was erected to commemorate the liberation of Buda from the Turks. The beautiful Baroque buildings, modern fountains, and outdoor terraces of cafés and restaurants make it a popular spot with locals and tourists alike.

Szent Ignác templom (St. Ignatius Church) – *Closed for renovation until further notice.* The church was built by the Jesuits between 1634 and 1641 to plans

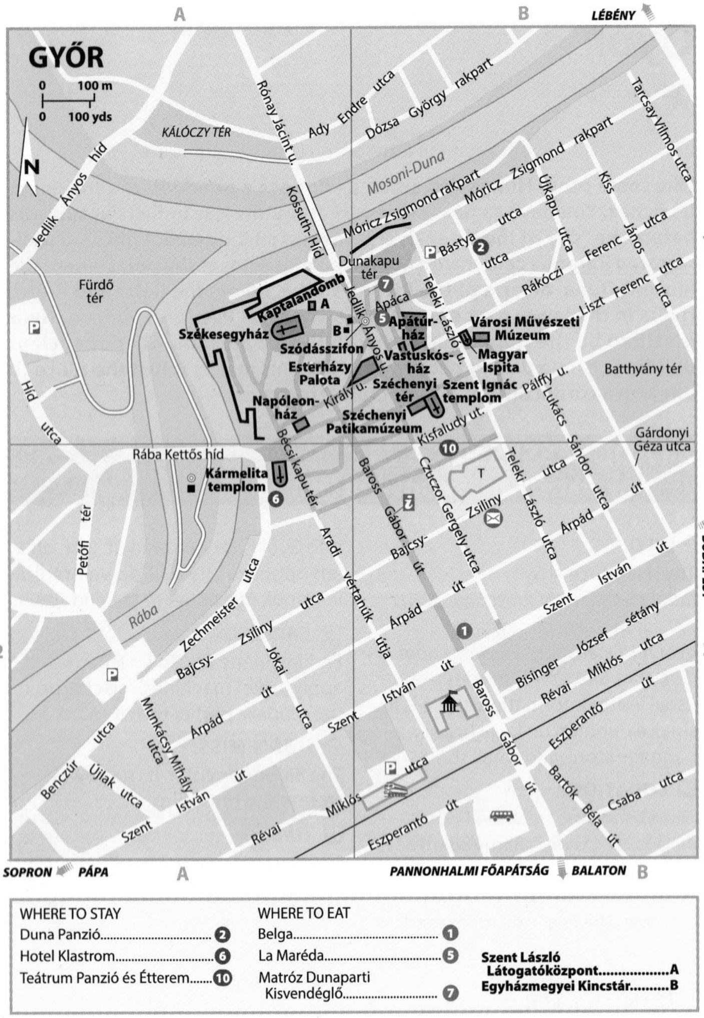

drawn up by the Italian architect Baccio del Blanco, who was inspired by the Church of the Gesù in Rome. The decoration inside the church is magnificent.

Széchenyi Patikamúzeum (Pharmacy Museum) – *Széchenyi tér 9. ☎ 550 348. Open 7.30am–4pm. Ft700.* Founded by the Jesuits in 1654, this still-operating pharmacy has retained its custom-made furniture, painted vaulted ceilings, and Baroque decoration dating from the end of the 17C.

Apátúr-ház – Xantus János Múzeum (János Xantus Museum) – *Széchenyi tér 5. Open Tue–Sun,10am–6pm. Ft800.* This beautiful Baroque palace formerly belonged to Pannonhalma Abbey (*see p230*). Now a museum, it presents the history of Győr, from prehistoric times to the 1950s. Philatelists will enjoy an exhibition of Hungarian stamps issued from 1891 onward.

★ **Vastuskós-ház – Patkó Imre Gyűjtemény** (Imre Patkó Collection) – *Széchenyi tér 4. ✆ 310 588. Open Tue–Sun, 10am–6pm. Ft700.* The museum is housed in Vastuskós ház (House of the Iron Butt, or stump), named after the tall, slender tree stump studded with iron nails attached to a corner of the building; at one time it was the custom for every craftsman who passed by to hammer a nail into it. The collection takes its name from the many objects and works of art brought back from his travels by journalist **Imre Patkó** (1922–83). As well as works by 20C Hungarian artists, there are others by Chagall, Rouault, Braque, and Picasso.
Continue straight on down Király utca.

Esterházy Palota – Rómer Flóris Művészeti és Történeti Múzeum (Rómer Flóris Art and Historical Museum) B1
Király utca 17. ✆ 322 695. romer.hu. Open Tue–Sun, 10am–6pm. Ft800.
Located in the Baroque Esterházy Palace building, this is the headquarters of the city's municipal museums and also exhibits in its own right—in this case, a private collection of 19C and early 20C Hungarian paintings. Temporary exhibitions are held here, too.
On leaving, turn left into Jedlik Ányos utca, heading toward the river.

Szódásszifon-szobor (Soda Bottle Fountain) B1
This quirky fountain is named after **Ányos Jedlik** (1800–95). Fans of fizzy drinks owe him a great deal as this inventor, engineer, and priest, who spent the last years of his life in Győr's Benedictine monastery, invented the soda (spritzer) bottle. He also earned his place in the annals of science by devising the precursor to the dynamo in 1827.

★★ **Káptalandomb** (Chapter Hill) A1
Walk up Káptalandomb from Bécsi kapu tér to explore this area above the point where the River Rába meets the Mosoni-Duna.
Szent László Látogatóközpont (St. László's Visitor Center) – *Káptalandomb 11. ✆ 20 251 3112. kaptalandomb.hu. No charge to enter.* This is the diocesan "tourist office" where you can find information on the sites managed by the church and buy tickets for the treasury. But you can also see the **Herm of St. László★★** (King Ladislas I), the amazing reliquary in the form of a bust containing the king's skull dating from the beginning of the 15C. The herm is on display here while restoration work takes place in the cathedral where is it usually kept.
Egyházmegyei Kincstár (Diocesean Treasury) – *Káptalandomb 11. ✆ 30 793 2959. kaptalandomb.hu. Open 10am–6pm. Ft1,000.* Numerous religious objects and illuminated manuscripts are on display; many are priceless.
Székesegyház (Győr Cathedral Basilica) – *Open 8am–noon, 2pm–6pm. Some parts are closed during restoration.* Dominating the neighborhood, the cathedral dates back to the 11C, but has suffered a great deal over the centuries. Restored in the Gothic style, damaged by the Turks, reconstructed in the Baroque style, and then completed in the 18C and 19C, the facade is neo-classical and the main door dates from 1938. However, this curious hybrid is not lacking in grandeur. Frescoes by Franz Anton Maulbertsch depict *The Assumption of the Virgin Mary* above the main altar and The *Transfiguration* on the vault of the nave. And above a side altar in the north wing, look out for an icon of the Virgin Mary. It found its way to Győr in 1655 in the hands of Bishop Lynch from Clonfert, Ireland, who had fled when Oliver Cromwell's parliamentary forces began persecuting priests in the English Civil Wars. The bishop died in Győr in 1663. Four years later, on St. Patrick's Day, the Virgin was seen to weep tears of blood and she has been honored on 17 March every year since then.

St. Ignatius Church, Győr
© JackF/iStock

A little further on, in the lovely Baroque square Bécsi kapu tér, pause to peep inside the **Kármelita templom** (Carmelite Church, 1721–25); the interior is magnificent with an imposing Baroque altarpiece.

Napóleon ház (Napoleon House) A1

Király u. 4. ✆ 314 552. Open Tue–Sun, 10am–6pm. Ft 700.

On 31 August 1809, the Corsican emperor himself spent a night here after the Battle of Raab (Raab is the German name for Győr), fought between Franco-Italian and Habsburg armies (Napoleon was victorious). Today the house is the **Győri Grafikai Műhely és Kiállítótér**, a small museum of graphic arts.

Városi Művészeti Múzeum (Municipal Museum of Art) B1

Nefelejcs utca 3. ✆ 318 141. Open Tue–Sun, 10am–6pm. Ft700.

The museum is located in the Magyar Ispita, the former Hungarian Hospice building and its chapel. In addition to the richly decorated interior, in particular the patio with its striking Tuscan columns, the museum exhibits a collection of fine Baroque and Renaissance furniture.

Excursions Regional map (p212–13)

★★ **Pannonhalmi Főapátság** (Pannonhalma Abbey) C2

14mi/23km south of Győr by Hwy 81. Leave your car in the covered parking lot (no charge) to the left of the Visitor Center. There are also two restaurants, an ice cream parlor (in summer), and a souvenir shop.

Founded in 996 by Prince **Géza** of the Árpád dynasty, the first Magyar ruler to convert to Christianity and father of the future Stephen I, Pannonhalma Abbey is one of the greatest Benedictine abbeys. In a majestic location on a hill overlooking the Pannonian Plain, it is well preserved and played an important part in spreading Christianity throughout Central Europe. It was listed as a Unesco World Heritage Site in 1996. Today there are around 30 monks living here, following the teachings of St. Benedict. Heir to the long tradition of monastic education, the abbey's private high school takes in more than 300 boarders, all of them boys.

Visitor Center – *Vár 1. ☎ 570 191. bences.hu. Open Jun–Aug, 9am–6pm; May & Sept, 9am–5pm; Oct–11 Nov (St. Martin's Day) & 21 Mar–Apr, 9am–4pm; 12 Nov–30 Dec & 3rd weekend Jan–20 Mar, 9am–3pm. Closed Mon, 24,25 & 31 Dec, and first two weeks of Jan. Ft2,400 (including audioguide in English).* It might be brand new, but the center's clean lines and contemporary architecture blend surprisingly well into the wooded hillside around the abbey. Buy entry tickets here; there is an interactive exhibition upstairs.

The abbey and library are close together but the rest of the monastic complex is very spread out (wine cellar, arboretum). During the summer months, a small tourist train takes visitors around the site *(no charge if you have a ticket for the abbey, ask for train times at the Visitor Center).*

Steps lead to a bridge that crosses the road, from where there is a path that climbs up to the abbey (around 10min walk).

Central Courtyard – A statue of Asztrik (Astrik), the abbey's first abbot, stands in the middle of the courtyard. Legend has it that it was Asztrik who presented Pope Sylvester II's gift of the famous Holy Crown to King Stephen *(see p297)*. From the **terrace** overlooking the Kisalföld (Little Plain), the view you gaze out at will be the same as the one the monks saw centuries ago. Before entering the basilica, a sundial in the cloister garden reminds visitors of their mortality, that one day one of the hours on the sundial will be their last—"Una Vestrum Ultima Mea."

★ **St. Martin's Basilica** – Construction of the present church began in 1224. The main entrance is through the beautiful south doorway, the **Porta Speciosa★**, the entrance that the monks would take to pass from the cloister to the church. Several alterations have been made since it was originally built in the 13C. The multiple columns are made of red marble, and the capitals and bases of white limestone. They were restored by Ferenc Storno in the 1860s, as was the fresco adorning the tympanum that depicts St. Martin sharing his cloak with a beggar. The Storno family—the Storno home in Sopron is open to the public *(see p215)*—came here from Italy at the end of the 18C and left their mark on numerous buildings in the western part of the country. They drew up the plans for the restoration of the cloister and abbey church and were also responsible for the church pulpit and "neo-Romanesque" altar in red marble.

★★ **Library** – The library was founded in the 11C during the reign of King Ladislas I (St. Ladislas), but the building you see today dates from the 19C and was designed by János Páckh, one of the architects of Esztergom Basilica *(see p108)*. The painted wood interior gives the illusion of marble and the lighting is cleverly designed, using a series of mirrors to reflect daylight around the room. It contains 400,000 works, including the Deed of Foundation of Tihany Abbey, the oldest manuscript in Hungarian which dates from the beginning of the 11C.

Painting Gallery – The visit concludes here with numerous works of art, notably from the 16C, 17C, and 18C, by the Dutch, Italian, and Austrian Schools. You can also see ceremonial objects and vestments.

Arboretum – Created at the same time as the abbey, the layout of the present arboretum dates from the 1840s and today contains 1,200 species of trees and aromatic herbs. The most famous is Pannonhalma lavender, which has been cultivated since the 17C. Dried flower arrangements, essential oils, and other products made from the lavender take pride of place in the monastery shop.

Wine Cellar – At the beginning of this century, the monks started making wine once more and it proved so popular that the abbey now produces 300,000 bottles a year. A visit and tasting can be arranged *(inquire at the Visitor Center).*

★ **Szent Jakab templom** (St. James Church), at **Lébény** C1

16mi/25km northwest of Győr. 30 255 1343. www.szentjakabtemplom.hu. Open Apr–Oct, 9am–6pm; Nov–Mar, 10am–5pm. Ft600 (children Ft400), buy tickets at the Visitor Center (Templom tér 2). Audioguide in English.

This stunning Romanesque church in the village of Lébény, consecrated in 1206 and beautifully restored, was first part of a Benedictine Abbey, and then was given to the Jesuits, before being burned by the Turks in 1683. The fine proportions of the western facade are especially noteworthy, as is the apse with three chapels, and the pretty frieze of small arches on the exterior of the building. The portal has particularly elaborate floral motifs.

ADDRESSES IN GYŐR

See Győr map (p228)

ARRIVAL/DEPARTURE

Railway station – *Vasútállomás. Révai Miklós utca 4–6.* There are fast trains between Győr and Budapest *(1hr15min)*. Vienna is only 1hr30min away (up to 8 direct trains a day). Luggage storage (Ft400/day).

Bus station – *Autóbuszállomás. Hunyadi utca 9–11 (south of the railway station).* One bus an hour to Budapest, Vienna, and Bratislava.

STAY

BUDGET

2 Duna Panzió – B1 – *Vörösmarty utca 1. 20 926 1778. dunapanzio.hu. P 13 rooms, Ft13,800.* The rooms might be a little basic, but they are in a charming building in the historic center, a short walk from the banks of the Danube. Plus there are reasonably priced family rooms and a covered play area for children.

10 Teátrum Panzió és Étterem – B2 – *Schweidel utca 7. 310 640. teatrum.hu. P 10 rooms (including 2 triples) from Ft16,900. Menus Ft1,200/1,500.* An elegant building with red walls houses this charming family guesthouse in the historic center. The restaurant attached to it is a favorite post-show meeting place after performances at the theater next door.

6 Hotel Klastrom – A2 – *Zechmeister utca 1. 516 910. klastrom.hu. P 40 rooms from Ft19,500. Restaurant, Ft2,100/4,200.* A magnificent 18C Carmelite cloister is the setting for this comfortable hotel. The bedrooms have recently been renovated and in summer there is a restaurant with a terrace in the garden.

EAT

BUDGET

1 Belga – B2 – *Árpád út 34. 889 460. belgagyor.hu. Open Mon–Sat, 10am–midnight; Sun, 11am–10pm. Ft1,500/2,500. Sun brunch Ft3,490.* A little bit of Belgium in the heart of Hungary. Belgian specialties are on the menu, with draft beer, mussels, and fries in pride of place, while the decor transports you straight to Brussels, too.

7 Matróz Dunaparti Kisvendéglő – B1 – *Dunakapu tér 3. 336 208. Open 11am–10pm (Fri & Sat, 11pm). Ft1,100/2,500.* A tavern that's popular with the locals who like its simple, hearty dishes, such as stews and breaded escalopes. A speedy service.

Pannonhalma Abbey
© markborbely/iStock

The terrace faces the river and is perfect for an aperitif or two.

AVERAGE

5 **La Maréda** – B1 – *Apáca utca 4. ✆ 889 460. lamareda.hu. Open Mon–Sat, 10am–midnight; Sun, 10am–10pm. Ft3,900/9,000.* One of the city's top spots, it attracts a friendly clientele. Chef Szilveszter Horváth has won numerous awards; he skillfully blends Hungarian produce with French cooking techniques, particularly from the Mediterranean.

Pannonhalma

Viator – *Vár 1. ✆ 570 200. hovamenjek.hu/pannonhalma/viator-apatsagi-etterem-esborbar. Open Tue–Sun, 11am–10pm (Sun, 6pm). Ft3,200/5,500.* The abbey's gastronomic showpiece was built in 2010. Futuristic in design and perched high up on a ridge, affording diners a superb panoramic view of the countryside. Benedictine traditions combine with contemporary cuisine, in perfect harmony with, of course, the abbey's own wines.

TAKING A BREAK

Kávébajusz – *Bécsi kapu tér 4. ✆ 20 330 4655. www.kavebajusz.hu. Open Tue–Fri, 8am–6pm; Sat 9am–6pm; Sun, 9am–5pm.* Sip a cup of good quality coffee in an elegant contemporary interior.

EVENTS AND FESTIVALS

Eurofest – A festival of dance and European Folklore held over one week end August/beginning September. *www.associationdance.com*

Győrkőc Fesztivál – A children's festival, first weekend of July, the biggest free outdoor festival in the country. Music, puppets, games, crafts, swings, animals.

Barokk Esküvő – A three-day Baroque wedding festival in August. Dancers, musicians, comedians, a costume procession, all in Baroque style.

Szent László Napok *(Ladislas Days)* – End June. Medieval life recreated. Knights, yurts, archery demonstrations, and horseback shows will delight young and old as the Middle Ages come alive.

Tata

★

Population 23,377 – Komárom-Esztergom county – area code ✆ 34

Tucked away between Mount Vértes and Mount Gerecse, Tata long ago attracted kings to its lakeside castle, some of whom made it their royal residence. With not just one but two lakes, water sports are well catered for in the town—Tata proudly hosts the training of the Hungarian swimming team. At one time it was also famous for its watermills. Their number has since dwindled but one or two still remain. Graced with tree-lined walks and lovely parks, this is a small but delightful town that will appeal to lovers of nature and history.

ADDRESSES PAGE 239
Stay, Eat, Taking a break, Events and Festivals

INFO:

Tourist Office – *Ady Endre út 9. ✆ 586 045. visittata.com. Open mid-Jun–end Aug, Tue–Sun, 9am–5pm (Sat, 8am–noon); Sept–mid Jun, Mon–Fri, 8am–4pm.* Small in size but big on information, and with a small shop.

LOCATION:

Regional map D2 (p212–13)

Close to the Slovakian border, Tata is 50mi/80km northwest of Budapest by Hwy M1.

PARKING:

Plenty of free places on the main streets. In the center you must display a blue disk, which can be bought at the tourist office (*Ft150).*

DON'T MISS:

A stroll by the two lakes; Fort Monostor; taking a break in Slovakia, with time for a drink in the main square in Komárno (Komárom), a town with a "foot" in two countries.

TIMING:

You can see Tata in half a day.

Walking tour

Tata's romantic charm derives from its two lakes: **Öreg-tó★★** (Old Lake), covering more than 618 acres/250ha, around which the town is built; and, a short walk from Öreg-tó, **Cseke-tó★** (Little Lake).

If you plan to spend an evening in Tata don't forget your insect repellent; they arrive in numbers as soon as the sun goes down.

★ **Öregvár** (Old Castle)

Váralja utca 1–3. ✆ 381 251. kunymuzeum.hu. Open Tue–Fri,10am–6pm; Sat & Sun, 9am–6pm. Ft800.

The castle's neo-Gothic silhouette provides a lovely backdrop to the lake. The building dates from the 14C, but only one tower remains from this time. The rest (19C) houses the small **Domokos Kuny Museum**, where, in addition to an archeological section, the life of the castle in the time of the Esterházy family is described *(most of the information is in Hungarian)*. The family lived in the neighboring Esterházy Palace (*see opposite)* from the 18C, and played a part in developing the town. The castle also regularly stages temporary exhibitions.

Take a break in the café upstairs to enjoy the stunning view over the lake.

Old Lake and the Old Castle
© Sebastian Szever/Shutterstock

Water mills

Water is a source of energy, hence Tata is also a town of watermills, the last of which, built in 1587, was in use until 1968. Several mills are still in existence here to a greater or lesser degree, among them Cifra-malom (Cifra Mill, *Bartók Béla u. 3)*, and **Nepomucenus Malom**, which has been well restored and now houses the **National German Minority Museum** *(Alkotmány u. 2; ✆ 381 251; kunymuzeum.hu; open Mon–Thu, 9am–4pm, Fri 9am–2pm, Sat 9am–5pm; Ft500).* As elsewhere in the area, a number of minority ethnic groups used to live in Tata, including some German-speaking communities. This interesting small museum presents a glimpse—through everyday objects (18C and 19C), carved furniture, traditional costumes, and agricultural tools—of a simple life, in which religious festivals also played a part.

Országgyűlés tér (Országgyűlés Square)

You can't miss the octagonal wooden bell tower in the center of the square, which dates from the 18C. It is proof of the many skills of Jakab Fellner, who also built **Esterházy-kastély** *(Esterházy Palace, Kastély tér, near the northern end of Öreg-tó; under renovation)*, which served as a hospital until the early 1990s. It was in the palace that the last Holy Roman emperor, Francis II, found refuge before signing the Schönbrunn Treaty with Napoleon on 14 October 1809, which effectively dissolved the Holy Roman Empire.

Szent Kereszt plébániatemplom (Parish Church of the Holy Cross)

This great church on Kossuth tér is another work by Jakab Fellner. One of the major architects of the Baroque era, Fellner settled in Tata in 1745 and lived here for most of the rest of his life until his death in 1780.

Kálvária-domb (Calvary Hill)

Fellner also built a chapel and 148ft/45m high tower on this hill. Climb to the top for a fine **view★** over the town, the Gerecse Hills, and sometimes as far as the Danube and Slovakia.

★ **Cseke-tó** (Lake Cseke)
This small, tranquil stretch of water covering around 30 acres/12ha is a lovely place for a walk, perhaps even a picnic, too. In the northeast of the town, it is bordered by an attractive wooded park of around 500 acres/200ha. People come here in search of fresh air and a little peace and quiet, with light and shade reflecting in the still water. If you venture into the park, you might come across an unusual church in the style of a folly, built using stones from an ancient abbey and Roman tombstones by French architect Charles Moreau. The national swimming team's training center is near the southern entrance to the lake.

Excursions Regional map (p212–13)

★★ **Monostori Erőd** (Fort Monostor), at **Komárom** D1
14mi/23km northwest of Tata. Duna-part 1. 540 582. fort-monostor.hu. Open Mar–Oct, 9am–5pm; Nov–Feb, 8am–5pm. Self-guided Ft1,600 (children Ft1,200). Guided tour Ft1,800. A café and souvenir shop.
Allow 3hrs for the visit and wear comfortable shoes as the fort is huge.
This is an interesting visit for two reasons. Firstly, for the town of Komárom itself (Komárno in Slovakian), the existence of which predates the fortress. The town is a curiosity since, cut in two by the Treaty of Trianon, it now sits on both banks of the Danube, straddling the Hungarian-Slovakian border. On becoming Slovakian, the northern part was named Komárno; this section retained the historic center, which is of interest for its cultural heritage. With free movement now possible between European countries, you can take a trip across the bridge into Slovakia and perhaps stop for a drink on a café terrace, before returning to Hungary once more.
Secondly, there is the immense Fort Monostor (also known as Komárom Fortress), which is awaiting classification from Unesco as a World Heritage Site. It was occupied until the end of the Cold War, as you can tell from the odd piece of rusty barbed wire that lingers beside the nearby Danube.
History of the fortress – Its construction took 21 years (1850–71). Occupying a site covering 143 acres/58ha, the building comprises 640 rooms and other

WELL FORTIFIED

The Romans built a number of strongholds in Pannonia, including **Brigetio**, one of the first and most important, which would eventually become the present-day town of Szőny, only 2mi/3km from Komárom. Many different remains were discovered during excavations of the area (fragments of frescoes and sarcophagi, as well as a collection of gold coins) that can now be seen in the National Museum in Budapest and the Domokos Kuny Museum in Tata's Old Castle (*see p234*).
Monostori erőd (Fort Monostor) was a sophisticated defensive complex built by and for the Habsburgs; it was to here that the Habsburg emperor Francis I and his court retreated in 1809 when Napoleon occupied Vienna. At the time the intention was to build a series of fortifications capable of housing 200,000 people. The northern section of this series of defensive structures is in Slovakia where the rivers Danube and Vág meet. Fort Monostor (to the west) is one of three forts that are at Komárom, along with **Csillag erőd** (Star Fort), to the east by the Danube, and **Igmándi erőd** (Igmándi Fort), which is south of the town.

Majk Camaldoli Hermitage
© Ferenc Ungor/age fotostock

spaces, divided into 14 sections. Two thousand stone masons and more than 10,000 laborers were involved in its construction. During the Second World War, it was used by the Germans as a transit camp to hold large numbers of Jews prior to their deportation. During the Cold War, the Soviets turned it into a secret munitions depot and for a time it even disappeared from the records. From the outside, sunken below ground level beside the Danube, the fortress is almost invisible.

Visit – Walking around the fort, the exhibition enables you to imagine the lives of the people who lived here, from the humble foot soldier to the senior officer. At the entrance you can learn about the commercial importance of Komárom in the 18C due to its ideal strategic position on the Danube. Various corridors lead off toward different exhibitions: military life and the blockhouses, the former stables, a collection of military vehicles dating from the Cold War (including some radar-trucks), the latrines, and a bread museum (in the fort's former bakery). The exhibits cover the different eras of the fort's history, including the Austro-Hungarian Empire and the Soviet era. These different areas are spread out across the fort so you can soak up the strange atmosphere of this now empty and abandoned space, which once would have been full of people.

If you want to make the most of your visit, it's best to book a tour with an English-speaking guide *(check the website for information on times).*

★ **Majk Kamalduli Remeteség** (Majk Camaldoli Hermitage) D2

12.5mi/20km south of Tata, between Oroszlány and Vértessomló, access is clearly signed. 560 690. Open Mon–Fr, 10am–6pm (closed Sat & Sun). Visit by guided tour only, every hour (last tour at 5pm). Ft2,000 (children Ft1,000).

If you take the road from Csákvár toward Vértessomló, take a turn off to the left to drive around the top of a small lake. A nice restaurant (Vendéglő a Négy Remetéhez) looks out over the lake and is popular with visitors to the hermitage and the local families who come to relax or fish here. Keep to the right through the trees (track suitable for vehicles) to reach the hermitage.

A chapel dedicated to the Virgin had been in existence at Majk since the 13C,

CAMALDOLESE ORDER

The Camaldolese Order was founded in Italy in the 11C by the hermit St. Romuald. Born in Ravenna, in Italy, in 952, Romuald was abbot at the nearby Basilica of St. Apolinare in Classe in 998 before founding a hermitage at Camaldoli in the Italian province of Arezzo. Romuald's teaching was originally based on the rule of St. Benedict, which advocated that the life of a monk should be lived within the community, but gradually became more austere. The headquarters of the order remained at Camaldoli and the monks could live in the monasteries or in the hermitages, depending on which path they chose to follow.

several hundred years before the land and the forests were purchased by Prince József Esterházy, provincial governor of Komárom county. The prince founded Camaldoli Hermitage in 1733. Included in his donation to the monks were part of the forest and hunting and fishing rights. The hermitage was designed by Franz Anton Pilgram and completed by Jakab Fellner, and features frescoes by Franz Anton Maulbertsch. Between 1715 and 1717, after the War of Independence against the Habsburgs, Prince Ferenc II Rákóczi took refuge at the hermitage.

The Camaldolese Order imposed silence on the monks, although they were allowed to speak two or three times a year. Each monk had a small cottage or hermitage with a basic level of comfort, paid for by the family whose coat of arms were carved above the door, and overlooking a small garden where the monks grew flowers and herbs. Each individual hermitage was entered from the garden and consisted of a decorated oratory chapel, a workplace where the monk could grade and dry herbs, a bedroom, and finally an area where he could eat and store food. The monks spent their days in fasting, silence, and prayer; many also studied the medicinal properties of plants.

The hermitage was closed down in 1781 by the Holy Roman emperor Joseph II as part of a move to reform the Church that saw the suppression of hundreds of religious houses. The whole complex was bought by Count Esterházy at the beginning of the 20C, who used it as a hunting lodge until 1945. Restoration of the estate was begun in 1980 and it makes for a very interesting and different kind of visit, especially if you are in the mood for a little peace and quiet. Of the 17 individual hermitages, only one is open to visitors although the rest are being restored. In the part that is open to the public, look out for a number of interesting frescoes depicting hunting scenes, while others house exhibitions on the Camaldolese Order, Prince Ferenc Rákóczi, and Count Móric Esterházy, who was born at Majk.

All that remains of the **church** is the bell tower, but you can climb to the top and look out over the trees to the surrounding countryside. In summer, concerts are held in this lovely tranquil setting.

★**Bokodi Horgászstég** (Bokod Floating Village) D2

2mi/3.5km west of Oroszlány, via Dózsa György utca. You will find this extraordinary fishing village a stone's throw from Oroszlány and the Majk Hermitage, on the eastern shore of Lake Bokod. A row of small wooden houses is mounted on stilts and connected by wooden walkways, looking very picturesque. To the rear is the Loszlány thermal power station, which warms the lake water, rich in fish.

ADDRESSES IN TATA

ARRIVAL/DEPARTURE

Railway station – *Vasútállomás, Révai Miklós utca 4–6.* There are frequent daily connections from Tata to Győr *(30min)*, Budapest *(1hr5min)*, and Sopron *(1hr30min)*.

STAY

AVERAGE

Sirály Panzió – *Tópart sétány 7. ✆ 30 313 2284. siralypanziotopart.hu. P 13 rooms, Ft19,500 ☕.* Recently refurbished, this charming guesthouse is conveniently located just a stone's throw from the lake. Half of its rooms overlook the lake, the other half a wooded park. Worth noting: the bedrooms have mosquito netting over the windows.

SPLASH OUT

Kristály Imperial Hotel – *Ady Endre utca 22. ✆ 383 614. hotelkristaly.eu. P ✕ 60 rooms, Ft33,000/49,000 ☕. Spa.* Designed by architect Jakab Fellner, this venerable hotel has been in business since 1770. It prides itself on being the oldest hotel still operating in Hungary and has welcomed many illustrious guests, including Archduke Franz Ferdinand and the writer Mór Jókai. It remains the jewel in the crown of the local hotel industry. The hotel restaurant, Esterházy Étterem, is worth a detour.

EAT

AVERAGE

Platán Restaurant & Café – *Kastély tér 6. ✆ 380 564. platanrestaurant.hu. Open Mon–Fri, 11am–10pm; Sat, 10am–10pm; Sun, 10am–8pm. Lunch menu Ft3,800/4,900 (Mon–Fri); à la carte Ft3,200/7,800.* Tata's top spot for elegance and gourmet food is close to the castle and the former Esterházy Palace. The food is as chic as the setting (and the clientele!). On sunny days, eat on the terrace by the lake under the shade of a 200-year-old plane tree.

TAKING A BREAK

Korzó – *Tópart utca 5–7. ✆ 597 623. korzotata.hu. Open 10.30am–9pm.* A combination of ice cream parlor, fast food outlet, and tea room, you might be surprised by the quality and tastiness of the food here, served in cardboard containers. Fairly low prices, too. In summer, there are some tables on the terrace by the lake (Öreg-tó). A good spot.

EVENTS AND FESTIVALS

Tata Baroque Festival – Held during the last week of August: concerts, exhibitions, and shows in period costume, in the town's beautiful Baroque buildings.

Őrség National Park

Őrségi Nemzeti Park

★

Vas county – area code ✆ 94

This undulating, wooded landscape has been a protected area since 2002, when it was declared a national park. The cottages in the villages still have their traditional thatched roofs and the fields are dotted with wooden bell towers. Hiking trails allow you to walk beside the River Rába, which skirts the north of the park. You might be lucky enough to see some European bison or Eurasian horses, whose presence is the result of the region's long isolation. It is like stepping back in time, a ferature that Őrség has turned into a strength, developing ecotourism and emphasizing the essence of this magical countryside.

ADDRESSES PAGE 245
Stay, Eat, Sports and Activities

INFO:
Őrség Tourist Office – *Városszer 57. Őriszentpéter. ✆ 548 034. orseginemzetipark.hu. Open Mon–Fri, 9am–4pm (15 Jun–24 Aug, also Sat & Sun, 10am–2pm).* An enthusiastic team, but not a great deal of information in English.

LOCATION:
Regional map A3 (p212–13)
Őrség National Park, in the extreme west of Hungary, covers 170sq mi/ 440sq km, on the borders with Austria and Slovakia.

PARKING:
Parking (no charge) is easy to find in the villages, which are not usually too busy. Stick to the designated zones in protected natural areas.

DON'T MISS:
The village of Magyarszombatfa; Szentgyörgyvölgy Church.

TIMING:
Allow a day to tour the national park, plus another day for a walking or cyling trip.

KIDS:
The Open-air and Pottery museums.

Exploring the park Regional map (p212–13)

A circular tour of 28mi/45km departing from Őriszentpéter. See the route marked on the Regional map.

Őriszentpéter

This village is conveniently located in the center of the park, so it makes a useful base if you are staying in the area or just want to pick up information about the park and its hiking and cycle paths *(many leave from the village, see Sports and Activities, p245)*, accommodation, and restaurants *(see tourist office above). Take the road going northwest in the direction of Szalafő.*

★ **Pityerszeri Skanzen** (Pityerszer Open-air Museum), at **Szalafő**
5mi/8km from Őriszentpéter. Pityerszer 12 (signposted). Open Apr–Nov, 10am–5pm (Jun–Aug, 6pm). Closed rest of the year. Ft1,200 (children Ft800). There's a restaurant, souvenir shop, and café. Information in Hungarian.

Bell tower in a field, Őrség National Park
© Volker Preusser/age fotostock

The museum complex consists of a dozen or so traditional white thatched cottages built in the first half of the 19C, grouped together to form a hamlet (*szer*, in Hungarian). The *szer* were once typical of the small Őrség communities. You can learn what traditional rural life was like from the furnished interiors of the cottages and farm tools of the period, which together with the farm animals and fruit trees around the site make it look very picturesque. In summer there are displays of breadmaking, pumpkin seed pressing, and traditional pastimes. The visitor center is housed in a "play barn" designed for children, where they will find a tree house and wooden toys depicting rural life. Before leaving, follow the signs to the field to see some European bison (an endangered species) and Eurasian horses grazing.

Return to Őriszentpéter and drive southwest in the direction of Magyarszombatfa (7.5mi/12km).

4

★ Magyarszombatfa

Leave the car to walk through this delightful small village with thatched country cottages to get a feel for the traditional rural communities of the area.

Fazekasház (Pottery Museum) – *Fő út 52. 30 865 1550. Open Apr–Sept, Tue–Sun, 10am–5pm. Closed rest of the year. Ft300 (children Ft200).* A workshop (1760, well preserved), where a guide will explain *(in Hungarian)* the village's specific area of expertise. In the past pottery was a way for the peasants to earn money to supplement the poor return on their land. By the beginning of the 20C, around 100 families were producing pottery here, but today the number is down to around ten.

Gödörházi harangláb (Bell tower in a field) – *Around 1.25mi/2km from the village. Gödörházi utca 74. No charge.* The practice of erecting bell towers made of wood in the middle of fields is special to the area. A decree from the Habsburg emperor restricted their height, but this one, with its "skirt" of wooden shingles, is one of the most striking (1790).

Continue in the direction of Velemér.

★ **Velemér Church** (Roman Catholic church)
Fő utca 54 (at the end of Fő utca, surrounded by trees, at the entrance to the village).
A lovely little Romanesque church (Church of the Holy Trinity) dating from the 13C. The beautiful 14C frescoes inside were painted by János Aquila.
Continue south to Szentgyörgyvölgy.

★ **Szentgyörgyvölgy Church** (Calvinist church)
Kossuth Lajos utca 33. Open Tue–Sun, 8am–4pm.
This church (1517) is unique in that its **painted ceiling** (1829), one of the most beautiful of its kind, is quite at odds with the conventional minimalist Calvinist style. The individual ceiling sections represent clouds in the blue sky above, while a central motif symbolizes the sun. The paintings are the work of an amateur, a retired teacher, who completed them at the age of 77!

Excursions Regional map (p212–13)

★★ **Ják Abbey Church** A3
26mi/42km northeast of Őriszentpéter by Rte 8.
The small community of Ják is home to a splendid Romanesque abbey church which, along with Zsámbék and Bélapátfalva, is one of the most outstanding examples of Romanesque architecture in Hungary. Work began in 1220 on the orders of Márton Jáki Nagy (who also gave his name to the village) and it was dedicated to St. George in 1256. Being responsible for the commissioning and building of ecclesiastical structures such as monasteries and churches at this time was a clear demonstration of an individual's power and importance. It also had a bearing on a building's design where, for example, a gallery might be reserved for members of the nobility. The church survived the Mongol invasion in the 13C intact, but it has undergone numerous restorations since then. The last was completed in 1904 by the architect Frigyes Schulek, who built the Fisherman's Bastion in Budapest. Most of the statues around the doorway, and those of the tympanum in particular, were replaced, stained glass windows were added, and some Baroque features removed.
The tiny (in comparison) Szent Jakab-kápolna (St. James Chapel) nearby was built for the (non-monastic) villagers.

Batthyány-Strattmann-kastély (Batthyány-Strattmann Mansion), at **Körmend** A3
9.5mi/15km south of Ják. Museum open May–Oct, Tue–Sun, 10am–6pm; Nov–Apr, Tue–Sat, 10am–4pm. Ft1,200.
Located right on the Austrian border, stop off at Körmend to see this splendid large mansion, a superb example of elegant, classic architecture. It houses the Dr. László Batthyány-Strattman Museum, which includes exhibits featuring the Batthyány family (it was their main residence 1716–1945) and a small shoe museum in the courtyard. Dr. Batthyány-Strattman was an eye specialist who would treat the less well-off free of charge. With a bit of luck you might also catch one of the music concerts that are sometimes held in the grounds.

Szombathely A2
19mi/30km north of Körmend.
Tourist Office, Király utca 1. 317 269. szombathelypont.hu. Open Mon–Fri, 9am–5pm; Sat, 10am–4pm.

Ják Abbey Church
© Laszlo66/Shutterstock

Szombathely is a lively and dynamic city. Founded during the Roman era, it can boast some impressive remains from that time, such as the shrine dedicated to the goddess Isis, where the Roman emperor **Septimus Severus** was crowned in AD193. The Romans named the city Savaria; it was situated on the famous Amber Road, several cobbled stretches of which can still be seen today. By the 18C and the reign of Queen Maria Theresa, the city had been elevated to an episcopal see. Szombathely took advantage of its new-found status as a religious center to build palaces and Baroque basilicas. However, this kind of grandeur was at odds with the Communist regime and the city sank into a kind of lethargy in the 1950s, before the fall of the Berlin Wall in 1989 had a reinvigorating effect.

Püspöki Palota (Bishop's Palace) – *Berzsenyi tér. ✆ 312 056. Open Tue–Sat, 9am–5pm. Visit by guided tour only: 9.30am, 11am, 12.30pm, 2pm, 3.30pm. Ft1,500 (children Ft700).* The Bishop's Palace and **Szombathely Cathedral** *(opposite the Bishop's Palace)* are the two principal buildings of interest. Commissioned by Bishop János Szily at the end of the 18C, they were designed by the Viennese architect Melchior Hefele, as were many of the buildings in the neighborhood, lending it an overall architectural harmony.

On the first (ground) floor of the Bishop's Palace, the Sala Terrena, Hungary's first lapidary collection, contains frescoes by István Dorfmeister depicting the city's Roman ruins. Religious objects and vestments, missals, and Bibles are displayed in the room, along with photographs of the cathedral before the destruction of the Second World War.

Romkert (Ruin Garden) – You can see some Roman remains (discovered in 1938) in a park behind the cathedral. Colonia Claudia Savaria, the colony founded by the Roman emperor Claudius in 43, grew until it became Upper Pannonia's principal city, and a number of important roads intersected here. You can still see some mosaics from the basilica dedicated to St. Quirin that also occupied this site.

Iseum (Temple of Isis) – *Rákóczi Ferenc utca 6–8. iseum.savariamuseum.hu. Open Wed–Sat, 10am–5pm. Ft1,600 (under 18s no charge).* A replica in concrete of the Roman temple to Isis, incorporating several original details. Operas and concerts are performed in this setting each year.

Opposite the Iseum is a former **synagogue**, with two onion domes. It is now the Bartók Concert Hall and hosts orchestral concerts amid superb acoustics.

Savaria Múzeum – *Kisfaludy Sándor utca 9. ✆ 500 720. savariamuseum.hu. Open Tue–Sun, 10am–6pm. Ft1,000.* The large museum building opens onto a pleasant garden. The exhibits focus on local history, with folk art and objects made by shepherds and herdsmen, as well as items and household utensils from the Roman era, glass vials, containers, and so on. It also traces the destruction wrought in the area during the Second World War.

Kámoni Arborétum – *North of the town center, which can be approached via either of two main roads, Paragvári út and 11-es-Huszár út. Visitor and Ecotourism Center and entrance on Szent Imre herceg útja. kamoniarboretum.hu. Open Apr–Sept, 9am–7pm; Oct–Mar, 9am–dusk.* An extensive area with more than 3,000 trees and plants; a great place in which to escape the heat of summer.

Vasi Múzeumfalu (Vasi Open-air Museum)– *Árpád út 30. savariamuseum.hu. Open Tue–Sun, 9am–6pm; Apr–May & Sept–Nov, 5pm. Ft1,200.* Learn about everyday life in the region between the 18C and 20C.

If you feel in need of some exercise (walking or canoeing), or a drink or snack overlooking some cooling water, there are two lakes nearby, **Horgásztó** and **Csónakázótó**.

ADDRESSES IN ŐRSÉG NATIONAL PARK

STAY

Magyarszombatfa

AVERAGE

Ginti Panzió – *Fő út 78. ✆ 30 903 5940. ginti-orseg.hu.* P ✕ *18 rooms, Ft19,000* . *Restaurant, Ft2,200/4,500.* An excellent guesthouse that is ideal for families. The rooms are warm and spotlessly clean, with pine furniture. There's a garden and swimming pool and games for children. A good restaurant with a choice of specialties that make use of local produce. Plenty of parking space, too.

A TREAT

Kosbor Panzió – *Fő út 6. ✆ 30 952 2478. kosborpanzio.hu.* P *4 suites and 5 rooms, Ft25,000/45,000* . Luxury, calm and … a rural location. This delightful place with its light, bright rooms, traditional Hungarian furniture, and embroidered linen is our personal favorite. It has the feeling of a warm and cozy family home, with sun loungers on which you can relax outside.

Szombathely

SPLASH OUT

Artis Boutique Hotel – *Hefele Menyhért utca 2. ✆ 900 600. artishotel.hu.* P ✕ *28 rooms* . *Restaurant, Ft2,790/5,990.* The design of this brand new hotel is unusual for provincial Hungary. The furniture is bespoke, the bedding high end, and the fittings are luxurious. This is a top quality hotel in the center of town, where staff upgrade you when space permits. A fashionable restaurant on the first (ground) floor. As well as brasserie-style dishes and meat grilled over a wood fire, a variety of tapas is also available.

EAT

Őriszentpéter

BUDGET

Bognár Étterem – *Kovácsszer 96. ✆ 30 237 2566. bognaretterem.hu. Open 10am–10pm. Ft2,190/4,890.* This tavern is popular with the locals and offers the chance to try Őrség specialties such as buckwheat soup or venison stew, all accompanied by Hungarian wines. The same family manage the restaurant in the Pityerszer Ecomusem at Szalafő *(see p240).*

A TREAT

Pajta Bisztró – *Templomszer 7. ✆ 70 416 3388. pajta.hu. Open Wed–Fri, 10am–10pm; Sat–Sun, 9am–10pm. A tasting menu Ft8,500/13,500.* Rural Hungarian meals are on the menu here. This "barn" (*pajta*, in Hungarian)—a modern building of brick, wood, and glass—has good views of the lush countryside and tables set up on decking. Dishes made with local produce and a superb wine list.

SPORTS AND ACTIVITIES

Hiking – A dozen or so marked walking trails set off from Őriszentpéter and are a good way to explore the area. Itineraries and brochures are available from the tourist office at Őriszentpéter *(see p240).*

Cycling – Various rental outlets are open during the summer months, mainly in Szalafő *(for information visit orseg.info/en).*

Debrecen and the Northern Great Plain 5

Michelin National Map 732

Hajdú-Bihar, Jász-Nagykun-Szolnok, Szabolcs-Szatmár-Bereg counties

Hungarian Grey cattle, Hortobágy National Park

© Manfred Mehlig/age fotostock

DEBRECEN AND THE NORTHERN GREAT PLAIN

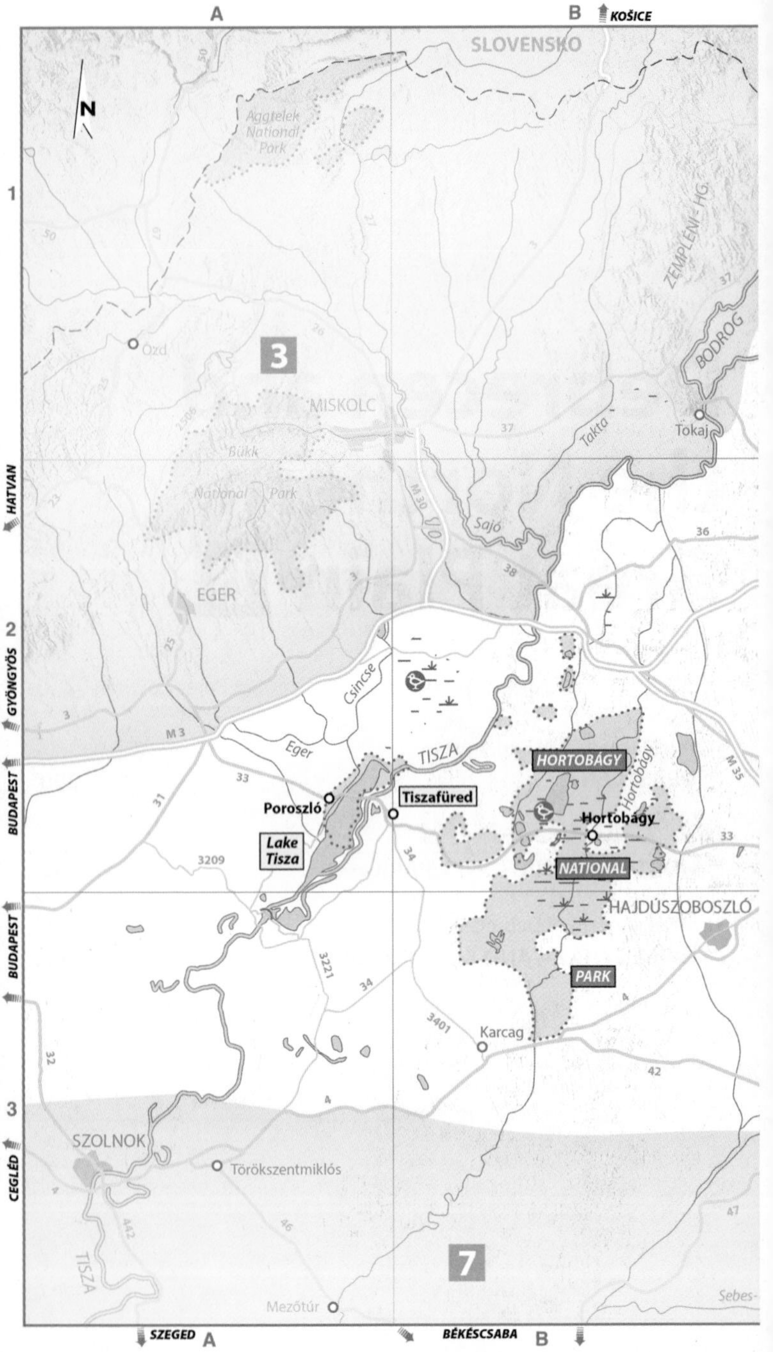

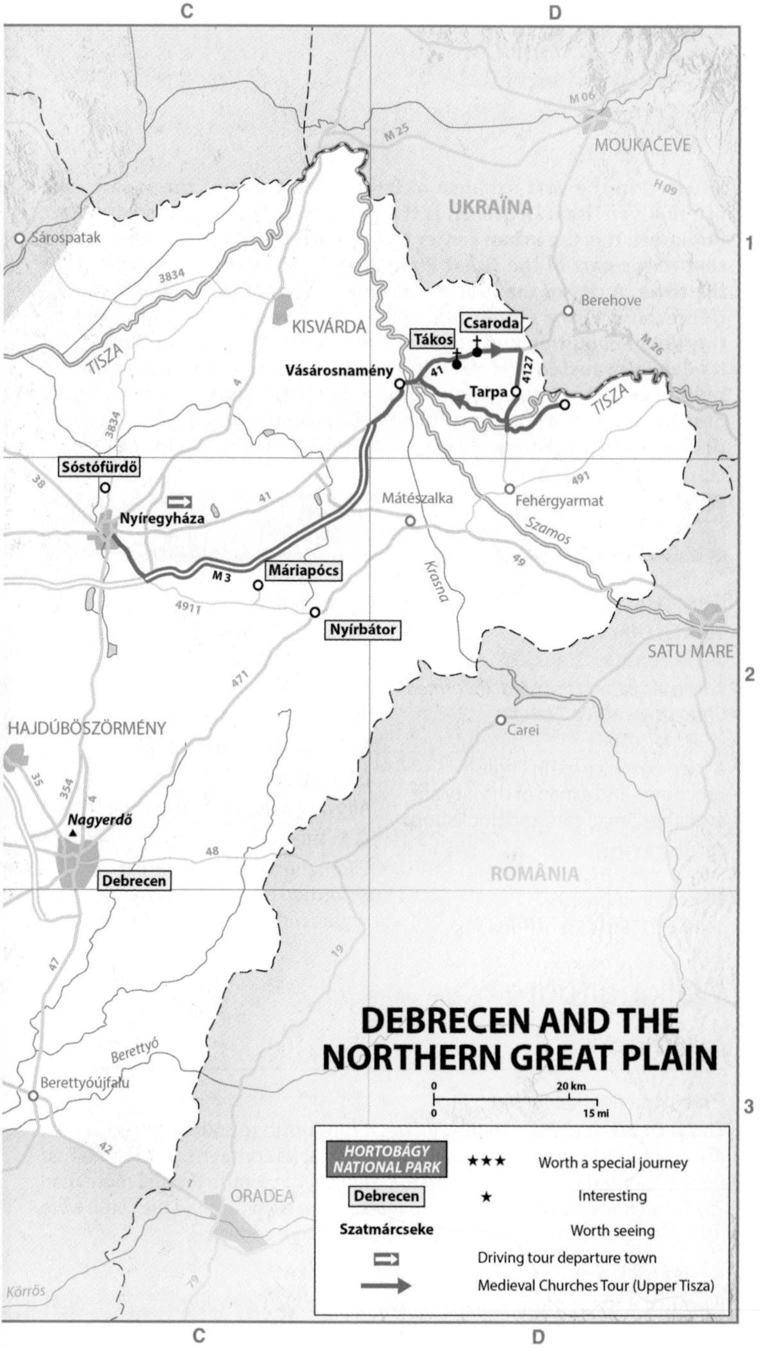
C
D
MOUKAČEVE
UKRAÏNA
Sárospatak
1
3834
KISVÁRDA
Berehove
Csaroda
Tákos
TISZA
Vásárosnamény
41
4127
Tarpa
TISZA
3834
4
Sóstófürdő
38
41
491
Mátészalka
Fehérgyarmat
Nyíregyháza
Szamos
Krasna
49
M 3
Máriapócs
4911
Nyírbátor
SATU MARE
2
471
Carei
HAJDÚBÖSZÖRMÉNY
35
354
4
Nagyerdő
48
Debrecen
ROMÂNIA
47
19
DEBRECEN AND THE NORTHERN GREAT PLAIN
Berettyó
Berettyóújfalu
0
20 km
0
15 mi
3
42
HORTOBÁGY NATIONAL PARK
★★★ Worth a special journey
Debrecen
★ Interesting
Szatmárcseke
Worth seeing
Driving tour departure town
Medieval Churches Tour (Upper Tisza)
ORADEA
1
79
Körrös
C
D

Debrecen

★

Population 202,214 – Hajdú-Bihar county – area code ✆ 52

Situated in the vast expanse of land in the heart of the region east of the River Tisza, Debrecen is the country's second largest city after Budapest. It is the urban center of the Hortobágy, the Puszta wetland that forms part of the Great Plain lying to the east and southeast of the town. A city of the Protestant Reformation, the "Calvinist Rome," Debrecen is also a city of the people. It served as the capital during the 1848 Revolution and again in 1944 during the Second World War. Its Calvinist austerity is reflected in the architecture of the imposing buildings lining the vast main square. But Debrecen is also a lively city of students, with a vibrant cultural life, epitomized by the fine museum dedicated to contemporary art (MODEM), which opened in 2006.

ADDRESSES PAGE 256
Eat, Stay, Baths, Bars, Events and Festivals

INFO:
Tourist Office
Debrecen map B1 (p252)
Kálvin tér, behind the Great Reformed Church. www.debrecen.hu. ✆ 20 450 0506.
A friendly welcome in English. Brochures and a map of the city are available. Small café and bookshop.

LOCATION:
Regional map C2 (p248–49); Debrecen map (p252)
145mi/233km east of Budapest.

PARKING:
Booking a hotel with parking is recommended.

DON'T MISS:
The Great Reformed Church; Déri Museum; and the MODEM.

TIMING:
Allow two days to explore the city.

KIDS:
Climb the tower of the Great Reformed Church; go swimming at Aquaticum.

Walking tour Debrecen map (p252)

CITY CENTER B1–2

Piac utca (Market Street)
This is Debrecen's main thoroughfare. It runs north to south from Kálvin tér, the city's main square, to the railway station at its southern end. It is named for the fairs and markets that used to be held in the area. In the 16C more than 75,000 animals would be brought to market here each year and the cattle were driven all over Europe by the *hajdúk* (shepherds or drovers).

★★ **Nagytemplom** (Great Reformed Church) B1
Piac utca 4–6. ✆ 614 160. www.nagytemplom.hu. Open Jun–Jul, 9am–6pm; Sept–Oct & Mar–May, 9am–4pm; Nov–Feb, 10am–3pm (Sat, 9am–1pm; Sun, noon–4pm). Church Ft700 and Ft800 to climb the towers. Combined ticket with the Reformed College Ft1,800.

From town to city

A PROSPEROUS PLACE

By the 9C the Slovaks had settled here and named the area **Dobre Zliem** (fertile earth), which eventually morphed into the name of the city we know today, Debrecen.

The town was promoted to the rank of city in 1218 by King András II and in 1361 was given franchise rights by Louis the Great. In 1405 King Sigismund awarded Debrecen the same rights as Buda and it became a free city. It was granted the right to hold three fairs per year, which within a hundred years had increased to eight. Debrecen prospered thanks to its trade in livestock, fur, salt, and the skill of its craftsmen, until it became one of the richest cities in Hungary. The city bourgeoisie owned great estates in the western plain that were worked by peasants. These farmers, who were horse and cattle breeders, would drive the animals traded at the fairs in Debrecen across hundreds of miles. The **hajdúk**, the drovers, would travel armed and were peasant-soldiers who also fought against the Habsburgs when the need arose.

After the construction of the railway line from Debrecen to Szolnok in 1857, the process of industrialization began, with the production of sugar, tobacco, and furniture contributing further to the prosperity of the city.

CALVINIST ROME

In 1536 the Debrecen population began to adopt Reformed Protestantism and the city became a Calvinist center. The **Reformed College** was founded in 1538 and three years later the university's first printing presses helped spread the word for the Protestant Reformation. From 1541 onward, the country was divided between the Ottomans, Habsburgs, and the Transylvanian princes, but thanks to skilful diplomacy, Debrecen managed to keep on good terms with each of them. In 1693 Leopold I granted Debrecen the status of an independent royal city.

Under the Habsburgs the city was threatened and burned several times. During the 1848 Revolution and the struggle for independence, it became the seat of the national assembly, which in 1849 voted to reject Imperial authority and dismiss the house of Habsburg. **Lajos Kossuth** was proclaimed governor of Hungary and for several months Debrecen was the capital of the country and the guardian of its liberty. However, after the eventual military collapse, the Austrians took power once more.

A BORDER TOWN

After the Treaty of Trianon (*see p354*), Debrecen became a border town, with an influx of thousands of people returning from other territories no longer part of Hungary. Two decades later, in the final days of December 1944, on the initiative of the Russians, a provisional government was installed at Debrecen. It was this government that organized the municipal and general elections in September and November 1945. The city's industrialization program continued in the 1950s and in October 1956 the Revolution began in Debrecen with demonstrations held in the city, even before those in Budapest.

Today Debrecen is eastern Hungary's economic, administrative, cultural, and educational center, with many companies based here, along with the 30,000 students who come to study each year at the University of Debrecen.

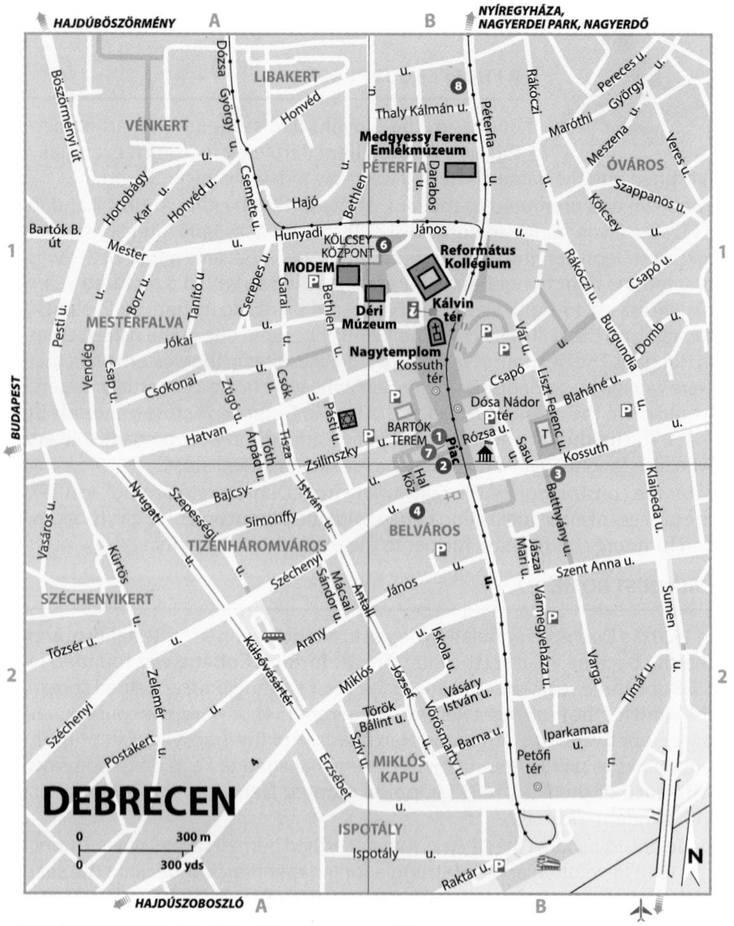

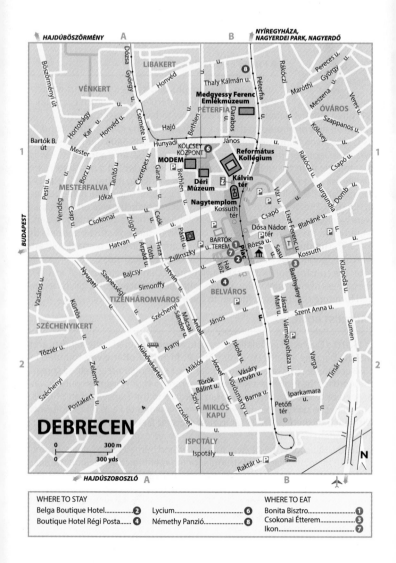

WHERE TO STAY		WHERE TO EAT
Belga Boutique Hotel ❷	Lycium ❻	Bonita Bisztro ❶
Boutique Hotel Régi Posta ❹	Némethy Panzió ❽	Csokonai Étterem ❸
		Ikon ❼

The Great Reformed Church is the largest Protestant church in Hungary. Able to accommodate close to 3,000 worshipers, it was built in 1822 and impresses mainly due to its size. The interior is white and understated, but includes a very fine organ that is often played at rehearsals, services, and concerts. The church has also preserved Lajos Kossuth's chair (*see p251*). The towers are accessible by elevator or by climbing the 350 steps. From close to 200ft/60m above the ground, you can enjoy a magnificent view of the city and see the Rákóczi bell that weighs more than 4 tons/3,800kg. Exhibits in the church and the towers trace its history and that of the congregation. Try the walkway between the two towers for some good views.

Great Reformed Church
© Egmont Strigl/imageBROKER/age fotostock

★ **Református Kollégium** (Reformed College) B1

Kálvin tér 16. ☏ 614 370. www.muzeum.drk.hu. Open Mon–Sat, 10am–4pm (Nov–Feb, closed Sat). Closed public holidays. Ft1,200. Combined ticket with the Great Reformed Church Ft1,800. Guided tour in English (reserve ahead) Ft5,000.

The present building was constructed in the neo-classical style between 1803 and 1816, and was then enlarged between 1870 and 1894. The Reformed College has enjoyed a first-class reputation since the Middle Ages. For many years it was the most important educational institution in northern Hungary, supported and maintained not just by the nobility but also by the financiers of the day and, of course, also by the Reformed Church. The present-day college was built on the site of the original 16C building. Until the end of the 18C, discipline was very strict with students having to get up at 3am.

★ **Museum** – This is primarily devoted to the history of the college, whose reputation was such that students came to study from almost every country in Europe. Also displayed on the first (ground) floor is a fine collection of **religious objects★**. Of particular note are the **kopjafa★**, a type of carved wooden pole that marks the location of graves. On the walls lining the staircase that leads to the library and oratory are frescoes (1938) depicting the college's history. A stained glass window on the second floor landing remembers a former student who became a famous mathematician, Oswald Thoroczkai, who was also head of the college's department of philosophy and mathematics.

★ **Library** – This contains the greatest number of documents concerning the Reformed Church. There are more than 500,000 volumes, among which are nearly 200 editions and different translations of the Bible.

★ **Oratory** – As the birthplace of Hungarian Calvinism, Debrecen is a city anxious to preserve its independence and has always asserted its desire for freedom. It is therefore not surprising that it was at Debrecen that the Hungarians proclaimed their independence from the Habsburgs and it was in the oratory that the Hungarian parliament announced that Hungary had passed this vote in May 1849. The names of the deputies who were present,

Library, Reformed College

including Lajos Kossuth, are inscribed on copper panels. A century later, in 1944, a provisional assembly was established at Debrecen while waiting for Budapest and Hungary to be liberated from Nazi Germany.

★★ **Déri Múzeum** (Déri Museum) AB1

Déri tér 1. ✆ 322 207. www.derimuzeum.hu. Open Tue–Sun, 10am–6pm. Ft1,800 (includes entrance to the Medgyessy Ferenc Emlékmúzeum).

Standing in front of the museum, you might like to pause to admire the four sculptures by Ferenc Medgyessy representing Science, Art, Archeology, and Ethnography. The museum takes its name from its principal donor, Frigyes Déri, who died in 1924. Born in Hungary, Déri studied in Vienna and manufactured silk fabrics. He had no particular connection with Debrecen but as an art collector he wanted to donate his collection to a public museum in a university city. The museum was built between 1926 and 1928 and has been renovated during the last ten years. It stages excellent permanent exhibitions. Once inside the museum, look out for the **Mihály Munkácsy triptych★★**, the museum's masterpiece, in a room specially dedicated to the three paintings that form it—*Christ before Pilate* (1881), *Golgotha* (1884), and *Ecce Homo* (1896). This monumental work (the canvasses measure more than 13ft/4m by 20ft/6m) depicts the Passion of Christ from the confrontation with his accusers and judges until his death on the Cross. Sadly Munkácsy (1844–1900) never saw his three canvasses exhibited together in his lifetime.

Archeological collection – This detailed exhibition (explanations in English) on funeral rites since the Neolithic period begins notably with remains found during local tumuli excavations. It continues upstairs with an exhibition of two superb Egyptian sarcophagi and their mummies, brought to Hungary by the Archduke Franz Ferdinand and then bought at auction in 1918 by Déri.

Japanese collection – On display are samurai swords, weapons, and armor from the Edo period (17–18C).

Weapons collection – The oldest weapons date back to the 15C and come from Europe. Other helmets and swords are from the Ottoman period.

Gallery of paintings – Here you can see canvasses dating from the 17–19C; they are principally portraits but there are also illustrations of some city buildings that are no longer standing.

Local life in the 19C and 20C – A street of small stores and craftsmen's workshops, which have been reconstructed to evoke everyday life as it was lived in Debrecen over the last 200 years.

★ **MODEM** (Center for Modern and Contemporary Art) A1
Baltazár Dezső tér 1. ✆ 525 018. www.modemart.hu. Open Tue–Sun, 10am–6pm. Ft1,200.
MODEM is the country's largest space dedicated to contemporary art outside the capital. Opened in 2012, the building provides a superb setting for exhibitions. There are no permanent collections as the aim is to keep things at the forefront of the contemporary art scene, presenting work by Hungarian and international artists through different temporary exhibitions and showcasing the visual arts.

★ **Medgyessy Ferenc Emlékmúzeum** (Ferenc Medgyessy Museum) B1
Péterfia utca 28. www.derimuzeum.hu. Open Tue–Sun, 10am–6pm. Ft1,800 (includes entrance to the Déri Museum).
This museum, housed in an attractive white building, is dedicated to local sculptor **Ferenc Medgyessy** (1881–1958) who, as well as being a native of Debrecen, was without doubt the greatest Hungarian sculptor of the 20C. His works include dancers in relief, equestrian statues, and bronze pieces such as a mother feeding her baby, and demonstrate a powerful understanding of humanity and human sensibilities. **Debrecen Irodalom Háza** is at the same address (Debrecen House of Literature, entry included in the museum admission ticket). It covers the life and work of the city's notable writers, although all the information is in Hungarian.

Pásti utcai Zsinagóga (Pásti Street Orthodox Synagogue) A1
Pásti utca 4. ✆ 415 861. www.dzsh.hu. Open Mon–Fri, 8am–4pm (Oct–Apr, 3pm). Closed public holidays. Ft1,200.
Built at the beginning of the 1880s, this Orthodox synagogue with its distinctive pink exterior was renovated in 2015 and turned into a museum dedicated to the history and traditions of Debrecen's Jewish community. A memorial in the garden pays hommage to the 6,000 Debrecen Jews who were victims of the Holocaust. Nearby, in Kápolnási utca, Debreceni zsinagóga is another synagogue that has been renovated, but remains a place of worship.

BEYOND THE CITY CENTER B1, off map

Nagyerdő (Great Forest)
A lovely landscaped wooded park in the northern outskirts of the city, with paths for walking and cycling beneath the shade of the trees, a lake with ducks, and facilities such as a children's play area. One part accommodates the university's faculty of medicine and another Aquaticum, the city's vast water park, hotel, and spa (*see Addresses p257*), plus an unusual water tower that can be seen poking out above the trees.
Nagyerdei Víztorony (Water tower) – *Pallagi utca 7. Open Fri, Sat & Wed 10am–1am, Sun & Mon 10am–10pm, Thu 10am–midnight. Ft900.* As well as carrying out the function for which it was originally intended, today this hundred-year-old water tower also houses a café, concert venue, and exhibition space, while the central column has been transformed into a climbing wall—plus you can admire the view out over the trees if you decide to climb to the top (112ft/34m).

ADDRESSES IN DEBRECEN

See Debrecen map (p252)

ARRIVAL/DEPARTURE

Train – Direct every hour between 5.55am and 6.55pm, from Budapest-Nyugati Station to Debrecen *(journey time 3hrs)*; return from 5.57am.

STAY

BUDGET

8 **Némethy Panzió** – B1 – *Péterfia utca 55. 444 480. www.nemethypanzio.hu. 13 rooms, Ft10,900. Ft1,300.* A little away from the center but not far from the Great Reformed Church, this smart little guesthouse has simple but very well-kept rooms. A warm welcome.

AVERAGE

10 **Boutique Hotel Régi Posta** – B2 – *Széchenyi utca 6. 325 325. www.regiposta.hu. 12 rooms from Ft16,800.* The name of this 17C building translates as "The Old Post Office" and refers to its original incarnation before it was turned into the hotel it is today. It has a pleasant ambience, with each room decorated according to a theme (Romantic Room, Tuscan Room, Cart Room with a bed in a Wild West-style wagon, …). The restaurant serves top notch Hungarian cuisine and also has a terrace.

A TREAT

2 **Belga Boutique Hotel** B1–2 – *Piac utca 29. 536 373. www.belgahotel.hu. 9 rooms from Ft22,900.* Opened in 2019 above a restaurant of the same name, this hotel has the advantage of an enviable location in Debrecen's main square plus brand new rooms. Parking (no charge) is available at the Boutique Hotel Régi Posta.

SPLASH OUT

4 **Lycium** – B1 – *Kossuth Lajos utca. 506 600. www.hotellycium.hu. (charges apply). 87 rooms, Ft49,000.* A modern hotel that is part of the Kölcsey conference center and adjacent to MODEM, offering comfortable rooms equipped to international standards. True, the breakfast room is rather impersonal, but the congenial pool-sauna-jacuzzi area on the top floor largely compensates for this.

EAT

BUDGET

1 **Bonita Bisztro** – B1 – *Piac utca 21. 216 816. Open noon–10pm. Pizza from Ft1,199.* Although you're not in Italy, there's no need to deny yourself a pizza. Here you can enjoy one that is so authentic and delicious it could have come straight from a Neapolitan wood-fired oven. They also serve good salads and tasty pasta dishes.

AVERAGE

7 **Ikon** – B1 – *Piac utca 23. (30) 555 77 66. Open Mon–Sat, 11.30am–11pm (Sun, 3.30pm). Main dishes Ft1,990/5,290, lunch menu Mon–Sat Ft3,290.* This fashionable city address deserves its good reputation. The tasty dishes are attractively presented, such as the spring risotto with spinach and wild garlic. The lunch menu is excellent value. And in addition there's a very pleasant terrace and a good wine list.

3 **Csokonai Étterem** – B2 – *Kossuth utca 21. 410 802. Open noon–11pm. Main dishes*

Ft2,690/4,690. This famous city restaurant is opposite Csokonai Theater, the oldest in Debrecen. You can eat in the restaurant's attractive vaulted cellar, decorated in a slightly glitzy style, or on the terrace. The Hungarian cuisine is excellent.

TAKING A BREAK

Black Sheep – *Csapó utca 23. Open 7.30am–7.45pm.* The coffee is roasted on the premises and customers can drink it outside on the terrace or inside amid exposed brickwork painted white, on which the black sheep in question looms large. Also on offer are homemade lemonades, some good sandwiches, and cakes.

Cut and Coffee – *Hal köz 3. Open 8am–10pm (Sat, 9am–10pm; Sun, 2pm–10pm).* An unusual combination in that this bistro, where the coffee is excellent, has a hair salon upstairs. Downstairs they serve tasty sandwiches and cakes, and face a pretty square where other coffee shops and eateries are compete to tempt you to their tables.

Levendula – *Csapó utca 25. Open 10am–7pm.* The house specialty is flavored with lavender, which also provides this small ice cream store with its name. Buy an ice cream to take out or sit on the terrace and enjoy it in peace.

Gara Cukrászda – *Kálvin tér 6. Open 9am–7pm.* For several decades, the citizens of Debrecen have been dropping in here for a coffee and a cake. Equally good are the excellent ice creams.

BARS

Roncsbár – *Csapó utca 27. Open Mon & Tue, 11am–midnight; Wed & Thu, 11am–2am; Fri & Sat, 11am–4am. Closed Sun.* In the style of Budapest's ruin bars with very eclectic decor (cymbals suspended from the ceiling, lots of bric-a-brac), this is the perfect place to have a drink, eat a huge burger, and listen to music (live bands at weekends).

Divino – *Piac utca 18. Open Mon–Thu, 5pm–midnight (Fri & Sat, 2am). Closed Sun.* In the heart of the city's main square, a wine bar offering a wide selection of Hungarian wines. A cool, young atmosphere.

BATHS

Aquaticum – *Nagyerdei park 1. ☎ 514 174. spa.aquaticum.hu. Open 11am–8pm (Fri–Sun & public holidays, 10am–9pm). Water park Ft3,200/day. A supplement for the thermal baths and saunas. A restaurant and hotel on site.* Fun and relaxation are on the agenda beneath the 217ft/66m diameter dome, where you can bathe in a tropical paradise. There are also children's pools, waterslides, Sauna World, and a wellness center. In addition to the covered baths, there some new baths, bringing the total surface area to nearly 7,176sq yds/6,000sq m.

EVENTS AND FESTIVALS

Campus Fesztivál
In the Great Forest (*see p255*) near Nagyerdő stadium, rock and pop concerts over 4 days in late July attracting big crowds. *campusfesztival.hu*

Virágkarnevál
The city is filled with flowers for a week in mid August. *debreceniviragkarneval.hu*

Bor-és Jazznapok
Wine and concerts for jazz lovers over 4 days in early August in the Great Forest (*see p255*). *boresjazz.hu*

The Hortobágy Puszta

A VAST PLAIN

The Hortobágy Puszta consists of the **Hortobágy National Park** (Hortobágyi Nemzeti Park), the first and largest national park to be created in Hungary, in 1973. The park was listed as a Unesco World Heritage Site in 1999; it covers 290sq mi/750sq km of protected nature reserve and is the largest wetland in Europe. Far from civilization and only sparsely inhabited, it is a sanctuary for animals and in particular for migratory birds, providing them with a vital stopover between September and November. In spring look up at the treetops or on top of the electricity poles in Hortobágy village to see the storks' nests. The village, which has a population of around 2,000 inhabitants, is in the center of the park.

A day trip to, or better still a stay in, this region will leave you with some lasting memories, especially if you manage to see the swirling spectacle of the *délibáb* ("mirage" in English). The way dark clouds suddenly appear to blot out the sky and hide the sun is strange and otherworldly.

ONCE POPULATED, NOW WILD

The first inhabitants of the Puszta, in around 2000BC, were nomadic tribes, traces of whom have been found in burial mounds. At the end of the 9C, the Magyar tribes arrived in the Carpathian Basin and settled in the area around the River Tisza. By the end of the 12C, numerous dwellings and places of worship had been established on the site of the present-day village of Hortobágy. These sheep-farming communities were then wiped off the map by the invading Mongols and Ottomans. The now empty plain was used as grazing land, peopled only by *pásztor* (shepherds), *csikós* (horse-herdsmen), *gulyás* (cowherds), and *kondás* (swineherds). *Csárdas* (inns) built for travelers and merchants began to spring up at the end of the 17C, although very few remain in existence today. During the 19C the Tisza was regulated for flood control, leading to a change in water levels. This solved the flooding problem but in turn dried out the land and turned it into a salty, sterile plain. In the 1950s, in order to bring fertility back to the barren areas, irrigation channels were cut and today crops are grown and livestock is farmed on parts of the Puszta once more. (*See Lake Tisza, p262.*)

IMMORTALIZED IN HUNGARIAN POETRY

The immense plain extends as far as the eye can see, with nothing to obscure the view. There are some gentle undulations in the land, each mound seemingly topped with a traditional T-shaped pendulum well (to bring up water), which stand out against the sky to dramatic effect. This impressive expanse seems to go on forever, like the sea, a place where the sky and the earth meet at the horizon. The landscape here fits perfectly the idea that many people have of Hungary—and duly appears on many postcards—a wild land carrying within it the soul of the nation. For Sándor Petőfi, a local boy and great Hungarian poet, it was a land of freedom:

"Puszta, Puszta, you are the image of freedom,
And freedom, you are the God of my spirit!
My God, freedom, I am only living in order to die once for you..."

Hortobágy National Park

Hortobágy Nemzeti Park

★★★

Hajdú-Bihar county – area code ✆ 52

Meaning "deserted" and "abandoned," Puszta is an apt name for this vast region of steppe, which is also Europe's largest plain. Pasture and wetland make up this area, a combination of salt marsh and sandy terrain, which the local inhabitants share with animals, mainly horses, and birds. The birdlife is indeed rich, with the chance to see many species, from herons and egrets to great bustards and cranes. In spring the ground is covered with wild flowers and the air fragrant with the scent of sweet briar roses. Unesco describes the Puszta as an outstanding cultural landscape, where there is harmonious interaction between people and the land, while to the Hungarians it is a symbol of freedom.

ADDRESSES PAGE 263
Eat, Stay, Shopping, Sports and Activities

INFO:

Tourist Office – *Petőfi tér 9, in the center of the village. ✆ 589 000. www.hnp.hu. Open Apr–Jun & Sept–Nov, 8am–4pm; Jul–Aug, 9am–5pm. Closed Dec.* In the Hortobágy National Park Visitor Center. There is a small exhibition on cranes and useful information on the park. You can also buy entry tickets to the park and hire bikes (Ft1,500/day). Plus a small souvenir store.

LOCATION:

Regional map B2–3 (p248–49)
Hortobágy is 25mi/40km west of the city of Debrecen.

DON'T MISS:

A horse-drawn carriage ride across the Puszta from Máta Stud Farm and then a walk around the Hortobágy Ponds to see the birds.

TIMING:

Allow a minimum of one whole day, more if you enjoy hiking and wide open spaces.

KIDS:

The Puszta Animal Park and the Bird Hospital.

Exploring the park from Hortobágy village

Regional map (p248–49)

HORTOBÁGY B2

The village of Hortobágy has given its name to the national park and provides some good opportunities to learn about the Puszta before you head off to explore it yourself. Within just a small area of the village you can visit several museums, get close to animals, and enjoy the atmosphere of a traditional inn. Only the Máta Stud Farm and the Great Fishponds are located a few miles from the center.

To explore the park (by bicycle or on foot), you will need to buy an entrance ticket at the tourist office *(see above, Ft1,000/1 day or Ft3,000/7 days).*

★ **Kilenclyukú híd** (Nine-arch Bridge)
This stone bridge is probably the most famous and also the longest (300ft/92m) in Hungary). Its long span with nine arches (*kilenc* = nine, *lyuk* = hole) is much photographed and features on the pages of many a book or magazine, having come to symbolize the Puszta wetland for many. Completed in 1833 to cope with the extensive flooding caused by the Tisza, it replaced a wooden bridge and gradually became so famous that each year, on 20 August, the Bridge Fair now takes place. There are displays of traditional dance, folk arts, and theater, while local dishes and the old livestock fairs of the 19C and 20C are recreated for visitors.

Ökumenikus Pusztatemplom (Puszta Ecumenical Church)
Built in 2016, this pretty little church in the center of the village has the distinction of being open to both the Catholic and Protestant faiths, hence its unusual bell tower where the Catholic cross and the star of Bethlehem sit one above the other. It was built on the site of a former forced labor camp and serves as a place to remember the deportees of the Hortobágy gulag. Between 1950 and 1953, the Puszta had the very dubious distinction of being the "Hungarian Siberia," a place where thousands of people were held captive in the work camps, as can be seen from the names listed inside the church.

★ **Hortobágyi Pásztormúzeum** (Herdsman's Museum)
Open 9am–5pm. Ft1,200 (includes the Round Theater and the Inn Museum).
This museum portrays the lives of the people who tended the livestock and lived in the area. You can see the embroidered felt clothes and the different objects made by the families, who spent several months on end with their beasts out on the plain. Their small reed huts have been reconstructed. Also on display are some *suba*, huge sheepskin cloaks that kept them warm in winter and served as beds in summer. And you can see wooden herdsman's sticks with carved handles.

★ **Körszínmúzeum** (Round Theater)
Next door to the Herdsman's Museum. Open 9am–5pm. Ft500 (including the Herdsman's and Inn museums, Ft1,200).
Displays of the local trades and crafts of days gone by can be found in this round building with a thatched roof. The work of local tradespeople such as blacksmiths, milliners, potters, and saddlers is explained through models, tools, and objects from the last century.

Hortobágyi Csárdamúzeum (Hortobágy Inn Museum)
Open Jul–Aug, 9am–6pm; May–Sept, 9am–5pm; Nov, 10am–4pm. Dec–mid-Mar closed. Ft500 (including the Herdsman's Museum and Round Theater, Ft1,200).
A small museum inside the **Hortobágyi Csárda** (inn), where you can also still have a meal (*see Addresses p264*). It explores the history of the inns that were dotted across the Great Plain in the 18C and 19C. They were located at intervals of a day and a half's walk apart, the distance a horse and cart would typically cover between stops for food and rest.

★ **Pusztai állatpark** (Puszta Animal Park)
1.5mi/2km south of Nine-arch Bridge (see above). ✆ 701 037. www.pusztaiallatpark.hu. Open 9am–6pm. Ft900.
It might be more accurate to describe this as a farm rather than a park, as the birds and animals on show are familiar domestic creatures, such as ducks, chickens, geese, and donkeys. Some, however, are typical of the region, such

Nine-arch Bridge
© Martin Zwick/age fotostock

as Racka sheep with their distinctive long, twisted horns, Mangalica pigs with their curly wool coats, and the famous Hungarian Grey cattle. Also take a look at the traditional hen houses. Children will enjoy being able to stroke some of the animals and there is also a play area.

Madárkórház (Bird Hospital)

369 181. Open 9am–6pm. Ft1,000.

Learn about the hazards faced by wild birds from human activity, such as poison and pesticides, traffic, and poaching. Wounded birds are cared for here and released back into the wild.

Hortobágy vadaspark (Hortobágy Wild Animal Park)

589 321. Departures by Land Rover every hour from the Herdsman's Museum: Mar & Apr, 10am–4pm; May–Oct, 10am–5pm/6pm; Nov–Feb, 10am–2pm, but call ahead to reserve. Closed Mon except in Jul & Aug.

See some of the animals that inhabited the Great Plain before humans arrived, safari-style from the vantage point of a 4x4. Look out for wolves, the rare and endangered Przewalski horses, foxes, golden jackals, wildcats, and eagles, among others. The ride lasts approximately 1hr 30min.

Cross Nine-arch Bridge and turn right toward Máta (about 2mi/3km).

★★ **Mátai Ménes** (Máta Stud Farm)

589 368. www.mataimenes.hu. Departures in a horse-drawn wagon: Mar–Oct, 10am, noon, 2pm (Apr–Oct, also 4pm). Minimum 10 people. Ft3,500. Reserving ahead is recommended.

With 250 powerful Hungarian Nonius horses, buffaloes, and Racka sheep, the stud farm evokes the Puszta of centuries past. Although the show is staged for tourists, you do get an idea of the life here and just how immense the plain is. The *csikós*, the famous Hungarian horsemen in traditional dress, put on exciting equestrian shows. One of the star attractions has to be a rider in control of five galloping horses, astride the backs of two with three others hurtling along just in front! They also perform tricks, the horses lying down at

the command of the crack of a whip. Visitors have the chance to get up on the back of a horse themselves—experienced horse riders can set off across the plain, while beginners remain in the riding arena (reserve ahead, from Ft3,600/hr). As the shows are performed outside, they are canceled during heavy rain.
Return to Rte 33 toward Tiszafüred and turn right at milestone 67 for the fishponds.

★★ **Hortobágy-Halastavi Kisvasút** (Great Fishponds)
Halászbárka Information Center. 4.5mi/7km west of Hortobágy village. ✆ 589 321. www.hnp.hu. Access on foot, by bike, or narrow gauge railway (3mi/5km trip). Trains depart: Jul–Aug at 10am, noon, 2pm, 4pm; Apr–Jun & Sept–Oct, Sat & Sun at 10am, noon, 2pm; Ft1,600 (children Ft1,000). Bicycle hire Ft1,500/day.
Not just ponds, but more an extensive area of lakes, paths, and dykes covering close to 4,950 acres/2,000ha. You can see thousands of birds (it is a famous bird wetland habitat), marsh plants, and grazing water buffalo. Climb the observation towers for a better view of both the landscape and the birdlife—in October the spectacle of 40,000 migrating cranes is breathtaking.

Excursions Regional map (p248–49)

★ **Tisza-tó** (Lake Tisza) A2–3
23mi/*37km west of Hortobágy.*
Historically the River Tisza has been beneficial to the region, providing irrigation for the land, but it has also created great problems through flooding. In the early 19C it was decided to address the problem by regulating the river (draining part and altering its course), work that was led by Count Széchenyi. In the 20C the decision was taken to dam the river and create Tisza-tó (Lake Tisza), which was completed in 1973. Today the lake, which covers 49sq mi/127sq km, extends in a succession of irregularly shaped stretches of water. Shallow, calm, and dotted with islands and creeks, it is a paradise for anglers. Ecotourism is the watchword here and respecting nature. Lake Tisza offers a complete vacation experience, with beaches, numerous campsites, entertainment, and water sports.

★ **Tiszafüred** AB2
22mi/35km west of Hortobágy.
The lake's main resort offering fishing, swimming, boating, and water skiiing or just the chance to relax in the sun after a dip in the warm water (since it is shallow it soon warms up under the sun). You can buy fishing permits, hire a boat, or buy tickets for trips on the lake from lakeside tourist agencies.
Keen cyclists can peddle the 34mi/55km around the lake, mainly along dedicated cycle paths. Good-quality bikes are available for hire from Tisza-Tavi Kerékpáros Centrum (*see Sports and Activities, p264*).
Walking around the southern part of the town you can see some traditional houses and potteries. The **Kiss Pál Múzeum** *(Tariczky sétány 8; ✆ (06) 59 352 106; www.kisspalmuzeum.hu; open Apr–Oct, Tue–Sat, 9am–noon & 1pm–5pm; Nov–Mar, closes 4pm; Ft500)* is devoted to local history and housed in a beautiful building dating from the first half of the 19C.

Poroszló A2
17mi/11km west of Tiszafüred (on the other side of the lake).
A lakeside resort, very popular since the Ökocentrum opened here in 2012.
★ **Tisza-tavi Ökocentrum** (Lake Tisza Ecocenter) – *Kossuth Lajos utca. ✆ 36 553 033. www.tiszataviokocentrum.hu. Open Jul–Aug, 9am–7pm; Apr–Jun &*

Sept, 9am–6pm; Nov–Mar, 10am–4pm. Ft1,990. Audioguide in English Ft800/2hrs. A café on site. This modern building beside the lake, with a lookout tower providing panoramic views, explores the flora and fauna of Lake Tisza and explains how the local biosphere functions. See some 50 species of fish that live in the lake up close as you walk through an amazing underwater tunnel in the aquarium.

In the 17 acre/7ha park you can wander from one enclosure to another housing pelicans, turtles, foxes, golden jackals, Racka sheep, and farm animals, which make it a popular place for families. There are also playgrounds for children and a traditional house to look around. Constructed in 1884, the house has been furnished and decorated in the style of that time. You can also take a boat trip on the lake.

ADDRESSES IN HORTOBÁGY

ARRIVAL/DEPARTURE

Train – Every 2hrs between Debrecen and Hortobágy *(journey time 1hr).*

STAY

Hortobágy

There are no hotels in Hortobágy, but there are a number of guesthouses and private homes that let out rooms.

BUDGET

Hajdú Lovasudvar – *Sarkadi utca 15. 1 mile/1.5km east of the village. 369 335. www.hajdulovasudvar.uw.hu. 4 rooms, Ft16,000.* The rooms might be a little basic but you will discover some true Hungarian hospitality here. The food, prepared by Judith (on request), is excellent. Albert, who speaks English, offers horse-drawn carriage trips in the Puszta (see website for prices). On your return, you'll be ready for dinner cooked in a pot over an open fire.

AVERAGE

Sóvirág Vendégház – *Czinege János utca 52–53. 1.2mi/2km east of the village. 369 130. www.soviragvendeghaz.hu. 6 rooms, Ft17,000.* With its flowering balconies, small sauna, and jacuzzi, this is a charming guesthouse. You can either use the barbecue in the garden or ask for a traditional Puszta dinner to be cooked for you. Bike hire is also available.

Tiszafüred

BUDGET

Aurum Vendégház – *Ady Endre utca 29. (59) 351 338. 5 rooms from Ft10,000.* The decoration of the rooms has not changed in 30 years but that only adds to the charm of the place. You might be greeted in German rather than English by the owner who lives on the first (ground) floor. Breakfast is not served but guests have use of a kettle, refrigerator, and microwave oven. A supermarket is nearby.

SPLASH OUT

Tisza Balneum – *Húszöles utca 27. (59) 886 200. www.balneum.hu. 68 rooms from Ft30,000.* Situated beside the lake, this is the nicest hotel in the area, with both indoor and outdoor swimming pools opening onto a very pleasant garden. From the hotel pier take a trip on the lake in a kayak or boat, or just sit on one of the benches beside the lake and watch the watery world go by. There is also a tennis court and a play area for young children. Minimum stay of two nights in the summer.

EAT

Hortobágy

As well as the two restaurants below, in summer there are stalls selling hot dogs and ice creams.

BUDGET

Hortobágyi Csárda – *In the center of the village opposite the Herdsman's Museum. ✆ 589 010. Open 11am–6pm (Sat & Sun, 8pm). Main dishes Ft1,090/3,790.* This 18C inn keeps local recipes alive, serving Mangalica pork chops and water buffalo or Racka lamb stews, often to the accompaniment of rather melancholic Romani music featuring the violin or cimbalom. Some good vegetarian dishes such as an unusual pasta with caramelized cabbage.

Pizza Sfera – *In the center of the village opposite the church. ✆ 369 06. Open 7am–midnight. Pizza Ft1,290.* As well as pizzas, there is a choice of classic Hungarian dishes, such as goulash and potato croquettes.

Tiszafüred

AVERAGE

Tisza Balneum – *Húszöles utca 27. ✆ (59) 886 200. Open 11am–9pm. Main dishes Ft1,200/4,200.* This restaurant, in the hotel of the same name, has a very pleasant terrace overlooking the garden and the lake. You may primarily come here for the location, but the portions are generous and they serve good, honest food (grills, gnocchi, and local fish).

TAKING A BREAK

Hortobágy

Nyerges Presszó – *Mátai Ménes. Open 9am–6pm.* The café at the stud farm serves coffees, cold drinks, snacks, and ice creams. A pleasant terrace.

Around Tiszafüred

Házi Rétes – *At Poroszló, 550yds/500m from the Ecocenter. Open 10am–5pm.* Before or perhaps after a visit to the Ecocenter, stop off at this delightful garden and sample delicious *rétes* (Hungarian strudels) with poppy seeds, soft cheese, or seasonal fruits such as strawberries, apples, and plums.

SHOPPING

Hortobágy

Puszta Souvenirs – *In the heart of the village.* The souvenirs are very typical of the area, but rather bulky to take home. They include sheepskins, buffalo horns and even skulls, cast iron cook pots, and wooden plates.

SPORTS AND ACTIVITIES

Cycling around Lake Tisza – *Tisza-Tavi Kerékpáros Centrum (Lake Tisza Cycling Center), Aradi utca 1 at Tiszafüred. Open 8am–6pm.* Bicycles to hire for between Ft2,000 and Ft4,500 for 2hrs, depending on the make. Electric bikes are also available.

Nyíregyháza and surroundings

Population 46,866 – Szabolcs-Szatmár-Bereg county – area code ✆42

Nyíregyháza lies in the center of the Nyírség, an area of the Great Plain that covers the northern part of Hungary. The River Tisza flows in a big loop here, after having crossed the eastern Hungarian/Romanian border, and skirts the Ukranian frontier before descending south and east, where it separates into the ponds and lakes of Hortobágy. In the 9C and 10C, settlers cleared the Nyírség (which translates as "land with birch forests") chopping down around 1,500 acres/600ha of trees to raise livestock and cultivate the land. Although the climate is cooler here than in the rest of the Great Plain, it is also sunnier and well suited to growing crops and farming animals. Few tourists venture as far as this region but it is precisely its rural aspect and remoteness that attracts those travelers who do come in search of deepest Hungary.

ADDRESSES PAGE 269
Eat, Stay, Shopping, Baths

INFO:
Tourist Office – *Kossuth tér 1. www.nyiregyhaza.info.hu. ✆ 310 735. Open Mon–Fri, 9am–5pm.* A warm welcome in English. Brochures and information on the city and region.

LOCATION:
Regional map CD1–2 (p248–49) 31mi/50km north of Debrecen.

DON'T MISS:
The Medieval Churches Tour in the Upper Tisza Region.

TIMING:
Allow two days.

KIDS:
The zoo and waterpark at Sóstófürdő.

Nyíregyháza Regional map C2 (p248–49)

This is an unpretentious but charming university town. A long ring road encircles the spacious center with its grand, tree-lined avenues, squares, and gardens that make it seem larger than it actually is. After the Second World War, Nyíregyháza became an important rail and road junction, close to the borders of Ukraine and Romania. The downtown area has several pleasant squares connected to each other by shopping streets and contains buildings that date back to several different eras. A stroll through its various squares, mainly named after illustrious figures (Kossuth Lajos, Hősök, Szabadság, Jókai, and Kálvin squares) makes for a pleasant short walk.

5

Jósa András Múzeum (András Jósa Museum)

Benczúr Gyula tér 21. Open Tue–Sun, 9am–5pm. Ft1,400.

You will find a fine selection of paintings, notably many by the Nyíregyháza-born artist Gyula Benczúr (1844–1920) and a room dedicated to the novelist **Gyula Krúdy** (1878–1933), one of the greatest writers of Hungarian literature. And as is convention with similar museums in Hungary, it also covers the history of the town and the Magyar conquest.

Excursions Regional map C2 (p248–49)

★ Sóstófürdő

3mi/5km north. Leave Nyíregyháza by Kossuth Lajos utca, then take Sóstói út.
In the 19C the area around Sóstófürdő was popular with walkers. It has since become a residential area, with a spa and leisure resort for visitors. Surrounded by lush, green vegetation, there are 1,200 acres/500ha of forest nearby. The thermal springs emerge from the depths at 122°F/50°C. The water contains sodium chloride and carbonates, recommended for the treatment of bone and joint complaints. The spa complex has an indoor swimming pool and other attractions, making it a good choice for families, and it's close to the zoo (*see p269*).

Sóstói Múzeumfalu (Open-air museum, *skanzen*) – *Tölgyes utca 1. Closed for building work. Currently due to reopen in 2020.* Learn about the lifestyle of the people who lived here in the past; some of their traditions are still carried on in very rural parts of the Upper Tisza region. Visit an old school, a barber's, various workshops, and other buildings. Many ethnic communities settled in this region, bringing their various skills and traditions with them.

★ **Nyíregyházi állatpark** (Nyíregyháza Zoo) – *Sóstói utca. www.sostozoo.hu. 479 702. Ft3,500.* The 86acre/35ha zoo was opened in 1998 and is divided into five "continents," each housing animals whose natural habitat corresponds to the relevant part of the globe. In total there are close to 500 species, including endangered animals such as the white tiger, Komodo dragon, and polar bear. There is also an aquarium, with tiger sharks being a notable attraction. It is one of the most popular Hungarian zoos after Budapest and Veszprém.

★ Nyírbátor

22mi/36km southeast of Nyíregyháza.
At the end of the 15C and the beginning of the 16C the fortunes of this small town in the Nyírség region increased greatly when two churches were built here by István Báthori (Stephen Báthory), prince of Transylvania. Each summer, in August, the town hosts the Nyírbátor Music Days festival. It is very popular with Hungarians who flock here from all over the country.

★★ **Református templom** (Reformed church) – *Egyház utca 1. Open Tue–Sat, 9am–5pm.* This Calvinist church is known as a late-Gothic masterpiece. Standing on a grassy mound, it is easily recognized by the wooden bell tower that stands slightly apart beside it. Inside, the beautiful vaulting of the nave has delicate ribbing and elegant columns, lit on one side by tall ogival windows. The carved wooden pulpit, the perfectly aligned prie-dieu benches, and the white walls combine to give the building an air of austerity, simplicity, and serenity. The **bell tower** beside the church has four turrets and a shingle roof, its dark wood contrasting starkly with the graceful, slender lines of the white-walled church. Several members of the Báthori family are buried in the church, including István V Báthori (1430–93), builder of the church, and István Báthori XII, who died in 1605.

Báthori Várkastély (Báthori Castle) – *Vár u.1 Open 9am–5pm.* A relatively small Renaissance building with white walls not far from the Reformed Church, this is the former Báthori Palace. The part you see today is the refectory and is all that remains of the original building. It now houses a small waxworks museum dedicated to the Báthori family, one of the most important noble families in Hungary with an intricate genealogy. Significant members of the family are portrayed as wax figures, dressed in the appropriate costume. Many became high-ranking state officials and some were princes of Transylvania. István Báthori (1533–86) was also king of Poland.

★ **Harangláb** (Church of the Minorites) – *Károlyi utca 19. Open 9am–5pm.* The original church was built by István V Báthori, but suffered damage over the years, before being finally destroyed by the Turks. It was rebuilt in the 18C in the Baroque style by the Minorite Order and is notable for its five altars and its pulpit, much of the elaborately carved wooden detail being the work of local craftsmen. The carving conveys deep sincerity through its simplicity. On the left as you enter the church, look out for the Krucsay Altar. It was commissioned by János Krucsay in memory of his wife, whom he had executed for adultery.

Báthori István Múzeum (István Báthori Museum) – *Károlyi utca 21. Open Apr–Sept, open Tue–Sun, 10am–6pm; Oct–Mar, Tue–Fri, 8am–4pm. Ft500.* Housed in a former monastery, the museum exhibits fossilized animals from the Ice Age that were discovered in Bátorliget marshland to the southeast of the town, as well as other items on local history.

★ Máriapócs

7mi/11km northwest of Nyírbátor on Rte 4911, then a small road to the right.

A popular place for pilgrimage, Pope John Paul II came here in 1991, as do people from all over the world to pray to the Weeping Black Madonna depicted on an icon in the Greek Catholic Church. The icon is in fact an 18C copy as the original is in St. Stephen's Cathedral in Vienna. The icon was first seen to be weeping in 1696, but she has not wept since her arrival in Vienna. However, the Máriapócs copy was seen to weep in 1715 and 1905. The interior of the church is highly decorated and the opulent iconostasis dates from the 19C.

Driving tour Regional map (p248–49)

MEDIEVAL CHURCHES TOUR (UPPER TISZA) D1

Circular tour of 125mi/200km departing from Nyíregyháza. See the route marked on the Regional map. Leave Nyíregyháza by Hwy M3.

The Bereg Region, close to the border with Ukraine, has remained very rural. It is famous for its plums, which are sold commercially as dried fruits, jams, and brandy *(pálinka)*. As the Turks never reached this outlying area, it is the only place in Hungary where medieval churches remain standing. Given that so few tourists venture as far as these small villages, to see inside you may need to ask around so they can be opened for you.

Vásárosnamény

This small town is the most important in the area. In summer you can relax on the beach by the River Tisza. For something to do indoors, try the 18C Tomcsányi Castle which houses the **Beregi Múzeum** *(Beregi Múzeum, Szabadság ter 31; open Apr–Oct, Tue–Sun, 8.30am–4.30pm; Nov–Mar, Mon–Fri, 8am–4pm; Ft600)*, a museum displaying local folklore items (embroidery, pottery, and painted Easter eggs).

Take Rte 41.

★ Református templom (Tákos Calvinist Church), at Tákos

Bajcsy-Zsilinszky utca 25. ✆ 70 22 21 996. Open 8am–6pm. Ft500.

A delightful small church, not much larger than a house, with wattle-and-daub walls and a wooden roof, which dates back to the 18C. Dubbed "Our Lady with Bare Feet" by the locals, it is famous for the colorful paintings of flowers

Medieval mural, Csaroda Calvinist Church
© Attila JANDI/Shutterstock

that decorate the ceiling. Look out also for the pulpit, painted wooden furniture, and traditional embroidered fabric decorating the stalls. A distinctive wooden bell tower stands next to the church.

★ **Református templom** (Csaroda Calvinist Church), at **Csaroda**
Kossuth utca 4. ✆ 20 44 47 624. Open 10am–6pm. Ft2,400.
Built at the end of the 13C, this delightful small Romanesque church is in two parts, comprising a rectangular nave and a square sanctuary, both decorated with murals in different styles and from different eras. The steeple on top of the tower is made of oak.

Tarpai Szárazmalom (Tarpa Mill), at **Tarpa**
Árpád utca 36. ✆ 20 35 82 938. Open 10am–6pm. Ft300.
Apart from the church, this unusual 19C mill made of wood is the star attraction. Circular in shape and with low walls, it is the roof that dominates. The tools used to weigh and crush wheat are on display. The **church** (Református templom/Calvanist Church, *Kossuth utca 15*) is 14C, although the coffered ceiling and pulpit are 18C. The beautiful 15C wall paintings are the church's main attraction, the largest of which shows Saint George fighting the dragon.

★ **Szatmárcsekei Temető** (Szatmárcseke Cemetery), at **Szatmárcseke**
Táncsics utca 14. Open daily and free.
The main draw in this village is not so much its church, but its extensive cemetery. With 1,200 carved wooden grave markers resembling the up-ended prows of boats, there is nothing quite like this ancient Calvinist cemetery anywhere else in the world. Some historians believe that the mysterious markers were a way of perpetuating the tradition of the Ugric tribes who buried their dead in boats. The poet, Ferenc Kölcsey, who composed the words of the Hungarian national anthem, is also buried in this cemetery.
Retrace your steps to Vásárosnamény, then return to Nyíregyháza.

ADDRESSES IN NYÍREGYHÁZA

ARRIVAL/DEPARTURE

Train – Trains run every 30min between Nyíregyháza and Debrecen *(journey time 30min on the fastest trains).*

STAY

Nyíregyháza

BUDGET

Un Pizzico di Italiano Étterem és Panzió – *Egyház utca 1. ✆ 797 474. www.unpizzico.hu.* P *10 rooms, Ft10,000.* ☕ *Ft1,300.* This guesthouse in the center of town takes its name from the very nice pizzeria downstairs. The bedrooms are simply furnished, but have reversible air-conditioning.

Sóstófürdő

SPLASH OUT

Hotel Pangea – *Blaha Lujza sétány 15. ✆ 479 702. www.pangeahotel.hu. 38 rooms from Ft39,000* ☕ *(including entrance to the zoo).* Having direct access to the zoo along with a garden and play area, this hotel is ideal for a family stay. The bedrooms are modern, light, and have been tastefully decorated. Some have a balcony that overlooks the lake. You can also stop here for lunch.

Tarpa

BUDGET

Kuruc Vendégház – *Táncsics utca 14. In Tivadar (3mi/5km south of Tarpa). ✆ 70 33 49 083. www.kurucvendeghaz.hu.* *5 rooms, Ft12,000.* This small, quiet guesthouse is not far from the river. Guests can hire bicycles and use the swimming pool. A good location for anyone wanting to prolong their stay by popping over to Ukraine as it is only a short distance from the border.

EAT

Nyíregyháza

BUDGET

John's Pub Restaurant – *Dózsa György utca 7. ✆ 500 808. Open 10am (Sun, 11am)–11pm. Main dishes Ft1,750/6,800.* The elegant exterior of this building in the center of town is painted yellow. Inside, in spite of an interior that is a cross between a British pub and a Wild West saloon, the menu is mainly Hungarian and serves a wide choice of whiskeys and local brandy *(pálinka).*

SHOPPING

Tarpa

Pitvar – *Kossuth u. 49/b Szódaház. Open Tue–Sat, 10am–5pm.* A small boutique selling homemade jams, notably plum (for which the region is famous), brandy *(pálinka)*, embroidery, and lace.

BATHS

Sóstófürdő

Aquarius Spa – *Szódaház utca 18. ✆ 500 106. www.sostort.hu. Open 9am–8pm. Ft4,200/day. Restaurant.* This lovely spa and water park beside the lake has indoor and outdoor pools that will keep the whole family happy (water play area, slides, and sun loungers).

5

Pécs and South Transdanubia 6

National Michelin Map 732
Baranya, Somogy, and Bács-Kiskun counties

130mi/209km south of Budapest:

South of Pécs:

Northeast of Pécs:

Zsolnay Fountain, Pécs
© Jon Arnold Images/hemis.fr

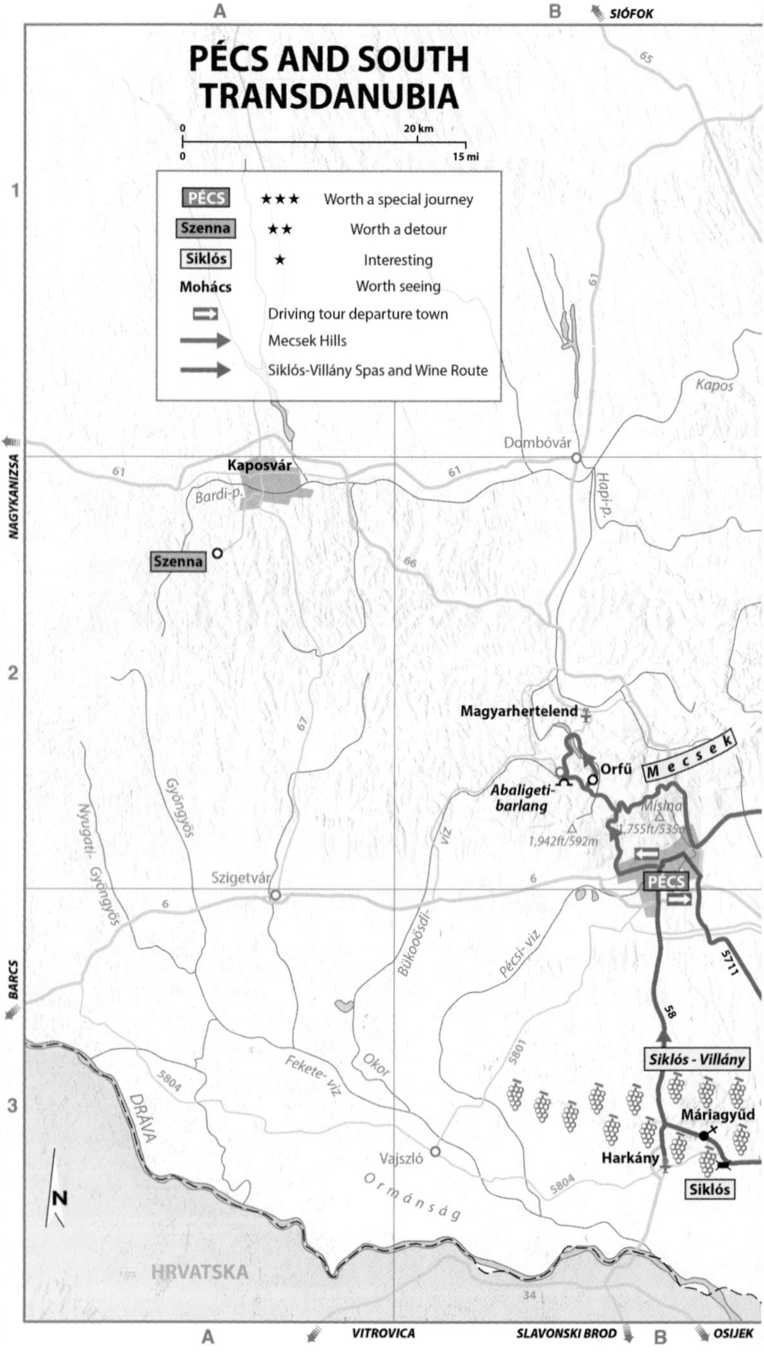
PÉCS AND SOUTH TRANSDANUBIA
0 20 km
0 15 mi
PÉCS ★★★ Worth a special journey
Szenna ★★ Worth a detour
Siklós ★ Interesting
Mohács Worth seeing
Driving tour departure town
Mecsek Hills
Siklós-Villány Spas and Wine Route
A
B
SIÓFOK
NAGYKANIZSA
BARCS
VITROVICA
SLAVONSKI BROD
OSIJEK
1
2
3
Kapos
Dombóvár
Kaposvár
Bardi-p.
Hapi-p.
Szenna
Magyarhertelend
Orfű
Abaligeti-barlang
Mecsek
Misina
1,755ft/535m
1,942ft/592m
PÉCS
Szigetvár
Gyöngyös
Nyugati-Gyöngyös
Bükkösdi-víz
Pécsi-víz
Fekete-víz
Okor
Siklós - Villány
Máriagyűd
Harkány
Siklós
Vajszló
Ormánság
DRÁVA
HRVATSKA
N

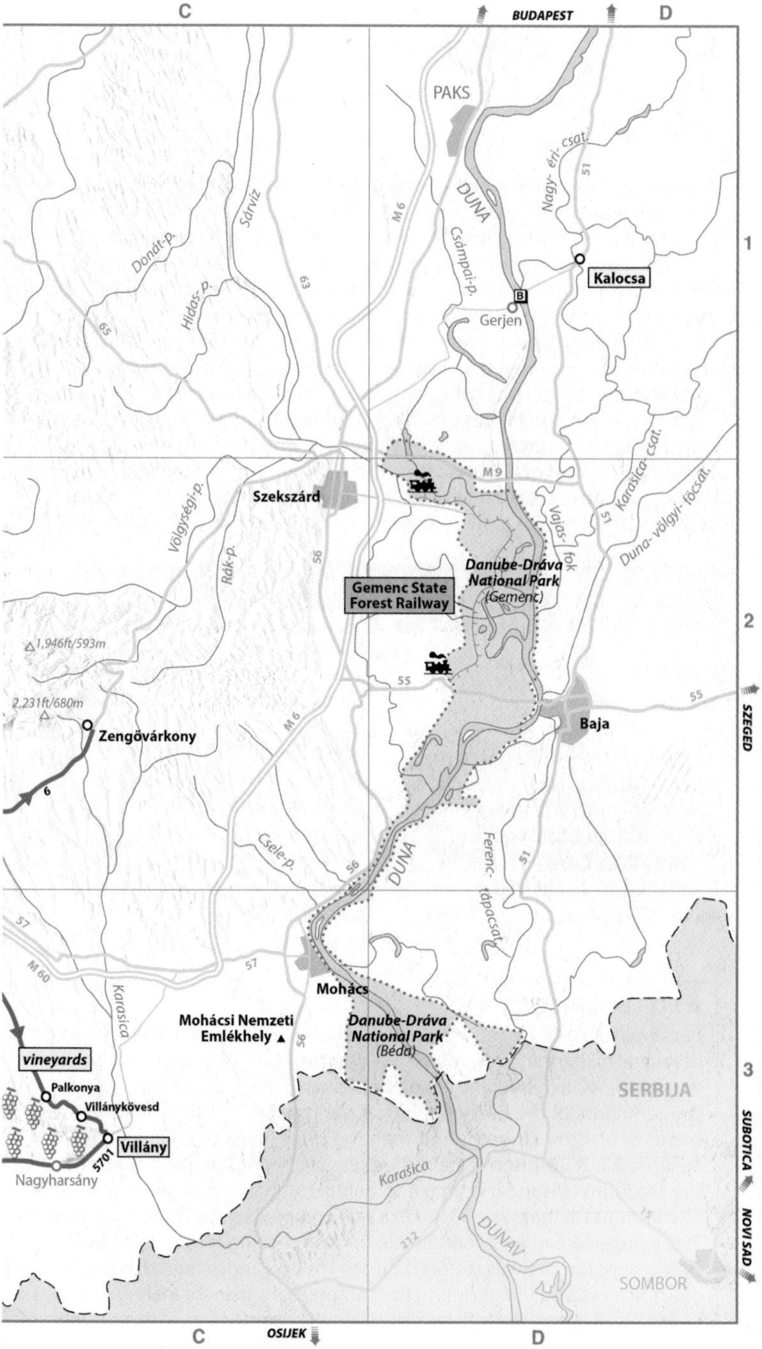
C
BUDAPEST
D
PAKS
Nagy-éri-csat.
51
DUNA
M 6
Sárvíz
Csámpai-p.
Donát-p.
1
Kalocsa
63
Hidas-p.
B
Gerjen
65
Karasica-csat.
M 9
Szekszárd
Völgységi-p.
Vajas-fok
51
Duna-völgyi-főcsat.
56
Rák-p.
Danube-Dráva National Park (Gemenc)
Gemenc State Forest Railway
2
1,946ft/593m
55
55
SZEGED
2,231ft/680m
Baja
Zengővárkony
M 6
6
Cséle-p.
DUNA
Ferenc-tápcsatorna
51
56
57
M 60
57
Mohács
Karasica
Mohácsi Nemzeti Emlékhely
56
Danube-Dráva National Park (Béda)
vineyards
3
SERBIJA
Palkonya
Villánykövesd
SUBOTICA
Villány
5701
Nagyharsány
Karašica
NOVI SAD
15
DUNAV
212
SOMBOR
C
OSIJEK
D

Pécs

★★★

Population 144,188 –Baranya county – area code ✆ 72

Tucked away in a hollow at the foot of the Mecsek Hills that protect it from the keen winds of the north, Pécs (pronounced "petch") lies stretched out in the sun, enticing visitors with a subtle hint of the Orient, a hang-over from the presence of the Ottoman Turks, who took their turn in the town between the Romans, Early Christians, Magyars, and Communists. As you walk past the buildings in their eclectic mix of styles that line the pedestrianized streets, you will hear Hungarian spoken, of course, but also German, Croatian (the border is very close), and even English, as almost a quarter of the student body comes from overseas. The painter Victor Vasarely, the father of Op art, and the architect Marcel Breuer, a member of the Bauhaus, were both born in the city, which was the 2010 European Capital of Culture. It is also a university center and home to museums, cultural organizations, and galleries galore. Buoyed up by its cultural vitality, Pécs can look the future squarely in the face.

ADDRESSES PAGE 284
Stay, Eat, Baths, Bars, Sports and Activities

INFO:

Tourist Office

Pécs map A1 (p277)

Széchenyi tér 1. ✆ 511 232. iranypecs.hu. Open Mon–Fri, 8am–6pm (Sat & Sun, 10am–6pm). In the city's main square, next to a café with wifi.

Irány Pécs Card – *Ft2,990/day + Ft500/day supplement (from the tourist office).* This discount card is valid for around 20 museums and tourist attractions, and includes free access to the guided tours of the city organized by the tourist office (*in English, only on reservation).*

LOCATION:

Regional map B2–3 (p272–73); Pécs map (p277) Centrally located, Széchenyi tér is a useful starting point for exploring the city.

A LITTLE HISTORY

Pécs was founded by Italian colonists, who settled here at the crossroads of several military and commercial routes in the 2C. The town grew rapidly and by the 4C had become a major Christian center, as can be seen from the remnants of the **Early Christian necropolis**. The city fell into the hands of first the Visigoths and then the Huns when the Roman Empire collapsed, but **Stephen I** established one of his ten bishoprics here when the kingdom of Hungary came into being. Hungary's first university was also founded in the city in 1367. Pécs was occupied by the Turks in the mid 15C, who remained until 1686. Left in ruins after being reconquered by the Habsburgs, the city was restored during the 18C and acquired a number of Art Nouveau buildings during the commercial and industrial expansion of the 19C. It is now the fifth largest city in the country and, with a student population of 20,000 (including 4,000 from abroad), has become one of the biggest tertiary education centers in Hungary.

Belvárosi Church – former Ghazi Kassim Mosque
© giulio andreini/age fotostock

PARKING:
You need a parking permit in the part-pedestrianized downtown area. Stick to the underground parking lots or suburban areas if possible.

DON'T MISS:
The old mosque; Cella Septichora Early Christian necropolis; the Vasarely Museum; the Zsolnay Cultural Quarter.

TIMING:
Allow a day for the attractions in Pécs and half a day for the Zsolnay Cultural Quarter.

KIDS:
Cella Septichora necropolis; Vasarely Museum; Zsolnay Cultural Quarter; the open-air museum at Szenna; Szigetvár Baths; Zselic Park of Stars, Orfű Aquapark (*see p286*).

Walking tour Pécs map (p277)

★★★ THE CITY CENTER

A circular tour starting from Széchenyi tér, marked on the Pécs map.

★★ **Széchenyi tér** (Széchenyi Square) A1
The beating heart of the city and the junction of several pedestrianized streets, this central square with its lively cafés and restaurants was restored and rejuvenated in 2010 in celebration of the city's appointment as European Capital of Culture. The square is surrounded by Baroque buildings, some of which are resplendent with Zsolnay ceramics, but its most striking and unique feature is the former Ghazi Kassim Mosque, an imposing building on the north side.

★ **Belvárosi templom – Dzsámi** (Belvárosi Church – former Ghazi Kassim Mosque) – *20 Széchenyi tér. ✆ 513 057. Open May–Sept, Mon–Fri, 9am–5pm; Sat, 9am–5pm & 7.30pm–10pm; Sun, 1pm–5pm. Oct–Apr, Mon–Sat, 9am–5pm; Sun, 1pm–5pm. Ft1,900.*
Built in 1543 at the behest of Pasha Ghazi Kassim, this mosque (the largest still in existence in Hungary) was constructed with stone salvaged from the demolition of St. Bartholomew's Cathedral, which was once located on this

site. When the Turks left in 1686, the building was converted into a church; inside, the only reminders of its previous incarnation are the mihrab, which points the way to Mecca, and a few verses from the Koran written on the wall. After being struck by lightning, the damaged minaret was finally demolished by the Jesuits in the 18C.

Szerecsen Patika (Saracen Pharmacy) – *Southwest of Széchenyi tér, on the corner of Apáca utca. ✆ (30) 543 6763. Open Tue–Sat, 10am–5pm. Ft500.* In 2017 this drugstore decorated with Zsolnay ceramics found a new role in life and it now houses a small pharmacy museum with a beautiful original interior. Before leaving the square, look out for the fountain **Zsolnay-kút** (1930), in front of the Hospitallers' Church. It has become a symbol of the city and was donated by the Zsolnays, the famous family of ceramicists (*see box p280*). It owes its iridescent beauty to the eosin process developed at the end of the 19C.

Continue down Ferencesek utcája.

★ Ferencesek utcája (Ferencesek Street) A1

This pretty pedestrianized street is lined with small pastel-colored houses and Baroque villas. It crosses **Jókai tér**, a square surrounded by stores, cafés, and restaurants, and carries on toward Váradi Antal utca, where the ruins of the **Memi Pasha Turkish Baths** come into view, slightly set back from the street. Next door stands the **Ferences templom** (Franciscan Church) with its elegant Baroque interior. The church was built in 1718 on the site of of an old mosque that once stood next to the baths, which were demolished, like many of the Turkish buildings in Pécs, when the Habsburgs retook the city.

Take a left turn into Rákóczi út.

★★ Jakováli Hasszán Dzsámi (Hasszán Jakováli Mosque) A2

Rákóczi út 2. This is the best-preserved Islamic faith building in Hungary. Built in the mid 16C, and once again a place of Muslim worship, it has retained its minaret, which features Turkish ceramics from Izmir. *Retrace your steps and walk up Szent István tér opposite. Walk across the park to Septichora Visitor's Center.*

★★ Cella Septichora Látogatóközpont
(Septichora Visitor's Center) A1

Szent István tér. ✆ 224 755. iranypecs.hu. Open Apr–Oct, Tue–Sun, 10am–6pm; Nov–Mar, Tue–Sun, 10am–5pm. Ft1,900 (ages 6–18 & students, Ft1,100).

One of Pécs' hidden treasures and not to be missed. This Early Christian necropolis was inscribed on Unesco's World Heritage List in 2000 and is one of the largest burial grounds dating back to the dawn of Christianity in Europe, and the biggest in Hungary. Imagine the many resting places lying beneath your feet—family tombs, mass graves, and dozens of burial chambers and chapels. The whole site is an exceptional example of Early Christian (4C) art and architecture. Excavations have been carried out here over more than two centuries. Having been reburied between digs (sometimes to protect them from acts of vandalism), some of the tombs were "rediscovered" and opened to the public at the turn of the millennium.

The necropolis is 13–20 ft/4–6m underground and is lit in places by daylight penetrating the glazed paving above. There is a labyrinth of corridors, stairs, and walkways that will delight children.

★★ **Cella Septichora** (Seven-celled Tomb) – The visit begins with a look around the ruins of this, the largest tomb building in the cemetery. You can still see traces of the seven apses in its stone walls (unique in Hungary), which are up to 6ft/2m high. It was built around 430 and, given its dimensions, was intended to be the last resting place of an important individual or a noble

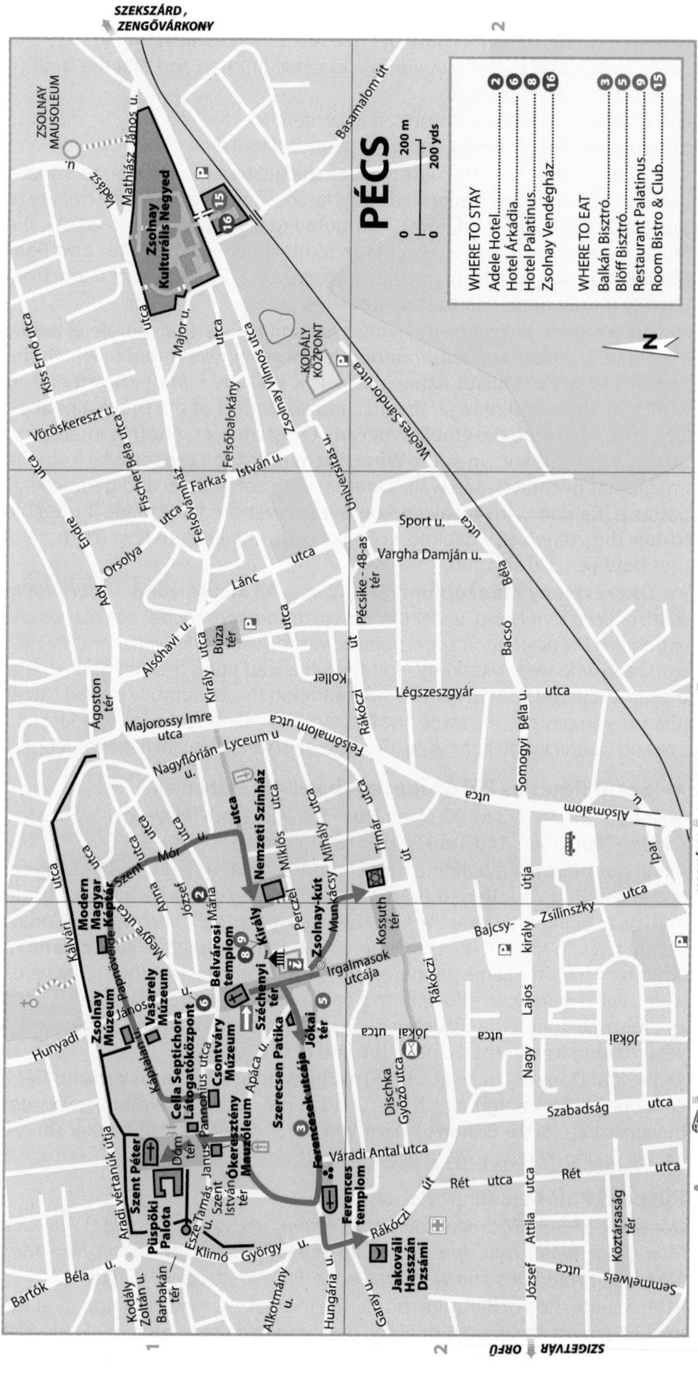
PÉCS
0 200 m
0 200 yds
WHERE TO STAY
Adele Hotel 2
Hotel Árkádia 6
Hotel Palatinus 8
Zsolnay Vendégház 16
WHERE TO EAT
Balkán Bisztró 3
Blöff Bisztró 5
Restaurant Palatinus 9
Room Bistro & Club 15
SZEKSZÁRD, ZENGŐVÁRKONY
HARKÁNY
BUDAPEST
SZIGETVÁR
ORFŰ
ZSOLNAY MAUSOLEUM
Zsolnay Kulturális Negyed
KODÁLY KÖZPONT
Zsolnay Múzeum
Vasarely Múzeum
Modern Magyar Képtár
Cella Septichora Látogatóközpont
Csontváry Múzeum
Ókeresztény Mauzóleum
Szent Péter
Püspöki Palota
Belvárosi templom
Széchenyi tér
Zsolnay-kút
Nemzeti Színház
Szerecsen Patika
Jókai tér
Ferencesek utcája
Ferences templom
Jakováli Hasszán Dzsámi
Dóm tér
Szent István tér
Barbakán tér
Kossuth tér
Ágoston tér
Búza tér
Pécsike - 48-as tér
Köztársaság tér
Rákóczi út
Zsolnay Vilmos utca
Weöres Sándor utca
Basamalom út
Felsőmalom utca
Alsómalom u.
Majorossy Imre utca
Király utca
Irgalmasok utcája
Bajcsy-Zsilinszky utca
Szabadság utca
Rét utca
Váradi Antal utca
Hungária u.
Garay u.
Alkotmány u.
Kodály Zoltán u.
Bartók Béla u.
Klimó György u.
Aradi vértanúk útja
Hunyadi
Kálvári utca
Papnövelde utca
Megye utca
Káptalan u.
János u.
Pannonius utca
Apáca u.
Janus u.
Esze Tamás u.
Dischka Győző utca
Jókai utca
Nagy Lajos király útja
József Attila utca
Semmelweis utca
Somogyi Béla u.
Légszeszgyár utca
Bacsó Béla utca
Sport u.
Vargha Damján u.
Lánc utca
Koller utca
Lyceum u.
Nagyflórián u.
Mór u.
Szent Mór u.
Anna utca
József utca
Mária utca
Perczel utca
Miklós utca
Mihály utca
Munkácsy Mihály utca
Timár utca
Ipar utca
Alsóhavi u.
Ady Endre utca
Orsolya
Felsővámház utca
Farkas István u.
Felsőbalokány utca
Universitas u.
Fischer Béla utca
Vöröskereszt u.
Kiss Ernő utca
Major u.
Mathiász János u.
Vadász u.
A B C
1 2

family. However, no tombs have been found during excavations (in 1939 and 2005), suggesting that the building was never finished and that the basilica took its place as a burial site.

Exhibitions, concerts, lectures, and conferences are regularly held on the site *(check the Visitor Center's homepage under Events).*

★★ **Burial chambers** – The route through the site takes you to around a dozen burial chambers, some decorated with frescoes similar in style and quality to those in the catacombs of Rome. Attributed to wandering Italian artists, the most interesting are to be seen in the tomb known as the **Peter and Paul Chamber**, which was the first to be discovered in 1782. It takes its name from the fine murals depicting the two apostles.

Also look out for Biblical scenes (which are unfortunately incomplete) below a painted Christogram. This monogram is a religious symbol in which the first two letters of Christ's name in Greek, X *(chi)* and P *(rho)*, are interlinked within an alpha and omega, the first and last letters of the Greek alphabet. It has since become the emblem of Early Christian Pécs. Another interesting burial chamber is known as the **Wine Pitcher**, and you can see why from the image that decorates one wall, together with some floral and geometrical patterns. Roman coins recovered during excavations have made it possible to date the site, which was almost certainly used for libations linked to funeral rites between 370 and 380.

★★ **Ókeresztény Mauzóleum** (Early Christian Mausoleum) – *330ft/100m south of Cella Septichora, under the ruins of the outdoor chapel, with a separate entrance in the neighboring park (joint admission with Cella Septichora).* In 1975 workmen who were repairing a fountain chanced upon this chamber, one of the largest in the Roman cemetery. In addition to a beautifully carved sarcophagus, you can also see some fine frescoes representing the Fall of Adam and Eve and Daniel in the lions' den. *Cross Szent István tér to reach the cathedral.*

★★ Szent Péter és Pál Székesegyház (Pécs Cathedral) A1

Dóm tér 1. ✆ (30) 373 89 00. Open Mon–Sat, 9am–5pm (May–Sept, + Fri & Sat, 7.30pm–10pm); Sun, 11.30am–5pm. Ft1,900 (children Ft1,100).

A real pot pourri of a building, this cathedral basilica dedicated to St. Peter and St. Paul is a curious neo-Romanesque building with a tower at each corner. It was built partly over the Early Christian necropolis and on foundations dating back to the 11C. During your visit, be sure to see the **subterranean church★★** from the same period, and climb the southeastern tower *(133 steps)*, which will reward your efforts with a panoramic view. The building was used as a mosque during the Ottoman occupation and has been added to over the years, taking its current shape at the end of the 19C.

West of Dóm tér you will find **Püspöki Magtár Látogatóközpont** (Pécs' Episcopal Visitor Center), which has found a home in an old farmhouse. Besides buying tickets for the Bishop's Palace, you can also visit the café, Magtár Kávézó *(see Taking a Break, p285). Follow the path down to the park.*

Püspöki Palota (Bishop's Palace) A1

Dóm tér 2. ✆ 513 057. Guided tours only (40min, audioguide in English): Apr–Oct, Mon–Fri at 10am, 2pm, 4pm; Sat & Sun at 9am, 10am, 11am, noon. Nov–Mar, Mon–Fri at 2pm; Sat & Sun at 10am & noon. Ft2,500 (children Ft1,700).

After a succession of Baroque rooms, the tour takes an exciting turn … at the exit! This reveals a secret tunnel the bishop would use to be sure of being far from prying ears during the Communist era. *Return to Janus Pannonius utca, which is just below Dóm tér, and follow it toward the center of the city.*

★★ Csontváry Múzeum A1

Janus Pannonnius utca 11. ✆ 30 313 8442. iranypecs.hu. Open Tue–Sun, 10am–6pm. Ft1,500.

Tivadar Csontváry Kosztka (1853–1919) was a former pharmacist who became a painter after a mystical experience. He was regarded as eccentric and only achieved recognition for his art after his death. His major works are exhibited here, including some large canvases such as *Lonely Cedar*, and *Baalbek*, and other scenes set in the Middle East. You can also see a collection of drawings and a striking gallery of portraits that includes a very touching study of Emperor Franz Joseph working at his desk. The artist casts a very human eye over his subjects, lending his pictures great power and a sense of authenticity. On discovering his work, Picasso is supposed to have said, in all modesty, "I did not know there was another great painter this century besides me."

Return to Káptalan utca.

★★ Vasarely Múzeum A1

Káptalan utca 3. ✆ (30) 934 61 27. Open Tue–Sun, 10am–6pm (Mar & Apr, 4pm). Ft1,500.

This museum was founded to celebrate the great legacy left by Győző Vásárhelyi, better known as **Victor Vasarely** (1906–97). Born near Pécs, he attained fame as the founder of Op art (optical art) and made use of all kinds of materials, including canvas, tapestry, metal, glass, and mosaics to play with geometric shapes and optical illusions. The museum explores his early work, influenced by the Bauhaus, at Budapest's School of Applied Arts where Vasarely studied. He then settled in France in 1930, where he created the remainder of his work. He went on to work as a graphic artist for several advertising agencies, and was notably responsible for the logo of the automobile manufacturer Renault (the diamond shape) in 1972. The museum has one of his best-known canvases, *Zebra*, in which the artist playfully explores the animal's stripes.

Around 0.5mi/1km from the museum is a small park named after the artist, where you can find his statue in Zsolnay ceramics.

★★ Zsolnay Múzeum A1

Káptalan utca 2. ✆ 514 045. iranypecs.hu. Open Tue–Sun, 10am–6pm (Mar & Apr, 4pm). Ft1,500.

Housed in a building which was also the home of Hungary's first public library (1440), this museum pays tribute to Miklós Zsolnay, founder of the Zsolnay factory (*see p280*). Among the exhibits are ceramics for both decorative and domestic purposes, along with extremely beautiful Art Nouveau pieces, in particular those with floral ornamentation and Oriental styling.

★★ Modern Magyar Képtár (Modern Art Gallery) A1

Papnövelde utca 5. ✆ 891 328. iranypecs.hu. Open Tue–Sun, 10am–6pm (Mar & Apr, 4pm). Ft700. A 19C villa housing a charming collection of works by the best-known Hungarian painters, including Rippl-Rónai and Gulácsy. You may find you are the only person inspecting some of the pictures as the gallery is not usually busy, and there is a delightful garden to enjoy at the end of your visit.

Continue along Papnövelde utca, turning right into Szent Mór utca.

Király utca (Király Street) AB1

This charming pedestrian street is an almost obligatory stop on the tour, with a continuous flow of locals, students, and tourists strolling past or settling down at one or another of its countless pavement terraces. **Hotel Palatinus**

SCINTILLATING CERAMICS

You'll find examples of Zsolnay ceramics, named after the renowned family of potters, just about everywhere in Pécs. Founded in 1853, the Zsolnay factory enjoyed its golden age between 1874 and 1914, exporting their wares around the globe. Things took off in 1878 at the World Fair in Paris, when Vilmos Zsolnay, the founder's son, unveiled an enamel of his own invention called **eosin**, made with a process that gave pottery a rainbow-like patina with a metallic sheen. The fashion for the Art Nouveau style also proved to be of benefit to Zsolnay, which supplied many of the faience tiles that decorate the facades of the great buildings in Pécs (notably the **Post Office**, *Jókai utca 10*).

The demise of the Austro-Hungarian Empire in 1918, the economic crisis of the 1930s, and then the Second World War caused the factory many difficulties until it was finally nationalized in 1948. While it is still a going concern today, the factory has never quite regained the glories of its past. There was some cold comfort to be had in 2010, as a part of the city's incumbency as European Capital of Culture, when the old factory was transformed into a cultural quarter *(see below)*; it includes the world's largest collection of Zsolnay ceramics, put together by an American-Hungarian engineer.

at No. 5 *(see Addresses, p284)* was at one time the city's smartest address, built in 1913. Stop by and drop in to see its Art Nouveau entrance hall. A little further on, look out for the Rococo exterior of **Nemzeti Színház** (National Theater), which was built at the end of the 19C.

★ **Zsinagóga** (Pécs Synagogue) B2

Fürdő utca 1. Open Apr–Oct, Sun–Fri, 10am–5pm (Nov–Mar, 10.30am–12.30pm).
This building holds memories of the painful history of the Jews in Pécs, 3,000 of whom were deported during the Second World War (with barely 10 percent surviving to return). There is a memorial to those who were killed. It was built in 1869 on the site of another synagogue dating to 1843. The Hebrew inscription around the clock on the front reads: "For my house, be called to the house of prayer for all peoples."

★★ ZSOLNAY KULTURÁLIS NEGYED (ZSOLNAY CULTURAL QUARTER) C1

Felsővámház utca 52. ✆ 500 350. zsolnaynegyed.hu. Site open 6am–1am. Visitor Center 9am–6pm (Nov–Mar, 5pm). Multi-entry ticket Ft5,500 (children Ft3,900), valid for 2 days. If you don't intend to visit each museum, you can also buy individual tickets (Ft1,300–2,000 per ticket). Parking in neighboring streets (no charge).
Installed within the former **Zsolnay factory**, this extensive industrial area was renovated to celebrate the city's year as the European Capital of Culture in 2010. It became a sort of mini-city within the city, retaining the old workshops, but also incorporating the villas owned by the various generations of Zsolnays who came and went at the helm of the family firm for more than a century. These various buildings now house several museums and galleries, a cultural center, planetarium, puppet theater, university campus, several designer boutiques, a guesthouse, and two restaurants.

When you buy your tickets at the visitor center, don't forget to ask for a map to find your way around the maze of buildings.

★★ The Golden Age of the Zsolnay – Gyugyi Collection

Open Tue–Sun, 10am–6pm (Nov–Mar, 5pm). Ft1,600 (children Ft1,000).
This magnificent private collection—the largest in the world of Zsolnay ceramics—is an absolute treasure trove, with 600 works of art that include unique pieces, undoubtedly inspired by Persian designs as well as Art Nouveau.

Also in the Cultural Quarter
The **Pink Exhibition** is a collection of pink pottery, a fashionable color at the time, used not only in unique art pieces but also in utilitarian crockery that was popular throughout Hungary. You can also see an exhibition about the **Zsolnay family**, its rich history of creativity and undeserved fate under the double burden of nationalization and imprisonment under Communist rule; a **leather glove-making** workshop, another Pécs specialty; and the children will like the "lab.game station," where they can play vintage video games.

Excursions Regional map (p272–73)

Kaposvár A2

40mi/65km north of Pécs on Rte 66.
Fő utca 10. (82) 512 921. tourinformkaposvar.hu. Open mid-Jun–end Aug, 9am–6pm (Sat & Sun, 2pm); rest of year, 9am–5pm (Sat & Sun, 2pm). The name of this small university city derives from the Hungarian words *kapu* (gate) and *vár* (castle), referring to the castle built in the marshy valley of the River Kapos. The river is still there but the castle was destroyed, like so many others, having been first attacked by the Turks and then its destruction completed by the Habsburgs. The statesman **Imre Nagy** *(see p361)* was born in the town.
Csiky Gergely Színház (Csiky Gergely Theater) – *Rákóczi Ferenc tér.* This immense wedding cake of a building named after a 19C Hungarian playwright was opened in 1911.
★ **Rippl-Rónai Múzeum** – *Fő utca 101. (20) 287 9323. smmi.hu. Open Tue–Sun, 9am–5pm. Ft700 (children Ft350).* In addition to an exhibition on local history, the municipal museum also features a gallery of paintings from 1860 to the present day, where you can see the works of József Rippl-Rónai *(see below)* and János Vaszary (1867–1939), two scions of the city who left their mark on Hungarian painting and were both influenced by Fauvism at one time or another.
★ **Rippl-Rónai József Emlékmúzeum** (József Rippl-Rónai Memorial Museum) *Fodor József utca 35 . (82) 510 049. ripplronaiemlekhaz.smmi.hu. Open Apr–Oct, Tue–Sun, 9am–5pm (Nov–Mar, 8am–4pm). Ft1,600.* This attractive yellow

WHITE STORKS
A colony of white storks *(ciconia ciconia)* returns to the region every March, before flying off, like clockwork, to warmer climes around the end of August. The birds have remained loyal to the area, which has become known for them. They selected **Nagybajom**, north of Pécs, in particular as the location of choice in which to settle and raise their young. It is much smaller and therefore doubtless a little quieter than Kaposvár. Nagybajom's proximity to wetlands also ensures there is an abundant supply of frogs and small fish on hand, and the local humans have proved to be very obliging, with the electricity company even installing some extra nesting sites on top of electricity pylons.

building set in its own grounds saw the last creative years of **József Rippl-Rónai** (1861–1927), who is now considered one of Hungary's greatest modern artists. Around a hundred of his pictures and personal items are on display. Rónai was a contemporary of the French sculptor Aristide Maillol, who introduced him to Gauguin, Toulouse-Lautrec, and Cézanne during his stay in France. Back then, you couldn't move in Europe for painters!

★★ **Szennai Skanzen** (Open-air Museum), at **Szenna** A2

50mi/80km northwest of Pécs on Rte 6 and then Rte 67. (26) 502 537. Open Apr–Nov, Tue–Sun, 9am–5pm. Closed Mon & rest of the year. Ft 900.

The village of Szenna is the setting for a charming open-air museum, unusually located in a living village. It features some 15 buildings dating from around 1850 in styles typical of the region, which have been dismantled elsewhere and reassembled here for conservation. During festivals and heritage days, costumed performers revive traditional skills such as bread making, wool spinning, and folk singing…

The buildings lie along a path just over 1 mile/1.5km long. Don't miss the **Református templom** (Reformed Church), which dates back to the 18C. It is still used by the villagers, but you can look inside and admire the canopied pulpit and painted coffered ceiling.

Szigetvár A3

22mi/35km west of Pécs on Rte 6. Underground parking near the center of town (no charge). This charming small provincial town spreads out around Zrinyí tér, the main square. It is closely associated with the siege of 1566 that left its mark on Hungarian history *(see box below)*. Relatively untroubled by tourists, it is a good place in which to take a break when traveling around South Transdanubia.

Szent Rókus templom (St. Roch's Church) – *Zrinyí tér.* Built in 1567, the former Ali Pasha Mosque has been transformed into a Baroque church. The frescoes depicting the siege of 1566 are the work of István Dorfmeister.

Zrínyi Miklós Múzeum (Miklós Zrínyi Museum) – *Vár utca 19 (5min walk from Zrinyí tér). (70) 702 8600. Open May–Sept, Tue–Sun, 9am–6pm; (Oct–Apr, 4pm). Ft1,850 (children Ft1,250).* After the 1566 Siege of Szigetvár, the castle was used by the occupying Turks who reinforced its walls and built a mosque in the

TWO TOMBS FOR A SULTAN

As part of a plan to take Vienna and continue their conquest of Europe, the Turks, led by **Süleyman the Magnificent**, attacked the castle at Szigetvár in 1566. As few as 2,500 Croatian and Hungarian soldiers held out against 100,000 Turks for a month. However, once their food and water had run out, the garrison had no choice but to set fire to the castle and make a hopeless attempt to fight their way out. Although defeated in battle, they managed to kill a quarter of the Turkish besiegers. Süleyman himself was also among the fallen, although he had in fact succumbed to a heart attack the day before the victory over Szigetvár. His demise was hushed up in order to preserve the morale of his troops. His body was taken to Istanbul, although his heart was interred in a mausoleum in Szigetvár. All trace of this was lost to history until 2015, when a new archeological excavation (still ongoing) was begun by researchers convinced they had located the forgotten mausoleum. If this turns out to be the case, the sleepy town of Szigetvár may well awaken to a second wave of Turkish visitors.

courtyard. It was rebuilt by the Hungarians in the 18C and restored in 1960, and now houses a museum dedicated to the siege. It is named after local hero and man of letters Miklós Zrínyi who led the Hungarian troops in the struggle against the Turks. This is rounded off with an interesting display (in English) about the Ottoman conquest.

Vigadó Kulturális Központ (House of Culture) – *József Attila utca 9.* This very striking building was constructed from concrete in 1985 to designs by Imre **Makovecz** *(see p314)*, master of Organic architecture.

Driving tour Regional map (p272–73)

★ **MECSEK HILLS** BC2

Circular tour of 43mi/70km starting from Pécs. See the route marked on the Regional map. Leave Pécs heading west along Rte 6 toward Szigetvár; turn right onto Páfrány utca and follow the road north for 12mi/20km to Orfű (signposted).

To the north of Pécs, the Mecsek Hills consist of uplands and forests that create a protective screen around the city. The high point is a modest 2,238ft/682m, but the contrast with Pécs below means that the hills could be taken for mountains. A pleasant place in which to enjoy a walk in the forest and countryside.

Orfű B2

Széchenyi tér 1. (72) 598 116 (72) 598 116. orfu.hu. Summer, 8am–6pm (Sat, 10am–4pm); rest of the year, Mon–Fri, 8am–4pm (Mon 1.30pm).

Nestling among pretty wooded hills, the village of Orfű has everything you could wish for in a vacation area: a large lake (Pécsi-to) that is ideal for swimming, and smaller lakes nearby where you can fish and go canoeing, as well as swim. Accommodation options include a large campsite (*see Addresses, p284*), guesthouses, and pensions. Orfű is very popular, not just for its many outdoor activities, but also for its mills (an old restored and now operating watermill and a reconstructed dry mill), and is famous for its local produce (cheese, lavender biscuits, wild garlic…).

Take Dollar út which runs along the western side of the lake, then a left turn toward Abaligeti-barlang (Abaliget Cave, signposted). Follow the road for 4mi/6km.

Abaligeti-barlang (Abaliget Cave) B2

(72) 498 766. Open mid-Mar–mid-Oct, 9am–6pm; rest of the year, 10am–3pm. Ft1,000 (children Ft800).

Take a subterranean walk through this cave (a walkway of 1,650ft/500m is open to the public) to see interesting rock formations (impressive dripstones). The temperature is constant with raised humidity levels. The caves are also home to various species of bat, which you can learn about in the Bat Museum, close to the entrance.

Return toward Pécs and follow Rte 6, heading northeast, for 13mi/21km, toward Bonyhád.

Zengővárkony C2

This charming small village is home to the delightful **Tojás Múzeum** ★ *(Kossuth Lajos utca 6. (72) 466 605. tojasmuzeum.ini.hu; open mid-Mar–mid-Oct, 10am–6pm; rest of the year, Thu–Tue, 10am–3pm; Ft600, children Ft400).* An amazing collection of several hundred eggs transformed into small works of art, painted, carved, and embossed. The weaving workshop next door is breathing new life into old trades and sells a range of toile fabrics and dinner services.

ADDRESSES IN PÉCS

See Pécs map (p277)

TRANSPORT

Train – Station: *Indóház tér 1.* A 15min walk from the center of town; rail connections to Szigetvár *(40min)*, Budapest *(3hrs)*, and Kaposvár *(1hr)*.

Bus – Bus station: *Zólyom utca (15min walk from the center and 0.5mi/700m from the railway station)*. Connections to Szigetvár *(50min)*, Orfű (in the Mecsek Hills, 40min), Budapest *(4hrs30min)*, Győr *(4hrs30min)*, Keszthely *(3hrs30min)*, Mohács *(1hr15min)*, and Szeged *(3hrs30min)*.

STAY

AVERAGE

16 **Zsolnay Vendégház** – C1 – *Zsolnay Vilmos utca 37 (in the Zsolnay Cultural Quarter). 500 390. zsolnaynegyed.hu. 11 rooms. Ft17 000.* A little away from the downtown area, but the position of this guesthouse in the heart of the Zsolnay Cultural Quarter has other advantages. Definitely one to consider.

6 **Hotel Árkádia** – A1 – *Hunyadi János utca 1. 512 550. hotelarkadiapecs.hu. (charges apply). 32 rooms, Ft19,900.* Good value for money in this small hotel, located a stone's throw from Széchenyi tér. Clean and modern rooms with air-conditioning. Good breakfasts.

8 **Hotel Palatinus** – A1 – *Király utca 5. 889 400. danubiusgroup.com/palatinus (charges apply). 100 rooms. €57/86.* This historic hotel's Art Nouveau decor will almost make you forget that the standard rooms are smallish and fairly plain. Go for the superior rooms instead, which are larger and better fitted out. You won't forget the generous breakfast, served in the splendid restaurant, nor your arrival in the entrance hall (1905).

A TREAT

2 **Adele Hotel** – B1 – *Maria utca 15. 510 226. adelehotel.hu. (charges apply). 19 rooms. Prices quoted in euros: €79/99 (US$88/110). Ask re prices in forints.* A boutique hotel within a protected historic (19C) building that has been admirably refurbished and decorated. Guests can enjoy its many facilities: sauna, fitness center, interior garden. Elegant, minimalist decor. Three apartments available also.

Kaposvár

AVERAGE

Hotel Dorottya – *Széchenyi tér 8. (82) 529 780. hoteldorottya.hu. 31 rooms. From Ft19,900.* Hands down, the most attractive place in town. It was built in the Art Nouveau style in 1911 but the 2012 renovation has retained a hint of its past while bringing the fixtures and fittings up to date. A good place to stay, with reasonable prices given its rating.

Mecsek Hills

There are numerous rooms to rent in private houses, especially in Orfű, the "capital." Information at the tourist office *(see p274)*.

BUDGET

Panoráma Camping – *Dollár út 1, Orfű (western shore of the big lake, Pécsi-to; head for the Aquapark when arriving from Pécs). (20) 341 1954. panoramacamping.hu. Chalets, Ft8,000/2 pers. (Ft13,000 /4 pers.).* In addition to pitches for tents, this campsite also boasts a series of chalets, ideal if you want a change from canvas, just a few minutes' walk from the Aquapark (see p286).

EAT

BUDGET

3 **Balkán Bisztró** – A1 – *Ferencesek utcája 32. 30 891 6809. balkanbisztro.hu. Open Mon–Tue, noon–10pm. Ft2,250/4,100.* The large map of the Balkans reminds you that this is the place to enjoy specialties from Bosnia, Serbia, and Albania. The flame-grilled (over wood) meat dishes come with crisp salads and aubergine caviar. A young clientele and a nice, shady garden.

15 **Room Bistro & Club** – C1 – *Zsolnay Vilmos utca 16 (in the Zsolnay Cultural Quarter). 20 777 7678. roombistro.com. Open Mon–Fri, 9am–4pm; Sat, 10am–3pm. Ft2,250/4,100*. You have to cross a four-lane highway (via a pedestrian bridge) to reach this modern-looking café in the heart of the Zsolnay Quarter. One slight downside is that the large terrace is a little noisy.

9 **Restaurant Palatinus** – A1 – *Király utca 5. 889 444. danubiushotels.com. Open 7am–10pm (winter 7am–3pm, 6pm–10pm). Ft2,990/4,990.* If you are not staying in the adjacent historic hotel, you can still enjoy its splendid Art Deco interior while you eat or enjoy a coffee break in the restaurant, under the watchful eye of a mosaic peacock. Opt for the dining room rather than the terrace if this is likley to be your sole visit, and never mind if the cooking isn't always quite up to the high standard of the interior decoration.

5 **Blöff Bisztró** – A1 – *Jókai tér 5. 497 469. Open 11am–noon. Ft2,200/3,900.* The atmosphere here is as warm as the brasserie cooking: burgers, salads, grilled meat. Nothing sophisticated, but it's good. This has become one of the hangouts of the young students of Pécs, who also enjoy chilling on the pretty terrace in summer and the calm of the pedestrianized street.

Mecsek Hills

AVERAGE

Almalomb – *Ormandi utca 19. Hosszúhetény (10mi/17 km northeast of Pécs). 793 680. almalomb.com. Open Wed–Thu, noon–9pm; Fri–Sat, noon–10pm; Sun, noon–4pm (closed Mon/Tues). Ft2,100/3,600. Menu Ft9,500 (for wines paired with the food, Ft3,000 supplement).*
An old 19C mill, bursting with charm and restored in a modern style by its owner. The bistro-style food showcases local produce and the large garden gives the whole place a rural feel. The owner is planning to open some apartments for rent, so watch this space.

TAKING A BREAK

Pécsi Kávé – *Irgalmasok utcája 6. Szent István tér 6. 951 586. www.facebook.com/pecsikave. Open 8am–6pm (Sat & Sun, 9am–6pm).* A fashionable café with a lovely inner courtyard in which to relax for a while in the sun. Enjoy Turkish coffee or a traditional cappuccino, both of which are excellent. Good cocktails made with fresh fruit.

Magtár Kávézó – *Szent István tér 6. 30 373 89 00. Open 9am–6pm (May–Sept, Sat & Sun, 10pm).* The former cellar of the bishops is now home to this nice café and wine bar, where you can sample some of the best regional wines available in Hungary.

Jókai Cukrászda – *Jókai tér 6. 20 929 2025. Open 10am–9pm.* If you are in search of the best ice cream in Pécs, this confectioner and tearoom is the place to come. Enjoy one on the spot or to take out. The choice of flavors is a little limited, but they are all very tasty and, best of all, seasonal, which is an excellent sign.

BARS

N-Eozin Grillterasz & Kultúrpark – *Esze Tamás utca 3. 30 276 86 69. Open noon–1am on fine days.* Draft beers and house cocktails that you can enjoy outdoors beneath the trees, on a large terrace looking out over the rooftops of Pécs in the distance. And if you start to get peckish you can order some grilled food.

Művész Presszó – *Kolozsvár utca 24. 30 769 7743. Open Mon–Sat, 2pm–midnight.* A beer bar in the railway station district that specializes in micro brews and is popular with students and local young people. The interior has vintage-style decor and there's a snug terrace that spills out onto the street in summer.

BATHS

Szigetvár

Szigetvári Gyógyfürdő – *Tinódi utca 1. (73) 510 485. szigetvarigyogyfurdo.hu.* With their Turkish domed roofs, these thermal baths have a distinct Eastern feel to them, reinforced by the decorative Zsolnay ceramics. Suitable for families and spa visitors, with a children's pool, waterslides, and shady areas for when it's hot.

Mecsek Hills

Hertelendi Termálfürdő– *Bokréta utca 1/A, at Magyarhertelend. 30 516 7978. www.hertelenditermal.hu. Open 9.30am–6.30pm (Fri & Sat, midnight). Sauna park open Sat–Mon, 12pm–6pm (Sat, 11.30pm), Wed, 2pm–10pm.* A great thermal baths complex, with both outdoor and indoor pools, and a fabulous sauna.

SPORTS AND ACTIVITIES

Mecsek Hills

Aquapark – *Dollár út 2, at Orfű. 70 399 1015. orfu-aquapark.hu. Open Jun–Sept only, 9am–7pm. Ft2,500 (6–14 years Ft1,300).* The secret of the success of this small waterpark is its seemingly endless supply of waterslides, but it also has a really good location with a view of the large lake at Orfű.

Near Kaposvár

Zselici Csillagpark (Zselic Park of Stars) – *At Zselickisfalud (9mi/14 km south of Kaposvár). (82) 505 180. zselicicsillagpark.hu.* Internationally recognized as a "dark sky" location (a starry sky with no light pollution), this public observatory in the Zselic hills puts on stargazing evenings and guided night walks beneath the stars. A planetarium and a meteorite collection also.

The vineyards of Villány and Siklós

★

Baranya county – area code ✆ 72

South Transdanubia, close to the border with Croatia, is where the Villány vintages vie with those of Szekszárd for the right to be named the best red wines in Hungary. Villány and Siklós have been a driving force in Hungarian wine production for some thirty years. The winemaking villages (of which there are eleven) have banded together to have their label protected in order to showcase the quality of their wines, and in 1996 they created the first wine route in Hungary. In successfully cultivating wine tourism, the region has also been smart enough to mix in a little water and also promotes the renowned spa resorts along the wine route.

ADDRESSES PAGE 290
Stay, Eat, Baths

INFO:
Villány-Siklós Wine Route Association – *Deák Ferenc utca 22, at Villány. ✆ 492 181. villanyiborvidek.hu.* Find out all you need to know about Hungary's premier wine route. You can organize your trip on the website (in English) before departure.

LOCATION:
Regional map BC3 (p272–73)
Villány is located 22mi/35km southeast of Pécs; Siklós is 19mi/30km to the south, via Rte 578. Croatia lies 12mi/20km to the south.

DON'T MISS:
The wine vaults of Villány; Siklós Castle; Harkány Spa.

TIMING:
Allow a day, followed by an overnight stay at a wine estate and a visit to a thermal spa, if you wish.

KIDS:
Siklós Castle; Siklós Spa (*see p290*).

Driving tour Regional map

★ THE VILLÁNY-SIKLÓS WINE ROUTE AND SPAS BC3

Circular trip of 52mi/84km starting from Pécs. See the route marked on the Regional map. Allow a day for the trip itself, and one or two additional days to enjoy the local hot springs. Leave Pécs, heading south on Rte 578.

The village and region of Villány are well known for their vineyards. The way of life here is still rooted in the lively folk culture of Swabian origin (a German community that settled in the region from Bavaria). The traditional festivals, music, and food (stifolder sausages and dumplings) all have a slightly old-fashioned charm as a result. The landscape is dotted with old farms and wine cellars which, when open for wine tasting, decorate their exteriors with beautiful floral wreaths. The history of viticulture in Hungary goes back to the Roman era, when the region was part of the Roman province of Pannonia. The southern slopes of the Villány Hills are the best suited for winegrowing, with the local **cabernet franc**, **merlot**, and **portugieser** grapes producing excellent wine, in particular reds of exceptional quality.

Palkonya C3
You can't miss the many small white buildings that are so typical of the region in this village, the northernmost in the winegrowing area. They are much bigger below ground than the building above would have you believe, concealing large wine cellars. Palkonya is also known for its church with a round dome. It might look like an ancient mosque, but it was built by the residents in 1816. Finally, there's one more thing to look out for—the large twiggy nests perched high up on the poles and lampposts, awaiting the return of the storks that built them.
Take Rte 578.

Villánykövesd C3
This charming village is also dedicated to winemaking, as you can see from the rows of the typical white buildings of the wine-tasting cellars that line the main road. The cellars are open from May to October; you can sample Cabernet Francs, Cabernet Sauvignons, Kadarkas, and Merlots, along with a few whites that include Olaszrizling and Hárslevelű.
Designated drivers should be careful, however, and resist the temptation to enjoy a little tipple, as there is a zero tolerance policy with regard to drink-driving in Hungary.

★ **Villány** C3
This small town is the so-called capital of the winemaking region of the south. It is on a main road full of the familiar white buildings with signs advertising *pince* (cellar), *bor* (wine), or perhaps *borház* (wineseller), and invitations to linger a while and taste the produce. The main attraction is the privately owned **Bormúzeum** (wine museum), which was opened by a winemaking family and is housed in one of the celebrated underground cellars (an immense space that is more impressive than the collection of equipment on display). There is no information apart from a few words in Hungarian *(slightly set back from the main road, access signposted, ✆ 30 335 5343, galpince.hu, Ft600)*. The best known of the region's cellars are on the main road *(Baross utca)*, where you will also find stores selling wine-related products and some cellars that offer dining and accommodation.

Siklós B3
Vajda János tér 8 (beside the castle ticket office). ✆ 579 090. infopontsiklos.hu. Open Tue–Sat, 9am–5pm.
As if keeping watch on nearby Croatia, Hungary's southernmost town lies at the end of a road lined on either side with immaculately groomed vineyards. You can spot the town from a distance as the imposing white walls of its impressive castle come into view.
★ **Siklósi vár** (Siklós Castle) – *✆ 579 090. siklosivar.hu/en. Open 9.30am–6pm (mid-Jun–Aug, 7pm). Ft1,900 (children Ft700). A café upstairs.* Consisting of a medieval (15C) section, with additional elements from the 16C and 18C, the old part of this castle is the best preserved in Hungary. Access is via a drawbridge and across a courtyard defended with murder holes (through which harmful substances could be dropped onto attackers). Enjoy views of the hillsides of Villány as you walk along the parapet and, once inside, don't miss the Gothic (15C) chapel with its fine arches, where you will also see several fragments of frescoes and a Renaissance window. Be sure also to see the Knights' Hall, the old prison, and the torture chamber with some reconstructions. Several exhibitions on the upper floors explore (in Hungarian only) the country's military history from the 16C to the 20C. There are costumes for the children to dress

Street lined with cellars, Villány
© Botond Horvath/Shutterstock

up in and, on certain days, actors in costume, some on horseback, put in an appearance to add to the medieval feel of the place.

Malkocs bej dzsámija (Mosque of Malkoc Bey) – *Vörösmarty utca 2. ℘ 885 370. Open 9am–5pm. Closed in winter. Ft350 (children Ft250).* The mosque was reconstructed from the ruins of a mid-16C building (using contemporary drawings and descriptions) in 1994, paying particular attention to its wooden ceiling. Now a cultural center, the building has on occasion been rediscovering its religious roots after the war in the former Yugoslavia, sometimes being used for services by Bosnian refugees.

Máriagyűd (Pilgrimage Church) B3

This pilgrimage site halfway up Tenkes Hill is the oldest in Hungary. The first chapel, housing a statue of the Virgin Mary, was built here in 1006 by the Benedictine monks of Pécsvárad. It was enlarged over the years and survived the Turkish occupation. In 1687 the Virgin appeared to two peasants and some 302 other miracles were recorded here between 1723 and 1799. In 1802 Pope Pius VII consecrated Máriagyűd as an official pilgrimage site, and in 2008 Pope Benedict XVI elevated the church to the status of minor basilica.

Harkány B3

What better way to round off your tour than with a short spa break (*see p290*) at this well-known resort, where the waters come bubbling up out of the ground at 140–144°F/60–62°C. The water contains fluorine and sulfur, as you may notice from the odor in the air. The mud baths here are said to be good for rheumatism, joint complaints, and some dermatological conditions. The hotels catering for tourists and spa-goers are almost all located opposite the main entrance to the spa on Bajcsy-Zsilinszky, while there are plenty of small restaurants, cafés, and cake shops along Kossuth Lajos utca, just as in every spa town. *Return to Pécs by Rte 58.*

ADDRESSES IN THE VINEYARDS

TRANSPORT

A **car** is the most practical way of getting around, but if you want to use public transport to get to Villány from **Pécs**, the **train** connection (around a dozen direct trains every day) operates more frequently than the bus (only one direct connection per day).
The **bus** is a more practical option for going to **Siklós**, however, with departures every 15–30min during the week, between 5.15am and 10.45pm.

STAY

There are plenty of rooms available in private houses and on the wine estates. Information from the tourist office (*see Info, p287*).

BUDGET

Flórián Vendégház – *Kossuth Lajos utca 12. Villánykövesd. 493 200. villanyvagyok.hu. 5 rooms, Ft15,500*. This is a lovely guesthouse in the heart of the village. The five large rooms are spotlessly clean and the beds are very comfortable. The owners are a charming couple who speak a little English. There's a pretty garden with flowers, too

AVERAGE

Hotel-restaurant Cabernet – *Petőfi utca 29. Villánykövesd. 493 200. hotelcabernet.hu. 25 rooms, Ft17,000/19,000*. Situated on the outskirts of the village but close to the wine cellars, this is a very popular place. The rooms are spacious, comfortable, and very clean. The restaurant is beneath the hotel in a cellar with a vaulted ceiling, serving grilled dishes made with local produce.

EAT

AVERAGE

Fülemüle Csárda – *Villánykövesd. (30) 220 7901. fulemulecsarda.hu. Open 11am–9pm (Sun, 8pm). Ft2,490/5,990.* This country inn has a warm family atmosphere, with its carved wooden furniture and sepia prints on the walls. Enjoy trying the regional dishes, mostly sourced locally, and sample the wines of Villány. At the end of the meal you will be offered some traditional *pálinka* (brandy); they don't speak English but they do speak German here.

BATHS

Siklós Fürdő – *Baross Gábor utca 6, at Siklós. 351 739. siklosfurdo.hu.* This modern spa complex is extensive, with 54,000sq ft/5,000sq m spread out over indoor and outdoor areas, including hot and cold pools, hot tubs, saunas, and more. It's nice and relaxing when there aren't too many people in the pools.

Harkány Fürdő – *Kossuth Lajos utca 7, at Harkány. 480 251. harkanyfurdo.hu.* Known as the place to go for sufferers from rheumatism. The story goes that it was workers draining the local marshes who noticed the therapeutic effects of the waters, finding themselves in better shape after completing the job than when they started it. Since then, spa tourism has proved a big draw here.

Szekszárd

Population 32,156 – Tolna county – area code ✆ 74

This small, pretty city has a history dating back by well over a thousand years. It is just the place to order a deliciously fruity red wine. As in Villány, you will find yourself in one of the oldest winemaking regions of Hungary, an area also cultivated by the Romans, who spotted the quality of the beautiful ocher-colored sand and silica strata that make up the local soil, creating a terroir particularly suitable for growing vines.

ADDRESSES PAGE 298
Stay, Eat, Shopping, Events and Festivals

INFO:
Tourist Office – *Garay tér 17. ✆ 315 198. visitszekszard.hu. Open Mon–Sat, 8.30am–4.30pm (Sat, 1.30pm).* Not far from Béla Király tér, the main square (at the junction with the pedestrianized area). You will find all the maps and information you need to explore Szekszárd.

LOCATION:
Regional map C2 (p272–73)
37mi/60km northeast of Pécs, on Rte 6.

PARKING:
Parking in the center (charges apply).

DON'TMISS:
A stroll in the Baroque downtown area; the forest railway at Gemenc.

TIMING:
Half a day is enough to walk around the town. Note the museums are closed on Mondays.

KIDS:
The forest railway at Gemenc; Petőfi Island and its leisure and sports activities, Baja (*see p299).*

Walking tour

It is difficult to imagine that until the turn of the 19C, this lovely little town was on the banks of the Danube. Since then construction projects on the river have altered its course, leaving Szekszárd high and dry, just as you see it today. As you approach the town, don't be fooled by the outskirts, a forest of large buildings; as is so often the case in Hungary, they conceal a beautiful historic heart (in the Baroque style, in this case) that is well preserved.

Start your walk at **Béla Király tér**, the main square, at the **Római Katolikus Plébánia** (Roman Catholic Church). Built in 1805, with a single tower, it is an example of the Zopf style (late Baroque). The white colonnaded building opposite is the **Megyeháza** (former County Hall), which was turned into a museum in 2011.

6

Vármegyeháza (County Museum)

Béla Király 1. ✆ (70) 491 1201. www.wmmm.hu. Open Tue–Sun, 10am–5pm. Ft600.

If you intend to visit several of Szekszárd's museums, you can buy a combined ticket for Ft1,200. Otherwise, entry to each museum is Ft600.

In the courtyard, note the foundations of a **Benedictine monastery** (1061), established by King Béla I. Various sections of the museum focus on the monastery and composer Franz Liszt's time in Szekszárd. Liszt used to give concerts regularly in the town and was famously commissioned by Baron Antal Augusz

Szekszárd vineyards
© Martin Zwick/age fotostock

to write his *Szekszárd Mass* for the consecration of a new church that was being built in the town.

Take the pedestrianized Garay tér.

At No. 26, not far from the tourist office, you will find **Garay Élménypince**, a privately owned cellar in an underground medieval vault *(see Addresses, p299)*. If you continue to No. 4, you will see the Art Nouveau building of the **Deutsche Bühne**, the only German-language theater in Hungary, which opened in 1994 to serve the town's German community of around 1,000. Continue along this road, which extends beyond its pedestrianized section. At the first crossroads, look out for **Augusz-ház** (Augusz House, now housing a music school) at No. 38 Széchenyi utca. Built in a Classicist style in 1820, it is immediately identifiable by the four windows in the roof that look as though half-open eyes are peeping out at you. Franz Liszt would stay here when he was in town, commemorated by a plaque fixed to the west wall.

★ Wosinsky Mór Megyei Múzeum

Szent István tér 26. ✆ (70) 491 1201. www.wmmm.hu. Open Tue–Sun, 10am–5pm. Ft600. This beautiful museum (named after an archeologist priest who carried out some important excavations in the area) was built at the turn of the 19C to house the collections that remain on display to this day. There are large numbers of Celtic and Avar coins, along with some jewelry, and upstairs an interesting exhibition illustrating life in Hungary at the turn of the 20C.

Babits Mihály Emlékház (Mihály Babits Memorial House)

Babits Mihály utca 13 (5min walk from the main square). ✆ 3 312 154. www.wmmm.hu. Open Tue–Sun, 10am–5pm. Ft600. **Mihály Babits** (1883–1941), one of the great Hungarian poets, known for writing on religious themes, was born in this modest house. He also translated some key international works into his native tongue, such as Dante's *Divine Comedy*.

Excursions Regional map (p272–73)

Baja D2

Drive 28mi/45km southeast along Hwy M6, then take Rte 55.

Szentháromság tér 11. (79) 420 792. baja.hu. Open Mon–Fri, 9am–noon & 1pm–5pm (Sat & Sun, 10am–2pm).

As they wind their way away from the main rivers, the various arms of the Danube and the Sugovica have created a number of islands, including Petőfi-sziget and Nagy-Pandúr-sziget, with the result that the town of Baja feels a little like a holiday resort.

Városháza (City Hall) – *Szentháromság tér.* On the west bank of the River Sugovica, Szentháromság tér (Holy Trinity Square) is enclosed on three sides by Baroque buildings, including the City Hall, which was built in the mid-18C by Count Antal Grassalkovich, who also built the Royal Palace of Gödöllő. It is not open to the public, but you can walk across the courtyard to emerge opposite the **Ferences templom** *(Bartók Béla utca 5)*, a Franciscan church that boasts a perfectly tuned Baroque organ.

★ **Türr István Múzeum** (István Türr Museum)– *Deák Ferenc utca 1. (79) 324 173. bajaimuzeum.hu. Open Tue–Sun, 10am–4pm. Ft800.* The museum is named after István Türr (1825–1908), the Baja-born hero of the 1848–49 War of Independence, who was sent into exile. Later in life he also helped to plan the Panama Canal and played a part in designing navigable canals between the Danube and the Tisza rivers in his home country. Among the museum's different sections is one dealing with life on and around the Danube, including models of water mills; these consisted of boats moored to the banks and fitted with a wheel turned by the river current. The equally interesting ethnographic collection examines the various peoples from Baja and the surrounding region.

On leaving the museum, retrace your steps toward Szentháromság tér, passing in front of City Hall and continuing as far as **Eötvös János utca**, Baja's main shopping street, which is pedestrianized.

LAST BRIDGE OVER THE DANUBE

Situated 96mi/155km from Budapest and south of Kalocsa, **Baja** boasts the last bridge over the Danube before the southern Hungarian border. On the eastern bank you will find a busy river port that has made the town a commercial center and a crossroads for people from far and wide. In centuries past, it was a meeting place for merchants who came to buy wine and grain, hence the many cellars and the local barrel-making industry. Grain, wine, and flour made their way up the Danube on small barges, while the wood to make the barrels was floated down from the north.

At one time at Baja, there were up to 70 watermills here on the Danube and its small tributaries. The millers, an affluent guild, celebrated the **Martyrdom of St. John** (St. John of Nepomuk, their patron saint), a feast day still observed in mid-May that has now also become a great folk festival. The bridge across the Danube is shared between rail and road, and Baja is a crossing point in every sense; to the west is Transdanubia—rich, wooded, and populous—and to the east, the interfluvial plain between the Danube and the Tisza, heralding the **Alföld** (the Great Plain of the east). Even here it already resembles the popular image of the **Puszta** with its vast landscapes, horses, dunes, and T-shaped well sweeps, and is a more sparsely populated region.

★ **Nagy István Képtár** (István Nagy Gallery) – *Arany János utca 1. ✆ (79) 325 649. bajaimuzeum.hu. Open Tue–Sat, 10am–4pm.* Once you are past Tóth Kálmán tér, take Vörösmarty utca to the eponymous square and you will find this museum, home to the works of several painters collectively known as the **Alföld School**, many of whom lived in this building after 1946. A stroll around the gallery provides a good insight into artistic activity in the provinces at the time.

Szerb ortodox templom (Serb Orthodox Church) – *Táncsics Mihály utca 21.* This is the more interesting of the two Serbian Orthodox churches in the town and features a beautiful 19C iconostasis.

Petőfi-sziget (Petőfi Island) – A bridge links the Baja's downtown area with this small island ringed with **beaches**. It is a really nice spot in which to take some time out from the museums, relaxing on one of the riverside beaches (busy in summer), or taking part in some water sports *(see Sports and Activities, p299)*. Much of the island is wooded so there is plenty of shade on offer.

★★ Gemenci Erdei Vasút (Gemenc State Forest Railway) D2

5mi/8km from Baja.

Pörböly Ecotourism Visitor Center, Bajai út 100. ✆ 491 483. gemenczrt.hu. Open daily in summer, 9am–5pm. Ask for opening times during rest of the year. On-site accommodation is available *(see Addresses, p298)**. Narrow-gauge train, 1 to 4 departures/day in summer (winter: trains run some Sat & Sun with enclosed, heated carriages, please inquire). Closed Jan & Dec. Round trip Ft2,700 (children Ft2,000).*

Take some insect repellent and wear appropriate clothing, particularly if insects are normally fond of you. As the area often floods, especially in spring, check ahead to be sure the train is running. In summer, this excursion can be combined with a boat trip on the Sió Canal, which links Lake Balaton to the Danube *(ask at the Ecotourism Visitor Center).*

Find out about the activities on offer (hiking, cycling, boating…) and see an interactive presentation about the local flora and fauna. Then jump aboard the small train for a journey of around 2hrs (allow half a day for the return trip). The train makes its way through the Gemenc Forest, a large floodplain forest unique in Europe. You will also see areas beside the Danube and Tisza that were once subject to flooding before they were regulated. From Pörböly, the train crosses the **Duna-Dráva Nemzeti Park** (Danube-Dráva National Park) to the canal at Sió (about 20mi/32km). There is an abundance of wildlife and the area is particularly famous for its colony of black storks. You may also catch sight of stags, boars, and water birds, and will see plants typical of wetlands.

Mohács C3

31mi/50km south along Hwy M6.

Széchenyi tér 1 ✆ (69) 505 515. mohacs.hu. Open summer Mon–Fri, 8am–4pm (Tue, 5pm); Sat, 9am–2pm; Sun 10am–12.30pm; winter Mon–Fri, 8am–4pm (Tue, 5pm).

Mohács is close to the borders with Serbia and Croatia in the far south of the country. It entered the history books with the defeat of the Hungarian army by Turkish troops on 29 August 1526 at the Battle of Mohács. It marked the beginning of a wave of Ottoman colonization that was to extend right across Hungary for more than a century and a half. "Our country was wiped out, the way a flourishing vineyard is laid waste by a wild boar," commented aristocrat and poet Miklós Zrínyi, who recorded the event.

Kanizsai Dorottya Múzeum (Dorottya Kanizsai Museum) – *Kisfaludy utca 9. ✆ (69) 306 604. kanizsaidorottyamuzeum.hu. Open Tue–Sat, 10am–4pm. Ft1,000 (children Ft600).*

A CARNIVAL WORTHY OF UNESCO

The **Busójárás**, a six-day carnival held at **Mohács** to mark the end of winter, is one of the best-known events in Hungary, indeed in Central Europe. It translates as "Busó-walking," in reference to the Busós, a gang of would-be invaders kitted out in scary costumes, wooden masks, and large, thick coats, who take over the town. More than 500 Busós range through the streets, accompanied by fantastic floats. The festivities include setting fire to a coffin symbolizing winter (a joyful event on the main square), feasting, and music throughout town. It originated with a Croat minority in Mohács (the Sokác, who still live in the region), and has since become a tradition for which the town and region are known. Having been handed down from generation to generation, it was inscribed on Unesco's Representative List of the Intangible Cultural Heritage of Humanity in 2009.

An ethnographic museum exploring the history of Hungary's Croat, Serbian, and Slovenian minorities. It also recounts the story of the famous 1526 battle and the history of the town. Don't leave without taking a look at the collection of masks from the town's famous carnival *(see above)*.

Busóudvar (Busó Court) – *Eötvös utca 17–19. ✆ (20) 222 9339. mohacs.hu. Open Mon–Fri, 9am–5pm; Sat, 9am–4pm; Sun, 10am–4pm. Ft1,300.* Now open to the public, this is the workshop where the carnival team creates the famous costumes and masks for the winter festival. There is also an exhibition exploring the lives of the Sokác minority.

Mohácsi Nemzeti Emlékhely (National Memorial of Mohács) – *5mi/8km to the south. Continue on Rte 56 then turn right after 4mi/6km. mohacsiemlekhely.hu. Open 9am–6pm (Oct–Mar, 4pm). Ft1,800 (children Ft1,200).* The memorial was consecrated at **Sátorhely** in 1976, on the site of the battlefield and where a mass grave was discovered in 1960. It is a huge site studded with strange, carved wooden memorial posts and an inscription on a large iron grille that reads: "This spot marks the beginning of the end of Hungary's power." There is also an exhibition exploring (in Hungarian) the battle from both the Hungarian and Turkish sides.

★ Kalocsa D1

30mi/48km northeast along Hwy M9 and Rte 51

Szent István király út 35. ✆ 30 467 8690. turizmuskalocsa.hu. Open Mon–Fri, 8.30am–4.30pm (Fri, 2pm). Kalocsa is the world mild **paprika capital**—it is grown on more than 11sq mi/30 sq km of land around the town. Kalocsa is also well known for its superb embroidery (decorated clothing and table linen), which you will have the chance to see and no doubt also buy. The quality and delicacy of the work is on show at the House of Folk Arts in particular.

Magyar Fűszerpaprika Múzeum (Hungarian Paprika Museum) – *Szent István király út 6. ✆ (78) 461 860. Open Apr–Oct, Tue–Sun, 9am–5pm; rest of the year by arrangement.* The museum presents the history of paprika, including how it arrived in Hungary (with the Turks), how it is cultivated, ground into powder, and put to many uses. After the harvest (carried out by hand, as the peppers don't all ripen at the same time), the paprika is dried during the month of September. Once stripped of moisture, the peppers are ground up with their seeds to preserve their beautiful dark red color. The museum is also where you can find out about how it was paprika that led Albert Szent-Györgyi, the Hungarian Nobel laureate for medicine in 1937, to first isolate vitamin C (*see p307*).

★ **Püspöki Palota** (Episcopal Palace) – The archbishop's palace dates from the end of the 18C. Built in a Baroque style to plans drawn up by Brother Gáspár Oswald, the overall effect is symmetrical, achieved with various architectural elements repeated at intervals, which combine to produce an attractive building that looks out over extensive parkland. During your visit you will be able to explore a library that includes such precious items as a Bible once belonging to Protestant reformer Martin Luther, annotated in his hand. There are 120,000 volumes in total, including some from the 13C. Upstairs in the great hall (when open) and the chapel are frescoes by Franz Anton Maulbertsch, the Austrian artist who decorated a considerable number of churches and religious buildings in Hungary.

Főszékesegyház (Kalocsa Cathedral) – A Baroque church (1735–54) designed by András Mayerhoffer. The crypt contains the last resting place of Asztrik, the archbishop who brought to King Stephen the crown given by Pope Sylvester as a token of the Holy See's recognition of his conversion. The donation of the crown also had the effect of strengthening papal authority over Christianity in Hungary. On display in the **Archbishop's Treasury** are priests' vestments and religious objects that include a bust of St. Stephen (1896) weighing 110lb/50kg (comprising 106lb/48kg silver and 4.5lb/2kg gold).

★ **Viski Károly Múzeum** (Károly Viski Museum) – *Szent István Király út 25. ✆ (78) 462 351. viskikarolymuzeum.hu. Open mid-May–mid-Sept, Wed–Sun, 9am–5pm; mid- Sept–Oct & mid-Mar–mid-May, Tue–Sat, 9am–5pm. Closed rest of the year. Ft500.* The museum explores the lives of the different communities (Hungarian, Swabian, Slovakian) who have lived in the region, through reconstructions of locations, dwellings, and the daily lives of the people. It shows how the communities evolved through the developments that took place in interior decoration and embroidery (both are arts for which the women of Kalocsa have acquired a reputation). There is also an interesting collection of coins.

Schöffer Gyűjtemény (Nicolas Schöffer Collection) – *Szent István Király út 76. ✆ (20) 409 5575. schoffergyujtemeny.hu. Open mid-Mar–mid-Oct, Tue, Thu & Sat, 10am–5pm; Wed & Fri by arrangement. Closed rest of year. Ft500.* Kalocsa-born sculptor and artist **Nicolas Schöffer** (1912–92) was one of the prime exponents of kinetic art, known for his sculptures using movement, light, and sound—the precursor of electronic and numerical art. Some of his sculptures are motorized. After studying in Budapest, he moved to Paris in 1936, where he lived until his death. When you leave the museum, look out for the nearby **Schöffer Fénytorony** (Tower of Light). Also by Nicolas Schöffer, this 72ft/22m high tower made of steel and mirrors is full of light and movement, and for a time was one of the symbols and signature pieces of the revolutionary Avant-garde in art.

Népművészeti Tájház (House of Folk Arts) – *Tompa Mihály utca 5–7. Open Tue–Sun, 10am–4pm. Ft600.* An exhibition of embroidery, decorated items, and murals painted by talented local artists. The shirts, also made in Kalocsa, are famous for the quality of the needlework.

Vasútállomás (Railway station building) – *Vasút utca. For times and prices, ask at the information office.* Although no train has stopped here since 2007, Kalocsa Station (1881) has been preserved for its beautiful decoration (particularly in the waiting room), which features floral garlands and painted foliage. A small exhibition recounts the story of the local railroad.

Kalocsa Cathedral
© karenfoleyphotography/iStock

ADDRESSES IN SZEKSZÁRD

TRANSPORT

Train – There is one direct train connection per day *(2hrs10min)* beween Szekszárd and Budapest.

STAY

BUDGET

Belvárosi Vendégház – *Garay tér 18. 317 002. belvarosivendeghaz.com. 4 rooms, Ft15,000.* Prices are spiraling rapidly in Szekszárd, which is not exactly overrun with good-quality accommodation. This guesthouse has the advantage of being right in the center, on the first (ground) floor of a pretty apartment block on a pedestrianized street. The rooms are rather dark but are very well maintained.

AVERAGE

Hotel Merops Mészáros – *Kossuth Lajos utca 19. 684 940. hotelmerops.hu. (see Eat). 30 rooms, Ft19,900/22,900.* One of the best hotels in Szekszárd is to be found adjacent to the wine estate of the same name. Comfortable rooms, but the spa and restaurant are the real attraction. A good find.

Away from the center

A TREAT

Takler Kúria – *Decsi Szőlőhegy. 5mi/8km west of the center. 20 429 2430. taklerkuria.hu. 24 rooms. From Ft22,800.* Enjoy rural chic at this elegant hotel-restaurant with a wellness center on a wine estate owned by a winemaker of some renown in Hungary. The rooms are furnished country-style, and some open out onto the garden. Swimming pool, spa, and contemporary Hungarian cuisine.

Gemenc Forest

BUDGET

Ecotourism Center – *Bajai út 100, at Pörböly. 491 483. gemenczrt.hu. Rooms for 2/6 persons, adults Ft5,500 (children Ft4,000). Chalet (up to 6 persons) Ft18,000. Café.* Simple and reasonably priced accommodation next door to the Ecotourism Center, in the middle of unspoilt countryside. Canoe and bike hire available.

EAT

AVERAGE

Merops Restaurant – *On the first (ground) floor of Hotel Merops Mészáros, Kossuth Lajos utca 19. 684 940. hotelmerops.hu. Open 11am–11pm (Sun, 9pm). Ft2,490/5,990. Dish of the day Ft1,150/1,440.* Gastronomic dining; the menu pairs local wines with local produce, such as duck breast in a merlot jus or sweet potato tart with blue cheese, for which a glass of 2016 Chardonnay is recommended. A culinary delight.

Szász Étterem – *Garay tér 18. 312 463. szasz–sorozo.hu. Open 11am–11.30pm. Ft 2,390/4,890.* A traditional tavern with wooden tables beneath a vaulted stone ceiling; draft beers and local wines. Good, honest, Hungarian brasserie cooking, with Wiener Schnitzel and homemade goulash on the menu.

There are two main types of **halászlé** (fish soup) in Hungary, named after the towns of Baja and Szeged. Baja fish soup is traditionally made from carp, while the Szeged variety is made from various kinds of fish and passed through a sieve.

TAKING A BREAK

A Kávé Háza – *Bátaszéki út 25. (70) 930 0950. Open Mon–Fri, 7am–7pm; Sat, 8am–3pm.* An unusual location for a café. Situated on an avenue lined with condominiums on the outskirts of town, it has been voted "the best café in Hungary," no mean feat in a country where even the local bistro serves excellent snacks. The young team knows its onions (not to mention its wines). Small snacks (sandwiches, salads, and homemade cakes), all in immaculate white surroundings.

SHOPPING

Garay Élménypince – *Garay tér 19. (20) 401 4651. garaypince.hu. Open Tue–Thu, 11am–6pm; Fri & Sat, 11am–11pm. Closed Sun & Mon. Ft700.* An interactive exhibition exploring the famous wines of Szekszárd in particular. There's also a shop where you can buy wine.

SPORTS AND ACTIVITIES

Baja

Petőfi-sziget – *Information at the tourist office (see p291).* This island in the River Sugovica is all about fun activities. You can take part in water sports in addition to enjoying its swimming pool and tennis courts. Or choose from canoeing, kayaking, and fishing, or go swimming from the beach equipped with amenities.

EVENTS AND FESTIVALS

Kalocsai Paprikafesztivál
A paprika festival, organized by the "paprika capital of the world," with a cooking competition based on hot peppers, of course!
kalocsaipaprikafesztival.hu

Bajai Halfőző Fesztivál
A festival dedicated to Baja's fish soup, held in mid July.
www. bajaihalfozofesztival.hu

Participants of Busójárás, a six-day carnival at Mohács
© csakisti/iStock

Szeged and the Southern Great Plain 7

Michelin National Map 732
Csongrád, Békés, Bács-Kiskun, Jász-Nagykun-Szolnok counties

Deutsch Palace, Szeged

© Funkystock/age fotostock

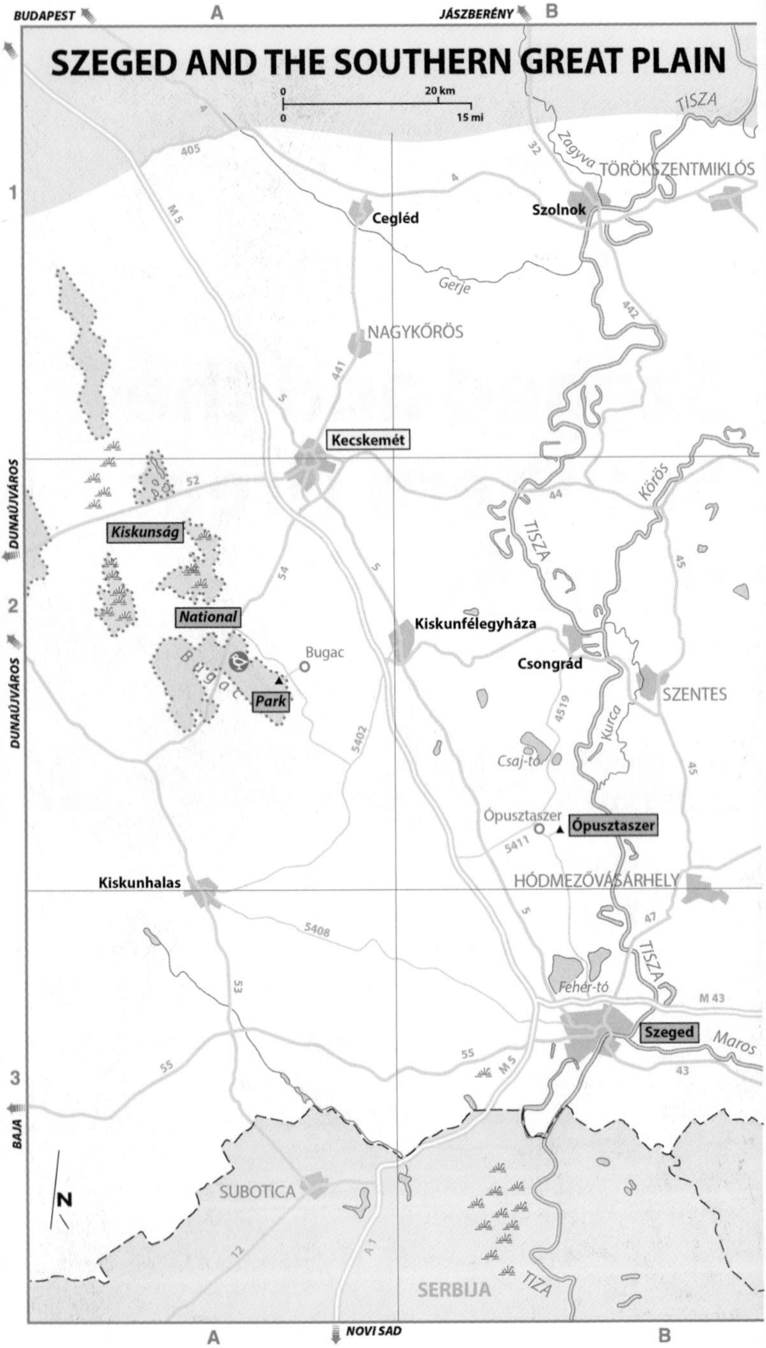
SZEGED AND THE SOUTHERN GREAT PLAIN
BUDAPEST
JÁSZBERÉNY
A
B
1
2
3
0
20 km
0
15 mi
TISZA
Zagyva
TÖRÖKSZENTMIKLÓS
Cegléd
Szolnok
Gerje
NAGYKŐRÖS
Kecskemét
Kőrös
TISZA
DUNAÚJVÁROS
Kiskunság
National
Park
Bugac
Kiskunfélegyháza
Csongrád
SZENTES
Kurca
Csaj-tó
Ópusztaszer
Ópusztaszer
Kiskunhalas
HÓDMEZŐVÁSÁRHELY
TISZA
Fehér-tó
Szeged
Maros
BAJA
SUBOTICA
N
SERBIJA
TIZA
NOVI SAD

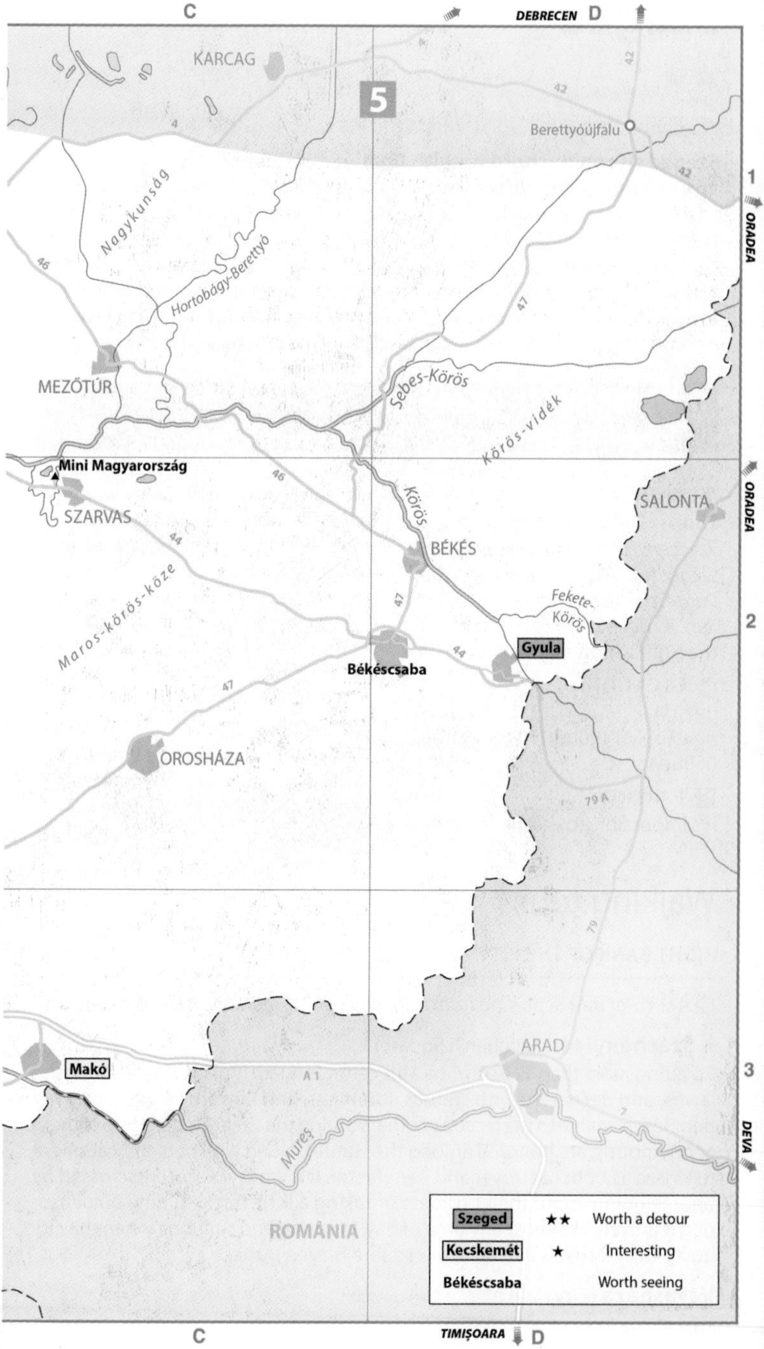
C
DEBRECEN D
KARCAG
5
Berettyóújfalu
1
ORADEA
Nagykunság
Hortobágy-Berettyó
MEZŐTÚR
Sebes-Körös
Körös-vidék
Mini Magyarország
SZARVAS
ORADEA
SALONTA
Körös
BÉKÉS
Maros-körös-köze
Fekete-Körös
2
Gyula
Békéscsaba
OROSHÁZA
79 A
ARAD
Makó
3
A1
Mureș
DEVA
ROMÂNIA
Szeged ★★ Worth a detour
Kecskemét ★ Interesting
Békéscsaba Worth seeing
C
TIMIȘOARA D

Szeged

★★

Population 161,122 – Csongrád county – area code ✆ 62

Szeged sits on the borders with Romania and Serbia and is a beautiful and engaging city. After the terrible flood of 1879, when water from the River Tisza destroyed the city, it had to be rebuilt. As a result, all the late 19C architectural styles, from neo-Baroque to Art Nouveau, can now be seen on the town's boulevards and squares and around its attractive gardens. A lively student city and the sunniest in the country, Szeged locals know how to enjoy life, relaxing on the many café terraces or enjoying a bowl of fish soup spiced with the famous local paprika.

ADDRESSES PAGE 315
Stay, Eat, Shopping, Baths, Events and Festivals

INFO:
Tourist Office – Szeged map A1 *Széchenyi tér 12. ✆ 488 699. www.szegedtourism.hu. Open Mon–Fri, 9am–5pm; Sat, 10am–4pm. Closed Sun.* A brochure in English detailing the sights and a map of the city.

LOCATION:
Regional map B3 (p302–303); Szeged map (p306) 106mi/170km southeast of Budapest.

PARKING:
It's impossible to escape the ticket machines in the city center, where charges therefore apply. Some hotels also have parking spaces.

DON'T MISS:
Reök Palace; the Votive Church; the New Synagogue.

TIMING:
Allow two days to visit the city.

KIDS:
The musical clock on the Votive Church; Ópusztaszer Heritage Park; Aquapolis Spa & Makó Baths *(see p316).*

Walking tour Szeged map (p306)

RIGHT BANK OF THE CITY AB1–2

A circular tour departing from the tourist office, marked on the Szeged map.

★ Széchenyi tér (Széchenyi Square) A1

Covering more than 12 acres/5ha, this central square is planted with trees and lawns, and decorated with statues, fountains, and flowerbeds. A number of people who came to the rescue of others during the Great Flood, some of them anonymously, are honored among the statues, along with personifications of the Tisza as both destroyer and benefactor. It is a busy place, crisscrossed by people going about their business or taking a little relaxing time out, ensuring it is lively at almost any time of day. In spring and summer, when the city hosts local festivals and fairs, the square is even busier.

Városháza (City Hall) A1

This is one of the key buildings in the square. Chimes ring out every quarter of an hour from the watchtower that stands high above the yellow-painted

Saved from the waters

BEFORE THE FLOOD

The name Szeged derives from the word *sziget* (island, in Hungarian), a hint at the part water was to play in its history. After the foundation of Hungary, the city became a distribution center for salt, for which it had a royal monopoly, a position it held for 200 years. Szeged was largely destroyed by the Mongols in the 13C. Then in the 16C, just as it was recovering, the Turks invaded the city, although it subsequently benefited from the presence of the sultan; he had his personal estate here until 1686, when the Turks eventually departed. However, it was not until the end of the 18C that prosperity returned.

DEVASTATION

A century later, on the night of 12 March 1879, the dikes (levees) that held back the River Tisza broke in several places. Within just a few hours the water had risen 24.4ft/8.06m above the normal level and by early morning the city had been engulfed and there was a scene of total devastation. The force of the water was so strong that it even disinterred the dead in the cemeteries. The toll taken by the flood was appalling, with around 160 dead and 60,000 of the 75,000 population made homeless (you can see the unfolding of the disaster in an illuminated model at the Ópusztaszer Heritage Park, *see p311*). Some districts remained under 10ft/3m of water for two months and Szeged almost disappeared off the map. Of some 7,000 houses, only around 300 remained standing and many thought the city would never recover.

A VOW TO REBUILD

Five days after the fury of the waters, Emperor Franz Joseph arrived from Vienna promising that "Szeged would be reborn more beautiful than ever." He sent **Lajos Tisza**, a royal commissioner, to coordinate and oversee the work. Many great European cities helped Sezeged financially with the task of rebuilding and the famous Hungarian composer **Franz Liszt** organized fund-raising concerts. Reconstruction began by replacing the narrow medieval roads with wide Parisian-style avenues. Between the end of the 19C and the beginning of the 20C, many of the leading architects of the day came to Szeged to design new buildings, notably in the Art Nouveau style that the city is famous for today. In grateful recognition of the assistance and donations received, the boulevards of the second ring road were named after the cities that had helped out, including Brussels, London, Paris, Rome, and Vienna.

In 1970 the waters of the Tisza rose once more, to 31.5ft/9.60m, but this time the levees held firm, although the consequences would not have been so great had they not held, since the new Szeged had been constructed at a higher level than the old city.

A GRATEFUL CITY

Szeged has never forgotten the support it received from other European countries and, in particular, France. The day after the dreadful fire in Notre-Dame Cathedral in Paris, in April 2019, the city donated €10,000 to help with its reconstruction "in a spirit of European solidarity."

exterior. In summer theater performances and chamber music concerts are held in the attractive interior courtyard, occasions that are known as **Városházi Esték** (City Hall Evenings).

Next door to City Hall, at No. 11, is the mayor's office, located in a building (Bérpalota) that predates the great flood. Look upward to see **Sóhajok hídja**, a small enclosed bridge connecting the two buildings, which spans the road below. It translates as the Bridge of Sighs, an allusion to its world-famous counterpart in Venice, or, as another story has it, because the townsfolk were sighing under the burden of heavy taxes. It was built in 1883 to allow Emperor Franz Joseph and his entourage, on their visits to Szeged, to walk directly from their apartments to City Hall.

Leave Széchenyi tér by Kárász utca to rejoin Klauzál tér, a long, rectangular "square," and take the pedestrianized street that leads to Árpád tér.

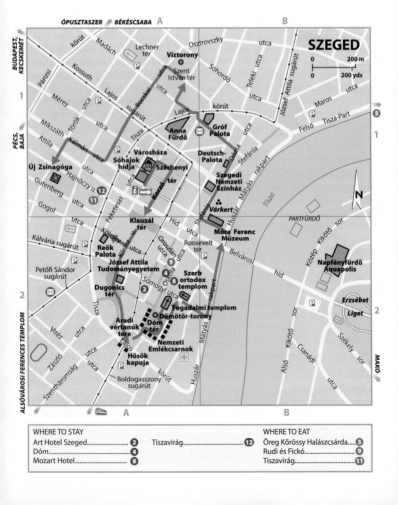

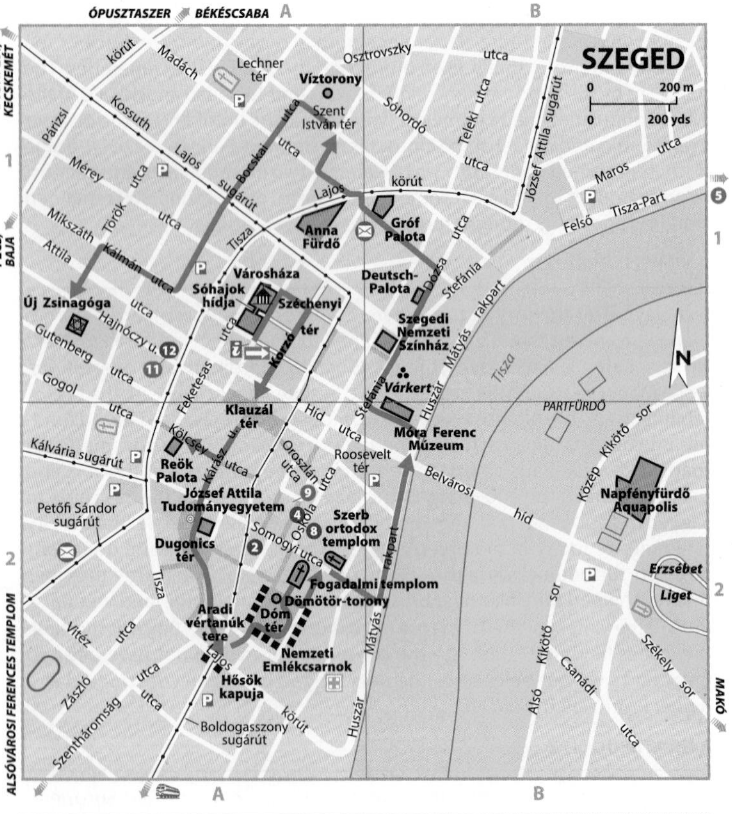

WHERE TO STAY
Art Hotel Szeged........ 2
Dóm........ 4
Mozart Hotel........ 8
Tiszavirág........ 12

WHERE TO EAT
Öreg Kőrössy Halászcsárda........ 5
Rudi és Fickó........ 9
Tiszavirág........ 11

★★ **Klauzál tér** (Klauzál Square) A1–2
Szeged's elegance is on show in Klauzál tér, a classically beautiful square. In the center is a statue of statesman **Lajos Kossuth**, who delivered his last speech here before going into exile. **Virág Cukrászda** (Virág Cake Shop) on the south side of the square is a real institution and has been indulging the locals' collective sweet tooth since 1922 *(see Taking a Break, p316).*

Korzó (Corso) A1
The citizens of Szeged named this busy and lively central path across Széchenyi tér the "corso," a place for promenading, while its continuation, Kárász utca, is known simply as "Kárász."
From Klauzál tér, carry on walking down Kárász utca and turn right into Kölcsey utca.

★ **Reök Palota** (Reök Palace) A2
Magyar Ede tér 2. www.reok.hu. 471 411. Open Tue–Sun, 10am–6pm.
This elegant palace, a typical example of Hungarian Art Nouveau, was built in 1907 by the architect **Ede Magyar**, who was dubbed the "Hungarian Gaudí." Commissioned by Iván Reök, a hydraulic engineer, the principal theme of its decoration is water—blue water lilies decorate the white exterior and there is a hint of the fluidity of water in the ironwork of the balconies and railings. Renovated very sympathetically in 2007, the building is now a cultural center where exhibitions, concerts, and shows are staged. There is a very nice large café on the first (ground) floor.
Retrace your steps to reach Dugonics tér, the main square.

★ **Dugonics tér** (Dugonics Square) A2
The university formerly named **József Attila Tudományegyetem** is on one side of the square. It bore the name of the great poet József Attila, who, while a student in 1925, was expelled for having written: "I have neither father, nor mother. I have neither God, nor country." It then merged with the University of Szeged. Biochemist **Albert Szent-Györgyi**, who was awarded the Nobel Prize in 1937 for his work on the vitamin C content of paprika, also worked in this building. It was also at the university that, in 1956, Szeged students met to ask that learning Russian should become optional and to demand a student organization independent of the Communist Party.
People often congregate around the **musical fountain**, built to mark the 100th anniversary of the flood. It plays a selection of tunes several times a day in spring and summer. Artistic events, concerts, and dance shows are staged in the square on the city's special day, 21 May, Szeged Day *(Szeged Napja).*

Hősök kapuja (Heroes' Gate) A2
This large archway beneath the building that straddles the street Boldogasszony sugárút leads to **Aradi vértanúk tere** (Square of the Martyrs of Arad). It commemorates the 13 Hungarian generals who were executed in 1849 on the orders of Austrian General Haynau, known as the "hyena of Brescia," who was brutal in his suppression of the 1848 Revolution. The gate is guarded by statues of two First World War soldiers, one depicted living and the other dead.
Two monuments in the square recall Hungary's struggles against the Habsburgs: an equestrian statue of Ferenc II Rákóczi *(see p179)* and a column in memory of the victims of the Battle of Szőreg (5 August 1849), on top of which is a **turul**, the mythological bird of the Magyars. There is also an obelisk commemorating the 1956 Revolution, which began with a student demonstration in Szeged.

Dömötör-torony (St. Demetrius Tower) A2
Dóm tér 16. www.szegedidom.com. (20) 385 5061. Open Tue–Sun, 9am–5pm. Ft800 or Ft1,800 with a visit to the Votive Church Tower and exhibition in the crypt.
The tower is the oldest building in the city and stands beside the cathedral. Its square base is 12C and the three octagonal floors above date from the 13C. It was almost destroyed to make way for the Votive Church, but it was spared the dynamite due to its proximity to houses. It was the decision to knock it down in the old-fashioned way, with sledgehammer and pickaxe, that led to the discovery of its 12C foundations, hence its restoration. Inside you can see an interactive exhibition recounting the story.

★★ **Fogadalmi templom** (Votive Church) and **Dóm tér** (Cathedral Square) A2
Dóm tér 16. www.szegedidom.com. 385 5061. Open 9am–7pm. No charge. Ft1,100 to visit the tower and the exhibition in the crypt (Tue–Sun, 9am–5pm). A café and restaurant beneath the church.
Szeged's imposing cathedral, also known as the Votive Church of Our Lady, is surrounded by university buildings on Dóm tér (4,350sq yds/12,000sq m). A cultural festival is held on the square in summer, when it is packed with people. A stage is erected together with stands that can hold 6,000 spectators. After a promise to build a cathedral in the wake of the flood of 1879, construction started on the red brick church in 1913, but was interrupted by the First World War, so it was not finished until 1930. The exterior is decorated with a mosiac depicting the 12 apostles, and is flanked by two tall neo-Romanesque towers. Inside are some large colorful frescoes, including one of the Virgin Mary in the traditional dress of the region. Also of note is the huge organ with its 9,040 pipes. In the **crypt** an exhibition traces the history of the church, including liturgical objects.
A walk around the perimeter of the square, beneath the arcades, will introduce you to the **Nemzeti Emlékcsarnok** (National Pantheon)—busts and statues of more than 80 celebrated Hungarians in the fields of art, culture, and history. There is one foreigner among these illustrious figures, the British engineer Adam Clark, to whom the people of Budapest owe the Chain Bridge.
If you are in Dóm tér at the right time (12.15pm and 5.45pm), wait to see the colorful musical clock perform (1936) on the wall of the building opposite the Votive Church's main entrance. The revolving figures represent students celebrating the end of their studies.

Szerb ortodox templom (Serbian Orthodox Church) A2
Somogyi utca 3. Look inside the 18C Serbian Orthodox Church to see its so-called "golden tree," a beautiful **iconostasis**★ created in the middle of the 18C. Suspended from its "branches" are 80 icons.
Walk down Somogyi utca toward the Tisza. Just before you reach the river and the road that runs beside it, take the path on the right. It runs along the river but is set back slightly between the trees and is a popular place for a stroll. Look out for the bronze figure sitting on a bench.

★ **Móra Ferenc Múzeum** (Ferenc Móra Museum) B1–2
Roosevelt tér 1–3. www.moramuzeum.hu.
The museum is closed for renovation work until at least 2020. In the meantime, you could visit **Fekete Ház** (Black House, *Somogyi utca 13, open 10am–6pm),* which is run by the museum; it has local history displays and holds occasional temporary exhibitions. The main museum is named after the man who ran it between 1917 and 1934, writer and museologist Ferenc Móra. It houses

Votive Church
© repistu/iStock

an ethnographic collection illustrating the **life of the Avars**★ (people originally from Mongolia who invaded part of Europe in the 8C). Another collection traces the history of the old city of Szegred via folklore exhibits, handicrafts (clothes embroidered with wool, and painted chests), and information about different trades (fishing, the cultivation of paprika, crafts, weaving, ...). There is also a gallery of paintings by artists from the Nagybanya School and region, as well as others by Hungarian masters from the early 20C, such as Pál Vágó, László Mednyánszky, and Mihály Munkácsy. An enormous canvas by Vágó depicts the flood of 1879.

Várkert (Castle Garden) B1

Due to the renovation work taking place at the Ferenc Móra Museum, the garden may be closed. There are still a few traces of the old 13C castle remaining; it was a prison before being destroyed in the flood *(visit by appointment only)*. On one side the castle garden overlooks the path by the riverbank, while the other side is bordered by the street named simply Stefánia. The large old building you see sandwiched between Stefánia and Dózsa utca is the once luxurious Kass Hotel, now abandoned.

On the other side of Dózsa utca, more or less opposite the old hotel, is **Deutsch Palota** (Deutsch Palace). It has an unusual orange and white exterior, with sea green and blue majolica decoration in the Secessionist style. The statue of a man with a long mustache clutching a violin in front of the building represents Pista Dankó, a native of Szeged, and a Romani composer and musician, who rose from poverty to achieve great fame, particularly after his death.

★ **Szegedi Nemzeti Színház** (National Theater) B1

Vaszy Viktor tér 1. www.szinhaz.szeged.hu. Built after the flood in 1883, the theater was damaged by fire in 1885 but reopened the following year. This creamy-yellow building looks particularly splendid in the evening when it is lit up, and is further proof of the ambitious reconstruction program that took place after the flood. It stages operas, dance shows, and theater performances.

★ **Gróf Palota** (Gróf Palace) B1

Tisza Lajos körút 20/b. This is the largest Art Nouveau building in the city. It was erected in 1913 and is an elaborate concoction of pediments, balconies, and ceramic bas-reliefs, flanked by two round towers on either side.

Víztorony (Water Tower) A1

Szent István tér. ✆ 558 844. Open Apr–Oct, first Sat in the month, 10am–4pm.
The tower was erected in 1904 and was Szeged's first structure to be built using reinforced concrete. It now looms 300ft/91m over Szent István tér. Still in use today, it offers a fine view over the city from the top.

★★ **Új Zsinagóga** (New Synagogue) A1

Jósika utca 10. ✆ 423 849. www.szzsh.hu. Open Apr–Sept, Tue–Sun, 9am–noon, 1pm–5pm; Oct–Mar, Tue–Sun, 10am–3pm. Ft1,200.
The Dohány Street Synagogue in Budapest might be bigger, but this is judged the finest synagogue in Hungary. Built between 1900 and 1903 to plans by Rabbi Immanuel Löw, it was designed by Lipót Baumhorn in the Art Nouveau style with Moorish features. The immense dome, supported by 24 columns, one for each hour of the day, represents the world. It is decorated with white roses symbolizing faith and blue stars to reflect the infinity of the universe. At the top, the Star of David shines like a sun. Miksa Róth, a celebrated stained glass artist who worked on many other buildings, including the Academy of Music in Budapest, created the stained glass windows here. Also of note is the altar stone made of Jerusalem marble and the door of the Ark of the Covenant carved from Nile acacia wood. The New Synagogue's excellent acoustics mean many concerts are held here. In the hall the names of 1,874 Jews, murdered during the Second World War, are engraved on white marble plaques and the symbolic tomb of the missing is set in a niche. The Old Synagogue still stands next door and is now a theater. Legend has it that during the flood of 1879 the waters rose, but when they reached the synagogue and were getting dangerously close to the Ark of the Covenant protecting the Torah, the flow suddenly stopped and the sacred book was saved.

ÚJSZEGED, ACROSS THE RIVER B1–2

Cross the river via Belvárosi híd (Belvárosi Bridge).
On the opposite side of the river, in Újszeged (New Szeged), the city is less-built up. The thermal baths complex **Napfényfürdő Aquapolis** (*see p316*) is a few minutes' walk to left after leaving the bridge.

Erzsébet Liget (Elisabeth Park) B2

To reach the park keep walking straight ahead after crossing the bridge.
The city's largest park (37 acres/15ha) was laid out in 1858 by an Imperial officer and his soldiers. Bordered by plane trees, ancient oaks, and maples, it is a lovely spot for walkers and there are good recreational areas for keen joggers. A theater festival is held here in summer.

ALSO SEE

★ **Alsóvárosi Ferences templom**

(Franciscan Church in the Lower Town) A2, off map

Take Szentháromság utca as far as Mátyás tér. Mátyás tér 26. ✆ 20 502 1953. www.latogatobarat.hu. Open Tue–Sun, 10am–6pm. Visit by guided tour only at 10am, noon, 2pm, and 4pm. Reserve ahead. Ft900 (Ft1,300 for visit in English).

Constructed from the remains of an old 12C building, the late Gothic Franciscan Church was consecrated in 1503. The pulpit and altars are Baroque and were installed at the beginning of the 18C. At the **Franciscan Visitor Center** next to the church, you can learn about the lives of the monks and the monastery, one of the most active in the country.

This neighborhood has retained its almost rural appearance in places and you can still see old houses with pointed gables like the rays of the sun.

Excursions Regional map (p302–303)

★★ **Ópusztaszer** (Ópusztaszer National Heritage Park) B2

19mi/30km north of Szeged (follow signs to Emlékpark), between Szeged and Csongrád. www.opusztaszer.hu. 275 133. Open Tue–Sun, 10am–6pm (Nov–Mar, 4pm). Closed Easter and Whit Monday (Pentecost). Ft2,500. Café.

Note that the park, which comprises a number of different sections that include the Panorama, is a popular excursion for Hungarians so the weekends are particularly busy.

Look out for the huge arrows protruding from a low mound, looking as if they have been fired from a massive bow pulled by a giant. Entitled *The Seven Hungarian Arrows* by artist László Morvay, they represent the seven original Magyar tribes.

Árpád Memorial – The centerpiece of the park was erected in 1896. It was here, according to history, that Prince Árpád received the oath of loyalty from the chiefs of the seven Magyar tribes who founded Hungary. It thus commemorates the Magyar conquest of the Carpathian Basin. This was later recorded by Anonymous (*see p62*), King Béla III's unnamed chronicler, who wrote the *Gesta Hungarorum* ("The Deeds of the Hungarians," a 24-page document preserved in the National Library). It was also here that on his return from Moscow in 1945, after the Second World War, Imre Nagy, who was at the time a committed Communist, attended the first symbolic ceremony for the distribution of land to Hungarian peasants as minister of agriculture. Countless Hungarians have been photographed beside this iconic monument over the years.

★ **Panorama – The Arrival of the Hungarians** – *Access every 30min.* On the first (ground) floor of the **Rotunda**, which resembles a large yurt. This is an impressive, well-mounted cyclorama, part of which is painted with a realistic foreground depicting different scenes from the Hungarian conquest in great detail. It reveals the skills of the artists, including the great landscape painter László Mednyánszky and Pál Vágó, whose ability to paint horses, oxen, and human figures is second to none. The scene unfolds beside the viewer as they follow a walkway around the painting. The commentary is given in different languages including English *(ask for the English commentary at the entrance)*, and is accompanied by music and the cries and sounds of battle. The most significant scene is where Árpád, astride his white horse and accompanied by the seven tribal chiefs, surveys his victorious troops from the top of a hill as they advance across the plain below. On his left, his wife sits resplendent in a chariot drawn by four gray oxen with large horns, protected from evil spirits by the skulls of two bulls on either side.

Another scene shows the Magyars settling on the edge of a forest and pitching their tents—an astonishing 2,000 people feature in the painting in total. Diametrically opposite the figure of Árpád, on top of another hill overlooking the plain and the Danube Valley, you can see men approaching the sacrificial white horse, the Táltos, beside which stands the Kádár, the man charged with its ritual slaughter. Young girls dance around with white smoke heralding

Ópusztaszer Heritage Park

STRANGE MOUNDS

The Ópusztaszer Heritage Park occupies one of the many mounds (of varying heights—up to 40ft/12m—and diameters) that are found at intervals right across the Great Plain. Many are burial mounds, sheltering the graves of tribal chiefs interred with their possessions. Others were border markers or guard stations. It is estimated that there were once three or four thousand of these mounds, although many have now disappeared, having been flattened in the quest for agricultural land. The park has a solemn atmosphere. Covering 136 acres/55ha, it aims to explore the history and conservation of the area, featuring displays and exhibits on a wide range of topics, including archeology, cultural history and society, art, and ethnography against a backdrop of the Hungarian Puszta.

THE FESZTY PANORAMA

Painted panoramas (or cycloramas) were popular in 19C Europe and were designed to display a circular 360-degree image. Artist **Árpád Feszty** was fascinated by a panorama he had seen in Paris and had the idea of creating one in Budapest to illustrate the Bible. His father-in-law, the celebrated romantic writer Mór Jókai, advised him to use the arrival of the Magyars as his subject instead, especially since Hungary's millennium anniversary was approaching. Árpád had an enormous canvas (395ft/120m long, 49ft/15m high) brought over from Belgium, which would form a continuous 360-degree painting encircling an area 125ft/38m in diameter. He chose to illustrate the landscape of the Valoci Valley in the Carpathians, which today is in Ukraine. A dozen or so artists took part in creating this huge work of art, including **László Mednyánszky**, who took care of many of the landscapes, and **Pál Vágó**, who painted the equestrian scenes and people. According to one story, Árpád Feszty offered himself as a model for the figure of his namesake, Prince Árpád. The panorama was created and viewed in a purpose-built venue in Budapest. After being exhibited in London in 1899, it was returned to Hungary and was installed in a new building in Budapest.

ON THE MOVE

During the Second World War, a bomb hit the building containing the panorama and it was damaged. Some well-meaning individuals decided it should be put out of harm's way. With the best of intentions, but unfortunately lacking the necessary experience, they decided to cut it into 26ft/8m wide strips for storage. These were rolled up, stored in poor conditions, and moved from one museum to another over the next 30 years. Almost inevitably the canvas was 60 percent destroyed, so a competition was launched to restore it. A team from Poland was recruited, who worked away using 660gals/2,500 liters of solvent and 8 US tons/7 tonnes of sawdust. It was a success and since 1995 has been exhibited in its present location in Ópusztaszer. Hungarians adore it and come in huge numbers to see it.

Building designed by György Csete, Ópusztaszer National Heritage Park
© Bertrand Rieger/hemis.fr

good omens. Victory is almost theirs—since the inhabitants of the valley have been defeated, the Magyars can settle on Szvatopluk's lands, the leader of the Moravo-Slavs. The beaten Szvatopluk has thrown himself into the Danube. Without tarnishing Árpád's glory, one story suggests that Szvatopluk (Attila's successor) was actually cheated of his lands rather than Árpád having won them in battle. Árpád sent his emissary Küsid to Szvatopluk to negotiate on his behalf. Szvatopluk was delighted, believing Küsid represented the leader of a peaceful people simply eager to cultivate some land. Satisfied with his welcome, Küsid returned to Árpád taking with him a gourd filled with water, a bag of black earth, and a sample of grass. According to Küsid, Árpád filled his drinking horn with water from the Danube, begged for God's blessing, and asked Him to allow these riches to be his (Árpád's) forever. Árpád then dispatched Küsid back to Szvatopluk to offer him a harnessed white horse in exchange for "his land, his grass, and his water." Szvatopluk happily accepted the magnificently decorated harnessed horse, thinking it was a sign of gratitude by these would-be settlers, and told Küsid that he and his companions could take as much earth, grass, and water as they pleased. Küsid returned with the news and Árpád, with his seven tribal chiefs, entered Pannonia as master of the territory. When Szvatopluk protested, Árpád told him: "Do not remain here for a moment longer as you have sold your land for a horse, your grass for a harness, and your water for a bridle."

Promenád 1896 (A Walk in 1896) – *Upper level of the Rotunda*. The promenade presents a cross section of Hungarian society in the year 1896 via different scenes. One shows a street with shops and figures representing people from the different social classes of the time: upper class gentlemen and their wives, servants, children both rich and poor, soldiers of all ranks, and craftsmen, many of whose crafts are now a thing of the past. At the time wearing black was a sign of elegance for women, while white and purple were associated with mourning.

Wax Museum – Wax figures of notable Hungarians are displayed on the top floor of the Rotunda—kings and queens and figures from the Renaissance.

Nomád Park – Learn about the daily lives of the nomadic peoples of the region during Prince Árpád's time by investigating yurts and trying your hand at archery.

Skanzen – An open-air museum featuring houses and farms from the early 20C, which have been reconstructed here showing what life was like at that time on the Southern Great Plain.

Dike-keeper's House – Near the lake, an illuminated model with sound that demonstrates the ruptures in the dikes (levees) that kept the River Tisza in check until one dreadful night in 1879. The ruptures caused the terrible flooding that almost totally destroyed Szeged.

There are a number of other exhibitions and things to see in the park, such as the archeological excavations of the medieval Szer Monastery, farm buildings from the Szegred region, and a display of local specialties.

Visitor Center – *Audioguide in English Ft800.* A new building containing a café and a movie theater where you can view a 30-minute film in 3D recounting the most important events in Hungary's history.

★ Makó C3

22mi/36km east of Szeged.

People have been living on this site since the 13C. The town was destroyed on several occasions by the Tartars, but has recovered each time to rise again from the ashes. Makó as we know it today was built at the beginning of the 18C and owes its rise to the cultivation of the **onion**—Makó onions are still considered the best in the country. There is even a fountain in the shape of an onion flower in the town center. **Imre Makovecz** (1935–2011), a highly creative pioneer of the Organic architecture movement, made the town one of his personal playgrounds. Thanks to Makovecz, in 1998 some extraordinary buildings started to appear on its streets, drawing on nature for their inspiration. Following in his footsteps, a children's nursery, elementary school, and library, which opened in 2019, were all designed and constructed according to the precepts of Organic architecture, which aims to promote harmony between human habitation and the natural world. However, any apparent connection between the name of the architect and the name of the town is purely incidental.

★ **Hagymaház** (Onion House) – This cultural center was the first building in the town to be designed by Imre Makovecz. Its two towers with glass panels symbolize the renewal of nature, resembling plants growing up toward the light. Inside you can see concrete pillars shaped like trees, while in the auditorium the wooden struts of the ceiling make it look as though you are inside a giant a rib cage.

★ **Hagymatikum Gyógyfürdő** (Thermal Baths) – This spa was completely rebuilt between 2007 and 2012 according to the principles of Organic architecture and the results are pretty extraordinary. Inspired by Roman and Turkish baths, the intention was that it should resemble a sacred temple, a place where people cleanse themselves both physically and spiritually *(p316)*.

Makói buszpályaudvar (Makó Bus Station) – We wouldn't normally pick out a bus station as a place of note, but with a roof designed to resemble the tree canopy in a forest, this one is certainly interesting.

József Attila Múzeum (Joseph Attila Museum) – *Open Tue–Sun, 10am–5pm. Ft800.* The museum explores the town's history from the 18C onward through paintings, objects, and furniture. The stand-out attraction has to be a Model T Ford car from the 1920s, as its chief designer, József Galamb, was originally from the town.

😊 ADDRESSES IN SZEGED

See Szeged map (p306)

ARRIVAL/DEPARTURE

Train – Every hour from Budapest-Nyugati Station to Szeged *(journey time 2hrs20min)*. The same for the return.

STAY

BUDGET

8 Mozart Hotel – A2 – *Oskola utca 16. ☎ 592 888. www. mozarthotel.hu. ✗ 15 rooms, from Ft16,000.* The rooms in this delightfully old-fashioned hotel are decorated in the style of a bygone era with wallpaper, patterned carpets, and portraits of Mozart on the walls.

AVERAGE

2 Art Hotel Szeged – A2 – *Somogyi utca 16. ☎ 800 040. www. arthotelszeged.hu. ✗ 🅿 charges apply. 71 rooms, from Ft21,000.* A hotel in a very good location, with cozy rooms and comfortable beds. Some rooms have a balcony.

A TREAT

4 Dóm – A2 – *Bajza utca 6. ☎ 423 750. www.domhotel.hu. ✗ 🅿 charges apply. 16 rooms from Ft25,000 ☕.* This boutique hotel, tucked away in the heart of the city, is close to all the attractions. The rooms are comfortable and the sauna-jacuzzi is very welcome after a day's sightseeing.

SPLASH OUT

😊 12 Tiszavirág – A1 – *Hajnóczy utca 1/b. ☎ 554 888. www. tiszaviragszeged.hu. ✗ 🅿 12 rooms from Ft32,000 ☕.* Each room in this beautifully restored mid-19C building is different and furnished with taste and style. The wooden furniture and marble bathrooms have clean, elegant lines. There

is also a pleasant lounge (shared with your hosts), a spa, and an excellent restaurant.

Makó

A TREAT

Grand Hotel Glorius – *Csanád vezér tér 2. ☎ 511 060. www.glorius. hu. ✗ 37 rooms, from Ft20,000 ☕.* The town's nicest hotel is close to the thermal baths and is modern and comfortable, with a slight 1920s Art Deco air about it.

EAT

BUDGET

5 Öreg Kőrössy Halászcsárda B1, off map – *Sárga Üdülőtelep 262. ☎ 495 481. Open 11.30am–10pm. Main dishes Ft2,050/3,450.* This restaurant by the river has been specializing in fish dishes since the 1930s, and in the city's signature dish in particular—fish soup with paprika.

😊 9 Rudi és Fickó – A2 – *Oroszlán utca 4 . ☎ 800 150. Open Mon–Thu, 8am–10pm (Fri & Sat 11pm). Pizza Ft2,490.* From breakfast (an excellent bakery) to dinner (eggplant caviar, soups, and pizzas), this warm, friendly café will make you feel good. There is also a terrace for relaxing on sunny days.

AVERAGE

😊 11 Tiszavirág – A1 – *Hajnóczy utca 1/b. ☎ 554 888. Open noon–3pm, 6pm–10pm. Closed Sun & Mon but the café stays open 7am–3pm. Main dishes Ft2,950/6,950.* The city's coolest address. Delicious Hungarian and international cuisine is served in a bright, contemporary setting. An excellent seasonal lunch menu and fast service. Sunday brunch is available in the café.

Makó

BUDGET

Silver – *Széchenyi tér 8. ✆ 264 799. Open 9am–11pm (Sat midnight, Sun 10pm). Main dishes Ft1,690/4,290.* Situated in the town center, this is a good place for a coffee. Simple meals are also served (fried cheese, burgers, pizzas) and there's a large terrace.

SHOPPING

Szeged is famous for its locally grown paprika, its salami, and *pálinka* (brandy).

TAKING A BREAK

Virág Cukrászda – *Klauzál tér 1. Open 9am–9pm.* A real Szeged institution serving generous portions of cake and good coffee out on the terrace or in the plush atmosphere of a 1930s salon. You can also get takeout ice cream.

Sugar & Candy – *Oskola utca 2. Open Mon–Fri, 8am–8pm; Sat & Sun, 9am–8pm.* The tempting smell of just baked scones and cakes will make you want to find a spot in this small, snug café, close to the Votive Church.

BARS

Maláta – *Somogyi utca 13. Open 2pm–11pm (Fri & Sat, noon–1am.* All types of craft beers are served on the really nice patio at this bar and grill, as well as salads and burgers made in house.

Nyugi Kert – *Vitéz utca 28. Open Mon–Fri, 9am–1am; Sat, noon–2am; Sun, 4pm–midnight.* This is a favorite hangout of Szeged's students and replicates the scene at Budapest's ruin bars with its mismatched furniture and vintage memorabilia.

BATHS

Anna Fürdő – A1 – *Tisza Lajos körút 24. ✆ 553 330. Open 6am–8pm (Sat & Sun, 10pm). Ft1,900.* Built in 1896 and renovated in 2004, these baths have retained their old world charm. The thermal water is excellent for muscle pain. You can try it from the fountain and people drink it for inflammation of the stomach.

Napfényfürdő Aquapolis – B2 – *Torontál tér 1. ✆ 566 488. www.napfenyfurdoaquapolis.com. Open 9am–8pm. Mon–Fri Ft3,450/day; Sat & Sun & school vacations Ft5,250/day.* A modern thermal spa complex with indoor and outdoor swimming pools, a play area for young children, 13 slides, a sauna, and a jacuzzi.

Makó

Hagymatikum Gyógyfürdő – *Makovecz tér 6. ✆ 511 220. www.hagymatikum.hu. Open 8am–8pm (Fri & Sat, 8am– noon). Mon–Fri Ft2,600, Sat & Sun Ft2,900.* This is everything a good spa complex should be and more. Numerous indoor and outdoor pools, water slides, a sauna, massages, and a restaurant.

SPORTS AND ACTIVITIES

Cycling – Bikes can be hired at the tourist office (*Széchenyi tér 12; Ft1,000/hr, Ft3,000/day).*

EVENTS AND FESTIVALS

Open-Air Festival – *Dóm tér. ✆ 541 205.* The country's biggest open-air festival, held in July/August, staging all kinds of events in the vast Cathedral Square (Dóm tér). *www.szegediszabadteri.hu*

Gyula

★★

Population 29,606 – Békés county – area code ✆ 66

Gyula (meaning chief and judge) was a colloquial name for the military leaders of the Magyar tribes. It is also the name of the settlement that for several hundred years was the county's principal town, before ceding that honor to Békéscsaba in 1950, when the latter became a major rail interchange. Water was an important feature in the town and Gyula still retains its canals, which provide a pleasant environment in which to walk, particularly in summer. Between visiting the castle and Almásy Mansion, you can also try out its baths and sample its delicious ice creams.

ADDRESSES PAGE 321
Stay, Eat, Shopping, Baths

INFO:
Tourist Office – *Kossuth utca 7. ✆ 561 680. www.visitgyula.com. Open Mon–Sat, 9am–5pm. Closed Sun.* A warm welcome in English, with a selection of leaflets and town maps.

LOCATION:
Regional map D2 (p302–303)
71mi/114km northeast of Szeged.

DON'T MISS:
Almásy Mansion; Százéves Patisserie; the Castle Baths.

TIMING:
Allow two days to explore and to make the most of the baths. Note the museums and castle are closed on Monday.

KIDS:
Gyula Castle; Mini Hungary at Szarvas; the outside waterslides at the Castle Baths (*see p321*).

Walking tour

★★ **Százéves Cukrászda** (The Hundred-year-old Patisserie)
On the corner of Jókai Mór utca and Béke sugárút. Open 10am–7pm (Fri & Sat, 8pm). This cake shop, confectionery, and museum combined is worth a peek inside for its ornate decoration and furnishings, a mix of 18C and 19C; the ceilings and walls are beautifully painted. There is also a small display of the equipment and utensils used by the pastry chefs of the past *(no charge)*. After feasting your eyes, it's all about satisfying the craving for something sweet that you are probably feeling by now, so try a mouthwatering pastry or several scoops of ice cream.

★ **Gyulai vár** (Gyula Castle)
Várkert utca 15. ✆ 650 218. www.gyulavara.hu. Open Tue–Sun, 10am–6pm (beg Jul–mid-Aug, 7pm). Ft1,900 (combined ticket with tour of Almásy Mansion and its exhibitions, Ft3,800). Guided tour in English, reserve 24hrs ahead
Built in the 15C, originally on an island, this is the only medieval brick castle in the Great Plain still standing. It fell into the hands of the Turks in 1566, then after over a century under Ottoman rule, became the property of the Harruckern family who turned it into a brewery and distillery. The castle building is in the form of a parallelepiped, with a similarly shaped tower, and was

THE WATER TOWN

Built in the heart of a wetland area, Gyula was crisscrossed with canals. The marshes were drained in the 19C and the rivers were regulated, but Gyula remains a water town thanks to its thermal springs, which feed eleven indoor swimming pools and nine outdoor pools. The water varies in temperature from 72°F to 102°F (22°C–39°C). **Várfürdő** (the Castle Baths, *see p321*) is a large spa complex near the castle, surrounded by high end hotels. A little further south of the castle is a wooded park bordered by a small waterway, Élővíz-csatorna (literally, "living water canal"). Crossed by bridges at intervals, you will find *panziós* and private homes offering accommodation dotted along its length.

restored in 2005. Tools, barrels, objects from daily life, and medieval weapons are on show in the castle's 24 rooms *(explanations in Hungarian)*. Displays of falconry and processions in period costume are held in the courtyard every Saturday. There is also the chance to try your hand at archery on weekends *(near the entrance, Ft300 for 5 arrows)*. The view from the tower is superb.

★ **Almásy-kastély** (Almásy Mansion)

Kossuth utca 15. ✆ 650 218. Open Tue–Sun, 10am–6pm (beg Jul–mid-Aug, 10pm). Permanent exhibition Ft2,200, temporary exhibition Ft800, to climb the tower Ft800; combined ticket for all three and Gyula Castle, Ft3,800. A good café.

Built in the 18C, this beautifully restored chateau offers a glimpse into the lives of Hungarian aristocrats living in the Great Plain during the second half of the 19C. Houses such as this were taken out of private hands after the Second World War and put to different uses. Under the Communist regime, this former family home became successively a business school, a nursing school, and then an orphanage. Thanks to meticulous research, Almásy Mansion has managed to track down furniture, clothes, everyday objects, old photographs, items of porcelain, and utensils from its heyday. As a result, you can now take a look behind the scenes at upper class life, especially the role played by the many servants it took to run such houses, including valets, laundresses, and cooks. The museum makes good use of interactive displays (including holographic projections) and the information panels include an English translation.

Erkel Ferenc Emlékház (Ferenc Erkel House)

Apor Vilmos tér 7. Open Tue–Sun, 10am–6pm. Ft1,000.

Ferenc Erkel, who composed the Hungarian national anthem, was a native of Gyula. The **house where he was born** has now been converted into a museum displaying photographs of the musician's life, his friends, and family, which open a fascinating window onto Hungarian society in the middle of the 19C. Some handwritten scores are also on display. Erkel also composed the famous opera *Bánk Bán*—the story goes that inspiration for it came to him while he was resting under a tree in the castle park.

★ **Kohán György képtár** (György Kohán Art Gallery)

Béke sugárút 35. Open Tue, Thu & Sat, 1.30pm–6pm; Wed, Fri & Sun 10am–1pm.

This small building, erected in 1889 in the middle of a wooded park, houses works bequeathed to the town by the painter **György Kohán** (1910–66). His paintings were inspired by the Impressionists and his drawings are a good example of the output of the artistic communities working in the Hungarian provinces at the time.

Gyula Castle
© paop/age fotostock

★ **Ladics ház** (Ladics House)
Jókai Mór utca 4. Open Tue, Thu & Sat, 10am–1pm, Wed, Fri & Sun 1.30pm–6pm. Closed mid-Oct–beg Apr. Ft600.
An early 19C Baroque townhouse, formerly the home of several generations of the middle-class Ladics family—György Ladics was a lawyer—with portraits, personal items, and original furnishings on show. The guided tours are in Hungarian (you may be given a transcript in English). Even so, there is plenty to enjoy in this beautifully furnished house.

Gyulai Kolbász Múzeum (Gyula Sausage Museum)
Kétegyházi utca 3/1. ☏ (30) 220 0290. Open Tue–Fri, 9am–3pm; Sat & Sun, 9am–1pm. Ft800.
A small museum celebrating one of the sausages for which Hungary is famous, the Gyula sausage, which has been gracing tables here in one form or another for 150 years. There is a display of butchers' tools and mincing machines dating from the end of the 19C, as well as cash registers and old-fashioned scales. The visit ends with a tasting of this local specialty, made with pork, garlic, cumin, and paprika, which produces the deep red color.

Excursions Regional map (p302–303)

Békéscsaba D2
9.5mi/15km west by Rte 44.
Appropriately, Békés county's principal town is a tranquil place (*békés* means "peaceful"), despite the region being known as the "land of storms" due to its turbulent history. In the 18C János György, Baron Harruckern, was sent by the Habsburgs to encourage people from Germany and Slovakia to move into the area. They arrived and settled in their own neighborhoods but lived peacefully alongside each other and Slovak is still spoken here today. Békéscsaba is also the birthplace of the great 19C painter, Mihály Munkácsy.

Canal, Gyula
© liptakrobi/iStock

★ **Munkácsy Mihály Múzeum** (Mihály Munkácsy Museum) – *Széchényi utca 9. Mihály Munkácsy's works are not on display until 2021 due to renovation work. Meanwhile there are temporary exhibitions on the first (ground) floor.* Apart from the artist's work, the museum has an interesting exhibition covering the region's different ethnic groups; visitors can discover the skill and richness of Slovakian, Romanian, German, and Hungarian craftmanship, among others.
★ **Munkácsy Emlékház** (Munkácsy Memorial House) – *Gyulai út 5. ✆ 442 080. Open Tue–Sun, 9am–5pm (Sat & Sun, 10am–4pm). Ft600.* The museum is housed in the former home of Mihály Munkácsy's uncle, where Mihály spent part of his childhood. Around 20 of the painter's works are on display, as well as several canvases by his contemporaries.
★★ **Szlovák Tájház** (Slovakian House) – *Garai utca 21. ✆ (30) 350 4423. Open Apr–Oct, Tue–Sat, 10am–noon, 2pm–6pm (Nov–Mar, 10am–4pm). Ft200.*
This is a fine example of a traditional rural Slovakian house—whitewashed walls, wooden furniture and utensils, pottery, floral decoration....
★★ **Meseház** (Fairy Tale House) – *Békési út 17. ✆ 326 370. Open Mon–Fri, 9am–4pm.* Children and adults alike will be enchanted by the different puppets on display here.

Mini Magyarország (Mini Hungary), at **Szarvas** C2

38mi/61km northwest of Gyula. I. Külkerület 9. ✆ 312 344. www.minimagyarorszag.hu. Open 8am–6pm. Ft1,500 (Sat & Sun Ft1,900); arboretum Ft1,500 (Sat & Sun Ft1,900); combined ticket Ft2,400 (Sat & Sun Ft3,000).

Not just a model village, but a model Hungary. The Chain Bridge in Budapest, Eger Castle, and Tihany Abbey ... there are almost a hundred detailed models in this park (covering 5 acres/2ha) of just about all the major Hungarian buildings and monuments. Some are interactive—children will enjoy being able to start the electric trains by pushing a button or ring the bells of the steam trains beside a mini Lake Balaton or mini Danube. New models are added each year, so that visitors can see even more of the country, in just an afternoon!

ADDRESSES IN GYULA

ARRIVAL/DEPARTURE

Train – There are no direct trains to Gyula from Budapest and Szeged. From/to both desinations you have to change at **Békéscsaba**. Allow at least 2hrs35min from Szeged and 3hrs from Budapest on the fastest connections.
Bus – There are six buses daily from Szeged to Gyula *(journey time 3hrs30min)*.

STAY

BUDGET

Lika Panzió – *Patócsy Ferenc utca 1. ✆ 30 363 9282. 3 rooms, Ft11,000.* Well-kept rooms, with comfortable beds, a small refrigerator, and coffee machine. The rooms and bathrooms are small but well designed. Ask for one of the two rooms on the upper floor rather than the one on the first (ground) floor, which only has one window opening onto the road and no air conditioning.

A TREAT

Elizabeth Hotel – *Vár utca 1. ✆ 529 110 . www.elizabeth-hotel.hu. 49 rooms, from Ft32,000 (Ft4,500 supplement for rooms with a castle view).* Comfortable and conveniently situated close to the castle and the baths. Decorated in the classic style favored by upmarket Hungarian hotels (thick carpets and wooden furniture). Guests can use the gym, small swimming pool, sauna, and jacuzzi.

EAT

BUDGET

Gusto – *Városház utca 19. ✆ 70 377 4450. Open 11am–9pm (Fri & Sat, 9.30pm). Main dishes Ft1,490/4,990.* Try Hungarian or international dishes at reasonable prices in the historic center. Not to be missed are their refreshing salads, such as Greek or Thai, with a base of mango and avocado. And there's a nice terrace.

TAKING A BREAK

Százéves Cukrászda (Hundred-year-old Patisserie) – *(See p317.)*
Kávézó Mansion – *Kossuth Lajos utca 15. Open Tue–Sun, 10am–6pm (summer 10pm).* This café located in Almásy Mansion serves drinks and cakes and has a delightful terrace overlooking the park.
Korzó Fagyizó – *Eszperantó tér 3. Open 9am–10pm.* Gyula has plenty of ice cream parlors but this is one of the best. Once you've bought your ice cream, you might like to take a stroll along the canal.

SHOPPING

Bor & Pálinka – *Városház utca 4. Open 9am–6pm.* A useful food store where you can buy Hungarian wines, craft beers, brandy *(pálinka)*, jams, paprika, and chocolate.

BATHS

Várfürdő (Castle Baths) – *Várkert utca 2. ✆ 561 350. www.varfurdo.hu. Open 8am–7pm, Ft2,500. Aquapalota open Mon–Fri, noon–7pm, + Ft1,600; Sat & Sun, 10am–7pm, + Ft1,800.*
With a choice of thermal and therapeutic waters, saunas, jacuzzis, swimming pools, and the recently opened Aquapalota (Aqua Palace) full of water slides, you could quite easily spend all day here.

Kecskemét

★

Population 110,638 – Bács-Kiskun county – area code ✆ 76

Situated between the Danube and the Tisza rivers, Kecskemét lies in the heart of the Puszta. To Brahms it was the loveliest city in the world and to Zoltán Kodály, the beloved town of his birth. It still has its fine Art Nouveau buildings and many churches. Also known as the "orchard of Hungary," fruit (particularly apricots) grows in abundance in the surrounding farmland and paprika fills the fields with color in summer.

ADDRESSES PAGE 334
Stay, Eat, Bars, Sports and Activities

INFO:

Tourist Office – Kecskemét map A2 – *Szabadság tér 5/a. ✆ 800 040. www.kecskemet.hu. Open Mon–Fri, 8.30am–5.30pm (Sat, 9am–1pm). Closed Sun.* Brochures in English and a map of the city.

LOCATION:

Regional map A1–2 (p302–303); Kecskemét map (p326) 53mi/85km southeast of Budapest.

PARKING:

Charges apply for all parking in the center (ticket machines).

DON'T MISS:

A walk through the historic center, City Hall, and the Cifrapalota.

TIMING:

Allow a full day for the city and another full day to explore Kiskunság National Park.

KIDS:

Leskowsky Musical Instrument Museum; Kecskemét Baths (*see p335*).

Walking tour Kecskemét map (p326)

A city with an eye for trade, Kecskemét conducted its business in its squares around which many buildings sprang up over the course of the centuries, cheerfully reflecting the different styles of Hungarian architecture. As a result, as you explore its steets and buildings, wandering from one leafy square to another, the center might feel more like a great urban park. In one of his *Gypsy Songs* Brahms described Kecskemét as "the loveliest village in Alföld." It is true that since the 19C and the time of Brahms the city has lost a little of its splendor, due mainly to postwar building, but it still retains a genuine charm.

A MIXTURE OF STYLES

Kecskemét is full of fine buildings from different eras and in different architectural styles that nevertheless merge harmoniously together. The contemporary period is represented by buildings such as Aranyhomok Hotel, close to City Hall, while **Luther Palota** (Luther Palace, A1–2), on the corner of Luther köz (Luther Passage) and Hock János utca, dates from the 1910s. Not far away, on Arany János utca, is the 19C **Kecskeméti Evangélikus Egyházközség** (Evangelical Church), designed by Miklós Ybl. Its white walls and simple interior create a serene and peaceful atmosphere.

Cifra Palace
© Funkystock/age fotostock

Nagytemplom (Great Church) A2
Kossuth tér 2. Open 6am–7pm (Mon, noon–7pm).
The Great Church, or Kecskemét Cathedral, inaugurated in 1806, stands in the main square and was designed in the late Baroque style. Its walls bear two plaques, one commemorating the victims of the 1848–49 War of Independence and the other a cavalry regiment from the First World War.

★ **Városháza** (City Hall) A2
Kossuth tér 1. Reserve ahead at the tourist office Mon–Sat, 10am–11.30am. Note that the building is closed for renovation until the end of 2021.
Construction on this large pink building, designed by Ödön Lechner and Gyula Pártos, began in 1893, and just over two years later the city's civil servants moved in. Compared with many Hungarian civic buildings, it is relatively sparsely decorated and is an example of what passes for Art Nouveau in Kecskemét.
The City Hall **carillon** chimes every hour. At 12.05pm it peals out Hungarian melodies by Kodály and Erkel, at 6.05pm snippets of Mozart, Handel, and Beethoven can be heard, while at 8pm it plays popular Hungarian music.
When you go inside, take the stairs that lead up to the Council Chamber. After two flights you pass through a series of arcades and arches. The Council Chamber was decorated by the painter Bertalan Székely, famous for his historic scenes in the Academic and Romantic styles.

Ferences templom (Franciscan Church) A2
Lestár tér 2. Open 6.30am–6pm.
Standing opposite City Hall, the Franciscan Church, or St. Nicholas's Chapel, is the oldest building in Kecskemét and dates from the 14C. Originally Romanesque in style, it has subsequently had Gothic and Baroque features added during various reconstructions over the centuries. Until 1564 it had the distinction of being used simultaneously by both Catholics and Protestants. To the left of the church are just a few remains of St. Michael's Chapel, which was the earlier Franciscan place of worship.

Musical notes

"SONG BEAUTIFIES LIFE AND THOSE WHO SING MAKE THE LIVES OF OTHERS MORE BEAUTIFUL"

A quote from Zoltán Kodály, one of the great names of Hungarian music of the 20C, revealing his main musical preoccupation, namely singing. He was one of the first, with his friend Béla Bartók, to collect the melodies and lyrics of folk songs to create a musical ethnography. His own compositions are a classical synthesis of Hungarian popular music and European heritage. As a music ethnologist, Kodály traveled beyond Europe, researching and working in North Africa, in particular Algeria. He wrote a number of works for the choral society in his home town of Kecskemét (*The Aged*, *Anna Molnár*, *Jesus and the Traders*). His great classical work, *Psalmus Hungaricus*, was written in 1923 to celebrate the 50th anniversary of the union of Buda and Pest. He composed it to a text by 16C poet Mihály Vég and added the words "of Kecskemét" after his own name in the credits.

KODÁLY THE EDUCATOR

Kodály made a significant contribution to music education in Hungary. He was a great teacher, not just of music, but also of composing and conducting, and he taught and trained many music teachers, too. He pioneered a method of teaching that came to be known as the "Kodály Method," which is still followed in Hungary today. As a result many Hungarians are familiar with traditional Hungarian songs and when singing spontaneously, such as at family celebrations or in community gatherings, are able to position their voice alongside those of their companions to create a harmonious whole—a true choir. Japan was the first country to adopt the Kodály Method and produces excellent musicians, while other countries have also been inspired by this Hungarian method of teaching music.

A MUSICAL CITY

Zoltán Kodály was born in Kecskemét. Although he did not live in the city for very long, he was very attached to it and confessed: "Somewhere in my bones I have always felt I belonged to this city, in the same way that those plants growing on sandy ground push their roots down under the sandy layer to reach the true nutrients they depend on." He studied violin and piano and sang in the cathedral choir in Nagyszombat, which introduced him to choral singing at a young age.

Since his death in Budapest in 1967, the birthday of this great musician and teacher has been celebrated each year with, alternately, an international choir festival and an international music festival. The Kodály Zoltán Zenepedagógiai Intézet (Kodály Institute, *see opposite*) was created in Kecskemét in 1975. Every two years the institute organizes the Kodály International Seminar (usually in July and August), offering an introduction to the Hungarian music teaching system and methods, along with a camp for international choirs. Musicians from more than 40 countries have taken part in the seminars to date.

Walk around the ruins to find Kéttemplom köz to the left, where a small bridge over a very shallow moat-like garden leads to the door of the Kodály Institute.

Kodály Zoltán Zenepedagógiai Intézet
(Kodály Institute of the Franz Liszt Academy of Music) A2
Kéttemplom köz 1. ☏ 481 518. Open 8am–4pm, reserve ahead. Ft150.
The school is housed in what was formerly a Franciscan monastery. It is open to the public but only partially since it is a full-time educational institute. It became a faculty of the Liszt Academy *(see p57)* in 2005 and hosts both Hungarian and international students. Along with the study rooms and a library, there is also some accommodation for foreign students on site. One side of the cloister can be accessed and has an exhibition on Kodály's life and work. You might be lucky enough to have your visit coincide with a concert. If so it will give you the chance to venture further into the building and share an exceptional musical moment.

Kossuth tér (Kossuth Square) A2
In fact there are two squares beside each other in this area—Kossuth tér and Szabadság tér. An Art Nouveau building between the two houses the well-known cake shop **Fodor Cukrászda** *(see Taking a Break, p335).*
And on one side of Szabadság tér you can find the 17C **Kecskeméti Református Egyházközség temploma** (Reformed Church), which was built under the Muslim Turkish occupation with the sultan's authorization. The church has since been remodeled several times.

Újkollégium (Calvinist New College) AB2
Szabadság tér 7. ☏ 500 380. It is possible to visit the college but reserve ahead.
Péter Lestár, a former mayor of the city and a key player in its development, is quoted as saying: "Even if we live in huts, we must build palaces for our schools." New College is a fine example of this philosophy. Built in 1912 by the architects Valér Mende and Lajos Dombi, its exterior achieves a skilful blend of the apparently contradictory ornate and the minimalist, with harmonious reliefs and decorations. For many years it was home to the Kodály School of Music and Singing, but after the break with the Communist regime it was returned to its former owners and today is a primary and secondary school belonging to the Reformed Church.
The **Ráday Múzeum** nearby *(Kalvin tér 1; open Tue–Sun, 10am–6pm)* traces the ritual of the Reformed Church through religious art and artifacts. It is located in what was previously the city's Calvinist College, the Ókollégium (Old College). The Bible Museum on Ráday utca in Budapest is also part of the institution.

★ **Cifrapalota** (Cifra Palace) B2
Rákóczi utca 1. ☏ 480 776. Open Tue–Sun, 10am–5pm. Ft700.
The exterior of this Art Nouveau masterpiece, built in 1902 and designed by Hungarian architect Géza Márkus, is decorated with beautiful majolica tiles featuring vividly colored and stylized flower motifs and ornamentation in the Moorish style. The result is a building of great freshness and joyful fantasy.
Cifra means "ornate" and this palace certainly lives up to its name. Venture inside to see an exhibition of paintings, among them some fine works by 20C Hungarian artists. Also definitely worth a look is the **Great Hall**, a former games room. Its decoration is in the same style as the exterior, but much more exuberant, with peacocks strutting about against a blue background of stucco waves. Some impressive Art Nouveau chandeliers hang from the ceiling.

Tudomány és Művészetek Háza (House of Science and Art) AB1–2
Rákóczi utca 2. ✆ 505 688. Open Mon–Fri, 8am–4pm.
This former synagogue, a beautiful white building constructed in 1871, has an interesting history. Just like many other buildings in the center of the city, it was damaged during the earthquake of 1911. It was rebuilt and was used as a stable for horses during the Second World War. Lacking the funds for its upkeep as a synagogue, it was converted in the 1970s into a conference center. Today it is also a cultural center hosting permanent and temporary exhibitions.

Katona József Színház (József Katona Theater) A2
Katona József tér 5.
Built in the 19C in the Eclectic style, the theater is named after the playwright József Katona, author of the historical tragedy *Bánk Bán*. It stages many productions and the Kecskemét Symphony Orchestra gives excellent concerts here.

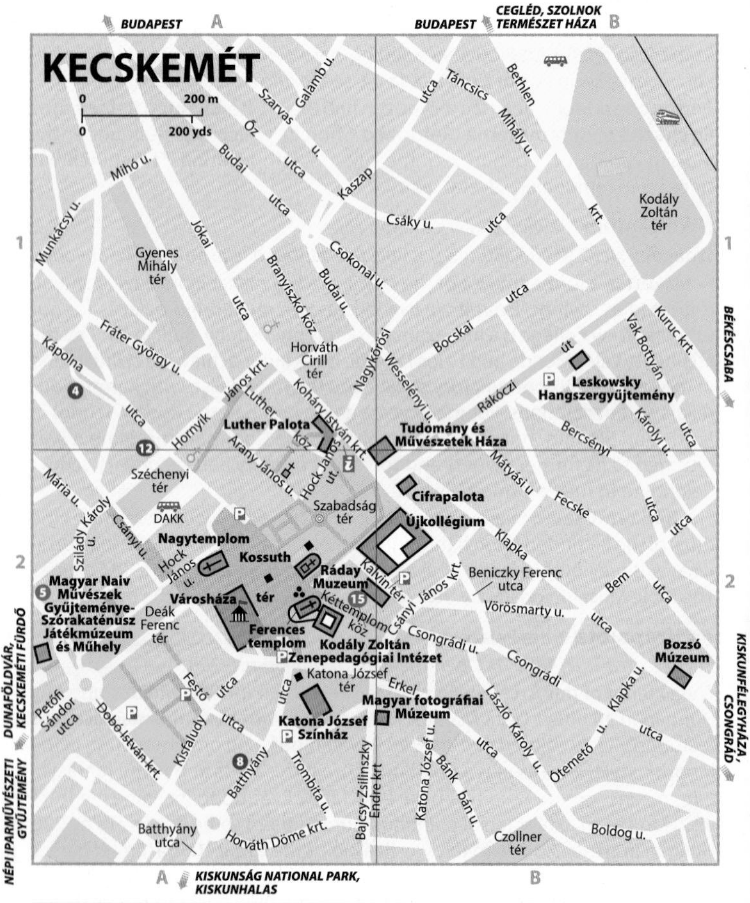

WHERE TO STAY		WHERE TO EAT
Fábián Panzió 4	Hotel Talizmán 12	Kecskeméti Csárda 5
Hotel Három Gúnár 8		Tepsi Gastropub 15

FOOD AND DRINK

Kecskemét's involvement with agriculture dates back to the 15C, a time when livestock farming played an important role in this part of the Alföld, the Hungarian Great Plain. Records indicate that by the mid-16C a third of the cattle crossing the Danube to Vác (north of Budapest) had been bred by farmers from Kecskemét. In the 18C, after suffering great privation during the struggles for independence from the Habsburgs, the resulting push toward the growing of crops, fruits, vegetables, and vines enriched the city considerably, enabling schools, churches, and houses to be built. In 1950, Kecskemét became the capital of the new Bács-Kiskun county (the largest in surface area in Hungary), created after the merging of two counties that adjoined it. Agriculture and the agri-food industry continued to expand and the breeding of cattle, sheep, horses, and poultry thrived. Today wide expanses of land are occupied by fields growing cereal crops, along with vineyards and orchards, and glasshouses growing young crops. Although the Kecskemét region accounts for about one third of Hungarian wine production, the local wines are not the finest the country has to offer. They are considered a little light and without great character, especially when compared to those of Eger. However, Kecskemét is celebrated in particular for its spirits, including apricot brandy or **barack pálinka**. Try a guided tour of the **Zwack distilleries** to sample some. *Matkói u. 2. www.zwackunicum.hu. Reserve ahead, min. 10 people, only in Hungarian. Ft2,100/ per person, tasting included.*

Magyar Fotográfiai Múzeum (Hungarian Museum of Photography) B2
Katona József tér 12. www.fotomuzeum.hu. ✆ 483 221. Open Tue–Sat, noon–5pm. Ft500.
This small museum in a former synagogue, contains an archive of around 275,000 photographs. As you would expect, Hungarian photographers such as László Moholy-Nagy, Brassaï, Robert Capa, and André Kertész are very well represented.

Bozsó Múzeum B2
Klapka utca 34. www.bozso.net. ✆ 417 130. Open Thu–Sun, 10am–6pm. Ft800.
Museums and galleries housing collections bequeathed to a local community by an individual are quite common in Hungary, but this has to be one of the most interesting. The collection of the painter **János Bozsó** (1922–98) is displayed in the magnificent old house where he used to live. As you make your way through the series of rooms, you will see not just some of his pictures, but also many domestic everyday objects. In the last rooms, including one upstairs, you can see a fine collection of sculptures and religious artifacts. A collection of watches has also been on show here since 2012.

Leskowsky Hangszergyűjtemény
(Leskowsky Musical Instrument Collection) B1
Rákóczi utca 15. ✆ 486 616. www.hangszergyujtemeny.hu. Open Tue–Sun, 10am–5pm. Ft1,000.
Musician Albert Leskowsky bequeathed this collection of musical instruments, unique in Hungary, to the city. It contains some 2,500 instruments, some from neighboring Hungarian regions, but others that come from the far corners of the world, both modern and up to 300 years old. Visitors are allowed to touch and play the majority of them. There is a one-hour presentation about the collection, in English if required.

Magyar Naív Művészek Gyűjteménye (Museum of Hungarian Naive Art) and **Szórakaténusz Játékmúzeum és Műhely** (Toy Museum and Workshop) A2

Gáspár András utca 11. Open Tue–Sat, 10am–12.30pm, 1pm–5pm. Ticket for both museums, Ft600.

The building houses two museums. The first displays around 2,500 canvases and sculptures by Hungarian Naive painters and artists from the early 20C onward. The second exhibits all kinds of toys, the oldest of which dates from the 19C, including dolls, wooden toys, trains, cars, and rocking horses, and some mechanical toys from the 1950s.

Népi Iparművészeti Gyűjtemény (Traditional Craft Museum) A2, off map

Serfőző utca 19/A. ✆ 327 203. Open Tue–Sat, 10am–4pm. Ft600.

In a former 19C brewery, this museum exhibits arts and crafts items from across Hungary's various regions (pottery, weaving, saddlery, textile printing). You can also see how modern artists and craftsmen are reviving old trades to design objects adapted to modern life or simply to enhance an object's appearance.

Excursions Regional map (p302–303)

★★ **Kiskunsági Nemzeti Park** (Kiskunság National Park) A2

21mi/34km southwest of Kecskemét. Access by car from Kecskemét on Rte 54; after about 16mi/25km, take a small road to the left as far as Bugac.

Before leaving Kecskemét, call in at the **Természet Háza** (Nature House, *Liszt Ferenc utca 19, knp.nemzetipark.gov.hu*), the park's administrative center, to pick up brochures about the park in English and possibly book a guided tour. A practical way to start your visit is to park your car in Bugac next to Karikás Csárda (inn), where you can have lunch (*see p335*) and also buy tickets from the office on site for the various activities. Either walk *(1 mile/1.5km,)* or opt for a ride in one of the carts *(Ft2,400 round trip; if you have a bad back note that the cart suspension leaves something to be desired)* to the Shepherds' Museum and an area where there is a farm and studfarm and horse shows are staged. (The cart rides and horse shows are cancelled in heavy rain.)

★ **Pásztormúzeum** (Shepherds' Museum) – *✆ 575 112. Open May–Oct, 10am–6pm. Ft950 for a combined ticket including the museum, entry into the park, and farm visit. Ft2,400 for the horse show (including the round trip cart ride, Ft4,000).*

The museum resembles one of the shepherds' huts in the Puszta: teepee-style dwellings covered with reeds and grouped together, and sometimes enclosed by a fence also made of reeds. The **pásztor**, the shepherds who guarded the Racka sheep with their long, corkscrew horns, lived in these temporary hamlets. It was here that they stored everything they needed while out on the Puszta to care for and watch over their animals. They were assisted by Puli sheepdogs, a Hungarian breed with a long, corded coat similar to dreadlocks. The dogs were dwarfed by the large sheep but their size did not prevent them from being highly effective sheepdogs. Working alongside the shepherds were the **csikós**, mounted horse-herdsmen, and the **gulyás** or cattlemen.

The exhibits in this well-renovated museum include items that the herdsmen made to pass the time, such as carved wooden pipes, decorated walking sticks, and everyday items carried about in small narrow carts, along with sheepskin capes. Look out for some evocative black and white photographs from the 1920s that capture the lives of these men living so close to nature.

Puszta Animal Farm – *Open May–Oct. Included in the entry ticket for the park. A short walk from the Shepherds' Museum.* Take a stroll around a farm that looks after animals typical of the region, such as Hungarian Grey cattle, Racka sheep, Mangalica pigs with woolly coats, horses, and donkeys.

Puszta "Cowboy" Show – *May–Sept at 12.15pm. Ft2,400. The ticket includes the Shepherd's Museum, entry into the park, and farm visit.* The show is staged next to the farm every day by the *csikós,* who look after the horses. Part of the show is the famous "five-in-hand," where a rider controls five horses galloping in unison while standing astride the two rear horses, whip cracking loudly in your ears. You will also see a herd of Grey cattle being driven from a distance toward you, led by dogs and *csikós*, and the magnificent sight of horses from the stud farm galloping across the Puszta together.

Szolnok B1

39mi/63km northeast of Kecskemét.

Szolnok, sitting on the right bank of the Tisza, is the principal town of this part of the Great Plain, known as the Central Plain. It developed as a market town in the 11C–14C and was later fought over by Ottoman Turks for its strategic position as a river port. Today it is an industrial and transport hub

THE GREAT PLAIN, THE PUSZTA

Think of the **Puszta** and what comes to mind? A tall pendulum well, stark against the horizon, a solitary hut, cattle grazing on endless grasslands, horses galloping across a vast plain? The word *puszta* does not mean "desert," despite the wooded sand dunes at Bugac, but rather "a place where there is nothing," encompassing the apparent emptiness of the plain. The Puszta is the Great Plain, the **Alföld** (lowland) that occupies the whole of the eastern and southeastern area of Hungary, from the Danube to the Romanian border and Hungary's southern border. The Puszta has many different aspects. Look at the great project for regulating the Danube and Tisza rivers, which profoundly changed the landscape of the Great Plain in the 19C. In other areas economic necessity and the development of agriculture have been eroding the uncultivated parts of this immense wilderness little by little, although fortunately the most typical areas are protected within the boundaries of the national parks *(nemzeti park)*, as at Kiskunság and Hortobágy.

It would be impossible to visit all the interesting sites in **Kiskunsági Nemzeti Park** on a normal visit, even by car. It covers a colossal 37,000 acres/15,000ha. The park itself is not concentrated in a single area, but is in 9 sectors forming a total of 2,000 acres/48,000ha spread throughout the wider territory, but the remainder of the area is a protected landscape and nature reserve. Two thirds of the park is classified as a biosphere reserve. The carbonate-rich lakes of Izsák Kolon-tó and Alkáli-tó are also protected. Birdwatching enthusiasts come to see the rare **great bustards**. The population of this protected species is the highest here in Europe (it has almost disappeared elsewhere in Europe). Many tourists come in the summer, while spring, fall, and late fall are quieter times when this flat, sandy expanse is covered with long grasses and conifers and is left more or less to itself.

(several international rail lines converge here), and spa town popular with Hungarians—a number of hotels and baths are located near the riverbank, over the thermal springs.

Damjanich János Múzeum (János Damjanich Museum) – *Kossuth Lajos tér 4. ✆ (56) 421 602. Open Tue–Sun, 9am–5pm. Ft1,000 for all the exhibitions.* The former Magyar Király Hotel (Royal Hotel) is now a museum named after General Damjanich, hero of the Battle of Szolnok, which was fought against the Habsburgs in 1849. Three sections of the museum are of particular interest: a display of archeological excavations that includes some fine pieces, an ethnographic section tracing the changing lives of the people who lived in the area from prehistoric times to the 20C, and the Szolnok Art Colony.

Szolnoki Galéria (Szolnok Gallery) – *Templom utca 2. ✆ (56) 513 640. Open Tue–Sun, 9am–5pm.* The gallery is located in a repurposed synagogue that was a place of worship until the 1940s and which now belongs to the main Damjanich János Museum. It holds permanent and temporary exhibitions and features pieces from the Szolnok Art Colony, which was established in 1902 in studios financed by the town. The artists lived and worked across the River Zagyva on Gutenberg tér; among them were some very talented painters such as Adolf Fényes and István Nagy. The building itself is also interesting for its architecture in the Moorish style.

Tisza Park and **Verseghy Park** – These two landscaped parks are adjacent to the River Tisza and close to the Tisza Hotel. The parks appear to merge into each other, providing a good place for a stroll beneath the shade of some trees.

Tiszaliget – Cross the river via Tiszavirág híd to the Tiszaliget district to find the small lake **Csónakázó-tó**. Nearby are a swimming pool and baths where you can relax.

Tiszavirág híd (Mayfly Bridge) Completed in 2011, the bridge was built for pedestrians and cyclists. Its graceful structure with outward leaning arches and cables is said to resemble a mayfly.

Cegléd A1

21mi/33km north of Kecskemét.

A small but charming town, Cegléd pays homage in particular to the memory of **Lajos Kossuth**, who made a rousing speech here against the Habsburgs on 24 September 1848. A statue in his honor was erected in Szabadág tér next to the large Reformed Church. The **Kossuth Múzeum** *(Múzeum utca 5; open Tue–Sun, 9am–5pm; Ft600)* traces his life through paintings and personal belongings.

Another significant historical figure, **György Dózsa**, is also honored with a statue, this time in the center of Kossuth Lajos tér. In 1514 the archbishop of Esztergom gave Dózsa the task of raising and commanding an army from among the peasants to fight the Turks. However, Dózsa encountered many problems organizing the battle and, conscious of the grievances and complaints of the peasants, he eventually took their part and turned against his patrons. He was defeated at Temesvár (Timişoara in present-day Romania), taken prisoner, and tortured to death.

City Hall facade, Kiskunfélegyháza
© Funkystock/age fotostock

Kiskunhalas A2–3

40mi/64km south of Kecskemét.

This otherwise ordinary town—also known simply as Halas—has achieved a reputation for its **lace making**. Halas lace first appeared at the beginning of the 20C thanks to Árpád Dékány, a teacher of drawing, and Mária Markovits, a lacemaker, who began to work together. Their collaboration flourished to the extent that their work eventually gained international recognition.

★ **Csipkeház** (Lace House) – *Kossuth utca 37. ☎ (77) 421 982. Open Mon–Sat, 9am–noon, 1pm–4pm (Jul & Aug, 5pm). Ft500.* Learn about the complexity of the lace-making process via the different stages involved in producing tablecloths, placemats, and other items. To be an expert lace maker you don't just need creativity, patience, and skill, but also an infinite capacity for attention to detail. The intricate Halas lace comprises 40 to 50 different stitches.

Thorma János Múzeum (János Thorma Museum) – *Köztársaság út 2. ☎ (77) 422 864. Open Tue–Sun, 9am–5pm. Ft1,000.* A museum exhibiting works by János Thorma (1870–1937), a local painter and member of the Nagybánya Artists' Colony, together with an important archeological collection.

Végh-kúria (Végh Mansion) – *Bajcsy-Zsilinszky utca 3. Open Tue–Fri, 9am–5pm.* This lovely house, built in 1840, displays paintings by Balázs Diószegi (1914–99), a relatively little-known artist who worked notably in black and used the contrast between black and white.

Kiskunfélegyháza AB2

19mi/30km southeast of Kecskemét.

This charming small town is no stranger to controversy. Was poet and revolutionary, Sándor Petőfi, really born here? He is said to have written that Kiskunfélegyháza was his birthplace, but that is strongly contested by the town of Kiskőrös, about 31mi/50km to the southwest. Either way, you can still see the house where Sándor Petőfi was born (theoretically or actually) and where he certainly did live, and then visit his other house in Kiskőrös, which, or so it is claimed, is the poet's true birthplace and also the small museum next to it. That way you are sure to be covering all bases.

Városháza (City Hall) – *Kossuth Lajos utca 1. Reserve ahead at the tourist office in City Hall. ☎ 562 039.* This fine example of the Art Nouveau style is the jewel in the town's crown and was built between 1910 and 1912 by Nándor Morbitzer and József Vass. The brick exterior is decorated with glazed tiles featuring plant and flower motifs. The interior expertly marries space with ornamentation. Painted garlands resembling embroidery wind their way across the stucco. The decoration, furniture, and lighting all come together superbly in the Great Hall. Look out for details such as the capitals, stained glass, doorways, integrated columns, and carved balustrades, not to mention the chandeliers. Outside look up to see some really lovely friezes on the facade in colorful majolica.

Kiskun Múzeum – *Holló Lajos út 9. Open Tue–Fri, 8am–4pm; Sat, 9am–5pm. Closed Jan & Feb.* This former military police prison, from the era of Empress Maria Theresa (you can see still some of the cells dating from that time), is now the departmental museum dedicated to the history of the town and surrounding area.

The museum's founder, Gyula Szalay, a local teacher, continued the work of novelist and museologist Ferenc Móra. One room is devoted to archeological displays, jewelry, and objects used by the people who lived in the region centuries ago, such as the Sarmatians and Avars. They were notable for the practice of inscribing their hierarchical rank on their belts. Look out for a pair of the first ice skates made from bone and a window painting that has three different images depending on the angle from which you view it. Also on display is the interior of a peasant dwelling showing what life was like for shepherds, including clothing and equipment for their nomadic life, a screen for hanging tools, and a stick on which to keep count of the number of animals in their care.

Csongrád B2

36mi/58km southeast of Kecskemét.

Csongrád lies on the on the River Tisza and was the "capital" of the county in the 11C. Probably ransacked by the Mongols in 1241, it lost its status to Szeged, but eventually regained it in the early 15C. After the failure of the War of Independence against Habsburg rule (1703–11) led by Ferenc II Rákóczi, Count Sándor Károlyi bought the town and the region and made Csongrád his capital. All kinds of trees line many of the roads, including linden and plane trees, which manage to mask the buildings, leaving you with the impression that you are walking in a park. The trees lining Fő utca have this effect. It leads into Kossuth tér, at the end of which you will find the imposing Gimnázium (high school), built in the Art Nouveau style with the obligatory majolica decoration. Csongrád also lays claim to being a town of grapes and wine (Kékfrankos, Cserszegi Fűszeres, and Irsai Olivér), which it celebrates every year when the wine festival is held 13–15 August.

★ **Tari László Múzeum** (László Tari Museum) – *Iskola utca 2, a turning off Kossuth tér. (63) 481 052. Open Mon–Fri, noon–4pm, Sat 8am–noon.* The museum is named after its founder, a dentist from Csongrád who was passionate about local history. Among its exhibits, it pays tribute to the many people who left their towns and neighborhoods to work on distant construction sites—such as the attempts to address the problem of persistent flooding—through the ordinary objects of everyday life. Although it is possible to admire István Széchenyi's vision, when he undertook the regulation of Hungary's rivers, in particular the Tisza, very little is known about the working conditions of those who actually carried out his grand plans. In the 19C, the unskilled workers *(kubikosok)* who excavated and transported thousands of tons of backfill to contain the river water, lived like slaves, working 12–16 hours a day in the mud or the dust, badly paid, malnourished, poorly housed, and far from their homes. An archeological collection of items discovered during excavations in the region is also on display.

In 1979 a statue representing an unskilled worker, by the sculptor Béla Tóth, was erected in Hunyadi Square in honor of the *kubikosok* and it has since become one of the defining symbols of Csongrád.

Belsőváros – Although *belsőváros* means inner city, this area is on the edge of town, near where the Tisza's tributary, the Kőrös, flows into the Tisza. The Holt-Tisza, a dead branch of the river, lies slightly inland further to the south. Belsőváros attests to the fact that fishing has long been a feature of the town. The fishing village is just as it was 200 years ago, with houses with earthen walls and roofs thatched with reeds.

From Fő utca, take either Gróf Andrássy utca or Gróf Apponyi Albert utca, and then Öregvár. Gyökér utca is a turning off to the right.

★ **Múzeum-Ház** (Museum village) – *Gyökér utca 1. (63) 483 103. Open May–Sept, 1pm–5pm.* Learn about Csongrád's long history of fishing in two old-houses connected by a thatched passageway. A room in one of them has an open fireplace and was kept for people passing on their way through the area, and contains objects from everyday life; in the other you can find the various equipment needed by a fisherman.

ADDRESSES IN KECSKEMÉT

See Kecskemét map (p326)

ARRIVAL/DEPARTURE

Train – Departures every hour between 6am and 9pm, from Budapest-Nyugati Station to Kecskemét *(journey time 1hr17min)*. The same for the return.

STAY

BUDGET

4 Fábián Panzió – A1 – *Kápolna utca 14. ✆ 20 257 1120. www.panziofabian.hu. 10 rooms from Ft9,000,* ☕ Ft2,000. A pleasant family-run guesthouse in the center of town, with very well-kept rooms beside a delightful garden.

AVERAGE

8 Hotel Három Gúnár – A2 – *Batthyány utca 1–7. ✆483 611. www.hotelharomgunar.hu.* P ✕ *54 rooms, Ft19,000/26,600* ☕. This hotel in the center of town underwent a complete renovation in 2010. It has lovely air-conditioned rooms beside a garden with a terrace, where you can relax and enjoy a drink. A good spot.

12 Hotel Talizmán – A1–2 – *Kápolna utca 2. ✆ 504 856. www.talizmanhotel.hu.* P *19 rooms, Ft20,000* ☕. A newly refurbished boutique hotel with smart modern rooms. The overall effect might be a bit soulless, but the hotel is contemporary and clean.

Kiskunság National Park

BUDGET

Gedeon Tanya Panzió – *II. körzet 150. Jakabszállás. ✆ (76) 722 800. www.gedeonfarm.com. 10 rooms from Ft8,000* ☕. Halfway between Hwy 54 and the village of Bugac in the heart of the countryside, this family-run *panzió* is a large rural house with a thatched roof. A newer building contains 3 apartments. It is also a working farm so there are plenty of animals about (horses, Hungarian cattle, goats, …) and you may be able to take a carriage ride. Traditional meals are served in the restaurant.

Csongrád

BUDGET

Pejkó Panzió – *Tanya 95. ✆ (70) 33 13 458. www.pejkopanzio.hu. 8 rooms, Ft14,000* ☕. A charming family-run guesthouse close to a stable of 16 horses … hence the chance to go horse riding from here.

EAT

AVERAGE

15 Tepsi Gastropub – A2 – *Kéttemplom köz 7. ✆ 508 558. Open Mon–Sat, 11am–11pm. Main dishes from Ft1,750.* Hungarian dishes and international favorites, such as delicious homemade burgers or tagliatelle with ceps and chicken, are served in a bright and comfortable environment. There is a large screen with video clips playing on a loop, which will appeal to some more than others.

5 Kecskeméti Csárda – A2 – *Kölcsey utca 7. ✆ 488 686. www.kecskemeticsarda.hu. Open noon–10pm (Sun, 5pm). Main dishes Ft2,600/5,900.* A traditional inn where the decoration has been sourced locally (barrels, pottery, and bottles of Hungarian wine), and you can feast on generous portions of dishes such as wild boar stew, occasionally accompanied by Romani music. There is also a nice terrace.

Kiskunság National Park

AVERAGE

Karikás Csárda – *At Bugac, entrance to the national park. ✆ 575 112. www.bugacpuszta.hu. Open Apr, 10am–4pm; May–8 Sept, 10am–9pm; 9 Sept–28 Oct, 10am–5pm. Closed Nov– Apr. Main dishes Ft1,900/5,900.* Specialties of the Great Plain are served in this vast inn (roast beef Romani-style, wild boar with forest mushrooms). The portions are so generous that they can easily be shared. There is a terrace in summer.

TAKING A BREAK

Vincent Bar & Pastry – *Szabadság tér 6. Open Mon–Fri, 8am–10pm (Fri, midnight); Sat & Sun, 9am–10pm (Sat, midnight).* This is a pleasant tea room during the day where you can enjoy cakes decorated with fancy icings, but it is also worth dropping in for a drink in the evening.

Fodor Cukrászda – *Szabadság tér 2. Open 9am–6.30pm.* This cake shop and tea room has retained its charming Art Deco feel. It serves generous bowls of ice cream and copious slices of cake.

BARS

DiVino – *Kéttemplom köz 14. Open Tue–Thu, 4pm–midnight; Fri & Sat, 5pm–2am. Closed Sun & Mon.* A branch of a wine bar chain, which is also in Budapest and several other Hungarian cities. It lives up to its promise with a large selection of Hungarian wines to sample, accompanied with platters of cheeses or cold meats.

SPORTS AND ACTIVITIES

Kecskeméti Fürdő (Kecskemét Baths) – *Csabay Géza körút 5. ✆ 500 320. www.kecskemetifurdo.hu. Open 6am–8pm. Ft1,100/3,600 depending on the day and zone.* This superb complex includes an Olympic-size swimming pool, a recreational area with water slides, and a pool with a wave machine, along with thermal baths, saunas, a spa, and a restaurant.

INTRODUCTION TO HUNGARY

Vineyards in the Lake Balaton region
© Hungarian Tourism Agency

Understanding Hungary

In its position at the heart of Europe, Hungary has long been a crossroads, a geographical intersection where people from all points of the compass have crossed paths. It has also been at times a place of confrontation, where one political power has given way to another, a country through which entire civilizations have passed, making their mark and leaving behind their culture and customs. However, Hungary's complex language is quite unique, with a grammar and vocabulary very different from the languages in the surrounding countries.

The population

Hungary has 9.8 million inhabitants (in 2017) with a population density of 277 people per square mile/105 people per square kilometer.

As in many European countries, the birthrate has been in steady decline for around 40 years. In 1920 some 49 percent of Hungarians lived in cities, a figure that has now risen to 63 percent. Thanks to the rapid industrialization of the postwar period, the rural workforce has been able to supply sufficient manpower for Hungary's requirements, without the need for any recourse to immigration.

Budapest now has 1.7 million residents, about a sixth of the country's total population; the capital saw its numbers swell in spectacular fashion at the end of the 19C, when it was at the political and commercial heart of a country three times its present size and on the rise economically. By comparison, the Hungary's other major conurbations lag far behind Budapest in terms of population numbers: Debrecen (pop. 202,214), Pécs (144,188), Miskolc (155,650), Győr (130,094), and Szeged 161,122).

THE MAGYARS

Hungary was a multiethnic society for many years, but lost 61 percent of its population under the terms of the Treaty of Trianon in 1920 (*see p354*). Today the country is largely ethnically homogeneous, with 97 percent of its population speaking Hungarian and of Magyar descent.

THE DIASPORA

Since the Treaty of Trianon put an end to the Austro-Hungarian Empire, there have been significant Hungarian minorities living in the states that are adjacent to Hungary: these expatriates number more than 1.2 million in Romania, some 520,000 in Slovakia, 300,000 in Serbia, 156,000 in Ukraine, and tens of thousands in Croatia and Slovenia. Besides Russia, Hungary is also the European country with the largest number of expatriate nationals living outside the country's borders.

"Shoes on the Danube Bank" memorial (2005) by Can Togay and Gyula Pauer, dedicated to the Jews killed during the Second World War, Budapest

© Konoplytska/iStock

THE ROMANI

The term Romani (or Roma) refers to a people who began to arrive in Hungary during and after the 14C in particular. These were originally mainly heterogeneous groups of ethnic peoples displaced in the wake of the eastern conquests of the Turkish-speaking empires; they now form the largest minority in Hungary and consist of three major groups: the Romungro, the Vlachs, and the Boyash. While their dialects may vary from one group to another, they generally speak Hungarian. Official statistics recorded 308,000 Romani in 2011, but there are actually likely to be many more; exact numbers are impossible to ascertain.

Porajmos: the Romani genocide

From the end of the 19C, and particularly during the Second World War, the Romani, who were sometimes considered outsiders and vagrants, were increasingly hunted down right across Europe. The Nazis began to intern them in Germany in 1933 and a third of Hungary's 100,000 Romani were exterminated in the concentration camps, either gassed or dying of starvation, illness, and exhaustion from forced labor. On the orders of Heinrich Himmler, the SS began the liquidation of the 2,897 Romani held in the Auschwitz-Birkenau camp in Poland on 2 August 1944. In memory of this act of genocide, 2 August was designated Roma Holocaust Memorial Day in 2015.

The goal of integration

The Council of Europe proclaimed the ten years from 2005 to 2015 the Decade of Roma Inclusion to ensure these European citizens would not remain marginalized in society. However, despite attempts at integration during the Communist regime, the Romani have been sidelined and are concentrated on the outskirts of the large cities, living precarious lives. They make up 15 percent of the population in Miskolc, an industrial city in the northeast, a figure shared with Debrecen and Nyíregyháza to the east of the country. The poorly educated Romani have also been hard-hit by unemployment since the introduction of a market economy in Hungary at the end of the 1980s.

THE JEWISH COMMUNITY

Jews have been living in Hungary since at least the 11C, with the community facing a struggle against discrimination throughout the Middle Ages. Viewed as having collaborated with the Turks during the Ottoman Empire's occupation of Hungary (1541–1699), they were massacred and expelled in the 17C; they did not return until the end of the 18C, when they were enticed back by the tolerant policies of Joseph II, the Holy Roman emperor. Two Jewish communities have coexisted since that time: one with its roots in Moravia and Germany, which settled in Budapest and the west of the country; and the other, principally made up of Hasidic Jews, wh0 settled in the northeast. In 1840 Hungary's Jewish community became the first to be able to trade freely in the Habsburg Empire and by 1910 there were 200,000 Jews living in Budapest.

In the dark days of the Second World War, having been robbed of all their possessions, 600,000 Hungarian Jews (of a total of 900,000) were deported to the extermination camps. Around 100,000 were saved thanks to the actions of a number of businessmen and diplomats, including the Swede Raoul Wallenberg, who was designated one of the Righteous Among Nations by Israel. He was born in 1912, but his date of death is unknown, he disappeared c. 1947 (*see p63*).

There are now between 50,000 and 100,000 Jews living in Hungary, mostly in Budapest, and it is here, in the former ghetto, that the capital's Jewish Cultural Festival is now held in summer, attracting thousands of spectators every year.

NOBEL LAUREATES AND INVENTORS

An impressive number of Hungarians have received the prestigious Nobel Prize in scientific fields, including **Philipp Lenard** (physics, 1905), **Robert Bárány** (medicine, 1914), **Richard Zsigmondy** (chemistry, 1925), **Albert von Szent-Györgyi** (medicine, 1937), **George de Hevesy** (chemistry, 1943), **Georg von Békésy** (medicine, 1961), **Eugene Wigner** (physics, 1963), **Dennis Gábor** (physics, 1971), **John Polányi** (chemistry, 1986), **George Oláh** (chemistry, 1994), and **Avram Hershko** (chemistry, 2004). **John Harsányi** shared the Nobel Prize for Economics with the American **John Nash** and the German **Reinhard Selten** in 1994, and **Imre Kertész** was recognized for his literary work with the award in 2002.

Many other Hungarians have distinguished themselves with ingenious ideas, lending their names to inventions that have enjoyed global success. **László József Bíró** (1899–1985) submitted a patent for a **ballpoint pen** in Paris in 1938. It was bought in 1949 by **Marcel Bich**, who then launched the famous Bic pen. Budapest architect and lover of puzzles **Ernő Rubik** (b. 1944), came up with a classic in 1974, the renowned Rubik's Cube. Hungarian-American engineer **Joseph Galamb** is credited with designing many of the parts for the pioneering Model T Ford car, launched in 1908.

The Hungarian language

THE FINNO-UGRIC FAMILY

The Hungarian language is almost unique in Europe, being quite separate from the Romance, Germanic, or Slavic tongues. It belongs to the Finno-Ugric family, much like Estonian, Finnish, and Karelian—in total around fifteen languages. The spawning ground for the Finno-Ugric languages was the steppe between the Urals and the central section of the Volga. The linguistic unity of the population across this vast territory was disrupted toward the middle of the 1C by migration, and differences now exist between the languages: a Finn and an Estonian can understand one another, but Hungarian remains a foreign language to both.

MODERN HUNGARIAN

The modern language bears the traces of a thousand years of contact between the Magyars and other peoples. In the Urals the language borrowed from the Indo-European tongue (descended from Indo-Iranian) that was spoken by peoples in the surrounding regions. Hungarian was later further enriched by thousands of words from the Turkic and Slav languages. The first document known to contain any Hungarian words is the charter founding the Benedictine monastery, Tihany Abbey. It was written in 1055, mostly in Latin, but contains several Hungarian words including place names.
The Hungarian language is low-pitched when spoken aloud. Latin was used for official purposes for many years, but began to be replaced by Hungarian after the Renaissance, notably in literature. Swingeing reforms, especially in grammar and spelling, were instigated at the turn of the 19C by **Ferenc Kazinczy** (1759–1831) and other writers. New terms and words were devised, taken either from dialects or created through analogy, enhancing Hungarian's stock of abstract expressions, with something approaching 10,000 words, which were integrated into the modern language. The complexity of this agglutinative language lies principally in the fact that it has an almost countless number of prefixes and suffixes—concepts are simply stitched together to make long words.
Useful Words and Phrases, p430. Names, p397.

Politics and geopolitics

The government of Hungary operates as a parliamentary republic with a single legislative chamber. The 1989 Constitution was replaced by the Fundamental Law of 2012. The country joined the European Union in 2004 and the Schengen area in 2007.

HOW THE STATE IS ORGANIZED

The **Hungarian parliament's** single chamber is made up of 199 members who are reelected every four years. The **Hungarian national assembly** has been presided over by László Kövér since 2010, and its immense Parliament Building is located in Budapest. The **president of Hungary** is elected by parliament every five years and has no executive power: János Áder (b. 1959) has been in post since 2012 in this essentially honorary role, although he is also commander-in-chief of the armed forces and responsible for nominating the prime minister. The president's official residence is Sándor Palace. The Hungarian government is

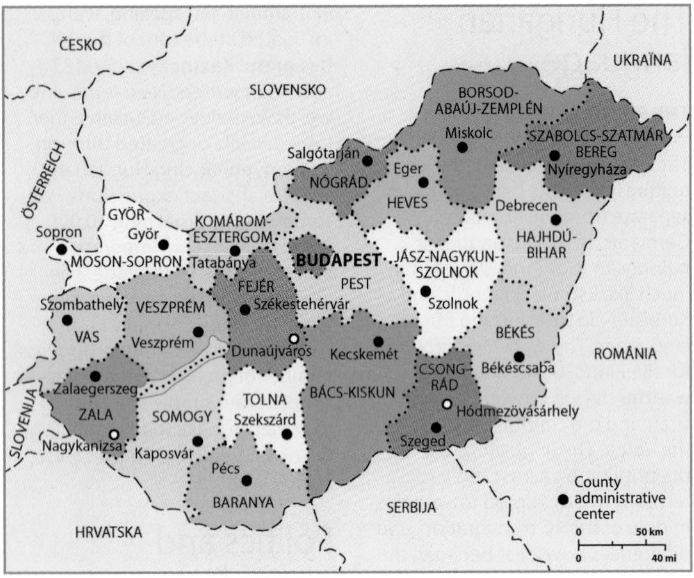

led by the **prime minister**, who is elected by the members of the assembly. After serving his first term between 1998 and 2002, Viktor Orbán was returned to power in 2010. The prime minister's offices have been located in the former Carmelite monastery building, which stands next to Buda Castle, since 1 January 2019.

The country was first divided into **counties** *(megye)* just after AD1000, a system that has endured to the present day as it guarantees the Magyar identity of the country in the face of centralized power. The 19 Hungarian counties now form an intermediary political subdivision between the state and local districts, but their administrative authority is strictly limited. By contrast, the 3,152 **local districts** (divided into municipalities, larger communities, towns, and cities with county rights) are locally run collectives headed by a district council and a mayor elected to an administrative role every four years under universal suffrage. The capital Budapest is subdivided into 23 districts.

NATIONAL SYMBOLS

The text of the **national anthem** was written by the poet Ferenc Kölcsey in 1828, entitled *Hymnus, a' Magyar nép zivataros századaiból* ("Anthem: From the stormy centuries of the Hungarian nation"), and was set to music in 1844. Although it begins with the words "Bless the Hungarians, oh Lord," this romantic poem is an appeal more to identity and history than to religion and was officially adopted as the national anthem in 1903.

It has eight stanzas, but only the first is played or sung at official ceremonies and at midnight on 31 December. In addition to the **National Day** (15 March), which commemorates the Hungarian Revolution of 1848, there are two other **public holidays** in Hungary: St. Stephen's Day on 20 August celebrating the founding of the state in AD1000, and 23 October, marking the anniversary of the 1956 Hungarian Uprising.

Inspired by the flag of the French Revolution, the Hungarian tricolor *(zászló)* first made an appearance during the uprising of 1848. It has been the country's official flag since 1867 and is comprised of three horizontal bands of red, white, and green. The red symbolizes power and recalls the banners carried by the tribes of Prince Árpád, who settled the Magyars in the heart of the Pannonian Basin; the white symbolizes loyalty and is the color of King Stephen, who ensured the kingdom remained independent; green is the symbol of hope and has been part of the royal coats of arms since Matthias Corvinus in the 15C. Hungary's historic **coat of arms** was adopted in 1990, after the fall of the Communist regime. The escutcheon-shaped shield is divided into two parts: the sinister (left) half features red and white bands, the symbol of the Árpáds, with the white bands symbolizing the country's major watercourses: the Danube, Tisza, Dráva, and Száva; the dexter (right) half features three mountains in green, representing the Mátra, Tátra, and Fátra ranges, with a golden crown and the Cross of Lorraine in white above. The Cross of Lorraine references the Christian kingdom and the Hungarian Catholic Church. On top of the shield is the Holy Crown of Hungary with its cross at an angle.

The **symbols of Hungarian sovereignty** (the crown jewels or the regalia) include the crown of St. Stephen, the scepter, the orb, the coronation mantle (an ornate cloak covered almost entirely in gold thread embroidery), and the sword. These medieval relics have been kept at the Hungarian Parliament since 1 January 2000, apart from the coronation mantle, which may be viewed at the Hungarian National Museum.

Parliament Building (p46); Hungarian National Museum (p52).

The economy

Hungary was hit hard by the financial and economic crisis of 2008, at a time when it was already weighed down by increases in public debt that were delaying its entry into the eurozone; the country benefited from an aid plan run by the International Monetary Fund (IMF), the European Union, and the World Bank, but the Hungarian government paid back the last tranche of this loan in 2016. Hungary now has a healthy economic situation, with 4.9 percent growth in 2018 and unemployment down to 3.7 percent.

AGRICULTURE

The abolition of collective farms and the rise of mechanization during the 1990s resulted in a dip in employment and national production in the agriculture sector, but it still plays a major role in the Hungarian economy, with the contribution made by farming to GDP rising to 3.3 percent in 2017, amounting to 4.8 percent of investment and 5 percent of employment. Production is diversified, with fruit, vegetables, and winegrowing alongside arable crops and livestock. Hungary is Europe's top producer of sweetcorn (and the second highest producer in the world). It is second only to France in the production of foie gras and is the fourth highest global producer of honey.

Winemaking is an extremely important sector for export and enjoys a very good reputation. The total surface area planted with grapevines has, however, shrunk

SPORT

"Sport is not only education of the body, it is also the most noble and efficient way to educate the spirit," according to Albert Szent-Györgyi (1893–1986), a Hungarian doctor who received the Nobel Prize in Medicine in 1937. In the field of top-level sports, water polo is the main discipline, followed by swimming, canoeing/kayaking, and fencing. The Hungarians took home 15 medals, including 8 golds, at the Summer Olympic Games in 2016, and the 2018 Winter Olympics saw the short track speed skating team achieve gold medals in the 5,000 meter relay.

by 11 percent since 2010, reaching 160,618 acres/65,000ha in 2019.

Animal husbandry is dominated by pork and poultry, with the principal products being milk, meat, butter, eggs, and wool, as well as a famous lard sourced from the Mangalica pig, a Hungarian species with a thick, woolly coat that once faced extinction. Because of the lack of competition, these sectors were affected first by the advent of a market economy in 1990 and then by Hungary's entry to the European Union in 2004.

Seal of quality – Hungary is aware of the importance of protecting and promoting its traditional products. Among the thirty or so that have been awarded a European Union label (such as PDO, Protected Designation of Origin, for wine) are Szeged paprika and salami, Hajdúság horseradish, wines produced in 22 historic winegrowing regions, Alföld chamomile, Makó onions, and Gönc apricots.

INDUSTRY AND SERVICES

Having been in slow decline since the fall of Communism, **industry** has since recovered as Hungary has become an indispensable link in the European production chain due to its low labor costs. Industry represents 26.44 percent of the country's GDP and employs just shy of 30 percent of the working population; it is extremely open to foreign investment, with the manufacturing industry almost always featuring in the top flight of direct outside investments. Manufacturers and equipment providers play a key role in exports and in the growth of the Hungarian economy, with the automotive sector attracting new investors—Suzuki, Audi, Daimler, Mercedes, and BMW already have plants in Hungary. **Services** are now the most dynamic sector, amounting to 54.85 percent of GDP and employing almost 65 percent of the working population.

Spas and thermal waters

Hungary could well be the thermal baths kingdom of the world. There is a truly exceptional number of curative hot springs in this part of Central Europe, with more than 200 spa localities and over 225 thermal baths open to the public and foreign visitors, including 100 approved thermal and curative spa resorts that are open to tourists and those seeking medicinal treatments. According to the

Széchenyi Baths, Budapest
© Hungarian Tourism Agency

legislation, thermal spring water must exceed a temperature of 86°F/30°C. These waters are used in specialized bathing establishments for purely medical purposes, but also in the swimming pools, lakes, and seasonal baths used for hydrotherapy and bathing for the public leisure market. Hungary currently has more than 270 approved medicinal waters, the majority of which are used in hydrotherapy, balneotherapy and/or, in certain cases, water cures.

A THOUSAND-YEAR-OLD RITUAL

The curative properties of the waters were known to the Romans, who made widespread use of them, as can be seen from the remains of the baths at Aquincum in Budapest *(see p68)*. In the 16C the Turks, who occupied parts of Hungary for more than a century, introduced public baths and built bathhouses, small architectural gems that have been carefully maintained to this day. Examples include Rudas Fürdő *(see p41)* and Király Fürdő *(p44)* in Budapest.

A hotbed of social life

The public baths are popular with many Hungarians, who visit them to soothe aches and pains, and to chat, play chess, or simply relax. The baths deliver a real sense of well-being and sessions often end in a sauna, massage, or just the obligatory shower. Don't leave Hungary without trying the experience, even if it's simply to admire the magnificent settings and interiors of some of the spas.

BEAUTIFUL SPA BUILDINGS

Some of the spa complexes are of unique architectural interest: Budapest's **Széchenyi Gyógyfürdő** (*see p62)* has more than a touch of the Baroque castle about it, while the Secessionist **Gellért Gyógyfürdő** *(p42)* is without doubt the most beautiful of the baths, with frescoes, mosaic tiles, and statues. The **Hagymatikum** spa resort in Makó, in southeastern Hungary, was designed in an Organic style; the onion-shaped building conceals a labyrinth of pools. The great attraction of **Hévíz** is its thermal lake *(p153)*; even in the coldest winters the water temperature never drops below 79°F/26°C and is constantly on the move, being refreshed in its entirety every 28 to 30 hours by the hot springs that feed into it. Hévíz is the largest thermal lake suitable for bathing in the world.

Nature

Hungary is a landlocked country that sits at the center of Europe, approximately equidistant from the Atlantic Ocean in the west and the Ural Mountains in Russia in the East, and the Mediterranean Sea to the south and the Baltic Sea to the north. Around 326 miles/524 kilometers in length and 155 miles/250 kilometers at its widest point, Hungary extends across the center of the basin of the River Danube, sharing borders that total some 1,248 miles/2,009 kilometers with seven other countries: Slovenia and Austria in the west, Slovakia in the north, Ukraine in the northeast, Romania in the east, and Serbia and Croatia in the south.

Countryside and climate

Hungary has no natural borders beyond four rivers: the Danube and one of its tributaries, the Ipoly, in the north, and the Dráva and Mura in the south. Plains cover two-thirds of its terrain, 2 percent of which are at an altitude of over 1,312ft/400m. Due to its geographical location, Hungary is subject to several climatic influences but it is the Continental climate that dominates. It has harsh winters, when the temperature drops to an average of 32–14°F/0°C–minus 10°C, but it also benefits from being one of the sunniest countries in Central Europe (averaging 2,000 hours of sunshine each year). It is hottest in July when the average temperature is 73°F/23°C. Annual rainfall is quite low (averaging 20in/500mm a year), with oceanic influences making the north and southwest the wettest regions (31–35in/800–900mm of rain), whereas in the center, the dry conditions of the Great Plain (the Great Hungarian Plain) are similar to the steppes of Eastern Europe.

Transdanubian Mountains

This mountain range, covering 3,089sq mi/8,000sq km, extends in a diagonal direction from the southwest to the northwest, linking the last foothills of the Central Eastern Alps with the Carpathians. Relatively low, it rises 1,640–1,969ft/500–800m and is made up of small crystalline massifs, limestone, and volcanic rock. It comprises three regions:

The western mountains – The small massifs to the west of the Danube include the Bakony, the Vértes, and the Pilis-Gerecse ranges.

The Danube Bend – After a stretch of 18mi/130km, which marks the border in the north between Hungary and Slovakia, the Danube winds between the mountains of **Börzsöny** and **Pilis**. It then changes direction by 90 degrees creating the Danube Bend *(Dunakanyar)*, before passing first Esztergom and then Visegrád, to carry on south between Buda and Pest.

The northern massifs – The Börzsöny range precedes the

Cserhát Mountains where the village of Hollókő nestles, with its wooden bell towers and whitewashed houses. Covered in oak and beech trees, the massif reaches its highest point in the **Mátra Mountains**, where Hungary's highest peak, Kékestető (Mount Kékes), rises to 3,327ft/1,014m. The rugged karst landscapes of **Bükk** and **Aggtelek**, enlivened by woods of juniper trees, stretch as far as the mountains of **Zemplén**, dominating the prestigious vineyard region of **Tokaj**, which graces the gentle slopes of the Hegyalja foothills.

In the basins that separate the massifs, towns have grown up around operations to mine coal, bauxite, and lignite. Miskolc, Hungary's third largest town, exploited the country's sole iron ore deposit (in Rudabánya). The only rare ore—manganese—was mined at Úrkút.

The massifs of this mountain ridge are constrained at the south by a major fault line that has led to the emergence of numerous thermal springs. Hungary has more than 1,300 **hot springs** and has exploited close to a hundred of them. The capital Budapest holds the world record with 118 springs that supply 12 approved thermal and medicinal baths.

The Great Plain

Bordered by the Danube and the northern massifs, the **Alföld,** as the Great Plain is known in Hungarian, extends as far as the borders with Romania, Serbia, and Croatia.

It covers more than half of the country (20,077sq mi/52,000sq km). Its highest point (597ft/182m) is in the northeast, close to Debrecen, and its lowest (256ft/78m) is in the south, near Szeged.

A LANDSCAPE SHAPED BY HUMANS

The Great Plain is crossed from north to south by Hungary's second longest river, the **Tisza**, which is very rich in fish. It rises in Ukraine and joins the Danube some 882mi/1,419km further on. It is known as the "blond river," due to the sand it churns up from the river bed as it flows, which is then driven into dunes by the wind.

The Great Plain was originally known as **Puszta**, meaning "bare earth," its landscape having paid a heavy price due to the Turkish occupation. Devasted by the Ottoman armies of Süleyman the Magnificent after the Battle of Mohács in 1526, the region was not returned to Hungarian rule until the end of the 17C. In the meantime, its marshy grassland had been sacked and its population decimated.

The Great Plain was on the verge of becoming barren wasteland until the 19C, when artists such as Sándor Petőfi (1823–49), drew attention to it in their work, celebrating its wild beauty. The dry, vibrant colors of János Tornyai's (1869–1936) paintings, recreate the aridity of this region before it was cultivated.

The scientific revolution in agriculture that has taken place over the last century has radically transformed the Great Plain. Dams built upstream on the Tisza in the 1960s have controlled the river's devastating floods, while developing irrigation for agriculture. Rice fields, acacias, and poplars have been planted to help anchor the sand and make the most of the poor soil, while developing the cultivation of cereals, fruits, and vegetables. A sign of this renewed vitality are the new houses that are now springing up around the existing villages.

Mátra massif
© Walter Bibikow/age fotostock

THE PUSZTA

Only two pockets of the original steppe now remain: Hortobágy National Park (197,684 acres/ 80,000ha) to the west of Debrecen, and Kiskunság National Park (39,537 acres/16,000ha) to the west of Kecskemét. These sandy heathlands, dotted with marshes and saltwater pools, retain their wild nature.

Hortobágy National Park is the largest area of steppe in Central Europe. Racka sheep with long, twisted horns are still reared in the traditional way here, as are an ancient breed of cattle, the Hungarian Grey cattle. With their reputation for strength and endurance, they provide a useful gene pool for crossbreeding. Herdsmen, mounted on Nonius horses, are accompanied by Puli, sheepdogs with long, curly, black or white coats. Other Hungarian dog breeds include the Pumi with bluish-gray coats, the Komondor with white coats, and the white and brown Kuvasz. The park is also home to more than 230 different species of birds, including ducks, herons, bustards, and geese.

The Bugac Puszta is the most visited part of the **Kiskunság National Park**. Cars are forbidden as the local shepherds who live here still get around on horseback in the traditional way; visitors can come and watch their exciting equestrian displays.

THE SOUTH, "HUNGARY'S ORCHARD"

Extremely productive in terms of agriculture, the Great Plain concentrates on high-yield farming and is one of the most fertile regions in the country.

Nagykunság (Greater Cumania), between Szolnok and Debrecen, benefits from loess soil, growing cereals such as wheat, maize, and rice. A green oasis, **Kecskemét** is surrounded by vines and apricot trees, from which the town produces its famous brandy *(barack pálinka)*. **Szeged**, on the southern

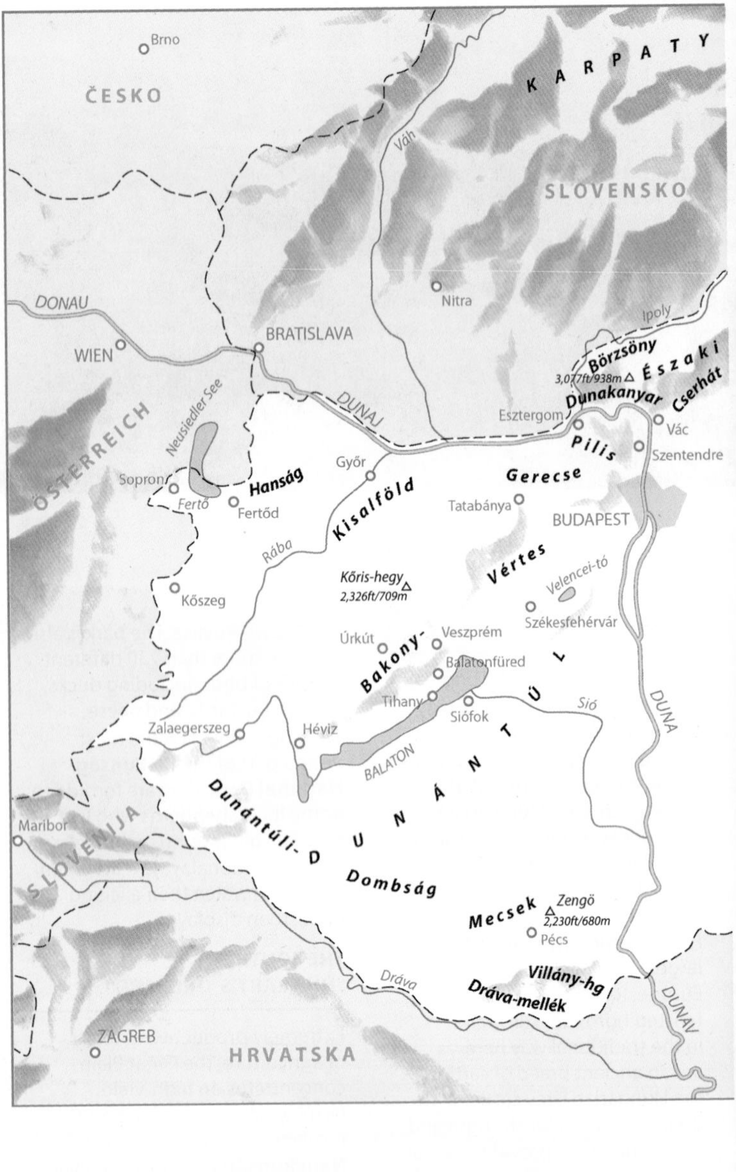

border, is the principal producer of paprika. During fall the windows in the villages are hung with garlands of the red peppers. Oil, natural gas, and geothermal energy are obtained from below ground (primarily used for farming and urban heating).

EAST OF THE TISZA

The **Nyírség** region here is home to industrial plants processing tobacco, wheat, sunflowers, and sugar beet, along with vast plantations of apple trees. Flocks of geese enjoy a breath

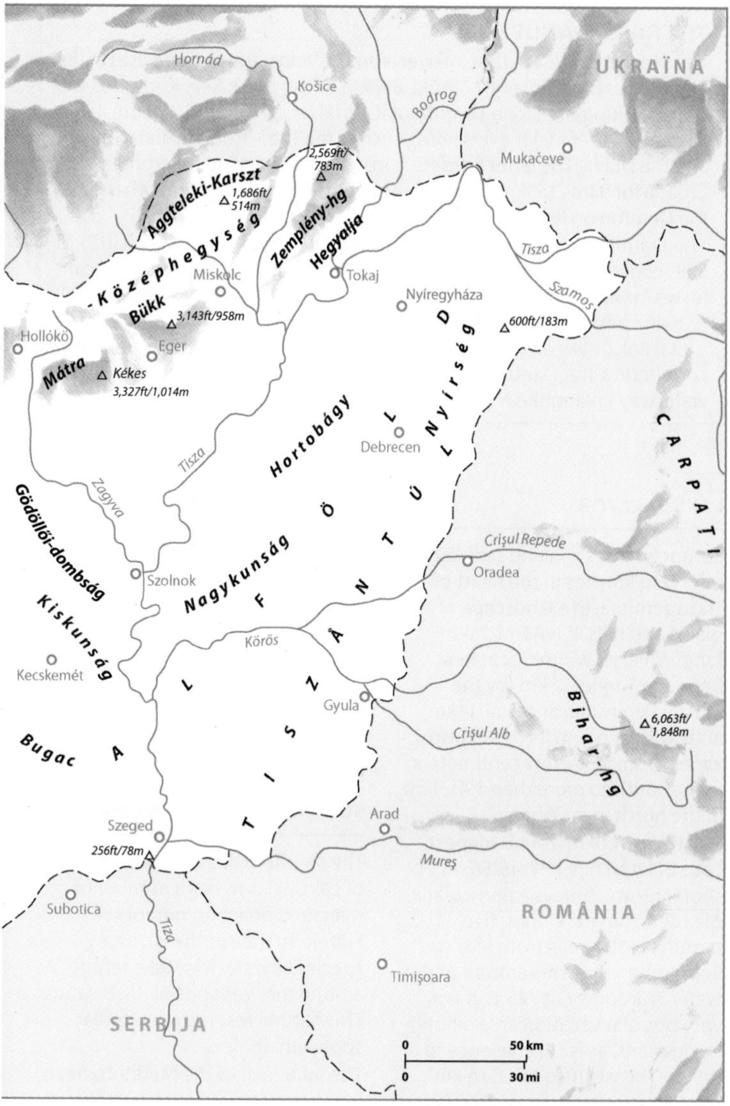

of cool air under the trees. The raising of pigs, ducks, turkeys, and guinea fowl completes the intensive development of the land. **Debrecen**, the regional center of the northern Great Plain, is to the northeast. It is one of Hungary's most important cities and the second largest after Budapest.

Transdanubia

Stretching from the alpine foothills to the Danube, this region, named **Dunántúl** in Hungarian (14,286sq mi/ 37,000sq km), lies in the west of the country. It was here that the Romans established the province of Pannonia (*see p354*).

THE RIVER DANUBE

The second longest European river after the Volga, the Danube rises in the Black Forest and flows 1,771mi/2,850km to the Black Sea. Known as the Duna in Hungarian, one seventh of its total length (266mi/428km) lies in Hungary. Other major rivers join it, such as the Tisza, from the Carpathians, and the Dráva. The latter borders Transdanubia, marking the frontier with Croatia for 93mi/150km. Most tributaries (the Váli-Viz, Sió, and others) join the Danube on its right bank.

The Danube is shallow, averaging only 10–13ft/3–4m, for a width of 328–656yds/300–600m. On its way across Hungary, it suffers significant losses in water volume due to infiltration and evaporation. However, it still remains perfectly navigable and since the Middle Ages has represented a vital link between East and West Europe. In 1992 the opening of a canal connecting the Danube with the rivers Main and Rhine created a new waterway linking the North Sea with the Black Sea.

LAKE BALATON

Europe's largest "inland sea" (229sq mi/592sq km) lies in the heart of Transdanubia, in a landscape of plains and hills. It is 46mi/74km long, while its width fluctuates between 1 mile/1.5km (by the Tihany Peninsula) and 9mi/14km at its widest point. Its depth also varies, from just a few centimeters in the south to more than 39ft/12m in the north, near Tihany.

Just 62mi/100km from Budapest, Lake Balaton has 159mi/256km of shoreline and enjoys a particularly pleasant climate. During five months of the year, from May to September, the temperature of the water is around 77°F/25°C. It is a very popular vacation area among Hungarians, as is Lake Velence to the northeast (10sq mi/25sq km).

Lake Balaton is home to 42 varieties of fish, among them *fogas* (a type of pike-perch), carp, sturgeon, bream, catfish, and eel. Together with the Biharian barbel and wels catfish (sheatfish), these are the most prelevant species.

The terrain north of Lake Balaton has the appearance of a succession of small massifs. Vines and fruit trees grow on its lush green shores. The **Tihany Peninsula** is one of the prettiest areas around the lake. Covered in poplars, acacia trees, and fields of lavender, it retains its wild allure.

The most famous of the thermal springs in the area is Hévíz, to the west of Lake Balaton, which supplies **Lake Hévíz**, the world's largest thermal lake (505,903sq ft/47,000sq m).

SOUTHERN TRANSDANUBIA

The southern, less rugged, shore of Lake Balaton has a number of managed beaches, notably at Siófok. To the southeast, many species of waterfowl take refuge among the wetlands of Kis-Balaton. This natural reserve is a popular spot with anglers.

The influence of the Mediterranean is apparent as you approach the city of Pécs. Built against the small karst massif of Mecsek, figs and almond trees merge here with vines, making the landscape reminiscent of Tuscany. As well as agricultural wealth, Transdanubia's land is also productive below ground, with the presence of natural gas, manganese, uranium, bauxite, and even some oil fields.

Basaltic wall, Káli Basin, Badacsony
© Fiedler Bernd J./age fotostock

The Little Hungarian Plain

Kisalföld (the Little Hungarian Plain, 3,244sq mi/8,403sq km) lies to the northwest of the Bakony Mountains and surrounds Sopron and Lake Fertő (122sq mi/315sq km). It marks the border with Austria, where it is known as the Neusiedler See—just 29sq mi/75sq km of the lake are in Hungary. Its relatively mild climate makes it one of the greenest regions in the country. Oak and beech trees grow in the poor soil, while farms are dedicated to the mass production of cereals, maize, sugar beet, forage crops for livestock, potatoes, cattle, and pigs. However, agriculture has disturbed the countryside here less than in the Great Plain as polyculture is predominant, farms are smaller, and the villages also operate as agricultural markets.

The Kisalföld was fortunate in being spared during the Turkish occupation, with the result that it has been able to preserve its cities with their medieval architecture almost intact, such as at Kőszeg and Sopron, along with Gothic churches and Baroque palaces such as Esterházy Palace at Fertőd. Culturally, this region remains close to Austria from which it has only been separated since the 1921 referendum, when it opted to remain in Hungary (*see p216*). The people here speak both Hungarian and German and the villages look virtually the same on either side of the border.

The Kisalföld's largest urban settlement is Győr, a town that is now a major national rail and road hub and where German automobile manufacturer Audi currently makes 90 percent of the engines installed in its vehicles.

History

Thanks to its central location between East and West, Hungary has attracted the acquisitive attentions of many other nations. Having offered centuries of resistance to the Ottoman Turks and the Habsburgs, it finally established a Hungarian state of its own, and from 1867 to the end of the First World War, in an empire shared with Austria, Hungary became a strong kingdom of 20 million souls spread across 125,483 square miles/325,000 square kilometers. However, after the signature of the Treaty of Trianon on 4 June 1920, Hungary found itself powerless, shorn of two-thirds of its territory and half its population. Budapest was occupied by the Red Army in 1945 and the Communist regime that subsequently established itself allied Hungary with the Eastern bloc. Left to its own devices after the fall of the Iron Curtain, Hungary turned toward Europe.

From Magyars to Hungarians

Originally from north of the Urals, the **Magyars** settled in the Middle Volga area during the first millennium, where they became semi-nomadic horsemen.
In 35BC the Roman legionaries of Octavian (the future Emperor Augustus) subjugated the Celts, occupied Transdanubia, and named it **Pannonia**. The province was Romanized and divided in two (Pannonia Superior and Pannonia Inferior). **Óbuda** (now a suburb of Budapest) became the capital of Pannonia Inferior in the 2C. The Romans withdrew during the 4C and 5C and first the Visigoths and then the Huns moved in. **Attila** (c. 406–53), king of the Huns, united the tribes into a vast empire that evaporated upon his death, and the country was given over to the Avars. After escaping the clutches of the Khazars in the 9C, the Hungarians settled between the rivers Don and Dniester in a region known as Etelköz, or "the land between the two rivers."

THE ÁRPÁD DYNASTY

In 896 Prince **Árpád** (c. 845–907) (whose name means "ogre") and the seven Magyar tribes conquered the Pannonian Basin. By the 10C, aided by the king of Germany, Arnulf of Carinthia, the Hungarians had brought down Svatopluk, ruler of Great Moravia, and Mojmir II. They gained fame for the raiding and pillaging that took them as far as Burgundy and Aquitaine, and Naples and the shores of the Bosphorus. In 955, however, the Hungarians were bested at **Lechfeld**, not far from Augsburg in Bavaria, by the Germanic king Otto the Great (912–73) and their chiefs were executed. This defeat put an end to their raiding and led them to settle down. **Géza**, great-grandson of Prince Árpád, became king in 972, had himself baptized, and asked Bruno, a monk from St. Gallen (in present-day Switzerland), to **convert the country to Christianity**. After his death, his son, Vajk, succeeded him. Vajk was baptized István (anglicized as Stephen) and reigned as **Stephen I** (r. 997–1038), continuing his father's work. Stephen was crowned at Esztergom on Christmas Day 1000 and is considered the true founder of the Hungarian state. He was canonized by Pope Gregory VII in 1083 and hence is also known as Saint Stephen, or King Saint Stephen. Further members of the Árpád dynasty followed Stephen and after long disputes over succession at the end of the 11C, László I (St. Ladislas) ascended the throne in 1077, to be succeeded in 1095 by Kálmán (Coloman), the Possessor of Books. The Hungarians extended their kingdom during this period, conquering Croatia-Slavonia, Dalmatia, and central Bosnia.

In 1222, during the reign of King **András** (**Andrew**) **II** (r. 1205–35), the son of Béla III (*see box p356*), the **Golden Bull** (*see p166*) gave the nobility the right to offer resistance (armed, if necessary) to the king if he encroached upon their privileges; the consequences of this charter of freedoms were to be considerable since all subsequent Hungarian kings had to swear to uphold its tenets.

In 1241 the **Mongols** carried out attacks on Central Europe, defeating the Hungarian army at Muhi. King Béla IV (r. 1235–70) just managed to escape and set up court in Trau (present-day Trogir in Croatia). After years of ransacking the country, the Mongol army was defeated in 1286 and the Árpád dynasty came to an end with the death of András III in 1301.

THE WARS AGAINST THE OTTOMAN TURKS

The accession of **Károly Róbert** (Charles I, r. 1308–42) in the first half of the 14C saw the first of a series of monarchs from foreign houses take the crown. It was Károly Róbert, born in Naples, who tackled the power of the great lords who "held

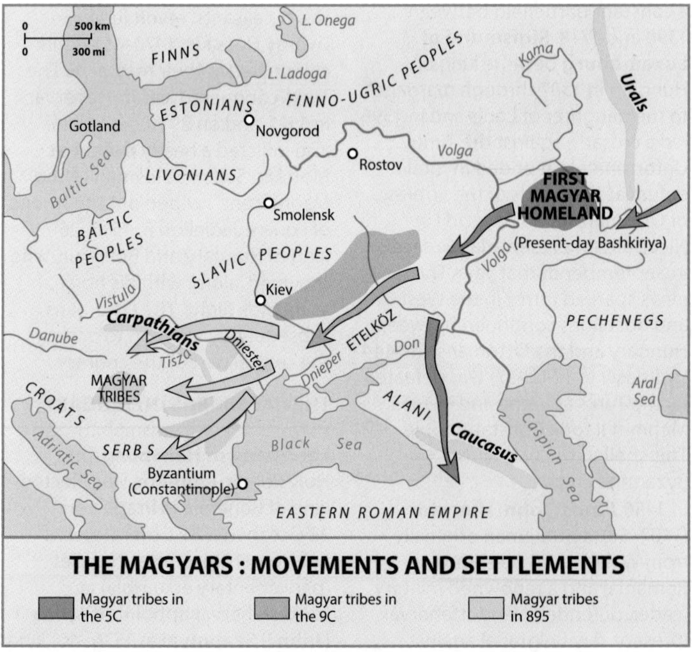

THE MAGYARS : MOVEMENTS AND SETTLEMENTS

Magyar tribes in the 5C | Magyar tribes in the 9C | Magyar tribes in 895

BÉLA III, A GREAT KING

King Béla III (r. 1172–96), who was great in both reputation and stature (6ft 3in/1.90m), governed by seeking a balance between his relations with the Eastern Byzantine Empire and the West. He based the organization of his state on the Western European model, appointing his first chancellor in 1180 and promulgating laws to make literacy obligatory. The Royal Council took shape and a new army and social class saw the light of day in the form of the *servientes regis* (king's servants), freemen living on royal property. The *jobagiones*, who commanded the castles, became landowners at the expense of royal landholdings, and peasants and slaves now formed a single serving class. Béla III also reformed the Church, basing it on the Cistercian Order (the abbeys and churches at Zsámbék near Budapest, Bélapátfalva, and Ják were built or extended). In 1189 Béla III played host to Frederick I, the Holy Roman emperor, during the Third Crusade; the visit marked the apogee of Béla's reign. Hungary's unique nature was upheld as the 12C came to a close—it never became Imperial territory or a vassal state.

almost the entire country against him." He reunited the kingdom, restoring its status and enriching it.

The **Ottomans** attacked Hungary for the first time in 1371, during the reign of Louis I (r. 1342–82), also known as Louis the Great. The country would virtually become a constant battlefield between 1390 and 1718. **Sigismund of Luxembourg** became king of Hungary in 1387 through marriage to the daughter of Louis and in 1396 led a crusade against the Turks. Unfortunately, it ended in total defeat at the hands of the armies of Ottoman sultan Bayezid I in Nicopolis (in present-day Greece), in September of that year. The news sparked terror in the West and hostilities continued between Hungary and the Ottomans. In 1444 Ladislas V (r. 1440–57) was defeated by the Turks at Varna and in 1453 Mehmet II took Constantinople. This spelled the end of the Byzantine Empire.

In 1456 **János (John) Hunyadi** (1407–56), a nobleman originally from Walachia (in present-day Romania) and a renowned military leader, defended Nándorfehérvár (present-day Belgrade) against the Turks. He died of the plague that same year and his son Mátyás was elected **King Matthias I**, also known as **Matthias Corvinus** (r. 1458–90). Interested in humanist ideas, Matthias introduced a number of reforms.

The year 1514, under Vladislaus II, saw a peasants' revolt led by György Dózsa (c. 1470–1514) that culminated in their massacre. The Turks conquered Nándorfehérvár in 1521, and on 29 August 1526 also inflicted a heavy **defeat at Mohács**; Sultan Süleyman I ("the Magnificent") wiped out the troops of Louis II Jagiellon (r. 1516–26), king of Hungary and Bohemia, who drowned, along with his horse, as he took flight. The Ottomans subsequently went on to occupy the central part of the country.

THE HABSBURGS IN HUNGARY

Ferdinand of Habsburg, the Holy Roman emperor, was elected king of Bohemia in Prague on 22 October 1526. Several weeks later, on 11 November, the diet (parliamentary assembly) at Székesfehérvár appointed **János (John I) Szapolyai** (r. 1526–40) king

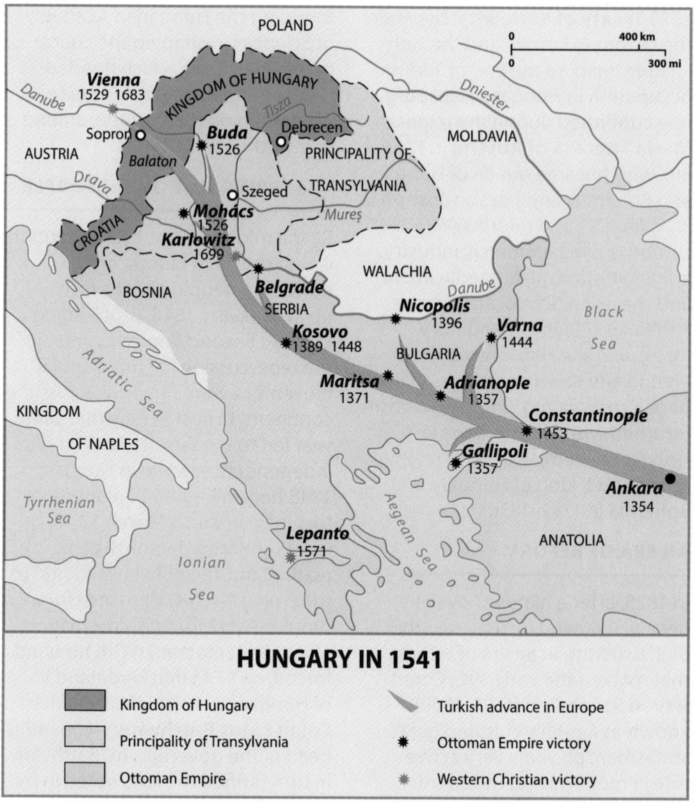

HUNGARY IN 1541

of Hungary. In the face of Habsburg might and despite Turkish support, János saw his kingdom reduced to the borders of Transylvania. In Pressburg, on 17 December, the Habsburg dynasty prevailed and **Ferdinand I** was elected king of Hungary. By 1541, some 15 years after the defeat at Mohács, only the north and the west of Hungary (Royal Hungary) remained in Ferdinand's hands, with **Süleyman** occupying the center and Buda also under Turkish control. **János Sigismund (John II) Szapolyai** (r. 1540–71) became the first prince of Transylvania. Süleyman died in Hungary on 5 September 1566, the eve of the **Siege of Szigetvár**, but his death was hushed up to preserve morale among his troops. The siege resulted in an Ottoman victory, but despite this Süleyman's death brought the Turkish advance toward Vienna to a temporary halt. In 1571 the **Holy League** of key Catholic states was founded to stem the advance west of the Ottomans, and on 7 October of that year, League troops (reinforced by Transylvanians) scored a naval victory over the Turks at the **Battle of Lepanto**. The Long Turkish War (1591–1606) was a series of conflicts conducted by the Habsburgs to try to oust the Turks from Hungary and Transylvania. By the end of the 17C, the Imperial army of the Habsburgs had occupied Transylvania and liberated Buda, and in 1687 the diet awarded the hereditary crown of Hungary to the Habsburgs. The

1699 **Treaty of Karlowitz**, between the Ottoman Empire and the Holy League, marked the end of Turkish occupation in Hungary. Habsburg rule continued during the reigns of **Maria Theresa of Austria** (r. 1740–80), who became queen of Hungary and Bohemia, and her son **Joseph II** (r. 1780–90), and reforms were carried out in commerce, industry, administration, justice, education, and the army. School attendance and taxes became mandatory for all, and the Habsburg court in Vienna and the Hungarian nobility began to work together. Absolutism returned with Francis II, the last Holy Roman emperor, who reigned as **Francis I**, king of Hungary and Bohemia (r. 1792–1830).

AN ERA OF REFORM

In 1825, after a hiatus of over a decade, Francis I reconvened the diet, ushering in an era of reform that marked the early 19C. Count **István Széchenyi** (1791–1860), known as a highly cultured great statesman, played a very active role in modernizing the country, founding the Hungarian Academy of Sciences, reshaping the course of the River Tisza which flooded regularly, and developing steam navigation on the Danube, among many other innovations.

THE SPRINGTIME OF THE PEOPLE

By the middle of the 19C, revolution was in the air in Europe once more. The people of Paris rose up in February 1848, proclaiming France's Second Republic, and the repercussions of this popular movement were felt right across the continent. Unrest in Italy that same year led to the First Italian War of Independence, while in Hungary 1848 became a year of revolution, too. In Pest, on **15 March 1848**, revolutionaries demonstrated, reading out their "Twelve Points" to the crowds—their demands for a program anticipating the creation of a civic democracy. With his hand forced, on 17 March Ferdinand V of Hungary (r. 1830–48) appointed Count **Lajos Batthyány** (1806–49) head of the government. Batthyány in turn ratified the laws voted in by

RESISTANCE TO THE HABSBURGS

Transylvania was the seat of resistance to the Habsburgs for much of the 17C, during which time three princes of Transylvania from three great Hungarian families came to prominence. The first, the Calvinist **István Bocskai** (r. 1605–06), achieved victory over the Habsburgs with the aid of battle-hungry troops, and in 1606 King Rudolph was obliged to accept independence for Transylvania and respect the privileges of the nobility, and to allow people the freedom to practice Protestantism. The centralizing policy of the Habsburgs had been stopped in its tracks.

Gábor Bethlen (r. 1613–29) pursued the same policy and after several concessions to the Ottomans expanded the principality's economy considerably. As the Thirty Years' War involving various European nations spread, he made an alliance with the Protestant princes against the Habsburgs, even managing to make himself king-elect of Hungary before signing a compromise with Vienna.

A third family, the Rákóczi, played a significant part in the history of Hungary for more than a century. Their most illustrious member was **Ferenc (Francis) II Rákóczi** (*see panel p179*), prince of Transylvania. He was the leader of the uprising and the War of Independence waged (1703–1711) against the Austrian domination of the Habsburgs.

the diet: the abolition of feudalism, the creation of a representative national assembly, freedom of the press, freedom of religion, and the return of Transylvania to Hungary. In September 1848 the Imperial Army marched on the Hungarian capital, only to be stopped in its tracks at Székesfehérvár. General von Lamberg was dispatched by the Imperial court in Vienna and killed by a mob in Pest.
Ferdinand V abdicated in December 1848 in favor of his nephew the Habsburg emperor **Franz Joseph I** (r. 1848–1916). However, due to the unrest, the latter was not officially crowned and instead the national assembly appointed journalist and political leader **Lajos Kossuth** (1802–94) head of a committee of national defense. Franz Joseph occupied the capital in January 1849 and the assembly, Kossuth, and the committee took flight to Debrecen. Kossuth passed a vote ending Habsburg rule in April and the Hungarian Army reconquered Pest and Buda. In August, however, after Franz Joseph had sought reinforcements from Tsar Nicolas I, the besieged Hungarian Army laid down its arms. Count Batthyány and 13 generals were executed, and Hungary was placed under Viennese authority once more.
After defeat at **Sadová** on 3 July 1866, during the Austro-Prussian War, the Habsburgs sought to appease Hungarian unrest and concluded a treaty with the Hungarian delegation led by **Ferenc Deák** and Count Andrássy Gyula in 1867, giving birth to the Austro-Hungarian Empire (or Dual Monarchy) that placed Austria and Hungary on equal footing. Hungary, Croatia, and Transylvania formed an independent state with its own government that recognized the emperor of Austria as its king.
The new state shared an army, subscribed to Imperial foreign policy, and had special financing for "common" affairs. A law was passed on nationality in 1868, establishing civic equality and the recognition of certain cultural and religious rights.

The modern era

FIRST WORLD WAR

As king of Hungary and emperor of Austria, Franz Joseph I was at the heart of the Austro-Hungarian Empire on the eve of the First World War. His wife, Empress Elizabeth (Sissi), was queen of Hungary. The empire was accused of having triggered hostilities to reduce the tensions created by the conflicting demands of its various nations. The Hungarian prime minister **István Tisza** (1861–1918) in particular played a direct role in triggering the First World War; his agreement was required for the empire to declare war and he hesitated, fearing, justifiably, that Hungary would be broken up in the event of defeat because of its multiethnic population, in which Slovaks, Romanians, and Croats lived side-by-side with Hungarians. However, he finally gave in to Austrian pressure, and in the upheaval following defeat, he was assassinated by Hungarian deserters at the end of October 1918. Austria-Hungary fought on the side of Germany and the Central Powers and suffered 1,500,000 deaths. Defeat and the end of the war led to the dissolution of the Austro-Hungarian Empire.

"THE WISE MAN OF THE NATION"
Ferenc Deák (1803–76) was a highly distinguished statesman and one of the most important Hungarian political thinkers and judicial reformers of the 19C.

THE INTERWAR YEARS

In October 1918, in the immediate aftermath of the First World War, during the three-day Aster Revolution in Hungary, **Mihály Károlyi** (1875–1955) became head of the government and a republic was proclaimed upon the abdication of King Charles IV (r. 1916–18), Franz Joseph's successor and the last king of Hungary. However, on 21 March 1919, the Communist Party, led by **Béla Kun** (1886–1938), established a Soviet republic that lasted just 133 days, a period of heightened tension and political suppression that came to be known as the Red Terror. With support from the Romanian Army, **Miklós Horthy** (1868–1957) established himself as regent of the Kingdom of Hungary in March 1920 and the White Terror ensued, during which many intellectuals and writers fled the country. The **Treaty of Trianon**, imposed by the Allied powers on 4 June 1920, stripped Hungary of two-thirds of its territory and half of its population. Fanned by the Horthy regime, which made the treaty the main target of its propaganda, Hungarian resentment hit new peaks, which both Hitler and Mussolini would later exploit.

SECOND WORLD WAR

The first law to disadvantage the Hungarian Jewish population was adopted in 1920 and limited their access to university education. Another law passed in 1938 as a result of pressure from Adolf Hitler's government in Germany limited to 20 percent the proportion of Jews permitted to take part in liberal and commercial professions and now completely forbade their access to university education. In 1941, under further pressure from Germany, Hungary declared war on the USSR, although Horthy was to make secret contact with the Allies in 1943. The **Arrow Cross** (Hungarian Nazis) took power on 15 October 1944, and the persecution and deportation of Jews soon followed; 700,000 were transported, mostly to Auschwitz-Birkenau. **Soviet troops** captured Budapest in February 1945, driving out the Nazis.

The provisional government of Béla Dalnoki Miklós (1890–1948) voted in agricultural reform and the Independent Smallholders' Party scored successes in the first elections. A **republic** was proclaimed in 1946 and Zoltán Tildy (1889–1961) became president between 1946 and 1948. The **forint**, which remains in circulation today, replaced the *pengő* as currency.

THE COLD WAR

Between 1946 and 1989, the Cold War reigned between East and West. The Red Army had a strong presence in Hungary and the countries of the East formed a homogeneous bloc with the USSR in 1948. In Hungary, conflict with the Church began and Cardinal Mindszenty (1892–1975) was arrested on 26 December and charged with plotting against the State. In 1949 **Mátyás Rákosi** (1892–1971), leader of the Hungarian Communist Party, also became head of the government. During these purges, the minister of the interior, **László Rajk** (1909–49), was accused of Titoism and his old friends, including János Kádár, deserted him; he was sentenced to death and executed.

Winds of change

The death of Soviet premier Joseph Stalin in 1953 initiated a thaw in relations as **Imre Nagy** (1896–1958), a Communist reformer, became prime minister. A troubled period ensued, marked by strife between reformers and hardcore Stalinists. In 1955 Nagy was expelled from the Hungarian Working People's Party and replaced by Mátyás Rákosi. By 1956 winds of change were

THE REVOLUTION OF OCTOBER 1956

A massive popular uprising began on 23 October 1956, with demands that included free elections, the withdrawal of Soviet troops, and the freedom of the press. In response, the state security police fired upon the crowd. **Imre Nagy** declared martial law on 24 October, announcing he was going to develop "national and independent socialism." The unrest spread throughout the country, however, and Moscow sent Anastas Mikoyan and Mikhail Suslov to report on the situation. **János Kádár** was appointed head of the Communist Party on 25 October and a general strike spread despite repressive measures. Nagy took up the cause of the protesters and on 1 November proclaimed Hungary's neutrality and its withdrawal from the Warsaw Pact. Soviet tanks moved into the capital on 4 November and crushed the uprising, resulting in 3,000 deaths and 200,000 people fleeing the country. Kádár (who had defected to the USSR) was appointed head of the "Hungarian revolutionary workers' and peasants' government." Nagy and his ministers were taken in by the Yugoslavian ambassador. Despite having been assured safe conduct, however, they were arrested by the Soviets as they left the embassy and taken to Romania. After a secret trial, they were sentenced to death and executed on 16 June 1958.

blowing, among intellectuals in particular. László Rajk's reputation was rehabilitated and Imre Nagy rejoined the party on 14 October. Revolution broke out that same month (see box p361).

Between 1963 and 1988, the Socialist Workers' Party, led by **János Kádár** (1912–89), operated a policy of leniency and introduced economic and agricultural reform. During his years in power, Kádár sought to avoid discord with the USSR while maintaining good relations with the West. Hungary encountered economic difficulties in the 1980s, amassing considerable debt and staying afloat mainly thanks to Western loans. In 1987 an economic crisis came to a head, dissatisfaction mounted, and Kádár was dismissed at an extraordinary meeting of the Communist Party on 22 May 1988.

1989: THE FALL OF THE IRON CURTAIN

On **3 May 1989** the minister of foreign affairs, **Gyula Horn** (1931–2013), met his Austrian counterpart at Hegyeshalom, the small village and main frontier post between Hungary and Austria, to cut—symbolically—the razor wire that separated the two countries. In June Budapest held a national funeral to reinter Imre Nagy and remember the victims of 1956. Hungary's supreme court officially announced Nagy's rehabilitation on 6 July, the same day that János Kádár died. On 23 October the Hungarian People's Republic became the **Third Republic**. The sudden fall of the Berlin wall on 9 November 1989 heralded the breakup of the Eastern bloc, and on 8 March 1990 an agreement was signed to arrange the departure of Soviet troops by 30 June 1991. The **first free elections** were held on 25 March and 8 April 1990, with the Hungarian Democratic Forum coming to power. József Antall (1932–93) took office as prime minister and **Árpád Göncz** (1922–2015) was elected president of the Republic by parliament. Hungary became a member of the Council of Europe in November and a general election in 1994 was won by the Socialist Party. **Gyula Horn** became prime minister and formed a coalition with the Alliance of Free Democrats. The Hungarians came out in favor of **joining NATO** in a referendum in 1997 and their membership was officially endorsed in 1999. Fidesz-MPP, a right-wing party, won at the polls in 1998 and **Viktor Orbán** (b. 1963) became prime minister. In 2000 parliament elected the conservative **Ferenc Mádl** (1931–2011) president of the Republic. The Socialists won the election of 2002 and Péter Medgyessy took over the reins as prime minister before being succeeded by **Ferenc Gyurcsány** (b. 1961) in 2004. That same year, Hungary joined the **European Union**. In 2005 the right-winger **László Sólyom** (b. 1942), became president of the Republic and a Socialist/Liberal coalition was reestablished in 2006.

Ferenc Gyurcsány, whose economic policies had been criticized when the country was hit by the global financial crisis, offered his resignation in 2009. He was replaced by Gordon Bajnai, until Fidesz's election victory in 2010; **Viktor Orbán** returned to office as prime minister and was reelected in 2018. He developed a **new constitution** that came into force on 1 January 2012 and the Hungarian Republic was henceforth to be known as **Hungary**. **János Áder** (b. 1959), one of the founding members of Fidesz, has been president of Hungary since 2 May 2012.

How the state is organized (p341).

Food and wine

Generous and spicy, but mellow on the palate, Hungarian cuisine is the culmination of a long journey that began with the Magyars from Asia. Adding to their nomadic traditions was a culinary melting pot with input from the Turks, Bavarians, and Bulgarians, along with a penchant for naming dishes after their creators ... while the Austro-Hungarians left an indelible mark on the art of making cakes and pastries. Today, street-food and "bistronomy" are becoming increasingly popular.

Hungarian flavors

KING PAPRIKA

Paprika is a spice used to prepare all kinds of Hungarian dishes. Onions and good quality paprika form the basis of the meals, which are typically named *paprikás*, such as with chicken *(csirkepaprikás)* and catfish *(harcsapaprikás)*. And not only is paprika used as a seasoning when preparing dishes, it also appears on restaurant tables as a condiment alongside pepper and salt. Cultivated in the regions of Kecskemét and Szeged, paprika comes in seven varieties, from the brightly colored extra-sweet to the strong variety.
The town of **Kalocsa** *(see p295)* is famous for the production of paprika, which it celebrates in its Paprika Museum. Women pick the ripe peppers and hang them to dry on the walls of their houses, after which they are collected to be ground in the windmills. These traditional methods of food preparation can still be seen in the towns and villages.

SNACKS

If you are feeling hungry when out and about, the quintessential Hungarian snack to munch in the street is **pogácsa**, which can be bought from a bakery. This small, savory treat is round and crusty and made from wheat flour, lard, and cheese or spices. Or try **lángos**, a type of raised dough, served with cheese, sour cream, or seasoned with garlic.

THE PEPPER OF THE POOR

Produced from red chili peppers, although originally from India and America, paprika is considered typically Hungarian, but in fact it was only in the 18C that it was introduced into Hungary. The story goes that it was only when Napoleon placed an embargo on produce, notably spices, coming from England, and pepper ran out, that the Hungarians invented "pepper for the poor." Paprika slowly earned its place in cookery books, before becoming of interest to the medical profession—it is very rich in vitamin C, as was demonstrated by the Hungarian biochemist and Nobel laureate, Albert Szent-Györgyi, who isolated the vitamin in the 1930s.

STARTERS AND MAIN COURSES

Soup is de rigueur

Meals generally start with a soup *(leves)*, such as *gombaleves* (with mushrooms), or a hearty broth such as *Jókai bableves*, made with white beans, diced meat, and smoked sausage. Chicken soup *(Újházi-tyúkhúsleves)*, made with peas, mushrooms, carrots, and pasta, is a specialty of the Great Plain.

Non-soup starters include, *hortobágyi húsos palacsinta*, a thick savory pancake filled with meat, paprika, and onions; and foie gras *(libamáj)*, served sliced or cut into large dice, deep-fried in goose fat, and garnished with garlic and onions. Duck foie gras in a pâté is a perfect accompaniment to late-harvest wine from Tokaj.

Charcuterie

Sausages come in infinite variety in Hungary. Two neighboring towns in the south of the country, Gyula and Békéscsaba, even argue over who makes the best sausage. The world's largest sausage fair takes place every year at Békéscsaba. Among the sausages on offer is the celebrated **salami Pick**, which has been produced on the banks of the Tisza river since the 1880s. It is made from natural ingredients, which include pork meat, pork fat, and a mixture of spices, the blend of which is a closely guarded secret. Its great flavor is mainly due to the mold that gradually covers the sausage as it matures.

Hurka means sausage; blood sausage is *véres hurka* and liver sausage is *májas hurka*.

Meat

The most famous Hungarian dish has to be **gulyás**, a beef soup with onions and paprika, accompanied by potatoes and carrots. Goulash as we understand it, however, is called **pörkölt** in Hungary, and is a braised beef hotpot with tomatoes and green bell peppers, strongly flavored with onions. In **tokány**, another version of the stew, the paprika is replaced with pepper.

In small restaurants roast shank of pork *(csülök)* is a specialty, along with a hearty assortment of meats *(fatányéros)*, including beef, veal, and pork served with different side dishes. Common stuffed dishes include cabbage leaves stuffed with minced pork and rice or peppers in a tomato sauce.

Game, roast or cooked in a sauce, is found particularly in the north of the country. The Great Plain provides poultry, including chicken. Cooked with paprika *(chicken paprikash)*, it is a great specialty.

Freshwater fish

The best known freshwater fish is silver **pikeperch** *(fogas)*. This lean fish, weighing 18–22lb/8–10kg, hides in the waters of Lake Balaton. It does not travel well, but its fine flesh is highly valued, so it is eaten, freshly caught, on the banks of the lake. It appears on good restaurant menus, either grilled or simmered in white wine. Another sought-after fish, **sturgeon** *(tokhal)* is caught in the Tisza and is prized for its flesh and its eggs, which produce a delicate caviar. The most common fish is **carp** *(ponty)*, eaten breadcrumbed or "Serbian style," dusted with the ubiquitous paprika.

Halászlé is a soup made entirely from freshwater fish, including carp, wels catfish (sheatfish), and pike, flavored with paprika. In certain restaurants, especially in summer, the soup is prepared in the open air in huge cookpots with a huge ladle to match and is often served highly spiced *(see p298)*.

Accompaniments

Dishes are served with rice, homemade pasta *(galuska)* that resembles gnocchis, or small dumplings made with flour and eggs, sautéed gently in lard

Hungarian paprika
© alxpin/iStock

(*tarhonya*). Most vegetables are added to casseroles or are served cooked or roasted as a side dish. **Főzelék** is a dish where vegetables are first boiled and then cooked in a flour and fat roux. Green salad is only served when it is in season and raw vegetable crudités are frequently served in the form of pickles.

Cheeses

Hungary produces several different varieties of cheese. Among the most well-known cow's milk cheeses are *pálpusztai*, a soft cheese typical of the Budapest region, *balaton*, another soft cheese from the region around the lake of the same name, and *trappista*, a hard cheese. Lovers of sheep's milk cheese can enjoy *kashkaval*, *monastor*, *brindza*, or *liptói* from Eastern Europe or northern Hungary.
Túrógombóc is a dish of dumplings made with cottage cheese. They are served, in their savory version, as an accompaniment to dishes in a sauce, or, in their sweetened version, as a dessert.

Desserts and sweets

Crêpes (*palacsinta*) are fairly common and are served in many different ways, such as generously filled with sweetened cottage cheese, chocolate cream, or apricot jam. Another favorite, the cottage cheese turnover (*túrós batyu*), appears modest when compared to the **Dobos torta**, created in Budapest at the end of the 19C by the pastry chef József Dobos. This great classic Hungarian cake consists of seven layers of genoese sponge, which are filled with chocolate buttercream and then topped with triangles of sponge coated in caramel.
Rigó Jancsi is a chocolate cake with a whipped chocolate cream filling. It takes its name from a Hungarian Romani violinist who in 1897 hit the headlines by marrying the wealthy American socialite Clara Ward, who was also known as Princess Caraman-Chimay from her previous marriage to a Belgian prince. The story goes that Rigó Jancsi created this irresistible gateau to win the lady's heart.

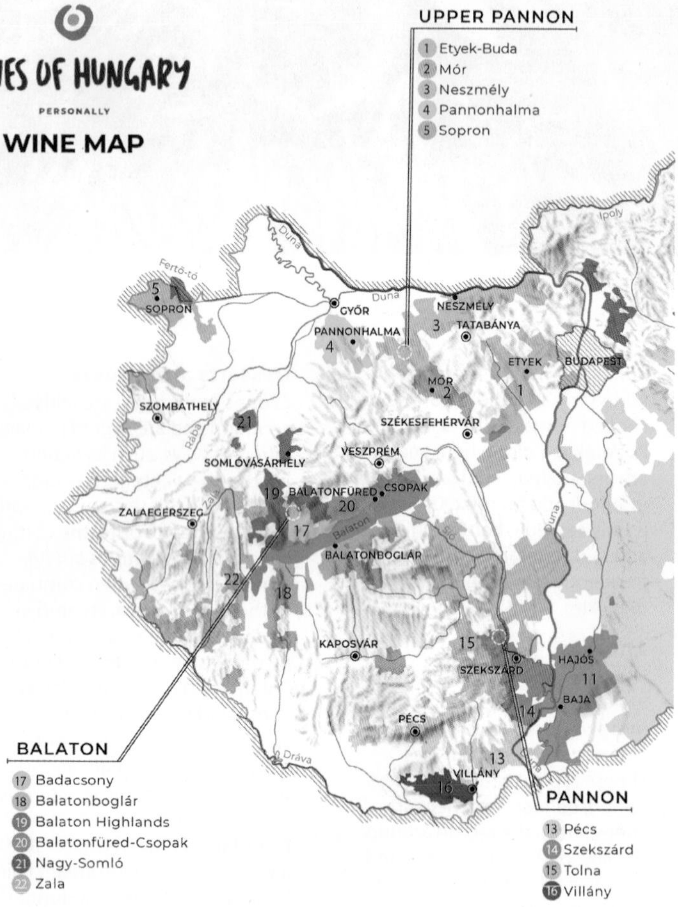
WINES OF HUNGARY
PERSONALLY
WINE MAP
UPPER PANNON
1 Etyek-Buda
2 Mór
3 Neszmély
4 Pannonhalma
5 Sopron
BALATON
17 Badacsony
18 Balatonboglár
19 Balaton Highlands
20 Balatonfüred-Csopak
21 Nagy-Somló
22 Zala
PANNON
13 Pécs
14 Szekszárd
15 Tolna
16 Villány
Fertő-tó
SOPRON
Duna
GYŐR
PANNONHALMA
NESZMÉLY
TATABÁNYA
ETYEK
BUDAPEST
Ipoly
MÓR
SZÉKESFEHÉRVÁR
SZOMBATHELY
Rába
SOMLÓVÁSÁRHELY
VESZPRÉM
BALATONFÜRED
CSOPAK
Balaton
ZALAEGERSZEG
Zala
BALATONBOGLÁR
Sió
KAPOSVÁR
SZEKSZÁRD
HAJÓS
BAJA
PÉCS
Dráva
VILLÁNY

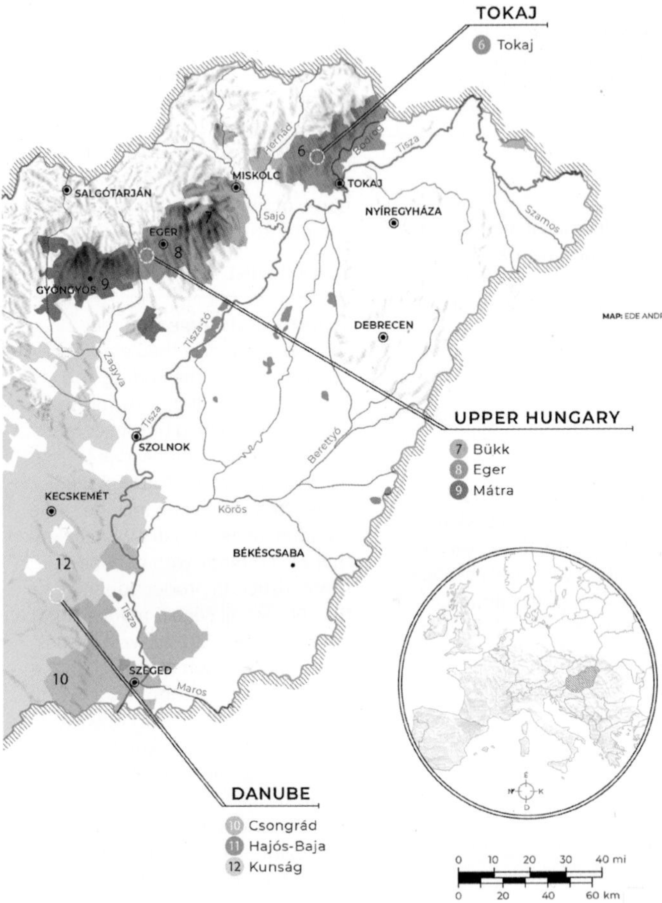

MAP: EDE ANDRÁS MOLNÁR

LATEST TRENDS

During the past few years, new restaurants, bistros, and wine bars have been opening their doors in Hungary. They offer excellent food and top quality service. Some of these establishments have been awarded food and drink accolades, such as *Onyx* in Budapest, which holds two Michelin stars. *See also p78 for the Michelin Guide selection.*

Somlói galuska is a melt-in-the-mouth sponge cake-based desert, flavored with rum and filled with walnuts and raisins, which is served topped with whipped cream and chocolate.

Rétes is a type of strudel made with layers of puff pastry filled with apples, cottage cheese, poppy seeds, or sour cherries. Also popular is **túró rudi**, a chocolate bar filled with cream cheese. **Kürtőskalács** ("chimney cake") is baked on an open fire; it is cylindrical in shape and made with pastry dough, served plain or with a sprinkling of sugar, cinnamon, chocolate, or coconut flakes.

Finally, one Christmas specialty that is well worth seeking out as it is easy to take home is **gingerbread** from Debrecen and Hajdúböszörmény; it is beautifully decorated with intricate designs piped in colored icings.

A world-famous wine region

The first vines were introduced into Hungary during Gallo-Roman times and it is now the largest wine-producing country in Central Europe, with vineyards covering close to 160,619 acres/65,000ha. The 31 PDO (Protected Designated Origin) zones in Hungary include the country's **22 wine producing areas**, which are attached to 6 large geographical areas. Just under 80 million US gal/3 million hl are produced there. The best-known grape varieties deliver 25 percent of the red and rosé wines and some 75 percent of the white wines (dry, sweet, and sparkling), which are the best known. The wines produced generally bear the name of the town or region of origin, to which is added a final "i," such as Badacsonyi, Egri, and so on. The name of the grape variety is also sometimes included.

TOKAJI WINE

In northeast Hungary, on the southern slopes of the Zemplén massif between the Bodrog and Tisza rivers, a region with volcanic soil covered in lœss produces one of the most exceptional sweet wines in the world, **Tokaji Aszú**. Wines from Tokaj also include some medium-sweet and dry white wines that are aromatic with mineral charactistics. In production since the 16C, Tokaji wine is made from hand-selected, late-harvest grapes that have been left to shrivel on the vine and develop "noble rot," which concentrates the sugar. Louis XIV of France baptized it "the king of wines and the wine of kings." Its aromas of quince, candied apricots, and honey are amazing, as is its intense golden color. It is also outstanding for its length on the palate and its unforgettable bouquet, making it the perfect accompaniment to foie gras, blue cheese, and desserts. The wine is made principally from **furmint**, a grape whose name comes from *froment*, the French word for wheat, due to its yellow color. It can also be produced from **hárslevelű**, a grape variety that gives a sweet, fruity

Street lined with wine cellars, Hajós
© Funkystock/age fotostock

wine, and from muscat blanc. **Szamorodni** is another type of Tokaji wine and in a category of its own, being produced from whole bunches of grapes and not from individual berries that have been carefully selected. Well structured, it is served as an aperitif or with dessert. The best is **Tokaji Aszú**, a mellow nectar, whose richness lies in the very ripe berries (*aszú* means "dried" in Hungarian), which are picked by hand, one at a time and on several occasions during late harvests. The crushed grapes are then tipped into large barrels containing dry wine. The wine can only be released after 3 years, including 18 months in oak barrels. The quantity of *aszú* grapes added to the dry wine is calculated in ***puttonyos*** (originally the name of the hod used to collect the grapes and carried on the backs of the pickers). **Essencia** is produced by collecting the syrupy juice from a pierced vat filled with only grapes affected by noble rot. No pressing is used, the juice just drips down under the weight of the grapes. The fermenting and aging lasts several years. This specialty is rarely bottled but is generally used as an ingredient to make Aszú wines. These wines have incredible longevity and the best vintages can last for up to 200 years.

EGER

On the edge of the Mátra and Bükk massifs, small producers make the famous **Egri Bikavér** (Bull's Blood of Eger). Spicy, full-bodied, and pleasant to drink, this dark rubin wine is a blend of grape varieties. Its major component is always kékfrankos, which is usually blended with kadarka, zweigelt, cabernet franc, merlot, or cabernet sauvignon grapes.
Another well-known wine of the region, **Egri Csillag** (Star of Eger), is a white wine in which half of the grape varieties must come from the Carpathian Basin.

LAKE BALATON

The six distinct winegrowing areas produce wines that are very typical of the region, mostly white, ranging from crisp, fresh, and fruity to aged white wines grown on volcanic, stony soil, along with sparkling wines. There are also some red wines. The soil on the gentle slopes around the lake is composed of clay and silt and delivers wines of character such as **Olaszrizling**, made from muscat ottonel, and **Szürkebarát** (Pinot Grigio/Pinot Gris), and a superb accompaniment to trout. You can also try soft reds, such as **Kékfrankos**, which are perfect with venison stew.

SOPRON

This region lies right on the Austrian border, at the point where the foothills of the Alps meet the Little Hungarian Plain. It produces red wines with a pronounced bouquet from kékfrankos, pinot noir, and zweigelt grapes. The sandy-gravel soil produces spicy white wines from veltliner.

SZEKSZÁRD AND VILLÁNY-SIKLÓS

The vines that grow here on the lœss and clay soil produce full-bodied reds from kékfrankos, kadarka, and cabernet franc grapes. **Szekszárdi Bikavér**, which was much enjoyed by the composer Franz Liszt, today competes with other vintages created from French grape varieties, such as merlot and cabernet, whose aromas evoke blackberries and prunes. These heady wines are best drunk with stews and grilled meats.

HAJÓS-BAJA

Kadarka was introduced in the 16C by the Serbians. This grape is best suited to loess soils and produces red wines with lightly spicy aromas and flavors of red fruit (cherry).

KISKUNSÁG

This region produces "sandy wines" typical of the Great Plain. They are usually dry. The region also produces some very good, refreshing rosé wines.

CSONGRÁD

The region that enjoys the most hours of sunshine in the country (2,100 hours a year). Its rosé and red wines are notable for the finesse of their bouquet. White wines, such as **Tramini**, have light acidity, and complement game dishes well.

OTHER ALCOHOLIC DRINKS

Schnapps – In addition to the wines discussed earlier, Hungarians enjoy drinking schnapps, known as ***pálinka***. Among the various traditional schnapps is the apricot-flavored ***barack pálinka***, in particular from Kecskemét, an excellent national spirit.

Unicum – This brown, spicy, and slightly bitter spirit, is made by distilling and blending together 40 medicinal herbs. Its reputation dates from 1790, when it was created by Dr. Zwack, physician at the court of the Habsburgs, for the Austrian Holy Roman emperor Joseph II, who pronounced it "ein Unikum," a "unique thing."

Beers – Draft or bottled, beer *(sör)* is very popular. Among the Hungarian brands, we would recommend Dreher, Soproni, Arany Ászok, and Borsodi. There are also some good Hungarian craft beers.

Arts and culture

Hungary has drawn on a wealth of different sources of inspiration, either homegrown or imported, thanks to the influence of civilizations such as the Romans, Ottomans, and Habsburgs. The Hungarian soul, with its love of tradition, has been eloquently expressed in every field of artistic endeavor: architecture, sculpture, painting, literature, and music, not to mention photography, cinema, and folk art. The arts are an indelible reminder of the irrepressible imagination of a people with a strongly defined identity.

Architecture

FROM THE ROMAN OCCUPATION TO CHARLEMAGNE

After arriving in the first century BC, the Romans remained in the region of western Hungary that they named Pannonia for nearly five centuries. As elsewhere in the world, they left their mark on the country and its population. Towns that have preserved significant remains from the period include **Intercisa** (Dunaújváros), **Savaria** (Szombathely), and **Aquincum**, the former capital of Pannonia Inferior, which is situated in the suburb of Óbuda in Budapest (*see p32)*. The Romans built **fortifications** along the *limes* (frontiers) and left behind a host of statues representing the gods they worshiped, as well as numerous gravestones. Several centers of Christianity were established during the 2C and 3C, but the Huns arrived in 492, at which point the by now Romanized population fled Pannonia.

ROMANESQUE ABBEYS AND CHURCHES

The end of the 10C and the dawn of the 11C saw the advent of the Árpád dynasty. The conversion of Géza in the 10C and the baptism of Vajk, his son, who became István (Stephen I) and received the royal crown from the hands of the papal envoy, resulted in Hungary becoming part of the Christian world. The country was organized into *vármegye* (counties). The statutes governing these administrative areas obliged their inhabitants to submit to baptism and build a church for every ten villages. During this period, the king bestowed considerable sums of money on the monasteries and churches, and clerics (both monks and priests) were invited to Hungary from France and Italy. Romanesque art spread throughout the country until the invasion of the Mongols. The impetus for this was at its greatest under **King Béla III** in the 12C, who wed Marguerite of France in a second marriage, after his first wife Agnes of Antioch died. Laborers and monks from Normandy and Burgundy, who were master builders, came to Hungary to build and decorate the palaces and churches. This period also saw construction begin on the abbey at **Bélapátfalva**, which was built by French Cistercian monks in 1232 and is one of the most

Siklós Castle
© Hungarian Tourism Agency

beautiful examples of Romanesque architecture *(see p190)*. **Zsámbék** monastery church near Budapest was built by the French Aynard family, who had followed in the footsteps of Marguerite of France (*see p124*).
See also: Benedictine Abbey Church at Tihany (p145); Ják Abbey Church (p243); Pannonhalma Abbey (p230).

THE GOTHIC STYLE

Hungarian Gothic architecture flourished a century later than its French inspiration and was plainer than its Germanic equivalent, in all likelihood for technical reasons. Few traces of the style remain today, with such original elements as have survived being incorporated into restoration work during the Baroque period. Gothic buildings of interest include the superb chapel of **Siklós Castle** (*see p288*).
Belvárosi plébánia templom, (**Budapest's Inner City Parish Church**) near the Elizabeth Bridge in Pest, was built on the ruins of a Romanesque church and houses a Gothic side chapel and boasts two steeples (*see p55*). The austere Református templom (**Reformed Church**) in **Nyírbátor** has a vault covered with beautifully interlaced Gothic ribbing *(p266)*.
See also: Bishop's Palace at Eger Castle (p185); Visegrád Royal Palace (p104); Matthias Church in Budapest (p38); Goat Church in Sopron (p217).

THE RENAISSANCE

Matthias Corvinus was crowned king at the age of 15 and lost no time in demonstrating the qualities of wisdom and strength attributed to the crow on his family's coat of arms, along with a taste for books and innovation, as he transformed the court into a hub of culture. He brought in artists from Italy, including the architect **Chimenti Camicia** (1431–?), the sculptor **Giovanni Dalmata** (c. 1440–c.1514). Matthias also transformed the castle at Buda (*see p31*), and the Royal Palace of Visegrád *(p104)*, buildings whose reputations spread far beyond the country's borders. Many of the features that were

introduced during this Renaissance era are still visible today, including chimneys, floors, and sculptures.
Bakócz Chapel at Esztergom, p110).

THE TURKISH PERIOD

This was to prove a sad time for many of Hungary's old monasteries, churches, and castles, with at best just a few stones of some of them still remaining as proof they once existed. The Ottomans turned some churches into mosques, although they were returned to Christian use in due course. The most visible signs of the Turkish occupation today include the purpose-built mosques, minarets, mausoleums, and bath houses that they left behind.
See also: St. Roch's Church at Szigetvár (p282); Belvárosi Church (p275) & Hasszán Jakováli Mosque (p276) in Pécs; the Minaret (p188) in Eger; Rudas Baths (p43) and Király Baths (p46) in Budapest.

THE BAROQUE

The enormously popular Baroque style spread throughout Europe between 1600 and 1800. In Hungary, what became known as **Early Baroque** (1630–1710) first saw the light of day in those parts of the country not occupied by the Turks. It was followed by High Baroque (1710–60) and Late Baroque (1760–1800).
It is worth bearing in mind that some buildings with Baroque facades are the result of the Habsburg Empire's desire to annex Hungary, and in the process to obscure beneath stucco work and various kinds of ornamentation and decoration any elements of Hungarian heritage that had so far escaped destruction.
Early Baroque is especially well represented in Sopron, which contains the Fire Tower (*see p215*) & Storno House *(p215); see also* St. Ignatius Church, Győr *(p227)*.
High Baroque Examples of the expressiveness of this style's rounded, dynamic structures are on show in every town and city in Hungary. Designs are based on curves in vertical sections, with twisted columns that serve to accentuate a building's dimensions. Decorative elements make use of the effects of light and shade and seek to surprise the viewer with false perspectives. Trompe-l'oeil, oversize dimensions, and interconnecting spaces all contribute to the final effect. The **Church of the Minorites** (the Minorites are members of the Franciscan Order) in Nyírbátor is one of the most significant Baroque buildings in Hungary (*see p267*).
See also: University Church (p53), Church of St. Anne (p45) & City Hall (p54) in Budapest; Regional County Hall in Eger (p185); the Royal Palace of Gödöllő (p120); Esterházy Castle in Fertőd (p220).
Late Baroque This style is a condensed expression of the Baroque, closely associated with the Zopf style, a Central European variant whose name derives from the fact that it uses *zopf* (festoons) as decorative elements. This style also strips back its architecture by reducing in size the profiles of facades and relief elements, to the point of replacing columns with pilasters or even just painting such elements on the walls. The style was brought to prominence by the well-known Austrian artist **Franz Anton Hillebrandt** (1719–97), architect to the royal court and supervisor of all the major building projects in Hungary from 1757 until his death.
See also: Royal Palace at Buda Castle (p31); Bishop's Palace at Székesfehérvár (p164); Szombathely Cathedral (p244); Vác Cathedral (p118).

CLASSICAL ARCHITECTURE

This style sought to integrate elements from the Classical school into architecture (columns, pediments, codified orders, and so on) and was prevalent in the first half of the 19C. It was an attempt to break away from the Baroque and the hegemony of the Habsburgs that had followed the Ottoman occupation. Hungary was resurfacing; the local nobility was making money in business and was keen to show it off. It was said that, "The Classical style in Europe was strict; in Hungary, it was full of spirit." This architecture marked the end of feudalism in all its different forms and saw the beginning of a period of activity and evolution. Two architects in particular made their mark during the period: **Mihály Pollack** (1773–1855), who worked in Szekszárd and Budapest, and **József Hild** (1789–1867), who built a large number of apartment blocks, public buildings, and cathedrals.

See also: Hungarian National Museum in Budapest (p52); Eger Cathedral Basilica (p186); Esztergom Basilica (p108).

THE ROMANTIC STYLE

This movement emerged at the end of the 19C as a challenge to the rigor of Classical architecture and sought to appeal to the imagination and emotions rather than reason, introducing a certain exoticism and a reminder of the past. **Miklós Ybl** (1814–91), who had trained in Vienna and Munich, initially worked in Mihály Pollack's workshop before striking out on his own and becoming the great architect of the era. He won the competition to build the **State Opera House in Pest** (*see p56*). Ybl's larger creations are well known, but some buildings of more modest dimensions particularly express his qualities as an architect, such as the **Reformed Church** in Kecskemét (*see p325*), whose simplicity and austerity conceal a highly condensed interior space.

Imre Steindl (1839–1902) was the architect of Budapest's Parliament Building (*see p46*), his most famous work. The building that he produced is a large, neo-Gothic construction with an ornately decorated and painted interior. Taking his cue from Gustave Eiffel, **Samu Pecz** (1854–1922) built market hall structures of iron, with infills of brick and glass. **Albert Schickedanz** (1826–1915) and **Fülöp Ferenc Herzog** (1860–1925) were also notable for creating several of the capital's buildings and monuments.

See in Budapest: Central Market Hall (p65); Millennium Monument (p59); Museum of Fine Arts (p59); Hungarian National Gallery (p35).

ECLECTICISM

Sometimes also known as **Historicism**, the Eclectic style in architecture draws inspiration from various different historical styles, an approach that is perfectly illustrated by **Vajdahunyad Castle** (*see p61*) in City Park in Budapest, designed by **Ignác Alpár** (1855–1928). At the time there was a desire to build quickly and cheaply, but people still wanted buildings that stood out and attracted attention, so they were built in brick and rendered in plaster to imitate stone. The inspiration for the work would come from the client's own preferences and the architect's predilection for a particular moment in history; it led to a flurry of neo-Gothic, neo-Roman, and neo-Renaissance construction.

See also in Budapest: Fisherman's Bastion (p39); Hungarian Academy of Sciences (p51); Museum of Ethnography (p61).

SECESSIONISM AND ART NOUVEAU

Academic architecture was largely rejected by the Hungarian art scene at the turn of the 20C, with 1896 seen as the year that marked the debut of Secession architecture: Budapest's millennial celebrations that year featured an **expression of national art** based on the Magyar origins of the Hungarian people. Art became a means of expressing an artist's social, ethical, and utopian ideas for the society of the future. Hungary was in a ferment, with the celebrations for the country's millennium bringing fresh impetus to the arts. Innovators in architecture dug deep into their creative impulses to investigate the relationship between a building's interior and exterior, seamlessly linking all its constituent parts. Architects "seceded" from their past, breaking with the "neo" styles and inventing their own way of thinking. The **Secession** style marks the appearance of fantasy, imagination, and color. This was architecture as a whole art form, with no separation between the various skills that combined to create the final work. Budapest can certainly look Brussels or Vienna squarely in the eye in this respect. Bursting with vitality, Art Nouveau was able to evolve and spread new ways of thinking; there are any number of examples in Budapest to illustrate this new form of architectural expression that prefigured the Bauhaus movement, associating art and a respect for its urban surroundings.

The leading figure was undoubtedly **Ödön Lechner** (1845–1914). His most striking creations in Budapest alone include the Museum of Applied Arts (*see p65)* and the former Royal Postal Savings Bank *(p50)*. Other architects designed with similar enthusiasm, with **Sándor Baumgartner** creating Kiskunfélegyháza City Hall *(p332)*, Kecskemét City Hall *(p323)*, and Cifra Palace *(p325)*, and **Ede Magyar** designing Reők Palace *(p307)* in Szeged. **Sámuel Révész** and **József Kollár**, the architects responsible for the apartment building at no. 11/b Váci utca in Budapest *(p53)*, were said to have been influenced by German Jugendstil and a degree of Orientalism.

The designer of the iconic tower in Paris, **Gustave Eiffel**, should also be mentioned. His studio designed the Nyugati Railway Terminal in Budapest (*see p50)*. The engineers and architects working for him carried on in the same spirit, building a number of covered markets along the same principles, including Central Market Hall in the capital (*see p65)*.

Influenced by ideas propagated by the **Bauhaus**, in the 1930s around twenty Hungarian architects worked on ingenious designs for villas and small apartment blocks that met the needs of the residents of the time. **Marcel Breuer (**1902–81) was a Hungarian architect and furniture designer, who helped to lay the foundations of the influential Bauhaus movement.

ORGANIC ARCHITECTURE

During the Communist period, several architects championed what became known as Organic architecture. The leader of this movement was **Imre Makovecz** (1935–2011), who built the Hungarian pavilion for the Seville Expo in 1992 and was an associate of **György Csete** (1937–2016). The Hungarian variation on this type of architecture is not based on the American designs of Frank Lloyd Wright (who coined the term "Organic architecture"), but is imbued with a kind of regionalist, even nationalist impulse.

© Spumador/Shutterstock

Interior, Orthodox Synagogue, Kazinczy utca, Budapest

© jacquesvandinteren/iStock

Detail of the facade, the former Török Bank, Szervita Square, Budapest

© Alex Timaios/age fotostock

Detail of the facade of the post office on Jókai utca, Pécs

See also: Siófok Evangelical Church (p135); the church in Paks (p 381); pavilions at Ópusztaszer Heritage Park (p311); the Onion House at Makó (p314).

Painting and sculpture

PAINTING

Battered by successive wars and occupations, Hungary has not always managed to conserve the work of its artists. There are few truly old works of art, apart from those preserved on walls or ceilings. Of the all-too-fragile medium of painting, only a few frescoes and canvases remain here and there. The most beautiful pieces created before the 10C can be seen at the **Hungarian National Gallery** in Budapest *(see p35)* and the **Christian Museum** in Esztergom *(see p112)*. The Hungarian National Gallery also features pieces by all the great Hungarian painters.
Miklós Barabás (1810–98) and **Bertalan Székely** (1835–1910), who arrived on the scene in the second half of the 19C, were both keen portrait painters, although Székely found equal fame as a painter of war scenes, depicting the history of Hungary. By the dawn of the 20C, Hungary had been gripped by a spirit of disruption and renewal, with young painters coming to the fore nationally and heading to Paris to study. As pioneers of the European Avant-garde, they took just a few years to invent an independent and original painting language: modernism with hints of a national tradition. **Gyula Benczúr** (1844–1920), who was also a student of history, was an excellent portraitist, producing images of Empress Elisabeth (Sissi), Count Andrássy, and István Tisza.
Pál Szinyei Merse (1845–1920) also produced some marvelous studies and sketches; the vibrant *Meadow with Poppies* (1896) is one of his best-known works.
Mihály Munkácsy (1844–1900), a trained carpenter, learned the basics of art from a journeyman painter before receiving help from two better-known artists, **Antal Ligeti** (1823–90) and **Mór Than** (1828–99). He was involved with the Barbizon School and is the creator of a triptych on display at the Déri Museum in Debrecen *(see p254)*.
László Mednyánszky (1852–1919) and **Károly Ferenczy** (1862–1917), who painted *October*, were skilful at working en plein air, much like **Adolf Fényes** (1867–1945), who was undoubtedly the most notable of the painters who emerged from the Szolnok artists' colony. His canvases reveal him to be a master of Hungarian light, shot through with lively color, as can be seen in *Early Morning in a Small Town*.
József Rippl-Rónai (1861–1927), the era's master painter, developed his own post-Impressionist body of work. Painted in 1894, *Woman with Black Hat* by **János Vaszary** (1867–1939) is on display at the Hungarian National Gallery, a youthful work that was doubtless influenced by the environment in Paris, where he was studying.
One name stands out in this long list of painters, however: **Tivadar Csontváry Kosztka** (1853–1919) created an original and highly personal body of work. His main pieces can be seen at the museum in Pécs *(see p279)*.
Having been rendered stateless by the Treaty of Trianon *(see p354)*, a group from the Nagybánya artists' colony came to settle in **Szentendre** at the beginning of the 20C. **Lajos Vajda** (1908–41) was instrumental in setting up the Szentendre school and the colony was to play a significant role in reinventing painting in Hungary.

ABC of Architecture

Religious architecture

JÁK – Abbey Church portal (13C)

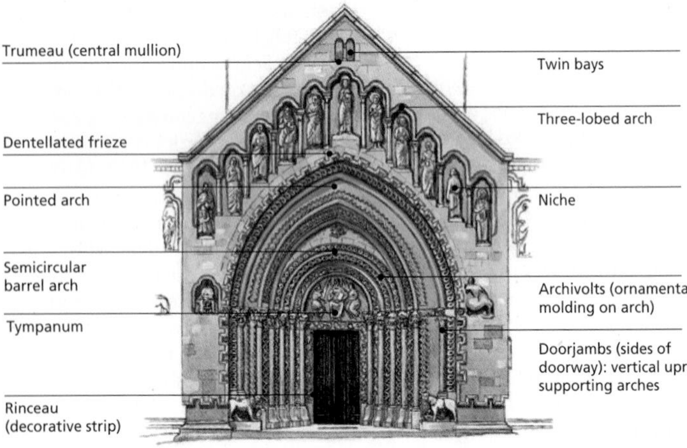

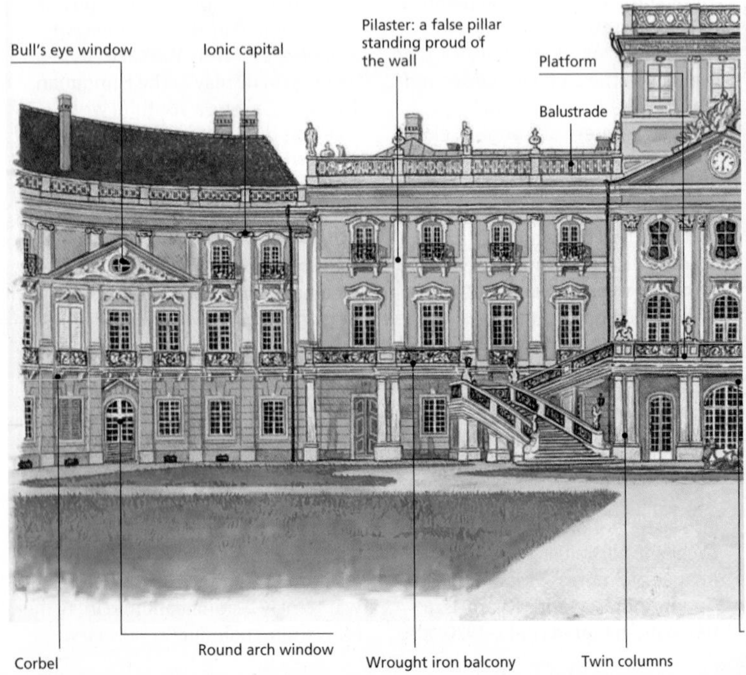

ESZTERGOM – Royal Chapel, Esztergom Castle (12C)

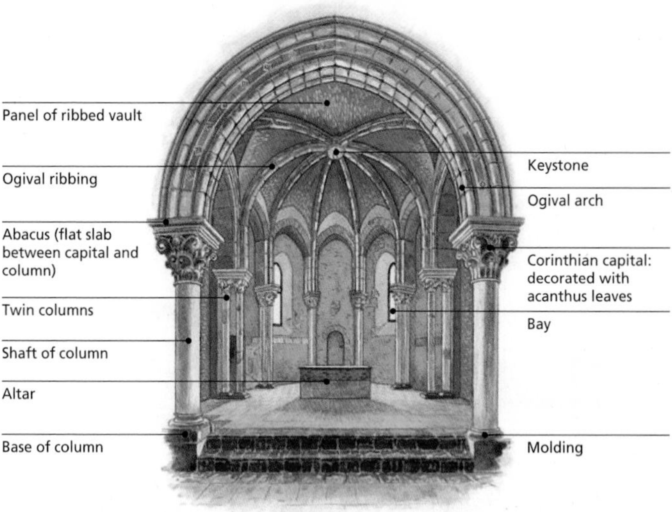

Civil architecture

FERTŐD – Esterházy Palace (18C)

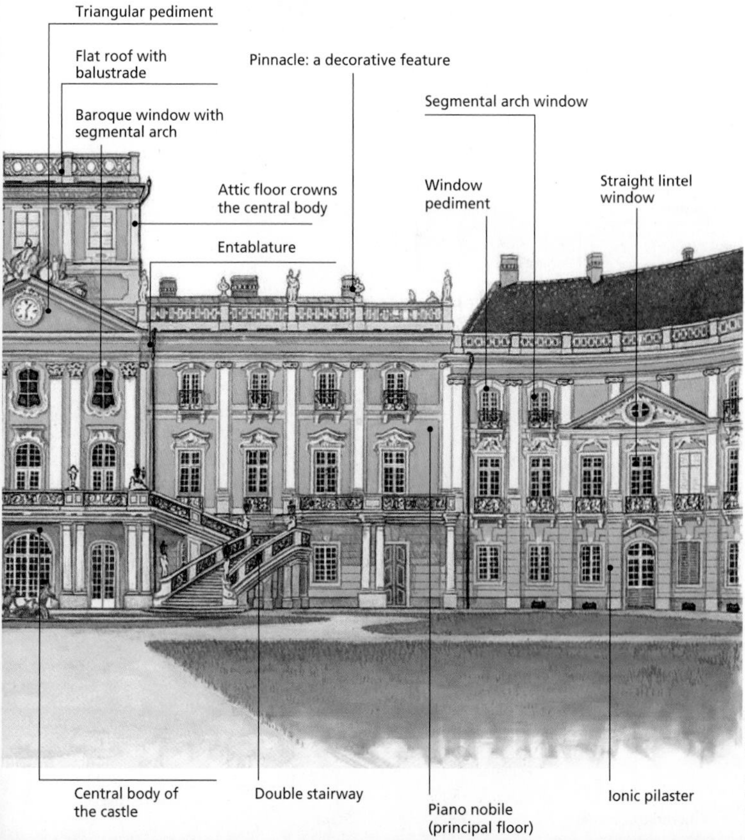

M. Guillou/MICHELIN

SÁROSPATAK – Covered staircase, Rákóczi Castle (16C–18C)

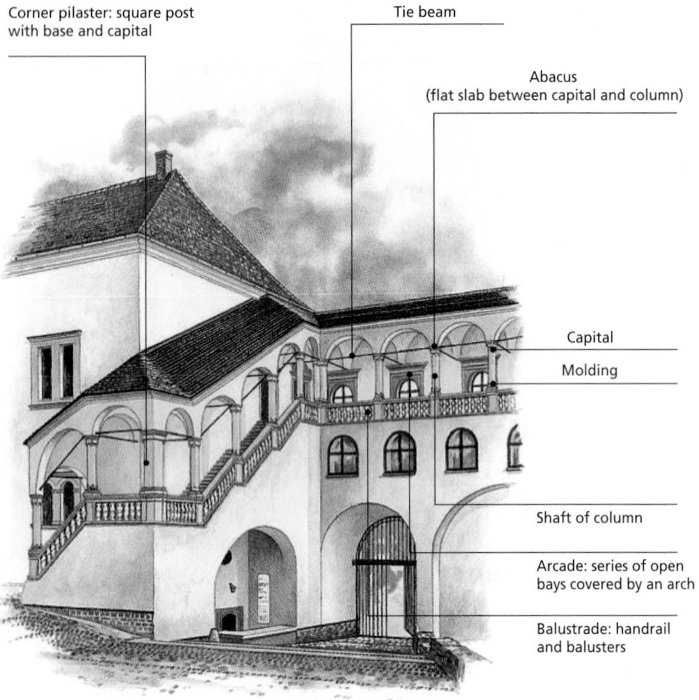

BUDAPEST – Opera House (end of 19C)

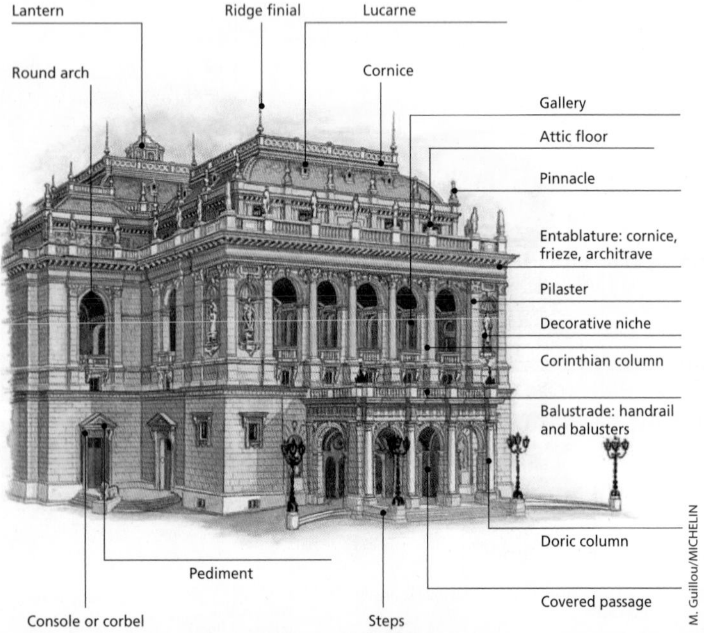

BUDAPEST – Former Postal Savings Bank (Secessionist style, 1901)

Roof in majolica: Zsolnay ceramics decorated with patterns, garlands, and coloured flowers

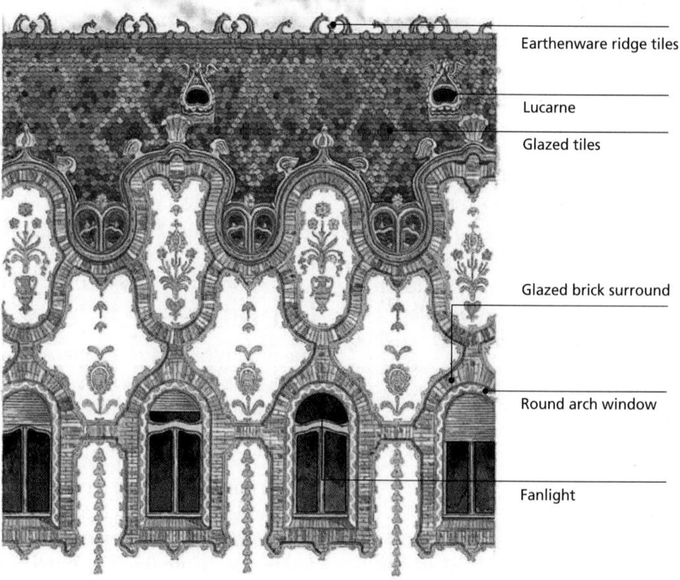

Religious architecture

PAKS – Church (20C)

Hungarian Organic architecture: a style whose symmetry was inspired by living beings, in particular the human body

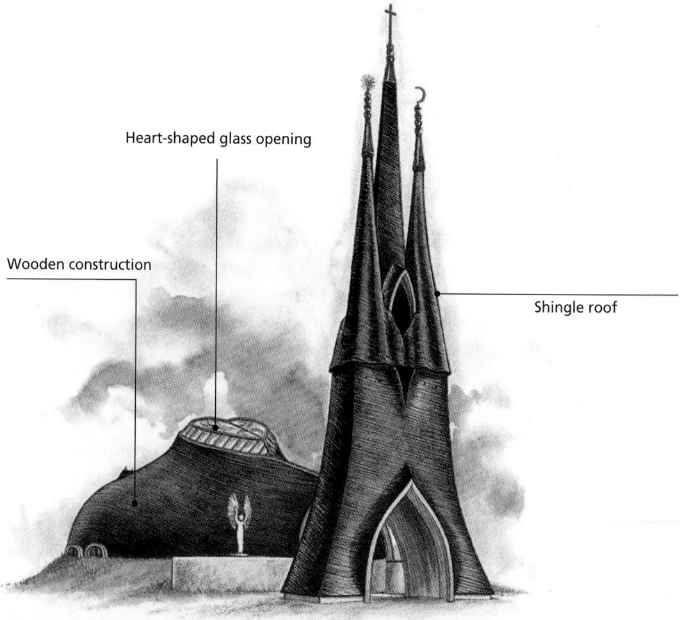

M. Guillou/MICHELIN

The Szentendre school was notable for introducing Avant-garde styles. Its famous names include **Károly Ferenczy**, the Constructivist **Jenő Barcsay** (1900–88), and the Cubist **János Kmetty** (1889–1975), along with **Anna Margit** (1913–91) and **Imre Ámos** (1907–1944).

Of the Hungarian artists living abroad, **Victor Vasarely** (1906–97), one of the leading figures in the Op art movement, deserves mention, along with the non-figurative painter **Árpád Szenes** (1897–1985) and **Tibor Csernus** (1927–2007), whose style was at once realistic and visionary.

SCULPTURE

Statues, jewelry, objets d'art … creating three dimensional objects has long been a means of artistic expression close to the Hungarian heart, as works from Roman times to the modern era reveal. The **Christian Museum** in Esztergom (*see p112*) has a very fine display of wooden sculptures. The Baroque period gave artists new possibilities of self-expression and by the 20C there were sculptors in every town. **Miklós Ligeti** (1871–1941) is known for his statue *Anonymous*, which can be seen in Vajdahunyad Castle in Budapest (*see p62*). **Imre Varga** (1923–2019) was a prolific sculptor whose work can be seen in a number of towns across Hungary, including *Saint Elizabeth*, an equestrian statue in Sárospatak, *Prometheus* in Szekszárd and, not far from the Great Synagogue in Budapest, the *Tree of Life Memorial*, which pays tribute to the victims of the Shoah (*see p63*). **Ádám Farkas**, born in 1944, has acquired an international reputation, and in addition to the numerous works on display in Hungary, his sculptures are exhibited in many other countries, including Japan and France. He also created the memorial at Recsk, the camp for political prisoners under the Communist regime.

You are most likely to see the sculptures and reliefs (generally in bronze) created by **András Lapis** (b. 1948) on the streets of Szeged. They include an equestrian statue of King Matthias and a woman seated on a park bench beneath the large, floppy brim of a hat.

Literature

The origins of Hungarian literature are as shrouded in mystery as its earliest history. Thanks to Hungarian chroniclers, historical works in Latin have passed down to us the epic poems and legends of the Magyar people, including the *Legend of the Wondrous Stag* and the *Legend of the Turul*. With the advent of Christianity, the written language of Latin soon came to dominate the predominantly oral culture and took over as the official tongue. Between the 11C and the 16C, chronicles, legends, and hymns were the principal literary genres of choice

The first Hungarian prose appeared in the form of a funeral oration in around 1200, while the oldest poem in Hungarian is undoubtedly *The Lamentations of Mary* (c. 1270), in which the Virgin laments the crucifixion of her son, Jesus. The first Hungarian versions of the Old and New Testaments are thanks to the efforts of two preachers, **Tamás Pécsi** and **Bálint Újlaki**, around 1430, but Calvinist **Gáspár Károli** (1529–91) produced the first full Hungarian translation of the Bible in 1590. **János Hunyadi** (c. 1407–56), conqueror of the Turks, who mobilized European diplomatic efforts against the Ottoman invaders, and his son, **Matthias Corvinus** (1443–90), were the first in Hungary to show an interest in humanism and the

Renaissance. The latter invited the greatest Italian scholars and artists to his court and created the famous Bibliotheca Corviniana, a library that was without equal in Europe.

POETRY IN THE SOUL

During the Renaissance, Hungarian literature produced lyric verse from the poet **Janus Pannonius** (1434–72); it became a major genre that endured until the 1970s. The cultural environment encouraged **Bálint Balassi** (1554–94) to develop an original lyric style that was at once Renaissance and Hungarian. His work largely consists of love poems (complete with the Petrarchan poetic clichés in fashion at the time), which reflected his amorous nature. Despite the subject of his poetry, he was also something of an adventurer and died of wounds sustained fighting the Turks in the Siege of Esztergom. The Reformation that took place in the 16C brought the Renaissance into contact with Protestantism, while the Catholicism that opposed it found its way into the spirit of the Baroque at the turn of the 17C. Inspired by the works of Italian poet Tasso, the statesman and epic poet **Miklós Zrínyi** (1620–64) wrote the famous saga *The Siege of Sziget*. Comprising 15 sections, it recounts the heroic struggle of the author's great grandfather and his troops against Süleyman I's army in 1566.

NEW IDEAS

The philosophical ideas of the Age of Reason and the French Revolution began to awaken national awareness from around 1755. The Hungarian Jacobin group that was formed at this time included pioneering champions of these ideas, such as its leader, philosopher and writer **Ignác Martinovics** (1755–95), the great reformer of the Hungarian language, **Ferenc Kazinczy** (1759–1831), and the poet **Mihály Csokonai Vitéz** (1773–1805). The lively poetic language and local color of his comic epic *Dorottya* led the great 20C poet Endre Ady to consider him one of the true precursors of modern lyric poetry in Hungary. **Dániel Berzsenyi** (1776–1836) took up the baton of Classical poetry to create a new context for odes and philosophical poems that showcased the ideas of the Enlightenment.
Literature enjoyed special status in the struggle for Hungarian independence: **József Katona** (1791–1830) died before his play *Bánk Bán* would come to be considered the greatest Hungarian drama of the 19C; it was based on historical events from the 12C and analyzed the problem of the presence of outsiders at the heart of power.

MAGYAR ROMANTICISM

The great era of political reform laid the foundations for the revolutionary literature of 1848. Four romantic poets were to dominate the period, including **Ferenc Kölcsey** (1790–1838), author of the national anthem. The works of **Mihály Vörösmarty** (1800–55) include his epic *The Flight of Zalán*, his poetic drama *Csongor and Tünde*, and his *Exhortation*, which best embodies the Romantic spirit. **János Arany** (1817–82) was an epic poet and author of the *Toldi*, a trilogy that wove a tale set in the time of King Louis the Great in the 14C. In the *Death of King Buda*, he takes readers back to the distant era of Attila, just before the mighty Hun ruler invaded the country. Although Arany supported the revolutionary ideas of 1848 and sought to justify them by evoking the past, it was his contemporary **Sándor Petőfi** (1823–49) who was to play a key role in the uprising on 15 March 1848, inspiring the citizens of Pest with his poem entitled *National Song*, an appeal to fight for liberty. Petőfi has since entered into legend as his body was never found after he took part in the Battle of Segesvár against the Russians and Austrians on 31 July 1849.

THE YEARS OF DISILLUSION

Hungarian literature entered a crisis after 1848, with writers and poets struggling to find a new path to assure the survival of the nation in the wake of the revolution. Among these, **Imre Madách** (1823–64) embodies this quest in his dramatic poem entitled *The Tragedy of Man*. **Mór Jókai** (1825–1904), a novelist and childhood friend of Petőfi, chose a path of reconciliation with Austria in the 1860s; his works *The Man with the Golden Touch, The Hungarian Nabob*, and *Zoltán Kárpáthy* promoted this approach, and exerted considerable influence on public opinion. **Kálmán Mikszáth** (1847–1910), who was considered Jókai's successor, conjures up the world of the landed gentry in small towns; the typically Hungarian realism of *St. Peter's Umbrella,* describes the rural life of the ordinary people.

> **NOBEL PRIZE**
>
> **Imre Kertész** (1929–2016), a Holocaust survivor whose writing had been overlooked for 40 years, received the Nobel Prize in Literature in 2002 for an oeuvre that "upholds the fragile experience of the individual against the barbaric arbitrariness of history" (Swedish Academy, Stockholm, 10 October 2002). He was the first Hungarian author to achieve this distinction.

A LITERATURE RICH IN INSPIRATION

The great turning point was to come at the beginning of the 20C with the founding (in 1908) of the literary journal *Nyugat* (in English, "West"), which brought together great literary minds such as **Dezső Kosztolányi** (1885–1936), **Endre Ady** (1877–1919), **Zsigmond Móricz** (1879–1942), **Mihály Babits** (1883–1941), **Árpád Tóth** (1886–1928), and **Frigyes Karinthy** (1887–1938).
While *Nyugat* managed to incorporate elements of Realism, Impressionism, Secessionism, Symbolism, and Naturalism, the Avant-garde literary movement did not get involved. Instead, **Lajos Kassák** (1887–1967) created another journal, *Tett* ("Act") in 1916, which encouraged modernism in literature, the fine arts, and music. Of the novelists who set the tone of the era, several names stand out: those of **Gyula Illyés** (1902–83) with his excellent autobiography *People of the Puszta*, and **János Székely** (1901–58), whose *Child of the Danube* recounts tales of life in the 1920s, not to mention the prolific **Gyula Krúdy** (1878–1933), whose mysterious world in the series *The Adventures of Sindbad* later inspired **Sándor Márai** to write *The Rebels*. Marai (1900–89) came to prominence in the 1930s and his work *Embers*, published in 1942, remains a literary bestseller to this day. **Miklós Bánffy** (1873–1950) is an excellent spinner of yarns, as demonstrated in his Transylvanian trilogy *They Were Counted*.
Many writers were obliged to hold their peace between 1948 and 1953 and, after the failure of the uprising of 1956 (*see p361*), a number were imprisoned. However, by the mid-1960s, efforts to impose ideological purity on the arts had largely been abandoned. **Lajos Grendel** (1948–2018) was known

State Opera House
© Hungarian Tourism Agency

for writing about Hungary and recounted the fall of Communism in *Einstein's Bells*. **József Lengyel** (1896–1975) produced a moving witness account of human suffering in Soviet labor camps. The greatest exponent of poetry in the first half of the 20C was **József Attila** (1905–37), who was celebrated for the expressivity of his simple yet profound language.

THE NEW GENERATION

Modern writers still play a part in the old tradition of exploring Hungarian national identity. The success of the novel as a genre from the 1970s onward would be unimaginable without **Géza Ottlik** (1912–90), **Miklós Mészöly** (1921–2001), and **György Konrád** (1933–2019), the uncompromising author of *The Case Worker*, as well as **Péter Esterházy** (1950–2016) with his sprawling novel *Celestial Harmonies*. The work of **Bodor Ádám** (b. 1936) is also noteworthy. It touches on the absurd and is not without humor, as in *The Sinistra Zone*. Among the top writers who gained an international reputation is **Magda Szabó** (1917–2007), winner of numerous prizes, most notably the Independent Foreign Fiction Prize, for the beguiling style she exhibited in *The Door*.

Literary life in Hungary is as fertile as ever in a society where books are still valued, poetry is still taught in schools, and history is ever present, and where cultural reviews are genuinely influential.

Books (see p427).

Music

MINSTREL POETS

In the late Middle Ages, the scribe of King Béla II (1109–41) enthusiastically recounted stories of the celebrations organized in honor of the chieftains of the seven Magyar tribes that arrived in Óbuda. These tales would have been related to the accompaniment

of ancient instruments such as the zither and chalumeau, a wind instrument that was the forerunner of the clarinet. The spirit of a people who had once been nomads, a roving warrior nation with an impetuous temperament that was also steeped in the melancholy of the steppes, was perpetuated in their music, alternating between *lamentoso* and *allegro*.
After the demise of the Árpád dynasty, kings from the French House of Anjou ruled Hungary for a time and brought a new dimension to secular music. The rise of exponents of the art of the epic poem, known as *regös*, was particularly notable during and after the reign of Sigismund of Luxembourg (1387–1437). Although little remains of the music of the minstrel poets (Minnesinger), who often came to the court from abroad, the names of the composers have come down to us, including Neidhart von Reuental, Tannhäuser (the great German lyric poet who inspired Wagner, thus becoming the hero of a popular legend himself), and Oswald von Wolkenstein. King Matthias Corvinus and his wife Beatrice of Aragon, the daughter of the king of Naples, invited musicians of international renown to their court in the 15C.

MUSIC IN THE 16C AND 17C

Ancient Hungarian legends of the Árpád era were revived in the 16C in the form of epic songs. After the Battle of Mohács in 1526, Turkish influences could also be heard in music, while the poems of the noted lutenist **Sebestyén Tinódi** (c. 1510–66) list the heroes of the past who fought the old Ottoman enemy. His great work, the *Cronica* (which first appeared in 1554), assembles 23 historical, biblical, and satirical songs. The most skilled lutenist and composer of the century was without doubt **Bálint Bakfark** (1507?–76). A true "citizen of the world," he traveled to various countries, including Poland, Italy, Germany, and France, where his first score appeared in 1552. The secret of his popularity lies in his individual style and sensual appeal, typified by intense rhythms and brilliant technique. Prince **Pál Esterházy** (1635–1713) was also a great musician, drawing inspiration from sacred music and bringing a Hungarian melodic twist to religious harmonies. His work *Harmonia* contains 9 chorales, along

© Hungarian Tourism Agency

Grand Hall, Franz Liszt Academy of Music, Budapest

with 50 concertos and cantatas, the majority of which are scored for instruments or an orchestra.

OPERA

Well received by the public from its first appearance, this genre quickly took on a specifically Hungarian character. The first domestically produced opera was *Prince Pikko and Jutka Perzsi* composed by **József Chudy** (1753–1813), but the entire score has been lost leaving only the libretto. The subject of *Béla Futása* ("Béla's Flight"), considered the first specifically Hungarian melodic work, harks back to the 13C and the era of the Tartar invasion. Its composer, **József Ruzitska** (1755–1813) adapted elements from popular music to the style of Viennese opera.

The 19C saw the rise of nationalist music, with **Ferenc Erkel** (1810–93) leading the charge. A composer and conductor who remained faithful to the traditions of Italian music, he founded Hungary's opera house, where he produced his first historical work, *Mária Báthory* (1840). In *László Hunyadi* (1844), Erkel reimagines the tragic story of the brother of King Matthias, but his most notable work was in 1860 for the premiere of his opera *Bánk Bán*, from the tragic play by József Katona. However, Erkel's name will also always be associated with the national anthem, for which he wrote the music.

HUNGARIAN MARCHES

During the struggle for independence against the Habsburgs, led by the prince of Transylvania, **Ferenc Rákóczi II** (1676–1735), the soul of the Hungarian people was expressed in the songs of the Kurucs. They were the soldiers who fought with Rákóczi against the Habsburgs. The Kurucs sang patriotic songs and recited satirical odes about the *labanc*, the nickname given to those Hungarians still loyal to the Habsburg court. A Hungarian translation of the French Republic's revolutionary anthem *La Marseillaise* was produced by **Ferenc Verseghy** (1755–1822), a musician and promoter of Jacobin ideology in Hungary. Drawing on Kuruc songs as a source, the stirring *Rákóczi March* delighted the public in the 19C, thanks to the dazzling technique of the Romani violinist **János Bihari** (1764–1827). One anecdote recounts how Hungarian soldiers made use of the melody in order to summon their courage before a battle against Napoleon's army in 1809.

Music in mid-18C Hungary came to be dominated by a new heroic style known as *verbunkos*, the "recruitment dance" (the German word *Werbung* means "recruitment"), accompanied by Romani "gypsy" music. The *palotás* dance (an imitation of the Polish dance, the Polonaise) interwove slow Hungarian motifs with hops and skips. The great exponent of these two types of dance was **János Lavotta** (1764–1820).

The traditions of *verbunkos* and *palotás* were continued in the ***csárdás***, a folk dance for couples, and Austrian composer Haydn (who spent many years in Hungary), Schubert, Liszt, and Brahms all composed in this idiom; the *csárdás* is still danced to this day.

RHAPSODIES

The most famous Hungarian composer is without doubt **Ferenc (Franz) Liszt** (1811–86), one of the greatest names in Romantic music. A prodigious composer and pianist, his pieces include symphonic poems such as the *Preludes* (1854), the famed *Hungarian Rhapsodies* (1846–85), and his *Historical*

Portraits (1884–86). It was in these last works of great melodic power that his musical genius paid homage to his home country. The Academy of Music was founded in Budapest in 1875 by Liszt himself and soon came to symbolize excellence in musical education throughout Europe. It served both as school and role model for artists such as **conductors** Ferenc Fricsay (1914–63), Antal Doráti (1906–88), Jenő Ormándy (1899–1985), George Széll (1897–1970), Frigyes Reiner (1888–1963), János Ferencsik (1907–84), and Sir George Solti (1912–97); along with **pianists** Ernő Dohnányi (1877–1960) and Annie Fischer (1914–95), among many others. And last but by no means least are the two great composers who turned musical theory upside down in the 20C, Béla Bartók and Zoltán Kodály.

POPULAR MUSIC

Much like **Zoltán Kodály** (1882–1967), **Béla Bartók** (1881–1945) juxtaposed popular song with the peasant music that he saw as the only medium that could preserve the origins of Hungarian music with any authenticity. Both men were interested in the origins of folk music and the cultural and social aspects that combined to produce it. They joined forces, traveling through the villages of Hungary and Transylvania collecting some 15,000 vernacular songs. Their paths were then to separate as Kodály, inspired by the popular tradition, went on to test his mettle as a composer, while Bartók incorporated elements of the music into his compositions as well, but also chose to analyze and classify the songs they collected. Kodály's orchestral works *Dances of Marosszék* and *Dances of Galánta* were completed between 1930 and 1933 and are characterized by motifs incorporated from folk music. A powerful fascination for French symbolism and a desire to uphold the traditions of Hungarian popular music meet in Bartók's first opera *Bluebeard's Castle* (1911). In 1916, at the request of Count Bánffy, the superintendent of the Budapest Opera, Bartók composed music for the ballet *The Wooden Prince*, while his Expressionist ballet entitled *The Miraculous Mandarin* premiered in 1919. His only choral work, the *Cantata Profana* (subtitled "Nine Enchanted Stags"), was composed in 1930; he based the music on an old ballad of Magyar origin (*see p390*). Bartók created music that was original and modern by forging links between European and Hungarian traditions. He was still researching his country's ancestral characteristics and the problems shared by people around the world right until the time of his death in New York. His humanism is discernible in each of his works. Many composers considered Bartók and Kodály to be their spiritual masters, including **Ferenc Farkas** (1905–2000) and **Endre Szervánszky** (1911–77), who set up a school of this new musical style. The **composers** György Ligeti (1923–2006), György Kurtágh (b. 1926), Rudolf Maros (1917–82), and András Szöllösy (1921–2007) each developed their own unique sound, along with the talented **pianists** György Cziffra (1921–94), Zoltán Kocsis (1952–2016), Dezső Ránki (b. 1951), and András Schiff (b. 1953). The most productive of the **Hungarian opera composers** include Emil Petrovics (1930–2011), Sándor Szokolay (1931–2013), Sándor Balassa (b. 1935), Attila Bozay (1939–99), and Zsolt Durkó (1934–97).

OPERETTA

The first great name in Hungarian operetta, which was to prove an extremely popular genre, was **Jenő Huszka** (1875–1960), the composer of *Prince Bob, Gül Baba,* and *Baroness Lili*. Another composer to attract interest was **Pongrác Kacsóh** (1873–1923), who wrote *János Vitéz*. Hungarian operetta gained worldwide recognition with **Imre (Emmerich) Kálmán** (1882–1953), who scored his first success in 1908 with *The Gay Hussars/ Autumn Manoeuvres,* followed by the well-known *Gipsy Princess* in 1915. However, it is the very popular *The Merry Widow* by **Ferenc** (**Franz**) **Lehár** (1870–1948), with its stream of memorable melodies, that has attained true immortality in this genre; his other notable works include *Gipsy Love* and *The Land of Smiles*. Switching from stage to screen, **Szabolcs Fényes** (1912–86) made a name for himself principally as a writer of Hungarian film scores, including *The Witness, One Night in Transylvania*, and *Lily in Love*.

MUSIC TODAY

The folk music scene is as lively as ever, whether in the open-air venues in towns and villages where *tanzas* is danced, or on the international stage, thanks in large part to the musical group **Muzsikás** and their singer Márta Sebestyén (b. 1957). Groups of talented musicians play at many special events and festivals, evoking the tales and legends celebrated in folklore. They are usually Romani musicians, who form traditional music groups—**Romano Drom** are a good example.

Rock music first came on the scene in the 1960s and, despite the bans issued by the Communist authorities in the 1970s, rock bands such as **Illés** (1960–73), **Omega** (formed in 1962), and **Locomotiv GT** (LGT, 1971–2016) achieved great popularity. Bands making a name for themselves on the Hungarian and international music scene today include **Turbo** (prog and psychedelic rock), **Shapat Terro**r (metal, who hail from Eger), **Fish!** (funk/rock/metal), **Grand Mexican Warlock** (psychedelic rock), **Amber Smith** (alt-rock), and **Óriás**.

Budapest has become a key center for modern European music, particularly **electronic dance** (EDM), demonstrating Hungary's ongoing capacity for musical creativity. **Balaton Sound**, one of Europe's largest open-air electronic music festivals, is held every July, while fans of all kinds of music congregate at the annual **Sziget Festival** in the Hungarian capital, the European Glastonbury or Woodstock. It is attracting more and more top international artists and features many cultural events. The **VOLT** Festival held over four days end June/beginning July in Sopron is multi-genre, ranging from urban and electronic to jazz, rock, and pop, with theater and film thrown in.

Cinema

BEFORE 1945

Projectograph, the first Hungarian movie production company, was established in 1898, and cinema played a key role in the country's cultural life, exerting considerable influence in the political arena. Copies of the first films to be made are still in existence and include *Chess Maniac*, made by Endre Nagy in 1898, and *Bánk Bán*, made in 1914 by Mihály Kertész, also known as **Michael Curtiz** (1888–1962).

Curtiz made 38 films in just eight years in Hungary before moving to America when Béla Kun nationalized the country's studios in 1919. Curtiz worked with many of the greats of Hollywood in its golden era and produced cinematic masterpieces such as the much-loved *Casablanca*. Other pioneers of Hungarian film include Sándor László Kellner, better known as **Sir**

Alexander Korda (1893–1956), who also spent time in America but went on to carve out a career in London, where he founded his own film studios; he was knighted by King George VI in 1942. There were few truly notable films made in Hungary before 1931, hampered by the fact that many of the best producers and screenwriters (André Kertész, László Benedek, André De Toth, George Pal, Pál Fejős, Emeric Pressburger, and Adolph Zukor, to name but a few) and actors (Peter Lorre, Béla Lugosi) left the country. There was a half-hearted reengagement with film in 1931 with the advent of the talkies, but fans had to wait for the end of the Second World War for any real renaissance in the movie theaters.

NEOREALISTS

The decade following the end of the Second World War saw directors shining a light on the truth about war and the national origins of Fascism. This era's most important production was *Somewhere in Europe* by **Géza von Radványi** (1907–86), a shocking indictment of man's inhumanity. Toward the end of Mátyás Rákosi's government, from 1953 onward, intellectual opposition bore fruit in **Félix Máriássy** (1919–75), who made a name for himself with *A Glass of Beer* in 1955 and **Károly Makk** (1925–2017), whose famous *Love* defined the Hungary of 1970.

THE NEW WAVE

Between 1960 and 1963, under János Kádár's regime, four studios were producing feature films, with the state underwriting all financing and distribution. The **Béla Balázs Studio**, founded in 1958, was a rare exception; filmmakers were allowed to express themselves "freely" using innovative equipment such as lightweight cameras, spotlights, and high-speed film, tools that allowed them to break free from studio shoots. These young directors included **Pál Gábor** (1932–87) and **István Gaál** (1933–2007), whose *The Falcons* and *Cserepek* castigate power and individualist society. Among the most notable of the era's movies are *Twenty Hours* (1964) by **Zoltán Fábri** (1917–94) and *Cold Days* (1966), a morality tale by **András Kovács** (1925–2017).

INTERNATIONAL RECOGNITION

After the General Amnesty proclaimed by Kádár in 1963, Hungarian cinema went on to carve out a place of its own among the former Eastern bloc countries, attracting significant recognition in Europe at film festivals.

Miklós Jancsó (1921–2014) achieved international renown and was a tireless inventor of new forms of expression in examining the history of his country. *The Hopeless Ones* (1965) evokes the post-revolutionary period of 1848 and *Silence and Cry* (1968) reveals the true nature of power in the form of allegorical montages. His film *Cantata* (1963) is a screen adaptation of Bartók's folk ballad *Cantata profana*, the story of a father no longer able to recognize his sons who have been transformed into stags, and uses it to interpret the events of 1956. His drama *Red Psalm* (1972) employs great lyricism to depict the agricultural workers' uprising at the end of the 19C.

András Vajna (1944–2019), who spent most of his career as a producer in Hollywood (the first *Rambo* films, several of the *Terminator* franchise), set up the **Korda Studios** in Etyek, west of Budapest, where *The Martian* (2015) and *Blade Runner 2049* (2017) were shot. These studios are now open to

Korda Studios, Etyek
© Jens Kalaene/dpa-Zentralbild/age fotostock

the public (kordastudio.hu), much to the delight of fans. Vajna never forgot his roots and played a role in facilitating the shooting of some films in Budapest (*Evita*, 1996).

BUDAPEST SCHOOL

After the great wave of cinema during the 1960s and 1970s, Hungary underwent an economic crisis, accounting for the dearth of productions after the golden years—a total of just eight films were made between 1987 and 1990. The **Budapest school**, a movement that took off in 1980, included a group of highly skilled documentary makers, who addressed social subjects such as housing and minority communities. They include the directors Lívia Gyarmathy (b. 1932) and Géza Böszörményi (1924–2004), who worked at Társulás Studio between 1981 and 1985. The best productions of the 1980s include *Diary for my Children* by Márta Mészáros (b. 1931), which was awarded the Grand Prix at the Cannes Film Festival in 1984—this screenwriter and director was also the first woman to win a Golden Bear at the Berlin Film Festival for *Adoption* in 1975; other fine productions include *80 Hussars* by Sándor Sára (b. 1933); *Mephisto*, *Colonel Redl*, and *Hanussen* by István Szabó (b. 1938); *Oh, Bloody Life!* by Péter Bacsó (1928–2009); *Another Way* by Károly Makk (1925–2017), which won an award at Cannes in 1982; and *Daniel Takes a Train* by Pál Sándor (b. 1939).

AFTER COMMUNISM

Many great directors emerged after 1989, but did not always succeed in getting their projects up and running due to a lack of financial means. The talent is certainly still there, with directors being recognized by prestigious awards: these include **Béla Tarr** (b. 1955), whose movie, *The Turin Horse*, won a Golden Bear at Berlin in 2011, and **László Nemes** (b. 1977), who won the Grand Prix at the 2015 Cannes Festival and the 2016 Oscar for Best

Foreign Film for *Son of Saul*, set in Auschwitz concentration camp. As with so many of his predecessors, Nemes has a deep love for his country and its history, which serves as a background for his films. In 2017 **Kristóf Deák** (b. 1982) won an Oscar in the Live Action Short Film category for *Sing*, made with non-professional actors.

Photography

The first daguerreotypes made in Hungary appeared in 1840, very soon after Jacques Daguerre had perfected his invention in 1838. The first images depicting conflict appeared during the Austro-Hungarian era, followed by photographs of the great events held to celebrate the Hungarian nation's millennium taken by **János Müllner**, the country's first photojournalist. Between the two world wars, photographers such as Rudolf Balogh (1879–1944), Frigyes Haller (1898–1954), and Tibor Csörgeő (1896–1968) developed a new **Magyar style** characterized by its rural settings in Hungarian villages. The finest exponents of **absolute photography** include Károly Divald (1830–97) and György Klösz (1844–1913), known for their superb compositions of nature and the countryside. The **realist style** burst upon the scene in the work of **Károly Escher** (1890–1966), who discovered the artistic value of depicting everyday life, Kata Kálmán (1909–78), Lajos Lengyel (1904–78), Lajos Tabák (1904–2007), and Judith Kárász (1912–1977).
The second half of the 20C saw **Károly Gink** (1922–2002), **Péter Korniss** (b. 1937), and **Tamás Féner** (b. 1938) working freely in a variety of styles across most fields, including sociography and applied photography.
The modern artistic photography movement is led by the **Hungarian Federation of Photographic Art**, which publishes an excellent resource in the journal called *Fotóművészet*. Its members include László Cseri (b. 1948), Tibor Hajas (1947–80), Péter Tímár (b. 1948), György Tóth (b. 1950), László Török (b. 1948), and Attila Vécsy (b. 1954).
Other artists of Hungarian origin have excelled in photography, gaining global recognition. **André Kertész** (1894–1985) produced his famous volume *Paris* in 1934 and won many awards. His contemporary **Brassai** (the pseudonym of Gyula Halász, 1899–1984), for his part, produced *Paris by Night* in 1932 and began his famous series *Graffiti*. The photojournalist **Robert Capa** (the pseudonym of Endre Ernő Friedmann; 1913–54) covered the great conflicts of the 20C and gave his name to Budapest's Contemporary Photography Center (*see p57*). Together with Henri Cartier-Bresson, in 1947 he was one of the founder members of the Magnum Photos cooperative in Paris. Capa hired the photographer **Ata Kandó** (1913–2017) to work in the Magnum laboratory, where she stayed for five years before pursuing her own career, most notably in the Netherlands.
Other notable names include **László Moholy-Nagy** (1895–1944), who worked with photograms (photographs made without using a camera) and used other artistic experimentation, and **Marton Munkácsi** (1896–1963), who came to be known as the "father of fashion photography" and worked for *Harper's Bazaar*. Whatever their style, they all helped to inspire a later generation of photographers, including Henri Cartier-Bresson, who never tired of repeating that "we all owe something to André Kertész."

Traditions and ways of life

The particular geographical, social, and religious circumstances of the 17C and 18C played a part in the development of very different regional styles. Today, Hungarian folk traditions represent a significant contribution to the country's enduring national culture, as trades and craft skills are handed down from one generation to the next.

A rural culture

"Peasant culture" is a term that has become synonymous with the culture and traditions of the Hungarian provinces since the 19C, preserving their ancient way of life. The **Palóc** people live in northern Hungary, in the area around the Ipoly and Sajó rivers, and in the Mátra, Bükk, and Karancs mountains; their folklore and traditions have been maintained with great care. Their distinctive buildings, carved furniture, and colorful embroidery and clothing as worn at folk festivals, can be seen in the region's many small villages. In 1987 the entire village of **Hollókő**, a hamlet of 450 people nestling in a valley on the rugged slopes of the Cserhát Mountains,

RURAL HOMES

The arrival of the Magyars in the Danube Basin ended a nomadic way of life that had been in existence for several centuries; it marked the beginning of a settled lifestyle, using locally sourced materials such as wood and stone to build dwellings. On the **Great Plain**, the traditional home was originally a single-story, earthen house, with mud compressed within frames to make the walls. The roof was made from reeds or straw. Inside, in the large communal room, smoke from the hearth would escape through the gaps in the roof (no chimney). Over time, porches were added to the exteriors, and later still, as agriculture developed further, summer farmhouses came to be built outside the villages. Scattered across the fields, these limewashed ***tanyas*** were later gradually transformed into permanent homes.

The traditions of the local people suffered greatly during the Ottoman invasion and were neglected during the Austro-Hungarian Empire, when industrialization arrived in Hungary with a vengeance. The earthen houses of small towns gave way to modern suburbs, with any homes that had survived outside the towns often being turned into country houses. However, this precious heritage has now been preserved and a number of traditional peasant homes have been conserved and rebuilt in open-air museums *(skanzen)* such as at **Szentendre** (*see p100*) and **Szalafő** *(p240)*.

was one of the first sites in Hungary to be included on Unesco's World Heritage List. The residents in some of these small villages make a living from traditional crafts, agriculture, and tourism. However, Hollókő is far from being a museum village of empty houses preserved in aspic; instead it is a small but busy community living in harmony with the landscape, an example of rural life as it was before the agricultural revolution of the 20th century. (See p205).

Holidays and festivals

Folk festivals are popular affairs in Hungary and many maintain the country's age-old traditions.

PALÓC VILLAGES

The **Festival of Palóc Culture** is held in the communities of Hollókő and Szécsény during the summer; Buják's **Sunday Festival** has become very well known, as have the fairs at Kazár and Felsőtárkány. The annual **Palóc Festival** in Parád sees villagers showcasing their traditional music, dances, and folk costumes, along with everyday items, tools and equipment, as used by the peasants and shepherds of the past.

An open-air mass is celebrated at the **Easter Festival** in Hollókő, followed by a ball. On Locsolkodás ("shower Monday"), in a somewhat one-sided tradition, men throw buckets of water over women or dunk them in troughs of water in return for shots of pálinka and cookies. Other traditional Easter customs include egg painting.

FOLK DANCE

Traditional folk music and dance have been kept alive thanks to the enthusiastic work of numerous organizations. These include the **Nógrád Folk Dance Ensemble**, which has achieved success on an international level, and the folk group Muzsla from Pásztó, the Kenderike children's group from Palotás, and the Vidróczki folk dance club from Gyöngyös. The **Szeged Open-Air Festival** has been held every summer since 1931, featuring plays, opera, and dance, and the town has also been hosting the **International Festival of Folk Dance** since 1966. In September, the **folklore festivals** in Kalocsa, Kecskemét, and Szeged see locals singing and dancing dressed in traditional costume just as in the past. At the **International Folklore Festival** in Pécs in August and the **Pentecost** celebrations in **Buzsák** in May, you can see more popular regional traditions in action. Folk songs are sung at the **Girls Fair**, which takes place in Pécsvárad in southern Hungary around St. Luke's Day in October. Another equally celebrated event is the **Folk Festival of the countries of the Danube**, which is held every three years and features a reenactment of a Sárköz wedding ceremony, with traditional folk dance and song.

Artisan skills

EMBROIDERY

The **Matyó** people live in Mezőkövesd and neighboring villages near the city of Eger in northeast Hungary. They have acquired a reputation for their traditional dress embroidered with elaborate floral motifs and their brightly painted wooden furniture. Having been inscribed on the Unesco Intangible Cultural Heritage List in 2012, the art of *matyó* embroidery is now kept alive by an association that teaches its skills and organizes folk dance events. The embroidery produced in the two Matyó villages of **Szentistván**

Folk dance on St. Stephen's Square, Budapest
© Andocs/Shutterstock

and **Tard**, which is richly decorated with floral motifs, leaves, small birds, hearts, and stars, has become equally well known—some of the most beautiful examples can be seen on display in the Matyó Museum (*see p190*).

The town of **Kalocsa** is also famous for its embroidery, with its distinctive floral motifs that form sumptuous multicolored bouquets decorating women's clothing and household linen. Having first appeared in the 19C, it was originally stitched by hand before developing into fine, interwoven lacework with the advent of the sewing machine. Highly decorative embroidered, hand-sewn slippers and shoes (known as ***papucs***) from Szeged hark back to the era of the Turkish occupation, while the celebrated needlework techniques of the **Kiskunhalas** area can be seen at the Lace House (*see p331*).

WOOD AND LEATHER

The shepherds who live and work on the Puszta (Pannonian Steppe) are well known for their woodcarving and for the folk items they make from leather and horn. Traditional items such as these can be bought as souvenirs at the **International Shepherds' Festival** held in **Hortobágy** in July. The Puszta is also the scene of the **Hortobágy Bridge Fair** (usually 20 August, folklore performances, dance, food). And the **Kurultáj**, a three-day festival, takes place in **Bugac** in August involving demonstrations of horsemanship, archery, folk music, and so on.

MASKS

A great deal of effort has been put into reviving a number of traditional trades in southern Transdanubia, one of the regions that is richest in folk traditions. These include painting on canvas, pottery, cabinet-making, carpet-weaving, and making frightening masks for the **Busó procession**, registered by Unesco as an event on the Intangible Cultural Heritage List. Busójárás (or "Busó-walking") takes place in February and is intended to chase away the rigors of winter,

HORSE SENSE

Hungary boasts one of the oldest equestrian traditions in the world and a number of stud farms are scattered across the country. **Prince Árpád** *(see p311)*, the country's semi-mythical founder, is often credited with introducing horses to Hungary. The outcome today is the beautiful historic breed of Shagya Arabians, a cross between Arab steeds and purebred Hungarian stock.

Holy Roman emperor Joseph II acquired the **Bábolna stud farm** in 1789 and set about breeding the most beautiful horses. Hardy and strong, the **Shagya** were originally intended as mounts for the cavalry. However, once mechanization took over in the army, as elsewhere, they were mostly used in equestrian sports and folklore displays.

The Shagya are also very popular for carriage driving and have been winning international plaudits for years. These spirited beasts also made a name for themselves carrying the mail for the **Hungarian Postal Service**. You can also see them in equestrian displays, the rider standing astride the rumps of the two stallions that form the rear pair of a team of between five and ten horses, as they gallop at breakneck speed across the **Puszta** *(see p329)*. These shows have become very popular, thrilling the crowds with the skill and daring of the horsemen.

in a tradition kept alive by the Šokci people of **Mohács**.

Arts and crafts

CERAMICS

The town of **Mezőcsát** in northern Hungary has become famous for its pottery. Decorated wine jugs, known as ***miskakancsó***, are just one of its specialties—the neck is in the shape of a man's head, on top of which is his shako (cylindrical military hat), which forms the spout.

The fine porcelain manufactured in **Herend**, where production began in 1826, is sold throughout the world. Herend specializes in hand-painted items made using several hundred different molds and thousands of different motifs. You can see some pieces at the museum in the Herend Manufactory near Veszprém, along with a practical demonstration in the mini workshop on site *(see p160)*.

The porcelain factory **Zsolnay** in Pécs was active on an international scale in the 19C and early 20C, when it played a leading role in the Hungarian ceramics industry. The Zsolnay name (after the founder Zsolnay Vilmos) achieved world renown thanks to the unique manufacturing techniques it developed. Zsolnay produced pyrogranite, a building material that is frost-resistant and invented the eosin process to coat ceramics, the secrets of which remain undisclosed to this day. The process produces a beautiful iridescent, metallic finish that changes color with the angle of reflection. *(See p280.)*

CRYSTAL GLASS

Ajka Crystal established its factory among the rolling hills of Bakony. The firm is the most famous manufacturer of crystal glass in Hungary. Founded in 1878 by Bernát Neumann, it is one of the largest companies in Central Europe and produces a wide range of unique items, especially of clear and colored glass, blown and cut by hand.

RELIGION

Just over a thousand years ago, change was afoot in the country that was shortly to become Hungary. The Magyar tribes were settling in the Carpathian Basin, leaving their nomadic way of life, and power was gradually becoming consolidated in the hands of the Árpád dynasty. The supreme Magyar chieftain, Géza, converted to Western Christianity in around 980, probably at first simply adding the Christian deity to the existing panoply of traditional pagan gods. His son Vajk was born a pagan in 970, but was subsequently baptized and raised a Christian. He took the Christian name Stephen when he became the first king of Hungary in 1000.

Hungary was to remain a Roman Catholic country until the 16C, when the authority of the Catholic Church in Europe was challenged and the Protestant Reformation took place. Many Hungarians adopted Protestantism and in particular Calvinism, one of its major branches. The Catholic Habsburg kings fought back with the Counter-Reformation and the two versions of Western Christianity continued to exist side by side among a relatively pragmatic population.

Judaism can also be added to this mix thanks to the Jewish community that was already present in Hungary as early as the 11C, if not before. Islam arrived with the invasion of the Ottoman Turks in the 16C, although Christianity was not prohibited during the Turkish occupation and Islam was not spread by force.

In common with other countries in the Eastern bloc, the church in Hungary was suppressed under Communism and land and property confiscated, although some participation in organized religions was permitted and many people retained a Catholic identity.

No accurate figures currently exist for religious affiliation in Hungary, but before the Second World War around 65 percent of the population were Roman Catholic and 25 percent Protestant. Today these figures are thought to have fallen to around 37 percent for Catholicism and around 14 percent for Protestantism (the majority belonging to the Reformed Church), with around 2 percent Greek Catholic (Orthodox), and around 18 percent agnostic or atheist, to which are added a small number of other groups (Buddhism, Judaism, Islam, …).

NAMES

Hungary is unusual in being one of the few countries in which a person's full name is given in the Eastern order, as in Japan and China, where names are presented in the order of surname followed by the given name. That is why you will visit the Liszt Ferenc Emlékmúzeum in Budapest, rather than the Ferenc Liszt Emlékmúzeum.

To confuse matters further for the unsuspecting first-time visitor, you will learn that some of the names of famous Hungarians with whom you are familiar are anglicized versions. Hence most English-speaking visitors will certainly know of Franz Liszt, but may stare blankly at mention of the name Ferenc Liszt. Many Hungarian first names have an English equivalent: Erzsébet (Elizabeth), István (Stephen), András (Andrew), János (John), and so on. However, apart from where they occur in the names of museums and other institutions, we have generally presented names in the more familiar order of first name/surname in the guide. (*Hungarian p341.*)

PLANNING YOUR TRIP

Rider standing on horses, Hortobágy National Park

© Manfred Mehlig/age fotostock

Getting there

Official name of the country: Magyarország
Capital: Budapest
Area: 35,919sq mi/93,030sq km
Population: 9,778,371 inhabitants
Currency: forint (HUF)
Official language: Hungarian

By plane

Hungary has five international airports: **Budapest Liszt Ferenc International**, **Debrecen**, **Hévíz-Balaton**, **Győr-Pér**, and **Pécs Pogány**. Most airlines fly into Budapest Airport. Scheduled and budget airlines all fly into Terminal 2 (Terminal 1 is closed indefinitely).

SCHEDULED AIRLINES

The major international airlines flying to Budapest include:
American Airlines (Philadelphia to Budapest direct): www.aa.com
Air Canada: www.aircanada.com
Air France: www.airfrance.com
British Airways: www.britishairways.com
Brussels Airlines: www.brusselsairlines.com
KLM: www.klm.com
Lufthansa: www.lufthansa.com
Norwegian Air: www.norwegian.com
Swiss International Airlines: www.swiss.com

BUDGET AIRLINES

Budget airlines are subject to change, with carriers coming on and off the market at intervals, but may include:
EasyJet: www.easyjet.com (London Gatwick)
Jet2: www.jet2.com (Manchester, Edinburgh, Leeds, East Midlands)
LOT: www.lot.com, direct flights from the UK and US (some US flights via Warsaw, several direct flights per week from New York to Budapest)
Ryanair: www.ryanair.com (London Stansted, Edinburgh, East Midlands, Bristol, and Manchester)
Wizz Air: www.wizzair.com (Luton, Birmingham, Liverpool, London)
www.google.com/flights allows you to research and compare the price/flight times/journey duration of different airlines.

By train

London to Budapest by train takes around 24 hours (Eurostar to Paris, high-speed TGV Paris–Munich, overnight sleeper Munich–Budapest). You can also travel via Brussels, Cologne, and Vienna, and Budapest has direct rail links with over 25 other European cities.

Budapest has three **main rail terminals**: **Nyugati** (in Pest, Teréz körút 55), **Déli** (in Buda, Krisztina körút 37/A); **Keleti** (in Pest, Kerepesi út 2–4). Keleti is the main international and intercity terminal. The metro serves all three stations.

The Interrail Hungary Pass (EU residents only) is a One Country Pass for a specific number of days. The Interrail Global Pass allows you to travel in 31 European countries. Non-EU residents can buy a Eurailpass, offering unlimited rail travel for a number of days over a certain period.

WOW HUNGARY
wellspring of wonders
wowhungary.com
wellspringofwonders
wow_hungary
wow_hungary
HUNGARY, THE WELLSPRING OF WONDERS.
Just go with the tide and let every path take you to a new wonder. Breathe with nature and get a taste of Hungarian cuisine.

DISTANCE IN MILES	Budapest	Debrecen	Eger	Győr	Gyula	Kecskemét	Keszthely	Pécs	Sopron	Szeged	Szombathely	Tokaj
Budapest	-	145	82	77	140	54	119	125	132	107	143	144
Debrecen	145	-	83	223	84	124	264	270	277	135	288	51
Eger	82	83	-	160	158	128	201	207	214	182	226	80
Győr	77	223	160		341	204	161	305	88	290	106	355
Gyula	225	136	255	212	-	87	250	190	266	71	273	134
Kecskemét	53	124	128	127	87	-	166	109	181	56	192	188
Keszthely	119	264	201	100	250	165	-	121	80	217	62	261
Pécs	126	270	207	189	190	109	121	-	190	121	172	276
Sopron	132	277	214	55	266	181	80	190	-	376	67	441
Szeged	172	218	293	290	114	90	350	195	234	-	245	190
Szombathely	143	288	226	66	273	192	62	172	42	245	-	281
Tokaj	144	51	80	221	134	188	261	276	274	190	281	-

Distances in miles: to convert to km, multiply by 1.6

Buy your ticket around three months ahead for the best deals.

Information:
www.eurail.com
www.interrail.eu/en; www.interrail.eu/en/interrail-passes/one-country-pass/hungary

Hungarian railways:
www.mavcsoport.hu/en

Transport within Hungary, p420.

By coach

The **main coach station** in Budapest (Népliget Autóbusz-pályaudvar) is in Pest (Üllői út 131), southeast of the city center and on the blue M3 metro line. London to Budapest takes around 28 hours. Book ahead for the best prices. Among the companies providing services to various destinations in Hungary are:

Eurolines: www.eurolines.eu
Flixbus: www.flixbus.co.uk
RegioJet: www.regiojet.com
Compare prices on:
www.busbud.com

By car

London to Budapest is around 1,100mi/1,800km by car so allow 2–3 days, depending on schedule and route. Consult **www.viamichelin.co.uk** to research your route, and to locate gas stations, hotels, restaurants, and sites worth seeing along your way. You will need a **Highway Toll Sticker** (a digital vignette for motorways and expressways) in Austria and Hungary. Buy online at www.asfinag.at/www.tolltickets.com. Driving is on the right. The most frequently used border crossing is via Austria (Nickelsdorf/Hegyeshalom).

General information: rac.co.uk/drive/travel/country/hungary/
Toll road information:
www.toll-charge.hu
Traffic information:
www.utinform.hu

Know before you go

When to go

Hungary has a temperate Continental climate (average 54°F/12°C). January is the coldest month (28°F/-2°C) and July the hottest (82°F/28°C). It has three major climatic areas: Mediterranean in the south, Continental in the east, and Atlantic in the west, and the temperature range can be significant. Seasonal differences are particularly marked in the Great Plain. The ideal time to visit is between late spring and early fall.

Spring

Although it can rain quite a bit during April and May, spring is still rather lovely wherever you go in Hungary, as temperatures are generally mild. And you can take advantage of the fact that the peak tourist season has not yet started.

Summer

Summers are hot, dry, and sunny. Tourist areas such as Lake Balaton can get very busy in July and August.

Fall

The heat of summer can last into early fall, especially in the hills around Budapest and in the Great Plain. November is one of the wettest months of the year in certain parts of the country.

Winter

Less popular, as the winters are often cold and rather harsh, with gray and overcast skies. The opening times of museums and tourist sites tend to be a little shorter in winter.

Useful addresses

EMBASSIES

Consulate General of Hungary, New York
223 East 52nd Street
New York, NY10022-6308, USA
(1) 212 752 0669
newyork.mfa.gov.hu

Embassy of Hungary, Ottawa
299 Waverley Street
Ottawa, ON K2P OV9, Canada
(1) 613 230 2717
ottawa.mfa.gov.hu/eng

Hungarian Embassy, London
35 Eaton Place
London, SW1X 8BY, UK
(44) 020 7201 3440
london.mfa.gov.hu/eng

Embassy of Hungary, Dublin
2 Fitzwilliam Place
Dublin 2, Ireland
(353) 01 661 3091/3092/3087
dublin.mfa.gov.hu/eng

Embassy of Hungary, Canberra
17 Beale Crescent
Deakin, ACT 2600, Australia
(61) 02 6285 3484
canberra.mfa.gov.hu/eng

Embassy of Hungary, Wellington
Legal House, Level 6
101 Lambton Quay, Wellington
6011, New Zealand
(64) 04 260 3175
www.mfat.govt.nz/en/countries-and-regions

Contact details for home country embassies in Budapest, p413

CULTURAL CENTERS

The **Balassi Institute** (Balassi Intézet, in Hungarian) promotes Hungary's cultural heritage. It operates in over 20 countries and develops cultural diplomatic relations between partner nations. The Balassi Institute organizes a wide spectrum of programs to promote Hungarian art and artists, with cultural exhibitions, seminars, literary events, festivals, debates, language classes, and conferences.

Hungarian Cultural Center, New York:
223 East 52nd Street
New York, 10022 NY, USA
(1) 212 660 7946
www.newyork.balassiintezet.hu/en/

Hungarian Cultural Centre, London:
10 Maiden Lane, WC2E 7NA, UK
(44) 020 7257 2023
www.london.balassiintezet.hu/en/

Other centers include:
Hungarian House of New York www.hungarianhouse.org
Hungarian Canadian Cultural Centre, Toronto www.hccc.org

USEFUL WEBSITES

British Council in Hungary: www.britishcouncil.hu

Bud News: independent website promoting Budapest. www.budnews.hu

Budapest Times: weekly English-language newspaper. www.budapesttimes.hu

XpatLoop: contemporary/classical, cultural and community events for ex-pats. www.XpatLoop.com

Tourist information

www.spiceofeurope.com: Hungary's official tourist website about Budapest.

wowhungary.com: presents each region of Hungary and its different tourist attractions, walks, spas, food & drink, and festivals. It might be a little low on practical detail, but nevertheless it's high on attractive images.

www.hongrietourisme.com: information on tourist sites.

www.welovebudapest.com: reliable and comprehensive website offering information on bars, restaurants, shopping, and nightclubs.

www.spottedbylocals.com: inside information on the best places to go in Budapest.

www.travelguide.michelin.com: offers a range of information on hotels, restaurants, route planning, and itineraries.

www.museum.hu: official website for Hungary's museums.

www.unesco.org: features Hungary's UNESCO World Heritage Sites.

TRAVEL AGENTS

Evaneos: creates tailor-made tours with local travel agents. www.evaneos.co.uk

Kirker Holidays: www.kirkerholidays.com

Quality Tours Hungary: www.qualitytours.hu

Trailfinders: www.trailfinders.com

Exploring by river

Several companies offer cruises on the Danube that take in Budapest and other European cities, as well as the Christmas markets:
www.rivieratravel.co.uk
www.rivervoyages.com
www.emeraldwaterways.co.uk
www.vikingrivercruises.co.uk
www.scenicusa.com/www.scenic.ca
www.amawaterways.co.uk

Organized nature tours, p415.

WOW HUNGARY

SPIRITUAL RECREATION AT THE WORLD HERITAGE SITE IN PANNONHALMA

The Benedictine Abbey of Pannonhalma has been towering above the Pannon countryside for a thousand years. It is an exceptional historical monument of Hungary, a church and art history centre, and is listed as a UNESCO World Heritage Site. It's only an hour and a half from Budapest by car.

The early 13th century Gothic basilica is one of Europe's richest monastic libraries and has a lovely arboretum and herb garden. Guests can also join Benedictine monks for a guided visit of the abbey's wine cellar and lavender distillery.

Following environmentally-conscious practices, the monks produce exclusive products including artisanal chocolates, liquors, premium quality white wines, and lotions and teas made from their own herbs and botanicals The monastery's restaurant is one of the most exciting culinary hotspots in the country.

ACCESSIBILITY

Most of the larger hotels have rooms for guests with reduced mobility or restricted vision but we recommend that you check with your hotel before you travel.

You may experience some difficulty getting around in the streets and entering certain restaurants, stores, and museums, or using public transport. However, the centers of some cities have been redeveloped and are equipped with Braille tactile signage.

If you are planning to travel in Hungary, you are advised to choose a specialized organized tour. The ♿ symbol used in this book indicates that the venue has facilities for disabled travelers.

Useful websites:
welovebudapest.com (in the English link, search for "mobility").
route4u.org/cities.html will help you plan your route.

Entry requirements

DOCUMENTS

Hungary has been part of the Schengen Area (allowing free movement between certain European countries) since 2007.

ID

American, **UK**, **Irish**, **Australian**, **New Zealand**, and **Canadian** citizens can stay for up to 90 days without a visa provided they are in possession of a valid passport.

For specific details, see your embassy's website.

For a stay in excess of these periods, you need to register with the local authorities. The Hungarian Ministry of Foreign Affairs' website (konzuliszolgalat.kormany.hu/en) will provide the necessary information.

Entry requirements and general advice for passport holders from:
USA: travel.state.gov/content/travel/en/international-travel.html
Canada: travel.gc.ca/destinations/hungary
UK: www.gov.uk/foreign-travel-advice
Republic of Ireland: www.dfa.ie/travel/travel-advice/
Australia: canberra.mfa.gov.hu/eng/page/vizum
New Zealand: wellington.mfa.gov.hu/eng/page/visa

Driving license

European and international driving licenses are accepted. If driving your own car, you must also be able to show the registration document for your vehicle and an insurance Green Card, an extension of the standard policy that covers all—or almost all—of Europe.

Cars, Car rental, p411–412.

Customs

Under the terms of the Schengen Agreement, there are no customs' controls when crossing the border from one country in the European Union to another.

If arriving from a **non-EU country**, you must declare items you are carrying in excess of the limits.

You are not allowed to bring firearms or more than €10,000 in cash or the equivalent in another currency into the country.

For persons aged over 17 traveling **from another EU member state**, there is no limit on the amount or value of goods you may import, providing they are for personal use and not for commercial sale.

For quantities deemed to be commercial see: budapest.com/travel/tourist_information/custom_and_vat_rules.en.html.

If you are arriving **from a non-EU country**, you may import the following without having to pay customs duty:

TYPICAL PRICES OF SOME SERVICES AND GOODS	AVERAGE PRICE IN FORINTS
cup of coffee	300
bottle of mineral water (2 US pts/ 1 liter)	250
glass of beer	400
cake in a café	400
takeout ice cream	300
entry ticket for a museum	800–1,500
2 US pints/1 liter of unleaded gasoline	450
postcard	200–300
postage stamp for USA/UK	470/400

Alcohol: 2.11 US pints/1 liter of spirits over 22% or 4.22 US pints/ 2 liters of spirits under 22%, 8.45 US pints/4 liters of wine, and 33.8 US pints/16 liters of beer.
Tobacco: arriving by air: 200 cigarettes or 100 cigarillos or 50 cigars or 0.55 US pounds/250g tobacco; arriving by other means: 40 cigarettes or 20 cigarillos or 10 cigars or 0.11 US pounds/50g tobacco.

For more information see: en.nav.gov.hu *(search for* Information for travellers*),* *or* www.iatatravelcentre.com

Insurance

Visitors from all countries are advised to have travel insurance to cover illness and eventualities such as hospitalization or repatriation. EU nationals should carry a European Health Insurance Card (EHIC) to cover them for any potential health care they may need locally. This needs to be requested from the national health department of their home country at least two weeks' prior to travel. Anyone planning to take part in extreme sports should check that such activities are covered by their insurance policy.

Health, p414.

Budgeting

PROJECTED EXPENDITURE

A trip to Hungary will cost less than a stay in some European countries, such as France or Italy, but the days of amazing bargain prices are no longer with us. Car hire from an international agency and accommodation are likely to constitute your major expense. A good hotel in Budapest will cost at least Ft23,000 a night but there are plenty of alternatives, such as booking rooms in private houses or renting an apartment.

Where to stay, p408.

On the other hand, restaurants and public transport remain cheap. Away from the tourist areas, restaurants will serve a main course of generous proportions for around Ft3,300.

Where to eat, p410.

ON A TIGHT BUDGET

If your budget is tight, remember that "living like a local" is the most economic option, so opt to stay in a room in a private home or guesthouse, take public transport, buy local produce, and eat in simple restaurants. As a general rule, accommodation away from the tourist areas is much cheaper than in the downtown part of a city. Hotels in Budapest and on the shores of Lake Balaton are two or three times more expensive than a provincial guesthouse. By taking trains and buses you can travel around the country more cheaply than by car, but public transport can be more costly in terms of time.

Concessions for EU nationals

People aged 6 to 26 years and 62 to 70 years benefit from a 5 percent reduction in the price of entry to State-run museums and many non-national museums. For children under 6 years and those over 70, entrance is free. EU citizens over 65 may travel free on public transport. To prove eligibility (student, senior citizen, etc.), carry your identity card or passport with you.

Telephones

To call Hungary from abroad, dial 00 (international code) + 36 (country code for Hungary), then the area code followed by a 7-digit number for Budapest and 6-digit number for other areas.

Telephone area codes, p 417.

Where to stay

Whatever your budget, accommodation is easy to find in the most popular towns and regions. Prices are higher in Budapest but the choice is increasing. You can find guesthouses in most locations; they often offer good value for money and provide a less impersonal environment than a hotel.

Hotel prices in this guide are given in forints (Ft). *See Money, p415.*

The addresses listed here are classified under four different price categories (*see table opposite*). The rates given are for a double room in high season (except for campsites and youth hostels).

Find our selection of places to stay under Addresses/Stay in the Discovering Hungary section of the guide.

RESERVATION

In summer it is advisable to reserve your accommodation well in advance **in tourist areas** (Budapest, Balaton).

Reserving a room online in a big hotel in Budapest or the provinces is easy. Prices are also likely to be more advantageous than if you book through a travel agency at home or pay the hotel direct.

TYPES OF ACCOMMODATION

Hotels

Hotels range from five star palaces to the more modest establishments that were built in the Socialist era. Under Communism each county had to have at least one hotel—an unmistakable Brutalist concrete block. The majority have been renovated, albeit somewhat unimaginatively, but they are comfortable and modern. In the most entrepreneurial cities, these hotels share the market with new commercial enterprises specializing in spa and wellness facilities and small hotels and guesthouses that have their own individual charm.

If you are seeking a little authentic Hungarian romance, try staying in one of the grand castle hotels (*kastély szállók*) or mansion hotels (*kúriák*).

Breakfast is often served buffet-style and is included in the cost of the room. Hotels in larger towns sometimes charge for parking.

Guesthouses

Less expensive than hotels in the same category and often more picturesque, these family-run pensions have a maximum of 25 rooms. You can find them in the countryside, towns, and cities,

USEFUL TERMS IN THE HOTEL

Hotel: *hotel, szálloda*
Guesthouse: *panzió*
Room to rent: *kiadó szoba*
Room: *szoba*
Single room: *egyágyas szoba*
Double room: *kétágyas szoba*
Double bed: *franciaágy*/**Twin beds:** *külön ágy*
Bathroom: *fürdőszobával*/**Shower:** *zuhanyzóval*
Air-conditioner: *légkondicionáló*
Breakfast: *reggeli*/**Included:** *reggelivel*
Do you have a room available? *Van kiadó szobája?*
Can I see the room? *Megnézhetem a szobát?*

ranging from traditional pensions to luxurious villas equipped with a sauna and restaurant. Unsurprisingly, the tourist areas have the widest choice.

Homestay

Kiadó szoba (spare room) is a very popular accommodation option and in summer around Lake Balaton, for example, you will see a many signs advertising *Zimmer frei* (room vacant, in German).

Campsites and motorhomes

The majority of campsites are open from April/May to September/ October, but campsites that are close to spas or baths are often open all year round. Campsites also sometimes have small bungalows or caravans available to rent.
Camping on unauthorized sites is forbidden in Hungary.

To locate and book campsites, visit: **www.eurocampings.com/ hungary**
Information regarding motorhome sites can be found at: **www. campercontact.com/hungary**

Youth hostels

There are at least a hundred youth hostels in Hungary offering overnight stays at reasonable prices. Book them online at: **www.hihostels.com**
Don't forget to take your HI (Hostelling International) card.

Other accommodation

As elsewhere in the world, you can also rent accommodation directly from an individual (www. airbnb.com), or search for free temporary accommodation (www. couchsurfing.com).

PRICE CATEGORIES

	Stay		Eat	
	Provinces	**Budapest**	**Provinces**	**Budapest**
Budget	up to Ft16,200	up to Ft22,700	up to Ft3,250	up to Ft5,000
Average	Ft16,200–22,700	Ft22,700Ft–39,500	Ft3,250–6,500	From Ft5,000–9,750
A treat	Ft22,700–29,200	Ft39,500–53,000	Ft6,500–9,750	From Ft9,750–16,500
Splash out	From Ft29,200	From Ft53,000	From Ft9,750	From Ft16,500

Restaurant in Sárospatak, Tokaj wine region
© Jacques Sierpinski/hemis.fr

Where to eat

You should be able to find somewhere serving food at most times of the day. Hungary has several types of restaurant:
– **étterem**: a traditional restaurant offering both set menus and à la carte;
– **büfé**: a fast food restaurant with counter service of sandwiches, cakes, and drinks;
– **vendéglő**: a brasserie and less formal restaurant.
When you are shown the menu you will be asked what you would like to drink.

A **traditional meal** includes soup, a main dish, a dessert, and a drink, with (generally excellent) coffee to finish. Main dish portions are usually generous, so you may find that making your way through three courses every time is impossible. And a soup such as a goulash can be just as filling as a main dish.

Opening hours – Some kitchens in the larger cities are open 11am–10pm (often until midnight in the more fashionable parts of Budapest), but hours do vary depending on location, and many kitchens close between lunch and dinner. Be aware that out of season and away from tourist areas, restaurants might close at 8pm or even 6pm, so check opening times ahead to avoid disappointment.

Tipping – A service charge is often included on the check (look for the words *szerviz díj* on the menu or the bill). If this is not the case, you can give a tip of around 10–15 percent of the total at your discretion, but don't leave it on the table.

The addresses in this guide fall into **four price categories** (*see table, p409*). The prices listed are the minimum/maximum a main course.

You will find our restaurant selection in Addresses/Eat in the Discovering Hungary section of the guide.

The **Michelin Guide: Main Cities of Europe** gives a selection of restaurants in Budapest, several of which have been awarded Michelin stars. To find them, visit: **guide.michelin.com**

Basic information

Birdwatching

Countless species of bird, can be seen in the Hungarian countryside, among them European Bee-eaters, European Rollers, eagles, and Red-footed Falcons. Good months for birdwatching are May and June when birds are nesting; or time your visit to coincide with migration periods (March–May and August–October), or overwintering months. Hortobágy and Lake Tisza are prime locations, but there are numerous other birding hotspots throughout the country. For more information and on birding tours: www.hungarianbirdwatching.com

Organized nature tours, p415.

Cars

A car enables you to explore further afield, including places away from the usual tourist areas.

ROAD NETWORK

Highways (motorways) are marked with the prefix "M" before the number of the road. From Budapest, the M1 goes to Vienna, the M7 to Lake Balaton, the M5 to Szeged, the M6 to Pécs and the south, and the M3 to the northeast. Highways that are also European routes are prefixed "E."

Expressways are the next class of high-speed road after the highways, followed by fast roads.

Take care when driving on secondary roads as they can be poorly maintained.

Table of distances between the country's principal cities p402.

Driving license, p406.

Road rules – Away from built-up areas, it is compulsory for car headlights to be on dipped beam at all times, both night and day.

The speed limit is 81mi/130km per hour on highways, 68mi/110km per hour on expressways, 56mi/90km per hour on rural roads, and 31mi/50km per hour in urban areas, unless specifically indicated. Note that signage may be patchy.

Wearing a seat belt is mandatory for the driver and passengers in both the front and back of a car.

Be aware that if you are stopped for speeding or are found to have a defective seat belt, you will be fined on the spot and will have to pay the penalty immediately.

The permitted level of **alcohol** concentration in the blood when driving is 0 percent. If you test positive at the wheel, your driving license will be immediately confiscated.

Using a **cell phone** while driving is illegal, except with a hands-free system.

You must carry reflective jackets and a warning triangle in your vehicle.

Rendőrség – The name of the Hungarian police, which appears on all their vehicles.

COMPULSORY FOR DRIVING ON HIGHWAYS

Highway (motorway) traffic requires an e-vignette that can be bought online at **toll-charge.hu** or at outlets throughout Hungary (see the website for a list). It is valid from 10 days to one year and is priced according to the type of vehicle. Make sure the e-vignette is clearly visible on the windshield so that it can be seen by the fixed cameras, toll control cars, and mobile toll booths. A hefty penalty charge awaits if you fail to display it.

Parking *(parkolás)* – Coins are required to pay for parking at a ticket machine or meter, or you can pay by cell phone (SMS).

Driving in Hungary, see: www.rac.co.uk/drive/travel/country/hungary/

Useful words:
Super: *szuper*
Super lead free: *szuper ólommentes*
Diesel fuel: *diesel*
Fill the tank, please: *tele kérem*
Service station/rest area: *töltőállomás / benzinkút*

Car rental

You must be able to produce a driver's license that is valid for more than one year and be at least 21 years old. You will generally have to pay a deposit. International car hire companies have outlets in Budapest (city and airport) and major towns and cities. They are more expensive than local agencies, where the quality of service and vehicle can be variable.

If you hire a car from a local agency, check the vehicle and its fixtures carefully and make sure you understand all the costs, any mileage limitation, and the level of insurance cover being provided. You can also book and pay for a hire car in advance, directly from a rental company before you travel.

Cultural heritage

Hungary is rich in cultural, artistic, and architectural heritage. There is a broad spectrum of museums, castles and monuments to see, from small village churches and rural dwellings to Baroque castles and mansions, via cathedrals and abbeys, and Hungary's amazing thermal baths—the colorful legacy of a fascinating history.

ABC of architecture, p378.

Folk villages

Folklore is very much alive and kicking in Hungary, and there's no need to restrict yourself to museums to discover it. The villages in certain areas in particular, such as Szeged, Hollókő, Nagykálló, Mohács, Badacsony, Balatonfüred, and Őrség, are very proud of their folk traditions.

There are a number of **open-air museums** *(skanzen)* such as the one at Szentendre (*see p94*), providing an insight into the diversity of rural architecture, traditional crafts, and everyday lives. And don't miss the Museum of Applied Arts in Budapest for a wealth of folklore artifacts (*see p65*).

Village and regional festivals, both secular and religious, are also a good way of discovering folk traditions on the spot.

See *Addresses/Events and Festivals in the Discovering Hungary section of the guide.*

Natural beauty

The diverse Hungarian landscape is shaped by its plains, hills, and mountains. The country has 10 national parks and 145 nature reserves, among them the well-known national parks of Hortobágy, Kiskunság, and Aggtelek, which form part of a designated Unesco world heritage biosphere reserve.

Nature, p347, Unesco sites p422.

Cycling

In recent years Hungary has made great efforts to meet the growing demand for cycle tourism, opening up more than 1,250mi/2,000km of cycle routes in the countryside and 125mi/200km in Budapest. Cycling is now permitted in a number of mountainous and wooded regions, including national parks, providing cyclists stick to the marked trails. Popular routes include the cycle path around Lake Balaton, the

Danube Bend, and the Buda Hills, as well as the Lake Tisza Tour, the trail across the Great Plain, and along the River Tisza. The Danube Bike Path is a stretch of the **EuroVelo 6** Rivers Route that runs from the Atlantic Ocean to the Black Sea. It sees the largest number of cycle tourists each year.

Cyclists must wear a clearly visible hi-vis vest from dusk onward and in bad weather.

Internet sites

www.eurovelo.com provides information (holidays, travel agencies) on cycling in Europe, in particular EuroVelo6.

www.bikemap.net/en/ provides marked routes.

Electricity

The voltage is 220V, as elsewhere in Europe.

Embassies

In the event of a serious problem or the loss of vital documents, contact your home country's embassy:

US Embassy
Szabadság tér 12, Budapest
(1) 475 4400
https://hu.usembassy.gov/embassy/

Embassy of Canada
Ganz utca 12–14, Budapest
(1) 392 3360
www.canadainternational.gc.ca/hungary-hongrie

British Embassy
Füge utca 5–8, Budapest
(1) 266 2888
www.gov.uk/world/organisations/british-embassy-budapest

Embassy of Ireland
Szabadság ter 7, Budapest
(1) 301 4960
www.dfa.ie/irish-embassy/hungary/

Australian Embassy
Now closed. Enquiries can be directed to the embassy in Vienna
https://austria.embassy.gov.au

+ (43) 1 506 740, or call the Consular Emergency Call Centre in Canberra direct + (61) 2 6261 3305

New Zealand Embassy
Enquiries can be directed to the embassy in Vienna.
+ (43) 1 505 3020
www.mfat.govt.nz/austria

Embassies in your home country, p403.

Fishing

Hungarians enjoy fishing and during the permitted season some foreign visitors can be spotted among them, hoping to catch zander, pike, catfish, carp, and giant wels catfish. The sheer size of the catches from the Danube is the stuff of every fisherman's dream.A special license is required, but fishing trips can be arranged from various guesthouses and hotels along the Danube, Tisza, and at the lakes of Balaton, Deseda, and Velence, among others.

Remember to take your license with you, so you only have to pay the local fishing fee at your chosen location.

For information on fishing season dates, licenses, and fish, visit: **gonefishing.hu**

Golf

A small selection of courses:

Zala Springs Golf Resort, Zalacsány – 18 holes. Designed by Robert Trent Jones Jr. zalasprings.hu/en/golf

Golf Club Imperial Balaton, Becehegy, Balatongyörök – 9 holes. golfclubimperial.hu

Pannonia Golf & Country Club, Alcsútdoboz-Máriavölgy – 18 holes. golfpannonia.hu

Greenfield Hotel Golf & Spa, Bük 18 holes. greenfieldhotel.net/hu

Sonnengolf, Zsira – 9 holes. sonnengolf.com/en

Health

Precautions

Vaccinations – No vaccinations are required to enter Hungary, but it is recommended that routine injections (in particular measles for young children and rubella for pregnant women) are up to date. The World Health Organization (WHO) also recommends cover for diphtheria, tetanus, mumps, and polio, regardless of destination (www.who.int).

Mosquitoes and ticks – In summer, the lake regions and areas near the Danube are breeding grounds for mosquitoes, so ensure you have an effective insect repellent. Ticks lurk in forests and among tall grasses, so at the end of a walk it's best to examine your skin to check if any ticks have attached themselves to you. The likelihood of contracting encephalitis or Lyme disease from a tick is low, but if you plan on staying for extended periods in rural areas, take the precaution of having a vaccination against tick-borne encephalitis (TBE) five months before you travel.

For more information visit: **www.cdc.gov** or **www.nhs.uk/conditions/tick-borne-encephalitis/**

Emergencies

Every Hungarian town has a hospital *(kórház)* and through its universal healthcare system everyone, regardless of their nationality or the length of their stay, is entitled to free emergency care in the event of an accident.

Treatments and medicines

For follow-up treatment or serious medical care, go to a medical center or private clinic. Your embassy may be able to help with advice/recommendation of an English-speaking doctor or clinic. Treatments and medicines normally need to be paid for, subject to any

ORGANIZED NATURE TOURS

Horse riding:

Unicorn trails – Discover the beauty of Hungary's Puszta on horseback. ☎ 44 (0) 1767 777 044. www.unicorntrails.com

Equus – Explore the Hungarian plain and experience Hungarian hospitality. ☎ 44 (0) 1905 388977. www.equus-journeys.com

Watching wildlife:

Nature Trek – Wildlife holidays and natural history tours of Hungary. ☎ 44 (0) 1962 733051. www.naturetrek.co.uk

Responsible Travel – Enjoy birdwatching in Hungary's national parks. ☎ 44 (0) 1273 823 700. www.responsibletravel.com

Bird Quest – Hungary & Transylvanian birding tours. ☎ 44 (0) 1254 826317. www.birdquest-tours.com

reciprocal agreement with your home country. *Insurance, p407.*

Pharmacies *(gyógyszertár)* are well stocked. Look for a sign with a green cross or a bowl with a snake.

Pharmacy business hours – Normal hours: Monday–Friday 9am–7pm. Some operate 24 hrs.

Horse riding

Hungary and horses: the two words are synonymous. Even though the Great Plain is still the number one location for equestrian shows (and stretching your legs on a long walk), each region has riding centers suitable for all levels.

www.ride77.com/hungary lists equestrian centers and riding schools in Hungary.

Internet

Wifi is free in most hotels and guesthouses. However, it is less widespread elsewhere, apart from in Budapest, which is ultra-connected. Bars, cafés, restaurants, and hotels in the capital generally offer free access (ask for the code if it is not displayed) and even the waterbuses have free wifi!

Languages spoken

Hungarian is a very difficult language for English speakers, but learning a few key words will sometimes make communication easier. Apart from in remote areas, many Hungarians speak or understand some English. Older Hungarians often speak German. *Hungarian, p341. Names, p397. Useful words & phrases, p430–31.*

Media

Television

Hungary has around 20 channels but larger hotels have satellite TV, so you should be able to access Sky, CNN, BBC World News, and so on (along with German channels).

Radio

You should be able to listen to your favorite English-speaking radio channels via wifi/specific apps, but be aware of the data usage on your portable devices.

Money

Currency

The monetary unit is the **forint** (abbreviated nationally to **Ft**, and internationally to **HUF**).

Notes exist in denominations of Ft500, 1,000, 2,000, 5,000, 10,000, and 20,000, and coins in Ft5, 10, 20, 50, 100, and 200. Keep an eye on the number of zeros on the notes—easily miscounted in haste.

Euro
Although Hungary has been a member of the European Union since 2004, it has not yet adopted the euro. Despite this, some hotels, restaurants, and other outlets will accept euros as well as forints, and some also quote prices in euros. However, if you pay in euros you may be given forints as change and find that you are in effect paying more than if you settle a bill in forints. We recommend researching the situation at the time of travel, to decide if it would be beneficial to take some euros with you.

Changing money
Money can be changed in banks, currency exchange outlets (cash), travel agencies, and hotels.
Under no circumstances change money in the street with people offering attractive rates, as these transactions are illegal.
Foreign currency exchange outlets in city centers and railway stations often offer the best rates. Banks have relatively favorable commission rates, while the rates at hotels and airports are the least favorable.
ATMs (automated teller machines) are a convenient way of obtaining cash in forints. (In Budapest Airport they are near the baggage reclaim area, but the rates are poor.)
A commission will normally be charged by your own bank so check with them before departure and the Hungarian bank may charge a transaction fee.
As always, it's wise to compare the various options to get the best deal.

Paying by card
Credit cards such as MasterCard, Cirrus, Visa, and JCB are accepted everywhere, American Express less so. Payment by card is very common. In case of theft or loss of your card, make a statement to the local police and retain a copy of it. Also remember to call the telephone number provided by your bank to block your card.

ATMs
These are indicated by the sign **Bankomat** and are plentiful in towns and cities. Instructions are often also given in English.

Bank business hours
Banks are usually open Monday–Friday 8am–4pm.

Museums
Opening hours – The majority of museums are closed on Mondays. Otherwise they generally open 10am–6pm, except when there are seasonal variations.
Concessions – As a rule, young people aged 6 to 26 years pay half the normal entry price. Hence we have not included this in the individual admission charges given in the guide. Where a child's rate is specified, it is because it differs from the usual half price rate.
Free over 70 – EU nationals aged over 70 years are entitled to free entry to museums (on presentation of ID showing proof of age).

Photography
Note that there is a charge to take photographs or film videos in museums (between Ft500–2,000).

Post
Magyar Posta (the Hungarian postal service) letter boxes are usually painted red and decorated with a hunting horn.
Stamps are only sold in post offices. A stamp for a letter or postcard to an address in the EU costs Ft400, and Ft470 to the USA. Allow around 5 to 9 days for a postcard to reach the UK and 1 to 2 weeks the US.
Business hours – Monday–Friday, 8am–6pm (or 7pm); Saturday 8am–1pm (in cities and large towns). **www.posta.hu**

Public holidays

1 January: New Year's Day.
15 March: National Holiday (anniversary of the 1848–49 Revolution, the struggle for independence against Austria).
Easter: from Good Friday to Easter Monday.
Pentecost and Pentecost/Whit Monday.
1 May: Labor Day.
20 August: St. Stephen's Day and the founding of the kingdom.
23 October: Republic Day, the anniversary of the October 1956 Uprising.
1 November: All Saints' Day.
25 and 26 December: Christmas.

Restrooms/Toilets

Public restrooms *(mosdó)* in Budapest are operated by several different companies. Restrooms in shopping malls and restaurants are often the best option. They are sometimes located in the basements of buildings and are identifiable by the usual pictograms. They generally cost Ft200.

To find restrooms away from towns and cities try **pee.place/en/l/Hungary**, but a listing on the site is not a guarantee of cleanliness.

Security

Hungary is a safe country, but as with anywhere in the world, you should take sensible precautions, such as keeping money or valuables out of sight, not leaving anything in your car, and not taking unnecessary risks.

Theft – Keep a close eye on your belongings when you are in crowded places (railway stations, markets, and so on). Keep photocopies of your documents somewhere safe so they will be easier to replace if stolen. Be extra cautious when withdrawing money and when using outlets for changing currency. Ask what the exchange rate is and calculate the sum due to you.

A police officer, whether in uniform or plain clothes, has no right to check your papers (let alone your money!) without justifiable reason. *Rendőrség* means police/Hungarian law enforcement.

Overcharging – In certain restaurants and bars tourists can sometimes be the victims of overcharging, so scrutinize the check/bill carefully. Watch out for overcharging in taxis, too—only use authorized taxis and make sure the driver switches the meter on at the start of the journey *(see p423)*.

Drugs – Never leave your food or drink unattended and do not ask strangers to keep an eye on them for you. And as in any unfamiliar environment, it is best to avoid accepting snacks, drinks, chewing gum, cigarettes, and so on from new acquaintances. Just a precaution against the unlikely event that they have been laced with drugs, putting you at risk of being robbed or sexually assaulted.

Senior discounts

Seniors benefit from reduced prices when visiting national museums (up to age 70, above that entry is free) and over 65s also enjoy free travel on public transport. Carry your passport or identity card with you as proof of age.

Shopping

Of all the country's many markets, Budapest's **Központi Vásárcsarnok** (Central Market, *p65)*, is definitely worth a visit. You will find fruit, vegetables, cold meats, and paprika, as well as embroidered tablecloths, dolls, jewelry, and more. But, markets apart, **Budapest** is still a great shopping city. It's also worth remembering Hungary's many **Christmas Markets**, where you can buy local handicrafts, drink mulled wine, and enjoy the folklore shows, such as those held in Budapest, Győr, Pécs, Szeged, and Sopron.

Souvenirs, see below.

Store business hours

Stores are generally open Monday–Friday 10am–6pm (Saturday 2pm). Some are open on Saturday afternoon and Sunday, mainly those in shopping malls and tourist areas.

Food stores are usually open 7am–7pm (Saturday 2pm). Small food outlets that are open 24 hours a day can normally be identified by their "Non Stop" sign.

Most stores are closed 26 December.

Smoking/Vaping

Cigarettes can only be bought from a tobacconist (identifiable by a green "T" logo) and sale is prohibited to under 18s.

It is forbidden to smoke or vape inside public places such as restaurants, cafés, pubs, and public transport (including transport stations and at stops for buses, trams, and so on), but it is still possible to light up on some terraces outside cafés and restaurants.

Souvenirs

Any Item marked **Hungaricum**, a combination of *Hungary* and *unicum* (unique), means it has been made in Hungary and represents Hungarian culture and style.

Alcohol – Brandies made from fruits such as Szatmár or Békés plums, Szabolcs apples, and Kecskemét apricots, have an alcohol level that fluctuates between 37 and 86 percent. Apricot brandy or *barack pálinka* is renowned and has been awarded PGI (protected geographical indication) status (OFJ is the equivalent in Hungary). Unicum, a bitter liqueur with 40 percent alcohol, is also popular.

Embroidery – The region of Matyó in the north of Hungary is known for its traditional folk embroidery on cotton canvas, frequently featuring floral motifs.

In the South, Kalocsa embroidery also features flowers and is very colorful, sewn on delicate openwork fabric. The pretty designs are used to decorate shirts, placemats, tablecloths, and T-shirts.

Ceramics – The factories of Herend, close to Lake Balaton, and Zsolnay in Pécs, produce fine porcelain and stoneware. Contemporary ceramics from Kecskemét and traditional pieces from Sándor Ambrus in Hódmezővásárhely make lovely souvenirs to take home.

Crystal – Ajka Crystal produces unique handmade pieces in leaded glass and various color combinations.

Paprika – Hungary is known across the world for its paprika. Historically, Szeged is the center of production, but afficionados prize Kalocsa paprika as well. However, you can now buy it almost everywhere in fresh, dried, or powdered form, or as a purée, or strung into garlands, and either sweet or hot.

Edible produce – Pick Szeged salami is made from Hungarian Mangalica pork and is very tasty, as are the sausages produced in Csaba and Gyula. The foie gras is excellent. The cake decorating store Mézesmanna in Budapest makes gingerbread cookies decorated to look like embroidery—edible works of art. The confectioner Szamos produces exquisite cookies and sweet treats in marzipan, along with chocolates and other products.

Rubik's cube – Classified as a Hungaricum product.

Wine – Hungary's rich wine culture dates back to the time of Ancient Rome. The top estates produce fine wines for maturing and aging. **Tokaji Aszú** is the most famous of the sweet wines, particularly the exceptional Szepsy Tokaji Aszú. The best white wines include Tokaji Furmint and Hárslevelű from the Tokaj region, while among the reds is Egri Bikavér from Eger … all well worth taking a bottle home.

Spas/Thermal baths

Spa etiquette

It's a good idea to plan ahead if you want to visit a spa. Most baths are mixed, but some still have have set times for men and women. Note that during single sex sessions, some people do not wear bathing suits. Remember to take your bathing suit, towel, and plastic sandals, although you can usually hire these on site if necessary. A bathing cap is sometimes needed for the swimming pool (this can normally be bought on site). A plastic bag will also be useful for carrying toiletries (shampoo, soap, hairbrush, …) from one pool to another. Blow-dryers/hairdryers are usually available.

Inside the baths there is a choice of pools: some in the actual spa area and others for recreational swimming. The complexes also normally include hammams and sometimes saunas. Most spas also have restaurants serving light meals and drinks.

For the complete experience, buy a massage at the entrance (reserve on arrival or, better still, book ahead on the spa's website, if possible).

After your session, always factor in spending a little time in the relaxation rooms so your body can gradually return to ambient temperature—important, especially during the winter months, when the cold north winds can be severe.

Telephone area codes

Hungarian numbers

A **landline** number comprises an area code followed by 6 digits in the provinces and 7 digits in Budapest. The **codes** corresponding to each of the cities, towns, and departments in the guide are listed at the beginning of each chapter of the Discovering Hungary section.

Cell phone numbers begin with the digits 20, 30, 31, 50, or 70, which must always be keyed in.

Calling within Hungary – From Budapest to the provinces, dial 06 + the 2-digit local area code + the 6-digit number.

From the provinces to Budapest, dial 06 +1 + the 7-digit number.

Within Budapest, just dial the 7-digit number you wish to call, (without any prefix).

Calling from Hungary – For the USA, dial 00 +1, for Canada 00 +1, for the UK 00 +44, for Ireland 00 +353, for Australia 00 +61, and for New Zealand 00 +64, followed by the number of the person you are calling, omitting the first 0.

Cell phones

Since the end of roaming charges within the European Union, calls made on a cell phone registered in any EU country will be charged at the same rate as those made in the cell phone owner's home country. No longer in the EU, UK visitors should check with their provider. Although most US cell phones can be used in EU countries without any problem, roaming charges can be very high. So it's a good idea to check the details of your plan with your cell phone provider before you travel, to find out about potential charges and to avoid any expensive and unpleasant surprises when you return home.

Telephones, p 408

USEFUL WORDS – TRANSPORT

Ticket: *jegy* (**round trip:** *oda-vissza menetjegy,* **one way**: *csak odaút*).
Departure: *indulás*. **Arrival**: *érkezés*. **Reservation**: *foglalás*.
What is the arrival/departure time...? *Mikor érkezik/indul...?*
How much is the journey to [place name]? *Mennyibe kerül az utazás...?*
Flying – Aeroplane: *repülő*. **Airport:** *repülőtér*.
Taking the train – Railway station: *állomás*. **Train:** *vonat*. **Coach:** *kocsi*.
Platform: *peron*. **Seat:** *ülés*. **Train with sleeping cars**: *fekvőhelyes kocsi*.
First class: *1. osztály*. **Second class:** *2. osztály*.
Taking the bus – Bus station: *buszpályaudvar*. **Bus:** *busz*.
In town – Taxi cab: *taxi*. **Tramway:** *villamos*. **Subway:** *metró*. **Stop:** *megálló*.
Ticket office: *jegyértékesítés*.
On the road – Car: *autó*. **Parking:** *parkolás*. **Garage:** *autószerelő*.
Tyre repair workshop: *gumis*.

Time zone

GMT + 1 in winter and GMT + 2 in summer: Hungary is on the same time as the majority of countries in the European Union using CET time (including France, Belgium, and Switzerland). Budapest is 5 hours ahead of New York (UTC-5).

Tourist offices

Most of the cities, larger towns, and tourist sites have a tourist office. The amount of information may vary, but it is often in English.
We have indicated the most useful tourist information points with the symbol at the beginning of each region in the **Discovering Hungary** section of the guide.

Tourist trains

A charming way of exploring parts of the country. Routes include:
Semmering Railway – Built in 1854, this was the world's first true mountain railway and today is on the UNESCO World Heritage List. The route passes through breathtaking scenery in Austria and Hungary.
The Danube Bend – The train follows the left bank of the river from Budapest to Szob, with beautiful views of the mythical river along the way.

MÁV Nostalgia – Information on special routes. (1) 269 5242. www.mavnosztalgia.hu

Transport within Hungary

Trains

A network of 5,000mi/8,000km of rail lines managed by MAV crisscrosses the country. Visitors can buy 7- or 10-day tickets for first or second class travel.
Suburban trains *(személyvonat)* – Passenger trains operating in outlying districts. They make frequent stops. No advance reservation required.
Express trains *(gyors)* – These cover longer distances than the suburban trains. No advance reservation required.
InterCity Trains – Hungary's fastest trains, they connect the major cities. Advance reservation is required.
EuroCity/EuroNight trains – A seat reservation is required for these international trains, which serve most of the countries bordering Hungary.
Reservations can be made up to 60 days in advance and tickets must be printed out. *Rail passes, p400.*

WOW HUNGARY

HEALTH TREATMENTS USING WATER AND HUNGARY'S UNIQUE CLIMATE

Hungary has 34 certified health resorts, unparalleled in Europe, inviting guests to feel healthy and relaxed. Treatments in these facilities typically use the natural healing properties of thermal water, mineral mud and the local microclimatic conditions.

With nearly 1,500 thermal water wells of more than 270 types of certified mineral water, Hungary is a thermal water superpower. These varying types of excellent mineral and thermal water are suitable for treating different health problems, and the country boasts no fewer than 98 certified health spas in which to do so.

These spas, health resorts, and wellness hotels provide everything guests need to truly relax: treatments with a diverse range of physiotherapy services, special therapies, saunas, various types of massage, and medicinal mud treatments. They also offer an array of delicious, healthy food options, highlighting local cuisine and ingredients.

Hollókő Castle
© Hungarian Tourism Agency

For timetables, visit:
www.mavcsoport.hu/en
See www.seat61.com for advice on travel across borders in Europe.

Buses

Volánbusz operates numerous lines serving major cities and resorts (yellow buses).
For information and reservations from Budapest:
Népliget Station (in Pest, the international bus station) – Serves destinations in the southeast (Monor, Taksony, Kecskemét, …).
Stadionok Station (XIVth District, in Pest) – Destinations in the east and northeast (Jászberény).
Árpád híd Station (the Pest side of Árpád Bridge) – Destinations on the Danube Bend and in the north (Vác, Szentendre, Dunakeszi, …).
Kelenföld Station (in Buda) – Destinations in the west and southwest of the country (Érd, Százhalombatta, …).
Adjacent to **Széll Kálmán tér** (in Buda) – Destinations in the west and northwest (Zsámbék).
www.volanbusz.hu/en

Unesco World Heritage Sites

Sites with designated World Heritage status:
– Millennary Benedictine Abbey of Pannonhalma and its Natural Environment
– Budapest, including the Banks of the Danube, the Buda Castle Quarter, and Andrássy Avenue
– Old Village of Hollókő and its Surroundings
– Early Christian Necropolis of Pécs (Sopianae)
– Hortobágy National Park – the Puszta
– Fertő (Hungarian side)/ Neusiedlersee (Austrian side) Cultural Landscape
– Tokaj Wine Region Historic Cultural Landscape
– Caves of Aggtelek Karst and Slovak Karst
whc.unesco.org
The Busó festivities in Mohács and the folk art of the Matyó community (embroidery) are inscribed on the Representative List of the Intangible Cultural Heritage of Humanity.
ich.unesco.org

Urban transport

A good public transport network operates in the big cities.
Budapest also has a subway system.
(Map inside the back cover).

Taxis

Taxi cabs are plentiful and are subject to strict licensing laws, which apply particularly to the tariffs they can charge. In Budapest licensed taxis are yellow, but watch out for unlicensed cabs. Check that the taxi bears the logo of its company on the front door and on the sign on top of the windshield (not simply "Taxi"), that it displays its license number, and that the meter is switched on at the start of the journey. (An unlicensed cab may be painted yellow, but may not bear a company name.) You can tip by about 10 percent if satisfied with the service.

You can hail a cab in the street in Budapest, but see above regarding unlicensed taxis.

Walking & hiking

Hungary's landscape of plains, wetlands, forests, and mountains, remains virtually unspoilt.
Its natural beauty makes it a delight to explore. Walkers can choose from among more than 6,200mi/10,000km of hiking trails. Large sections of the protected areas are open to walkers, as are the national parks, although in some areas you have to be accompanied by a guide. Trails are normally well signposted and there are excellent maps available.
As with any walk, check the weather forecast before setting out and ensure you are equipped for the length and difficulty level of your chosen trail. Remember to inform someone of your departure time, destination, and estimated time of return if embarking on a long hike.
The symbol in the guide indicates a walking trail or path.

Water sports

Water sports, including windsurfing and sailing, play a major part in Lake Balaton with Keszthely, Badacsony, Siófok, and Balatonfüred the principal centers.
Sailing – Sailing is popular on Lake Balaton, where it is possible to rent a boat as well as the services of a skipper at one of the marinas.
Water skiing – Available off the beaches of Balatonfüred, Vonyarcvashegy, and Siófok.

Wine tourism

Exploring the Villány, Tokaj, and Eger wine regions, and enjoying the wine festivals are all a great way to discover Hungarian wine.
www.hungarianwines.eu is a website for Hungarian wine enthusiasts who love to share their knowledge and enthusiasm. You will find information on individual wines and recommendations on estates/cellars to visit.

EMERGENCY NUMBERS

The Europe-wide emergency number): **Ambulance, fire brigade, police** 112

Plus Hungary's internal emergency numbers: **Police:** 107; **Fire** 105 **Ambulance:** 104 (in English 311 1666).
SOS Medical Service in Budapest (urgent medical care in English, private paid): 01 240 04 75.

Activities with kids

THINGS TO DO AND SEE WITH THE FAMILY			
Section in the guide	**Nature**	**Museums/castles**	**Activities**
Aggtelek National Park	Baradla Cave		
Badacsony	Tapolca Caves	Sümeg Castle	
Lake Balaton	Kányavári Island; Little Balaton Buffalo Reserve	Szigliget Castle; Sphere Lookout, Balatonboglár; Szántódpuszta Tourist & Cultural Center, Szántód; Siófok Water Tower	Balatonudvari Beach; Zalakaros Spa complex
Balatonfüred	Lóczy Cave	History Museum	Beach
Budapest	Zoo	Memento Park (statues from the Communist era)	Funicular to the castle; Városliget Ice Rink; Palatinus Beach on Margaret Island; Children's Railway in the Buda Hills
Around Budapest		Gödöllő Palace; Grassalkovich Mansion	
Debrecen			Swimming at Aquaticum
Eger		Castle blockhouses & Astronomy Museum; Equestrian Museum & Stud Farm, Szilvásvárad; Diósgyőr Castle, Miskolc	Baths or Thermal Spa; narrow gauge railway to Szilvásvárad
Esztergom		Danube Museum	
Gyula		Mini Hungary, Szarvas; Fairy Tale House, Békéscsaba	Castle Baths
Lake Hévíz	English Garden, Keszthely		Beaches
Hollókő		Museum of Palóc Dolls	Palóc play-house
Hortobágy National Park	Puszta Animal Park; Bird Hospital		

THINGS TO DO AND SEE WITH THE FAMILY			
Section in the guide	**Nature**	**Museums/castles**	**Activities**
Kecskemét		Leskowsky Musical Instrument Collection	Baths
Mátra Mountains		Mátra Mountains; Coach Museum, Parád; Sirok Castle	Oxygen Adrenalin Park, Mátrafüred
Nyíregyháza	Sóstófürdő Zoo		Aquarius Spa, Sóstófürdő
Őrség National Park		Open-air Museum, Pityerszer; Pottery Museum, Magyarszombatfa	
Pécs		Cella Septichora; Vasarely Museum; Zsolnay Cultural Quarter; Open-air Museum, Szenna	Szigetvár Baths; Zselic Park of Stars; Orfű Aquapark
Siklós		Castle	Baths
Sopron		Storno House; Mining Museum; Bakery Museum	Lake Fertő
Szeged		Musical clock; Ópusztaszer Heritage Park	Aquapolis; Makó Spa complex
Székesfehérvár			Beaches of Lake Velence
Szekszárd			Gemenc–Pörböly Forest Railway; Petőfi Island, Baja
Szentendre		Marzipan Museum; Skanzen (open-air museum)	
Tihany	Echo Hill	Lavender House	
Tokaj			Boat or kayak trip on the River Tisza
Vác		Tragor Ignác Museum	
Veszprém	Zoo		
Visegrád			Medieval tournament reenactment

Calendar of events

The key events in each region also appear at the end of the Addresses sections under Events and Festivals.
Public holidays see p417.

FEBRUARY

Mohács – Busójárás Carnival Festival: a masked parade with torches that takes place before Mardi Gras. www.mohacs.hu

MARCH

Gödöllő – Chamber Music Festival in the palace.
www.kiralyikastely.hu

Győr – Spring Festival: classical music concerts and dance performances.
http://hellogyor.hu/en/esemeny/spring-festival-of-gyor/

APRIL

Budapest – Spring Festival: classical and contemporary music, theater, opera, operettas, folk music, Hungarian and foreign ballet, film.
www.btf.hu/events

Gyula – Pálinka Festival: a gastronomic event in celebration of Hungarian brandy.
www.gyulaipalinkafesztival.hu

Hollókő – Easter Festival: parades in traditional Palóc dress and Easter egg decoration.
www.holloko.hu

JUNE

Budapest – Danube Carnival International: a dance and music festival (classic, modern, traditional Hungarian folk, world).
www.dunakarneval.hu

Budapest – The Night of Museums: free access to museums and entertainment 6pm–1am, around 20–25 June (dpending on the year).
www.muzej.hu/en

Sopron – VOLT: Volt Festival: one of Hungary's biggest rock and electro music festivals. www.volt.hu/en

JUNE–AUGUST

Budapest – Summer Festival: classical, klezmer, and traditional Hungarian Romani music concerts in various locations. eng.szabadter.hu/

JULY

Badacsony – Wine Festival: traditional folk performances, demonstrations, and concerts.
www.programturizmus.hu

Baja – Fish Soup Festival: as it sounds, a celebration involving thousands of cauldrons of fish soup!
bajaihalfozofesztival.hu/index.php/en/

Miskolc – Medieval festival at the castle; tournaments, plays, and a fair.

Visegrád – International Palace Games: medieval games and tournaments.
www.palotajatekok.hu/en

Zamárdi – Balaton Sound Festival: electronic music festival.
www.balatonsound.com

AUGUST

Balatonfüred – Wine Weeks: tastings and traditional folk events.
welovebalaton.hu/events/balatonfured.wine.weeks.1

Budapest – Sziget Festival, mid August: a Glastonbury/Woodstock-style music festival attracting young people from around the world to Óbuda Island.
www.szigetfestival.com

Budapest – Festival of Folk Arts: in Buda's Castle district, including the city's famous firework display on 20 August.
www.mestersegekunnepe.hu

Bugac – Kurultáj ("tribal meeting"): assembly of people descended from ancient nomadic Huns. www.kurultaj.hu
Debrecen – Jazz Days: festival of wine, music, and food in early August. www.debrecen.hu/en/tourist/events/debrecen-wine-jazz-days-1
Debrecen – Flower Parade: mid August, with a procession of floats.
Nagykálló – Festival of Folk Arts: singing, dancing, and traditional crafts.
Szombathely – Savaria Historical Carnival: events performed in traditional costume; plus food and wine. www.karnevalsavaria.hu

SEPTEMBER

Budapest – Budapest International Wine Festival: second week; a celebration of wine with auctions, harvest parade, and concerts on the terraces of Buda Castle. aborfesztival.hu/en
Budapest – Jewish Cultural Festival: concerts, dance, arts, food. www.zsidokulturalisfesztival.hu

OCTOBER

Békéscsaba – Csabai Sausage Festival: visitbekescsaba.com/en/sausage-festival/
Budapest – CAFe Budapest Contemporary Arts Festival: experimental contemporary art (films, music, exhibitions). cafebudapestfest.hu/events
Gödöllő – International Harp Festival and Liszt Festival in the palace. www.kiralyikastely.hu

DECEMBER

Budapest
– Christmas markets in the center of the city.
– Gala Concert, 30 December: with the Gypsy Symphony Orchestra. budapestconcert.com
– Gala and Opera Ball: the big New Year's Eve concert and party.
Győr
Winter Festival: classical and contemporary music concerts; Christmas markets.

Books

HISTORY AND GENERAL BOOKS

A Concise History of Hungary, Miklós Molnár, Cambridge University Press, 2001.
Twelve Days: Revolution 1956, Victor Sebestyen, Weidenfeld & Nicolson, 2007.
The Will to Survive: A History of Hungary, Cartledge, C Hurst & Co, 2011. From the Magyar tribes to NATO and the EU.
Hungary, A Short History, Norman Stone, Profile Books, 2019.
Danubia, A Personal History of Habsburg Europe, Simon Winder, Picador, 2015.

NOVELS

Miklós Bánffy – *The Transylvanian Trilogy*, Everyman Library, 2013. A classic written in the 1930s. Intrigue, conspiracy, and the Belle Epoque.
Péter Esterházy – *Celestial Harmonies*, Harper Perennial, 2005. The destiny of the author's family, one of the most ancient and powerful in Europe, serves as the novel's backdrop.

Imre Kertész – *Kaddish for an Unborn Child,* Vintage Classics, 2017.
Fateless, Vintage Classics, 2017. The life of a 15-year-old living in Budapest and sent to Auschwitz. Semi-autobiographical novel.
Dezső Kosztolányi – *Skylark,* Central European University Press, 1995. A Hungarian literary classic—one extraordinary week in the otherwise uneventful life of an elderly couple in provincial Hungary in 1899.
Anna Édes, New Directions Publishing, 1993. A fine but dark novel; the cruelty and emptiness of bourgeois life.
László Krasznahorkai – *Satantango,* Atlantic, 2013. A poetic journey across the Great Plain.
War & War, Tuskar Rock, 2016. A Hungarian archivist, only partly in possession of his sanity, and a mysterious manuscript.
Seiobo There Below, Tuskar Rock, 2016. A reflection on art and creativity.
Gyula Krúdy – *The Adventures of Sindbad,* Central European University Press, 1998. A great seducer recounts his life in Hungary.
Sunflower, NYRB Classics, 2010. The contrast between the old and new Hungary in 1918 and the story of the vicissitudes of love.
Sándor Márai – *Esther's Inheritance,* Vintage, 2009; *The Rebels,* Knopf, 2002; *Casanova in Bolzano,* Vintage, 2005; *Embers,* Vintage 2002; *Portraits of a Marriage,* Vintage, 2012. Five great novels from a great writer and insightful chronicler of the world.
Péter Nádas – *A Book of Memories,* Vintage, 1998. A colossus of a novel in three first-person narratives, featuring a romantic triangle in East Berlin and a novel within a novel.
Magda Szabó – *The Door,* Harvill Press, 2005. Included in *The New York Times* 10 best books of 2015. What secrets lie behind the door?
Abigail, NYRB Classics, 2020. A coming-of-age novel.
Krisztina Tóth – *Pixel,* Seagull Books, 2019. Thirty stories that tell a complicated tale of relationships.
Lajos Zilahy – *The Dukays,* 1500 Books LLC, 2008. A saga set in the gilded twilight years of the European aristocracy.

Thrillers

Dan Brown, *Origin,* Transworld, 2018. Set in Bilbao and Budapest, university professor and sleuth, Robert Langdon, is in pursuit of the discovery that "will change the face of science forever."
Jessica Keener, *Strangers in Budapest,* Algonquin Books, 2017. A thriller full of seduction and intrigue.
Julian Rubinstein, *Ballad of the Whiskey Robber,* Back Bay Books, 2004. A gentleman burglar in Budapest.

TRAVEL, MUSIC, FOOD & DRINK

Travel

A Poet's Bazaar, Hans Christian Andersen, Forgotten Books, 2018. The author tells of the journey during which he met Franz Liszt.
Blue River, Black Sea, Andrew Eames, Black Swan, 2010. A journey along the Danube.
Between the Woods and the Water, Patrick Leigh Fermor, NYRB Classics, 1986. Fermor's account of a journey on foot in Europe in 1933–34.

Music

Hungarian Rhapsody: The Life and Loves of Franz Liszt (A Historical Novel), Zsolt Harsányi, Pannonia Publishing Company, 1955.
Redefining Hungarian Music from Liszt to Bartók, Lynn M. Hooker, OUP USA, 2013.

Food & drink

Culinaria Hungary: A Celebration of Food and Tradition, Aniko Gergely, Ullmann, 2015.
The Food & Cooking of Hungary, Silvena Johan Lauta, Aquamarine, 2011.

The Hungarian Cookbook: Pleasures of Hungarian Foods and Wines, Susan Derecskey, Harper Perennial, 1987.

Films

The films listed below are available on DVD with English subtitles.

Béla Tarr – *Damnation* (1988), *Family Nest* (1977), and *The Prefab People* (1982).

*The Turin Horse (*2011). His last film is a powerful drama. Silver Bear winner at the Berlin Film Festival.

Péter Gothár – *Time Stands Still* (1982). A young Hungarian wants to rejoin his father, who was forced to leave the country in 1956.

Ferenc Török – *1945* (2017). Drama set in 1945 when two Jews arrive in a Hungarian village. Winner of 8 awards in 2017.

László Nemes – *Son of Saul* (2015). Life in the Sonderkommandos (work units of prisoners in the Nazi death camps). Grand Prix winner at Cannes Film Festival 2015.

Márta Mészáros – *The Heiresses* (1980). Set in 1936, a young, sterile woman bribes her friend to have a child with her husband.

Diary for My Children (1984). An autobiographical film.

Ildikó Enyedi – *My 20th Century* (1989). The amorous adventures of twin girls separated in childhood. Filmed in black and white.

On Body and Soul (2017). A love story set between the worlds of dreams and reality. Golden Bear winner at the Berlin Film Festival, 2017.

Károly Makk – *Love* (1972). A portrait of two women's suffering due to the absence of one man. Inspired by two short stories by Tibor Déry.

Tamás Yvan Topolánszky – *Curtiz* (2018). The dilemmas of a director filming the legendary *Casablanca*.

Music

You may find it cheaper to buy music by Hungarian artists (vinyl and CDs) on your trip to Hungary rather than from outside the country or online.

CLASSICAL

Rákóczi March, an iconic piece of music in Hungary, revived by Liszt in his *Hungarian Rhapsody.*

The Merry Widow, a famous operetta by Franz Lehár. Another notable operetta is *The Csárdás Princess* by Emmerich Kálmán.

Franz Liszt – *Faust Symphony,* conducted by Leonard Bernstein, 1996; *Lieder,* sung by Diana Damrau and Helmut Deutsch, 2012; *Danse Macabre,* played by pianist Pascal Amoyel, 2002.

Béla Bartók – *44 Duos for Two Violins*, by Sarah and Deborah Nemtanu, Naïve, 2014; *Concerto for Orchestra* with Zoltán Kocsis conducting the Hungarian National Philharmonic Orchestra, 2005; *Music for Strings, Percussion, and Celesta,* conducted by Pierre Boulez, 2009.

Zoltán Kodály – *Háry János Suite, Psalmus Hungaricus, Dances of Galánta and Marosszék*, interpreted by Ferenc Fricsay, 1999.

FOLK MUSIC

Hungarian Gypsy Music, Ferenc Santa, 1995.

Csík Zenekar is a traditional Hungarian folk music group, featuring singer Marianna Majorosi.

Ungarische Volkstänze (Hungarian Folk Dances), by the Choir & Orchestra of the Hungarian State Folk Ensemble, 2017.

Lakatos Bela & the Gypsy Youth Project Celebrating a New Generation of Gypsy Music, 2006. This group aims to keep traditional Romani music alive.

PRONUNCIATION

Hungarian differentiates between short and long vowels. Accents signify long vowels. Stress falls on the first syllable of the word.

a = aw as in "raw"
á = ah as in "past"
c = ts as in "tsar"
cs = ch as in "church"
e = eh as in "less"
é = ay as in "say"
gy = j as in "duke"
h = huh as in "hi"
i = i as in "thick"
í = ee as in "leave"
j = y as in "yoga"
ly = ee as in "ill" (but do note that the l is not pronounced)
ny = ni as in "new" or "onion"
o = oh (short) as in "force"
ö = uh as in "purr," but without the "r"
ó = oh (longer) as in "awe"
ő = ur, but longer
s = sh as in "chocolat"
sz = s as in "say"
ty = st as in "stew"
u = ou (short) as in "foot"
ú = ou (longer) as in "food"
ű = u (with umlaut) as in "few," but longer
zs = zh as in "measure"

NUMBERS

0	nulla	**20**	húsz
1	egy	**30**	harminc
2	kettő	**40**	negyven
3	három	**50**	ötven
4	négy	**60**	hatvan
5	öt	**70**	hetven
6	hat	**80**	nyolcvan
7	hét	**90**	kilencven
8	nyolc	**100**	száz
9	kilenc	**1000**	ezer
10	tíz		

COMMON WORDS

yes/no .... igen/nem
good, okay .... jó
please .... kérem
thank you .... köszönöm
hi, hello .... szia
good morning .... jó reggelt kívánok
good evening .... jó estét kívánok
goodbye .... viszontlátásra
sorry/excuse me .... elnézést
today .... ma
yesterday .... /tegnap
tomorrow .... holnap
entrance/exit .... bejárat/kijárat
open .... nyitva
closed .... zárva
post office .... posta
stamp .... bélyeg
police .... rendőrség
pharmacy .... patika, gyógyszertár
hospital .... kórház
doctor .... orvos
dentist .... fogorvos

TOURIST AND HISTORICAL SITES

abbey .... apátság
basilica .... bazilika
beach .... strand
bridge .... híd
castle .... kastély
cathedral .... dóm
cave .... barlang
cemetery .... temető
chapel .... kápolna
church .... templom
forest .... erdő
fortified castle .... vár
fortress .... erőd
garden .... kert
hill .... domb
house .... ház
lake .... tó
market .... piac
mountain .... hegy
monument .... emlékmű
palace .... palota
river .... folyó
ruin .... rom

IN A CAFÉ/RESTAURANT

eat .... enni
drink .... inni
menu .... étlap
vegetarian .... vegetáriánus
the bill, please .... a számlát kérem

MEALS

breakfast .... reggeli
lunch .... ebéd
dinner .... vacsora

CUTLERY etc.

fork .... villa
knife .... kés

spoon ... kanál
cup ... csésze
glass ... pohár
napkin ... szalvéta
plate ... tányér

COMMON FOODS

bread ... kenyér
butter ... vaj
cheese ... sajt
egg ... tojás
foie gras ... libamáj
jam ... lekvár
salad ... saláta
salt ... só
soup ... leves
sugar ... cukor
tomatoes ... paradicsom

VEGETABLES ... zöldség
beans ... bab
cauliflower ... karfiol
corn ... kukorica
lentils ... lencse
mushrooms ... gomba
pepper ... bors
potatoes ... burgonya
French/string beans ... zöldbab

FISH

fish ... hal
carp ... ponty
catfish ... harcsa
pike ... csuka
pike-perch ... fogas
trout ... pisztráng

MEAT ... húsételek
beef ... marhahús
chicken ... csirke
duck ... kacsa
game ... vadételek
goose ... liba
ham ... sonka
lamb ... bárányhús
pork ... sertés
poultry ... szárnyasok
turkey ... pulyka
veal ... borjú
roast ... sült
very rare (blue) ... alig sütve
rare ... félig átsütve
medium ... közepesen átsütve
well done ... jól átsütve

FRUIT ... gyümölcs
apple ... alma
grape ... szőlő
melon ... sárgadinnye
orange ... narancs
peach ... őszibarack
pear ... körte
water melon ... görögdinnye

DESSERTS

dessert ... édesség,desszert
ice cream ... fagylalt
pastries ... sütemények

DRINKS ... italok
beer ... sör
coffee ... kávé
fruit juice ... gyümölcslé
hot chocolate ... forró csokoládé
milk ... tej
hot ... meleg
cold ... hideg
tea ... tea
wine ... bor
red/white wine .. vörösbor/fehérbor
bottle ... üveg
half bottle ... fél üveg
water ... víz
mineral water ... ásványvíz
sparkling water ... szénsavas ásványvíz
still water ... szénsavmentes (ásvány)víz
ice cubes ... jégkocka
Cheers! ... egészségére

DAYS/MONTHS

day/month ... nap/hónap
week ... hét
Monday ... hétfő
Tuesday ... kedd
Wednesday ... szerda
Thursday ... csütörtök
Friday ... péntek
Saturday ... szombat
Sunday ... vasárnap
January ... január
February ... február
March ... március
April ... április
May ... május
June ... június
July ... július
August ... augusztus
September ... szeptember
October ... október
November ... november
December ... december

Transport, see p412, p420; In the hotel, p409.

GENERAL INDEX

In Budapest, individual places of interest are indexed by Hungarian and English names.
Places of interest (incl. religious buildings) in other towns/cities are not indexed individually: please see the relevant town/city described in the guide, e.g. Győr, etc.
Places of interest not in towns/cities described in the guide are indexed by name, e.g. Fort Monostor.
Baths, castles, caves, national parks, open-air museums, palaces: see under relevant heading, e.g. "Baths," "Castles" (key references).
Names of significant figures from history (e.g. Béla Bartók): key references are indexed.
General topics (e.g. vineyards, the Baroque): key references are indexed.

A

B

C

D

E

F

V

Y

Z

GENERAL MAP

REGIONAL MAPS

THEMATIC MAPS

TOWN PLANS

LEGEND: MAPS AND PLANS

Attractions and landmarks

- Tour
- Tour departure point
- Church
- Mosque
- Synagogue
- Temple
- Buddhist - Hindu
- Building
- Monastery - Lighthouse
- Fountain
- Viewpoint
- Castle, historic house
- Ruins, archeological site
- Dam - Cave
- Megalithic monument
- Genoese tower - Mill
- Temple - Greco-Roman remains
- Other place of interest - Summit
- Distillery
- Palace, villa, house
- Cemetery: Christian - Muslim - Jewish
- Olive grove - Orange grove
- Mangrove
- Youth hostel
- Rock carving
- Runestone
- Stave church
- Wooden church
- National park or reserve
- Country house

Sports and leisure

- Swimming pool: open-air covered
- Beach - Stadium
- Marina - Sailing
- Diving - Surfing
- Trail refuge hut – Walking, hiking
- Horse riding
- Golf - Leisure center
- Amusement park
- Wildlife park, zoo
- Gardens, park, arboretum
- Bird reserve/sanctuary
- Windsurfing, kitesurfing
- Fishing
- Canyoning, rafting
- Campsite – Hostel
- Arena
- Leisure center, sailing/canoeing center
- Canoeing/kayaking
- Boat trips

Practical information

- Tourist information
- Parking - Park-and-ride
- Station: rail - bus/coach
- Railway
- Tram
- Departure point: carriage
- Metro - Suburban train - Tram
- Metro (subway) station
- Cable car, ropeway
- Funicular, cog/rack railway
- Tourist train
- Ferry: cars and passengers
- Foot passenger ferry
- Waiting in line/queue
- Observatory
- Service station - Shop
- Post - Telephone
- Internet
- City Hall
- Bank, Bureau de change
- Law courts - Police
- Police station
- Theater - Museum
- University
- Open-air museum
- Hospital
- Market - Covered market
- Airport
- Hotel/Accommodation run by the state
- A Agricultural office
- D District council
- G District government office
- L Local government offices
- P Provincial capital
- Spa, thermal center
- Thermal/hot spring

Roads

- Highway/motorway or primary route
- Interchange/junction: full - partial
- Road
- Pedestrian street
- Steps - Path, track

Topography, borders

- Active volcano - Coral reef
- Marsh - Desert
- Border - Nature Park